THE MINORITY RIGHTS REVOLUTION

THE MINORITY RIGHTS REVOLUTION

JOHN D. SKRENTNY

The Belknap Press of Harvard University Press

Cambridge, Massachusetts, and London, England

2002

Library of Congress Cataloging-in-Publication Data

Skrentny, John David.
    The minority rights revolution / John D. Skrentny.
      p. cm.
    "The Belknap Press of Harvard University Press."
    Includes bibliographical references and index.
    ISBN 0-674-00899-5 (alk. paper)
    1. Minorities—Civil rights—United States—History.
  2. Minorities—Legal status, laws, etc.—United States—History.   I. Title.

JC571 .S62978 2002
323.1'73—dc21   2002068615

PREFACE

If readers are expecting an attack on minority rights policies, they will not find it here. Neither will they find a defense. This book is motivated by a desire to understand American politics during a crucial formative period. I want to understand modern American political and moral culture and the meaning of "Left" and "Right." I want to show how weak groups often win big in American politics. I want to trace the genesis of various controversial policies and America's current tendency toward "identity politics." In doing so, my aim is to cut through the shrillness of political rhetoric and improve American democratic deliberation by informing participants in policy debates how we arrived at our current situation. This may in turn enhance the care with which decisions are made about what kinds of rights Americans should have and ultimately what kind of country they want. This last goal may be a stretch, but that is what I hope to do here.

Full disclosure requires that I admit to identifying mostly with the Left, though there is much on that side of the political spectrum that I have trouble supporting. Most important is that I disagree that the minority-rights policies of the 1960s and 1970s always must be defended to the point that nothing new is tried. I disagree with the practice of labeling any criticism of those policies as racist, sexist, anti-immigrant, and so forth. Such labels end debate, or horribly stifle or distort it by declaring that those in disagreement have a psychological problem. These policies were means to an end; they may have been the best means at the time, but they very well may no longer be. Too often, the Left has stopped looking for new ideas, leaving it to the Right to generate them. If the Left is to claim its role as a progressive force, it has to continually think afresh.

Other biases creep into the pages that follow. I am on record as saying we need a national commission to carry out a massive study of which groups—when, where, and how—are actually the victims of discrimination in American life. This sounds critical of nonblack minority inclusion, as well as the exclusion of potential minorities not so designated by the government, but it is in the interests of defenders of affirmative action because the current list of America's official minorities has no justification and is legally vulnerable, and may be politically vulnerable. Those who want to include some nonblack ethnoracial minorities need a persuasive and legal reason for doing so (at this time the "diversity" rationale only has legal standing in university admissions).

If I appear especially sympathetic to the rights claims of African Americans, it is probably because I am, for reasons explained in Chapter 10. If I appear critical of rights for Latinos and the disabled, it is because I want to understand how they won new policies so easily despite weak mobilization. If I appear especially sympathetic to women's rights and rights for gays and lesbians, it is because the issue to be explained there is the greater resistance or exclusion their advocates faced in getting involved in minority-rights policies. If I appear especially sympathetic to white ethnics, it is because I do believe this group got a raw deal.

A note on terminology. I have written this book for academics and nonacademics alike. There is some jargon here to address and engage in social science debates, but I have tried to minimize it. I have also endeavored to make the book as welcoming as possible to readers of all political persuasions. This is hard to do because certain words carry heavy ideological freight for some readers (for example, the Left recoils at the notion of the "victimization" of groups while the Right rolls their eyes at the notion of group "oppression"). I try to switch back and forth between these words or use both. Near the completion of my writing this book, there developed a backlash among the Left (in my current home city of San Diego, no less) against the word "minority" because it may connote inferiority. I continue to use it because it is ubiquitous in the documents of the period and I know of no synonym to link together groups disadvantaged on diverse but nonclass bases.

Then there is the issue of the ever-changing group names. I use a variety of contemporary terms but let the old terms stand in quotations and documents. I mostly use "blacks" and "African Americans" interchangeably, though some documents that I quote use "Negro." I use "Latino" in place of "Hispanic" for no reason other than it seems to be the norm in academia, though in the discourse of the period other terms pop up, such as "Spanish-surnamed" and "Spanish-speaking" Americans. I use "Asian American" in the text, though some documents use "Oriental." I use "American Indian" because it seems to be making a comeback after years of "Native American." This conforms to the 1965–75 group term. I considered using "ethnics" rather than the more traditional "white ethnics," because the latter term implied a denial of Latino whiteness, but some colleagues urged me to stick with the traditional term since "ethnics" was ambiguous. I use both. I also use both "whites" and (following Orlando Patterson) "Euro-Americans," most often the latter rather than the cumbersome "non-Hispanic whites."

This book was at least seven years in the making (it started as a chapter of my last book, *The Ironies of Affirmative Action*), and along the way I benefited from wisdom and guidance of so many people I cannot possibly remember them all. I would like to give special thanks to those that helped the most, but then I would have to draw a line between the special and the less so, and that would be difficult as well as unpleasant. So I thank the following as a much-appreciated group and apologize to those I do not mention: Richard Alba, Edwin Amenta, Dana Barron, Ed Berkowitz, Rick Biernacki, Erik Bleich, Alfred Blumrosen, Thomas Borstelmann, Clem Brooks, John Bukowczyk, Tom Burke, James Button, Keith Bybee, Karen Chai, Jack Citrin, Elisabeth Clemens, Clark Cunningham, Gareth Davies, Paul DiMaggio, Mary Dudziak, Steve Epstein, Paul Frymer, Christina Gomez, Amy Gutmann, Jeff Haydu, Gerald Horne, Jerry Jacobs, Christian Joppke, George Kateb, Stan Katz, Peter Katzenstein, Jason Kaufman, Phil Klinkner, Michele Lamont, George La Noue, Marc Landy, Catherine Lee, Jennifer Lee, Martin Levin, Robert Lieberman, Glenn Loury, Doug McAdam, Deborah Malamud, Doug Massey, Bud Mehan, Shep Melnick, David Meyer, Kelly Moore, Ewa Morawska, Francesca Polletta, Catherine Rymph, Abigail Saguy, Kim Scheppele, Peter Schuck, David Sears, Stephen Shapin, Peter Skerry, Stanley Skrentny, Brian Steensland, Thomas Sugrue, John Sullivan, Steve Teles, Carol Swain, Jonathan Tilove, Roger Waldinger, James Q. Wilson, Mayer Zald, Steve Zimmers, and the anonymous reviewers for Harvard University Press.

I was able to present portions of this work in several supportive and constructively critical environments. These included the Institute on Race and Social Division at Boston University, the Departments of Sociology at the University of Arizona, Case Western Reserve University, UCLA, Indiana University, UC-San Diego, Princeton University, and Stanford University, the Departments of Political Science at Boston College and Brandeis University, the Gordon Public Policy Center at Brandeis University, the Institute of Governmental Studies at UC-Berkeley, the Program in Ethics and Public Affairs at Princeton University, the Fellows' Seminar at the Center for Human Values, the Workshop on Power, Politics and Protest at New York University, and the Contentious Politics Seminar at Columbia University. Thanks also go to audience and panel members for my presentations at the conferences of American Sociological Association, the American Political Science Association, the Journal of Policy History, the Social Science History Association, and Central European University's Annual Conference on the Individual vs. the State.

The project benefited from support from the University of Pennsylvania, UC-San Diego, and a grant from the Lyndon Johnson Library. It also benefited from a group of talented research assistants. At the University of Pennsylvania, Laura Protzmann did a lot of great work, joined by Keren Polsky and Melissa Vanouse. At UC-San Diego, I received expert help from Faye Gibson and Sara Samuels. At Harvard University Press, Michael Aronson, Benno Weisberg, David Bemelmans, Mary Ellen Geer, and Sheila Barrett gave the book first-class treatment, and I am grateful.

I thank the following individuals for allowing me to interview them or for answering my correspondence: Birch Bayh, Derek Bok, Alfred Blumrosen, Martin Gerry, Herbert Hammerman, Aileen Hernandez, Charles Markham, Harold Orlans, Leon Panetta, and Leonard Walentynowicz.

I thank librarians and archivists at the University of Pennsylvania, UC-San Diego, Harvard University, the Lyndon Baines Johnson Library, the John F. Kennedy Library, the National Archives, and the Library of Congress.

Special gratitude also to my parents, Stanley and Marie Skrentny, for their unconditional and enthusiastic support. Younghae Choi's support went beyond the call of duty. Finally, Hyokyung Stella Jeong's irrepressible spirit, warmth, and pursuit of excellence always inspire me.

This book is dedicated to my teachers who helped me to form the ideas, the skills, and the ambition to write it. They were all especially generous with their intelligence, time, and encouragement and I am indebted to them. These include, at Indiana University, Abhijit Basu, David Brain, Donna Eder, Paul Eisenberg, Robert Eno, Paul Gebhard, Tom Gieryn, Reinhardt Grossman, David James, David Pace, Bernice Pescosolido, and Whitney Pope, and the incomparable Brian Powell; at Harvard University, Daniel Bell, Nathan Glazer, Liah Greenfeld, Peter Marsden, David Riesman, Theda Skocpol, Yasemin Soysal, Mary Waters, and especially my adviser Orlando Patterson. Outside of these institutions, a few people were extraordinarily helpful and were informal teachers. These include Frank Dobbin, Jennifer Hochschild, and Alan Wolfe.

Another teacher, the great historian of modern American politics, Hugh Davis Graham, graciously responded to my mail when I was a doctoral student, thus beginning a correspondence and friendship that lasted almost a decade. Hugh was uncommonly generous with encouragement and comments on this and my earlier books. He was invaluable in building my confidence. As I write these words, it has been less than a week since his death. I was lucky to have known him.

All of these individuals, and others I have undoubtedly neglected to mention, helped me to reach professional standards, not be afraid, and love what I do. The old cliché of book acknowledgments of course applies here: they and the others named above deserve credit for the strengths of this book, but I am responsible for its weaknesses.

CONTENTS

ABBREVIATIONS

AAUP	American Association of University Professors
AAMC	Association of American Medical Colleges
CCOSS	Cabinet Committee on Opportunities for the Spanish-Speaking
EEO-1	A form used by the EEOC to count minorities in a firm's workforce
EEOC	Equal Employment Opportunity Commission
ERA	Equal Rights Amendment
ESEA	Elementary and Secondary Education Act
ESL	English as a Second Language
FEPC	Fair Employment Practices Commission
HEW	Department of Health, Education and Welfare
LEP	Limited English Proficiency
LSAT	Law School Admissions Test
LULAC	League of United Latin American Citizens
MALDEF	Mexican American Legal Defense Fund
MAPA	Mexican American Political Association
MCAT	Medical College Admissions Test
NAACP	National Association for the Advancement of Colored People
NDEA	National Defense Education Act
NEDA	National Economic Development Association
NEA	National Education Association
NOW	National Organization for Women
NPEA	National Project on Ethnic America
OCR	Office for Civil Rights
OFCC	Office of Federal Contract Compliance
OMB	Office of Management and Budget
OMBE	Office of Minority Business Enterprise
PAC	Polish American Congress
PCCR	President's Committee on Civil Rights
PCEEO	President's Committee on Equal Employment Opportunity

PCSW   President's Commission on the Status of Women
PEER   Project on Equal Education Rights (part of NOW)
SBA   Small Business Administration
UNESCO United Nations Educational, Scientific and Cultural Organization
WEAL   Women's Equity Action League

THE MINORITY RIGHTS REVOLUTION

INTRODUCTION:

HOW WAR AND THE BLACK CIVIL RIGHTS

MOVEMENT CHANGED AMERICA

On January 6, 1969, Senator Barry Goldwater, Republican of Arizona, sent a letter to the new presidential administration of Richard M. Nixon. Goldwater personified the right wing of the Republican Party, argued passionately for limited government, and had previously written a book entitled *The Conscience of a Conservative*.[1] He had also famously stuck to his principles and voted against the Civil Rights Act of 1964, the landmark law that ended racial segregation. On this day, however, Goldwater offered a lesson in political savvy for dealing with a disadvantaged group. The senator reminded the new administration that Nixon had promised a White House conference on Mexican American issues during his campaign, and that Nixon wanted to have "Mexicans" serve in his administration. Goldwater explained that this group preferred to be called "Mexican-Americans" and that the administration should avoid referring to them as Latin American—save that term for South America, coached Goldwater. The White House conference should occur "at the earliest possible time because these people are watching us to see if we will treat them the way the Democrats have." He reminded them that New York was the largest Spanish-speaking city in the United States and that nationwide there were 6 million in this category. "You will hear a lot on this subject from me," the strident, states' rights conservative warned, "so the faster you move, the less bother I will be."[2]

A few years later, Robert H. Bork, who would become a famously right-leaning federal judge and author of the 1996 book *Slouching towards Gomorrah: Modern Liberalism and American Decline,* also promoted the cause of federal recognition of disadvantaged groups. In 1974, Bork was Nixon's solicitor general, and in that year co-authored a brief to the Supreme Court arguing that the failure to provide special language education for immigrant children was racial discrimination, according to both the Constitution and the Civil Rights Act of 1964. The Supreme Court agreed with the statutory argument, though it did not wish to go as far as Bork and create constitutional language rights in schools.[3]

Goldwater and Bork were not alone in promoting rights for minorities. The 1965–75 period was a minority rights revolution. After the mass mobilization and watershed events of the black civil rights movement, this later revolution was led by the Establishment. It was a bipartisan project, including from both parties liberals and conservatives—though it was hard to tell the difference. Presidents, the Congress, bureaucracies, and the courts all played important roles. In the signature minority rights policy, affirmative action, the federal government went beyond African Americans and declared that certain groups were indeed "minorities"—an undefined term embraced by policymakers, advocates, and activists alike—and needed new rights and programs for equal opportunity and full citizenship. In the parlance of the period, minorities were groups seen as "disadvantaged" but not defined by income or education. African Americans were the paradigmatic minority, but there were three other ethnoracial minorities: Latinos, Asian Americans, and American Indians. Immigrants, women, and the disabled of all ethnic groups were also included and won new rights during this revolutionary period.

Bipartisanship was not the only notable aspect of the minority rights revolution. Consider also the *speed* of the development of its laws and regulations. While they appeared to have global momentum on their side, it still took two decades from the first proposition in 1941 that blacks be ensured nondiscrimination in employment to the law (Title VII of the Civil Rights Act of 1964) guaranteeing that right. Similarly, it took about twenty years between the first efforts to allow expanded immigration from outside northern and western Europe and the Immigration Act of 1965, ending all national origin discrimination in immigration. Following these landmarks, however, the government passed other laws and regulations almost immediately after first proposal. In most cases, it took only a few years to have a new law passed and there was little lobbying pressure. Bilingual education for Latinos, equal rights for women in education, and equal rights for the disabled all became law within two years of first proposal. Affirmative action expanded beyond blacks almost immediately. Such rapid success in American politics is rare. It is especially rare when achieved by groups that were defined precisely by their powerlessness and disadvantage in American society.

The rapidity and ease of the minority rights revolution brings up another puzzle. If minority rights were so easy to establish, why were not more groups included? For example, government officials perceived eastern and southern European Americans (Italians, Poles, Jews, Greeks, etc.) to be discriminated against, economically disadvantaged, or both. These "white ethnics" also had strong advocates. Yet they were never made the subjects of

Table 1.1 World and American rights developments

World developments	U.S. developments
1941 "Four Freedoms"	1941 Executive Order 8802
1945 UN Charter	
	1947 President's Committee on Civil Rights
1948 UN Universal Declaration of Human Rights	
1950s–60s Emerging nations in Africa and Asia	1954 *Brown v. Board of Education*
	1964 Civil Rights Act
1965 International Convention on the Elimination of All Forms of Racial Discrimination	1965 Voting Rights Act; Immigration Reform Act
1966 International Covenant on Economic, Social and Cultural Rights; International Covenant on Civil and Political Rights	
	1968 Bilingual Education Act, developing Affirmative Action policies

special policies for aid, protection, or preference. Despite widespread perceptions of their oppression, gays and lesbians similarly failed to gain a federal foothold in the minority rights revolution. Some members of Congress first submitted a bill to protect Americans from discrimination on the basis of sexual orientation in 1974. There still is no law ensuring this protection.

Another curious aspect of this minority rights revolution is that the 1960s recognition of the right to be free from discrimination was not just an American phenomenon. Nondiscrimation was quite suddenly a *world* right, a *human* right. That is, the United States was anything but alone in its recognition of minority rights.[4] Consider the dates of major American minority-rights developments and United Nations conventions and covenants guaranteeing human-rights protections (see Table 1.1). Though usually (and notoriously) unperturbed by world trends, Americans were guaranteeing nondiscrimination and other rights at the same time that much of the world was coming to a formal consensus on these same issues. Was it just a coincidence that America and many other nations traveled on parallel paths? Moreover, was it happenstance that Africans and Asians simultaneously threw off the yoke of colonialism and their new nations joined the UN while American citizens of third-world ancestry also gained more control of their destinies?

The minority rights revolution is not only an intellectual puzzle. It was an event of enormous significance. It shaped our current understanding of American citizenship, which is more inclusive than ever before, while also drawing lines of difference between Americans. It was a major part of the development of the American regulatory state, later decried by those same conservatives who joined with liberals in building it up. And it offers a unique look at American democracy. When the stars and planets line up in just the right way, politicians, bureaucrats, and judges can offer a range of efforts to help disadvantaged Americans—even if those Americans did not ask for them.

What Do We Know about the Minority Rights Revolution?

The minority rights revolution was a sudden growth of federal legislation, presidential executive orders, bureaucratic rulings, and court decisions that established nondiscrimination rights. It targeted groups of Americans understood as disadvantaged but not defined by socioeconomic class. Many of these laws and regulations, especially affirmative action, were novel in that they created the new category of "minority" Americans and sought to guarantee nondiscrimination by giving positive recognition of group differences.

There is much research debating the fairness or efficacy of minority-rights laws. But how did we get them in the first place? American scholarship lacks a comprehensive treatment.[5] Several approaches are possible to understanding this important process.

Readers will almost certainly expect a book on the spread of minority rights in the 1960s and 1970s to be a study of social movements. The image that comes to most Americans' minds when they think of the period is angry protest—radical blacks, feminists, and Latinos shouting slogans, a white ethnic "backlash," newly assertive disabled and gay people, all joining Vietnam War protesters in creating a climate of upheaval. These images exist because there was, of course, a very large amount of social-movement activity. One account of the minority rights revolution might therefore emphasize the role of grassroots mobilizing.

Social-movement researchers such as the political scientist Sidney Tarrow offer this "bottom-up" view. Tarrow refers to the period as a "protest cycle" that used the "rights frame" elaborated in the 1960s black civil rights struggle.[6] Various minority groups observed the success of the black civil rights movement and they adopted similar collective action "repertoires," or styles of protest, and their "frames," or ways of understanding their (unjust) place in society. Therefore, "the American 'rights' frame" spread to women, gay men and lesbians, and other groups.[7] Elites become involved because "opportunistic politicians seize the opportunity created by challengers to proclaim themselves tribunes of the people." "Reform is most likely," Tarrow continues, "when challenges from outside the polity provide a political incentive for elites within it to advance their own policies and careers."[8]

Much of what I describe in the pages that follow does not contradict this model. But a social-movement approach also leaves many questions unanswered. Most important, because social-movement theories are mostly about the emergence of social movements, they offer little guidance on the outcomes of social movements or the *content* of reforms.[9] Second, they cannot explain why some groups during the same time period had to exert more pressure than others, some did not have to lobby at all, and still others failed completely despite lobbying and pressure. Why are "opportunistic politicians" so selective? Groups representing white ethnics and gays and lesbians found little and no success, respectively, during the revolution. Latinos succeeded marvelously despite small numbers, weak organization, and inconsistent demands. Women, who had better organization than Latino groups and ostensibly promised greater votes to opportunistic politicians, struggled for some of their new rights. A movement seeking rights for the disabled did not exist when the first disabled-rights law was passed. Other differences are detailed in the chapters that follow.

This book fundamentally challenges the social-movement approach to understanding the late 1960s and early 1970s. One theme throughout this study is that while white men dominated government, by no means were social movements and minority advocates excluded. Scholars almost always assume social movements are discrete entities that exist *outside* of government.[10] There are "challenges from outside the polity" confronting "elites within it." In the late 1960s and early 1970s, however, formal members of social-movement organizations held positions of power in Congress and the bureaucracy, and strong advocates also worked out of the White House. They played crucial roles in formulating and pushing new rights. The images conjured up in this book are therefore mostly not of angry minority protests, raised fists, pickets lines, and placards. The images of the minority rights revolution are mostly of mainstream Euro-American males and minority advocates, wearing suits, sitting at desks, firing off memos, and meeting in government buildings to discuss new policy directions. While these are not romantic images, they are the images of power.

The minority rights revolution also presents a puzzle for a strand of scholarship on American politics that has sought to explain how the American state grew and why it did not become a welfare state like many similarly industrialized European nations. A dominant issue in the field known as American political development, these studies have generated insights that show how difficult it is in the United States to establish comprehensive old-age pensions, health-care insurance, unemployment insurance, and support for the poor. Most emphasize the complexity of the American federal government, with its numerous checks and balances that offer seemingly endless opportunities for opponents of legislation to erect roadblocks and exact concessions.[11] Comprehensive, sustained, coordinated lobbying campaigns have been necessary to accomplish welfare policies, usually coupled with domination of the White House and Congress by the Democratic Party.[12] The limitations of this approach are obvious in the present case: If it is so hard to accomplish anything in American politics, how did we get a minority rights revolution notable precisely for its sudden, rapid, bipartisan policy development? Insights from the study of welfare states highlight the significant differences of the politics of social regulation from the politics of social provision. In some periods and with some policies, America's fragmented governmental system and undisciplined political parties, long identified as the bane of strong welfare policies, do not pose any obstacles at all.

From the perspective of rationalist studies of policy development, the minority rights revolution also presents a mystery. While not normally identified with the rational-choice approach, James Q. Wilson offered a lasting contribution to the study of policy development that generally conforms to the rationalist premise that people behave according to their self-interest. Wilson argued that the politics of public policy can be understood with reference to perceptions of how widely or narrowly a policy's costs and benefits are distributed.[13] In Wilson's theory, a policy perceived to narrowly target a beneficiary but distribute costs widely is usually in for smooth sailing in American politics. Wilson termed this kind of politics "client politics" and contrasted it with other combinations, such as policies with diffuse benefits but concentrated costs. In client politics, the beneficiary greatly cares about the policy and supports its passage and maintenance, while the majority who pays for it does so on such a small per-capita basis that there is little resistance or opposition. The costs are just too little to bother with. The opposite scenario, "entrepreneurial politics," is much more difficult, where the concentrated costs go to a small group that is therefore motivated to fight, while the broad class of beneficiaries who share in the policy's benefits are less motivated to mobilize for passage or maintenance.

Though Wilson's theory is broad and includes a role for perceptions to go along with its rationalist premises, in the present case it is the perceptions and not the rationalism that are doing most of the work. Purely rational politicians should have *always* treated minority politics as client politics. Instead they ignored or oppressed most of the groups later defined as minorities. Even in the 1965–75 period, when they suddenly behaved differently, not all groups won benefits; and for those that did, the picture still does not look like client politics—because many of the policies were not demanded by the "clients." Politicians simply anticipated that they would like them, and pushed them through based on this perception.

Last, because these approaches are focused on national politics, none of them seriously addresses the linkage between America's rights revolution and the world's. How were the two linked? If global developments aided the American minority rights, did it aid all groups equally? If not, why not?[14]

Dynamics of Change: Understanding the Minority Rights Revolution

To explain the minority rights revolution, this book emphasizes the importance of two factors: the perceived needs of national security and the various legacies of the black civil rights movement. I show *how* these factors were important through a detailed study of processes and mechanisms of political change in America. Significant themes throughout are the ways that prior policy developments and cultural meanings matter. Initial policymaking can make later policy development possible, easy, and quick. But understanding rapid policy development requires seeing the political importance of meanings—perceptions of what a thing, person, policy, or action *is*.

The Sequence of History and the Legacies of National Policy

An important concept used to study historical sequences in politics is the policy legacy (sometimes called "policy feedback").[15] The basic idea is simple: new policies remake politics. Government leaders, interest groups, and the public adjust their interests to take into account the existence of the new policy. This sometimes requires greatly changing their preferences. Policies may even call into being entirely new political organizations. This all means that the sequence of historical events matters greatly. For the present case, World War II and the Cold War helped make the minority rights (especially black) revolution possible, and the black civil rights movement helped make the rest of the revolution possible—and rapid.

National security and equal rights

The minority rights revolution could not have occurred without the prior world battle against the Nazis and Japanese and the Cold War struggle with the Soviet Union.[16] World War II and especially the Cold War's broadly defined "national security" policy had important legacies in domestic politics. In some ways this was direct and obvious: the perceived need for national security led to great investment in the means of warfare, driving a large part of the economy and building up firms that created weapons and other equipment. But there were other, more far-reaching effects.

During this dynamic period, war threats were staggering and horrifying, and national security prompted policies that included everything from education to highways to racial and ethnic equality. The latter became part of national security because American strategy in World War II set in motion the creation of global human-rights norms that gave a cause for the Allies and a structure to the later Cold War struggle with the Soviet Union. World War II marked the beginning of an unprecedented global cultural integration and the establishment of a global public sphere, held together by the UN and a few basic premises. The sanctity of human rights was one. At the top of the rights list was nondiscrimination. Race or ethnic discrimination, especially when practiced by those of European ancestry, was wrong. In short, geopolitical developments set into motion a dynamic where policies defined as furthering the goal of national security by fighting Nazism or global communism—including equal rights policies—found bipartisan support and rapid change in political fortunes.

Legacies of black civil rights

The legacies of black civil rights policy were complex and varied. One important legacy was the creation of new "institutional homes" (to borrow Chris Bonastia's term) for rights advocates to have positions of real policymaking power.[17] Most important here were the Equal Employment Opportunity Commission (EEOC), the Department of Health, Education and Welfare's Office for Civil Rights, and the Department of Labor's Office of Federal Contract Compliance. All were created to enforce rights laws for blacks, and all attracted employees who supported equal-opportunity rights. Though they usually kept black rights as their priority, this was not uniformly true. The EEOC played a crucial role by implicitly designating four ethnoracial groups, plus women, as America's official minorities to be given special attention and included in affirmative action. These new sites of rights advocacy allowed the designated groups to concentrate their lobbying efforts to a sometimes very receptive audience, usually out of the public view.

Other policy legacies of the black civil rights movement were more cultural in character, though equally important. The Civil Rights Act of 1964, as well as other efforts to help blacks, created a tool kit or repertoire of policy models that could be extended again and again and adapted to deal with the problems of groups other than black Americans.[18] Through their own initiative, or when pressured by nonblack minority advocates, civil-rights bureaucrats responded with affirmative action—regardless of the specific demands of the minority advocates. Policymakers sometimes simply anticipated what minority constituents wanted. They created an "anticipatory politics" based on these policy tools and the new legitimacy of minority targeting.[19] Activist members of Congress used the Civil Rights Act's Title VI, barring federal funds for any program that discriminated on the basis race, national origin, or religion, as part of a policy repertoire when seeking votes or social movement goals. Congress thus created Title IX of the Education Amendments of 1972, barring sex discrimination on the part of educational institutions receiving federal funds, and Section 504 of the Rehabilitation Act of 1973, which addressed discrimination on the basis of disability also by using the Civil Rights Act model.

Meanings as the Foundation of Politics

There are limits to the use of a policy as a model. The constellation of strategic interests that political actors have in particular contexts are based on the *meanings* they perceive in certain things. Meanings are constitutive—they tell us the identity of a person or thing. They tell us what it is. These meanings are the foundations of the legitimacy rules or "logics of appropriateness" analyzed by neoinstitutionalist organizational scholars and the moral boundaries and norms studied by cultural sociologists such as Michèle Lamont and international relations scholars like Peter Katzenstein.[20] Meanings may make a policy acceptable for one goal or group, but not for others. The foundational role of meanings is highlighted throughout the book. Cultural meanings help us understand the speed of the revolution as well as its limits.

This approach is both similar to and different from developments in the social sciences regarding the role of culture in political life. In political science and especially in sociology, there is a growing literature on "frames." Most of this work defines frames as coherent pictures of the world that can motivate and facilitate the development of social movements.[21] Social movements typically have a frame that defines and explains the genesis of some grievance, labels it as an injustice, and offers goals and strategies for change. More recently, the term has migrated into political sociology and political science but retains its basic meaning, referring to coherent ways of seeing the political world.[22] Other sociologists emphasize the explanatory utility of "narrative" or the stories people use to make sense of their actions.[23] Political scientists often discuss culture as such, or as "ideas" that affect policymaking in some way. Some ideas are said to have particular persuasiveness or power.[24] Some thinkers in political science and sociology have emphasized the importance of "traditions" to understanding politics.[25]

All of this work has made important contributions and is relevant to the case at hand. To fully understand processes of policymaking, however, we

need a more disaggregated approach focusing on meanings or understandings of specific things. The concepts "frames," "ideas," and "traditions,"
while offering their own useful insights, frequently do not fit because they
imply a level of conscious development and coherence that I believe rarely exists in the minds of political actors or in a nation's culture.

A more realistic conception recognizes that our perceptions of a thing or
person need not be related to other things in any coherent way, and may appear illogical if subjected to close scrutiny. To make this point most clearly,
consider some aspects of the diet of Americans. Many if not most Americans
consider certain crustaceans—lobster, crab, or shrimp—to be delicacies. On
the other hand, their stomachs will likely turn if offered tarantula, beetle, or
grub. But both groups of creatures are members of the phylum *arthropoda:*
entities with hard exoskeletons, jointed limbs, and soft, protein-filled insides.
Perhaps in America we draw a distinction between sea-dwelling arthropods
and those on land. But why? In many parts of the world, people attach different meanings to insects and spiders and they are regular components of
healthy meals.[26]

The American preference for some arthropods and the quite different feeling for others cannot properly be said to be based in "ideas," "frames," "traditions," or a people's "narrative." All of these terms seem too grand to capture what is going on. Most Americans have not given much thought why
they do not eat the centipede that might race across their living room floor
on a warm summer evening. There is no coherent American philosophy, idea,
or frame that explains the consumption of some animals but not others.[27]
People respond to meanings on a preconscious, almost unthinking manner.
On a very basic level, they understand the meaning of the centipede, perhaps
even while munching on a bowl of the similarly shaped popcorn shrimp: the
centipede is an unpleasant thing (that must be squashed).

The example of the inedibility of insects shows this constitutive or foundational role of meanings, and is additionally helpful because it shows that the
variability of meanings is not simply or always a function of power struggles
in society. Public policy is obviously more complex but is similarly rooted
in such meanings. Continuing with the same example, the food industry and
its accompanying regulations are based on the same distinction: most bugs
should be killed, none should be eaten. Nearly everyone in the West operates
with these meanings; they are so strongly held that discomforting physiologi-
cal reactions may occur if someone challenges them. Significant hunger problems the world over may be allayed by the mass consumption of bugs, but no
one in the West proposes this because, for Westerners, bugs are not food.
Consider another example: political scientist Marc Landy has pointed out

that people seem much less willing to tolerate very low risks to their health from toxins in the environment than the relatively greater risks from driving a car.[28] Meanings shape our analogic reasoning—which things are "like" other things—and divide the world into categories that are not necessarily coherent. These categorizations are rooted in the correspondence of some features of prototype objects or phenomena. They highlight similarities while sometimes obscuring great differences.[29]

Meanings are generally stable but they can change, turning a particular stance toward a policy anachronistic. In some cases, strategy and effort shepherd change. Certain individuals act as "meaning entrepreneurs," actively promoting new meanings for objects or social groups, often without pushing any particular set of norms or policies—these follow from the meaning shifts.[30] In other cases the changes occur rapidly and almost consensually, as if a veil has been lifted or an imposter unmasked. It is akin to what Doug McAdam referred to as the "cognitive liberation" that precedes the collective action of a social movement.[31] This process has been and remains mysterious.[32]

Meaning and the Minority Rights Revolution

Both promoted and rapid meaning changes are on display in Chapter 2, showing how black civil rights and nondiscrimination in immigration were categorized as national security.[33] To attract support for the Allied side during World War II, President Franklin Delano Roosevelt strongly promoted the United States as a symbol of human rights and race equality. These efforts then invited first the Axis and then the Soviet Union's propaganda strategies highlighting American racism and ethnic inequality. Especially with the parts of government aware of this propaganda and engaged with foreign audiences, specifically presidents and State Department officials, there was a rapid recategorization of domestic nondiscrimination as part of foreign policy and national security. This is apparent in both Democratic and Republican administrations. Comprehensive policy change, however, required convincing Congress and the American public, and both government leaders and rights groups actively promoted the meaning of nondiscrimination as national security. Change was incremental and needed mass mobilization for black civil rights and lobbying campaigns for immigration reform before breakthrough victories finally came in the mid-1960s.

Other rights could not be categorized as easily as national security. Women, for example, made few gains because gender was not a dividing principle in geopolitics as was race. Gender equality was not a part of Nazi, Japanese, or Communist propaganda and therefore served no national security interest. Social rights and welfare state development similarly did not become part of national security policy, even during the Cold War when America confronted an ideology based on economic egalitarianism. This was in part because many business and professional interest groups and Republican party leaders could quite plausibly argue that excessive interference with the market economy and market-based wealth distributions would push America *toward* socialism, rather than save it from this threat.

Recognition of the role of meanings is necessary to understand aspects of the minority rights revolution besides national security linkages and categorizations. If meanings are the foundations of the logics of appropriate action, then politicians will consciously or unreflectively use similar or different policies to appeal to different groups depending on their deservingness or some other meaning.[34] A key theme throughout Chapters 4–9 is that different categories of Americans varied in their analogical similarity to African Americans, creating boundaries of appropriate or legitimate policies relating to them.

This was not only a matter of simple voting power, lobbying, or protest strength. Success and the speed at which it was achieved in the minority rights revolution depended greatly on the meaning of the group in question. After advocates for black Americans helped break the taboo on targeting policy at disadvantaged groups, government officials quickly categorized some groups as "minorities"—a never-defined term that basically meant "analogous to blacks." These classifications were *not* based on study, but on simple, unexamined prototypes of groups.[35] Most obviously, government officials saw the complex category of Latinos (then usually called "Spanish-surnamed" or "Spanish-speaking") in terms of a simple racial prototype, obscuring the fact that many Latinos consider themselves white. Racialized in this way, Latinos needed little lobbying to win minority rights. Women, who faced ridicule like no other group, needed significant meaning entrepreneurship. Their advocates pushed hard to make the black analogy. Though Asian Americans presumably possessed a clearer group racial definition than did Latinos, the analogy between Asians and blacks was weaker than that between Latinos and blacks. Policymakers sometimes dropped Asian Americans from their lists. This was apparently just a cognitive forgetting—it required only small reminders for them to be included in minority policy, at least formally. While rights for the disabled were included easily and without debate, gay rights were a political nonstarter. Government officials saw white ethnics in a multifaceted way that shifted policy away from the minority-rights paradigm, despite the efforts of ethnic advocates. Moreover, though seen as disadvantaged, policymakers saw white ethnics as insufficiently disadvantaged to be categorized as minorities. In fact, federal government officials never spelled out what were the necessary and sufficient conditions or qualities for minorityhood. They classified groups just the same, and had little trouble doing so.

Meanings of groups also greatly affected the types of justice each group received.[36] Being analogous to blacks served as an initial classification, but groups retained distinctiveness. Equal opportunity meant different things depending on the group in question. In the late 1960s, equal opportunity in education for blacks meant a rejection of the "separate-but-equal" policy of the Jim Crow south. It meant zealous integration of schools, the bussing of students around cities so that blacks and whites could learn together. For Latinos, it meant *rejection* of the zealous integration practiced in some southwestern schools which included forced English-language usage. Instead, Latino children were to receive special bilingual education. For women, it meant a combination of different approaches, including integration in classrooms while segregated dormitories, sororities, and sports teams flourished. Readers may protest that these differences in policies were based on "real" differences between groups, yet this claim neglects the fact that lawmakers see some differences as real and relevant and others as not.[37] For example, the one-drop rule (which until recently was broadly taken for granted) defines anyone with any black ancestry as black and the European ancestry in an estimated 75–90 percent of African Americans as unreal.[38] The whiteness of Latinos is similarly denied reality. Despite the footnotes that may appear at the bottom of census tables, federal policy and national debates do not acknowledge that many Latinos are physically indistinguishable from Euro-Americans and consider themselves white. Orlando Patterson was thus able to point out the absurdity of ubiquitous news media predictions of a decline in the percentage of US citizens who are white due to the 2000 census's reports of the growing Latino presence.[39]

A focus on meanings is not a radical innovation. In the study of policymaking, and especially in the setting of policymaking agendas, meanings have also been center stage, though usually discussed in a way similar to frames and labeled as "problem definition."[40] The approach in this book is similar to studies of problem definition, as well as studies relying on "frames" and "ideas," but uses a more disaggregated way of discussing meanings, referring to the meanings of specific things or actions, and allowing for their possible incoherence.[41] This approach requires an attention to detail and an appreciation of contingency that many social scientists may find alien. The payoff is a fuller understanding of the complex processes of policy change.

Meanings for Whom?

The foregoing should not suggest that politics is "determined" by culture and that political results can be accurately predicted by reference to meanings. What it does suggest is that successful policymakers understand, if only subconsciously, everything that I have described. They may choose to play it safe and not challenge their perceptions of social standards, or they may choose to take risks, innovating by testing the boundaries of meanings and morality.[42]

Either strategy takes skill, even a little artistry. Not everyone will share the same definition of a thing or an assessment of appropriateness. Of course, we all know this: whenever we meet a new group of people, especially when we want to make a good impression, we will want to find out about those people, what they take for granted, what they expect, how they understand the world. If we do not learn enough, or guess wrong, we may commit a crushing, delegitimizing faux pas. Different audiences or publics will have different cultural rules and meanings, and successful politicians know this. They rely on their own skills, or hire cadres of political consultants to help them understand. Thus, propounding equal rights for gays and lesbians will likely be a safe, even popular political strategy in a large city or college town; but before a rural community, or before the entire nation, the issue is more safely avoided or approached with trepidation. Consequences of violating cultural rules vary from just a few arched eyebrows to total disgrace, delegitimization, and temporary or permanent banishment from politics.

Joycelyn Elders, President Clinton's first surgeon general, learned this the hard way. After first evoking outrage by mentioning that a drug legalization policy should be studied, she then affirmatively answered a question at a 1994 UN forum about whether masturbation could be taught to reduce exposure to AIDS among young people. She was a newcomer to national politics, she violated two (unrelated) taboos, and Clinton fired her before her presence compromised his own legitimacy. Sanctions for violation depend on the reputation or understanding of the violating politician or official and the strength of the taboo (in part created by interest group mobilization and media reporting practices).[43]

While I stress the importance of policy legacies and meanings, creative, willful people are at the center of this story, though their identities and power may be constituted by institutions and meanings. Policy elites make decisions and those decisions matter. This approach shares with rational-choice approaches an appreciation for strategic action and the importance of the choices of individuals.[44] After the meanings of certain groups shifted, and the groups became "minorities" and legitimate targets of policy, presidents, bureaucrats and members of Congress behaved in ways that rational-choice theorists would expect. Following a "logic of consequences," they pursued support from and justice for these groups with public recognition and targeted policies. But these policymakers were always basing their appeals in the universe of social meanings, especially the black analogy, and using policy and discourses originating in black civil rights. This is clear because, once started, the expansion of minority rights policies could have gone further than it did. Instead, creativity and risk taking reached limits.

Studying Meanings in Policymaking

Some social scientists reading this book might be surprised by the methodology employed here: I reconstruct meanings and tell the story of the minority rights revolution relying almost exclusively on internal government documents, congressional debates and discussions, interviews with key players, and legal documents. This methodology is based on the notion that the context in which something happened or was said—who said it, to whom they said it, and how eloquently it was phrased—are of great importance. This premise obviously makes the book more interpretive and less scientific than many would prefer.

I chose the more interpretive, historically grounded approach partly as a matter of necessity. Much policymaking regarding minority rights came out of the White House, and here there is little data to analyze systematically. White House memos and letters reveal great amounts, but their writing is idiosyncratic. Furthermore, by closely examining the discourse of the most powerful government actors—the ones who actually made and justified policy decisions—I can offer an image of the world that *they* likely perceived, the meanings and thus the political reality of the time. This can offer, obviously, insights into policy causation. For example, if a social movement engages in a series of protest actions on a particular issue, but those actions *never* show up in the discourse of government leaders on the same issue, a reasonable conclusion is that they did not matter very much in the decisionmaking process.

Other possible sources for policymaking are the arguments of intellectuals or journalists. As with social-protest actions, this study makes no attempt at a systematic analysis of journalist or intellectual activities. For both, I register their impact only where they actually lobby the government or officials specifically discuss or respond to their writings.

The premise that discourse gives insight into how political leaders viewed their world informs the style of this book: it is filled with quotations from many well-known political leaders. It also contains quotations from the lower-level, less well-known government officials who actually make many of the policy decisions in America. There are a lot of names of White House aides and civil rights administrators here that the reader will not be familiar with, but these names nevertheless identify enormously important players in American history. The book also pays close attention to the words of advocates of minorities in order to show exactly what they were demanding when they interacted with the federal government. These words provide a window into the world as it existed during the minority rights revolution.

Comparative Analysis and the Design of the Book

The book is divided into two parts—the first consisting of Chapters 2 and 3, and the second of Chapters 4–9—and is organized into various cases. I have chosen these cases for a variety of reasons. To some extent, the cases represent understudied aspects of the minority rights revolution. Most also show the development of policies that were controversial and thus hold intrinsic interest—why would policymaking elites support controversial policies to benefit weak groups? Finally, the cases are chosen for methodologically strategic reasons: they are meant to present the dynamics of the policymaking process, the relative workings of different factors, and to show the limits of the revolution.

The first part of the book describes the prehistory of the minority rights revolution, focusing on the 1941–65 period. It explains how the American and the world rights revolutions were linked through the categorization of (some) rights as national security. Chapter 2 shows successful cases where world culture and geopolitics gave national-security meanings to equal rights. Presidents Truman, Eisenhower, Kennedy, and Johnson and their State Departments all saw black civil rights as a matter of national security, and promoted rights reforms to combat enemy propaganda. The independent effects of national security are obscured in the case of black civil rights because reform occurred at a time of increasing African American electoral clout and mass mobilization. However, a nearly identical national-security dynamic in the case of reforming immigration policy to end discrimination based on national origin suggests the power of national-security meanings in promoting reform. Immigration reform mostly helped Asians, though Asian Americans were a small part of the population and did not apply great political pressure for change. Chapter 2 buttresses the point by showing that the Soviet Union had a similar policy of promoting domestic ethnic equality to further geopolitical interests.

In Chapter 3 I show that national-security interests did not always aid rights of disadvantaged groups. The goal of stopping the spread of Communism sometimes led to such policies as FBI harassment of civil-rights leaders who were or were suspected of being Communists and the maintenance of European colonies in unstable parts of Africa and Asia. Women's rights were not a priority in Asia or Africa, were not a part of Soviet propaganda strategy, and therefore had no national-security meaning. Economic rights for America's poor failed because many believed they pushed America toward Communism, rather than holding off this threat. Together, these two chapters show how the American minority rights revolution was linked to the world-rights revolution and why they happened concurrently. They underscore the importance of meaning changes while showing how they are also linked in complex ways to international and national contexts, especially the actions of foreign powers.

The book's second part does not offer detailed analyses of the much-studied development of black civil rights in the late 1960s and 1970s, such as the development of bussing to achieve school integration, affirmative action for blacks, and voting rights for blacks. Nor does it devote attention to Nixon's "southern strategy"—his attempt to appeal to the south by slowing down the effort to secure black civil rights. Yet black civil rights are still the major factor in these chapters, which explore how the various policy legacies of black civil rights allowed for the development of rights for other groups.

Chapters 4–6 consider the expansion of affirmative action to include groups other than black Americans. Chapter 4, focusing on employment affirmative action, is the most detailed and most important, for it is in this context that the government designated America's official minorities. Despite the sweeping prohibitions on all race, national origin, religion, and sex discrimination in the 1964 Civil Rights Act's Title VII, the government decided only to monitor the equality of a handful of "minorities": blacks, Latinos, Asian Americans, American Indians, and women of all ancestries. The chapter shows how this decision was made, and how and why federal bureaucracies expanded the policy of affirmative action to include these groups. It is a story of administrative politics where the appropriateness of minority selection was rooted in assumed meanings of certain groups. After that formal selection, advocates for Latinos and women demanded more government attention, but made no consistent demands for affirmative action. They got it anyway, as administrators simply took the policy designed for blacks and offered it to other minorities.

Chapter 5 examines the development and expansion of affirmative action for minority capitalists, from the policy's origins as an effort to control black rioting in the late 1960s to part of an effort by the Nixon administration to reach out to minority voters and campaign contributors, especially Latinos. Here the expansion of affirmative action was also rooted in group meanings, most prominently the racialized vision of Latinos, but I show that democratic politics could push the minority rights revolution just as the inner workings of bureaucracies did. Moreover, the case is important because it demonstrates most clearly the "anticipatory politics" that characterizes the whole period.

Chapter 6, on the expansion of affirmative action in higher education, is shorter since the policy is not based on federal actions. Still, it shows how the federal government was complicit in the independent decisions of universities to create affirmative admissions, giving preference to mostly the same minorities designated by the federal government. It was in the context of affirmative admissions that the Supreme Court affirmed the minority rights revolution. It did not, however, speak with one voice and at least one justice evinced concern at the unsystematic process of minority designation.

Together, the three affirmative action chapters make it clear that government officials saw Latinos, American Indians, and to a lesser extent, Asian Americans, despite very different histories, as analogous to blacks and therefore categorized them as minorities. Group meanings shaped expansion of policy designed for African Americans. Civil rights advocates used positions of power in new government bureaucracies to expand affirmative action without debate. Chapter 4 also shows that women's advocates were burdened by a weaker analogy with blacks. They had to push harder, engaging in meaning entrepreneurship, to be given a meaning similar to blacks. They eventually succeeded, as they also gained coverage in employment affirmative action regulations.

In Chapters 7 and 8 I examine Latino politics and women's politics, respectively, in more depth. Chapter 7 explores the movement to accommodate language differences in the public schools, exemplified by both the Bilingual Education Act and the decision to interpret the Civil Rights Act of 1964 as requiring accommodation of language differences in schools to ensure nondiscrimination. Advocates for Latinos, including many government officials, again had a surprisingly easy time of it. Bilingual education was made possible by both national-security policy and legacies of the black civil rights movement, but for simplicity's sake, the whole story is told in Chapter 7. In the late 1950s, for the first time, Americans saw that speaking foreign tongues *contributed* to national security rather than threatened it because it allowed better communication with allies and enemies. This new national-security meaning eased passage of the Bilingual Education Act. This law also benefited from black civil rights, especially the Supreme Court's *Brown v. Board of Education* decision's linking of educational practice to equal rights when striking down school segregation. Just as segregation hurt black children's self-esteem and thus their education performance and opportunity, advocates for Latinos argued, forced English usage had the same effects on Latino children. In a parallel development, officials of the Office for Civil

Rights, with cooperation from the Nixon administration and the Supreme Court, needed very little persuading to find a right to language accommodation and bilingual education in Title VI of the Civil Rights Act, originally intended to end segregation of African Americans.

Chapter 8 examines the origin of Title IX of the Education Amendments of 1972, which granted women equality in all educational institutions that accepted federal aid. Title IX was important because it mandated equality in a setting that formerly was a bastion of sex discrimination. Its reach to athletics challenged head-on some of the most traditional—even cherished—practices of sex inequality. Again the Civil Rights Act's Title VI was a model, and the law passed with ease. The story of Title IX, however, shows that the trouble women had getting the black analogy to work for them was not limited to the affirmative-action case. The faltering black analogy resulted in a low level of enforcement extending even to situations of blatant discrimination. Advocates for women, representing half the nation's population, had to struggle at the implementation stage to have women treated the same as blacks in government policy. They succeeded in preserving the most far-reaching aspects of the implementing guidelines of Title IX, but they also allowed exceptions that would not have been tolerated for blacks.

Chapters 7 and 8 both show the importance of group meanings, but with a new twist not apparent in the affirmative-action cases: Latinos and women were like blacks and also unlike blacks. They were properly the beneficiaries of black civil rights policy models, but those models had to be modified for their group differences. The Title IX case also shows that the black analogy could break down when it was given a close look, deeper thought was required, and actual resources were at stake.

In Chapter 9 I present comparisons to highlight the dynamics, possibilities, and limits of the minority rights revolution. Specifically, I examine whether "white maleness" was a barrier to inclusion in minority rights policies. The chapter describes one very successful and two failed cases of rights developments. The successful case is rights for the disabled, Section 504 of the Rehabilitation Act of 1973.[45] Disability is obviously a category that includes Euro-American men but was nevertheless analogized with blacks. Section 504 was also based on Title VI, and led to a sea change in how America treats its disabled. Disability rights meant accessibility rights and recognition of difference that sometimes required great cost. Section 504, however, was passed very easily and with no opposition whatsoever. The black analogy worked well in Congress, where lawmakers only thought superficially about what nondiscrimination meant for the disabled. Again the black analogy ran into problems at implementation, when civil-rights administrators saw how different disability was from blackness.

Two cases of the failure of the minority rights revolution highlight the importance of group meanings in shaping its limits. First, white ethnics, or the immigrants from eastern and southern Europe and their descendants, organized for action and were recognized as a disadvantaged and important political constituency. They nevertheless did not gain policy recognition and remained categorized outside the minority rights revolution. Ethnic rights failed primarily because the meaning perceived in white ethnics as a group. On the one hand, government officials did not see ethnics as being within a threshold of oppression or victimhood that while unspoken, undebated, and unlegislated, nevertheless powerfully shaped policy. Additionally, politicians saw ethnics in multifaceted ways—as ethnic minorities, but also as Catholics, union members, and anti-Communists. These different perceived identities sent policy appeals off in directions other than those derived from black rights. Second, gays and lesbians, though undeniably discriminated against, victimized, oppressed, and newly organized for power, also were left out of the rights revolution during the 1965 to 1975 because of the meaning of homosexuality. The analogy with blacks again hit a wall: this group was different—too different. The basis of group difference—same-gender sexual attractions—remained taboo as a target of protective policy recognition, and gay rights bills in Congress went nowhere.

In Chapter 10 I bring the story up to date, and explain the varying fortunes and surprising resilience of the minority rights revolution policies despite a rights counterrevolution, mostly led by Republicans. I offer an assessment of the present, which ironically shows increasing signs of the unique disadvantage of black Americans despite their role as the model for all other groups' rights policies. Finally, I offer some possible visions for the future. Not all policies of the rights revolution are equally likely to survive, but American political culture has been changed forever. Americans now take for granted that political leaders will support equal opportunity for all, and this was not always true.

2

"THIS IS WAR AND THIS IS A WAR MEASURE": RACIAL EQUALITY BECOMES NATIONAL SECURITY

Shortly before the passage of the Civil Rights Act of 1964, the Republican Senate minority leader, Everett Dirksen of Illinois, said he finally supported equal rights for blacks. He explained, "No army is stronger than an idea whose time has come."[1] Dirksen was right. Any resistance to federally guaranteed black civil rights by a national political leader was anachronistic. The following year, Congress passed the Voting Rights Act, giving African Americans in the southern states the right to vote, and the Immigration Act, ending decades of discrimination against Asians and eastern and southern Europeans in their ability to come to the United States.

But why were federally guaranteed nondiscrimination rights such a powerful idea? The brilliant strategies and sacrifices of the black civil rights movement were certainly part of the story, as was their growing political strength in conventional electoral politics. These factors cannot explain, however, the establishment of immigration and naturalization rights for Asians, who had little political clout and no major lobbying or protest activities. Moreover, racial supremacy and blatant racial discrimination were anachronisms the world over, not just in the United States. This was not a coincidence. The development of minority rights in the United States was connected to their development elsewhere in the world.

This chapter describes this important linkage by showing how nondiscrimination rights became categorized as American national-security policy. For this to happen, there first had to be a new standard of legitimacy for a country aspiring to be a world leader. This occurred when officials in both the United States and Britain saw that equal rights should be a war aim of the Allies as part of their strategy to fight racist regimes in Nazi Germany and Imperial Japan. President Franklin Delano Roosevelt was an especially effective meaning entrepreneur, promoting the image of the United States as a racial egalitarian and force for democracy.

21

The strategy was a spectacular success and attracted the support of both Western peoples and those in Asia and Africa. But it also allowed criticism of discriminatory practices at home, highlighted in German and Japanese propaganda. With this, protection of equal rights at home became national-security policy and gained unprecedented bipartisan support. After World War II, the UN institutionalized the rules relating to human rights in its charter, declarations, conventions, and covenants. Though scholars usually see the Cold War as a period of rights retrenchment, the pace of reform picked up when the Soviet Union replaced the Axis powers as America's threat. The USSR followed the same propaganda strategy as the Axis, and government officials, especially in those parts of government engaged with the world through foreign policy, continued to see nondiscrimination rights for ethnic minorities as a matter of national security. They gave support for those rights in a way that had been lacking before World War II and the Cold War. Advocates for equal rights promoted the national-security meanings to parts of government and to American citizens who did not see the new categorization.[2]

This chapter describes the origins of the world rights culture and America's meaning within it primarily through the ambitious actions of President Franklin Delano Roosevelt. I then show the political impact of America's meaning within the world human-rights culture with three case studies. First, I consider these international impacts on black civil rights, emphasizing that the White House and the State Department, most engaged with the world at large through foreign relations and aware of the importance of nondiscrimination for national security, were at the forefront of reform. (Congress, the more provincial institution, tended to show less engagement and less sensitivity for the world audience.[3]) This led to an elaborate presidential propaganda strategy on the issue of civil rights, and to civil-rights activists with a distinctly global perspective. This case only sketches the general themes of the process in view of a recent flourishing of research on this important topic.[4] The second case study shows that immigration policy also took on national security meanings, as propaganda strategies based on rights violations created interests in reform. Again, the White House and the State Department were active in promoting change, as they directed a refugee program, based on geopolitical considerations, that gradually eroded the national-origin discriminations in the immigration law. By 1965, they could compare immigration discrimination with discrimination against blacks, make analogies between blacks and immigrants, and declare that both discriminations were anachronisms. In the third case study, I show that the Soviet Union, vying with the United States for world leadership, also promoted nondiscrimination rights for ethnic minorities and presented itself to the world as a racial egalitarian.

The End of Isolationism and America's Promotion of a World Human-Rights Culture

Human Rights and Black Rights after World War I

Before World War II, the views, meanings, and cultures of publics outside the United States were not significant factors in American domestic politics, at least regarding domestic race relations.[5] While some international egalitarian and humanitarian norms shaped international relations, such as prohibitions against slavery and rules of war institutionalized in the Geneva Convention, these were very specific and a hierarchical approach prevailed in Europe as well in the US.[6] This is obvious from the maintenance of colonies and the standard of "civilization" in international law relating to these colonies.[7] World War I resulted in the creation of the League of Nations, but the United States never joined. It is unlikely the League would have affected American domestic race politics had it joined, since the League, though concerned about minority ethnic populations in central and eastern Europe, did not express concerns outside this area. It rejected Japan's attempt for an official statement on racial equality. The term "human rights" does not appear in the Covenant of the League of Nations. James Frederick Green has pointed out that even "the wholesale and systematic suppression of human liberty in Communist Russia, Fascist Italy, and Nazi Germany went officially unnoticed by the League."[8]

If there were no global institutions or world audiences demanding fidelity to equal-rights norms, American politicians also had little incentive at home to pursue African American rights. The problem was that from the very beginning of the Republic, many Americans tended to assume that being black meant being inferior.[9] Of course, blacks made up a significant numerical proportion of the population in the south, but as an audience impressing their own meanings of African Americanness, they were irrelevant. For the most part, blacks were disenfranchised and their views simply had no political consequence. In 1940, only 5 percent of African Americans in southern states had voted in the past five years.[10]

The rest of the country reflected a basic indifference to the plight of blacks, and at worst they shared the culture of white supremacy. When Woodrow Wilson brought segregation to the federal civil service, few complained.[11] As late as 1942, a National Opinion Research Center survey found that only 47 percent of white respondents thought that blacks were as intelligent as whites, only 36 percent felt it would make no difference if a black of equal education and income moved onto the same block, and only 46 percent said no when asked if there should be segregated transportation.[12]

Southern conceptions of the undeservingness of African Americans were an especially powerful force in politics at the federal level because the southerners in Congress were a dominant force. De facto one-party rule in the region led to long congressional careers and thus seniority on congressional committees, which doomed civil rights legislation. During the depression, President Roosevelt deferred to the racism of southern committee chairmen in order to gain passage of his New Deal legislation.[13] There was little reason to expect a significant change in minority politics until events overseas changed the political calculus.

Hitler, Roosevelt, and Black Civil Rights

American blacks would get help from an unlikely source. In response to the threat posed by Nazi Germany, the United States defined itself before the world as a force for equality, human rights, and democracy to win allies. Franklin Roosevelt played a crucial role in promoting America as the champion of human rights, but he did not invent the modern notion of international human rights. In the 1930s, several experts in the area of international law as well as the British author H. G. Wells began to promote the concept of an international declaration of human rights. Wells was especially active; in October of 1940 he pushed the idea as a war aim to Roosevelt and other world leaders.[14]

On December 29, 1940, Roosevelt gave the United States a new international meaning by declaring it to be an "arsenal of democracy" that would give industrial aid to Great Britain, then looking increasingly vulnerable to the Nazis.[15] On January 6, 1941, Roosevelt told the world that those fighting the Axis powers were fighting for "a world founded upon four essential freedoms"—freedom of speech and expression, religious freedom, freedom from want, and freedom from fear. These were "a definite basis for a kind of world attainable in our own time and generation" and not a "vision of a distant millennium." "Freedom," Roosevelt explained, "means the supremacy of human rights everywhere. Our support goes to those who struggle to gain those rights and keep them."[16] The Four Freedoms garnered considerable domestic and international attention, and provided the United States with the background of meaning and purpose for its entry into the war.[17]

The United States and its allies elaborated and institutionalized the Four Freedoms. Under Secretary of State Sumner Welles later recalled that in June of 1941 Roosevelt told him that, since the United States and Britain stood for freedom and justice, they should commit themselves to "a new world order" based on those principles "that would hold out hope to enslaved peoples."[18] Minutes of a meeting in May 1941 of Roosevelt's closest advisers describe a perceived need for a "statement of our alternative to Hitler's new order, a definition of the New Order of the Ages proclaimed on the Great Seal of the United States" and something with "real propaganda value for bringing peace." The notetaker's minutes summed up, "The need for a vigorous lead was repeated over and over . . . Without outspoken leadership, we are in the position of fighting something with nothing."[19] In July, Stalin urged the United States to use its global influence to give moral strength to Hitler's opponents.[20]

Roosevelt then issued with Britain the Atlantic Charter on August 14, 1941. To avoid needlessly bringing up the issue of colonialism, however, Roosevelt wanted the first draft to come from Churchill. Thus it was Churchill's first draft that introduced the idea, uncontroversially, of a basic human right: the United States and the United Kingdom "respect the right of all peoples to choose the form of government under which they will live." The final version added two of FDR's Four Freedoms. The two nations "hope to see established a peace . . . which will afford assurance that all the men in all lands may live out their lives in freedom from fear and want."[21]

America's formal entry into the war in December of 1941 did not change this strategy. Further elaboration came in the Declaration by United Nations of January 1, 1942. The United States, Britain, China, and the USSR (joined by twenty-two other countries on January 2) gave support to the principles of the Atlantic Charter and for a preamble stating they were "convinced that complete victory over their enemies is essential to decent life, liberty, independence and religious freedom," and wished "to preserve human rights and justice in their own lands as well as in other lands."[22]

Picking up where H. G. Wells had left off, a small group of legal specialists in the US State Department set about drafting an international bill of rights, beginning in 1942. In their view nondiscrimination was "the heart of any modern bill of rights, national or international." They included in their final draft the sentence, "These human rights shall be guaranteed . . . without discrimination on the basis of nationality, language, race, political opinion, or religious belief, any law or constitutional provision notwithstanding."[23]

Human Rights and the United Nations

Roosevelt died in 1944 but his vision of human rights lived on in the Truman administration.[24] Various nongovernmental organizations—notably, black civil-rights groups—played a crucial role in keeping the commitment to equal rights part of the world order. At the founding UN meeting in San Francisco, black leaders such as the NAACP's W. E. B. Du Bois and Walter White lobbied for the inclusion of a bill of human rights, as they "huddled constantly" with officials from such diverse countries as the United States, France, the Philippines, Haiti, and Liberia.[25] They sought to equally benefit both non-American nonwhite people and their fellow citizens. Du Bois and White saw these fates as linked. For example, Du Bois told the *San Francisco Chronicle* that the world's colonies were similar to "slums," and explained that a world bill of rights would hold all nations accountable for their discriminatory treatment of human beings. The historian Brenda Gayle Plummer credits these efforts with getting "human rights" mentioned in the official UN charter.[26] Also, in a move that American representatives considered a calculated effort of "playing up to the small nations," the Soviet Union prominently endorsed the principle.[27] The result was that the UN charter mentions human rights seven times, including a mention in the preamble and in Article I, affirming human rights and racial equality as major purposes of the organization.[28]

Another result was a commitment to produce a universal declaration of human rights. In 1946, President Harry Truman appointed Eleanor Roosevelt to represent the United States and chair a new UN Commission on Human Rights charged with creating the declaration. Despite conflicts (the Soviet Union was concerned by the inclusion of French- and Anglo-American-style liberties, and the State Department opposed the inclusion of socialist-style social or economic rights, such as a right to employment and health care), the UN ratified the declaration on December 10, 1948.[29] Though unenforceable, this was a grand statement of worldwide moral principles. The General Assembly stated on December 10, 1948 that the declaration was "a common standard of achievement for all peoples and all nations."[30] Its very "universal" character implied an ethic of nondiscrimination. The words "all" and "everyone" are ubiquitous in the document. Article 7 specifically prohibited discrimination, stating, "All are equal before the law and are entitled without any discrimination to equal protection of the law. All are entitled to equal protection against any discrimination in violation of this Declaration and against any incitement to such discrimination."[31]

Controversy regarding the declaration continued in the United States. Conservatives and isolationists grew suspicious of the UN and its projects. Former president Herbert Hoover called for Communist countries to be banished from the organization if the United States was to remain. In 1953, Senator John Bricker (R–OH) sought legislation to prevent the United States from ratifying human-rights covenants so the country would not sacrifice its sovereignty to a "super-state."[32]

Yet these were activities on the margins. Grumbling in the United States could not change the fact that whether he originally intended to or not, President Roosevelt helped create and institutionalize a remarkable world moral culture. Despite the kaleidoscopic diversity that existed then and now in the world, all nations recognized the UN Universal Declaration of Human Rights as a political and moral standard. Furthermore, they understood from its beginning that the United States sought to represent that standard.

Black Civil Rights as National Security

Perhaps the first event bringing together black civil rights and national security was a precedent-making executive order issued by Franklin Roosevelt. As soon as he promoted America's image as champion of human rights, black civil-rights leaders made black equality an issue of national security. A. Philip Randolph, the head of the Brotherhood of Sleeping Car Porters, called for African Americans to join in a massive march on the capital on May 1, 1941 to make Roosevelt's arsenal of democracy begin to practice fair hiring practices in government and wartime industries. With an international loss of legitimacy a distinct possibility and with encouragement from some in Congress and in his administration, Roosevelt signed Executive Order 8802 on June 28, 1941. This prohibited employment discrimination in government and war industries on the bases of race, creed, color, and national origin, and created a Committee on Fair Employment Practices (FEPC) to investigate complaints of discrimination.[33]

Advocates for blacks and equal rights continued to promote the national-security meanings of racial equality during World War II. Civil-rights leader Walter White told Roosevelt that the FEPC would help black–white relations at home and also "have its effect upon the colored peoples of the world, who constitute four-fifths of the world's population, through its demonstration that no longer will black, brown, and yellow peoples be treated as inferior or exploited by white peoples."[34] Gandhi reminded Roosevelt in a letter that Allied statements of being on the side of freedom and the individual sound "hollow, so long as India and, for that matter, Africa are exploited by Great Britain, and America has the Negro problem in her own home."[35] Black newspapers made the same connections, as did the NAACP in a 1943 legal brief dealing with a riot in Detroit.[36]

Roosevelt would not need this friendly urging to see links between race equality and national security. Nazi and Japanese propaganda strategy highlighted lynchings and other evidence of black oppression through leaflets and broadcasts to the nonwhite world.[37] Roosevelt recognized the threat of Nazi propaganda in his 1942 state of the union address, when he told Americans, "We must be particularly vigilant against racial discrimination in any of its forms. Hitler will try to breed mistrust and suspicion between one individual and another, one group and another, one government and another."[38]

Events during World War II were the beginnings of political patterns that would characterize the next few decades. By 1945, the US and the USSR became established as rivals and competitors for "zones of influence" in Europe and also in the developing world. Soviet leaders did not simply storm into the Third World with military force and impose Communism and Soviet influence. They were careful to respect (or give the appearance of respecting) the emerging nations' sovereignty and sought influence by sowing seeds of distrust of the Americans through propaganda. The emerging nations—mostly nonwhite—had developed an acute racial consciousness after years of colonialism and already tended to be distrustful of Western powers. Soviet propaganda showing American race discrimination provided confirming evidence that Americans did not respect the rights of people of color.

During the Truman administration, three themes in the national-security politics of civil rights stand out. First there was the continuing concern with propaganda. As early as June of 1945, Truman wrote in his diary, "Propaganda seems to be our greatest foreign relations enemy. Russians distribute lies about us."[39] In the early 1950s the State Department estimated that nearly half of Soviet propaganda was on racial equality.[40]

The second theme was the desire of foreign policymakers to counteract this propaganda. The State Department and the White House concentrated reform efforts in ways that had maximum value for communicating to foreign and especially Third World audiences the message that America was racially egalitarian. Beginning immediately after World War II, the State Department often had someone of high profile lobbying for civil rights. In a May 8, 1946 letter to the FEPC (before Congress killed it that year), frequently cited by later civil-rights advocates, Acting Secretary of State Dean Acheson communicated the national-security implications of equal rights. Acheson, never an advocate for black rights in his public life, nevertheless argued "that the existence of discriminations against minority groups in the United States is a handicap in our relations with other countries" and explained that "the Department of State, therefore, has good reasons to hope for the continued and increased effectiveness of public and private efforts to do away with these discriminations."[41] From World War II to the Civil Rights Act of 1964, State Department officials lobbied Congress and other bodies for reforms.[42]

The reason foreign-policy officials were promoting reforms in domestic policy was that these officials were most aware of the national-security meanings of these reforms. Research by Mary Dudziak and Paul Lauren accumulated masses of evidence attesting to the State Department's concern for black civil rights, based on State officials' meetings with world leaders in the UN and meetings with citizens and diplomats on the streets and government buildings of foreign capitals. The Soviet Union used the UN to attack the United States on race equality, working to establish a Subcommission on the Prevention of Discrimination in 1947 to draw attention to America's failings.[43] When the Americans sought to have it abolished, the Soviet Union told the world that the Western powers wanted only to make it easier to oppress minorities within their borders.[44] The State Department's global outposts reported that from India and Ceylon to the Netherlands, Britain and Italy, the Soviet Union, Mexico and Iraq, there was great interest in African American racial inequality. Evidence of this interest also came from the local newspapers, which breathlessly reported on American racial inequality.[45]

Not surprisingly, in 1951 the State Department accepted the demand of Randolph and other civil-rights leaders that it prove to the world in a direct way that America respected the rights of people of color by increasing the numbers of black appointments to the department and to embassy staffs. By 1953, the department had added almost sixty blacks to the foreign service, including an ambassador, and seven Asian Americans.[46]

Meanwhile, the Truman administration pursued other civil-rights reforms. Truman's Justice Department submitted a series of briefs to the Supreme Court on discrimination cases, arguing that civil-rights protection was a matter of national security. It was victorious in cases such as 1948's *Shelley v. Kraemer*[47] (striking down court enforced racially restrictive covenants in housing),[48] and in 1950's *Henderson v. United States*[49] (striking down segregation in interstate train dining cars).[50]

Because racial progress had no foreign policy effects unless the rest of the world knew about it, White House meaning entrepreneurs broadcast to the world any movement that could be interpreted as progress on civil rights. Given that European nations appeared to be almost as concerned as the emerging Asian and African nations about American racial practices, these positive messages had wide exposure. For example, in June of 1947, when Truman addressed the NAACP at the Lincoln Memorial on civil-rights issues, the State Department oversaw the short-wave transmission of the message to the entire world.[51] Similarly, a 1948 administration report assured Truman that America's propaganda radio, Voice of America, gave his strikingly progressive Civil Rights Message to Congress "top place, and covered it fully, giving all main points" and for "twenty-four hours, the Message received full play in all areas." In addition, "the Wireless Bulletin carried 610 words to all missions, including all the recommendations made by the President" and "editorial comments were airpouched to London and Paris."[52] Truman also created some institutional machinery for meaning entrepreneurship. In 1950, he developed a "Psychological Strategy Board" to bring "the race problem" in international propaganda to his attention.[53]

A major area of bipartisan focus on civil rights that shows the importance of creating a positive global image was the high priority given to integrating Washington, D.C. Beginning with Truman, several presidents perceived that integration of the nation's capital, by then a symbol of a nation in the modern world system and thus a focus of international attention, was important to national security. Integrating the capital was an early concern of Truman's President's Committee on Civil Rights, created on January 6, 1947 to study and make recommendations on civil rights.[54] Minutes of the committee's earliest meetings show that the group quickly decided there should be a specific Civil Rights Act for the District of Columbia. The primary reason was that the "nation's capital symbolizes the United States both to the world and to our own people."[55]

The third major theme of Cold War civil-rights/national-security politics was civil-rights advocates' exploitation and promotion of the categorization of civil rights as national security to create reforms. A. Phillip Randolph used this strategy when pressuring the Truman administration to end segregation of the military. In a modification of his World War II strategy, Randolph threatened a black boycott, and argued that American moral authority in the world was tightly linked to the military's openness to blacks. His efforts led to a Truman executive order in 1948 ending segregation in the military, though full implementation took several years.[56]

Another strategy was to bring complaints to world attention at the UN. In 1946 the National Negro Congress, made up of various black fraternal and veterans groups, assembled a petition seeking "relief from oppression" for presentation to the UN.[57] On October 23, 1947, the NAACP filed a petition to the Commission on Human Rights entitled *An Appeal to the World: A Statement on the Denial of Human Rights to Minorities in the Case of Citizens of Negro Descent in the United States of America and an Appeal to the United Nations for Redress.* The document offered detailed information regarding "barbaric" race discrimination and the suppression of political rights. The NAACP's W. E. B. Du Bois traveled to twenty different countries to publicize the *Appeal.* Greek, Soviet, French, Italian, Indian, Danish, Chinese, English, and Norwegian journalists requested copies in preparation for stories.[58] The UN did not act on the petition, though in the Subcommission on the Prevention of Discrimination the Soviets, with Du Bois's help, pushed a proposal to investigate the treatment of blacks in America, losing 4–1, with the United States the lone vote against and seven abstentions.[59] In 1951, the Civil Rights Congress followed in the NAACP's footsteps with another appeal to the world through the UN. This time the charge exploited the December 9, 1948 UN adoption of the Convention on the Prevention and Punishment of the Crime of Genocide, which America ratified on December 11. The charge was that American treatment of African Americans violated the convention—it was geno-cide.[60]

Government advocates for civil rights used links between world opinion and national security in propaganda aimed at American citizens. The strategy was to get Americans to think of the global audience and the different poli-cies that could help in the fight against Communism. Truman's President's Committee on Civil Rights used this strategy prominently in its high-profile report, *To Secure These Rights.* After detailing the various rights being denied to blacks, the report concluded with justifications for federal action, includ-ing the "moral reason," the "economic reason," and the "international rea-son." Here the report explained that "our position in the postwar world is so vital to the future that our smallest actions have far-reaching effects." The re-port concluded, "The United States is not so strong, the final triumph of the democratic ideal is not so inevitable that we can ignore what the world thinks of us or our record."[61]

National-security meanings also shaped campaign strategy and political speeches at home that discussed civil rights.[62] Nongovernmental groups rep-resenting business and religious faiths argued for the same recategorization. The Advertising Council had embarked on a publicity campaign entitled "'United America' (Group Prejudice is a Post-War Menace)" designed to en-courage Americans to respect human rights.[63] The Institute for Religious and Social Studies—a graduate school created at the Jewish Theological Seminary of America, but which united Jewish, Catholic, and Protestant scholars—published lectures in a 1949 series called *Discrimination and National Wel-fare.* Leading scholars such as the sociologist Robert K. Merton as well as po-litical activists such as Roger Baldwin of the ACLU and Adolph A. Berle, a leading member of the Roosevelt administration's "brains trust," contrib-uted to the collected lectures. Readers encountered reasoned arguments that mostly stressed the cost of discrimination in terms of business, foreign policy, and national security. Adolf Berle, in "Race Discrimination and the Good Neighbor Policy," argued, "It is no exaggeration, I think, to say that the habit of race discrimination practiced in considerable parts of the United States is the greatest single danger to the foreign relations of the United States, and conceivably may become a real threat to American security."[64] In "Our Standing in the Orient," Baldwin argued that

> Communist influence in the Orient, however dangerous to democracy, at least impresses Orientals with one aspect of democracy flouted by the West—the equality of all peoples regardless of race. The principles of the United Nations affirming racial equality and freedom from discrimina-tion have made a profound impress on the Orientals, and their new na-tions in the U.N. press their application to the limit.[65]

All of these themes—concern for Communist propaganda, desire to counteract it, and the advocates' strategy of exploiting national-security meanings of civil rights—could also be seen in the Republican Eisenhower administration, though the world was changing. As Baldwin's point suggests, decolonization had begun by the time Eisenhower took office in 1953. The emerging nations, mostly in Africa and Asia, were not aligned with the East or the West, and Cold War competition for their allegiance intensified. Especially when Khrushchev took control of the USSR in the 1950s, the developing world began to play a major role in the superpower struggle.[66] Watching these developments closely were White House and State Department leaders. They— and black civil-rights leaders who would travel to the new African nations for independence ceremonies—linked global developments with domestic civil rights.[67]

Like Truman, Eisenhower agonized over the propaganda wars with the USSR. He appointed a special committee to study how best to combat Communist propaganda; predictably the committee reported that integration, especially of the armed forces, promised to be effective, since it would seem to put America on the side of Third World nations in their drive for national identity.[68] Eisenhower built on Truman's institutional machinery for controlling the international meaning of America, pushing hard for the creation of the United States Information Agency to help control the nation's global meaning.[69] In his "Annual Budget Message to the Congress: Fiscal Year 1956," Eisenhower warned of "Soviet efforts to divide the United States from other nations of the free world by twisting our motives, as well as its efforts to sow fear and distrust." He declared that it was of "the highest importance that our programs for telling the truth to people of other nations be stepped up to meet the needs of our foreign policy."[70]

Despite the switch in party affiliations with the election of Eisenhower, the new president and his secretary of state, John Foster Dulles, followed Truman's strategy based on the national-security meaning of black equality. They sought more blacks for State Department jobs and embassy appointments in the nonwhite nations.[71] This strategy extended to White House jobs with international visibility.[72]

While less active than Truman in seeking civil rights legislation, Eisenhower also acted as a meaning entrepreneur, promoting America as racially egalitarian in international propaganda. He had some excellent material to work with in the historic Supreme Court decision *Brown v. Board of Education*. The president himself was ambivalent about the decision[73] and worried about how it would play before the American south.[74] Nevertheless, Eisenhower shared the concern over America's international meaning, and he grandly told the world that the United States stood for "human rights" while the USSR represented "force,"[75] and Voice of America broadcast details of the *Brown* decision to the world less than an hour after it came down.

Eisenhower shared Truman's recognition that civil rights mattered more in Washington than in any other part of the United States, since the capital should be "the showpiece of our nation"[76] and the "showplace of peaceful civil rights."[77] In his 1952 campaign, Eisenhower referred to discrimination in the nation's capital against nonwhite, foreign visitors as "a humiliation" to his nation and argued that this was "the kind of loss we can ill afford in today's world."[78] His administration therefore focused on halting discrimination and segregation in the District of Columbia government. He issued an order mandating equal opportunity there and used behind-the-scenes persuasion to protect civil rights in private businesses. He had some success, as many of the capital's hotels, motels, theaters, and restaurants stopped segregating.[79]

More so than during the Truman presidency, the Eisenhower years and those following saw violent civil-rights conflicts that would provide the USSR with its most powerful propaganda—photographic evidence of American racial injustice. Especially worrisome were photos of southern repression of civil-rights demonstrations that filled the pages of the world's newspapers.[80] Dudziak has written, for example, of Eisenhower's great distress regarding the international consequences of his order to send troops into Little Rock, Arkansas when disorder and violence threatened to engulf efforts at school desegregation.[81] In recounting the incident in his memoirs and in private communications, Eisenhower revealed how he construed the crises in terms of national security and the moral boundaries then taken for granted in the UN. On national television, the president implored the American people to see the incident in terms of national security:

> At a time when we face grave situations abroad because of the hatred that Communism bears toward a system of government based on human rights, it would be difficult to exaggerate the harm that is being done to the prestige, and influence . . . of our nation . . .
>
> Our enemies are gloating over this incident, and using it everywhere to misrepresent our whole nation.[82]

By 1960, the black migration northward created a larger pool of black voters, and both presidential candidates—Republican vice president Richard Nixon and the eventual winner, Democrat John F. Kennedy—sought the black vote.[83] Both also often invoked the national-security meanings of black equality as a reason to support civil rights at home.[84] In this regard the presidential candidates were in lockstep with civil-rights leaders. The Committee to Defend Martin Luther King and the Struggle for Freedom in the South placed an ad in the *New York Times* on March 29, 1960 for contributions for King's mounting legal bills. "As the whole world knows by now," the ad began, "thousands of Southern Negro students" were fighting for their constitutional rights, "which the whole world looks upon as setting the pattern for modern freedom." After detailing various repressive acts by southern authorities, readers were reminded that America's "good name hangs in the balance before a watchful world."[85]

The Kennedy years saw both the cresting of the civil rights movement at home and the growth of nonwhite independent nations. The pattern of presidential and State Department interest in foreign propaganda and domestic civil-rights reform continued. Kennedy's secretary of state, southerner Dean Rusk, was very candid about efforts for black equality in an interview for the Kennedy Library. He explained that the State Department tried hard to recruit blacks for foreign service, searched in universities, upgraded where they could, and appointed black ambassadors.[86] When an African American passed the written part of the Foreign Service qualifying exam, "he was almost a surefire appointment because there was such a premium on blackness that a black would pass the oral part of the examination usually very promptly."[87]

Notwithstanding Eisenhower's earlier efforts, African diplomats continued to encounter discrimination in Washington and while traveling between New York and Washington through the segregationist state of Maryland. The Kennedy White House and the State Department worked together to find solutions.[88] Officials from the State Department persuaded Maryland businesses to stop discriminating and ultimately coaxed the Maryland legislature to outlaw segregation in public accommodations. Rusk also set up an "International Club" for black diplomats in Washington to have a place to relax, and "hospitality committees" in other parts of the country to mitigate discrimination if a diplomat traveled.[89]

Though the most diligent efforts were targeted at helping black foreigners, Rusk also supported broader strategies. He fought for civil rights legislation in congressional hearings, as the Department of State "threw full weight behind the civil rights proposals of President Kennedy and President Johnson."[90] He later recalled,

> I tried to make clear in my testimony that the foreign relations aspects of our civil rights problems in this country were secondary to the constitutional and domestic impact, that we should move on civil rights for our own domestic reasons to give effect to the Declaration of Independence and the Constitution. But then I went on to add that how we handle this problem did have a considerable bearing upon our relations with the rest of the world.[91]

Throughout the early 1960s, civil-rights leaders continued their effective strategy of directing world attention to black inequality and linking black civil rights to national security. They traveled to Africa and seized opportunities in the UN.[92] Martin Luther King Jr. encouraged the nation to think globally, often stressing the links between the struggles of black people in the United States to those in Africa.[93] And any time civil-rights leaders met white repression, the story made international headlines.[94]

Following the bombing of a black-owned motel and the home of Martin Luther King's brother, severe racial violence erupted in Birmingham, Alabama in 1963. The Soviet Union broadcast 1,420 anti-American commentaries about US rights violations in the wake of the racial crisis.[95] House hearings on "Soviet Covert Action (The Forgery Offensive)" later highlighted the ongoing use of faked pamphlets, leaflets, bank statements, and government documents meant to show the world that the United States was an illegitimate leader. For example, one forgery operation involved the creation of phony *Newsweek* magazine issues for November 18 and December 18, 1963. The magazines looked real from the outside, but on the inside they were completely devoted to attacking the United States on the race issue and were filled with (real) pictures of black protesters and white repression of protesters. The photographs had captions in both English and French explaining "Negro demonstrators battered half-dead by the New York police" and "The policeman is handcuffing a Negro knocked down." Troubling quotes from American statesmen appeared next to the photos, such as one by Senator Barry Goldwater stating, "No one has the right to impose their ideas on the southerners."[96]

In this domestic and international context, and with domestic public opinion supporting civil rights at an all-time high, Kennedy sent legislation (later to become the Civil Rights Act of 1964) to Congress.[97] Fearing more racial violence, he worked behind the scenes meeting with business leaders and other elites in an attempt to gain control of the racial situation. In a July 11, 1963 meeting with approximately seventy members of the Business Council, Kennedy, Vice President Lyndon Johnson, Attorney General Robert Kennedy, and Secretary of State Dean Rusk all urged these business leaders to help by employing more black Americans.[98] Minutes of the meeting sent to all members of the Business Council reported that President Kennedy stressed national security. He told the business leaders that potential for more racial violence existed and that "clear evidence exists that the problem is being exploited abroad and has serious implications in our international relations."[99]

Lyndon Johnson presided over great propaganda triumphs for the global image of the United States. His time in office saw the Civil Rights Act of

1964, the Voting Rights Act of 1965, and the Civil Rights Act of 1968 (for equal rights in housing)—all crowning jewels of the black civil rights movement. Meanwhile, pressure in the UN continued to intensify. American laws barely preceded major UN human-rights initiatives in the same area. African and Asian nations and the Soviet bloc helped push new efforts for human rights. These included, most prominently, the International Convention on the Elimination of All Forms of Racial Discrimination (1965), but also the International Covenant on Economic, Social, and Cultural Rights (1966) and the International Covenant on Civil and Political Rights (1966).[100] All were founded on the bedrock UN principle of the equal dignity of persons.

The civil rights movement played the global angles in its efforts at domestic progress during these years. King's selection to receive the internationally recognized Nobel Peace Prize provided more strategies for using a global stage.[101] In October of 1966, a new radical group, the Black Panthers, adopted the tried-and-true strategy of appealing to the UN, drawing a comparison between the plight of American blacks and former Third World colonies, as they requested the UN to oversee "a plebiscite to allow American blacks to determine their national future."[102]

While the world press gave much positive attention to the historic US civil rights legislation, it also cast light on the black urban riots of the middle and late 1960s. There were literally hundreds of incidents of violence involving blacks in cities across America, with the worst incidents of arson and clashes with police and the National Guard occuring in Los Angeles, Detroit, and Newark. Between 1966 and 1968, 169 persons were killed, 7,000 wounded, and 40,000 arrested.[103] Administration reports told President Johnson of Soviet and Chinese propaganda that argued that the riots showed the American system was a racist failure. The *New Times,* a USSR propaganda magazine with worldwide distribution, published articles linking the riots to the Vietnam War. Both were said to be the result of "brute force American imperialism." These articles had titles such as "Washington's Other War," "From the Great Society to the War Society," "The Negro Ghetto in Revolt," and "A Sick Society."[104] While Johnson received his own reports on Soviet propaganda and world opinion about the violence, other media brought the global view to the American people. Both *Newsweek* (August 7, 1967) and *U.S. News & World Report* (August 7, 1967) carried special reports on the perspective taken by the international press. Johnson later wrote in his memoirs that he agonized over the prospect of American soldiers shooting American citizens, spilling blood that would be shown on television news and pictured on front pages of newspapers around the world.[105]

As a House subcommittee would learn in July 1968, the riots, along with the Vietnam War and the assassinations of Martin Luther King and Robert

Kennedy, seriously damaged US prestige in the world. Witnesses at subcommittee hearings testified that not repression but positive government action was the best response.[106] In fact, Johnson and American elites in businesses and universities were already pursuing various efforts at affirmative action to respond to the black riots in ways that did not hurt the United States internationally (some of which are discussed in Chapters 4–6).[107]

By the late 1960s, it was clear that Roosevelt's effort to promote America as a stalwart for equal rights set in motion the creation of a global-rights culture. This in turn allowed for a recategorization of African American equal rights as national security. While not all government officials were equally inclined to see black civil rights in this light, American presidents and State Department officials did: domestic reform was for them a matter of national security. Their prominence helped promote acceptance among the American public of new civil rights. Black leaders and other civil-rights advocates also prominently promoted civil rights as national security and forced presidents' hands with strategically organized civil-rights demonstrations and UN appeals. The Nazis, the Imperial Japanese, and the Soviet Union were all unwitting accomplices, as they created the threats to national security that made domestic meaning entrepreneurship both necessary and compelling.

The Case of Immigration Reform

One difficulty with assessing the impact of war and geopolitics on minority rights is that in the case most often studied, that of black Americans, the impact of war coincided with growing organized black protest and increasing black voting power gained through migration to the northern states.[108] Did national-security meanings really have any independent prorights impact? Evidence that it did comes from an examination of rights reform in the area of immigration and naturalization, a case where, at least in the early stages, there was no mass mobilization pressure and few electoral benefits for reform-minded lawmakers.

American immigration and naturalization policy used race and ethnic discrimination from the nation's founding.[109] In 1790, Congress limited the right of naturalization to free whites. Blacks gained naturalization rights during Reconstruction, but Asians remained excluded. Limitations on the immigration of various "undesirable" ethnic groups were imposed shortly after these groups came to America. Restriction was motivated by concerns of immigrant inferiority, cultural incongruity, a perceived lack of democratic values, and economic competition. Thus, a few decades after Chinese began to come to the United States in large numbers, Congress excluded them through various measures, culminating in the Chinese Exclusion Act of

1882.[110] The Immigration Acts of 1921 and 1924 combined Asian exclusions beyond the Chinese with strict limitations on immigration from eastern and southern Europe.[111] The 1921 law stated that the number of immigrants to be admitted from each European nation should be 3 percent of the number of persons from that nation living in the United States in 1910 (blacks were not counted).[112] The 1924 law excluded all Asians, including Japanese, who had formerly been exempt from exclusions as part of a negotiation with the Japanese government. It established national quotas based on a country's representation in the 1890 census. This was before the great influx of eastern and southern Europeans.[113] By 1929, as Peter Schuck has described, the United States allowed 154,000 visas for Europeans. About 76 percent went to British, German, Irish, and Scandinavians. The rest went to "Poles, Italians, Dutch, French, Czechs, Russians, Swiss, Austrians, Belgians, Hungarians, Yugoslavs, Finns, Portuguese, Lithuanians, Rumanians, and Greeks in that order; no other group received more than 300 and most received only the token minimum of 100."[114] These ethnically targeted restrictions of the 1920s had a profound effect: Asian immigration, already very small, declined to nearly zero, and immigration from eastern and southern European countries fell precipitously.[115] The exclusionary law reigned, with minor modification in 1952, until 1965.

Beginning in World War II and continuing over a period of slightly more than two decades, nondiscrimination in immigration took on a national-security meaning. The same themes in the national-security politics of black civil rights are apparent in the immigration case: concerns over propaganda, leadership and advocacy from foreign policymakers, and the use of national-security arguments by groups pushing reform. Nondiscrimination in immigration gained bipartisan support in White House administrations, the State Department, and sometimes even in Congress. This categorization was a crucial factor in reform, first eroding Asian exclusions, then creating a strategically open refugee policy that rendered the remaining restrictions irrational. With the help of a large lobbying campaign coming from the White House, the State Department, elite groups outside of government, and the disfavored ethnic groups themselves, an unexpectedly revolutionary compromise reform measure finally passed in 1965. This effort also benefited from the analogy of immigrants with blacks: If discrimination against blacks was unacceptable in 1965, then should not discrimination in immigration policy be unacceptable too?

World War II was not the beginning of openness on the part of US presidents to immigration. They acted to preserve immigration opportunities in the late nineteenth and early twentieth centuries, but were stymied by Congress. White House occupants, oriented to a world constituency, did not want such restrictions to interfere with negotiations with other nations. President Hayes vetoed the Chinese Exclusion Act, but was overridden by Congress. Presidents Cleveland, Taft, and Wilson all vetoed bills creating literacy tests and other restrictions for immigrants.[116]

In the 1930s, presidents were still hamstrung. Though many in Europe were trying to flee Hitler, American laws did not even recognize refugees as a category of immigrants.[117] Reformers could not point to any international obligation to help; the League of Nations was doing virtually nothing to help refugees from Hitler's Germany.[118] Fascism provided even more reasons to restrict immigration because the rise of totalitarianism in Europe exacerbated concerns that fascist immigrants compromised national security.[119]

The depression, with an unemployment rate of 30 percent, shifted the focus from national origins to absolute numbers of immigrants. With so few jobs available, it seemed to many lawmakers not only that immigrants and refugees should be barred as before, but that some immigrants should be expelled. The government jettisoned approximately four hundred thousand Mexicans in the 1930s.[120]

Wartime Brings War Measures: Ending Chinese Exclusion

Some Americans, especially missionaries and those with business interests, tried but failed to reform national origin exclusions such as those against the Chinese during the 1920s and 1930s.[121] Groups pressing for repeal of Chinese exclusion gained new leverage during World War II because the meaning of Chinese immigration changed.[122]

The meaning of immigration could change because of a complex array of geopolitical interests and understandings. Franklin Roosevelt, as described previously, defined the United States as a champion of human rights to win allies in the war against the Axis powers. Because China was an important ally in this global conflict, there was now foreign propaganda criticizing the United States before China and the nonwhite world for its hypocrisy regarding human rights in immigration. If America believed in equality, then why did it exclude the Chinese? This led to fears of an American loss of legitimacy, a morale collapse in China, and a weakened position in the war. These linkages combined to categorize nondiscrimination in immigration as a matter of national security. Responsible members of Congress voted to repeal the restrictions on Chinese immigration. Once this succeeded, advocates for change pressed for new and expanded reforms, arguing that all racist exclusion undermined national security.

In 1942, the new effort at allowing Asian immigration began, led by a small but elite group of sympathetic, non-Chinese New Yorkers. Magazines such as the *Christian Century,* the *New Republic,* and Richard Walsh's *Asia and the Americas* tried to raise awareness of the issue by publishing such articles as "Our Great Wall against the Chinese," "Repeal Exclusion Laws Now," "Are We Afraid to Do Justice?" and "Justice for the Chinese."[123] Walsh was the husband of author Pearl Buck, whose novel of China, *The Good Earth,* won a Pulitzer prize in 1932. He formed a Citizens' Committee to Repeal Chinese Exclusion, which first met on May 25, 1943. This organization, what political scientist Frederick Riggs called a "catalytic group," was a small but active pressure group that encouraged larger forces to lobby.[124]

Lobbying for repeal was old. The new element was the war. Only four days later, a State Department official wrote up a report on his conversation with the Chinese ambassador to the United States:

> The Chinese Government is interested in removal of our discriminations against the Chinese as Chinese; they are eager for recognition, technical at least, of China and the Chinese on a basis of "equality." The fact, however, that the Ambassador twice expressed a hope that something might be done without undue delay causes me to speculate as to the possibility that he had the present military and economic situation in unoccupied China—which situation is becoming acute especially from point of view of morale—much in mind. What the Ambassador said, together with other indications, causes me to believe that it is desirable from the point of view of the war effort for us to work along as liberal lines as may be possible and as expeditiously as may be possible toward doing something constructive with regard to the solution of this question.[125]

Representatives Martin Kennedy (D–NY), Vito Marcantonio (D–NY), and Warren Magnuson (D–WA) were among those submitting a bill to give the Chinese some immigration rights during this propitious time for action. Magnuson's bill became the eventual law. The desired immigration reform was meager, almost laughably so. The bills would have given China slightly more than the standard congressional token quota—105 of 400 million Chinese would be allowed to come to the United States. Yet this low number was comparable to the standard quota given to smaller disfavored groups from Europe. Moreover, even such a weak beginning could—and did—have an impact on changing the meaning of immigration and opening possibilities for other groups and greater reforms. Last, the bill would make the Chinese eligible for naturalization, a right denied to all other Asians.[126]

As with the failed efforts, the lobbying forces for repeal of the exclusion included business interests and religious groups. Business interests did not want cheap Chinese labor, or if they did, it was not mentioned. Some American business leaders argued that *total* exclusion and the general mistreatment of Chinese by immigration officials were bad for business. Even the tiny quota could serve as a symbol to help aid American commerce with China. Religious groups, not surprisingly, made moral arguments. These sorts of claims had been made before.

Chinese officials applied pressure in less public ways. Two representatives, Magnuson of Washington and Republican Noah Mason of Illinois, reported that Chinese officials had personally told them that they supported the move, but did not want to beg for it. Madame Chiang Kai-shek, wife of the Chinese leader, held a private dinner for key members of the House Immigration Committee. At the dinner, according to Mason, Chiang and the guests discussed the possibility of repeal. Chiang pointed out that repeal would aid Chinese morale during the war and thus should be considered part of the war effort.[127]

This was the new element that made lobbying successful where it failed before. Numerous witnesses in House hearings established early on the meaning of Chinese immigration as national security, beginning with Representative Samuel Dickstein (D–NY), the chairman of the House Committee on Immigration and Naturalization. Discounting business interests, he argued that war and concerns over Japanese propaganda highlighting America's Chinese exclusion were more important than future trade.[128] Advocates for Chinese immigration such as Dickstein were able to cite Japanese radio broadcasts from Tokyo and Hong Kong that repeatedly used the Chinese exclusion as a symbol of American racism, imperialism, and illegitimacy. In December 1942, Tokyo radio declared:

> The Chungking authorities must certainly know that Chinese are rigidly prohibited from emigrating to the United States and that this ban on Chinese immigration was established in the latter portion of the last century after a campaign of venomous vilification of the character of the Chinese people . . . The Chinese are rigidly excluded from attaining American citizenship by naturalization, a right which is accorded to the lowliest immigrant from Europe . . . Far from waging this war to liberate the oppressed peoples of the world, the Anglo-American leaders are trying to restore the obsolete system of imperialism by which they hope to prolong their iniquitous exploitation of the best portions of the earth.

A month later, a Tokyo radio broadcast scoffed at a new, ostensibly equal agreement between the United States, Britain, and China: "If the British and American Governments intend to accord equality to Chungking, why don't they [start by repealing] the immigration law now in force in the United States."[129]

Admiral H. E. Yarnell, former commander of the Navy's Asiatic station and a member of Walsh's lobbying group, pointed out the deleterious effects of such Japanese propaganda. It mattered because "allied success against Japan requires the continuance of China in the war" since mainland China "was the only area from which long-range bombers can reach Japan." The small quota would have "a very great effect" on efforts to keep China stable and fighting. Reform was in the interests of the United States, and would be "necessary in post-war time especially."[130] Yu Pin, a Chinese Catholic bishop, agreed that Chinese morale was linked to war strategy.[131] Representative Walter Judd (R–MN) argued that though problems of famine, disease, and the economy threatened China's viability as an ally, it was the people's unsteady morale that was the biggest threat to its war efforts. And though there were a variety of factors that hurt Chinese morale, such as the American failure to aid China or to disavow Britain's plans to maintain its empire, disillusionment about American morality was a crucial issue.[132]

Advocates for reform made use of Roosevelt's efforts to promote America as racially egalitarian. In the Citizens Committee's attempt to round up support from larger lobbying groups, it emphasized the contradiction between the stated purpose of fighting the war—to preserve the Four Freedoms—and the discriminatory Chinese immigration laws.[133] A representative for the Post-War World Council of New York City and the National Peace Conference (the latter body made up of thirty-seven other organizations, including the National Council of the Y.M.C.A. and the Federation of Business and Professional Women's Clubs) argued in congressional hearings that repeal of exclusion was "an acid test of the sincerity of ourselves and our allies," without which "the whole avowed moral structure of the United Nations collapses." "Our whole pretense that we are fighting for democracy and the 'four freedoms,'" he continued, "will crash to the ground."[134] Similarly, Dr. Taraknath Das, a history professor of Indian descent at the College of the City of New York, argued that "as long as Anglo-American power would continue to practice racial discrimination against the peoples of the Orient, the vast majority of the Orientals will not have any genuine confidence in the professions of promotion of world democracy and world brotherhood." He added that reform "will be a great antidote against anti-American propaganda in the Orient."[135] The Congress of Industrial Organizations also formally passed a resolution supporting the repeal at its national convention in Philadelphia on November 2, 1943 stating all of the familiar reasons making the national-security linkage: Chinese morale, Japanese propaganda, and the need to eliminate "a bar to acceptance by our Oriental allies of the sincerity of our war aims and equality among men."[136]

Nondiscrimination as a matter of national security was a powerful rebuttal to southern critics. Representative A. Leonard Allen (D–LA) expressed concerns that ending Chinese exclusion was a precursor to ending other Asian exclusions, and tried to keep the focus of the hearings on the perceived unpleasantness of race equality. When he confronted author Pearl Buck with the question of whether she believes in "full social equality of the races," she avoided the question. Pressed further by Allen, she responded, "This is wartime and this is a war measure. I do not think social equality has one thing to do, at this moment, with war. I think repeal of these acts has a lot to do with war measures."[137]

President Roosevelt expressed similar concerns in his letter to Congress dated October 11, 1943.[138] He regarded the immigration bill "as important in the cause of winning the war and of establishing a secure peace" and an effort "to correct an injustice to our friends." The tiny quota in the bill was not enough to create employment competition, but it was enough to "silence the distorted Japanese propaganda" as well as supply, with legal changes allowing Chinese naturalization, "another meaningful display of our friendship."[139]

The fading opposition forces—who could argue for losing the war?—included various patriotic societies, southern and some western congressmen, the American Federation of Labor (AFL), and some veterans' organizations. The concerns of the latter organizations focused on numbers of immigrants, not ethnicity. The American Legion, for example, wanted a suspension of all immigration until each veteran had a job.[140] Usually avoiding racial or cultural arguments, others argued that sending military equipment was the way to aid China, or that Chinese immigration was the thin end of a wedge to open up more immigration that would damage the American economy.

The bill's quota of 105 was based on ethnicity, not national origin. This meant that Chinese coming from elsewhere, such as Latin America or other Asian countries, would count as part of the quota tally. An ethnicity-based immigration quota was not duplicated anywhere in Europe. When the committee reported its bill for House and Senate debates, the familiar arguments received a replay. National-security understandings continued their prominence. Even a southern immigration restrictionist saw the logic of this position. Echoing Pearl Buck, Representative Ed Lee Gossett (D–TX) argued that the bill "is not an immigration bill. This bill is a war measure and a peace measure."[141] The war measure passed.

As some southerners feared, soon after repeal of Chinese exclusion passed, in 1944 and 1945, members of Congress introduced new bills to allow for immigration from India, Korea, the Philippines, and Siam (Thailand). With the exception of the Philippines, there were very few persons with ancestry from these nations in America, little business interest, and even less lobbying. But the meaning of all Asian exclusion was changing, and resistance to reform was weakening. As with Chinese immigration, concerns over the new proposals regarding national security, foreign policy, and propaganda issues were paramount. After quoting from a Roosevelt statement on the war aims of the Allies, Representative Emmanuel Celler (D–NY) told the House that allowing Indian immigration and naturalization was important because oppressed nations looked to the "United States for justice and equality." The United States simply could not criticize Nazis and still completely exclude Indians. "Our breaking down of immigration and naturalization barriers may do much to dull the edge of this Jap propaganda against us and our Allies."[142] Congress needed little convincing and little debate. Hearings in 1945 gave the bill, granting India a quota of 105, near unanimous support.[143] Surprisingly, however, the House immigration committee decided to table the bill, but the White House lobbied for action, sending William Phillips, the president's representative to India, to offer secret testimony. This apparently convinced the committee to act. Though originally introduced in 1944 amid concerns of "Jap propaganda," the bill retained its usefulness for foreign policy purposes but was now also a weapon against Communist propaganda. The Senate version tacked on an amendment allowing Filipinos also to become naturalized citizens and granting them a quota of 100. Both houses passed the bill easily.[144] President Truman declared that the Philippines had a quota of 100 on July 8, 1946, four days after the Philippines became an independent nation.[145]

Congressional Parochialism: The McCarran-Walter Act

Reform momentum slowed, but only briefly. The next major immigration legislation was the McCarran-Walter Immigration and Naturalization Act of 1952. Named after its two Democrat chief sponsors, Senator Pat McCarran of Nevada and Representative Francis Walter of Pennsylvania, it was based on conflicting premises of national security. One was that total exclusion of some groups sacrificed American legitimacy and this damaged national security.[146] A more prominent concern was that America must closely monitor the political backgrounds of the immigrants that did enter the country for signs of disloyalty. The new law made no change to the overall discrimination framework. It created the "Asia-Pacific Triangle," assigning quotas of only one hundred to the nations of South and East Asia, and charging to their quotas immigration of persons of at least one-half Asian ancestry, even if they came to the US from Latin America or the Caribbean.[147]

The bill had its origins in a massive 1947 congressional study of immigration. Five years in the making, the report disavowed Nordic superiority, avoided overt racist language, but declared the ethnic discrimination desirable "to best preserve the sociological and cultural balance in the population of the United States."[148] An alternative bill proposed by liberal Democrats offered little better for disfavored ethnic groups. It retained the national origins formula, and would allow few Asians to enter the United States. Since both bills ended total Asian exclusion and would allow all Asians who did enter to become naturalized citizens, and since McCarran-Walter had a greater chance of passing, Asian American groups joined southern Democrats and supported McCarran-Walter.[149] Though the "Asia-Pacific Triangle" concept had racist premises, the State Department was satisfied that the bill would end all Asian exclusion and also supported McCarran-Walter.[150] As Dean Acheson told President Truman, "Our failure to remove racial barriers provides the Kremlin with unlimited political and propaganda capital for use against us in Japan and the entire Far East."[151]

President Truman vetoed the bill, demanding that the entire national origins model be scrapped and objecting strongly to the internal security measures of the bill. Congress, however, promptly overrode the veto and the bill became law on June 27, 1952. Perhaps going beyond the normal powers of a lame-duck president, Truman then created a President's Commission on Immigration and Naturalization on September 4 to examine (and promote) the need for further immigration reform.

Though not running for president, Truman continued to support reform, as did Republican candidate Dwight Eisenhower.[152] The Truman commission's report, issued January 1, 1953, kept the pressure on. It devoted much space to the redefinition of an open, nondiscriminatory, and friendly immigration policy as a measure of national security. It based its conclusions on principles that mirrored those of the Truman committee for black equal rights. That is, immigrants from all lands should be welcomed for moral, economic, and foreign-policy/national-security reasons.

Titled *Whom We Shall Welcome,* the report argued that in hearings held across the country, the commission discovered a basic consensus for reform of immigration that was at odds with the McCarran-Walter Act. The new immigration policy should abolish the national-origins system, set an over-all maximum annual quota for immigration that "should reflect the needs and capacity for absorption of the United States" (this figure was said to be 250,000 in 1952), and base priorities on emergency situations abroad "such as continued distress and suffering among refugees, expellees, escapees, displaced persons and other victims of communism and other forms of totalitarianism."[153]

The economic reasoning did not offer clear support for ending national-origins discrimination. It was Chapter 3 of the report, on "Immigration and Our Foreign Policy," that contained the note of urgency and arguments categorizing discrimination as national security. The commission argued that Japanese exclusion in the 1924 Immigration Act "contributed to the growth of the nationalistic, militaristic, and anti-American movement in Japan which culminated in war against the United States." The Japanese ambassador had warned that the exclusion could have serious consequences, and Secretary of State Charles Evans Hughes had similarly warned Congress that it should not "affront a friendly nation" with a stigma such as total exclusion.[154] The commission then extended this line of argument to the present situation in which the United States, as a world leader, should show "a decent respect to the opinions of mankind" if it wanted to win the struggle against Communism.[155]

The report buttressed this view with strong support from a variety of participants at hearings, from labor organizations to women's organizations to religious organizations to officers of the foreign service. This last group made arguments virtually identical to those used to support civil rights for black Americans. Secretary of State Dean Acheson maintained that "our immigration policy, with respect to particular national or racial groups, will inevitably be taken as an indication of our general attitude toward them, especially as an indication of our appraisal of their standing in the world." W. Averell Harriman, director of Mutual Security, argued that "the kind of immigration policy we adopt is a factor in the world struggle between democracy and totalitarianism." The U.S. special representative in Europe, William H. Draper, said that "in endeavoring to strengthen the economic and military defense of the free world, and particularly of the North Atlantic Community, we should recognize immigration policy as one of the elements in achieving economic and political stability as well as social equilibrium." Edward M. O'Connor, consultant to the Psychological Strategy Board, also argued that immigration policy was an important foreign policy tool and "must at all times, and particularly in times of international crisis, be geared to a dynamic, purposeful, and farsighted policy of world leadership."[156]

The categorization of immigration policy as national security was successful in part because these meaning entrepreneurs could point out that, like the Japanese, Communists in Asia used the exclusions against the United States in propaganda, such as in a July 5, 1952 message that Radio Moscow broadcast in Korean. This message stated that the McCarran-Walter Act "is very similar to the Nazi theory of racial superiority" because of the "inferior category" used for Asian people, which also spread prejudice against Asians among the American people.[157] Acheson claimed that current American policy would lead to resentment and suspicion in Asia and that new quotas in West Indian former colonies had led to resolutions denouncing the new American law. The law was feeding the "propaganda mill" in emerging African nations and resentments in Europe, especially in Italy and Greece.[158] The report also alleged that American propaganda encouraged or lured people behind the Iron Curtain to try to escape, but the current law did not allow them to enter America.

Refugee Admissions as National Security

In vetoing McCarran-Walter, a major concern of Truman's was his desire for an immigration policy that would allow entry of refugees from Communist countries in Eastern Europe (he created his own President's Escapee Program in 1952 to help those fleeing Communism).[159] A presidential desire for open admissions for refugees from Communism was constant throughout the Cold War. Refugees then had a national-security meaning. American openness to this category of immigrants was a sign to the world audience that America respected human rights and had the superior political system. Thus, the perceived national-security imperatives of Cold War competition cast the McCarran-Walter restrictions into oblivion. Refugees, let in the through legal loopholes, would significantly shape immigration policy because national security favored certain populations—those coming from Communist countries.[160] Each refugee admission from a Communist country was a Cold War victory, and buttressed the American system. From the 1950s through the 1970s, Hungarians, Cubans, and Indochinese, among others, became Americans without lobbying or grassroots mobilization.

Congress, despite the passage of McCarren-Walter, understood the national security purpose of refugees. As Republican senator Alexander Wiley of Wisconsin declared in 1948, refugee policy was an "ideological weapon in our ideological war against the forces of darkness, the forces of Communist tyranny."[161] Representative Harold Donohue (D–MA) explained, "In world leadership we can speak more convincingly for freedom everywhere when we have done our fair share to bring real freedom to those who have suffered most." Representative John Fogarty (D–RI) chimed in: "We do ourselves and our democracy a great deal of good by show[ing] to all the world that we are in truth champions of freedom and that we shall aid all those who rally to our cause."[162] One result of this concern, the Displaced Persons Act of 1948, let in four hundred thousand refugees from Eastern Europe.[163]

It was thus not only the White House that saw refugee admission as a matter of national-security policy. The admission of refugees for the purposes of foreign policy had strong, consistent support, converting even die-hard immigration restrictionists. As the Cold War heated up, Congress gave increasing support for the International Refugee Organization and the principle of a selectively open refugee policy.

The pattern continued in the Eisenhower administration. Eisenhower, like the presidents before him, favored fairer immigration and in the Cold War context he was able to find loopholes for refugee admissions as part of his war strategy.[164] In 1953, only a year after McCarren-Walter, Congress passed the Refugee Relief Act, allowing for more than two hundred thousand persons fleeing Communism to enter the United States outside the quota system.[165] Eisenhower supported the policy for reasons of national security. A National Security Council memo identified the Refugee Relief Act as a way to "inflict a psychological blow on Communism" and drain away brain power.[166] Increasingly, Republicans also saw refugee policy as a cheap and easy way to appeal to ethnic voters.[167]

In 1956 and 1957, the United States admitted thirty-eight thousand Hungarians who fled their country after an attempted revolution—encouraged by the Eisenhower administration—failed. The Hungarians had expected military support from the Americans, but received nothing. More than two hundred thousand left, settling in a wide variety of countries. Eisenhower was able to exploit a loophole in McCarran-Walter that allowed the attorney general to use a "parole" power to admit special cases of nonquota immigrants. Once admitted, Eisenhower then arranged to have a President's Committee for Hungarian Refugee Relief create housing and job opportunities in the communities where the Hungarians settled.[168]

The categorization of refugees as elements of national security is also clear in the response of the Kennedy administration and the Congress to the Cuban refugees. Kennedy established the Cuban Refugee Program on February 3, 1961, which built on the precedent of Eisenhower's policies regarding the Hungarians, but offered more. Kennedy's program "provided reception, resettlement, welfare payments, job and language training, help in a job search outside of Miami, education support (including subsidized college loans), and health care services, well above what was available then to U.S. citizens and residents or to other migrants to the United States."[169] The US government offered *very* generous means for Cuban exiles to enter the United States: there were twice daily flights from Havana to Miami on Pan Am Airlines, and flights twice weekly on KLM. Both airlines would forward ticketed passengers' names to the government for a visa "waiver"; these passengers were granted indefinite parole six months after arrival. Only 1 percent faced rejection.[170]

Toward the 1965 Reform

Politically, the Hungarian and Cuban refugee programs appeared to have been achieved easily. The State Department initiated action, the president approved, and Congress added a rubber stamp when necessary.[171] The strategic welcoming of refugees from Communist lands and other exceptions left the national-origins system in tatters. It existed on paper, and frustrated many would-be immigrants, especially from Asia, but it hardly existed in practice. No one looking at the origins of the persons actually admitted would have concluded that the system was based on Nordic preference from Europe and selective immigration from Latin America for cheap labor. As a result it became increasingly easier to support the formal abolishment of the national-origins system. After the perceived imperatives for national security prompted immigration reform in the 1950s, it merged into normal interest-group politics as ethnic organizations began to lobby Congress.[172] By the early 1960s, ending discrimination on the basis of national origin was a way to appeal to the ethnic groups that were disadvantaged by the current system. The success of the black civil rights movement further eroded the legitimacy of national origin discrimination in immigration. During the 1960 election, both parties supported immigration reform in their national party platforms.[173]

"Such a system is an anachronism": Reform efforts in the Kennedy and Johnson administrations

Like the two presidents before him, President Kennedy lent the prestige of his office to the cause of immigration reform. He was a supporter of immigration (he even published a book on the subject in 1958),[174] and was almost certainly aware of the electoral benefits of immigration reform. The State Department pressed for change as it did with black civil rights.[175] By 1961, various nationality groups, especially Chinese, Polish, and Italian groups, were regularly sending letters in support of immigration reform.[176]

While Kennedy and the State Department wanted reform, the initiative for legislation came in the person of Democratic Senator Philip A. Hart of Michigan, who urged support for his bill from the Kennedy administration. Before he submitted his bill in 1963, Hart asked Kennedy aide Theodore Sorensen for help in the form of a section on immigration reform for the coming state of the union address. Hart informed Sorensen that the numbers of immigrants admitted were less important than having "a system which will select the best immigrants without prejudice because of race or nationality." Hart claimed his bill had "the support of the major religious groups in the country, Protestant, Catholic and Jewish, and has been formally endorsed by a number of official bodies in each of them. I believe that this is the first time that a concensus [sic] on immigration policy has been reached by these groups." Worried about arguments that stressed the negative economic impacts of immigrants, Hart requested that the Labor Department develop material on the relationship between immigration and employment.[177]

The irrationalities created by the national-security/refugee policy created a new climate for reform and added momentum to the struggle. When Hart submitted his immigration reform bill in February of 1963, he was able to claim that reform would "update our basic statute to conform more with our actual practice since 1952." Of the 2.5 million foreigners who had been admitted since that year, 1.5 million were nonquota immigrants, including 750,000 refugees (the others being the immediate relatives of US citizens or resident aliens or those coming from independent Western Hemisphere nations). At the same time, one-third of the 1.5 million authorized quota visas were not even used by northern and western European countries. The cumulative effect of the various temporary admissions policies was that "the act of 1952 is no longer an accurate measure of American policy."[178]

In addition, Hart now had an impressive list of supporters of immigration reform to put into the record. Hart and the numerous sponsors of the bill worked closely with a new organization called the American Immigration and Citizenship Conference. This group included the American Civil Liberties Union, twelve Jewish organizations, nine Christian organizations, three Italian groups, three labor unions, and a large number of international organizations, refugee support groups, and other nationality groups.[179] By April, Hart staffer William B. Welsh was informing the Kennedy administration of the coordinated effort to sell the bill, with various senators making speeches in Detroit, Toledo, New York, Bridgeport, and along the West Coast.[180]

Kennedy joined the effort with his own bill and a letter to Congress on July 23, 1963. He explained that "the most urgent and fundamental reform" was elimination of discrimination. Reform would not solve all problems, but

> it will, however, provide a sound basis upon which we can build in developing an immigration law that serves the national interest and reflects in every detail the principles of equality and human dignity to which our nation subscribes . . . The use of a national origins system is without basis in either logic or reason. It neither satisfies a national need nor accomplishes an international purpose. In an age of interdependence among nations, such a system is an anachronism, for it discriminates among applicants for admission into the United States on the basis of accident of birth.[181]

The Kennedy bill would eliminate the national-origin quotas incrementally by transferring each country's quota into a world quota pool. These quotas would be allocated on a first-come, first-served plan. Fifty percent of these quotas would go to persons with special skills or training, 30 percent to unmarried sons and daughters of US citizens who were ineligible for nonquota status because they were over the age of twenty-one, and 20 percent to spouses and children of aliens already granted permanent residence.[182]

The State Department continued to be an important influence on the process, stressing the foreign-policy and national-security implications of nondiscrimination in immigration. A State Department proposal pointed out that though most nations in the Western Hemisphere did not have quotas as an "outgrowth of our good neighbor policy," McCarran-Walter made sure that newly independent nations such as Jamaica had minimum quotas, and "this has become a highly charged political issue in Jamaica since its independence." The State Department also carried out a study of the effects of the elimination of the discrimination against Asia with the cooperation of American missions and "certain key consular posts," concluding that

> as far as the impact of the proposed change on the foreign relations of the United States is concerned, the great majority of posts reported that the change would have a most favorable effect on our posture abroad . . . The uniformly favorable reports are not limited to countries with a large Asian population but include such areas as Finland and Ireland. Some posts which anticipate a favorable reaction from the enactment of the proposed change, stress the potentially adverse effect if the proposed becomes a matter of public record and is not acted upon favorably by the Congress. Observations to this effect were made by: Abidjan, Asuncion, Brazzaville, Cairo, Hong Kong, Montevideo, New Delhi, and Tripoli.[183]

Kennedy would not live to see reform, but his successor Lyndon Johnson maintained the pattern of past presidents in supporting reform, as did Secretary of State Dean Rusk in 1964 congressional hearings. Rusk pointed out that the national origins system "results in discrimination in our hospitality to different nationalities in a world situation which is quite different from that which existed at the time the national origins system was originally adopted."[184] Rusk would make the familiar foreign-policy arguments, but in 1964, there were differences. For one, there was the momentum supplied by the black civil rights movement: "We in the United States have learned to judge our fellow Americans on the basis of their ability, industry, intelligence, integrity and all the other factors which truly determine a man's value to society."[185] In addition, there was the irrationality of maintaining the national-origin quotas while the government simultaneously admitted hundreds of thousands of refugees from some of those disfavored countries. Rusk saw that the exigencies of American foreign policy had already created immigration policy that disregarded national origins. Various refugee and other measures meant that "only 34 percent of the 2,599,349 immigrants who came to the United States from 1953 through 1962 were quota immigrants."[186]

Eliminating that national-origins system, and especially the racist program for Asia, would therefore eliminate a millstone and fight enemy propaganda while only technically changing policy. Rusk explained, "We deprive ourselves of a powerful weapon in our fight against misinformation if we do not reconcile here, too, the letter of the law with the facts of immigration and thus erase the unfavorable impression made by our old quota limitation for Asian persons."[187] Reform would answer complaints heard around the world:

> I would say that more than a dozen foreign ministers . . . have spoken to me in the past year, not about the practicalities of immigration from their country to ours, but about the principle which they interpret as discrimination against their particular countries.
>
> In other words, they seem to be more concerned about the principle than about the actual immigration, because this is picked up by people unfriendly to the United States and made an issue in their countries, and because of this, it causes political disturbances in the good relations which we would hope to establish. This has been a matter of frequent discussion by me with foreign ministers of other countries.[188]

Abba Schwartz, a prominent aide in the Kennedy administration during its efforts at immigration reform, sent a copy of Rusk's testimony to Jack Valenti, gushing, "As I indicated to you on the telephone, the Secretary was brilliant and made a great impression not only with this statement but in answer to the questions posed to him during one and a half hours."[189]

The final push

If national security was not enough motivation, the desire to eliminate a contradiction with the drive for black civil rights was an added interest for Johnson. He linked immigration reform and black civil rights in his 1964 state of the union address, and the new vice president, Hubert H. Humphrey, also made the analogy.[190] Thus, while World War II and the Cold War both contributed new national-security meanings to black civil rights and immigration reform, the two policies also interacted with each other. Immigrants were analogous to blacks and deserved the same equality guarantees.

The timing for reform was otherwise auspicious. Both parties again supported reform in their 1964 platforms. The deaths of the major Democratic supporters of national-origins discrimination, McCarran and Walter, removed major stumbling blocks in Congress. McCarran had died in 1953, and Walter died a decade later. McCarran's replacement at the head of the Senate immigration subcommittee was Mississippian James O. Eastland, who was also hostile to reform. But Walter's replacement atop the House Judiciary Immigration and Nationality Subcommittee was Michael Feighan, and the Ohio Democrat was more willing to compromise. This led to discussions characterized by logrolling and tinkering with the provisions of the bill. Contention centered around preferences for skills versus family reunification (a possible proxy for national-origins preferences, given the relatively smaller numbers of disfavored groups then in the population), and whether or not the Western Hemisphere would be included in an overall immigration quota.

Momentum for reform was strengthened by the formation of the National Committee for Immigration Reform. It included two former presidents (Truman and Eisenhower) and some leading figures of corporate America, among them Robert Murphy, chair of Corning Glass International, who was also a former under secretary of state and US ambassador. George Meany, president of the AFL-CIO, was a member of the organization, as well as a host of ethnic organizations. The group worked as high-profile meaning entrepreneurs, giving its support for reform in global and national-security terms, but also emphasizing an interest in immigrants' well-being. At a June 1965 news conference, Murphy called reform "a three-pronged weapon that can help to wage the peace":

> First, it will reveal to the world at large that humanitarianism is a foremost principle in our American tradition. The moral principle involved in family reunion is one in which we believe.
>
> Second, I feel that this long overdue reform can make an important contribution in our relations with other countries. It can prove to the world that we are determined to ban ethnic and racial bigotry.
>
> Third, it is to our own best self-interest in gaining skills to advance our scientific and technical progress . . .
>
> It is difficult for me to believe that any American fears the small numerical increase in immigrants who will come into this country under the Administration's proposal. The issue is not one of numbers—the issue is *how* we bring these people in.[191]

In its published materials, the National Committee for Immigration Reform stated as its first reason for reform that "by discriminating among nations on the basis of birthplace, the national origins provision is detrimental to our international interests, breeds hatred and hostility towards the United States, blocks comity among nations, and is a hindrance to our nation's policy of peace among nations, without serving any national need or serving any international purpose of the United States."[192] This group worked closely with the Johnson administration—Johnson even thanked Murphy for forming the group—helping with the public relations campaign.[193]

As Gabriel Chin has shown, members of Congress supporting reform also continued to voice the same arguments used in 1943 categorizing immigration reform as a national-security measure. A new twist were the links to the growing struggle in Vietnam, a nation with a quota of only one hundred. For example, Tip O'Neill (D–MA) pointed out that "current policy . . . presents the ironic situation in which we are willing to send our American youth to aid these people in their struggle against Communist aggression while at the same time, we are indicating that they are not good enough to be Americans."[194]

What did the American people want? Some ethnic groups and citizens groups were pushing the new law.[195] The State Department assembled a summary of American newspaper editorial opinions, showing an overwhelming majority of newspapers offering support for immigration reform, usually stressing the simple injustice of McCarran-Walter, the need for equality, and the need for rationality, as the current policy was "a crazy quilt."[196]

Public opinion polls showed majority support for reform. When a July 1965 Gallup poll asked "What is the most important criterion for admitting new immigrants to the U.S.?" those favoring occupational skills numbered 71 percent, having relatives in the United States was selected by 55 percent, and country in which one was born was chosen by only 33 percent. In response to the question "The U.S. currently has a quota system based on the country of origin. Should this policy be changed to one of occupational skills rather than the country in which the immigrant was born?" the numbers for reform were somewhat less overwhelming, but a still-solid 50 percent chose "should change." Thirty-three percent said "should not change" and 17 percent had no opinion. On the issue of whether or not immigration should be kept at the present level, 40 percent said yes, only 7 percent wanted an increase; 32 percent said decrease, while 20 percent chose "don't know."[197]

Who still supported discrimination in immigration? There was little organized lobbying against the reform bill. Only two small conservative groups lobbied against reform—the Liberty League and the American Committee on Immigration Policies.[198] A State Department report showed that some conservative publications, including the *Washington Star* newspaper and the *U.S. News and World Report,* as well as smaller newspapers challenged the national-security meanings of immigration.[199] Conservatives in Congress expressed similar doubts about the need for nondiscrimination, also tending to deny the national-security meanings rather than defend discrimination. For example, the section for minority views in the Senate report on the 1965 immigration bill (H.R. 2580), written by southern Democrats James O. Eastland (D–MS) and John L. McClellan (D–AK), asked:

> Why is it that of all the nations of the world the United States is the only one that must answer to the rest of the world and be apologetic about its

immigration policy? Certainly no other country that we are aware of seems to be concerned about its "image" in other countries. All other countries consider their self-interest first. They are realists, who are far too astute to compromise their own national interests in quest of an illusionary and vague "symbol" in the eyes of the rest of the world.[200]

But the United States was not like other countries any more. It aspired for world leadership in the fight against Communism by trying to prove its system was superior to that of the Soviet Union. Unlike the State Department and each president since World War II, Eastland and McClellan were insulated from the front lines of that battle. They did not perceive the stinging propaganda highlighting American discrimination and its national-security implications. By 1965, immigration reform was an idea whose time had come. Support for discrimination in the middle 1960s was, as Kennedy had said, an anachronism. It still existed, but had to be hidden to maintain legitimacy in mainstream politics.

Feighan, chair of the House subcommittee on immigration, was finally willing to compromise and bargain. Assistant Attorney General Norbert Schlei told President Johnson that

> Mr. Feighan appears to be looking for a way to justify a vote to abolish the national origins system. The justification has to make sense to the traditional supporters of the national origins system (veterans groups, patriotic societies, conservative nationality groups, etc.), whom Mr. Feighan regards as his constituency. He wants to be able to say that in return for scrapping the national origins system-which never really worked anyway—he has gotten a system that for the first time in our history puts a limit on *all* immigration, not just immigration from "quota" areas (original emphasis).[201]

Such a compromise would be problematic, however, for geopolitical reasons. Valenti told Johnson, "According to Secretary Rusk, if we go along with Feighan we will vex and dumbfound our Latin American friends, who will now be sure we are in final retreat from Pan Americanism. The immigration project, on top of Santo Domingo [where the United States was then intervening in a revolution], will be, in the opinion of Rusk too much too quick for them to take." Rusk suggested adding a line to the bill: "In the event total immigration goes beyond 350,000 annually, the President is requested to make recommendations to the Congress." Valenti explained, "What this will do is keep non-quota status for Latin America—but allow Feighan to tell his right-wing friends that the Congress and the President will act if immigration looks like it is getting out of hand."[202]

Opponents of reform, such as Sam Ervin (D–NC), also wanted more pref- erence given to family reunification than for job skills, not for humanitarian reasons but because this would more likely preserve America's ethnic mix.[203] In the end, opponents of reform such as Feighan, the southern Democrats like Eastland, Ervin, and McClellan, and Republican leader Everett Dirksen, were able to gain concessions from the Johnson administration, including the limits on Western Hemisphere immigration and the first preference going to family ties.[204]

Nearly everyone agreed that the preference for families over skills would work to preserve America's ethnic mix without overt discrimination. In a September 17, 1965 letter to Senator Thomas Kuchel (R–CA), the Japanese American Citizens League leader Mike Masaoka expressed both strong sup- port for the bill but also his "fear" regarding its consequences. It would allow the immigration pattern to "remain approximately as it is—and has been— because of past restrictions and exclusions of those of Asian ancestry." Since the bill would give so much preference to family reunification ("74 percent of the authorized annual numerical ceiling from Old World countries shall be made available to members and close relatives of American citizen and resi- dent alien families" while "only 26 percent is available for professionals, for skilled and unskilled labor in short supply, and for 'conditional entries' or refugees"), and since "the total Asian population of the United States is only about one-half of one percent of the total American population," then "the very arithmetic of past immigration now precludes any substantial gain in actual immigration opportunities for the Japanese, Chinese and other Asians."[205] Masaoka was willing to look beyond this problem for his national- ity group and still support the bill, and paraded his indignation to allay the concerns of those who wished to exclude more like him.

In the final version of the bill, the national-origins system was to be com- pletely eliminated over a three-year period, as national quotas were gradually transferred to an open pool of visas. There was now an overall quota of 120,000 visas for Western Hemisphere immigrants without regard to coun- try and 170,000 for Eastern Hemisphere immigrants with a limit of 20,000 on every nation. These quotas did not count immediate relatives (minor un- married children, spouses, and parents of a US citizen). Preference classes emphasizing family reunification divided up the quota of 170,000 Eastern Hemisphere immigrants. Seventy-four percent of all quota immigrants were restricted to family members of US citizens or resident aliens. Ten percent of quota visas went to professionals or persons with special talents or education, and another 10 percent to skilled or unskilled laborers filling a specified la- bor need in the United States. The remaining 6 percent went to refugees fleeing a Communist or Communist-dominated country or from the Middle

East, but the law also allowed refugees admittance under parole without limitation.[206]

The Immigration Act of 1965 is strangely neglected in studies of American politics and minority rights. Even major figures instrumental to its passage appear to think little of it. Momentous and hard fought, it is not discussed at all in Johnson's memoirs of his presidency—not a single mention.[207] Dean Rusk, a star player in its passage, gave the topic only one paragraph in his memoirs, saying, "We at State helped promote it."[208]

Still, it was a major policy development—much more so than was intended, as discussed in Chapter 10. The point here, however, is that reform happened at about the same time as other major nondiscrimination laws and declarations in America and in the UN. By mostly benefiting Asians, it benefited a group that, in the initial stages at least, were unlike African Americans in that they were tiny parts of the population, promised few electoral benefits, and did not mass mobilize. But regardless of party, presidents and State Department officials were active players in the reform of immigration; mindful of foreign propaganda, they therefore saw nondiscrimination in immigration as they did black civil rights—as national-security policy.

The Cold War and Equal Rights in Other Nations: The Soviet Union's Minority-Rights Strategy

Another comparison highlights the importance of equal rights as national-security policy. If race and ethnic equality was categorized as national-security policy for the United States in part because of the struggle for world leadership, we would expect the same to be true for the Soviet Union. The important question to ask is simple: Did the Soviet Union try to present itself to the world as a committed racial and ethnic egalitarian?

The answer is yes. While a full analysis is beyond the scope of this study, available evidence suggests that the Soviet leaders tried hard to give the impression of ethnic equality in the USSR, using some of the same strategies of the United States and many original strategies as well. The goal was to actively demonstrate to the world that the Communists, not the capitalists, offered the road to modernity that respected norms of racial and ethnic equality.

The leaders of the Soviet Union, faced with overseeing a multiethnic society, had in fact preached equal rights for minorities since its founding. This could be seen in Leninist nationality policy, which justified a value on ethnic harmony in the USSR. Lenin argued for equal treatment and a respect for national differences while trying to build international proletarian solidarity.[209] As Frederick Barghoorn and Thomas Remington have written, "Internationalism—meaning tolerance and brotherly affection for peoples other than one's own in the Soviet Union—[was] a cornerstone of political indoctrination."[210]

After the revolution, according to the proud Soviet representative at a UN seminar on the "multinational society," the Soviet leaders told Muslims and peoples of the USSR's eastern republics that

> from now on, your beliefs, your customs, your national and cultural institutions, which were repressed by the Czarist authorities, are free and inviolable. Organize your national life freely and without any hindrance. You are entitled to this. You should know that your rights, as well as the rights of all the peoples of Russia, are guaranteed by the might of the Revolution and its organs—the Soviets of workers, soldiers, and peasant deputies.[211]

Though this statement is an exaggeration, it shows that the Soviets knew how to exaggerate strategically. And with those words—they claimed—came actions. The new government leaders, for example, made anti-Semitic activities a crime.[212] The Soviets appeared to be precocious multiculturalists and protectors of language rights. They gave rights to preserve ethnic cultures, and the 1936 Constitution promised a right to education in a person's native language.[213] While not always respectful of cultural differences, the central government made a major effort to industrialize the Asian republics and to bring literacy to the peoples there. Certainly, great efforts were needed—only 0.5 percent of the Kirghiz and 2 percent of the Kazakhs could read in 1900. The Soviet leaders built schools in these areas and succeeded in making the populations literate.[214] The central government moved such major industries as textiles, paper factories, sawmills, and canneries from Russia to far-flung republics including Georgia, Armenia, Azerbaijan, and Turkmenistan, among others.[215] The Soviet representative proudly told the UN seminar on the multinational society seminar that between 1913 and 1964, industrial output had increased by a factor of 42 in Byelorussia, 41 in Tajikistan, 72 in Kazakhstan, and 26 in Turkmenistan.[216]

In politics, Slavic citizens, especially Great Russians, were overrepresented in the Politbureau and the Secretariat of the Party (the main power centers of the Communist Party). They constituted 75 percent of these bodies in the years 1919–62, but only 54.6 percent of the population. However, Lenin feared a lack of prestige in Asia if the USSR did not integrate its elites.[217] Allaying this concern was a federal system that ensured representation of the Asian minorities. Russians were actually underrepresented in the Supreme Soviet, the main lawmaking body.[218]

Egalitarian efforts on behalf of the USSR's ethnic groups were a celebrated part of Soviet policy, understood to have a national-security meaning. Nikita Khrushchev wrote in a 1949 *Pravda* article titled "Stalinist Friendship of Peoples, Guarantee of Our Motherland's Invincibility" that "all the peoples of the world see the fraternal friendship of the peoples of the USSR . . . as a great example for them. They are becoming convinced that the Soviet, the Stalin way, of solving the national question is the only correct way." Similarly, Lavrenty P. Beria, a member of the Central Committee of the Communist Party, made a prominent speech at the Nineteenth Party Congress in October 1952 extolling the condition of the non-Russian peoples in the USSR by contrasting the central Asian Soviet republics with Egypt, Turkey, Iran, and many others. He argued that the world saw in the Soviet Union the path "from the denial of rights to freedom and independence, from discord and enmity among nations to fraternal friendship among peoples, from hunger and poverty to a prosperous life, from illiteracy and cultural backwardness to the flowering of culture, science and the arts."[219]

In the 1950s, the Soviets tried hard to impress foreigners—especially Asian and African peoples—with the Communist commitment to ethnic minority rights. Of course, the USSR and other Communist countries had been trying to impress visitors generally for decades, often going to great trouble and expense to ensure hospitality and selective exposure to prestige-enhancing aspects of Communist life.[220] What was new in the years following World War II, especially during the 1950s, was the attention given to people of color.

Soviet leaders devoted great effort and expense creating propaganda to show the Soviets' un-imperialistic respect for peoples of the developing world (the Soviets preferred this term to "Third World," which they only used in quotation marks).[221] Part of this strategy was to take Asian and African observers to witness the relatively good conditions in the minority areas of Transcaucasia, Central Asia, and Siberia; also they often sent Soviet citizens of Asian ethnicities to Asian and African nations as technical specialists[222] and in cultural exchanges.[223]

India and Indonesia were two giant nations that were important strategically and seemed especially vulnerable to Communist propaganda. Khrushchev seized every opportunity to appeal to these countries. He told the Indian parliament in 1955 of the equal rights given to Soviet citizens "regardless of nationality" and that rights violations committed on the grounds of "race or nationality" were "punished by law." In Indonesia, Khrushchev invited students to "come to the Soviet Union and see . . . how our country lives and develops," emphasizing that "more than one hundred nationalities and peoples live as one family" (this was clearly a statement no American president could make). During a 1960 visit to Indonesia, Khrushchev again trumpeted the equal rights in the fifteen Soviet republics. Similar to the American State Department's diversity strategy, he pointed out that his entourage contained Russians, Byelorussians, and representatives of the Ukraine, Azerbaidzhan, Tadzhikistan, Georgia, Armenia, and other republics.[224]

Soviet leaders devised elaborate youth exchange and friendship programs, including the Afro-Asian People's Solidarity Organization and various other Third World friendship societies, to ensure that Africans and Asians could see the USSR for themselves. The themes of the Soviet friendship societies and other forays into multiculturalism were celebrations of diversity, the dignity of nonwhites, and equal human rights. In April of 1959, the USSR created the Soviet Association of Friendship with African Peoples to "arrange meetings, social events, talks, and exhibitions devoted to the national holidays of the African peoples, to anniversaries of people outstanding in the cultural field in Africa, and to other important events in the life of the African nations."[225] In 1970 the USSR began to sponsor a biannual Festival of Afro-Asian and Latin American Film Makers, and sponsored regular meetings of African and Asian writers. These meetings always took place in the Asiatic Soviet republics, and were always exploited for propaganda purposes, stressing Soviet respect for nonwhite peoples. An internationally distributed magazine quoted an obviously happy Senegalese delegate at the 1972 festival who stated, "The very existence of the Soviet state helps the young African states to hold their own against imperialism and to develop everything on our own continent which can be called progressive."[226]

Like the United States, the USSR also sought to make its capital a welcome place for non-Western peoples. It was during the 1955 visit to Indonesia that Soviet officials announced the establishment in Moscow of a special university—called the University of the Friendship of the Peoples—exclusively intended for African, Asian, and Latin American students. The government changed the school's name in 1961 to Patrice Lumumba Friendship University. The new name was to honor the anti-Western prime minister of the Congo who assumed power after Belgium relinquished colonial control, and whom the Soviets alleged was then murdered in a CIA plot.[227] Similar to the efforts to make Washington the "showplace of democracy," Soviet leaders also tried to promote Moscow to uncommitted India as an "international meeting place."[228]

Friendly overtures to people of color were not limited to visits to Third World countries or visits by Africans, Asians, or Latin Americans to the USSR. The Soviet Union engaged in a costly program of military and economic aid to nations fighting colonialism. The amount of aid was so great that the historian Gerald Horne has commented that "this assistance to those fighting racialized systems of oppression was no small factor in sparking an economic and political crisis that led to the collapse of the USSR."[229] The Soviet leaders also used the UN and its peripheral institutions to present itself as honoring racial equality. Inis Claude Jr. has written of the consistent support for minority rights from the Communist countries in the Soviet bloc, stating, "The Soviet Union has been an indefatigable producer of draft formulations of minority rights and of speeches extolling the virtues of Soviet nationality policy, representing the minority rights movement in the United Nations as an effort to universalize the benefits enjoyed by Soviet minorities, and scolding its opponents for claiming to worry about the security risks involved in such an innocuous matter as allowing minorities to speak their own language and maintain their own schools."[230] Soviet UN representatives submitted almost all of their proposals with attacks on the US treatment of minorities.[231]

In November of 1964, Moscow was able to host a UNESCO-sponsored seminar at which twenty-two biologists, geneticists, and anthropologists signed an historic statement denying that human behavior was linked to race.[232] In 1960, during trips to the UN in New York City, both Khrushchev and Cuba's Fidel Castro visited Harlem. Khrushchev pointed out the fact (well known to American officials) that African and Asian delegates were subjected to racial discrimination, and argued that therefore the UN should be moved from New York.[233]

In short, the Soviet Union adopted—and even went beyond—many of the same strategies as did the United States to show the world its commitment to the equality of ethnic groups. This is exactly what one would expect if a world culture of human rights shaped national-security interests embedded in racial equality.

Conclusion

The categorization of black civil rights as a matter of national security was a major development for the minority rights revolution. For the first time, there was a reason and interest beside that of simple justice for progressives and conservatives, Democrats and Republicans, northerners and southerners to support ethnic and racial equality. Many, especially parochial political figures in the south, still resisted, but now they were standing up against the world and—as Everett Dirksen said—the tide of history. America and the world changed together.

Were arguments connecting equal rights and national security only rhetoric, a verbal window dressing? Did the shift to equal rights result only from the domestic social movement that sought them and the increasing electoral benefits of support for black civil rights that came with the great migration northward? The case for an independent effect of the national-security categorization is strengthened when we see that World War II and the Cold War helped minorities who were not black and did not have either significant electoral power or a social movement. Skillful meaning entrepreneurs linked national security and nondiscrimination to pursue reform of America's discriminatory immigration laws, helping at first the Chinese, where electoral benefits were miniscule, and later other Asians and immigrants from eastern and southern Europe. American Cold War propaganda strategy in the 1950s and 1960s reinforced these efforts, shaping a strategically open refugee policy that further undermined continuing national-origin discrimination in immigration policy. By the middle of the 1960s, concerns over national security combined with the analogy drawn between immigrant rights and black civil rights to ease passage of Immigration Act of 1965.

A cross-national comparison shows that the United States was not alone in supporting minority-rights efforts aimed for world display. But not every nation should be expected to see ethnic equality in terms of national security.[234] World War II and the Cold War imbued human rights with strong national-security meanings, but nations were not simply complying with norms to symbolize modernity and be accepted as members of the modern international community. If so, South Africa would have ended apartheid sooner than it did. World attention focused most on nations seeking global leadership, and it was these nations that pursued international propaganda strategies. The United States and the Soviet Union were under the most pressure, and developing nations (which mainly played the role of audience) the least. That the Soviet Union tried to show its legitimacy on the matter of minority rights in ways similar to the American efforts suggests the importance of these cultural factors.

A few questions remain regarding the ways national-security meanings facilitated policy development. First, was the dynamic limited to ethnic rights, or did policies in areas outside of nondiscrimination rights find greater fortunes when defined as national security? Second, why did national security meanings of nondiscrimination rights decline in the late 1960s?

Not all of the domestic policies emerging from perceived national-security imperatives were related to equal rights for blacks or other ethnic groups. Wartime has been a period for domestic federal policy growth and development throughout the history of the United States.[235] But as the sociologist Gregory Hooks has written, World War II produced a shift that continued throughout the Cold War from a concern for "defense" to "national security." The difference is that the latter meant that "U.S. strategic interests are at stake in developments throughout the world, even when U.S. sovereignty was in no way threatened."[236] With the role of the federal government in areas of national security unquestioned, policies that could be defined as national-security measures had an advantage over others.

In a direct way, of course, lavishly funded military bases had beneficial effects on some local and regional economies.[237] Money poured into projects said to promote national security. Many are unknown today, while others made a lasting impact. One of these, a computer networking system called ARPANET, became the foundation for the Internet and allowed the explosive growth of the Internet-based economy thirty years later.[238]

The national-security gravy train went to areas further removed but still understood as national security. As Michael Sherry commented, "The Cold War and other great-power rivalries had long been waged as total struggles embracing all forms of power, but now the embrace seemed bigger than ever—*everything* counted in the global struggle (original emphasis)."[239] Eisenhower told America in his first state of the union address that there was a connection between America's military strength, economic strength, and the health and education and welfare of the people.[240] In his 1958 state of the union address, he stated that the country "could make no more tragic mistake than merely to concentrate on military strength," explaining that

> what makes the Soviet threat unique in history is its all-inclusiveness. Every human activity is pressed into service as a weapon of expansion. Trade, economic development, military power, arts, science, education, the whole world of ideas—all are harnessed to this same chariot of expansion.[241]

Examples are plentiful and they are not limited to the Eisenhower administration. Perhaps the most spectacular is the development of the space program and the effort to get a man—an *American* man, and an *American* flag—on the moon. After the USSR sent the first man-made satellite, Sputnik, into space, Eisenhower's National Security Council argued that "the USSR has . . . captured the imagination and admiration of the world," and that this could undermine the prestige and thus the security of the United States.[242] On May 25, 1961, President Kennedy announced to Congress his belief that the United States should land a man on the moon. This was part of "the battle that is now going on around the world between freedom and tyranny."[243] The projected global meaning of American success in moon exploration was that the American political system was superior to the Soviet, hence other nations would be less likely to become Communist, and thus less likely to isolate and weaken the United States. This was essentially the same logic that made equal rights for blacks and immigrants part of national-security policy. The progressive effects of wartime national-security measures and meanings are also clear in other areas, such as the development of federal aid to education through the National Defense Education Act (see Chapter 7) and even the creation of the interstate highway system.[244]

A second issue regards the decline of national-security meanings in policy related to equal rights. The international dimension of equal rights and its categorization as national security lasted from World War II until about 1968. After that year, government officials less frequently expressed great concern for the security implications of the national performance on racial equality. This disengagement was the result of the convergence of several forces.

First, and most simply, there was a "thaw" in relations between the Western and Communist countries. The futility of a nuclear missile buildup, the growing animosity between the Soviet Union and China, and a growing constituency for peace in the United States led to changes in the stark Cold War relations. Nixon's policy of "détente" did not eliminate but lessened Cold War tensions, reducing greatly the power of national-security meaning to catalyze policymaking in all areas.[245]

Second, by the time of the Nixon administration the United States had a strong answer to foreign criticism of American race problems: it had enacted the three major pieces of legislation for blacks, had waged a War on Poverty, and had developed affirmative action. In an interview, former secretary of state Dean Rusk explained that Soviet propaganda on the race inequality issue would have hurt more if the United States was not doing something about it. In contrast, South Africa, as well as Rhodesia, became more obvious targets. American actions to protect black rights meant there was "no real steam behind the idea [of sanctioning America] in the United Nations." "I think the efforts made particularly by our Presidents deflated that possibility very effectively," he added, and African ambassadors saw "we were on the move."[246]

Third, in a related factor, civil-rights mobilization and related violence declined. As Doug McAdam has shown, the number of public actions initiated by the civil rights movement peaked in 1963 and again in 1965, and then went into decline. The urban racial violence peaked in 1967.[247] Consequently, there were fewer new incidents to use as anti-American propaganda.

Fourth, the nations of Africa and Asia were less available to be courted, as they settled into self-conscious neutrality. They disavowed allegiance to American or Soviet ideology. The Indonesian dictator Sukarno said in Belgrade in 1961 that "the ideological conflict is not, I repeat, not the main problem of our time. It is not a problem which affects the majority of mankind, such as poverty, disease, illiteracy and colonial bondage." Cambodia's Prince Sihanouk agreed that "we can only be indifferent to foreign ideologies." In 1960, the Congo's Patrice Lumumba, whose name the Soviet Union used for political purposes following his martyrdom, stated, "les questions idéologiques ne nous intéressent pas."[248] These nations tended toward a proud nationalism, or toward forming regional subgroups such as the Arab

League and the West African National Secretariat.[249] Declarations of neutrality could go too far; if the new nations were not going to join the Soviet or the American sphere of influence, why worry about their opinions at all?

These nations also appeared to lose legitimacy as an important audience to many US officials. Through sheer numbers, the African and Asian countries took control of the UN Commission on Human Rights and waged a campaign against white racism, but ignored racism in nonwhite countries and other Third World human rights abuses (see Chapter 3). The commission also strongly pushed—and the United States openly resisted—resolutions that declared Zionism was racism.[250] By the early 1970s, some politicians saw *opposition* to world opinion as righteous and courageous. When the UN General Assembly passed a resolution declaring that "Zionism is a form of racism and racial discrimination," the American ambassador to the UN, Daniel Patrick Moynihan, defiantly voted nay, maintaining that passage was an "infamous act" and that the resolution "drained the word 'racism' of its meaning."[251]

Perhaps most important of all for understanding the decline of the international impact on civil rights and the national-security meanings of black equality is the fact that American views on racism caught up with the world. Legitimacy rules are not simply reducible to public opinion poll data—there must be enough anticipated intensity to the sentiments that violation will produce great response from a large or privileged segment of the population—but the data do suggest a profound change in the United States. For instance, when asked, "Do you think white students and black students should go to the same schools or separate schools," only 32 percent of Americans responded with "same" in 1942. This figure jumped to 50 percent in 1956, 73 percent in 1968, and was 90 percent in 1982. Questions regarding support for equal opportunities for blacks at jobs increased from 45 percent in 1944 to an astonishing 97 percent in 1972, and the percentage of Americans supporting integrated public transportation increased by 42 percentage points between 1942 and 1970.[252] Some doubt the sincerity of this support and suspect that whites simply learned the "right" answers to pollsters' questions, but this view still strongly supports the idea of a change in taken-for-granted cultural rules. Public support for racial discrimination was an anachronism. "Civil rights" and the principle of racial equality thus became a solidly legitimate part of American political culture.[253] Even if the national security concerns were still there, they were no longer needed to persuade Americans of the righteousness of the cause of race equality.

3

NATIONAL SECURITY AND EQUAL RIGHTS: LIMITS AND QUALIFICATIONS

Is war always such a good thing for disadvantaged people? Obviously not. Elite Americans' understanding of the best way to achieve national security could also work against or fail to work for the rights and equality of disadvantaged groups. Some groups found no benefit to categorizing their struggle as part of the World War II or Cold War victory effort. This chapter examines four such cases of harm or limited help from national-security meanings. While a general formula for success may be impossible to discern, one can see some factors that help clarify when national security helped the cause of minority rights, and how it did so.

For example, in the cases of FBI harassment of civil-rights leaders and the lingering existence of Third World colonies, political elites saw national security costs to human rights. FBI harassment and maintenance of colonies were anti-Communist, national-security efforts, just as nondiscrimination rights were in the areas of black civil rights and immigration reform. FBI harassment was secret and carried few risks; on the other hand, government officials greatly feared the unpredictable civil-rights leadership and the prospect of Communist infiltration. In the case of colonies, American leaders tried to persuade European powers to grant freedom to their colonial territories, but ultimately both sides saw that a hasty withdrawal risked Communist takeovers in the colonies. They both saw this risk as a greater and more direct threat to national security than the propaganda battering the West took because of its colonialism. Even so, the Western powers *did* begin to relinquish control, and decolonization was mostly complete by the time the major American civil-rights laws passed.

Two failed cases of national security to promote equal rights—women's rights and social rights (such as rights to health care, a job, a guaranteed income)—also help clarify the political dynamics of the period. These cases highlight the importance of global priorities, foreign propaganda, and the strength of US resistance to reform. The reason policymakers or activists did not categorize gender equality as a matter of national security was that it was a low priority in the Third World—racial equality with whites was by far the most valued human right there, clearly beating out gender equality with whites and even political rights, social rights, and civil liberties. Put another way, race and ethnic minority rights gained a national-security meaning in midcentury American politics because the emerging nations in Asia and Africa cared most about white oppression of people of color. For this reason, the USSR hammered away on this point incessantly in its propaganda. There was comparatively little international propaganda on women's rights. Though World War II and the United Nations did in various ways aid women's rights, the Cold War national-security policy did little for them.

National security also did little for the poor, though there were some efforts by the Roosevelt administration to use war to change the meaning of poverty policy and social rights, categorizing them as national security. It was a tough sell. The emerging nations did not exhibit much interest in income inequality in the United States, and Soviet propaganda on this point therefore was not a concern. More important, social rights faced much greater resistance than any other case examined in this book because of the great economic stakes in the matter. Moreover, opponents were able to point out a basic irrationality in the argument that national security required social rights: if America ended its embrace of a market economy in order to ward off Communist expansion, then it was only accelerating Communist expansion—social rights meant losing the Cold War, not winning it.

The Negative Effects of National Security on Rights: Political Repression and Colonialism

While national-security meanings aided the struggles of blacks and other groups, there is no necessary positive impact of categorizing equal rights as national security, and it could also lead to harm.[1] Indeed, the Cold War's negative effects regarding political rights and liberties are better known than its positive effects on ending racial discrimination. Paradoxically, in some cases, national security led to rights violations, just as in others it led to rights protections.

The FBI and the Civil Rights Movement

FBI surveillance of black leaders began at least as early as 1919 and did not stop after creation of the UN or the Universal Declaration of Human Rights. FBI director J. Edgar Hoover had a mandate to root out Communists, and toward that end American presidents, including John F. Kennedy and Lyndon Johnson, authorized and approved wiretaps of civil rights leaders. Regardless of any personal, political, or national-security desire for progress in civil rights, these presidents, according to Kenneth O'Reilly, were also genuinely concerned about possible Communist infiltration of the civil rights movement. In addition, various White House administrations viewed the activities of the organized movement for civil rights with trepidation, as these amounted to a massive campaign of demonstration, protest, and civil disobedience occurring on their watch. Not surprisingly, those in the role of federal executive wanted to avoid being in a position where they could only react to this activism; rather they wanted information about the plans of the civil rights movement.[2] Indeed, they felt that knowledge of and preparation for movement plans (and southern responses to them) might aid in a careful and coordinated projection of an image of minority rights legitimacy to the world.

Still, the contradiction is obvious: the wiretaps and surveillance schemes were serious violations of rights of blacks authorized by ostensible defenders of rights.[3] Furthermore, Hoover turned this anti-Communism crusade into a sordid, frequently bizarre attack on civil-rights advocates, both black and white, that included recordings of sexual encounters and various leaks calculated to damage their legitimacy and image. While some of this activity went beyond White House authorization, no one in the White House tried to stop Hoover. Some civil-rights leaders, such as the NAACP's Roy Wilkins, sometimes cooperated.[4]

Several points are relevant to this puzzle. The crucial point is that the FBI activity was for the most part secret—it was generally not openly done and was not part of an American or Soviet propaganda strategy. Hoover explained to the American public that the FBI watched over the civil rights movement for the good of its leaders. He was simply protecting the groups from Communist infiltration and protecting the civil-rights demonstrators.[5] Thus, though there was a racial component to the FBI activities, these activities did not have high visibility.

Second, what was known about Hoover's campaign did not necessarily make good propaganda for the Soviet Union. Though the USSR would sometimes forge documents in an attempt to show American conspiracies for propaganda purposes (as described in Chapter 2), reports that the American police spied on blacks would not be as compelling as propaganda that showed photos of obvious, undeniable rights violations perpetrated by white authorities against black citizens. There was no shortage of these. At a time when there was ample photographic evidence of segregated schools, trains, buses, drinking fountains, and so forth, and news footage of white police officers physically beating black activists, FBI activities were but a footnote.

Third, the USSR had a considerably worse record on abuses of power by secret police than did the United States. Unlike the issue of ethnic equality, on which the Soviet Union had a positive record they could point to, drawing attention to illicit activities of a national police force could backfire as a propaganda strategy.

Last, and perhaps most important, even if the USSR had a clean record on civil liberties and secret police activities, the FBI's violation of civil liberties still might not have been a serious vulnerability for the United States because of a hierarchy of rights American policymakers perceived in the moral culture of the emerging nations (or at least of their leaders). All rights were not equal. In the words of the historian Paul Lauren, as early as 1947, "the Department of State . . . began to recognize that the Iron Curtain of political repression actually might present fewer difficulties for many in the world than the Mason-Dixon Line of racial segregation."[6] In other words, using the federal police to inhibit political activities was not as egregious a violation of world morality as was everyday or brutal racism and discrimination.

It is not surprising that the emerging nations appeared to care more about a right to be free of Caucasian people's racial discrimination than any other. Many of these nations were emerging from the control of Europeans who believed themselves to be superior to the Africans and Asians. This conflation of imperialism with racism was a major theme in the work of the Algerian intellectual Frantz Fanon.[7] Further, the rejection of white people's racism was a cause that could unite nations as diverse as Ghana, Libya, Cambodia, and India. It found great support also from the Soviet Union.[8] Though these developing nations often gave rhetorical support to a panoply of UN-recognized rights, even putting some of them in their constitutions,[9] they did not necessarily honor them, and ethnic relations within the new nations themselves were often far from harmonious. In general, their primary interests were in eradicating colonialism and racism practiced by persons of European descent against Africans and Asians, and in furthering economic development.

This could be seen in the actions of the UN, where the growth of nonwhite nations was explosive. The United Nations began with fifty-one nations, including only three from Africa and three from Asia, and seven from the Middle East. By 1955, twenty-five new countries entered the organization, and forty-one more joined in the following ten years, including seventeen African countries in 1960 (see Tables 3.1 and 3.2).[10]

At first the numbers of nonwhite delegates to the UN were not large enough to make much of an impact. For example, when the General Assembly decided in 1958 that 1968, the twentieth anniversary of the Universal Declaration of Human Rights, would be a year for human rights, the Economic and Social Council killed a resolution sponsored by Afghanistan, In-

Table 3.1 Growth of new nation representation in the United Nations

Year	Total UN membership	New nations in UN	Percentage of UN that are new nations
1950	60	5	8.33
1955	76	10	13.15
1960	99	33	33.33
1961	104	37	35.57
1962	110	43	39.09
1963	113	46	40.70
1964	115	48	41.73
1965	118	51	43.3
1966	122	55	45.0
1967	123	56	45.5

Source: David A. Kay, *The New Nations in the United Nations, 1960–1967* (New York: Columbia University Press, 1970), p. 3.

Table 3.2 New nation representation in the United Nations, by region

Date	African	Asian	East European	Latin American	West European and other	No group
Original members (Oct. 1945)	1	6	6	9	6	1
1945–1949	4	7	2	12	8	1
1950–1959	6	8	2	0	6	0
1960–1969	32	5	0	5	1	0
1970–1979	8	11	0	5	1	0
1980–1989	1	2	0	3	0	0
1990–1995	2	5	17	0	4	0
Total	54	44	27	34	26	2

Source: Michael Banton, *International Action against Racial Discrimination* (Oxford: Clarendon Press, 1996), p. 27. © Michael Banton, 1996. Reprinted by permission of Oxford University Press.
Australia, Canada, and New Zealand are grouped with the "West European and other." The United States is not a member of any group.

dia, and Pakistan for a Freedom from Prejudice and Discrimination Day.[11] But these nations continued to press this theme. In David Kay's study of the "new nations," he classified and counted speeches made in the UN General Assembly between 1961 and 1966, and found that the dominant priorities were decolonization, South Africa, economic development, and human rights (linked to race discrimination).[12] Actions specifically on race discrimination first included educational seminars on the topic, and in 1963 there was a proposed resolution to the General Assembly for a Declaration on the

Elimination of All Forms of Racial Discrimination. This stated that "any doc-trine of racial differentiation or superiority is scientifically false, morally con-demnable, socially unjust and dangerous, and that there is no justification for racial discrimination in theory or in practice."[13] The UNESCO resolution in Moscow, described in Chapter 2, announcing that racism was a false doctrine came in 1964.

In 1965, the Third World nations went beyond their 1963 declaration with the International Convention on the Elimination of All Forms of Racial Discrimination. This was an attempt to give some enforcement power to the Universal Declaration of Human Rights. The race discrimination convention stated that "the term 'racial discrimination' shall mean any distinction, exclu-sion, restriction, or preference based on race, color, descent, or national or ethnic origin which has the purpose or effect of nullifying or impairing the recognition, enjoyment or exercise, on an equal footing, of human rights and fundamental freedoms in the political, economic, social, cultural, or any other field of public life." The convention, based on an unassailable principle, was (on paper at least) strong medicine: a legally and morally binding docu-ment to ensure elimination of racial discrimination, requiring nullification of any national or local laws that maintained racial discrimination. It included measures for punishment of advocates of racial discrimination or hatred, and requirements of annual reports of progress.[14] The International Covenant of Economic, Social, and Cultural Rights and the International Covenant on Civil and Political Rights, both with nondiscrimination provisions, followed in 1966.

Even this was not enough to satisfy the demand in African and Asia for ra-cial equality. In 1969, the General Assembly accepted a resolution of the "Measures to Be Taken against Nazism and Racial Intolerance" and an-nounced that 1971 would be the International Year for Action to Combat Racism and Racial Discrimination. But was a year enough? In 1973, the Gen-eral Assembly announced the Decade for Action to Combat Racism and Ra-cial Discrimination—to begin immediately. Within the year, Third World na-tions focused attention on South Africa, and the next UN initiative was the International Convention on the Suppression and Punishment of the Crime of Apartheid.[15]

UN activities were not the only forums for Third World attacks on white colonialism and racism. Official statements of international meetings and as-sociations in Africa and Asia also denounced the West for its racial and colo-nial policies. For example, the Asian-African Conference in Bandung, the All-African Peoples' Conference in Accra, the formation of the Organization of African Unity in Addis Ababa, and the meetings of the Afro-Asian Peoples' Solidarity Organization in Cairo all offered speeches and pronouncements criticizing racism.[16]

Throughout all this, the primary concern of the developing nations was not eradicating racism within their own borders or bringing to a halt Third World colonialism practiced by Indonesia and India. While the UN focused on South Africa during the 1970s, it gave comparatively little attention to the tragic genocide in Cambodia or Idi Amin's atrocities in Uganda. Developing nations ignored discrimination against lower castes India, anti-Chinese discrimination in Malaysia, and oppression of native tribes in Brazil and the Philippines. Similarly, the USSR's white-on-white domination of eastern European peoples evoked no great concern.[17]

Meanwhile, the countries in Africa and Asia began to openly maintain that civil liberties were a luxury for already developed nations. With the Soviet Union, they disagreed with the Western emphasis on individual rights exercised against the state. For many, as Michael Banton has written, "states came first."[18] Economic development had priority over civil liberties. In a challenge to liberal capitalist nations, the 1968 Human Rights Commission's Proclamation of Teheran stated that "the full realization of civil and political rights without enjoyment of economic, social and cultural rights is impossible." Though the United States and Sweden disagreed, Commission delegates from Iran, the USSR, Egypt, Ecuador, India, and Argentina all in various ways openly subscribed to the notion of a hierarchy of rights, with civil liberties such as those violated by Hoover's FBI having the lowest priority.[19]

Why Didn't America Act to End European Colonies?

Because of the importance of racial and ethnic equality, it was of great importance that the United States eliminate white racism, both domestically and internationally, if it was to maintain world leadership and defeat Communism. The continuing existence of European colonies was therefore not only a great injustice but a public relations disaster for the United States. But if national security, if defeating Communism, was the ultimate goal, the Western powers also saw the defense of empire as the best way to achieve that goal— even though it came with considerable cost.

By not immediately relinquishing their empires, European countries including Britain, Belgium, and France faced withering criticism for violating sovereignty norms held by most of the world. By not severely criticizing colonialist friends and working against colonialism, the United States violated these same norms and the developing world and the Communist nations criticized the United States most of all. The Soviet Union zealously attacked the West on this point in its propaganda directed to Africa and Asia. The Soviet media rarely referred to the United States or the West without the scathing modifier "imperialist."

In the UN, colonialism was a dominant issue. For example, in 1960, forty-three African and Asian nations proposed to the UN a Declaration on the Granting of Independence to Colonial Countries and Peoples, which stated that colonialism must be ended immediately and unconditionally as it violated both the Universal Declaration of Human Rights and the UN Charter. The Soviet bloc joined the nonwhite nations in giving thumping support to an idea that no one could oppose. And no country did oppose it. The United States, Portugal, Spain, South Africa, Britain, Australia, France, and Belgium meekly abstained.[20]

The United States, in fact, had no great love of European imperialism, and Franklin Roosevelt quietly worked against colonialism as he helped construct the postwar world order. One difficulty in fashioning common Allied war aims for Roosevelt was that he believed colonialism to be an anachronistic institution and at odds with any reasonable moral pact for the battle against Hitler. In early meetings with Churchill, Roosevelt expressed his discomfort at the rather obvious contradiction. Hitler was conquering nations, and the Allies were clearly for a people's self-determination. Yet Churchill would not countenance any relinquishing of empire. Roosevelt told aide Rexford Tugwell that Churchill "doesn't see things as you and I do," and was "amazingly unreformed." "He wants this war to result, as others have, in another extension of the Empire," he complained. "And he wants us to back him up."[21]

Not surprisingly, the Atlantic Charter led to questions regarding Britain's intentions with colonies in India, Malaya, and elsewhere. Churchill responded by telling Parliament that, despite the grand words, the Charter was aimed at restoring self-rule to European nations "now under the Nazi yoke" and that the Indians, Malayans and others constituted "quite a separate problem."[22] Moreover, Churchill's talk of postwar international organization during speeches and radio addresses tended to leave out China as a great power. Roosevelt was not happy with this, as he believed that the inclusion of China as one of the "Big Four" (joining the US, USSR, and UK) was an important symbol to nonwhite peoples that the war was not simply for the Western powers to maintain colonial domination. Roosevelt wanted the world to know that independence was at hand for these nations.[23] In November of 1943, Roosevelt proposed future independence for Indochina from France, with a Four Power trusteeship overseeing Vietnam, Laos, and Cambodia in the initial stages. Stalin agreed, but Churchill refused to go along.[24]

Churchill thus let it be known that if sovereignty was a principle worth fighting for, it would not apply to British colonies. The British asked if Roosevelt was serious about his anticolonialism, and he said he was. Indochina, the president told Secretary of State Cordell Hull on January 24, 1944, was "worse off than they were at the beginning" as a result of French domination, and sensed that the British were not defending the French so much as "they fear the effect it would have on their possessions and those of the Dutch"—specifically, "future independence."[25]

In the end, Roosevelt deferred to Churchill. He was not a forceful speaker for the rights of nonwhites to the British because the American south was still thoroughly dominated by racist laws and institutions. And Roosevelt was willing to go along with Britain because—similar to the case of harassment of civil-rights leaders—the policy was based on calculations of security. A major fight on this issue would weaken the war effort even more than Britain's failure to renounce colonialism.[26]

This pattern continued after World War II, with American leaders giving support to the maintenance of colonies in certain areas. There was then a global threat of Communist expansion arising from *within* countries rather than being forcefully imposed from without. The United States and other Western powers harbored the great and quite reasonable fear that pulling out of their colonies would be destabilizing, making them vulnerable to Communist influence and infiltration. Security considerations thus shaped the strategy of colonial withdrawal, which all Western nations realized was inevitable. Scholars of decolonization are nearly unanimous in agreeing that the pace of decolonization was in part dictated by the strength of Communist movements in the colonies and the strategic position of those colonies.[27] As the historian Thomas Borstelmann has shown, this logic led to America's much-criticized support of South Africa. It was "a hard, inescapable fact," an assistant secretary of state explained in 1953, "that premature independence can be dangerous, retrogressive and destructive."[28] Or as Paul Lauren succinctly put it, "Ironically, the same Cold War that actually assisted the movement for racial equality in the United States thus helped retard decolonization in the world at large."[29]

There is a final point about the apparent contradiction presented by the maintenance of the Western colonies after America's global self-promotion as racially egalitarian: the colonies did not last long. To be sure, some lasted longer than others. But even with an interest in maintaining colonies for the stability they appeared to provide and the Soviet Union's shaky moral authority on this issue, it is important to note that by the middle 1960s, most colonies, like officially sanctioned race discrimination in the United States, were gone.

Why Only Race and Ethnic Equality for National Security?

The ways that national-security meanings promoted equality can be further clarified and understood by comparisons with groups other than blacks and immigrants. Women and the poor, for example, did not benefit from policies to create more equality because there was no strong strategic interest in women's rights or poverty. Therefore, State Department and White House officials did not categorize women's rights and social rights for the poor as matters of national security.

The National Security Irrelevance of Women's Rights

The failure of national-security policy to aid women's rights is perhaps surprising when one considers the fact that women's labor was essential for victory in World War II, and that women's advocates were active in the UN. Labor shortages led to an interest among government and business elites in opening up areas of endeavor where cultural rules previously made them unwelcome. Estimates of positions that women could reasonably apply for went up from 29 to 55 percent of new jobs. The federal government actually encouraged women to work with a major public-relations campaign. The Office of War Information led the effort by encouraging contests to communicate the new message, and the War Labor Board said women would be paid at a rate equal to men. But with military victory came loss. Just as quickly as women had been encouraged to work, they were asked to leave. Though four of five women in industrial jobs wanted to keep their jobs, they did not have a choice. War industries shut down, and new plants refused to hire women. In the auto industry, women's proportion of jobs fell from 25 to 7.5 percent. The jobs that remained available to them paid less than half what they were making during the war.[30]

A similar transition occurred in the Soviet Union, though somewhat more lasting gains were made, especially for women as doctors. Although approximately 27 million (presumably mostly male) citizens died in World War II, the Soviet government encouraged women to stay in their traditional role to ensure family stability.[31] The Soviet Union, despite Marxism's promise of liberation and a 1936 constitution that granted women "equal rights with men in all spheres of economic, state, cultural, social and political life," held deeply institutionalized beliefs of women's appropriate roles as defined by domestic responsibilities: child rearing and homemaking.[32]

There were signs of progress at the UN. International women's groups had been active since the late nineteenth century, and in 1938 they successfully lobbied the League of Nations to create a Committee of Experts on the Status of Women.[33] They also lobbied the UN for attention in its Charter, even trying (as did American advocates for blacks) to take advantage of conflict between the United States and the Soviet Union on the matter.[34] These efforts met with some success. Though twenty nations gave women no political rights at all, the preamble of the UN Charter mentioned equal rights for men and women, as did four different articles. The UN established a Commission on the Status of Women to study and promote women's equality, and sponsored various seminars in the 1950s and 1960s focusing on women's rights.[35]

In December of 1952, the UN General Assembly adopted the Convention on the Political Rights of Women, to ensure equal voting, equal access to elected office, and equal access to public office. In 1945, twenty-four member states granted full or limited political rights for women. By 1954, women had equal voting in sixty nations, limited in six, and denied completely in seventeen—including several in the developing world: Afghanistan, Cambodia, Colombia, Egypt, Ethiopia, Honduras, Iran, Iraq, Jordan, Laos, Libya, Liechtenstein, Nicaragua, Paraguay, Saudi Arabia, Switzerland, and Yemen.[36]

Yet these developments, while significant, were spotty and lacked the urgency of the racial-equality issue. Consequently, the superpowers did not show great interest in women's rights and remained preoccupied with racial equality. The Soviet Union, seeking to highlight American illegitimacy on racial equality, unsuccessfully tried to add to each article of the Convention on the Political Rights of Women the phrase "without any discrimination on the grounds of race, colour, national or social origin, property status, language or religion."[37] The United States voted for the convention but did not sign it. Secretary of State John Foster Dulles told the Senate Foreign Relations Committee that his administration approved of it in principle but did not see treaty coercion as appropriate, explaining, "We do not see any clear or necessary relation between the interest and welfare of the United States and the eligibility of women to political office in other nations."[38]

UN efforts to halt sex discrimination never became an issue in American domestic politics.[39] The American women's movement was significantly hampered by factions in the 1940s, 1950s, and early 1960s, but had it been strong, global geopolitics still would not have presented women's advocates with the same opportunities that black civil rights advocates and immigration reformers had. The emerging nations cared most about race equality. And without interest from the emerging nations, there was no Soviet propaganda on women's equality. And without the propaganda, it was difficult for meaning entrepreneurs to sell women's rights as national security. It is especially revealing that on the rare occasion when women prominently entered into Cold War discourse and propaganda, it was in the context of the "kitchen debate" between Vice President Richard Nixon and Soviet leader Khrushchev on how America provided wonderful kitchen appliances for happy homemakers. Neither side questioned whether women belonged in the kitchen. Nixon stated, "I think that this attitude toward women is universal. What we want to do is make easier the life of our housewives." Khrushchev called this "the capitalist attitude toward women" but offered no alternative.[40]

The Cold War was therefore a period of "doldrums" for the effort to secure women's rights.[41] Though the American public was increasingly supportive of equal rights for women (71 percent of men and 81 percent of women in a 1946 poll expressed support for equal pay),[42] Truman and Eisenhower did little for women. Both offered only lukewarm support for the Equal Rights Amendment and for increased appointments of women to government jobs.[43] It was not until the 1960s that women's advocates won significant policy developments (as described in Chapters 4 and 8).

The American Poor and National Security

Linking social rights and national security: the NRPB
Even before his presidency, Franklin Roosevelt was interested in establishing a guaranteed standard of living for Americans. In his 1932 campaign address at the Commonwealth Club of San Francisco, Roosevelt suggested that government should attend to citizens in ways beyond what had been the norm. Specifically, it should protect them from the threats to their livelihoods arising from giant capitalist enterprises and great market fluctuation.[44]

In 1940, he expanded that theme by linking social rights and national security. He promised a radio audience that "the strength of this nation shall not be diluted by the failure of the government to protect the economic well-being of its citizens."[45] Roosevelt then argued in his 1941 state of the union address that the Four Freedoms constituting the war aims of the Allies included "freedom from want." This was to at least suggest that government was the guarantor of economic or social rights. Inspired by recent arguments in the press that economic inequality led to hatred and war, he emphasized then that America was fighting for economic democracy as well as political democracy.[46]

The National Resources Planning Board (NRPB), chaired by Roosevelt's uncle, Frederic A. Delano, made this explicit in 1942 when it linked the new social goals to war needs. The NRPB was Roosevelt's short- and long-term policy planning team.[47] In its 1942 report on "National Resources Development," the NRPB stated,

> We are intent on winning this war, not only to safeguard our lives and our liberties, but also to make possible the "pursuit of happiness"—the full fruition of our hopes and plans for progress and development. We must fight the dictators and all their forces, not only with greater force, but with ideas and faith. We must develop with our own people and hold

out to the enslaved people now under the heel of the dictators a better way of life than we or they have had.[48]

The report outlined "A New Bill of Rights" that, along with the Four Freedoms and the Atlantic Charter (see Chapter 2), were statements of "our national objectives." The new rights list was comprehensive, including rights to a job, health care, and basic necessities of life. The NRPB sold social rights as part of national security, warning that "if the victorious democracies muddle through another decade of economic frustration and mass unemployment, we may expect social disintegration and, sooner or later, another international conflagration." Further, the report argued that "democracies, if they are going to lead the world out of chaos and insecurity, must first and foremost offer their people opportunity, employment, and a rising standard of living."[49] Aid for the poor, in other words, was a national-security measure.

Though the arguments were similar to those for minority rights, the link to enemy propaganda was still missing—but not for long. In 1943, the NRPB fleshed out the geopolitical implications of social rights:

It is increasingly apparent as the world goes on in this conflict, that we must not only provide the physical things with which to carry on the war, but also to make clear the things for which we are fighting. A nation carrying on total war must have a reasonable assurance of a livable world and satisfactory conditions when the war is over. We have got to provide through planning the means for sustaining the American concept of living, for full employment, security, and the pursuit of happiness, and for giving a reasonable assurance to our people and to other peoples that the Four Freedoms and the New Bill of Rights will be implemented and made real for all persons "everywhere in the world." The enemy is making very large use of propaganda to misinform our people and our allies of the United Nations—saying the Axis can provide a better world order than we can. It is important that we combat this propaganda with realistic and effective plans of our own for winning the peace.[50]

The new bill of rights

In 1944, President Roosevelt prominently featured these ideas linking rights for the poor and national security. In his state of the union address on January 11, he argued that "security" was the "one supreme objective for the future . . . for each Nation individually, and for all the United Nations." He clarified that for him, security meant "not only physical security which provides safety from attacks by aggressors. It means also economic security, social security, moral security—in a family of Nations."[51] He maintained that a "basic essential to peace is a decent standard of living for all individual men and women and children in all Nations. Freedom from fear is eternally linked with freedom from want."[52] A "lasting peace" required provision for all, since "people who are hungry and out of a job are the stuff of which dictatorships are made."[53] In his speech to the nation, Roosevelt went on to present a simplified version of the NRPB's New Bill of Rights. It was nevertheless a grand and ambitious statement:

> In our day these economic truths have become accepted as self-evident. We have accepted, so to speak, a second Bill of Rights under which a new basis of security and prosperity can be established for all—regardless of station, race, or creed.
>
> Among these are:
>
> The right to a useful and remunerative job in the industries or shops or farms or mines of the Nation;
>
> The right to earn enough to provide adequate food and clothing and recreation;
>
> The right of every farmer to raise and sell his products at a return which will give him and his family a decent living;
>
> The right of every businessman, large and small, to trade in an atmosphere of freedom from unfair competition and domination by monopolies at home or abroad;
>
> The right of every family to a decent home;
>
> The right to adequate medical care and the opportunity to achieve and enjoy good health;
>
> The right to adequate protection from the economic fears of old age, sickness, accident, and unemployment;
>
> The right to a good education.
>
> . . . America's own rightful place in the world depends in large part upon how fully these and similar rights have been carried into practice for our citizens. For unless there is security here at home there cannot be lasting peace in the world.[54]

Roosevelt would go on to promote this theme, connecting his domestic program of social security with the war effort's national security. "Some people," he told a crowd in Chicago, "have sneered at these ideals [of the Economic Bill of Rights] as well as at the ideals of the Atlantic Charter, the ideals of the Four Freedoms." But, said Roosevelt, these people ("I need not name them") had less faith than the American people in their abilities. Roosevelt linked his opponents to "the Nazis and the Japs," who also failed to recognize that the American people had "the habit of going right ahead and accomplishing the impossible."[55]

A special section of the April 19, 1943 issue of the *New Republic* threw support behind the NRPB's vision in a twenty-page article entitled "Charter for America" (the reference to the Atlantic Charter was only implicit). The article argued that a comprehensive system of social rights would be a "powerful weapon" for "demoralizing the enemy." While "the Nazis have told their people that they must sell their birthright of freedom in return for security," the German people only lost freedom. An American plan that preserved freedom and achieved security would eliminate "much of the reason for their resistance against our armies." Fulfilling the promise of Roosevelt's Four Freedoms with this American Charter would "also be a weapon in heartening our friends in the countries still under Hitler's domination."[56] This logic, linking domestic welfare to the war effort, was the same as that categorizing African American and immigrant equality as national security.

The failure of social rights as national security

After presenting this ambitious agenda linking social rights and national security, however, Roosevelt could do little to make it a reality. During the war, the New Deal's future was uncertain and faced growing resistance.[57] Roosevelt died shortly after winning an unprecedented fourth term. His vice president and successor, Harry S Truman, attempted to pick up where Roosevelt left off, calling for Roosevelt's "economic bill of rights."[58] Although he did put greater emphasis on the national-security meanings of minority rights than did Roosevelt, Truman did not maintain the linkage between national security and social rights that Roosevelt had worked to achieve. Without strong meaning entrepreneurship promoting social rights as national security, Truman failed to secure the bipartisanship necessary to achieve much in the way of Roosevelt's new bill of rights. Efforts to create a full employment law and federally guaranteed health care both failed. Eisenhower did not continue the struggle. Despite support for race equality and immigration reforms, and strong efforts for federal aid to schools (Chapter 7) and highways as national security, Eisenhower did not show any interest in making America a model of social rights for the world.

Would Roosevelt have succeeded if he lived, or would Truman have succeeded had he continued with Roosevelt's national-security strategy? It is possible, but not likely. The case highlights a significant difference from the cases in Chapter 2: organized, massive lobbying in opposition.

As a generation of scholarship on "American exceptionalism" has shown, it is extraordinarily hard to create comprehensive policies of social rights—a "welfare state"—in the United States. This is true because of the nation's history as well as the rules of its political institutions. Work by the sociologists Edwin Amenta and Theda Skocpol on the failure of the United States to develop comprehensive programs of social provision during World War II nicely exemplifies some of the themes in this strand of American exceptionalism literature.[59] Other nations, they point out, *did* develop social rights during World War II. British leaders, for example, actually used the same strategy as the NRPB: they defined reform as part of the war effort. Indeed, the very term "welfare state" was created by a British writer who was demonstrating the British war aims and how it differed from the Nazi "warfare state."[60]

Amenta and Skocpol argue that by World War II Britain had an institutional base and fiscal capacities already in place on which to build their welfare state. During the 1910s and 1920s, Britain created social insurance programs financed by both general public revenues and payroll taxes, and then gave relief to the unemployed during the depression by expanding these programs. The United States created Social Security during the depression, but made it a contributory program based on payroll taxes. For the unemployed, the New Deal created emergency work and relief programs. Where postwar planning for social provision was concerned, the British already had a strong base and a history of programs to assess and British leaders worked to strengthen the more successful ones. In contrast, the NRPB had little to build on except emergency programs. The lack of experience led to bureaucratic rivalries. Big players included the Social Security Board, which favored payroll taxes to generate revenue, and the Veterans Administration, which had a major say in postwar planning and worked to keep veterans separate from the general population.[61]

Amenta and Skocpol also point to the different electoral systems in the two countries to explain the failure of American social rights. Britain has a parliamentary system, where a formal coalition of the Conservative Party and the Labour Party ran the government with little partisan bickering during World War II. Many Labour officials headed key ministries. The government secured strong controls in wartime planning and employment, setting the stage for postwar welfare state development. The government also suspended elections during the war. In contrast, the bipartisanship in the American government was informal and achieved with clenched teeth, and elections were held during 1942. This allowed Republicans to exploit wartime grievances and win fifty seats in the House, almost all from liberal northern Democrats.[62] With increased power, Republicans and conservative Democrats were able to thwart Truman's efforts to create rights to full employment and health care.

Other scholars' work elaborates on these points. Another factor inhibiting social rights is the enormously complex legislative process that offers many "veto points" for opponents.[63] There are multiple steps to a bill's being enacted into law by Congress, and at any one of them opponents of the bill can stop its progress or exact so many compromises that the bill becomes ineffectual or meaningless. Such was the case, for example, with the so-called Full Employment Bill in 1946.[64]

The comparison with black civil rights and immigration reform, however, highlights some basic differences between the politics of social provision and regulatory politics that are lost in the tight focus of the American exceptionalism literature on social provision. First, efforts to create social rights call forth stronger, more diverse, and more determined resistance and lobbying than nondiscrimination regulations.[65] Precisely during the period that national-security meanings were changing policies in other areas, business groups, for example, created a massive public relations and political effort to defend the free-enterprise system from encroachments by prolabor and prowelfare state policies.[66] But business groups have rarely put up a fight on civil-rights regulations, and in the case of immigration reform, many businesses supported an end to discrimination based on national origins. In some areas with national security meanings outside of equal rights, such as the space program and the construction of highways, businesses won big, and did not fight federal largesse that went to them.

Second, the threat of Communism easily works *against* social rights and help for the poor. If defeating Communism means the United States must move away from a market economy, then the national-security logic breaks down. Social rights more easily lend themselves to charges of "creeping socialism" than do regulations to guarantee equality between groups on bases other than class. Minority rights—in either their classical liberal, difference-blind formulation or understood as a hard affirmative action guaranteeing "equality of results"—are always about guaranteeing that there are proportionally as many minority poor as there are majority poor. Minority rights never aspire to eliminate "the poor" as a class or the market as an institution.[67]

And so, for example, despite Roosevelt's goals, Congress's resistance on social rights was fierce. For its efforts, Congress abolished the NRPB in 1943.[68] Business groups lobbied strongly against the NRPB's recommended efforts to guarantee a right to work, and they were joined by major newspapers, including the *New York Times*, in condemnation.[69] They criticized the bill as an attack on the American system of free enterprise. The political scientist Stephen Kemp Bailey writes, "The argument that full employment and freedom were incompatible took a number of forms. Some opponents adopted the simple syllogism: Russia is a tyranny, there is full employment in Russia, full employment means tyranny."[70] Attempts to create a right to health care, or "socialized medicine," similarly met fierce resistance, as the sociologist Paul Starr has shown. The powerful American Medical Association said the plan would make doctors into slaves.[71] Republicans also fiercely resisted. When Senator James Murray (D–MT) introduced Truman's national health care plan in 1946, Robert Taft (R–OH) interrupted: "I consider it socialism. It is to my mind the most socialistic measure this Congress has ever had before it." Taft stated that the plan had its origins in the Soviet constitution, and that Republicans would refuse to participate in hearings.[72] Starr writes, "As anticommunist sentiment rose in the late forties, national health insurance became vanishingly improbable."[73] In Senator John Bricker's (R–OH) attempts to limit UN influence in the United States, he directed his contempt to UN efforts that would further economic and social progress, complaining that they would make the United States a "socialistic state."[74]

While resistance to equal rights for minorities was strong, it was more localized. Southerners and their way of life stood to lose from black equality, and southern members of Congress strongly resisted race equality of any kind. Though Congress killed Roosevelt's Fair Employment Practices Committee upon the end of World War II, just as it abolished his NRPB, Truman went ahead and created his own civil rights agency that though weak, maintained a precedent followed by every president through the Johnson administration. And when Congress would debate civil rights bills in Congress, it did so without much input from big business organizations such as the National Association of Manufacturers and the Chamber of Commerce.[75] Business leaders have very rarely lobbied strongly against minority-rights measures. Black civil rights and equality in immigration both needed categorization as national security measures to become policy, but these national security meanings were never contested by powerful business groups. Indeed, business leaders helped promote these meanings.

Conclusion

That national-security categorization had inconsistent effects on rights does not mean that it was not a powerful progressive force. The United States did not risk much by harassing civil rights leaders when it was thought they might be cavorting with Communists. Emerging nations showed little interest in civil liberties, as did the USSR, and the Soviets did not make it a major propaganda issue. On the other hand, the Americans risked much if they pulled out of the totally illegitimate European colonies; the colonies could destabilize and fall into Communist hands. There were other instances where the rights of ethnic minorities suffered due to similar calculations of national security. The internment of Japanese Americans during World War II is another example where government leaders decided that national security required rights to be denied rather than protected.[76]

Women's rights failed as a compelling national-security concern because neither the Soviet Union nor nations in the developing world gave women's rights a high priority. While some women's groups fought for progress on nondiscrimination issues in the UN, their efforts remained on the sidelines of the superpower struggles for the hearts and minds of the developing world. Instead, these new nations showed a laserlike focus on white racism against people of color. The developing world similarly did not give high priority to social rights for the poor, or at least the American poor, and therefore Soviet propaganda on poverty in America did not threaten the State Department or White House as did propaganda on American racism. While there were efforts in the Roosevelt administration to define aid to the poor or the unemployed as part of national-security policy, no subsequent administration sustained those efforts.

In part, the case regarding social rights highlights the contrast between the politics of social provision and the early politics of regulation: advocates for the poor met with stronger resistance than did those advocating the more successful cases. This brought into play an array of political institutions that made it difficult to pass comprehensive social-rights legislation. Equally important was that arguments about preventing Communist expansion did not have the same force—these legions of powerful critics could plausibly say that social rights *were* Communism. Establishing guaranteed jobs, income, and health care to win the war against Communism would be a Pyrrhic victory—an America with such rights guarantees would not really be America at all.

For the most part, the cases of national-security meanings or categorizations of black civil rights and immigration reform exemplify the development of "difference-blind" minority rights and liberal citizenship. The United States moved in step with the world in the development and institutionalization of difference-blindness and equality of ethnic and racial groups. As America prohibited discrimination in public accommodations, employment, schooling, housing, and immigration in the 1960s, its guiding principles were as much the world's as its own. In the same period of American reform, the UN made similar declarations, and over a period of years European nations relinquished control of their colonies. American reform was thus linked to world reform in an interactive process. Minority rights took on national-security meanings in light of the global culture of world rights that America did much to create.

Because these reforms were classically liberal, however, the new laws did not identify any particular minority groups. The initial civil rights gains of blacks, for example, in fact protected *any* and *all* Americans. These were simple nondiscrimination provisions. The following chapters explore the question of how America went beyond the general reach of these reforms to specifically identify minority groups and recognize their rights in special policies and programs. The key dynamic of this development was hinted at above in the late stages of immigration reform: the initial gains of the black civil rights movement created opportunity for advocates of other groups.

4

"WE WERE ADVANCING THE REALLY REVOLUTIONARY VIEW OF DISCRIMINATION": DESIGNATING OFFICIAL MINORITIES FOR AFFIRMATIVE ACTION IN EMPLOYMENT

Who are America's minorities, and how were they decided upon? The designation of official minorities was a consequence of affirmative action, which makes it the most important policy in the minority rights revolution. In the regulations of affirmative action America formally moved away from "difference-blind," classically liberal policy toward an approach that specifically divided America into the majority and the minorities, the privileged and the oppressed.

Affirmative action developed in three main domains in the United States—employment, business ownership, and university admissions. Since African Americans were at the vanguard of the minority rights revolution, both because of their own mobilization and the national-security implications of their subjugation, policies to ensure equality in all three domains were first developed to accommodate blacks, but all quickly expanded to include Latinos, Asian Americans, American Indians, and women of all backgrounds. It happened first in employment and the primary goal of this chapter is to explain how and why it happened there. I give a brief overview of the origins of employment affirmative action for African Americans. I then focus on how some other groups became America's official minorities, implicitly equal and implicitly sharing similar backgrounds and disadvantages.[1]

In the period of the minority rights revolution, there were two efforts at affirmative action in employment. First, there was the vague but expansive pressure from the Equal Employment Opportunity Commission (EEOC), created by the Civil Rights Act of 1964. Second, there were the regulations for government contractors administered by the Office of Federal Contract Compliance (OFCC) of the Labor Department as well as the Department of Health, Education and Welfare (HEW), the enforcement agency for educational institutions. Both expanded to include the same four ethnoracial blocs plus women.

A significant theme in this chapter, as in the chapters that follow, is that the policies that developed for groups other than African Americans are policy legacies of the effort to protect the rights of African Americans. In every case, the prior creation of rights for blacks greatly eased and accelerated policy development for other groups. Without the efforts of the black civil rights movement and the policy responses to that movement, affirmative action for other groups would not exist.[2]

The chapter describes two main factors to explain affirmative action's expansion. First, the expansion was made possible because government officials and bureaucrats as far back as the late 1940s saw some groups as analogous to blacks; in the language of 1965, "Spanish Americans," "Orientals," and "American Indians" had meanings that were similar to "Negroes." The Eisenhower administration, with nudging from some minority advocates in Congress and in advocacy groups, established the first survey form implicitly declaring these groups to be America's minorities. While the forms were not part of any major program at that time, they mattered because the 1960s civil-rights agencies copied them and institutionalized them as part of affirmative-action employment policy. The EEOC would collect and analyze data on discrimination against these official minorities. This form's collection of data was absolutely necessary for affirmative action to develop because it revealed the varying representation of minorities throughout the nation's workforce. The form made some inequalities more real and others invisible. It reinforced whatever notion already existed that Latinos, Asian Americans, and American Indians were indeed minorities—like blacks—and sent a different message regarding groups that were not deemed official minorities. For these reasons I explore the form's inclusion of groups beyond blacks in some detail.[3]

The second major factor allowing rapid expansion of affirmative action is that after the EEOC had established it as an effective and efficient means to enforce black rights, affirmative action became part of an administrators' policy repertoire to attend to the demands of other groups—regardless of the content of those group advocates' demands. Affirmative action was a cheap, easy, and available way to appeal to and appease the EEOC-designated official minority lobbying groups, whatever their grievances. It became a part of a policy and public relations repertoire to preempt or assuage quickly developing minority constituencies and to quiet criticism.

If the analogy with blacks allowed bureaucrats to expand affirmative action, it did not mean that it was equally easy for all groups to have affirmative action enforced. The EEOC tended to neglect Asian Americans and American Indians, but these groups did not make an issue of it. The EEOC neglected Latinos at first, but after a few nudges, Latinos gained the EEOC's attention. Women had the most difficulty in getting the black analogy to work for them. Advocates for women faced the barrier of simply not being taken seriously—they were ridiculed and their "alleged" inequality was ridiculed. Beyond this barrier, there was another problem. Many government officials rightly or wrongly believed that women were simply different from men and from other minorities in the sort of jobs they would seek, whereas black, Latino, Asian American, American Indian, and Euro-American men would all share identical career preferences and aspirations. Women's advocates, both within and without the government, had to fight hard and persistently push the black analogy in their efforts to be treated seriously by the EEOC. They did not have to fight long, however, before the commission began to include women in affirmative-action policies. In the OFCC's contract compliance program in the Labor Department, where the nonblack minorities were immediately included in affirmative action, women's advocates also had to lobby in the face of strong resistance to be included in the regulations governing affirmative action. In a few years, they were successful.

This chapter is divided into four main sections. It first defines affirmative action and then briefly describes the origins of employment affirmative action for blacks. Next, it examines why and how the EEOC expanded "minority" to include Latinos, Asian Americans, American Indians, and women, showing that these groups were not significant players in the struggle for Title VII or the Civil Rights Act as a whole, and also presenting the origins of the EEOC's EEO-1 form and the reasons it included groups other than blacks. The third section shows how some of these nonblack groups lobbied to have their government-granted official minority status be respected with better treatment by the EEOC, and how they won affirmative action without making a priority of this policy. The last section examines affirmative action in the government contract compliance program, showing how the OFCC included the official minorities from the beginning, and also showing the greater struggles of women to be categorized as a minority like blacks and win a place in affirmative action regulations.

African Americans and Affirmative Action's Beginnings

A defining characteristic of affirmative-action policies is that they bestow a positive meaning on some noneconomic group difference. This distinguishes them from both welfare programs for the poor of any race, gender, ethnicity, and so forth, and also from policies that bestow negative meanings to racial differences in order to segregate, deny opportunity, or stigmatize some group. Another hallmark of affirmative action is the attempt to achieve proportional representations of certain groups in economic, educational, or political endeavors. In this sense, affirmative action first developed in two government organizations: the EEOC and the OFCC.[4]

Title VII of the Civil Rights Act of 1964 created the EEOC.[5] Section 703(a) of Title VII states that "it shall be an unlawful employment practice for an employer to fail or refuse to hire or to discharge any individual, or otherwise discriminate against any individual" regarding terms of employment "because of such individual's race, color, religion, sex, or national origin." It was also unlawful for an employer "to limit, segregate, or classify his employees in any way which would deprive any individual of employment opportunities or otherwise adversely affect his status as an employee, because of such individual's race, color, religion, sex, or national origin." The title covered employers with at least one hundred employees (later reduced to fifteen), employment agencies, and unions. Title VII assigned to the EEOC the job of investigating complaints of discrimination, but allowed it only the power to investigate and attempt to conciliate if it found discrimination. Failing this, the EEOC could refer the case to the attorney general.

Congress created a weak EEOC to make Title VII palatable enough for passage. In 1964, advocates for African American civil rights wanted an agency with cease-and-desist authority, the legal power to enforce its own rulings. They continued to press for this as the EEOC stumbled along in its first few years. Another problem for the EEOC was the legally mandated difference-blind model of justice. Given the small staff and budget, the operating procedure required time-consuming and cumbersome investigations into the intent of an accused firm. Since people are routinely denied jobs or promotions due to inadequate qualifications, lack of fit, or a lack of openings, rooting out denials based on discrimination was (and is) extremely difficult. To make matters more challenging for the EEOC, the agency was immediately overwhelmed with complaints of discrimination. A backlog of unexamined cases quickly developed that soon reached more than ten thousand, and the average time of investigation far exceeded the legally defined limit of two months, sometimes extending to two years. Civil-rights leaders demanded something be done, though they did not offer any policy alternatives other than demanding for cease-and-desist authority for the EEOC. Meanwhile, African American unrest, often on a massive scale, erupted in cities across the nation (see Chapter 2). All of this added to pressure on the EEOC and OFCC.

The most far-reaching developments first occurred in the EEOC, where officials, behaving like typical American bureaucrats, decided to rationalize the enforcement process, first by developing quantitative indicators of the discrimination problem of blacks. The goal was to attack the discrimination problem in the most effective and efficient strategy possible. To this end, the EEOC developed the EEO-1 form, a way for employers to send information regarding the racial makeup of their workforces so the government could focus attention on the most serious discriminators: employers who hired almost no blacks. This also would free the EEOC from having to wait for complaints to come from individuals (more on the EEO-1 form below).

This process occurred in the years 1965–66. The EEOC used this data for an important development for the establishment of affirmative action, the 1966 agreement with the Newport News Shipbuilding and Drydock Company, which the EEOC believed discriminated against blacks. The agreement featured the first remedy for discrimination that sought a more proportional representation of blacks.[6] By 1967, the EEOC had collected and analyzed information from thousands of employers. In January of 1967, it expanded the affirmative action approach, meeting with representatives from the textile industry in North and South Carolina. The region had very large numbers of blacks and a strong textile-manufacturing base, but almost no black textile workers. The EEOC confronted industry representatives with statistics showing the low underutilization of blacks in the workforce, and demanded an explanation. The commission then used this "forum" technique with other industries and regions. Notice was served: employers—if they wanted to avoid such unpleasant encounters with the federal government—should hire percentages of qualified blacks that came near to their proportions in the population.

Through a similar process of administrative pragmatism, the Labor Department's OFCC also came to affirmative action for African Americans. Beginning first with a trial project for government construction contracts in St. Louis in 1966 (the St. Louis Plan), and continuing through further refinements in the San Francisco Bay Area Plan and the Cleveland Plan, the administrators in the OFCC finally developed a winning civil-rights enforcement formula for a set of Philadelphia construction contracts—the Philadelphia Plan. Its distinguishing feature was the "goals-and-timetables requirement": a contractor had to promise to try to hire certain predetermined percentages of minorities at specified occupations in specified time periods. After a few legal snags in 1968, Nixon's Labor Department resurrected in 1969 what they then called the Revised Philadelphia Plan, complete with the goals and timetables requirement. From these origins in plans to provide equal opportunity for African Americans in the construction business, the OFCC then expanded this affirmative-action model from construction to all contracts of at least $50,000 in its terrifically obscure but important Order No. 4.

How Did the EEOC Decide to Recognize Some Groups as Minorities?

Though the first efforts at affirmative action focused on African Americans, the EEOC would come to add Latinos, American Indians, women of all ethnicities and races (*qua* women), and to a lesser extent Asian Americans to their enforcement efforts. This minority selection process was not based on mass mobilization but more on a simple understanding of which groups were analogous to blacks.

"The Bill Has a Simple Purpose": Title VII and Discrimination against African Americans

One simple hypothesis is that the EEOC chose as the official minorities the groups that lobbied the most for the Civil Rights Act, and were thus the original targets of the law. In this view, grassroots mobilization established in the early 1960s the identities of America's minorities.

The problem is that all available evidence indicates that Congress and President Lyndon Johnson intended Title VII and the entire Civil Rights Act of 1964 for black Americans. From the 1940s through the middle 1960s, advocates for groups other than blacks were a minor part of the civil-rights struggle. Discrimination on the bases of national origin and religion were part of that law only because of early elite support and generally their being taken for granted in civil rights legislative proposals. And the law came to prohibit discrimination on the basis of sex only through a bizarre sequence that underscored the unique meaning of women even while women's advocates took advantage of the opportunities afforded by law designed for blacks.

Nonblack groups and civil-rights advocacy

Officially classified as white for the purposes of naturalization law, Mexican Americans, the largest Latino group, nevertheless sometimes experienced economic discrimination, segregation in schools and limitations on political rights.[7] This varied considerably in kind and severity within and between the southwestern states where they were concentrated.[8] Latinos were a very minor part of the pre-1964 struggle for equal employment opportunity, but they had some high-profile support (especially in Congress) that likely helped reinforce the importance of fighting national-origin discrimination and the notion that Latinos, or at least Mexican Americans, were a minority in federal politics. Only on rare occasions did Mexican American leaders testify to the wartime Fair Employment Practices Committee (FEPC) or, after urging from Truman's President's Committee on Civil Rights, in hearings for a permanent FEPC after World War II.[9] Some Mexican advocacy groups did emerge before the 1960s. For example, The League of United Latin American Citizens (LULAC) formed in 1929 and the GI Forum, an organization of Mexican American veterans, formed in March of 1948. They fought for classical liberal goals like the black civil-rights groups.[10] Both groups, however, were small and concentrated on local issues.

There was hardly mass unrest among Latinos regarding the employment discrimination they suffered. Mexican American citizens were not mobilizing to use the legal protections afforded by the FEPC, though this may have been in part due to geographical concentration of Mexican Americans in rural states.[11] Mexican American senator Dennis Chavez (D-NM) was nevertheless a strong defender of the program.[12] He and a Roosevelt administration official tried to organize a Latino pro-FEPC lobby, but found among that population little knowledge of the FEPC or enthusiasm for the idea of forming a lobbying group. Chavez would later complain that he received no letters at all from Mexican American constituents on the subject.[13] Without backing, Chavez still worked to ensure that Latinos were a part of the national discrimination picture in the 1940s.

Chavez had significant help in establishing Mexican Americans as a minority group from Truman's President's Committee on Civil Rights (PCCR), described in Chapter 2. While the final report of the committee, *To Secure These Rights,* dealt mostly with black rights, it also briefly discussed other groups that the PCCR considered "distinctive." The PCCR recognized that rights violations occurred in all regions of the country and to "practically every group." It downplayed differences in treatment between blacks and other minority groups, defining "minority" as "a group which is treated or which regards itself as a people apart," based on physical or cultural characteristics. Though there were white ethnic groups from eastern and southern Europe who had experienced severe discrimination in the past and during World War II (see Chapter 9), except for a brief discussion of Jews, *To Secure These Rights* ignored these groups. It gave most attention to blacks, Mexican, Chinese and Japanese Americans, and American Indians, and officially sanctioned a norm for the later development of affirmative action: Latinos, Asians, and American Indians were analogous to blacks.

The PCCR distinguished blacks from other groups explicitly only in terms of size. While being ambiguous, the report also gave official sanction to the notion that Mexican Americans were a distinct race. It explained that "groups whose color makes them more easily identified are set apart from the 'dominant majority' much more than are the Caucasian minorities" (there was no discussion of the fact that many Latinos are white Caucasians). "Our other racial minorities are all much smaller than the thirteen million Negroes," the report continued. "But these groups, identified by physical appearance, unique culture traits, or both, are often geographically concentrated. As a result, irrespective of their small number in the population, theirs are the predominant civil rights problems in particular localities" and were in "particular danger."[14] By separating "unique cultural traits" from "physical appearance," the committee seemed to suggest that Mexican Americans were a white national-origin group. By then classifying them as a racial minority, it simultaneously undermined this notion. There were occasional mentions of discrimination against Jews (and two mentions of Jehovah's Witnesses), and one mention of a medical school admissions officer who testified that he was prejudiced against Irish Catholics.[15] But otherwise a line was drawn that separated the report's minorities "of physical appearance or culture or both" from everyone else.[16]

Implicitly, the PCCR indicated that blacks had the worst or most important problems by devoting the vast majority of space to them. But given the lack of mobilization and lobbying by Mexicans, Indians, and Asians, it is notable these groups received any attention at all. *To Secure These Rights* described denial of jury duty to Mexican Americans and American Indians, the wartime evacuation and loss of property suffered by the Japanese, citizenship limitations on Chinese and Japanese, limitations on the voting of Indians, school segregation of Mexican American and Indian children, restrictive covenants against a variety of groups, and statistics indicating poor health care for Chinese, Indian, Japanese, and Mexican Americans.[17]

To Secure These Rights helped establish the need for federal civil-rights laws, but it did not provoke widespread activity from nonblack pressure groups on employment civil rights. At the level of the federal government, there was little visible politics from nonblack minorities in the 1950s, but Mexican Americans, as voters and as organized pressure groups, made their presence known in the 1960 election. In a close election with Richard Nixon, John F. Kennedy and his running mate, Texas senator Lyndon Johnson, made a targeted effort to win the Mexican American vote. Mexican American members of Congress and Kennedy campaign officials created the "Viva Kennedy" program to aid the campaign. Senator Chavez and Representative Henry González (D-TX) actively shaped "Viva Kennedy." As Juan Gómez-Quiñones has written, "Mexican American voters seemingly responded to a candidate who appeared to take them seriously, was charismatic, addressed issues in Latin America, shared with most of them a Roman Catholic religious heritage, and had a wife who spoke to them in Spanish."[18] Kennedy won 85 percent of the Mexican American vote.[19]

The political activity during the 1960 election did not mean that Mexican or Latino groups were fighting for their civil rights alongside African Americans. In their massive study of Mexican Americans undertaken in the middle 1960s, Leo Grebler and his colleagues found group leaders quite unconvinced of the black analogy. To many leaders interviewed in 1964, the Grebler team's labeling of them as a "national minority" "seemed threatening," since it seemed "to classify all Mexican Americans with the least acculturated people in the group," "to slight traditional Mexican culture," and "implied unsettling comparisons with Negroes and their new militant tactics." Grebler wrote, "Indeed, merely calling Mexican Americans 'a minority,' and implying that the population is the victim of prejudice and discrimination, has caused irritation among many who prefer to believe themselves indistinguishable white Americans."[20]

Not surprisingly, the sociologist Paul Burstein found that only 9 of 433 witnesses at congressional hearings for employment civil rights from 1940 to 1972 represented national-origin groups (see Table 4.1).[21] Still, Title VII and all parts of the Civil Rights Act of 1964 prohibited discrimination on the basis of national origin. It had been prohibited in Franklin Roosevelt's executive order creating the wartime FEPC, and nearly all FEPC bills sponsored in Congress continued to prohibit national-origin, race, and religious discrimi-

Table 4.1 Pro- and anti-rights interest group activity, 1940–1972

Type of group or organization	Number of witnesses testifying before Congress on EEO	
	Pro	Anti
Black	69	0
Other racial	2	0
Jewish	37	0
Catholic	7	0
Nationality	9	0
Women	6	1
Protestant or nondenominational	27	0
Employers	11	11
Employment agency	1	0
Labor	54	2
Public interest	33	1
EEO	14	0
Federal government	103	41
Other government	48	8
Other covered organizations	2	0
Other	10	2
Total	433	66

Source: Paul Burstein, Discrimination, Jobs and Politics (Chicago: University of Chicago Press, 1998 [1985]), p. 106. © 1985 by the University of Chicago Press.

nation from 1941 through 1964. Executive orders designed to create equal employment opportunity among government contractors signed by Presidents Truman, Eisenhower, and Kennedy all routinely included national origin (plus race and religion) as forbidden grounds of discrimination. Possibly from the early efforts of Chavez and the good fortune of having national-origin discrimination included in the first executive order, it was a taken-for-granted part of civil rights, a part of the repertoire of civil rights policy. It is unclear if Latinos were significant intended beneficiaries as their inclusion was almost never discussed. Early state-level antidiscrimination laws, such as New York's 1945 State Law against Discrimination, also continued the familiar protections, and other states and cities followed suit.[22] Therefore, a meager showing at hearings or in lobbying groups simply did not matter. Antidiscrimination laws prohibited discrimination on the basis of national origin as standard operating procedure.

If Latinos were low-profile players in the struggle for civil rights, Asians and American Indians were even less visible. American Indian and Asian American representatives were virtually absent: only two witnesses for race groups other than African Americans appeared (see Table 4.1). Much more active in the employment civil-rights struggle, but left out of affirmative action, were religious groups. Representatives of Jewish organizations were major players, arguing for nondiscrimination as a moral principle and also stressing their concern, supported with statistics, for discrimination against Jews.[23] According to Paul Burstein's research, from the 1940s to the early 1970s, 37 of 433 witnesses in hearings on discrimination in employment were representatives of Jewish organizations, while seven witnesses representing Catholic groups appeared. Twenty-seven Protestant or nondemoninational witnesses also appeared, primarily arguing that discrimination was morally wrong.

In summary, Latinos, Asian Americans, and American Indians did not become involved in affirmative action because they "earned" a place through grassroots mobilization for the Civil Rights Act. Instead, concern for discrimination against them had elite support (in the case of Mexican Americans) and a taken-for-grantedness. If mobilization for Title VII was the source of inclusion in affirmative action, then Jews and Catholics would have been included before any of the groups other than African Americans.

Discrimination against women

Women's groups also were absent in lobbying for Title VII. Discrimination against women was actually gathering more attention by 1964 than discrimination against Latinos, Asians, or American Indians. But sex discrimination was a concern running on a separate track. One factor keeping women's rights separate was the conflict over the so-called protective legislation, which had splintered the women's lobby for decades. Many states had passed laws mostly during the Progressive Era that limited job possibilities and maximum hours women could work. The public justifications were that women were weaker than men and that their health should be maintained for their important roles as mothers.[24]

Many women supported these laws because they helped prevent exploitation of working-class women. Others opposed them on the principle that the law should treat women and men equally, and because they believed many laws were passed to eliminate women from job competition. This conflict was most obvious in the struggle over the Equal Rights Amendment (ERA), first proposed in 1923, which would have struck down all laws denying rights on the basis of sex.

These factions, and the lack of national-security meanings of women's rights (see chapter 3), kept women's equality off the political agenda. However, after President Kennedy broke with the tradition of courting women's support with job appointments (he preferred a search for the "best and the brightest" as part of his "New Frontier" campaign theme), he found himself under significant pressure from women's advocates in the Democratic Party (including the vice president, Lyndon B. Johnson) and in the press to do something for women.[25] Kennedy responded by creating the President's Commission on the Status of Women (PCSW). The PCSW's widely read and publicized report, *American Women,* came out just six months after Betty Friedan's best-selling protofeminist book, *The Feminine Mystique.* It took a step toward unifying women's leaders by delicately avoiding the conflict over the ERA and protective legislation even while suggesting a progressive agenda of equal employment opportunity, equal pay for equal work, and other causes.[26] The commission's report also led to an executive order for women's equality in government jobs, and helped in passage of the Equal Pay Act in 1963.[27] The states immediately formed their own commissions. By 1967, *all* states had a women's status commission.[28] But the PCSW mostly denied the categorization of sex with race discrimination, explicitly stating that "discrimination based on sex . . . involves problems sufficiently different from discrimination based on the other factors listed to make separate treatment preferable." For example, *American Women* demonstrated the complexity of sex discrimination by asking whether it was discriminatory for a firm to give more training resources to men on the assumption that "women will not be in the workforce continually."[29] And though its discussion had hints of gender consciousness, its recommendations did not directly lead to the development of affirmative action.

Shortly after *American Women* appeared, Kennedy created the Citizen's

Advisory Council on the Status of Women. He also created an Interdepartmental Committee on the Status of Women, made up of federal officials. Both would serve as institutionalized sources of advocacy for women's opportunities. Before any further action took place, however, Kennedy was assassinated. His successor, Lyndon Johnson, did not pursue the PCSW's agenda or any women's rights legislation. Instead, he chose the traditional strategy of seeking the support of women's advocates in early 1964 through government appointments, promising to appoint fifty women in thirty days.[30]

Women and Title VII: "Riding the coattails"

For women to gain employment civil rights in 1964, they needed extraordinary circumstances and new political opportunity. They did not need demonstrations and protest, and they needed almost no lobbying. The story of the 1964 addition of sex discrimination to Title VII is well known, but I tell it here to emphasize a less-acknowledged part of the story. The rights of women had a different meaning than Latino rights or rights for other groups. Women's rights, unlike those for other minority groups, encountered a unique resistance. Black rights also encountered resistance, obviously, but it had a different character. Black nondiscrimination rights were simple but threatening. Women's rights were complex but funny. This suggests that when policymakers considered women as a group and the discrimination they faced, the black analogy was less salient than other aspects of the meaning of women. What made women funny is not clear, but was almost certainly based on disparaging stereotypes and the folklore of marriage.

It is the basic plot that is well known: Democratic representative Howard Smith of Virginia offered an amendment to Title VII to add sex discrimination to the bill in hopes of *preventing* passage of the entire bill, thus thwarting African American civil rights. The cynical linkage of sex and race—premised on a sense of their very incongruity—had a long history. Amending civil-rights bills designed to help African Americans with presumably outrageous or incongruous prohibitions of other kinds of discrimination, especially sex discrimination, was a standard practice of legislative sabotage. Thus, in 1945, Howard Smith had tried to kill a Fair Employment Practices bill by seeking a sex discrimination amendment. In 1950, Democrat Dwight Rogers of Florida had successfully added "sex" to a similar bill that passed the House but went on to die in the Senate.[31] Not all such linkages were cynical. In 1962, James Roosevelt, a Democrat from California, had proposed an equal employment opportunity bill that would have protected against both race and sex discrimination, but the NAACP and the Justice and Labor Departments expressed opposition. Edith Green, Democrat representative from Oregon and member of the PCSW, then motioned in the House Committee on Education and Labor to eliminate the sex-discrimination protection.[32]

By the time Smith acted in 1964, there had been previous attempts by another devious southern Democrat, John Dowdy of Texas, to add sex discrimination protections to other titles in what became that year's Civil Rights Act. Attorney General Nicholas Katzenbach had recruited Edith Green to reprise her role as fighter against the mischief. Green believed, with many others, that discrimination against blacks was much more severe than that against women, and was concerned that the sex amendment would kill the bill.[33]

In 1964, other elite Democratic women opposed adding sex discrimination to Title VII. Esther Peterson, director of the Labor Department's Women's Bureau, later recalled, "I myself opposed that at the time—1964—because I was afraid it might endanger the civil rights bill. I just felt as an American woman I didn't want to ride the coattails of an issue that I thought was more important at that time."[34] Mary D. Keyserling, an economist Johnson appointed to head the Women's Bureau after Peterson left, felt similarly. She recalled, "[W]e were so deeply concerned with the problem of larger opportunities, equality of opportunities, on the basis of race—where perhaps the hardest problem has resided—that we did not want to introduce any issue which might impede the progress of the civil rights legislation. It was a deliberate hold-back on that ground, and I think it is a very important aspect of the legislative history."[35] No one believed that grouping national origin and religious origin with race discrimination would "impede the progress" of the bill.

The resistance to the amendment in the House revealed the unique factor affecting women's rights. In contrast to any other group's civil rights, in 1964, women's rights could be very funny. As Jo Freeman has pointed out, "Despite their many disagreements, both Smith and the liberal opponents played the provision for all the laughs it was worth and the ensuing uproar went down in congressional history as 'Ladies Day in the House.'"[36]

On the day the sex discrimination amendment was added, the atmosphere in the House was already less than serious. Southerners were seeking any maneuver to cause delays. One amendment would specifically allow employers to discriminate against atheists. It passed. Texas Democrat John Dowdy suggested adding age as a forbidden ground of discrimination. The eighty-one-year-old Smith said that "this is a right serious amendment for some of us," but it lost, 123 to 94.[37] And it was on this day that Smith introduced his amendment on sex discrimination.

Smith had help from Michigan Democrat Martha Griffiths, who did not share the prevailing view among women's leaders that this was not the appropriate time to push for women's rights. Others played a part. Though

Griffiths had no contact with any lobbying group,[38] the National Women's Party (NWP), upset that Kennedy's PCSW had recommended against the ERA, encouraged Smith. On December 16, 1963, the annual convention of the NWP passed a unanimous resolution declaring that sex discrimination should be a part of the new civil rights bill. In language that a southern opponent of civil rights could understand, the resolution stated that without this addition, the law would not provide "to a *White Woman,* a *Woman of the Christian Religion,* or a *Woman of United States Origin* the protection it would afford to Negroes (original emphasis)."[39] In Congress, however, pressure from the NWP was light at best.[40]

Griffiths let Smith introduce the amendment, explaining later that "to have Smith offer it would guarantee that you would get more than a hundred votes" and southern support might be lost if a woman introduced it.[41] Smith suggested women were entitled to nondiscrimination in employment with a light-hearted, joking style that characterized the day and the treatment of women's issues throughout the decade of the birth of feminism and women's rights. He wanted "to prevent discrimination against another minority group, the women, but a very essential minority group, in the absence of which the majority group would not be here today . . . Now, I am very serious about this amendment." In justifying his amendment, Smith explained that women suffered from employment discrimination, insisted again that he was serious, but then read from a constituent's letter complaining that there were not enough husbands to go around and asked for government action. Smith asked, who was going "to protect our spinster friends in their 'right' to a nice husband and family?" Smith thus introduced women's rights and insulted women at the same time.

Edith Green, joined by Emmanuel Celler (D–NY), led the Democratic resistance to the amendment on the House floor. Celler added to the comic atmosphere with his own knee-slapper. "[W]omen, indeed, are not the minority in my house," he announced, and explained that harmony was maintained there even though Celler himself always had the last two words in his household: "yes, dear." Celler then said he opposed the amendment, reading a letter from the Labor Department quoting Esther Peterson on the PCSW view that sex discrimination "involves problems sufficiently different from discrimination based on the other factors listed to make separate treatment preferable." Celler then raised the utterly irrelevant tangle of complexity that the ERA was supposed by some to produce ("What would become of the crimes of rape and statutory rape?"), and warned that the amendment would strike down women's protective legislation. Edith Green also argued that it jeopardized women's protective laws, pointing out that no group testified in support of it at hearings and repeating several times that "for every discrimination that has been made against a woman in this country there has been 10 times as much discrimination against the Negro of this country." This language indicates that when lawmakers said "woman" they thought "white woman." The message was that race discrimination did not equal sex discrimination, though even in opposition, the analogy was irresistible: Green admitted that she might appear to be "an Uncle Tom—or perhaps an Aunt Jane."[42]

Despite the opposition from many liberal Democrats and the lack of lobbying on the issue, Griffiths, joined by some women legislators, fought hard for passage. The primary foe was the hilarity of women's rights. She later recalled:

I can remember that just before I went up there, once the amendment had been offered, there was uproarious laughter. Now we had been debating this bill since Tuesday, and this was now Thursday, and Lee Sullivan [Leonor Sullivan, Democrat of Missouri] looked back at me—there had never been any laughter on the rest of the bill, but when the amendment was offered, there was tremendous laughter, there was uproarious laughter—and Lee looked back, and she said, "Martha, if you can't stop that laughter, you're lost."[43]

On the House floor, Griffiths pointed out the significance of the hilarity: "I presume that if there had been any necessity to have to point out that women were a second-class sex, the laughter would have proved it." Griffiths brought up various examples of sex discrimination, argued that the law without the amendment would leave white women unprotected, and that "a vote against this amendment today by a white man is a vote against his wife, or his widow, or his daughter, or his sister." Griffiths and New York Republican Katharine St. George both argued that the so-called protective legislation often was a tool used by men to keep women from some high-paying jobs.[44]

Southern Democratic congressmen, such as George Andrews of Alabama, saw the possibility of racial preference in the bill without the sex amendment. In language that would become familiar in debates over affirmative action, Andrews said, "If a white woman and a Negro woman applied for the same job, and each woman had identical qualifications, the chances are about 99 to 1 that the Negro woman would be given the job because if the employer did not give the job to the Negro woman he could be prosecuted under this bill. Failure to employ the white woman would not subject the employer to such action." J. Russell Tuten of Georgia, Lucius Rivers of South Carolina, Ezekiel Gathings of Arkansas, and Howard Smith all agreed with this preferential logic. Smith said starkly, "[I]f I do not hire the colored woman and hire the white woman, then the Commission is going to be looking down my throat and will want to know why I did not. I may be in a lawsuit." The amendment passed, 168 to 133.[45]

The entire bill passed the House 290 to 133, and the Senate passed the same bill 73 to 27. There was almost no discussion of the sex amendment in the Senate. One exception was buried in a list of questions submitted to the Democrats by Senate minority leader Everett Dirksen (R–IL). The question was introduced in a jokey manner (Dirksen wrote, "Now I turn to discrimination on account of sex. Frankly, I always like to discriminate in favor of the fairer sex. I hope that the might of the Federal Government will not enjoin me from such discrimination"). Dirksen brought up the potential conflict of Title VII with protective legislation, but then immediately shifted to another issue—whether women could be preferred for jobs requiring manual dexterity, such as building radios. Senator Joseph Clark (D–PA) simply responded that such preferences could continue as a BFOQ, or "bona fide occupational qualification," a loophole that allowed hiring on the basis of religion, gender, or national origin but not on the basis of race. Clark ignored the protective legislation inquiry.[46] Public debate was over, and the final bill included sex among the other forbidden grounds of discrimination.[47]

Title VII: a civil rights law for American blacks

Despite the inclusion of sex, religion, and national origin, the early discussion of other ethnic minorities by Truman's Civil Rights Committee, and the presumably broad meaning of the prohibition on race discrimination, it must be emphasized that American citizens and political elites saw Title VII and the entire Civil Rights Act of 1964 as being a law for African Americans. The model for Title VII and the EEOC grew out of the old wartime FEPC that A. Philip Randolph had fought for in 1941. Civil-rights advocates both in and outside the government had fought for a similar bill ever since. In lobbying Congress, the motive forces for Title VII were the African American civil-rights groups, federal government officials, and religious groups concerned with discrimination against African Americans. The sociologist Paul Burstein found that the *New York Times* reported on almost 3,800 demonstrations in favor of civil rights between 1940 and 1972, and that 95 percent of these were related to discrimination against African Americans. Some protests occurred in the 1940s regarding anti-Semitism, but other groups did not register in the nation's newspaper of record until the late 1960s and early 1970s, and then only barely.[48] Regarding general *Times* coverage of discrimination issues, Burstein sums up: "Beginning in the 1950s . . . an increasing proportion of media attention to civil rights was devoted to blacks, and by 1961 coverage of civil rights and of blacks had become virtually synonymous. At least through the beginnings of the 1970s, neither women nor minorities other than blacks had succeeded in gaining much attention from the *New York Times*."[49]

Other evidence shows the overriding salience of African American issues in the making of civil-rights law. Much of the discussion of the bill in Congress emphasized its targeting of blacks. Senator Hubert Humphrey stated bluntly that "the bill has a simple purpose. That purpose is to give fellow citizens—Negroes—the same rights and opportunities that white people take for granted."[50] Lyndon Johnson only mentioned discrimination on the bases of race and color (naming no nonblack minority groups and making no mention of national origin, sex, or religious discrimination) when he signed the Civil Rights Act.[51] The EEOC shared this perception. Its first annual report, for example, stated plainly, "The chief thrust of the statute was, of course, aimed at discrimination against the Negro."[52] The basic orienting materials gathered for the five new commissioners had only limited references to sex discrimination, and when the new commission started on July 2, 1965, there were no women in the highest "super-grade" level appointments.[53]

Institutionalizing Minority Recognition at the EEOC: The EEO-1 Form

The first step in the expansion of affirmative action was the most important and far-reaching. It was also the easiest and least discussed. The key to the process of group recognition was inclusion in any government analyses of discrimination. This meant deciding which groups were to be counted as minorities for the government's EEO-1 form, which employers used to record the racial, ethnic, and gender breakdowns of their workforces. The EEO-1 institutionalized the prevailing view that Title VII, though formally quite broad, was really about race discrimination. It further erased lines within minority categories, and established the black analogy for Latinos, Asian Americans, and American Indians.

Precursors of the EEO-1

The facts surrounding the origins of the EEO-1 remain hazy, but research by Harold Orlans points to a magnificently obscure bit of political activity during the late 1950s and early 1960s. President Eisenhower had followed Roosevelt and Truman in issuing an executive order to prohibit discrimination by government contractors on the bases of race, national origin, and religion. The order established the President's Committee on Government Contracts to oversee the program. In 1956, this committee began using a survey requiring contractors to count their "Negro," "other minority," and "total" employees. If there were many "other minority" employees, the survey added that "the contractor may be able to furnish employment statistics for such groups" including "Spanish-Americans, Orientals, Indians, Jews, Puerto Ricans, etc." Except for the inclusion of Jews, the enigmatic "etc.," and the inexplicable separation of Puerto Ricans from the seemingly broad "Spanish-Americans" category, these administrators in 1956 quietly established the official minorities for the rest of the century and beyond.

They also established the principle—in contradiction to discrimination law, if not logic—that the problems of blacks should be privileged. There were "Negroes," to be counted by every government contractor, and then there were "other minorities." Noticing the hierarchy, some Mexican American groups demanded that they be promoted from "other minorities" and placed on every form, along with blacks. The League of United Latin American Citizens (or LULAC, a mostly Mexican American group that had campaigned to have Mexicans labeled as Caucasians in the 1930s),[54] the GI Forum (a group of Mexican American veterans), the Mexican-American Political Action Committee (MAPA), and Alienza, a group based in Arizona, argued that Mexican Americans had suffered discrimination on a par with blacks. They worked with Mexican American legislators Edward Roybal (D–CA), Henry Gonzales (D–TX), and Joseph Montoya (D–NM). Accordingly, the broad and ambiguous "Spanish-Americans" category was elevated to the standard form.[55]

Through the efforts of advocates for Japanese and Chinese Americans, the administrators of President Kennedy's more active agency, the President's Committee on Equal Employment Opportunity (PCEEO), similarly elevated the entire category of "Orientals." The Japanese American Citizens League asked for equal attention, and when Hawaii became a state in 1959, its congressional representatives, Senator Hiram L. Fong (R–HA) and Representative Daniel K. Inouye (D–HA), supported inclusion of a category for Orientals. In response, David Mann, the director of surveys for Eisenhower's committee and Kennedy's replacement, added the broad and ambiguous "Oriental" category in 1962.

Mann went ahead and added American Indians to the form as well, though Indian advocates had not lobbied. He later recalled believing that they suffered discrimination and suffered from a "woeful economic state." On the other hand, black groups objected to the inclusion of Jews because Jews had done relatively well economically. Jewish groups did not press the matter, and Mann had them removed from the form (see Chapter 9). Though the categories were blunt and unscientific, in Mann's view they had the virtue of simplicity. America's official minorities were born.[56]

While some lobbying played a role in this process, it is easy to overstate its importance. The form was created for blacks. The administrators, apparently on their own, then created a list of "other minorities." This prior development made it very easy for other groups to be placed next to blacks after just a few meetings—or none, in the case of American Indians. *They were already designated as minorities.* The taken-for-grantedness of America's minorities, even in the 1950s, was the crucial factor in this process. There was something self-evident to administrators about the plausibility of these particular groups. They did not see any need for independent studies of relative discrimination. The groups included in the 1950s were also the groups given the most prominent mention in the 1947 report of the President's Committee on Civil Rights, as described above. While lobbying played a role, it is by no means certain that other groups could have successfully lobbied. As I show in Chapter 9, some of the groups left off of the later EEO-1 form tried to be included, but did not succeed.

It should also be underscored, however, that the Eisenhower committee paid most attention to blacks, at least as shown by public-relations documents. For example, "Five Years of Progress," a report on the Eisenhower committee's activities for 1953–58, almost completely ignores the "other minorities." The report included twenty-four photos of successful minority employees in their work environments. While embarrassingly patronizing from a contemporary perspective, it is worth noting that twenty-three of the photos depicted only black men and women at work (often with apparently satisfied white supervisors watching them). Only one photo included some Asian American women together with a Latina employee. A section of the report on "Compliance Surveys" and "Areas Opened to Minority Group Members" mentions only "Negroes." The broader inclusiveness of the program was only suggested by some of the descriptions of "Records of Progress," in which a few companies presented statistics of their "other minorities," including numbers for Spanish-Americans, Orientals, Indians, and Jews.[57]

If the first listing of minorities occurred during the Eisenhower administration, the full equal billing on a government form occurred on Kennedy's PCEEO's "Standard Form 40." The PCEEO used Form 40 for monitoring purposes but did not integrate the form into enforcement activities. An identical form, the "EEO-10," was used by Plans for Progress, a parallel program, in which certain mostly large employers worked with the government on a voluntary basis to improve job opportunities for African Americans. The government used Form 40 and EEO-10 simply to measure the levels of minority hiring by government contractors or by Plans for Progress firms. Neither program used the forms for anything except information gathering. It is not clear what the program officials did with the information, if anything, but both forms went beyond the then-prevailing concern for discrimination against African Americans only. They included—under the heading "Minor-

ity Groups"—categories for "Negro," "Spanish American," "American Indian," "Oriental," as well as gender breakdowns for each race. Form 40 included a category for women, even though the PCEEO had no jurisdiction
over sex discrimination.[58] The EEO-1 was basically Form 40 with a different
name.

Congress and the EEO-1

What did Congress have in mind regarding minority counting forms?
Though it intended the Civil Rights Act for black Americans, as described
above, it is possible that Congress offered some guidance on which groups
should be counted. Title VII of the Civil Rights Act of 1964 specifically em-
powered the EEOC "to make such technical studies as are appropriate to ef-
fectuate the purposes and policies of this title and to make the results of such
studies available to the public."[59] In addition, the law stated that the EEOC
"shall, by regulation, require each employer, labor organization, and joint la-
bor-management committee subject to this title . . . to maintain such records
as are reasonably necessary to carry out the purpose of this title."[60] While
some in Congress appeared to have had in mind monitoring of the racial
composition of workforces, the focus of the debate was so focused on African
Americans that no one thought about which groups should be included. In
their interpretive memo, Senators Joseph Clark and Clifford P. Case barely
hinted at something like the EEO-1:

> Requirements for the keeping of records are a customary and necessary
> part of a regulatory statute. They are particularly essential in title VII be-
> cause whether or not a certain action is discriminatory will turn on the
> motives of the respondent, which will usually be best evidenced by his
> pattern of conduct on similar occasions.[61]

Everett Dirksen raised possible reporting forms in his own memorandum,
showing both a concern and expectation that the form would go beyond race
to include religion:

> What of the conflict between State and Federal record requirements? Il-
> linois prohibits any reference to color or religion in employers' records.
> Title VII would require this information to be kept. Are we now to force
> an employer to violate a State law in order to comply with a Federal stat-
> ute, each of which has the same purpose?

Clark replied that state laws "would yield to the supremacy of the federal law,
since it is necessary to have this data to determine if a pattern of discrimination exists." Dirksen pressed again, asking why the bill did not specifically
state what the forms would be like, and suggesting that Congress and not

a federal agency should create them. Clark deflected, saying vaguely that "Congress cannot set definite recordkeeping requirements and should not try to write them in the statute, because it is not yet known what records will be needed."[62]

Members of Congress seemed aware that some kind of designation of minorities would be required. But there is little evidence Congress was passing the buck to avoid making a difficult decision. There was no real decision here. With the focus of the civil-rights debate squarely on African Americans, Dirksen never questioned which groups should be on the forms, and neither Clark nor Case, nor anyone else, showed much interest, at least not in the public record.

Expert opinion on counting official minorities

The idea of race-reporting forms was, in short, hardly discussed during congressional lawmaking and the issue of which groups were to be counted and designated as America's official minorities was not discussed at all. Still, the leading analysis of the Civil Rights Act's Title VII, provided by the Columbia University law professor Michael I. Sovern, predicted the use of race-counting forms. Sovern pointed out that some unnamed critics found them "reminiscent of Hitler's Nuremberg Laws," "unwholesome," and "potentially divisive." But on balance he approved of them, and said it was "a good guess" that the EEOC would require reports like Form 40.[63]

Why? Sovern argued that such a form supplies information that is of "incalculable value," since it showed firms and the government where firms were likely discriminating: "A report that shows no Negroes above the level of unskilled labor may not be the report of a discriminator, but it is suggestive enough to warrant further checking." Such reports could also show that African Americans are available to be hired. "For example," he explained, "a contractor can hardly continue to maintain that no qualified Negroes are available when the reports of other contractors in the area show Negroes doing comparable work." Sovern admitted that "the risk that companies will engage in quota hiring in order to impress government officials that they are not discriminating is less easily dismissed." However, since a company with "about the 'right' proportion of Negroes" is "virtually invulnerable to a charge of discrimination," Sovern argued that this type of "insurance" was a part of any equal opportunity program regardless of race statistics forms, and "[f]air administration" was needed to minimize the quota-hiring defensive tactic. For all of these reasons, "expansion of compliance reporting seems inevitable."[64]

What was remarkable about Sovern's otherwise thoughtful analysis was the complete absence of attention to the number or nature of the groups on the existing form, and the inclusion of gender statistics. Though his book reprinted Form 40 so that it accompanied his analysis, it was as if the three other ethnoracial groups and the male and female categories were not even there. His discussion only mentioned "Negroes." He did approve of the omission of religion ("The limitation to race means . . . that companies need not inquire into their employees' religion—a subject that many of us firmly believe to be no one's business but our own"). But he did not explore the legal or moral implications of the elimination of one ground of discrimination from an agency's "incalculably valuable" tool for fighting discrimination. Also ignored was that the form was *not* limited to race. It included gender. Moreover, no biology books stated that "Spanish American" was a race—it was an extremely complicated national-origin grouping that spanned the globe and included arguably three races and various mixtures. Sovern's myopia was broadly shared, even by Form 40's creators. The PCEEO, which collected Form 40, only used it to create "zero lists" of firms with no African American employees, and "underutilization lists" of firms with very few African American employees.[65]

The very easy process of declaring America's official minorities

The EEOC soon came to the same view as Sovern. The reporting system would be a valuable tool in measuring progress in the eradication of discrimination, and by identifying firms that were likely discriminators, it would make the most efficient use of the EEOC's limited personnel and resources. Rather than being limited to federal government contractors, the EEOC had jurisdiction over all firms with more than one hundred employees. In developing what became the EEO-1 form, however, EEOC officials simply copied Form 40, making only minor changes. When the proposed regulation that would require the form was printed in the *Federal Register*, allowing Americans who happened to read the new regulation to respond with their comments about it, an explanatory note stated that the form was nearly identical with Form 40.[66] This meant that it retained the four official minority groups, plus male and female categories for all groups.

This similarity was strategic. According to Herbert Hammerman, the EEOC's chief of reports, and Charles Markham, the director of research and reports, the EEOC wanted to keep its form as much as possible like the one already used in the established (and very obscure) practice. Changing the forms risked adding controversy where there had been none. As Markham recalled, "Basically we decided that this is what employers are used to, let's just stick with it."[67]

In addition, everyone "knew" that, despite the wide scope of Title VII, race discrimination was the key issue and Form 40 matched the EEOC administrators' view of which groups were American minorities and which suffered the most discrimination. Markham recalled later, "We just felt the thrust of the problem was black, Hispanic, and Native Americans."[68] In his interview with me, Markham made no mention of Asian Americans, a group that the EEOC included apparently because they had previously been included. There was brief discussion of dropping them from a later form (see below).

In addition to publishing the regulation in the *Federal Register*, EEOC officials had some other roadblocks and veto points to navigate, including Congress, the Bureau of the Budget, and the civil-rights groups. It was not the issue over who would be counted as minorities that was most troubling; EEOC officials were more concerned about having the legal authority to require employers to fill out the forms in states that already had antidiscrimination agencies. The law was ambiguous on this point.[69] They sought to clear the new form with Dirksen, the Senate minority leader and a major figure in getting Title VII passed. Charles Markham recalls visiting Dirksen's office along with EEOC chair Franklin Delano Roosevelt Jr. and general counsel Charles Duncan, "and he [Dirksen] didn't make any loud objections and so we went ahead with it."[70]

Markham and Herbert Hammerman also met with African American civil-rights leaders, including representatives of the Leadership Conference on Civil Rights and Marion Barry of the more radical Student Non-Violent Coordinating Committee. In a meeting in the EEOC office, Markham quickly convinced the dashiki-clad Barry that the form was needed. Other civil-rights leaders were more difficult to persuade. For instance, Washington NAACP lobbyist Clarence Mitchell had spoken against color-conscious methods, arguing that "the history of the reason why we do not include [racial identification] is sadly and surely proven, that the minute you put race on a civil service form, the minute you put a picture on an application form, you have opened the door to discrimination and, if you say that isn't true, I regret to say I feel you haven't been exposed to all of the problems that exist in this country." For Mitchell of the NAACP, "keeping racial statistics" was "the crevasse which has no bottom."[71] Those who opposed the EEO-1 resisted the idea of maintaining official firm-level statistics of African American employment. Some suggested alternatives, such as an occasional "audit" of a firm's minority hiring.

There is no record of civil-rights leaders addressing the issue of which groups to include on the form, except for handwritten notes made on a copy of the EEO-1 in the files of the Leadership Conference on Civil Rights (LCCR), an umbrella group of civil-rights organizations. The notes apparently were made after a meeting with Markham and Hammerman. They describe the reason for the form ("in absence of a charge, we [EEOC officials] have no right to get any evidence"), offer suggested alternatives ("can commission send investigators in for routine checks?"; "universal reporting v. sampling"), and include a very rare expression of the form's scope. The LCCR official noticed a curious omission. "Catholic," the note taker wrote; "doing nothing about *creed*" (original emphasis).[72] But the issue was dropped. The absence of religious discrimination from the chief enforcement tool was a point not pursued by the LCCR or any other group. Black groups similarly did not seek to restrict scope to blacks.

Within the EEOC itself, there is no record of discussion of who was to be included on the EEO-1. Hammerman recalls the focus was simply on obtaining maximum information while not being overly complex, and that "minority groups, sex data, and job categories were carried over from Form 40 without discussion."[73] Markham recalls EEOC vice chairman Luther Holcomb bringing up the issue of native Alaskans, and wondering where they might fit. No one at the time raised the issue of adding religious groups to the form, and no one questioned inclusion of all four groups. A representative of Polish Americans asked that a category of "Polonians" (the term used by Polish leaders to refer to Polish Americans) be added, but the EEOC held firm on their EEO-1 minorities (see Chapter 9).

Instructions for the EEO-1 stated that employers were not to ask employees to which group they belonged, but rather were to rely on visual identification. The importance of relying on visual surveys came as a result of consultations and compromise with African American civil-rights groups. Hammerman later stated:

> I recall vividly a group conversation with the [NAACP's] Washington representative, Clarence Mitchell. He angrily declared that he had fought the tendency of employers to ask applicants for employment to state or write their race for several years and was not about to change his mind now. We were at a crossroads. With the opposition of the NAACP, the EEO-1 would be dead. It also seemed obvious to me that it made sense for employers to identify minorities in the same way that they were discriminated against, by observation. After all, employers were not sociologists.[74]

Appeasing the NAACP by relying on a visual basis for minority categorization had important consequences. Perhaps most important, it meant government policy would mirror basic social patterns of discrimination. It meant reinforcing the "one-drop rule" by which Americans have long categorized African Americans. Anyone who looked remotely black was black. Thus, as Hammerman has commented, "there could be no discussion of interracial or interethnic marriages," including American Indians or Asian Americans, two groups not normally subject to the one-drop rule, but that have high rates of intermarriage with Euro-Americans. Employers might use the one-drop rule for making minorities of persons of any combination of mixed ancestry, or they might not categorize them as minorities (though it would be in their interest to count them as minorities to increase the minority percentages in their work forces).

There was also no clear way of identifying the "Spanish-Americans," who might be of any race. This suggests that the policymakers—if they thought about it at all—had in mind a distinctly racialized prototype with the category, and presumed the nonsociologist employers could discern a Spanish surname from sometimes similar Italian or Portuguese surnames. Visual identification reinforced the exclusion of white ethnics and religious groups from the form (see Chapter 9). Visual identification, reliance on surnames, and the form categories also erased any differences on the basis of national origin within minority groups: a white Cuban would be grouped with a dark brown Mexican *indio* as Spanish Americans; a Japanese American would be grouped with a Laotian; and an immigrant from Jamaica or Kenya would be grouped with an American descendant of slaves.

These sorts of issues were invisible in 1965, since massive discrimination against African Americans was such an obvious and urgent priority and immigration policy and global developments had not yet allowed great numbers of Latinos and Asians to come to the United States. The intermarriage issue came up only when Markham received letters from South Carolina arguing that there had been considerable black–white racial mixing there in the past, and this made it difficult for employers to fill out the EEO-1. Markham, who with Hammerman had helped devise the method of determining group classifications, simply pointed out that the South Carolinians could rely on the method that they had been using for decades to segregate and discriminate against the African Americans—simply looking at them.[75]

After these initial consultations, on December 16, 1965, the EEOC held public hearings on the race-reporting system. Support for the system was strong, especially among those involved in civil-rights administrative enforcement. Like Professor Sovern, these individuals felt that the form would help administrators measure progress toward equal opportunity.[76] Again, in the hearings, there was almost no discussion of the EEO-1's level of inclusiveness.

The lack of discussion on inclusiveness is especially remarkable regarding women, as few administrators at the time had any idea of what the expected level of female employment should be. The issue of counting women only came up only once, and then in jest. Willis Bullard, representing the Kelly

Girls temporary employment service, gave testimony that showed the overriding emphasis on African Americans: "I have no comment to make upon sex. I think I am the first one today to have used that three-letter word. We do of course, when we send out a Kelly Girl, it is going to be a real shock to some customer when he finds a man appearing as a Kelly Girl!"[77] The EEO-1 passed the scrutiny of the public hearings intact and unmodified.

These decisions, if they could be called that, were of great importance. The EEO-1 was a public, if implicit, federal declaration of the nation's minorities. The EEO-1 made certain types of underrepresentation more visible, more discernible, and more outrageous than others. On paper, discrimination against women of all groups, Latinos, Asian Americans, and American Indians was the same as blacks, and all became, with no debate, eligible for affirmative action. With these groups, discrimination would be measured and assessed. The rest of the population collapsed into a monolithic "white male" category.

From the EEO-1 to Affirmative Action

Being listed on the EEO-1 was a crucial prerequisite for benefiting from a difference-conscious justice. But it was perfectly possible for the EEOC to gather statistics on many groups, but pay most attention to only one. This is indeed what happened, as EEOC officials focused their attention almost exclusively on African Americans. They simply neglected Latinos, Asian Americans, and American Indians and treated gender discrimination as a nuisance.

African Americans were emphasized because the Civil Rights Act, and thus the EEOC, was created for blacks. But the EEO-1 also quickly showed that the different minorities were not equal. The 1966 *Equal Employment Report No. 1,* a nationwide analysis based on the new EEO-1 data of forty-three thousand employers and 26 million workers, generally revealed that minority-group workers were concentrated in lower-paid occupations, with African Americans and Spanish-surnamed men and women doing generally the worst. Assuming that all disparities were the result of discrimination, however, the EEO-1 showed a clear hierarchy of group exclusion: "A male Oriental has a little better than half as good a chance of becoming a manager or official as an Anglo; the American Indian's prospects are slightly lower than the Oriental's; the chances of a man with a Spanish surname are only one fifth as good as that of a member of the majority group; and for Negroes, the figure is one twelfth."[78]

But group inequality and minority status were not this simple. The reports showed that while underrepresented in managerial positions, other measures showed Asian American men and women on average had a higher occupational standing than did Euro-Americans: "More than 1 out of every 4 Oriental men is a professional compared to 1 out of 11 Anglos (and 1 out of 100 among Negroes)." Asian American women also did better than Euro-American women on the occupational scale.[79] The EEOC's own data, then, told them that blacks had the worst of it.

Officially identified as victimized minorities but then neglected, lobbies for the two largest groups—women and Latinos—developed to join African Americans in pressuring the EEOC. None of the groups, however, made affirmative action or any kind of difference-conscious hiring a priority. As described previously, African Americans focused on simply more effective enforcement (cease-and-desist power), and the EEOC responded with an affirmative action model of justice. As I describe below, women primarily fought for classically liberal goals and for the inclusion of more women on the EEOC staff and elsewhere in policymaking positions. Latinos wanted similar increases in staff representation. These groups would not be completely satisfied, but they would get relatively quick and positive responses. The EEO-1's official minorities could now make policy gains by focusing attention on a civil-rights bureaucracy and not complex, democratically elected branches of government. EEOC administrators, some of whom were themselves activists in rights organizations, could respond to the pressure with the ready-made policy of affirmative action.

"Boos from Lady Fans"

Many members of Congress and even some women's leaders understood gender discrimination as a lesser priority, and women were an almost absent force in lobbying for the Civil Rights Act. Nevertheless, there were a surprisingly large number of sex discrimination complaints. In 1966, for example, the EEOC received 2,053 charges of sex discrimination (34 percent of all complaints), compared to the 3,254 charges of race discrimination (56 percent of all complaints).[80] Such a large number of complaints required immediate, if reluctant, attention.

Early controversies in women's equality

If the EEOC was to act on women's rights, it would do so without support from the liberal media. For the *New York Times*, discrimination against women was a low priority—and an opportunity for jokes. In an editorial titled "De-Sexing the Job Market," the *Times*, smug and satisfied, brought up "the bunny problem," the general label for such burning issues as "the quandary of how you rule if a man applies for a job as 'bunny' in a Playboy club." Misinterpreting the law and misusing words like a stumbling drunkard, the nation's newspaper of record predicted that "everything has to be neuterized," that "the Rockettes may become bi-sexual, and a pity, too" and concluded its inquiry with mock indignation: "Bunny problem, indeed! This is revolution, chaos. You can't even safely advertise for a wife any more."[81]

The conservative *Wall Street Journal* echoed the same take on the issue, though treated women with a bit more respect. In an amazingly prescient article, Monroe Karmin predicted on October 13, 1965 that the EEOC would "draw cheers from Negroes, boos from lady fans, and cries of 'foul' from conservatives." Karmin foresaw for African Americans a "two-fisted barrage against almost any suspected discrimination, aiming for an early knockout," and this effort would call for preferential treatment. "On behalf of the ladies," however, the EEOC would only offer "a succession of light jabs against unchivalrous treatment, just enough to qualify as effort though far short of enthusiasm." One commissioner told him, "We're not going out on our charger to overturn patterns [of sex discrimination]." The *Journal* highlighted a few sex discrimination issues (such as protective legislation and whether companies would have to provide women's restrooms) where the EEOC was keeping "an open mind," and declared "the 'Bunny' is safe."[82]

Commission chairman Franklin Roosevelt Jr. seemed unsure how to approach the issue of sex discrimination. At his first press conference in July 1965, he said sex discrimination was a "terribly complicated" issue.[83] In Roosevelt's letter to President Johnson concerning the first one hundred days of the new commission, he said implementation of the sex discrimination prohibition was "particularly challenging" and "continues to occupy a great deal of the Commission's time and effort."[84] On the other hand, Roosevelt showed an early belief that the commission's responsibility in prohibiting sex discrimination could be a vehicle for gaining new allies. In December of 1965, he asked fellow commissioner Richard Graham for ideas regarding review of "existing state 'protective' legislation." "I realize this is a pretty big undertaking," Roosevelt continued, "but I think that it would be one which would give the Commission great status as a leader in this field and, of course, I am confident that the women's groups would enthusiastically endorse such an effort."[85]

It is typical for a government agency to behave in ways meant to secure its legitimacy and value to a particular constituency.[86] There is evidence, however, to suggest a level of resentment among EEOC administrators at having to trouble themselves with sex discrimination. Most showed little interest in gaining political support from women's groups. The bizarre circumstances of the sex discrimination amendment led many to view that provision as illegitimate.[87] Consequently, most EEOC administrators viewed women's rights as a low priority or a distraction.[88] Though Title VII and the commission's own EEO-1 form suggested otherwise, most EEOC officials did not at first believe that sex discrimination was analogous to race discrimination. In a line often quoted by historians of women's rights, EEOC executive director Herman Edelsberg said in 1966 that the sex discrimination protection was a "fluke . . . conceived out of wedlock," implying the law had no legitimate standing. Showing brazen contempt for the idea of women's rights, he declared that "men were entitled to female secretaries."[89]

Many EEOC staffers shared this low regard for women's rights. The commission staff attorney David Zugschwerdt recalls, "Given that . . . sex discrimination came in as essentially a ploy by the opponents to try to derail the legislation, it is quite understandable that it was not . . . even on the radar."[90] Women who worked in the EEOC in those early years complained of the lack of priority or respect given to women's rights. Sonia Pressman Fuentes, an EEOC attorney, recalled that the commission's general counsel (and African American) Charlie Duncan "called me a 'sex maniac' because I was interested in enforcing the prohibition against sex discrimination. That made me a sex maniac at the commission." She later remembered "walking on the street to my car, and the tears would be rolling down my face because I felt like . . . I was battling the whole commission, basically, except for the few people who felt as I did."[91] Another staff attorney, Susan Deller Ross, similarly recalled later that "the people [at EEOC] viewed it as an agency whose only serious mission was really to work on black civil rights . . . I think there was an overtone of hostility with some as much as it was not having thought out the issues."[92]

In September 1966, Aileen Hernandez, an African American woman married to a Latino and the lone female EEOC commissioner, had enough of the negative attitude. She sent letters to the other commissioners and EEOC counsel Richard Berg, explaining "I am well aware that there is a difference of opinion within this agency as to the extent and kind of discrimination against women . . . That brings me to our long-range responsibility—assuming the role of attitude changer." She reminded them that they were not bound by "conventional wisdom" on race questions, and should take a similar attitude on gender. "Just as in the race question," she pointed out, "we can start the change in attitude, by forcing a change in behavior."[93]

The message did not get through. As late as March 1967, a progress report of an EEOC Task Force on Staff Relations, Efficiency and Morale commented that "morale is low, and evidence indicates that it is declining" but it was unclear why. To help, the task force suggested, among other things, an orientation program that would give a history of the civil rights movement and its current status, but no mention was made of women's rights or any other minority group.[94] Also in March, when Berg received a letter from a woman's group demanding some action, he passed it on to Pauli Murray, an African American woman and fellow counsel at EEOC, with a small note attached saying, "Why don't you answer this? They're *your* friends" (original emphasis).[95]

Meanwhile women were sending in complaints around three main issues: women's protective laws (about which Title VII said nothing), the airlines' desire to hire women as stewardesses while forcing them to resign when they married or reached a certain age (varying between thirty-two and thirty-five), and sex-segregated classified advertisements for job openings.[96]

These were complex issues because there was, of course, no tradition at all of laws intended to protect African Americans from long work hours or dangerous occupations. There also were no companies that cared about the age or marital status of black employees. And whereas the EEOC ordered that classified advertisements segregated by newspapers on the basis of "white jobs" and "black jobs" were immediately (and uncontroversially) illegal, advertisements that separated male and female jobs appeared sensible and continued after Title VII went into effect. To the EEOC administrators these issues seemed different from race discrimination, and they were unsure how to handle them.

Not much interested in the question of protective legislation for women, the EEOC flip-flopped on the issue, though the courts were beginning (in 1968) to get involved, mostly striking down the laws.[97] It also flip-flopped on the stewardess problem. Alfred Blumrosen recalled that "when the stewardesses first came to the EEOC, in the form of two very attractive women, it struck me that the staff was probably more interested in their attractiveness than the nature of their complaint."[98] After three years, the agency finally agreed that customer preferences did not justify the discrimination.[99]

It was the EEOC's position on sex-segregated advertisements that would attract the most attention. This controversy was significant because it highlighted the tenuousness of the black–woman analogy, and because it came to dominate the women's agenda, keeping issues like affirmative action a much lower priority.

The main problem was that the EEOC believed blacks and women were different.[100] Blumrosen recalled that "if you had asked the senior staff 'is it okay to have "help wanted-white,"' they would have thrown up their hands in horror. But when the question was can we have help wanted male and help wanted female, they said we better call a conference of the newspaper publishers."[101] The EEOC's initial position on sex-segregated job advertising was the product of a special committee appointed to consider the issue, consisting of thirteen men and four women, and including ten representatives of newspapers or advertising agencies.[102] On September 22, 1965, the EEOC ruled that "for the convenience of readers" the practice was acceptable as long as the advertisement itself stated the job was open to both sexes and a disclaimer notice was placed on every other page stating "Many listings in the 'male' or 'female' columns are not intended to exclude or discourage applications from persons of the other sex." Still, the American Newspaper Publishers Association (ANPA) complained, fearing lost revenue from firms that preferred the segregated advertisements, and because the disclaimer notice took up ad space. The EEOC responded by revising the policy, removing the need for any disclaimer.[103]

The change in policy came as a result of political pressure, but the perceived reasonableness of sex-segregated ads, and an assumption that race and sex discrimination were essentially different, made the pressure effective. The EEOC commissioner Luther Holcomb (who assumed the position of acting chair when Roosevelt resigned) told Lyndon Johnson's aides James Jones and Marvin Watson on March 25, 1966 that "few times in their entire history have they [ANPA] been as disturbed as they have been by the [EEOC] interpretation" and confided that "this has been my most delicate undertaking since coming to Washington." However, Holcomb—apparently unconcerned about the views of women—announced that "I am glad to be able to report to you that the task has been accomplished to the complete satisfaction of the Publishers." Holcomb reported that Stanford Smith of ANPA "feels that this is going to be of great significance in creating a new climate of goodwill for President Johnson and the Administration," and recommended that Johnson speak at the upcoming annual meeting of the association, since "the way has been cleared now for the Administration to really cinch some mileage with an all important group." Though Johnson could not attend the meeting, Jones and Watson expressed their satisfaction at Holcomb's actions.[104]

The double standard outraged Congresswoman Martha Griffiths, who had stood up to a laughing House of Representatives in 1964. On May 19 she wrote to Holcomb, pointing out that Section 704(b) of Title VII states: "It shall be . . . unlawful employment practice for an employer . . . to print or publish . . . any notice or advertisement relating to employment . . . indicating any preference, limitation, specification, or discrimination, based on race, color, religion, sex, or national origin." Griffiths added that "I assume you will agree that advertisements under the heading 'white' or 'Negro' or 'Protestant' would be prohibited by the statute, and therefore I have difficulty seeing how advertisements under the headings of 'male' and 'female' could be in compliance with the very clear prohibitions of section 704(b)."[105]

Holcomb responded on June 1, explaining that "it is primarily the reading habits of job seekers which presently dictate the placement of ads," and denied the race–sex analogy:

> We do not regard the classification of help wanted advertising by sex as completely analogous to such classification by race. While some job categories are and are likely to remain of particular interest to members of one sex or the other, this cannot be said of job classifications by race, and accordingly where an advertiser places his ad in a column classified to one race we would be compelled to the conclusion that his purpose is to exclude applicants of other races.[106]

Griffiths printed both letters in the *Congressional Record,* accompanied by her own scathing indictment of the EEOC. She compared the ads to "colored only" signs in the waiting rooms of bus and train stations, and pointed out that the Citizens' Advisory Council on the Status of Women declared that the sex-segregated ads should be illegal. Griffiths cited a law review article by Pauli Murray and Mary Eastwood—"Jane Crow and the Law"[107]—on the "obvious fact that the rights of women and the rights of Negroes are only different phases of the fundamental and indivisible issue of human rights." She also claimed the support of the UN Charter, the Universal Declaration of Human Rights, and the US Constitution. Griffiths described the attitude of the EEOC toward sex discrimination as "specious, negative, and arrogant," accused it of "shilly-shallying" and "wringing its hands," and said its policies on the airline stewardess issue were so foolish that the EEOC headquarters should be called "Fantasyland."[108]

This was powerful women's rights advocacy coming from within the government. Griffiths was urging the analogy between blacks and women, though she did so in a classically liberal, difference-blind formulation.

Women's groups and the EEOC

It was clear that the EEOC would respond to interest-group pressure. By 1966, African American civil-rights groups and ANPA had pressured the agency to some effect.[109] But what about women's groups? The National Women's Party, remotely involved with the effort to include sex discrimination protection in Title VII, was not organized and had no interest in a sustained lobbying effort to ensure that the newly created EEOC honored and enforced the law.[110] Other women's groups, such as the League of Women Voters and the American Association of University Women, were similarly not interested in a sustained fight for women's rights—and earning the dreaded "feminist" label—despite urging from EEOC commissioner Richard Graham.[111] But as former EEOC commissioner Aileen Hernandez has written, many women saw the agency as "the enemy," and "in a very real sense, therefore, government agencies can bear some of the responsibility for stimulating the growth and development of the 'second wave of feminism.'"[112] New groups emerged to fill the void.

The dynamics of this process could be seen at the third National Conference of State Commissions on the Status of Women in 1966. State commissions had sprouted up all over the country, following Kennedy's lead with his PCSW, and the national conferences were a chance for women's advocates from across the nation to assemble and compare notes. At the 1966 conference, twenty-eight delegates expressed concern about the lack of a lobbying group for women.[113] The fires of discontent were stoked when copies of Griffiths's blistering floor speech denouncing the EEOC were distributed to delegates.[114] Sympathetic EEOC officials, especially Commissioners Richard Graham and Aileen Hernandez, teamed with Mary Eastwood of the Justice Department and Catherine East of the Citizens' Advisory Council on the Status of Women to encourage formation of a new women's group; they recruited Betty Friedan to be its head. At the conference, Friedan and Kathryn Clarenbach, of the Wisconsin commission, along with thirteen other women, met over two tables at a conference luncheon. There they formed the new women's rights group, penning its name on a paper napkin—National Organization for Women (NOW).[115]

NOW quickly became the pressure group for women that many had desired. NOW's leaders, many from within the government, clearly understood the dynamics of administrative politics and the need to establish women as an audience to judge the EEOC. Betty Friedan described NOW's first order of business as making "clear to Washington, to employers, to unions and to the nation that someone *was* watching, someone *cared* about ending sex discrimination" (original emphasis).[116] NOW's leaders immediately sent telegrams asking the EEOC to reappoint Graham to the commission (his term was soon to expire), and mailed letters asking the EEOC to cancel its directive on "help wanted" listings in the newspaper.[117]

NOW's official stated purpose was "to take action to bring women into full participation in the mainstream of American society now, assuming all the privileges and responsibilities thereof in truly equal partnership with men." NOW vowed opposition to "all policies and practices—in church, state, college, factory, or office—which, in the guise of protectiveness, not only deny opportunities but also foster in women self-denigration, dependence, and evasion of responsibility, undermine their confidence in their own abilities, and foster contempt for women." If Griffiths in Congress and the commissioners in the EEOC provided the immediate spark for the organization, the African American civil rights movement provided the model. NOW would be

a "civil rights movement for women" that would create a "fully equal partnership of the sexes, as part of the world-wide revolution of human rights
now taking place within and beyond our borders."[118]

NOW rapidly became *the* voice of women's rights, patterned after the African American civil rights movement. But did NOW pressure the EEOC to
promote affirmative action? On November 11, 1966, representatives of
NOW sent a letter to the EEOC commissioners with a list of eight demands.
Complaining of a lack of serious effort by the agency, the letter called for (1)
limiting EEOC appointments to those who "recognize the legal mandate" to
fight sex discrimination; (2) an EEOC statement prohibiting many airlines'
policy of mandatory retirement of stewardesses who marry or reach the age
of thirty-two; (3) revision of the EEOC sex-segregated advertising policy; (4)
comprehensive guidelines on maternity leave with financial compensation
through insurance; (5) a legal statement nullifying women's protective legislation; (6) guidelines on retirement and pension plans that discriminate on
the basis of sex; (7) public conferences with civic organizations on the topic
of sex discrimination; and (8) a vague demand that the EEOC "develop,
in conjunction with other agencies such as the Department of Labor, affirmative action programs and technical assistance projects to bring women
into the mainstream of employment opportunities."[119]

The call for affirmative action, last on the list of priorities, was not soon followed up. Later communications with the EEOC stressed the segregated advertising issue and the need to rule women's protective legislation illegal under Title VII. Protest activity also focused on issues other than affirmative
action from the EEOC. NOW drafted a Bill of Rights for Women in 1967,
advocating increasing societal responsibility for child care, child care centers
to allow more employment and education, extension of maternity leaves, social security benefits, tax deductions for child-care expenses, legal birth control, and abortion on demand for control over reproductive lives.[120] In 1967,
it held a national day of picketing against the EEOC for allowing the sex-segregated ads, with demonstrations in New York City, San Francisco, Pittsburgh, Washington, D.C., and Chicago. NOW also organized pickets and
demonstrations (and filed a formal complaint) against the *New York Times* for
printing sex-segregated want ads. NOW lobbied to get sex added to Executive Order 11246 (see below), and continually put pressure on EEOC to re-
sponsibly do its job.[121]

NOW was successful. On May 2–3, 1967, the EEOC held hearings on
what were considered by the new chairman Stephen Shulman to be "quite
controversial" areas of sex discrimination, including protective laws and the
segregated advertisements. Shulman told President Johnson that "any decision the Commission might make on any one of these issues will doubtless be

wrong in the eyes of many," but "the hearings will enable us to say that all views were at least considered."[122] The hearings attracted women's groups, labor, and business representatives.[123] On August 6, 1968, the EEOC finally ruled that sex-segregated advertisements were in conflict with Title VII.[124] By 1969, the EEOC ruled that the protective laws were also in conflict with Title VII,[125] after which they gradually faded from the states' statute books.[126]

The focus of NOW's work as a pressure group was on eliminating any relevance of perceived sex differences and equating sex discrimination with race discrimination. Major support would be given to the capstone of feminist classical liberalism, the Equal Rights Amendment, which stated simply that "equality of rights under the law shall not be denied or abridged by the United States or any state on account of sex." Though women became beneficiaries of EEOC affirmative-action policies, it was not because they applied significant or consistent pressure for these policies.

"We Are America's Invisible Minorities": Latinos and the EEOC

Unlike women, there was never any question that discrimination against Latinos, under either the category of national origin or race, would be covered by the Civil Rights Act. Like women, they were not a significant presence in lobbying for the law. Title VII was the sort of law they wanted, however. Latino organizations and Latinos in Congress had traditionally supported the difference-blind justice of the Civil Rights Act.[127]

Though there was no question that discrimination against Latinos would be covered by the Civil Rights Act, few perceived that law as directed in any significant way at Latinos, and the EEOC and others mostly ignored Latinos and their discrimination problems. As mentioned above, Lyndon Johnson made no mention of Latinos or national-origin discrimination when he signed the Civil Rights Act, and the otherwise prescient *Wall Street Journal* article that analyzed EEOC politics ignored this group entirely. Like the case of women, this dismissive treatment helped mobilize a new Latino lobby.

It was easier to ignore Latinos because their advocates in Congress were not speaking up as Griffiths did for women. In another contrast with women, the Latinos were simply not filing discrimination complaints in any significant numbers. In fiscal year 1966, for example, only 2 percent of complaints were based on national-origin discrimination, or 131 of 6,133.[128] Of the first 3,773 complaints earmarked for investigation, only 25 were from Mexican Americans (0.66 percent). None were identified to be from Puerto Ricans.[129] Furthermore, Latinos had no organized groups helping individuals in the complaint process at the local level. The EEOC administrator Alfred Blumrosen recalled that his first complaint to investigate came from a Mexican American in Corpus Christi, Texas. Instead of meeting the person in the offices of a local civil-rights group such as the NAACP, as was typical with complaints from African Americans, Blumrosen met the complainant in a doctor's office. The Latino rights movement in Corpus Christi consisted of one doctor who saw both patients and the occasional person with discrimination problems.[130]

Despite this lack of appeals or complaints made to the EEOC, a Latino lobby quickly developed. It focused demands on what is probably the most traditional identity politics in America: group representation in government. For example, Johnson administration officials invited Mexican American delegates to a 1965 White House Conference on Equal Employment Opportunity even though the conference was almost totally devoted to the problems of African Americans. The angry delegates later demanded "fuller utilization of the talent resources of qualified Mexican Americans in government service today."[131] When EEOC officials eventually met face to face with Mexican American leaders, their demands were similar.

Like activists for women's rights, Latino leaders felt they were not being treated seriously by the EEOC, but much more than the women's groups, they demanded changes in EEOC personnel rather than specific policy changes. They felt that the 1966 lineup of the five EEOC commissioners—consisting of three Euro-American males, an African American male, and an African American female (Aileen Hernandez, who was married to a Latino)—could not understand Latino discrimination problems.

As he did with women, EEOC chairman Franklin Roosevelt Jr. showed early interest. On December 24, 1965, he told Herman Edelsberg that he was concerned about an anticipated manpower shortage in the United States, and he wanted a memo on what the EEOC was doing for the Spanish-speaking population. "This should include not only a method of education with regard to complaint filing procedures, but also an affirmative action program (what are we doing, for example, about the 800 companies in the southwest who employ minimal numbers of Spanish-speaking citizens)." Roosevelt wanted Puerto Ricans involved in any advisory committees, and wanted to identify the Puerto Rican leadership in New York and Chicago to discuss their special problems.[132] In early 1966, Roosevelt also arranged for creation of a Spanish-language poster explaining how to use the new civil-rights agency.[133]

But these were rare gestures of concern for this group. Edelsberg, the EEOC official who had expressed annoyance at women's demands, did the same with respect to Latinos at a March 18, 1966 meeting in San Francisco with the Mexican American Political Association (MAPA), a group organized in 1959 specifically for political empowerment.[134] MAPA's San Francisco chapter president, Robert E. Gonzales, asked Edelsberg what the EEOC was doing about Mexican Americans' language barrier. According to MAPA's account, Edelsberg responded that little was being done for their special problems, including those regarding language difficulties, but blamed Mexican American "disorganization" for the problem. He pointed out that up until that time the EEOC had received only twelve complaints by Mexican Americans, arguing that this showed "Mexican Americans are basically distrustful of agencies." He explained to the leaders that their culture did not seem to understand the proverb "the wheel that squeaks the loudest gets the grease."[135] Though MAPA felt insulted by Edelsberg's comments, taken another way they were a government invitation and a strategy outline for Latino lobbying and protest. To get something done, make some noise.

It was not long before Latinos would take Edelsberg up on his suggested strategy. George Sánchez, an education professor at the University of Texas and former president of LULAC, wrote to Chairman Roosevelt complaining about the Edelsberg comment, saying "the number of complaints, and the ratio of Negro to Mexican-American, is a very lame and illogical excuse for inaction. By this line of reasoning we would render public health service only to those who called in a doctor!"[136] Later that month, at a conference in Albuquerque with EEOC commissioner Richard Graham and other agency officials, Mexican American delegates representing several groups (LULAC, the Latin-American Civic Association, the Political Association of Spanish-Speaking Organizations, and the American G.I. Forum) were angry and confrontational. Apparently confident of their status as analogous to blacks, they instead emphasized their differences. One Mexican American leader, Luis Garcia, complained of neglect by the EEOC, and claimed that Roosevelt himself had stated, "Spanish-speaking minority groups suffer some of the nation's highest unemployment rates and live in the most abysmal housing, perpetuated by an educational system that makes no provision for the unique problems and the unique needs of this different ethnic group." At the conference, the leaders demanded the appointment of a Latino to the EEOC who would bring, in the words of Augustin Flores, national president of the G.I. Forum, "his special insight into the unique employment problems of our bilingual, bicultural group."[137] The Mexican American leaders then marched out before sixty minutes had passed.

They later sent a list of eight demands to President Johnson. Instead of emphasizing greater enforcement or attention to Latino employment problems, their overwhelming interest was for increased Mexican American representation or participation in government. The activists clearly believed that co-ethnic representation was necessary for any successful advocacy. They demanded no specific policy rulings or legal interpretations. The final two demands, however, did call for affirmative action, with the eighth specifying the policy by name though limiting it to government. The Latino leaders demanded:

1. That at least one Mexican American, with full understanding of the unique employment problems of America's second-largest minority, be appointed to the five-member Equal Employment Opportunity Commission.

2. That staff hiring practices of the EEOC—an organization which should serve as a model for all of our nation's employers, be investigated and changed to eliminate current ethnic imbalances which work against the Mexican American.

3. That the Commission send knowledgeable representatives to any future conferences involving federal agencies and the Mexican American community.

4. That regional offices of the EEOC be relocated into areas where employment discrimination is most severe.

5. That the entire program of the EEOC be reoriented, and new procedures be established to reach the Mexican-American community.

6. That the Mexican American be allowed full participation in the upcoming June White House Conference on Civil Rights, and in all other civil rights programs and activities engaged in or sponsored by the federal government.

7. That the EEOC take immediate steps against some 800 major national companies in the Pacific Southwest which have more than 600,000 employees on their payrolls, yet hire no Mexican Americans.

8. That the hiring practices of all governmental agencies be reviewed and that affirmative action be taken to rectify present imbalances against Mexican Americans and all other ethnic minorities.[138]

These low-priority demands for affirmative action would soon be eclipsed almost totally by the demands for political representation and patronage. The Mexican American leaders were unhappy with new EEOC acting chairman Luther Holcomb, who assumed the lead after Roosevelt resigned. Holcomb met with the GI Forum attempting to mend relations. Senator John Tower (R–TX), who only a few years earlier had voted against the Civil Rights Act, kept up the pressure, proposing a bill to expand the EEOC board of commissioners by two to allow Latinos to have a voice. Commissioner Dick Graham offered to resign and said in an April 14 letter to the White House, "I am increasingly convinced that this commission should have a Mexican-American Commissioner." Graham's family even joined Mexican Americans in picketing the White House on Easter Sunday in an act of solidarity with the striking National Farmworkers Association.[139]

Poor treatment by the EEOC and lack of representation on the agency staff (only 3 of 150)[140] continued to be the focus of Mexican American lobbying. On April 28 and 29, two hundred Mexican American leaders in Los Angeles held a "Mexican American Unity Conference" in Los Angeles. The purpose, according to a Johnson administration observer, was to "(a) honor the 50 who walked out on the Equal Employment Opportunity Commission at Albuquerque, New Mexico, (b) plan action regarding an upcoming White House Conference on "black" civil rights, and (c) press for a meeting with the President." The group considered a march on Washington to protest "exclusion of Spanish-Americans from the White House Conference," but the idea was dropped "because it was feared that such action would be interpreted by the press as anti-Negro." Still, they planned "to continue the agitation as leverage for a similar conference for Spanish-speakers." They sent a telegram to President Johnson urging a meeting and filed a formal complaint with the Civil Service Commission charging discrimination against Mexican Americans by the EEOC.[141]

In May 1966, Johnson met with leaders from the G.I. Forum, LULAC, and MAPA. They complained about EEOC treatment, asked for a Mexican American White House aide and for inclusion in White House conferences, and extracted from Johnson a promise to help (see Chapter 7 for discussion of the White House conference).[142] LULAC's new, more radical leader, Alfred J. Hernández, sponsored a banquet in honor of the Albuquerque walkout where he declared, "In spite of our number we are America's invisible minority. Because we have not demonstrated, because we have not cried out when we have been abused and exploited, we have been ignored."[143]

By October, the demands were similar, but there was a new rationale. Rudy Ramos of the G.I. Forum sent a letter to the White House that was passed on to the EEOC with a demand for an explanation. Ramos made the familiar charges, mostly about the lack of Mexican Americans at the EEOC, and argued that the lack of complaints filed with the agency (he cited thirteen complaints from Latinos out of the first three thousand received) showed that the "complaint procedure is not geared to solution of Mexican American discrimination in employment problems." Was a policy of affirmative action for Latinos the answer? Ramos suggested no clear policy preference. He demanded "at least one Mexican American commissioner to be appointed," more representation at the EEOC, and "revamping of EEOC procedures so that they are more conducive to correcting Mexican American discrimination in employment problems, considering that the present procedures and policies have ended in utter disaster and failure."[144] In others words, Latino leaders demanded that their problems be solved, but did not offer a solution.

Despite such concerns and activity, Latinos remained a lower priority for the EEOC. As late as November 1966, a report on "Mexican Americans in the United States" by Lamar Jones, an economist at the Virginia Polytechnic Institute, all but told the EEOC to give low priority to Latino problems because blacks and Latinos were very different. The report (containing a note warning it *"should not be circulated outside of the Commission* [original emphasis]), declared that "equal employment opportunity is greater" for Mexican Americans than for blacks, a statement it supported with statistics. For example, even with lower education, Latinos had higher incomes than blacks. Jones also reported, apparently to preempt any political strategizing, that Mexican Americans did not vote in blocs and tended to vote according to the personalities of candidates. Should any administrators still feel *something* should be done, Jones had another argument: most of the problems for this group resulted from illegal aliens who were willing to work for almost nothing. In other words, Mexican American problems were the result of immigration policy, not discrimination.[145]

Still, the Mexican American groups were to obtain their sought-after representation, as President Johnson appointed G.I. Forum member and Texas Democrat activist Vicente Ximenes to be EEOC commissioner in June of 1967. Johnson also appointed Ximenes to chair a new Inter-agency Committee on Mexican American Affairs. By 1970, the EEOC also appointed a Latino, Eliseo Carrasco, to be "Special Assistant to the Chairman" for Latinos and American Indians. To respond to the issue of few complaints from Latinos, the EEOC established new district offices in places that had high Latino concentrations, such as Denver and Phoenix, recruited investigative personnel fluent in Spanish, and printed EEOC literature, charge forms, and instruction booklets in Spanish.[146]

The EEOC Takes Affirmative-Action Policy beyond Blacks

The EEOC responded to all the various minority group demands with a blanket strategy. In answering the basic and general demand from African Americans for more effective enforcement, *all* official minority groups could gain—they would gain a new legitimate vehicle for fuller participation in the economy and a politics of identity. The government would henceforth pressure private firms to hire more African Americans, Latinos, and women *qua* African Americans, Latinos, and women. After already using the "forum" technique to pressure firms to hire more blacks, it was cheap and easy to expand this policy to the other groups. This affirmative-action approach was simply part of the EEOC's tool kit, and since women and Latinos were already designated as minorities, and their advocates made some noise on other issues, they won the policy without asking for it. EEOC officials began to pay attention to the proportional underrepresentation of Latinos and women, and at the forums where they showed their data to industry representatives, they began to focus the firms' attention on that proportional underrepresentation—sometimes including Asian Americans and American Indians, too.

The EEO-1 form made this wonderfully effortless and natural: right there alongside the racial hiring statistics were the female hiring statistics, as well as Latino hiring statistics. Thus a 1967 report from the EEOC Office of Research and Reports, "White Collar Employment Opportunities for Minorities in New York City," focused on African Americans and Puerto Ricans. It was also able to give "special attention . . . to women, regardless of whether they are members of these (Negro and Puerto Rican) minority groups or not." The report was an early usage of affirmative action: in examining hiring statistics, it sought not an end to discrimination per se but "an expansion of minority employment in white collar occupations," partly based on the logic that "the more members of minority groups that can be elevated to white collar jobs, the less will be the competition for blue collar jobs, increasing the chances for the unemployed to gain employment."[147]

A 1968 forum pushing affirmative action in white-collar employment thus made blacks, women, and Puerto Ricans points of focus, despite this Latino group's lack of lobbying and miniscule contribution to the EEOC complaint docket. According to the more than 160 invitational letters sent to New York City executives, the EEOC sought testimony from major companies "who have been successful in locating and utilizing relatively large numbers of minorities for white collar positions." The agency promised a statistics-based presentation to "clearly illustrate the extent of minority underutilization." The "principal objective" of the entire undertaking was proportional representation; it was "to facilitate greater utilization of minorities in white collar jobs."[148] At the forum, statistics on blacks, Latinos, and women were highlighted as "facts of underutilization."[149] In a surprise move, the EEOC also presented some data on the utilization of Jews and pressed for more opportunities for this group (see Chapter 9).

There is no record of any serious discussion whether it was valid to deduce discrimination from employment statistics, but there is some evidence that it was seen as not entirely legitimate or necessary in the case of women. Despite their presumable availability in every labor market, there was a tendency to drop the women category from the analysis. Thus a forum with the Washington, D.C. pharmaceutical industry concentrated only on the "participation rates" for Negroes and "Spanish surnamed" Americans.[150] The EEOC also targeted forums in places with large Latino and Asian American populations. Forums in New York, Los Angeles, and Houston especially allowed for attention to Latinos. Similarly, as the commission became more aggressive, a "Project Outline" in July 1968 described an "action project" whose aim was "to increase the proportion of the minority group individuals participating in the labor force as well as the numbers of minorities actually hired and to do so by eliminating the discriminatory practices and patterns which have excluded them." The latter point, justified by a pragmatic logic, had in mind groups outside of African Americans: "The project is designed to obtain a maximum return for the investment of limited governmental effort; the return will be measured in the form of new hiring of numbers of minority employees, including, but not limited to Negroes and Spanish Surnamed Americans." The project involved investigating firms with lowest utilization rates of African Americans, Latinos, American Indians, and Asian Americans.[151]

In the 1970s, the EEOC increasingly began to emphasize women's status in the workplace. By this point, the women's movement had established a solid base in the formerly black-oriented EEOC. In 1970, the commission initiated a case against AT&T for alleged sex and race discrimination. David Copus—a thirty-one-year-old Harvard Law graduate, former Peace Corps volunteer in India, and women's advocate—was the instigation for the case. Copus later told the *New York Times* that when he read about AT&T's asking the Federal Communications Commission for permission for a rate hike, he saw it as a chance "to get at discrimination in the Bell System."[152] Copus, an activist described by the *Times* as uniformed in denim pants, a denim jacket, and a shirt weighted down by feminist campaign buttons (to go with shoulder-length brown hair), successfully persuaded EEOC chairman William H. Brown to pursue the case. The EEOC charged "that because AT&T's operating companies engage in pervasive and unlawful discrimination in employment against women, blacks, Spanish-surnamed Americans, and other minorities, the rate increase proposed and filed by AT&T with the Commission is unjust and unreasonable," citing Title VII, among other laws and orders, as authority.[153]

By this point, the EEOC had developed an affirmative-action-oriented definition of discrimination, one in which the intent of the discriminator was not necessarily relevant. The crucial question in this "adverse impact" theory of discrimination was simple: Did AT&T's hiring practices have an adverse effect on minority hiring? The data from the EEO-1 forms clearly showed statistical underrepresentation. But there were also many complaints from individuals, as Copus was well aware. Phyllis A. Wallace, a former EEOC technical expert, later explained that one of the reasons for the EEOC's charge was that "AT&T accounted for five to six percent of all such charges pending before EEOC" and the affirmative action approach was "a cost-effective way of reducing the backlog."[154]

EEOC officials had finally learned that women's advocates could be valuable allies. After Copus's feminist fervor and Wallace's administrative pragmatism led to the initial charge against AT&T, EEOC officials worked closely with NOW leaders. Brown assigned Copus to head a task force for the case and NOW aided in fleshing out the EEOC's concept of sex discrimination.[155] As Copus enthusiastically told the *New York Times,*

> we were advancing the really revolutionary view of sex discrimination. We took more or less hook, line and sinker the feminist view as espoused by the National Organization for Women—their view of institutionalized sex discrimination—and we said we wanted to attack it at its roots in the Bell System. Not just equal pay for equal work, etc. We wanted to present the whole sociology and psychology of sexual stereotypes as it was inculcated into the Bell System structure.[156]

The EEOC's final report on the charge claimed that "the Bell monolith" was "without doubt, the largest oppressor of women workers in the United States."[157] The heart of the EEOC sex discrimination charge was that 92.4 percent of all employees were shown by the data to be concentrated in jobs where the workers were 90 percent or more of the same sex. In its defense, AT&T argued that the problem was not "discrimination" but that women did not have an interest in the "male" jobs or did not have the necessary training.

In 1973, AT&T and the EEOC ended the formal hearings and agreed to an historic consent decree. It was a triumph for the new, expanded affirmative action. AT&T, which employed nearly eight hundred thousand workers at the time, agreed to an affirmative-action plan that was "to achieve within a reasonable period of time, an employee profile, with respect to race and sex in each major classification, which is an approximate reflection of proper utilization . . . This objective calls for achieving full utilization of minorities and women at all levels of management and non-management."[158] Though the charge focused on African Americans, women, and Latinos, the consent decree went beyond these groups in a well-balanced effort to bring about better representation of the official minorities. According to a Wharton School study of the decree:

> As a result of the decree, the Bell System labor force was partitioned into fifteen separate job classes ranging from management . . . to service workers . . . The labor force was further segmented into ten race-sex

groups, or five racial groups (Caucasian, Black, Hispanic, Asian Pacific, and Native American), for each sex.

Ultimate employment goals or ultimate objectives were then set for each of these ten groups in every job class . . . the race-sex profile of the AT&T labor was eventually supposed to approximate that of the relevant labor pool.[159]

Most controversially, the consent decree called for $15 million in back pay to be paid to thirteen thousand women and two thousand minority men and wage adjustments for thirty-six thousand other minority and women workers that eventually totaled $30 million.[160] These were considerable sums, but much less than the $175 million that the EEOC originally requested.[161]

It was not long before the EEOC negotiated more consent decrees with other large employers. For instance, negotiations between the federal government, nine steel companies, and the United Steelworkers of America resulted in a plan in April 1974 that included goals and timetables as well as $30.9 million in back pay for forty thousand minority and female employees. Other consent decrees involved trucking, banking, and airline companies.[162]

Affirmative action for America's government-designated minorities had arrived. To preempt such actions, some companies began to reach out to the growing industry of consultants on equal employment opportunity. Most of these companies had little resistance to implementing the difference-conscious affirmative action part of the plan, except for some concerns about convincing white male workers to quietly accept the promotion of minorities ahead of them. Companies were especially concerned with the back-pay requirements, and sought assistance on developing hiring and promotion practices to make them immune to litigation that would affect their profit margins.[163]

What about Asian Americans and American Indians?

While the analogy with blacks was enough to get Asian Americans and American Indians onto the EEO-1 form, the EEOC gave these two groups less attention than the others. In 1970, a report of the US Commission on Civil Rights explicitly stated that the EEOC had set priorities on African Americans, Latinos, and women.[164] Neither Asians nor American Indians exerted significant pressure on the commission, though this factor should not be exaggerated: Puerto Ricans gained considerable attention without pressing for it or filing many complaints. With Asians and American Indians, the main reasons for their neglect were more likely the small size of both groups, and the perception that Asian Americans—despite their continued existence on the EEO-1—were not significantly disadvantaged. It would have taken significant meaning entrepreneurship to promote Asians as analogous to blacks, and no Asian groups were making this effort.

In 1967, the EEOC's Herbert Hammerman even sought to remove the two from forms similar to the EEO-1 but designed for unions, arguing that the groups were very small, the Asians did not show great discrimination, and American Indians on reservations were not technically under the purview of Title VII anyway. No one disagreed with Hammerman's reasoning, but Chairman Stephen Shulman kiboshed the effort, anticipating that such an action would mobilize these groups and produce a loud outcry.[165]

Though rarely the focus of much direct attention from the EEOC, the two groups still benefited from being official minorities in ways that Jews, Italians, Poles, Arabs, or others could not. EEOC administrators could at any time ask a firm to explain low numbers of Asians in various positions, and an individual claiming discrimination on the basis of being Asian or American Indian could, in court, easily present statistics of how many of their group a firm hired and in what positions. At their affirmative-action forums, EEOC officials occasionally grilled company representatives on their hiring of "Orientals" and American Indians. The company representatives were—when possible—armed with their own data to exonerate themselves. For example, Harvey A. Basham Jr. of New York's Chemical Bank boasted that one in five employees were either Negro, Oriental, American Indian, or Spanish-surnamed, with Orientals very well represented.[166] In the Los Angeles forum, EEOC Chairman Clifford Alexander demanded officials from companies such as Lockheed, TRW, and Universal Studios to show how many "Oriental" employees, along with blacks and Mexican Americans, they had at management and clerical levels.[167] Even in Houston, far from centers of Asian American population, firms such as Gulf Oil described their affirmative-action program that included Asian Americans and American Indians, and without prompting Texas Instruments reported data on all of the official minorities.[168] The pressure exerted by the EEOC regarding the status of Asians and American Indians was never all that strong; part of the problem for a zealous advocate of Asian American rights was that the firms often reported higher numbers of Asian American employees at the professional, management, and official levels than they did African Americans and Latinos. Still, America's larger employers learned to pay attention to and to value increasing numbers of Asian American and American Indian employees. In contrast, nonofficial minorities or victims of religious discrimination would have to either find smoking-gun evidence of discrimination or somehow assemble their own statistics, as described in Chapter 9.

Expansion of Affirmative Action in the Contract Compliance Program

The designation of the official minorities and the beginnings of the affirmative-action model of justice occurred in the EEOC, but affirmative action as a policy would gain its most explicit regulatory formulation in the hiring goals and timetables requirements of the Labor Department's Office of Federal Contract Compliance (OFCC). Here, as in the EEOC, the focus of affirmative action was on African Americans, and developed following a logic of administrative pragmatism. From the beginning, however, despite the emphasis on blacks, this affirmative action included the EEOC's ethno-racial minorities. Sex discrimination, though not originally covered by the executive order establishing affirmative action in government contracting, did become so through amendment. It took meaning entrepreneurship by women's activists inside and outside the government who pushed for the analogy with blacks, and the political opportunity afforded by the law's formal equivalence of race and sex discrimination, to overcome the reluctance of Labor Department bureaucrats and other government officials to treat women as a minority.

Sex Discrimination in the Executive Order and Affirmative Action

NOW's concern with equal employment opportunity was not limited to pressuring the EEOC. One of its earliest actions was to ask President Johnson to add "sex" to the list of forbidden grounds of discrimination in his 1965 Executive Order 11246, requiring nondiscrimination and an undefined "affirmative action" by all government contractors on the basis of race, color, religion, and national origin. The executive order mirrored Title VII in its coverage, but was missing sex discrimination. NOW demanded that this inconsistency be rectified.

NOW had demanded the change in its 1966 letter to Johnson (described earlier). Though the organization was new and had almost no membership, its representatives met with officials of the Justice Department and the Civil Service Commission and persuaded Labor Secretary Willard Wirtz to accept the idea.[169] With some additional support from the Business and Professional Women Clubs and the General Federation of Women's Clubs, Johnson signed Executive Order 11375 on October 13, 1967 (usually referred to as "11246 as amended").[170] With that, women could now benefit from federal pressure on contractors to use affirmative action.

What were women's advocates hoping to achieve? Did they want to aggressively root out discrimination—or have women hired preferentially? Mary Keyserling, director of the Labor Department's Women's Bureau, interviewed in October of 1968, shared thoughts that expressed no clear idea of what women had won for themselves. Though formerly a relatively conservative women's advocate, by 1968 her views fit with the incipient ideology of NOW. She seemed to avoid advocating overt difference-conscious policy, but also sought increasing proportions of women in employment. In her view, OFCC officials could

> say quite flatly, just as they have in relation to the problem of race discrimination, "We expect affirmative action on the part of federal contractors and on the part of government supervisors." This means recruiting people on the basis of ability. Where sex isn't relevant, and it almost never is, you recruit people, and all people who are qualified are open to appointment.

She admitted that it was hard to find discrimination, "but general employment patterns are detectable. The firm that never has any women in certain of its jobs where women are skillful and qualified—and I believe that women are skillful and qualified in the full range of jobs—the firm that establishes this pattern is clearly discriminating."[171] Apparently without even being aware of doing so, Keyserling then began to talk in terms of affirmative action. She claimed that Johnson had "a very real concern with the under-utilization of woman-power"[172] and argued that

> a new approach to meeting the needs of women in our society has emerged. The emphasis was very largely on correcting underutilization. It turned from mere declaration of rights to the actual opening of the doors of opportunity. There was still much door-opening to be done, and it was done through law. But it was also—"Let's find out *why* people aren't going through those doors and if there are barriers that are keeping them from realizing the opportunities now released through change in law. Let's meet those problems specifically."[173]

For Keyserling, as for many civil-rights advocates, the only way to know if an opportunity existed was if someone successfully pursued it. In this view, women could not, therefore, simply miss an opportunity or prefer not to seize it.

Despite the high hopes, impatience, and pressure of women's advocates such as Keyserling, the OFCC behaved toward women much as the EEOC had. The transition to the new administration of Republican Richard Nixon, who appointed African American Arthur A. Fletcher as assistant secretary of labor, was not a favorable change for women's advocates. Fletcher, as well as labor secretary George Shultz and his successor James Hodgson, resisted the women–blacks analogy. The familiar pattern of delay and indecisiveness kicked in; the OFCC issued *proposed* guidelines—not official—implementing 11246 for women in January of 1969, and eight months later (August 4–6) the office held public hearings on the issue. These guidelines required contractor recruiters to make trips to women's colleges and to include female students when they visited coeducational colleges, technical schools, and secondary schools. They also required an undefined "affirmative action" to eliminate sex-segregated departments where females were paid less than males to do similar work.[174]

Meanwhile, the Labor Department's affirmative action for ethnoracial minorities was developing on a different track, as described previously. At the OFCC, affirmative action began in the Philadelphia Plan, which was aimed at blacks in the construction industry. Though women were covered by the executive order that authorized the Philadelphia Plan, the plan did not include women. It did include the other official minorities. A June 1969 memo to the "Heads of All Agencies" justified the plan's minority hiring goals with references to the underutilization of black workers in seven skilled construction trades: iron workers, plumbers/pipe fitters, steamfitters, sheetmetal workers, electrical workers, roofers and water proofers, and elevator construction workers. African Americans constituted less than 0.5 percent of these trades in the Philadelphia area, despite a black population in 1970 of 33.6 percent.[175] Though it only discussed the facts of African American workers, the Philadelphia Plan ordered that bids for contracts must include "specific goals of minority manpower utilization." The meaning of "minority" was the same as in the EEOC definition: "Negro, Oriental, American Indian and Spanish Surnamed American." This last category included "all persons of Mexican American, Puerto Rican, Cuban or Spanish origin or ancestry."[176]

The original Philadelphia Plan thus nominally included the EEOC's official minorities, but emphasized African Americans. The groups were soon equalized. Only three months later, the next order gave details on implementation of the plan and did not mention African Americans separately from the other groups. It gave aggregate statistics only for "minorities."[177] There is no evidence of debate, lobbying, or protest in the process of reproducing the official minorities of the EEO-1. If there was any pressure from advocates for the ethnoracial groups, it was very light.

Women and sex discrimination, however, remained marginalized by their perceived incongruity with the situation of blacks. Part of the neglect of women may have resulted from the focus of the Philadelphia Plan on construction employment, an area few feminists saw as an important frontier for women's utilization. However, the OFCC soon expanded on the Philadelphia Plan by requiring something like it for *all* contractors, not just construction, and not just Philadelphia. On February 5, 1970 the OFCC—without any apparent lobbying from outside civil-rights groups—issued Order No. 4, requiring government contractors to supply hiring goals and timetables for the ethnoracial minorities, thus leaving out religious minorities, European ethnic groups, and women. Contractors with at least a $50,000 contract and more than fifty employees were to make efforts to "correct any identifiable deficiencies" in the utilization of minorities. Utilization was "having fewer minorities in a particular job class than would reasonably be expected by their availability." Order No. 4 required minority-hiring goals and timetables based roughly on "the percentage of the minority work force as compared with the total work force in the immediate labor area."[178]

This was a remarkable flowering of minority rights, happening without significant lobbying, without controversy—without anyone noticing at all. That is, *almost* no one was noticing: women's groups again felt the sting of second-class treatment. The OFCC was denying the validity of the analogy between blacks and women, keeping equal-opportunity regulations for the two completely separate, and ignoring women as much as possible. The sex discrimination guidelines were still languishing in the proposal stage.

Women's advocates, both inside and outside of government, mobilized to push for the equality of women with the other minorities. The effort started small. Bernice Sandler, a member of a NOW spin-off group called the Women's Equity Action League (WEAL), believed she was unfairly denied a position for which she was qualified in the department of counseling and personnel services of the University of Maryland, where she was told that she "came on too strong for a woman." Title VII and the EEOC could not be of help, since educational institutions were exempted from its coverage. Encouraged by an OFCC official, she sought remedy through the only legal means—the new, amended 11246.[179]

Because of the way discrimination law had developed in response to discrimination against African Americans—focusing on statistics of employment discrimination—it was not difficult for a few women's advocates to have a large impact. The goal was to show that women were victimized like blacks. Sandler and her colleagues at WEAL only needed to assemble statistical data showing disparities of women being hired as compared to men.[180] Sandler may have been an individual victim, but she sought a broad attack on discrimination in higher education. Women's advocates did not need great funding or organization. They only needed to send their statistics to the OFCC, which was responsible for affirmative-action guidelines, and the Department of Health, Education and Welfare (HEW), which was responsible for the regulation of educational institutions.[181]

Sandler led WEAL on January 31, 1970 to a class-action sex discrimination complaint against all universities and colleges with federal contracts.[182] This was not a case where women's leaders faced a uniformly uncaring government—an OFCC official helped draft the initial complaint.[183] Support also came from Martha Griffiths, herself a member of WEAL, who declared that the men running the universities were "the most bigoted, the most provincial group of people in the country."[184] Later, WEAL helped organize specific complaints directed at more than 250 institutions of higher education, including Columbia University, the University of Chicago, and the state university and college systems of California, Florida, and New Jersey.[185] WEAL had little interest in finding discriminatory intent. Following the logic of affirmative action, this was a rationalized, numbers-based drive for equality. While blacks had needed decades of protest before passage of laws and regulations ensuring equal rights, things were now much easier for women. Sandler wrote:

> One of the most useful aspects of the Executive Order is that any individual or group can file a complaint, and the complaint can be filed on the basis of a pattern of discrimination . . . The complainant need not be the individual or group suffering discrimination . . . In some instances complaints have been based on extensive reports; in others, simply the number and percentage of women at each rank in several departments of an institution has served as the basis of a complaint.[186]

WEAL sent letters of complaint to the secretaries of the Departments of HEW and Labor. It also sent letters to approximately forty members of Congress, chosen because they represented the state where the complaint was based or because they sat on education committees. The letters included requests for the congressmembers to write the Labor and HEW secretaries for additional pressure. Typical letters highlighted facts such as an absence of female full professors at a university, and discrepancies between the percentage of doctorates in a field awarded to women and the number of female faculty in that area. The letters demanded a "full-scale compliance review" and suspension of pending contract negotiations "until such time as all inequities are eliminated and an acceptable plan of affirmative action is implemented."[187]

The WEAL campaign, then, was a well-orchestrated push for affirmative action for women. Its immediate accomplishment was to validate the analogy drawn between women and blacks. As Sandler stated, "By filing charges under the Executive Order we have been able to 'legitimize' the issue and confirm the suspicion that there really *is* discrimination."[188] WEAL encouraged women's groups from campuses across the country to file complaints with the "basic data necessary," which consisted of "minimal-statistics showing that women were underrepresented in various departments at various levels."[189]

Though some in government had encouraged the pressure, other officials did not appreciate it. HEW asked its Office for Civil Rights to handle the complaints of the women's group, expecting them to go away in a few months. But twenty members of Congress responded to WEAL's request for help. It was not difficult to get this help—Congresswoman Martha Griffiths was a member of WEAL, along with fellow members of Congress Edith Green, Shirley Chisolm (D–NY), and Patsy Mink (D–HI). Griffiths helped lead the effort with a speech in the House of Representatives that explained the WEAL complaint and chastised the Labor Department for not enforcing the executive order for women. Other women associated with WEAL or higher education wrote letters to their representatives in Congress.[190] Even President Nixon's Task Force on the Status of Women (see Chapter 8) called for the "immediate issuance by the Secretary of Labor of guidelines to carry out the prohibitions against sex discrimination by government contractors" in their April 1970 report.[191] Sandler then got a closer look at the administrative goings on: HEW offered her a job in 1970, though she continued to lend her leadership to the pressure brought about by WEAL in her spare time.[192]

On June 2, 1970, the OFCC finally issued its Sex Discrimination Guidelines for Government Contractors and Subcontractors. Separate guidelines for race and sex discrimination were justified, according to the guidelines, because "experience has indicated that special problems" were related to implementing the executive order for women. The guidelines, to be effective on June 9, contained most everything women's groups had lobbied for in the previous four years: no discrimination unless sex was a BFOQ, no sex-segregated job advertisements, no distinctions between married and unmarried, no validity to state protective laws, no refusals of leave for child bearing, and so on. In the area of affirmative action, the guidelines were even weaker than before. They kept women separate from the other minorities by not requiring hiring goals and timetables. Instead, they offered only vague extra effort to recruit and promote women. No numerical goals were required.[193] Badly misinterpreting the political climate, Nixon's domestic policy adviser Leonard Garment was proud of the guidelines and expected political mileage from a dramatic release.[194]

Whereas the guidelines would have been a boon in 1967, in 1970 they were totally inadequate. Women's leaders felt that affirmative action for women was not taken seriously by the federal government; some even called the guidelines "useless."[195] A week after the guidelines went in effect, Ann Scott of NOW's Federal Compliance Committee sent a letter to Assistant Secretary of Labor Arthur Fletcher, a major architect of the Philadelphia Plan for the other official minorities, pointing out remaining loopholes. She argued that "NOW recognizes no valid bona fide occupational qualifications in the kind of work done by federal contractors, nor in any kind of work except for sperm donor and wet nurse." In addition, Scott rejected the distinction the OFCC made between the other official minorities and women, demanding that "the affirmative action goals and timetables required by Order No. 4 must be enforced in regard to women."[196] Meanwhile, NOW continued to apply pressure, filing on June 25 a formal complaint against thirteen hundred government contractors, charging sex discrimination.[197]

Labor Department officials in charge of affirmative action were wringing their hands, clearly uncomfortable with the women–blacks analogy but unable to make a final decision about it. Lobbyists for women, as part of their campaign against inequality in higher education, had met with Arthur Fletcher several times. As Sandler later wrote, Fletcher had "assured women orally at several meetings that the order [No. 4] did indeed apply to them." This never appeared in writing. According to Sandler, "the department wavered, for at one point an internal memorandum was circulated within the department stating that Order No. 4 covered women workers; a few days later the memorandum was withdrawn." Replacing Shultz (whom Nixon moved to the Office of Management and Budget to use his talents on a wider variety of issues), new secretary of labor James D. Hodgson then reiterated—despite contrary urgings from Patsy Mink—that Order No. 4 in fact did not apply to women.[198] On July 25, Hodgson told a meeting of ten women's organization leaders that though job discrimination against women was "subtle and more pervasive than against any other minority group," the Labor Department still had "no intention of applying literally exactly the same approach for women" as that used for the other minorities. NOW's Ann Scott, clearly believing that subtlety and pervasiveness did call for exactly the same approach, told the press after the meeting that "women had been left out again" by Nixon.[199] Representative Florence Dwyer (R–NJ) joined Scott in urging Hodgson to categorize women with the other minorities and include them within the ambit of Order No. 4.[200] Scott and Bernice Sandler threatened to use Mink, Edith Green, and Senator Margaret Chase Smith (R–ME) for all communications with the OFCC and raised the spectre of "disruptive activities."[201] In the face of mounting criticism, Hodgson waffled some more, saying a few days later that "some kinds of goals and timetables applying to some kinds of federal contractors" would be a part of new guidelines.[202]

On July 31, 1970, Green, chair of a House Special Subcommittee on Education, was concluding her comprehensive hearings on sex discrimination (see Chapter 8). Speaking that day were Jerris Leonard, assistant attorney general of the Civil Rights Division of the Justice Department, and Elizabeth Duncan Koontz, the director of the Labor Department's Women's Bureau.

They were to explain why women were different from the other minorities for purposes of the affirmative-action guidelines. Green, who in 1964 had argued that race and sex discrimination were very different, now clearly was angry that women were treated differently: "Now, it is my understanding that the Labor Department, and we have, I hope, someone who can respond to this question today, has made this Order No. 4 apply only to minorities and not to discrimination on the basis of sex. Now, is that not stating an [illegal] administrative preference under title VII?"

After Leonard told her that there *were* guidelines for affirmative action for women, Green correctly pointed out that "Order No. 4 is far stronger in requiring the contractors to have an affirmative action program," and argued again that "the Government has, by administrative action, placed enforcement in ending one kind of discrimination above all others, when Congress did not in any way say that was to be the case."[203] Of course, Congress had nothing to do with Order No. 4; it was a regulation designed to implement an executive order. Moreover, neither the Civil Rights Act nor the executive order said anything about hiring goals and timetables. Green also paid no attention to the religious minorities and countless ethnicities that were also left out of Order No. 4.

But the focus that day was women. To answer Green's complaints, Koontz read into the record an explanatory statement from outgoing Labor Secretary Shultz that displayed considerable sociological sublety on the issue of women's employment patterns—a wariness that was completely lacking in the area of ethnicity and race. Shultz sought to show equal commitment by arguing that "the Federal Government is convinced that the under-utilization of women in employment throughout the nation constitutes a waste of national resources and talent." Though there were sex discrimination guidelines separate from Order No. 4, "both documents are directed to the same result and both require affirmative action on the part of Government contractors to attain that result." The main difference was that for Order No. 4, contractors were to "analyze their work force and their potential work force recruitment area and where deficiencies in the utilization of minorities exist, that goals and timetables be set to which the contractor's efforts shall be directed to eliminate those deficiencies." Shultz's letter argued that though "it is clear that utilization of the concept of goals and timetables as an anti-sex discrimination tool is appropriate," the procedures under Order No. 4 did not apply, primarily because "many women do not seek employment. Practically all adult males do."[204] In short, taken-for-granted gender roles made women different.

Green dismissed the sociological assumptions of the Labor Department, declaring, "I am getting more and more discouraged about any real deep concern or intention to act." Koontz could only respond, "Well, please don't," and continued reading Shultz's statement, which is worth quoting in detail, both because of Shultz's reasoning and Green's reaction. Shultz argued not only that many women did not seek employment, but that those who did might not want all occupations: "Many occupations sought after by all racial groups may not have been sought by women in significant numbers." While all races and ethnicities were fundamentally the same, then, this was not true of men and women:

> Now, accordingly, different criteria must be employed in examining work force patterns to reveal the deficiencies in employment of women than are used in revealing racial deficiencies. Such criteria may well include the availability of qualified women in the employer's own force and the interest level expressed in respective occupations, as evidenced by applications for employment in those occupations. It will be necessary to examine whether the interest among women for certain occupations might be changed by effective affirmative action programs, and to properly examine these criteria and review suggestions regarding them or regarding the other applicable criteria. The Department plans to engage in an immediate series of consultations with interested parties. Representatives of women's groups, employers, and unions as well as acknowledged authorities on human resources will be invited to participate . . . The information thus obtained will be utilized by the Department in expanding and further defining its approach toward employing affirmative action to achieve an equal employment opportunity for women among Government contractors and by applying the concept of goals and timetables.[205]

Green's response to Shultz's plan was unequivocal: "I just have to say it is the biggest bunch of gobbledygook I have heard for a long, long time." Green may have heard nothing in Shultz's bureaucratese other than that women's rights in the workplace would receive different—lesser—enforcement. Referring to an earlier proposal by Koontz that the Women's Bureau be given authority to investigate and report on discrimination against women, Green forcefully rejected the idea "because it seems to me that you would still be under the Secretary of Labor, who in only one instance, back in FDR times, was ever a woman. And the Labor Department—you know, after a hundred years, has apparently yet to find out the widespread pattern of discrimination on the basis of sex."[206]

Even after this confrontation, the Labor Department continued to delay, as it met with Sandler and Scott but also business groups and labor unions.[207] In August, Hodgson told speechwriter William Safire there were benefits to appeasing women but also that "women's Lib groups are obviously trumpet-ing some absurdities."[208] Weeks stretched into months. October brought more vague Labor Department denials of the women–black analogy to WEAL members in Congress.[209]

How were women's rights viewed behind the scenes at the Labor Depart-ment? An incident at the University of Kansas in February 1971 reveals the dismissive attitude toward problems faced by women, especially Euro-Ameri-can women. It showed that the top OFCC officials continued to be at odds with women's advocates on the question of the sociology of women's em-ployment and the analogy drawn between women and race minorities. Assis-tant Secretary of Labor Arthur Fletcher, an African American male and a ma-jor figure in the development of affirmative action for racial minorities, was giving a public lecture as part of a course on labor relations. The professor had introduced Fletcher as the person in charge of four divisions, including the Women's Bureau, which the professor derisively said was concerned with "women's lib, and these kinds of things." Fletcher did not rebut this charac-terization. Unknown to Fletcher, Karen Keesling, executive director of the Intercollegiate Association of Women Students, was part of the class and re-ported this and other transgressions to Senator Bob Dole (R–KS) and the White House. Fletcher apparently had a very circumscribed idea of fair em-ployment, focused only on the official ethnoracial minorities. Keesling ex-plained that during the question-and-answer period,

> a Mexican-American student asked if Mr. Fletcher was referring to blacks only when he spoke of minority groups. His answer was that a mi-nority group is any group which is discriminated against economically because of its color. He stated that [white] ethnic groups are not in-cluded in his definition of minority groups. After this comment I asked if women were included in his definition of a minority group. He replied that "women were legislated their minority status." I assume he was re-ferring to the addition of the word "sex" in Title VII of the Civil Rights Act of 1964.
>
> Following this explanation I asked if he felt that women were the vic-tims of economic discrimination. He said, "Yes, some of them, but they were thrown in with all the rest of the women." This leads me to believe that Mr. Fletcher thinks there are very few women who are economically deprived, and that these few did not justify the inclusion of the word "sex" in Title VII.

According to Keesling, Fletcher expressed the view that only women who were heads of households faced significant discrimination, and their discrimi-nation was based on color, not sex. Dole requested clarification of the matter from the department, and in response, a legislative affairs aide from the Labor Department, Frederick Webber, informed Dole how best to respond to Keesling. In doing so, he supplied the clearest explanation (devoid of Shultz's bureaucratic "gobbledygook") of why women were different from racial minorities and should not receive the same affirmative action.

First, Webber told Dole to inform Keesling that federal officials make numerous speeches in a week and a "slip" occasionally occurs. Additionally, Webber said Fletcher was a strong supporter of women's rights, and "the OFCC under his leadership is proceeding to get affirmative action goals for women in employment established and implemented." But this affirmative action had to be specially tailored:

> You will recognize that women, per se, cannot be considered one of the groups having minority status. For example, Order 4 . . . specifying the obligations of government contractors with respect to equal employment opportunities for minorities, cannot be applied to women because one of the factors setting goals and time tables [sic] is the percentage of minority population in the area surrounding the employer. For women this percentage would usually be more than half. No one has yet proposed that every employer's payroll should be more than half women.

This was the crux of the matter: the proportional model of justice at the heart of affirmative action was just too revolutionary to include women, which would lead to apparent absurdities such as a requirement that employers strive for a 51 percent female workforce. But nothing in the civil-rights laws or executive orders, and nothing in the concepts of "civil rights" and "equal opportunity," suggested there should be different models of justice for different groups. The result was a conflict between the way civil-rights law was being implemented for ethnoracial minorities and what the administrators believed was appropriate for women.

Dole was to explain that Labor is "currently forming an advisory committee, including representatives of women's organizations as well as the National Association of Manufacturers, Chamber of Commerce, etc. to determine the relevant factors needed to secure an Order affecting women's employment similiar [sic] to Order 4 for ethnic minorities." In a comment sure to only increase Keesling's anxiety, Dole was to add that Fletcher was helping in this current effort.[210]

When Labor officials did meet with women's groups in April and May of 1971, the dam finally broke: the government accepted the understanding that women as a minority were analogous to blacks, Latinos, Asian Americans, and American Indians. The result was a "Proposed Order No. 4," published for comment on August 31, 1971. The final version, the "Revised Order No. 4," equalizing women and racial minorities with respect to goals and timetables, became binding on December 4, 1971—a full year and a half after Koontz promised immediate action.[211] Still, a year and a half was far shorter than the many decades it took blacks to win civil-rights protections. Women would henceforth be a part of government contractor affirmative-action plans. Contractors would have to promise to hire certain percentages of women within given time periods (though these would be based on studies of the pool of women workers and rarely be 50 percent).[212] Women's advocates had won their affirmative action, and an officially recognized victim status equal to African Americans and the other official minorities.

Conclusion

Employment affirmative action for Latinos, women, Asian Americans, and American Indians was made possible and—compared with the black civil-rights struggle—relatively easy by the prior development of law, bureaucracies, and regulations designed to help black Americans. The Civil Rights Act of 1964 and Title VII within it, the EEOC, the OFCC, the EEO-1 form that made difference-conscious affirmative action possible, and affirmative action itself were *all* created to prevent discrimination against black Americans and prevent black unrest in America's cities. The protections against national origin and sex discrimination in Title VII, the designation and counting of nonblack official minorities in the EEO-1, and the inclusion of the official ethnoracial minorities in the OFCC's affirmative action were all basically free rides, requiring virtually no lobbying or protest at all. EEOC officials defined the official minorities mostly undisturbed by representatives of any groups except blacks. This was possible because the government's experience with black Americans had legitimated racial or ethnic targeting in public policy, and because these minorities had meanings that made them analogous to blacks. Indeed, that was the very meaning of minority in the American context: analogous to blacks.

Once they were formally included in affirmative-action regulations, some of the other groups needed to apply pressure for significant action on their behalf. At the EEOC, it was not necessary for Latinos and women to lobby specifically for affirmative action to be included in the agency's efforts in that area. What was needed was meaning entrepreneurship aimed at the bureaucrats. The message was that Latinos and women were oppressed like blacks, and that their advocates cared. When EEOC administrators saw these groups as analogous and as politically active, they included them as part of affirmative-action policy. Over at the OFCC, Latinos and the other nonblack minorities identified on the EEO-1 form were integrated without controversy into the program for affirmative action. Here, however, there was reluctance to include women. Labor Department officials had trouble with the woman–black analogy.[213] Women's advocates had to apply significant pressure and lobbying to have the policy designed for African Americans extended to them. While the resistance they encountered was very great relative to other nonblack groups, this should not obscure a simple fact: it took less than two years of pressure before they found victory. Their efforts were significantly eased because discrimination law developed for blacks, relying on statistics, made unnecessary individual women complainants.

What occurred here was not typical of the politics of disadvantaged groups in America. The advocates for women and Latinos were not representing organized, mass constituencies as had civil-rights groups representing disenfranchised southern African Americans. For Latinos, there was never anything remotely like the mass marches on Washington organized by leaders of the black civil rights movement. Latino groups were poorly funded, poorly organized, and lacking in mass mobilization capabilities. It did not matter—their leaders had clout. Similarly, NOW and WEAL were not originally groups with mass memberships, and their influence predated their grassroots activities. NOW had influence literally days after it was planned on some paper napkins at a luncheon. The mass mobilization of the black civil rights movement helped create agencies for civil rights that obviated any similar need among other groups. A nonparticipatory minority-rights politics became possible, where self-appointed leaders could pressure and have impact. Civil-rights bureaucrats practiced anticipatory politics. They anticipated that the millions of women, Latinos, Asian Americans, and American Indians wanted affirmative action.

Though political leaders and advocates for disadvantaged groups had used the term "minority" before the EEOC's EEO-1 form, this form—based on determinations made in the 1950s without study or analysis—gave the term real political meaning. For the first time, there was an official government document that stated the identities of the nation's minority groups, separating them from the "majority," and joining this designation to policy with real impact and implications. The OFCC copied the EEOC's determinations in its own affirmative-action regulations. These quiet designations of official minorityhood shaped the trajectory of American politics and the structure of opportunity for the next several decades. The same official minorities, with only minor changes, would be replicated in other affirmative-action programs, as shown in Chapters 5 and 6.

5

"IN VIEW OF THE EXISTENCE OF THE OTHER SIGNIFICANT MINORITIES": THE EXPANSION OF AFFIRMATIVE ACTION FOR MINORITY CAPITALISTS

Employment affirmative action was not the only way to help African Americans and other minorities. That policy sought to help minorities be hired and advance through established—that is, white male-owned—businesses. Another possibility was to help the minorities become owners of businesses. This could be done through minority preference in the provision of government contracts, where billions of dollars flowed from the federal agencies to construction companies or suppliers of various goods and services. A struggling black-owned construction business, for example, could get a multimillion dollar road improvement contract even though that business offered to do it at a price higher than white-owned businesses. Minority preferences were also possible through favorable loan terms or even technical assistance. In this way, the black-owned business could develop, become stronger, and eventually graduate out of the preference program.

The Johnson and Nixon administrations created programs of this type during the minority rights revolution. The goal of this chapter is to explain why they did so, and why and how they expanded the program to include the other official minorities of the employment affirmative-action regulations. The dynamics here are different than in the case of employment. That was mostly an administrative process shielded from electoral politics. Programs for minority capitalism, on the other hand, were developed for blacks as a way to mitigate the urban riots of the 1960s and also in part to win their votes.

Unlike employment affirmative action, which was always premised on fighting discrimination against minorities or remedying past discrimination, minority capitalism did not (originally, at least) have a discrimination rationale. There is no evidence that the government, in establishing such programs, was responding to complaints of discrimination or to studies showing why some groups were not setting up their own businesses in rates similar to Euro-Americans. There was no clear public rationale other than the intrinsic

143

or self-evident good of creating proportional fair shares for government-designated official minorities.

Democratic and Republican White House officials expanded the program beyond African Americans in part because of the compelling analogy drawn between blacks and other minorities. This analogy worked marvelously for Latinos and American Indians. It worked so well that when the Johnson White House supported minority capitalism to mitigate black rioting, it was extended to these other groups even though they were not involved in the violence. White House officials saw these groups as having a meaning similar to blacks. In addition, not only did the Nixon team perceive Latinos as being disadvantaged like blacks, they also saw them as potential key members of the Nixon coalition—they were numerous, their votes were winnable, and they lived in key electoral states. Minority capitalism thus became an arrow in the quiver of political strategists, now freely targeting groups with ethnicity-based policies, and Nixon increasingly directed his own program of minority capitalism to Latinos as part of a presidential coalition building strategy. It was the purest case of anticipatory politics. Though Latinos were not demanding it, this program devised for blacks was presumed to be something they *would* want. So Nixon gave it to them.

There is little evidence of any lobbying against minority capitalism, though labor unions did complain about it initially. There is no evidence at all of resistance to expanding it beyond blacks. The tendency for one official minority group—Asians—to be left out of these programs was the result of the failure of the black analogy to work for them automatically. Policymakers tended to drop Asian Americans from the programs apparently because they simply forgot that Asians were minorities. However, it took just a few nudges from Asian American advocates to have them reinstated. Programs for minority capitalism also did not originally include women. In employment, women's advocates needed significant meaning entrepreneurship to convincingly make the analogy between women and blacks, and in the area of minority capitalism, they simply did not make the effort.

The major focus of the expansion of minority capitalism was Latinos, and this chapter details that story. Latinos did not receive this attention simply because of their greater similarity, as a minority group, to blacks. Political meanings also played a role . This is a story of how democratic politics could work to promote a minority rights revolution.

Origins of Minority-Capitalism Affirmative Action

During the late 1960s, as American cities were rocked by a series of black racial uprisings, many black leaders, both moderates and radicals, began to argue that blacks needed more control over their communities.[1] The vast majority of businesses in black neighborhoods, both industrial and retail goods and services, were Euro-American owned and operated.[2] Business leaders and Johnson administration officials heard little in the way of specific demands; the task at hand was to stop the rioting in the cities, restore order, and prevent damaging international propaganda showing the failure of American justice. Working separately and together, they developed various programs for empowering blacks in poor neighborhoods that could serve as riot control: special poverty aid, employment training, targeted recruitment and employment of ghetto residents, and various schemes to have residents "buy in" to their community so they would have incentives to preserve rather than burn down local businesses.[3]

The Small Business Administration (SBA) as well as other agencies became involved in these targeted efforts in 1965. The Small Business Act created the SBA in 1953. This law, as the name suggests, was designed to protect and encourage small businesses. Affirmative-action-style preferences for minority capitalists began quietly, in the summer of 1965, when Johnson's vice president Hubert H. Humphrey and the US Commission on Civil Rights asked the Small Business Administration (SBA) to gather information on minorities applying for loans. The SBA, originally intended to protect and encourage all small businesses, was now to target special help to minority-owned businesses. Though it was black neighborhoods in cities that were by then already showing signs of serious crisis, the vision of "minority" here was broader. Humphrey's directive was focused on "minority groups which are significant in size . . . and which are known currently to be subject to discrimination." It listed as categories "Negro, American Indian, Mexican-American, and Puerto Rican." The SBA then added the category "Asian," which included "Japanese, Chinese, Korean or Polynesian."[4] In late 1967, Lyndon Johnson appointed Howard Samuels, an energetic New York entrepreneur active in the civil rights movement, to head the SBA. Samuels pushed the SBA farther along toward minority capitalism, injecting new life into the Small Business Act's "Section 8(a)" program. Section 8(a) authorized the SBA to be a sort of middleman to aid small business by allowing it to contract with federal agencies to provide various goods and services. It would honor those contracts by subcontracting with small businesses, allowing them to share in the bounty of federal procurement. Samuels developed rules to channel these subcontracts to "socially or economically disadvantaged persons," a formally broad category but in fact targeted to help blacks. He called the program "compensatory capitalism."[5] Congress helped the effort along by giving the SBA funds for formally color-blind efforts to help the poor that boosted its budget from $650 million to $2.65 billion in 1967.[6]

Clearly, African Americans were the focus of this effort, as they were the only minority group involved in the urban violence. Still, without lobbying or any debate, Latinos and American Indians also were early beneficiaries. Policymakers apparently took it for granted that these groups were sufficiently analogous to blacks that their inclusion needed no explanation. A black riot, as a minority riot, was taken as evidence that riots by analogous minority groups should be expected. Asians, as mentioned earlier, initially were left out of the 8(a) program without explanation.

Unlike employment affirmative action, these first moves to minority-capitalism affirmative action did not have a pretext of preventing current discrimination. No one thought much about why all ethnic groups were not equally involved in business. For example, William Welsh, an assistant to Vice President Hubert Humphrey, assembled a report on March 26, 1968 entitled "A National Program for Promoting Minority Entrepreneurs." Though Humphrey was running for president (Johnson having decided not to seek a second full term), Welsh did not discuss the campaign implications or electoral benefits of the new program. He explained that the programs were appropriate "because they are right and just" and "because all Americans are entitled to participate in all vital aspects of our nation's life." "More pragmatically," he explained, "the harnessing of the energies of all parts of our society can substantially improve the economy." These two arguments, morality and economic growth, were prominent in the report advocating color-blind non-discrimination laws by Truman's Committee on Civil Rights twenty years earlier, as discussed in Chapter 2. But rather than further grounding the policy in Cold War geopolitics and national security, as Truman's committee had done, Welsh's report argued that riot prevention was a further justification: "Furthermore, we must move forward in this area because economic control is one of the critical issues underlying tension in our ghettoes." Though only blacks were rioting, the program defined minority as "Negroes, Spanish-speaking Americans and Indians." The program was oriented toward "results" rather than "opportunity," which figured so prominently in the language used for American civil rights and poverty policy discourse. Rather than preventing discrimination, "the principal objective . . . must be to create minority owned and operated businesses of a substantial nature in both urban and rural areas." To this end, Welsh reported, the Office of Economic Opportunity (OEO) created small-business development centers in ghettoes, the Department of Commerce had an affirmative-action program to obtain franchises for minority persons, and the SBA provided special counseling for small businesses.[7]

Meanwhile, Humphrey's main opponent, Richard Nixon, began to promote a program that he explicitly called "black capitalism."[8] It is not clear whether Welsh and Humphrey were aware of Nixon's plans, or whether

Nixon was aware of what Welsh and Humphrey had in mind. It is possible that Nixon independently came to advocate a similar program. On April 25, 1968, he proposed special help to build "the bridge of black capitalism." He explained that "what we need is imaginative enlistment of private funds, private energies, and private talents, in order to develop the opportunities that lie untapped in our own underdeveloped urban heartland," adding that "it costs little or no government money to set in motion many of the programs that would in fact do the most, in a practical sense, to start building a firm structure of [black] economic opportunity."[9] In a television commercial, Nixon sold the program as riot prevention, saying, "More black ownership of business and land and homes can be the multiplier of pride that will end our racial strife."[10] Nixon, still fighting the fallout from the disastrous Barry Goldwater loss in the 1964 election, was experimenting with new coalition possibilities while showing part of his response to the ghetto violence.[11] Advocating black capitalism also gave Nixon a prominority policy to counterbalance his "southern strategy," which sought to win the south by advocating "law and order" and slowing school integration.

A few months later, there was more momentum for affirmative action. Here there is evidence of an indirect role played by black civil-rights groups, as well as some impetus from Johnson. In a June 1968 memo, the SBA administrator Howard Samuels told President Johnson that a good strategy for responding to the multiracial Poor People's Campaign (the last brainchild of Martin Luther King Jr., assassinated the previous March) was to explain that the federal government already had an affirmative-action program to help the poor. The campaign was led by King's successor, the Rev. Ralph Abernathy. Samuels told Johnson to have a meeting with Abernathy and then announce programs that were already in existence: "One possibility would be an announcement that you have organized a new Federal response to the urgent need" for the poor to become "owners and managers, as well as workers. The call for 'a piece of the action' is the clearest message coming from the poor." More specifically, "you could announce publication of a memorandum to the Departments of Labor and Commerce, OEO and SBA to unify their eligible lending, grant, guarantee and technical assistance activities, under the leadership of the latter, into a comprehensive national program to increase opportunities for disadvantaged Americans to be come [*sic*] full participants in the economy."[12]

In fact, though some leaders were calling for "black control," Abernathy was demanding nothing of the kind. He was then advocating cross-race coalitions of the poor. Abernathy pushed issues that he later described as "issues of common interest to all of the poor." He demanded job training, food stamps, housing aid, a minimum wage, and full employment as part of his

Poor People's Campaign. It is hard to see how ethnoracially targeted policies fit into that project. It was arguably a perversion of it.[13] Johnson, who never publicized support for such programs, nevertheless apparently encouraged further development along ethnoracial lines. The next day, Samuels reported on "efforts to meet your mandate 'to take the lead in the development of minority entrepreneur programs through the available resources of the Federal Government and the cooperation of American business.'" If Johnson did indeed utter these words (I can find no record that he did), it was a rare departure from his preferred color-blind language of the need to help "the poor," "the disadvantaged," "the hardcore unemployed," and so on.[14] Samuels described successful efforts of working with the American Bankers Association to develop programs for "disadvantaged areas of the country," though he meant minority areas.[15] These efforts were substantial: in the last six months of 1968, the SBA directed 5.7 percent of its money to minorities.[16] Though the Johnson administration used the broad term "minority," it is clear from the concerns with ghetto tensions that blacks were the original intended beneficiary.

Richard Nixon assumed the presidency in 1969 and pushed along the SBA's nascent interest in helping minorities. He appointed a Mexican American, Hilary Sandoval, to head the SBA. His Executive Order 11518 in March of 1970 directed the SBA to "particularly consider the needs and interests of minority-owned small business concerns and of members of minority groups seeking entry into the business community."[17] These actions led to the section 8(a) program that exists to this day, otherwise called the "Minority Small Business and Capital Ownership Development" program. It allowed the SBA to act as prime contractor with the government, and to subcontract with "socially disadvantaged" firms. This program increased quickly and steadily, targeting contracts to the official minorities of the EEO-1 form, including Asian Americans (though Puerto Ricans mysteriously were put in a category separate from "Spanish Americans").[18]

"Discrimination" had little to do with the creation of the program, and SBA officials did not try to understand why minority firms often did not get government contracts without special help. It just tried to give more contracts to minority-owned firms. A Senate report later explained that "the 8(a) program simply evolved . . . in response to the 1967 Report of the Commission on Civil Disorders . . . The finding that triggered the 8(a) effort was that disadvantaged individuals did not play an integral role in America's free enterprise system, in that they enjoyed no appreciable ownership of small businesses and did not share in the community redevelopment process."[19] The Section 8(a) program was based on a proportional model of justice to a degree that disturbed even the liberal US Commission on Civil Rights. It complained in 1975 that "when queried about program goals and objectives, SBA officials responded in terms of a dollar volume of 8(a) contracts to be awarded . . . No mention was made of such objectives as developing bidding and negotiating skills of the participants, despite the importance of these factors in developing the competitive status of the firms concerned."[20]

Nixon also followed through in a more distinctive way with his campaign promise to promote black capitalism. On March 5, 1969, he issued Executive Order 11458, creating the Office of Minority Business Enterprise (OMBE). Under Nixon, OMBE never replaced the SBA programs for minority capitalism. They ran on mostly parallel tracks, though there was some intersection and conflict.[21] Like affirmative action in the SBA program, OMBE developed without a clear antidiscrimination rationale. It was directed simply at giving more opportunities for designated underrepresented groups. As Nixon explained, "I have often made the point that to foster the economic status and the pride of members of our minority groups we must seek to involve them more fully in our private enterprise system."[22] To appeal to Euro-American pocketbooks, he stated, "the first need is to replace dependence with independence."[23] In his personal notes, Nixon framed the program as a way to bring "dignity, pride, self-respect" to blacks. It promised votes, at least among the 20 percent (Nixon's guess) of the black vote that was middle class.[24]

OMBE's development was slow and sloppy, but by 1975 it evolved four main responsibilities. According to the US Commission on Civil Rights, OMBE's jobs included "(1) coordinating Federal procurement with minority firms, (2) promoting mobilization of State and local resources for aiding minority enterprise, (3) serving as a data collection center and an information bureau, and (4) funding organizations to provide training and technical assistance for minority entrepreneurs and conducting special pilot demonstrations projects."[25]

Minority-group leaders gave Nixon little encouragement. What little support he had came from black separatist leaders, such as Roy Inniss and Floyd McKissick of CORE. McKissick argued that "handouts are demeaning. They do violence to a man, strip him of dignity, and breed in him a hatred of the system." (How black capitalism was less of a handout than the job-training programs that many Democrats then favored was not clear.) The Leadership Conference on Civil Rights offered no support. This stalwart integrationist organization—either unfairly partisan or oblivious to the similar Johnson administration efforts—said of Nixon's effort that it was "saddening" to watch "the old seemingly discredited doctrine of 'separate but equal' manifesting itself anew in some of the current plans for enterprise, education, and housing." Civil rights movement veteran Julian Bond said "black capitalism" was a "pitifully underfinanced public-relations gimmick." He called instead for "community socialism."[26] Andrew F. Brimmer, a black Federal Reserve governor, said the program was "one of the worst digressions that has attracted attention and pulled substantial numbers of people off course."[27] The AFL-CIO was appalled, calling the program "apartheid, antidemocratic nonsense," and part of self-destructive "attempts to build separate economic enclaves."[28] Despite the criticism, Nixon enlarged the program.

Expanding Minority Capitalism beyond Blacks

The SBA efforts had expanded beyond blacks in the Johnson administration. The same expansion would occur in Nixon's OMBE. How and why Nixon became convinced that the program should be broadened from its original application to "black capitalism" to include the official minorities besides African Americans is not clear, but there is little evidence of struggle, lobbying, or protest. It happened quietly early in 1969.

Nixon picked an enthusiastic Maurice Stans, secretary of commerce, to run the black-capitalism program. Stans, a former Chicago businessman and Eisenhower administration official, was the likely instigator of the expansion. He used the passive voice in a memo to Nixon's chief domestic policy aide John Ehrlichman, obscuring exactly who pushed for the expansion while also giving the impression of a smooth process. He simply stated that "in view of the existence of the other significant minorities, the program was given the title of Minority Enterprise and the other ethnic groups were brought into it."[29]

In an interview two decades later, Stans attributed the expansion to his desire simply to put the program in line with previous designations of official minorities. He recalled a meeting with Nixon in which he explained that "we have to enlarge the scope of this, because there are more than blacks involved; there are four ethnic groupings of people in the United States that are considered by the Congress to be minorities: blacks, Hispanics, Asians, and American Indians. I'd like to wrap them all together into one program and call it 'Minority Business.'" According to Stans, Nixon agreed to the change without discussion: "All right; let's do it that way."[30] In Nixon's signing statement for Executive Order 11458, however, he only mentioned blacks, Mexican Americans, Puerto Ricans, "and others."[31]

It is not clear what congressional designation regarding minorities Stans was talking about, and it is unlikely Congress had anything to do with it (I can find no such official congressional designation). But Stans probably knew of the other regulations that were part of affirmative action in employment and the SBA minority program, and knew that they included other groups—

what he called "the other significant minorities." It appears that Stans felt that all of the groups were equal or analogous in their "significance," and a legitimate minority program had to include *all* of the official minorities.

"The Republican Party can Champion the Spanish-speaking Groups": Pursuing Latino Votes with Minority Capitalism and Other Programs

Seeing the minority-capitalism program as a form of riot control faded along with the riots in 1970. Increasingly its wider scope and political benefits came to the fore. The Nixon administration began to understand minority-cap-italism affirmative action as one of many tools to appeal to minority voters. The administration also began to differentiate between minority groups, but only in terms of their political value. Though originated for African Americans and nominally including all of the official minorities, the Nixon team began to promote minority capitalism in a bid to win support from Latinos. They saw the rapidly growing Latino group as a possible coalition partner for Nixon's reelection and for Republicans generally. Government officials arguing this point put the number of Latinos at 9 million, 12 million, and 16 million. While there was no agreement on actual numbers, there was little disagreement that they were political gold and became a recurring focus of campaign strategy.

As described in the Introduction, Senator Barry Goldwater (R–AZ) impressed on Nixon, even before the Nixon presidency began, how politically valuable Mexican Americans in particular were. By the fall of 1969, Nixon was a believer. When the Republican National Committee (RNC) created various offensives to target certain demographic groups in American society, Nixon believed these efforts were misguided, and counseled his political aides that the RNC activities "are not putting nearly enough emphasis on the *key* ethnic groups—Italians, Poles and Mexicans." These were the areas that could "be really politically productive."[32]

Other conservative Republicans also sought political support from Latinos with appeals recognizing them as a distinct group. One congressional effort transformed Johnson's old Inter-Agency Committee on Mexican American Affairs into a congressionally sanctioned Cabinet Committee on Opportunities for Spanish-speaking People (CCOSS). CCOSS was to coordinate government activities in various cabinet departments that could benefit Latinos. The bill had several Latino congressional sponsors and supporters, including Jorge Cordova (New Progressive, Resident Commissioner of Puerto Rico in the House), Rep. Edward Roybal (D–CA), Rep. Joseph Montoya (D–NM), and Rep. Manuel Lujan (R–NM). They were joined by Barry Goldwater (R–AZ), George Bush (R–TX), Paul Fannin (R–AZ), George Murphy (R–CA), and John Tower (R–TX). All received Nixon's pens from the December 31 signing ceremony.[33]

Nixon's statement on the occasion of the bill's signing promoted his administration's interest in programs for Latinos, including affirmative action. In an address prepared by speechwriter William Safire, Nixon introduced the language of equalizing opportunity into the minority-capitalism program. He declared that CCOSS would increase attention for a group that had been denied "good jobs and a real share in American Business Enterprise." What or who did the denying, Nixon did not say. His minority capitalism would "open doors to better jobs and the ownership and management of business." CCOSS would help by working "closely with the Department of Commerce's Office of Minority Business Enterprise in assisting Spanish-speaking people to launch their own businesses and generate new job opportunities." Such help was part of classically liberal citizenship: "I sign this bill con gusto—with the enthusiasm and determination to make equal opportunity a reality in these United States."[34]

As the 1972 presidential election drew nearer, Latinos loomed larger in the political calculus. For example, Ehrlichman informed Nixon in April of 1970 that a meeting with Latino appointees was a good idea to "demonstrate Presidential concern for the interests of the Spanish-speaking minorities." Ehrlichman referred to the advice of Martin Castillo, former chair of the Inter-Agency Committee on Mexican American Affairs, to argue that most important was "presidential awareness that Negroes are not the only minority in the country."[35] One 1970 effort along these lines was for the SBA and CCOSS to create a mini-OMBE specifically for Latinos—the National Economic Development Association (NEDA). Beginning with a $600,000 grant from SBA and later funded by OMBE, the NEDA's purpose, despite its vague name, was to generate financial assistance packages to create or expand existing Latino-owned businesses. From 1970 to 1972, it generated 821 assistance packages amounting to $43.5 million.[36] The Nixon administration also made major efforts in 1970 in the area of language rights and bilingual education (see Chapter 7), Latino employment in government (see below) and forced a "Hispanic origin" question onto the 1970 census, literally stopping the presses to make the change after the original census forms had already been sent to the printers.[37]

The Nixon team increasingly tried to make Latinos feel special, making efforts to bring them onto the national agenda. When asked at a May 1971 news conference how he felt about many African Americans perceiving him as opposed to civil rights, Nixon responded by defending his record with this group, but then changed the subject: he would meet with African American leaders "and with representatives of other parts of our society, because we have got to move forward not only with black Americans; we have very significant problems . . . in the Mexican American community."[38]

Later that month there was another sign that Latinos mattered. Administration officials heard rumblings that the Latino members of Congress would follow the lead of the new Congressional Black Caucus and form a caucus of their own. They immediately felt a meeting with these congressmembers was warranted—though the administration had refused to meet with the black caucus. Their reasoning was simple: "There are some twelve million Spanish surnamed Americans . . . Most of this population is strategically located in politically doubtful states."[39]

A few days later, a strategy memo reiterated "there are some twelve million Spanish surnamed Americans," that their demands "are now accelerating," that "most of this population is strategically located in politically doubtful states," and "if we get or can get momentum going with these people, they will be very loyal and at present they feel neglected." With policy recognition and ethnic targeting now taken for granted as a legitimate part of the policy repertoire, equating blacks and Latinos was simply a part of the coalition-building calculus. The Nixon administration considered preempting demands from Latinos in Congress. Policy for African Americans should beget policy for Latinos, since "one of the battle cries of the Spanish speaking community is that they want the same type of opportunities as Negroes, and do not want 'to play second fiddle to any minority.'" "It seems advisable," the memo continued, "that any action toward Black demands should be taken with subsequent Spanish speaking requirements in mind, and with awareness that the Spanish speaking will ask for parity in treatment. Perhaps package proposals should be considered."[40] The memo said nothing about affirmative-action regulations, but their expansion perfectly fit this strategy of showing Latinos that Nixon cared about them as much as (or more than) African Americans.

In July of 1971, the Nixon team began to explore in some depth the nature and dynamics of the Latino population. One strategy memo showed rare subtlety, breaking down the group into "Chicanos," "Puerto Ricans," and "Cubanos," and identifying variations between the groups. It pointed out that only "Anglos" and Latino leaders group all three ethnicities together. But it did not strongly contrast Latino disadvantage with black disadvantage. In politics, these did not really matter. It was more important that "The Democratic Party appears to be the champion of the Blacks. This does not go down well with the Spanish speaking. The Spanish speaking are beginning to call themselves 'the second largest minority.' They now see themselves as competing with the Blacks. It is possible the Republican Party can champion the Spanish speaking groups.[41]

Another strategy memo explained (with questionable word choice) that Latinos were "much more open to penetration by the President than their 80 to 90 percent Democratic registration would indicate." The political opportunity was "wide open" because

> Spanish-speaking Americans will take what they can get from whomever will give it. Because it is relatively costless to give them more than what they have had in the past, we should accelerate what we are doing and, where it is insufficiently publicized, work to gain it visibility in Spanish-speaking communities. At the same time, we should exploit Spanish-speaking hostility to blacks by reminding Spanish groups of the Democrats' commitment to blacks at their expense.[42]

These political considerations finally led the Nixon administration to give CCOSS a boost as the 1972 election drew nearer. It had languished after its creation but was dusted off for its first official meeting on August 6, 1971, when Nixon told the group that Latinos were not "getting their fair shake with regard to other groups," and declared "that is going to change. It can only change if the members of the Cabinet get off their duffs." Every group in the United States, he argued, should "have an equal chance to develop their capability." The Spanish speaking did not have equality, and that this was going to change "or the people in the personnel offices in every department are going to change." In a rambling set of remarks, Nixon essentially gave CCOSS encouragement to be a progressive force. He did not just want antidiscrimination efforts but he wanted his administration to show that "we are making positive moves to rectify the situation."[43]

Emboldened by this meeting, Henry Ramirez, acting CCOSS chairman, blanketed administration officials with letters. Ramirez suggested that Thomas Kleppe of the SBA develop "an affirmative action plan . . . to insure that the Spanish-speaking contractors receive their proportional share of the contracts from the various agencies of government" as part of the Section 8(a) program. Ramirez also sent a letter to Maurice Stans, suggesting that 25 percent of OMBE grants go to the Spanish speaking. Affirmative action for Latino capitalists was not the only focus of Ramirez's efforts; letters also went to Secretary of Labor James Hodgson, EEOC chairman William H. Brown, Civil Service Commission head Robert E. Hampton, Attorney General John Mitchell, Treasury Secretary John Connolly, Director of OEO Frank Carlucci, Housing and Urban Development (HUD) Secretary George Romney, Agriculture Secretary Clifford M. Hardin, and Health, Education and Welfare Secretary Elliot Richardson. All of the letters emphasized Nixon's support for pro-Latino efforts. At the August 6 meeting, "the President stated in very explicit terms his dismay and concern at the lack of effort being directed towards meeting the needs of the Spanish speaking/Spanish surnamed," and Ramirez was acting to comply with Nixon's instructions.[44]

There were others in the administration pursing Latino voters with affirmative action for Latino capitalists. A few weeks later, Stans suggested to John Ehrlichman in an "EYES ONLY" memo that the minority-business program should be expanded and oriented more toward Latinos. The memo did not mention lobbying, protest, preventing discrimination, or compensation for past discrimination. Instead Stans included census data showing the number of blacks (22.6 million), Spanish-Americans (9.2 million), and Indian and other (2.9 million, presumably including Asian Americans) and data on the number of minority-owned businesses in the United States. To justify more resources for the programs, he argued that since minorities made up 17 percent of the population but only 4 percent of the businesses in the United States—accounting for only seven-tenths of 1 percent of the total sales in the economy—"the equity of doing something is readily apparent."

But the thrust of the argument was politics, not principle. The placement of Latinos in large cities and states (New York City, Texas, California) meant that an expanded program "could have real political value." Stans found support for his view from Senator John Tower of Texas, quoting the conservative Republican as saying "I am particularly concerned with the lack of economic opportunity afforded the Mexican American population." Tower explicitly equated the situations of blacks, Mexican Americans, and Indians:

> While I do not want to depreciate the problems of the Blacks in gaining adequate economic opportunity, I do want to urge the business community to help foster greater opportunity among the less publicized minorities such as the Mexican Americans. They and the American Indians have suffered from the same lack of opportunity, yet have not come to the forefront of the expanded-opportunity campaign.

Stans admitted that blacks "are not very friendly toward the Administration" and that "actions deemed desirable by the Blacks leave many whites unhappy, and vice versa," but the program for blacks should not be ended. He cited Senator Bob Dole (R–KS) for the belief that 10 percent of African Americans could still be "won over." This would involve "reduc[ing] vocal criticism where possible" and pointing to specific accomplishments. In summarizing the political significance of the minority-capitalism program, Stans first mentioned the "distinct vote-getting potential among the Spanish-Americans in an expanded program." Unlike programs for blacks, Stans saw no political liabilities with ethnic targeting of Latinos.[45]

In the increasingly tight fiscal climate of the early 1970s, Stans's proposal encountered considerable resistance, but none of it related to ethnoracial targeting or orienting the program to Latinos. In September 1971, Stans wanted a commitment of at least $100 million, but the Nixon administration wanted to keep the figure at $60 million. When Stans wanted to personally appeal to the president, George Shultz of the Office of Management and Budget explained the issues to Nixon. Shultz saw much potential for waste in the program, which was still mostly untested, and he and Ehrlichman suggested that Nixon hold at $60 million. Newly appointed HEW Secretary Caspar Weinberger counseled retrenchment to $40 million, while Attorney General John Mitchell, a major player in the upcoming campaign to reelect Nixon, suggested deferring to Stans's proposed heavy spending. But Shultz added a separate information sheet on the "distinct vote-getting potential among Spanish-Americans in an expanded minority business enterprise program" for California, Texas, Florida, Arizona, New Mexico, Chicago, and New York. Shultz explained without evidence that "the Spanish-speaking population responds well to the economic development programs" and that "past experience indicates that a strong new thrust to the Minority Business Enterprise Program will go along [sic] way to further enhance the favorable impression of you and the Administration in the Spanish-American Community." Nixon wrote on the memo that efforts for the Latinos should be strengthened, but "keep the black about where it is."[46]

In the end, Nixon requested only $43.6 million for OMBE, mainly for technical assistance, but wanted another $700 million for grants, loans, and guarantees. This was all considerably more than what he originally said the program would cost—zero. His strongly worded message to Congress was more significant for its legitimation of the minority-capitalism concept, in which he recited statistics of the underrepresentation of blacks, Latinos, and Indians in business—Asians were either left out accidentally or their statistics of underrepresentation were not compelling. He described the increases from 1969 to 1971 in grants and loans to minorities ($200 million to $566 million) and a growth in government purchases from minority companies from $13 million to $142 million. Nixon sold the preferences for minority capitalists as self-help for the poor: "The best way to fight poverty and to break the vicious cycle of dependence and despair which afflicts too many Americans is by fostering conditions which encourage those who have been so afflicted to play a more self-reliant and independent economic role."[47]

Meanwhile, SBA efforts continued at a somewhat slower pace. Exact figures regarding which groups were benefiting are difficult to find, but Nixon presided over an increase in Section 8(a) contract awards from a 1969 total of 30 contracts and $8.9 million to 351 new contracts in the first three quarters of 1971, worth $29.5 million.[48] A confidential Nixon administration document on strategy to win votes from Latinos stated that in fiscal year 1971 the SBA awarded contracts in excess of $57 million. Further, "SBA made over

2,500 loans totaling nearly $58 million to Spanish speaking businesses, an increase of nearly 50 percent in number and 60 percent in dollars over the previous period."[49]

Adding to the momentum, Charles Colson, Nixon's designated coalition builder, sounded nothing like a conservative as he advocated efforts to win the Latino vote for 1972. Colson told Ehrlichman, "We could see some significant movement in the voting preferences of Spanish-surnamed Americans next year. I think we should do everything possible to encourage it." Colson suggested possible policy initiatives, including a computerized network to assist locating Latino contractors and subcontractors for the minority capitalism program. Better public relations through utilization of the Latino press and organization also was a good idea, according to Colson, who concluded his memo with a favorite expression of the Nixon administration, "There is much in the way of fertile ground to be plowed hard."[50]

In this case, "plowing hard" meant doling out minority rights policies that the "fertile ground" was not demanding. Apparently following up on Colson's December 1971 initiative, in January of 1972 domestic policy aide Ken Cole sent a series of urgent memos through the White House, explaining that "the President has a strong interest in program development of assistance to Spanish-speaking Americans," and that "we would like to get things out and rolling in a very short time." Ideas related to the minority-capitalism program included stationing an SBA development officer in Latino areas and Colson's idea of a computerized Spanish-speaking minority enterprise capabilities directory.[51]

Nixon's zeal for using minority capitalism for political purposes ultimately became a sidelight to the ethics investigations by the congressional Watergate committee. This committee exposed particularly brazen uses of the OMBE minority-capitalism affirmative action to appeal to Latinos.

It began in early 1972. William H. Marumoto, a Japanese American apparently uninterested in advocating for Asian Americans as a minority, moved from a position in the White House involved with recruiting to work on Latino issues under Colson. He headed weekly meetings with his deputy, Antonio Rodriguez, a Latino White House aide named Carlos Conde, Henry Ramirez, head of CCOSS, and Alex Armendariz, director of the Committee to Re-elect the President. (Marumoto originally called this group the "Brown Mafia" until he was told by his immediate supervisor, Fred Malek, that this name would "look bad if it ever got out.") Marumoto's group was one of several designed to develop strategies to win the votes of a subsection of the electorate. His group got into hot water because it used minority capitalism to win and reward support from Latino business persons—while withholding support from political enemies.[52]

Part of the responsibility with which Marumoto had been charged was called "Capitalizing on the Incumbency." This meant he was to find ways to use the executive branch's grant-making and hiring powers to secure Latino support.[53] Though OMBE was formally designed to help minority businesses generally, the Nixon team narrowed the focus to helping black and Latino minority businesses that supported Nixon. This practice had support from the White House. In a memo from Fred Malek to Bob Brown and Paul Jones, who worked on black issues, and Marumoto and Armendariz on the Latino side, Malek wrote

> Each of you has expressed concern to me recently about the use of OMBE grants. This, obviously, represents an excellent opportunity to make a contribution and gain headway in the Black and Spanish-speaking areas.
>
> I have discussed this situation with Ken Cole, and we are in agreement on the importance of the program to our efforts.[54]

Marumoto's 1972 "Weekly Activity Report(s) for Spanish Speaking" were sprinkled with embarrassingly incriminating comments. These included having an administrator on March 24 "set aside $300,000 for one of *our* Spanish speaking contractors" (emphasis added). An April 7 entry described "reviewing with [Nixon staffmembers] John Evans, Bob Brown and Wally Henley proposals and grants at OMBE to make sure the right people are being considered and receiving grants from OMBE." On May 19, Marumoto wrote, "Rodriguez is assisting Ultrasystems, Inc., of Long Beach, California with a $200,000 grant from OMBE. This organization strongly supports the administration."[55] The transfer of Armendariz from the Committee to Re-elect the President, where he was already pushing minority capitalism for Latinos, to become head of OMBE made it even easier to use minority capitalism for political purposes.[56]

The Nixon administration's use of the SBA Section 8(a) program to secure support from Latino Republicans also ran into trouble with the Watergate committee. Benjamin Fernandez, who ran a program to gain financial donations from Latinos to reelect Nixon, told the Watergate committee that "nationally there was a major effort on the part of the administration to award contracts to Spanish-speaking businessmen" from the Section 8(a) program.[57] Fernandez did not mention the other political uses of the program, formally designed to aid struggling minority-owned businesses. Marumoto's team, for example, arranged to have an outspoken Democratic firm "graduated out" of the Section 8(a) program. In other words, the firm was told it no longer needed the government preferences. In what would have been the most dramatic progress of minority politics from pre-1960s taboo to 1970s "pork barrel" politics, several officials met in March 1972 to discuss "ways of improving coordination and more effective means of getting political impact in the grant-making process." Their discussion emphasized "the tremendous need for a centralized computer facility for all Departments and Agencies whereby one could obtain data regarding grants to any congressional district and/or organization."[58]

Did Latino Leaders Demand Minority-Capitalism Affirmative Action?

It is clear that the Nixon team wanted Latino support and would use minority capitalism programs to win that support. But were the Latino leaders demanding minority capitalism? There is no evidence of any group demanding it in their communications with the White House. This is not to say that Latinos did not in fact greatly desire such programs or that street-level leaders did not ask for it.[59] But throughout both Nixon administrations, Latino lobbying remained almost obsessively focused on their representation in government. Getting their fair share of government attention and government jobs dominated their concerns. In other words, Latinos lobbied hard for affirmative action, but *only* in government employment.

The archives are filled with papers relating to this issue. One of the earlier efforts came in August of 1969, when the GI Forum, a Latino veterans group, complained to Nixon about a lack of "equal employment opportunities in Federal agencies." "It is rather ironical," the Forum mused, "that we are good enough to serve in leadership roles in the military, but not good enough to serve in subordinate roles in civilian government."[60] The next month, Martin Castillo, chairman of the Interagency Committee on Mexican American Affairs, sent a memo to John Ehrlichman regarding "prejudice against some minority groups within the Civil Rights Commission." The problem was that "the staffing pattern of the Commission indicates that five of the Executive Staff are Jewish-American, the remaining two are Black. Staffing patterns below indicate similar proportions. The Mexican American and the Indian are virtually unrepresented. Budget allocation, outlays and programs reflect similar imbalance."[61] The following summer, there was pressure to meet with Latino groups that organized a petition asking "that your office implement a Philadelphia Plan (specifically for Mexican Americans and other Spanish surname Americans) for employment within the Executive Branch of government."[62]

Nixon responded to these criticisms by offering in November of 1970 his "Sixteen-Point Program," geared entirely to hiring Latinos in government. Nixon instructed Civil Service Commission chairman Robert E. Hampton to appoint a full-time official to ensure equal opportunity for Latinos; begin an intensified recruitment drive for Latinos in Latino areas and in universities;

specially target Latinos for recruitment for those programs in OEO, HEW, and HUD that deal with the Latino population; as well as a variety of other efforts of recruitment, training, planning, and reporting.[63]

Latino leaders were not satisfied. The issue of government hiring was the main concern when Latino members of Congress communicated with Nixon. Representatives Herman Badillo (D–NY) and Edward Roybal (D–CA) contacted Nixon in August 1971 to complain about the president's long delay in appointing a chairman for CCOSS, noting that "the Spanish-speaking people in this country, numbering more than 16 million, are experiencing massive problems in housing, job training and employment, education, welfare, health, equal justice under the law and basic human dignity." But the problem they chose to highlight was government employment: "Consider, for example, that although Spanish speaking Americans represent over 8 per cent of the nation's population, only 2.8 per cent are employed by the Federal Government, and only one third of one per cent are found in top managerial positions."[64]

When Henry Ramirez, the chairman of CCOSS, complained in 1972 that Latino appointments to federal positions were being blocked by middle-level bureaucrats, Nixon aides immediately assembled a report that showed that Nixon's Sixteen-Point Program was showing progress. As assembled for Nixon, the summary stated that Latinos had "a doubling of jobs in the GS-13 and above salary grades in 34 agencies and 12 departments since December 1970," "a doubling of full-time Presidential appointees since December of 1970," and "over twelve-hundred jobs have gone to Spanish surnamed Americans in the lower GS levels from November 1970 to November 1971." On the report, Nixon wrote *"good"* when told that "to get recognition we deserve we are instructing Chuck Colson's staff to get our record out to the Spanish speaking community."[65]

While Nixon worked on minority capitalism and bilingual education for Latinos (see Chapter 7), the Latino lobby maintained its focus on the issue of government jobs through to Nixon's second term. A new organization formed—IMAGE—that described itself as "a Spanish Speaking Organization Concerned with Government Employment." Though it was not clear whether its name was an acronym, there was no doubt what IMAGE wanted: strong implementation of the Sixteen-Point Program to correct underutilization of Latinos in government.[66] By 1973, the Nixon team had learned how to manage Latino relations. When Anne Armstrong, a Nixon aide assigned to deal with Latino concerns in the second Nixon administration, arranged a meeting with Latino leaders and the president, the paramount "talking point" was for Nixon to emphasize "continued expansion of employment opportunities for the Spanish speaking in Government through improved implementation of 16 Point Program."[67]

The leaders were not satisfied. The Mexican American Political Association (MAPA) wasted its political capital by lobbying Armstrong for help in the case of an individual Latina who was denied a promotion by the Postal Service in the town of Milpitas, California.[68] The Mexican American Issues Conference, a group of various Latino organizations, passed two resolutions in October of 1973 that were communicated to the White House—one dealt with the Latina in Milpitas, and the other expressed "that this conference objects to the total lack of implementation by the Postal Service of its own Affirmative Action Plan, the Federal Womens Program and the 16 Point Program for Spanish Speaking Americans."[69]

Internal White House battles over the Latino-targeted policies described above, such as that regarding funding of the OMBE program and how much focus should be placed on Latinos at OMBE, took place with minimal input from the Latino organizations. Latino leaders continued to press for federal government hiring until the end of the Nixon's presidency and the close of the era of the minority rights revolution. During a January 1974 luncheon meeting with Latino leaders, Armstrong made nine commitments in response to the leaders' concerns. Five related directly to Latino representation in the federal government; two others related to meetings with and recognition by the White House. Only one (number nine), which had to do with the administration's position on a bill to provide health services for migrant workers, related to policy to aid Latinos, while another related to the GI Forum's efforts to help veterans.[70] The Latinos pushed so hard for government employment that, while happy in principle to comply with their wishes, it reached the point in June 1974 that domestic adviser Ken Cole was forced to tell Armstrong, "I think it important to be sure that the President is not placed in the position of saying that Spanish speaking Americans should be accorded a position *more* equal than that of other minorities."[71]

Expansion of Minority Capitalism after the Nixon Administration

After Nixon won election in 1972, some advocates for Latinos perceived a loss of support for the group.[72] Bill Marumoto even resigned over the matter.[73] The minority-capitalism program, however, saw no retrenchment. Operating concurrently, the SBA, the OMBE, and other programs such as the National Economic Development Association (NEDA) all sought to target special help to race and ethnic minorities. While the NEDA specifically targeted Latinos, the minority-capitalism programs were intended for the official minorities. In practice, Asians were a lesser priority, but they were eligible to participate under the programs, and received aid and funds. In a surprising development, some minority-capitalism programs in 1974 included Hasidic Jews (see Chapter 9).[74] Nixon and Stans, as well as the SBA officials, left women out of the program entirely. Women's advocates eventually asked for women to be included in the SBA programs and discussed the possibility with SBA officials, but the SBA resisted, and women's groups did not make an issue of it the way they did with employment affirmative action.[75]

Unlike affirmative action in employment, minority capitalism saw considerable expansion through the 1970s and 1980s. Congress began to show support for the effort. In 1972 and 1975, House subcommittees described (for the first time) how past discrimination led to difficulties for minority entrepreneurs to compete.[76] Congress acted in 1977 with another obscure minority-capitalism effort, Section 103(f)(2) of the Public Works Employment Act of 1977.[77] It declared that applicants for local public works project grants had to promise to reserve at least 10 percent of the amount of each grant for minority business enterprises. The law thus set aside 10 percent of $4 billion for the official minorities of the EEO-1. There was no debate on the nature of the minorities or whether to expand or contract this list.

Parren Mitchell, an African American representative from Maryland, was the motive force behind the set-aside. Mitchell dropped the discrimination rationale when presenting the bill. He described the program as an effort to combat minority unemployment and the dissolution of minority-owned construction firms, which he claimed had reached 20 percent. He pointed out that Congress already accepted "Buy American" provisions to encourage targeted growth, and argued that helping minority businesses would help cities, crime problems, and unemployment. Moreover, it was "ridiculous" not to set aside funds for minority-owned businesses since the SBA and OMBE were spending a lot of congressionally appropriated money to get minority businesses off the ground. Again, the issue was not discrimination but underrepresentation—only 1 percent of federal contracts went to minority firms. Mitchell explained that they had trouble offering competitive bids because they were too new, too small, and usually underbid by larger, older nonminority firms. Another African American representative, John Conyers (D-MI), added that "the bidding process is one whose intricacies defy the imaginations of most of us here" and minorities "usually lose out." The only issue that came up in Congress was what to do in states such as Idaho or New Hampshire with few minorities (Congress decided they would not have to reach the 10 percent set-aside).[78]

In 1978 Congress acted to give the SBA program a statutory basis with the

Small Business Investment Act. The law organized participation in Section 8(a) set-asides based on "social and economic disadvantage." It presumed that businesses owned by blacks, Latinos, and American Indians were socially and economically disadvantaged, and they automatically qualified. But businesses owned by other Americans could qualify if they could show that their group had suffered prejudice, bias, and discrimination; that these conditions led to economic deprivation similar to the official minorities; and that these conditions produced barriers in business that were unique to the group.[79]

Originally, Mitchell did not include either American Indians or Asian Americans in the bill. The House–Senate conference committee added American Indians but no one noticed (or cared) that Asian Americans had been dropped from the official minorities. Mitchell later said the omission was "inadvertent."[80]

Asian groups, however, immediately lobbied the SBA to reinstate the Asian–black analogy, and the SBA quickly responded by adding the category of Asian Pacific Americans. This category specifically included persons with ancestry from Cambodia, China, Guam, Japan, Korea, Laos, the Northern Marianas, the Philippines, Samoa, Taiwan, the US Trust Territory of the Pacific and Vietnam. The Asian Pacific Americans category had more room to grow: from 1982 to 1989, the SBA added to the list persons with ancestry from India, Tonga, Sri Lanka, Indonesia, the Marshall Islands, Micronesia, Nepal, and Bhutan.

The SBA did not allow everyone to be minorities. It rejected Hasidic Jews, women, disabled veterans, Iranians, and Afghans.[81] (Women capitalists were included in congressional set-asides in appropriation bills.[82]) In an analysis of the petitions from members of these groups and SBA decisions, George La Noue and John Sullivan found that the process of designating presumptively disadvantaged groups was messy and inconsistent, as the SBA sometimes applied its own rules and sometimes did not. They conclude that the SBA, consciously or unconsciously, employed a "people of color" rule, though neither the law nor their guidelines state nonwhiteness as a determining factor.[83] However, this rule makes sense only if we pretend—as many Americans do—that Latinos are a "nonwhite" category, and that there is no such thing as racial mixing.

Conclusion

Minority-capitalism affirmative action developed for black Americans primarily as a riot control measure and as a way to attract support from black voters. It was for blacks that the SBA even considered making its Section 8(a) program into a program for nonwhite capitalists, and that Nixon signed an exec-utive order creating the OMBE. And yet, from almost the very beginning, government officials included other minority groups as well.

Why did minority-capitalism programs expand beyond blacks to include the other minorities? The case shows both similarities and differences regard-ing the expansion of affirmative action in employment. Minority capitalism, like employment affirmative action, is the story of the newly found legitimacy of ethnic targeting with social policy, and it shows the ease with which the analogy between blacks and other minority groups was drawn. African Amer-icans were *the* minority, but there were others. Everyone just assumed that to be true. It was not a matter of study or contention. Though only blacks had rioted, the other minorities were brought along in the program because they were like blacks.

Minority capitalism differs from employment affirmative action in that its expansion is a story of electoral politics. Though some government agencies were involved (the OMBE and the SBA), the expansion of minority cap-italism, once established through the workings of the black analogy, was rein-forced by an electoral dynamic. In the words of Charles Colson, there was fertile ground to be plowed hard.

Minority capitalism exemplified an anticipatory politics—politicians of-fered a group a new policy because they anticipated the group would like and reward them for doing so. There was little lobbying for the policy and, except for African Americans, certainly no mass mobilization. Except for the case of Asian Americans, who sometimes had trouble having the black analogy work for them, no meaning entrepreneurship was necessary. Minority capitalism was a political tool that the Nixon team used to help build a winning coali-tion for 1972.

But if minority capitalism was a political tool, the tendency to overlook Asian Americans is mysterious. Did Nixon not want Asian American votes? One possibility is that there was little census data on them and their participa-tion in business. However, both the 1960 and 1970 censuses had questions about Asian origin.[84] Another possibility is that policymakers saw Asians as politically unimportant due to their small numbers. But then why include the similarly small American Indians? The likely answer is that policymakers saw Asian Americans as somewhat different from blacks in degree of disadvan-tage. If this is so, the decision may have been unreflectively based on simple perceptions of Asian Americans, that is on cultural prototypes. I can find no evidence of study on the issue. It should also be noted that Asian *were* similar enough to blacks that it only took a bit of lobbying to have them included in the program. And no one resisted. Still, it was clear that when government officials thought "minority," they did not always think of Asian Americans.

6

"RACE IS A VERY RELEVANT PERSONAL CHARACTERISTIC": AFFIRMATIVE ADMISSIONS, DIVERSITY, AND THE SUPREME COURT

The federal government's policymakers were not alone in thinking that affirmative action was a good idea. The nation's universities, including both undergraduate colleges and professional schools, became strong supporters of affirmative action. They did so on their own initiative. University affirmative-action programs, giving preference to some groups in admission because of race, are mostly voluntary.

Because this book is about the government's role in the recognition and protection of minority groups, this chapter does not offer a full analysis of the development of "affirmative admissions." I do want to show, however, that the admissions programs had a similar genesis and largely mirror the federal affirmative actions in the choice of groups preferred. They apparently copied the federal official minorities or took for granted that the same groups were minorities. This is true despite the unique rationales in this type of preference. It is in admissions that the "diversity" justification for affirmative action first evolved. Though this concept is logically expansive, affirmative admissions have not gone beyond the official minorities designated by the government.

This chapter also shows that the Supreme Court has been the only institution to look closely at the question of who is a minority and why. This occurred in the context of the important "reverse discrimination" case, *Regents of the University of California v. Bakke,* which offered constitutional approval for the minority rights revolution. However, at the same time, the deciding opinion in the case—that of Justice Lewis Powell—expressed serious doubts about the foundational project of officially designating some groups of Americans as "minorities."

"The Blacks Have Dramatized the Failure of Our Colleges": The Origins of Affirmative Admissions

The black violence in the nation's cities that spurred the other affirmative actions also fostered an interest among university administrators in affirmative admissions. In this crisis climate, universities took the initiative and did their part to reach out to African Americans and integrate them into mainstream society. In February of 1967, for example, representatives of the New York Board of Education, the Manhattan and Brooklyn Catholic Archdioceses, and thirty-nine New York metropolitan colleges and universities created a program to give two to three thousand "disadvantaged" high school students special help to get into college. The program would place promising students in a special academic track, offer an enriched academic program, an extended school day, special tutoring, financial aid, scholarships, work-study money, and loans. Jacob Landers, New York's assistant superintendent of schools, told the *New York Times* that they expected mostly blacks and Puerto Ricans to participate in the program, though they would take in other students. Remedying discrimination was not a prominent part of the program. Richard Plaut of the National Scholarship Service and the Fund for Negro Students explained that the reason for the great effort and expenditure of money was simply so "the kids will have some place to go."[1]

The cosmetic color blindness of the policies soon gave way to more overt color consciousness as a way to deal with the violence in the inner cities. Black admissions were on university policy agendas across the nation. As one somewhat inarticulate officer for the College Entrance Exam Board put it in 1969, "A few years ago, we did not have the problem of black students because we did not have the students and did not know enough to worry about not having them. We still do not have the students but we worry about it a great deal."[2] The University of California system created "Educational Opportunity Programs" designed to bring in more low-income students, predominately from minority backgrounds, and the regents of the UC system decided to allow for race and ethnicity as factors in admitting students under a policy of "special action" admissions, where standards could be lower.[3] *Newsweek* casually reported in 1969 that "in recent years the trend at both the sought-after liberal-arts schools in the Northeast and the multiversities of the Midwest and Far West has been to seek more black students as well as bright, socially committed white students."[4] Numbers of black students in colleges and universities were still very small, but growing. Harvard doubled its black admissions in 1969 over 1968, to 109 students. Dartmouth increased from 50 to 120. The colleges of the "Seven Sisters" admitted a new class that was 13 percent black. The University of Michigan admitted 200 minorities, mostly blacks, in 1969, pushing their total to 1000. Indiana University created a special program for mostly black disadvantaged students, as did the University of Illinois. The latter institution accepted 250 blacks out of a freshman class of 5,630. Princeton had 111 blacks, and 30 other minorities (including Mexican Americans, Cuban Americans, and Puerto Ricans) in an entering class of 1,346.[5]

While black violence in the cities likely contributed to this trend, so did violence, or the threat of it, on the campuses themselves. On some campuses, black students organized for protest and on occasion brandished weapons for effect. Preferences or quotas in admissions, however, were not always on their agenda. In one of the more dramatic actions, black men and women students at Cornell University, wearing bandoliers and carrying rifles, took over a campus building to protest various incidents of racism on campus, including insensitive remarks from a professor and harassment by white students. Among the student demands were "black studies" courses and an African American student center on campus. They got their wishes.[6]

The demand for black studies was a militant identity politics that alienated veteran civil-rights activists such as Bayard Rustin, a former associate of Martin Luther King Jr. Like King, Rustin preferred a focus on bread-and-butter issues that he believed could directly improve economic status, though this logic did not necessarily lead to a demand for affirmative action, either. "Stop capitulating to the stupid demands of Negro students," Rustin told university administrators. He explained that the students

are suffering from the shock of integration and are looking for an easy way out of their problems. The easy way out is to let them have black courses and their own dormitories and give them degrees. But what in hell are soul [black] courses worth in the real world? No one gives a damn if you've taken soul courses. They want to know if you can do mathematics and write a correct sentence.[7]

But students did not limit their demands to blacks studies courses and campus cultural centers. At some schools, they demanded that admissions standards be lowered or changed so that more blacks could attend. And though blacks were the most vocal in expressing this demand, other groups sometimes joined in the protest, unified by the notion that they were all "Third World" peoples. The global context and the Cold War struggle that had been so important in the early stages of the minority rights revolution made an impact in the late 1960s by—with the help of the Vietnam War—supplying a frame for aligning the official minorities. As emerging nations of Africa, Asia, and Latin America had unified in the anticolonial movement and the fight against capitalist imperialism, American students who were black, Asian, and Latino found inspiration and solidarity in Third World nations' struggles against domination by persons of European descent.[8] Some of the most serious incidents of campus unrest occurred at San Francisco State College, UC-Berkeley, UC-San Diego, Harvard, and City College of the City University of New York.[9] If their focus on race kept them separate from the mostly white antiwar movement, the minority student activists shared their militancy.[10] *Newsweek* described the situation in an article entitled "Campus '69: Riot, Fire and Blood."[11]

While these student demands were usually local, their impact was national. Princeton University's admissions director John T. Osander said, "The blacks have dramatized the failure of our colleges to seek out the talented young people who, for one reason or another—their race, or their economic background—have not applied or even considered applying to the best schools."[12] Affirmative admissions for undergraduates, then, began as a voluntary measure in response to generalized black discontent in the cities and some specific (mostly black) demands on campus. No federal guidelines or legislation have mandated affirmative action in admissions.[13]

While they began with a focus on lower- or working-class blacks, and were inspired to some degree by black violence in the cities, undergraduate colleges tended to include the other minorities designated in federal affirmative action whether they took part in campus protest or not. Why they did so is not clear, though the Office for Civil Rights, enforcing Title VI of the Civil Rights Act of 1964, required admissions data for the official minorities. By doing so, OCR communicated which groups mattered.[14] As with affirmative action programs for minority capitalism, however, there was a tendency to overlook Asian Americans. This was not simply due to an unconscious failure of the black analogy in their case. From the perspective of university administrators and other education professionals, readily observable admissions data showing strong performance changed the meaning of Asian Americans, severing the black analogy. A report by the Carnegie Commission on Higher Education specifically counseled against including at least some Asians, declaring that "the Japanese-Americans and Chinese-Americans are well represented in higher education and are not now educationally disadvantaged."[15] Women also fit poorly in undergraduate affirmative admissions, since their educational performance was on average superior to that of men.[16]

Meanwhile, the move on the part of university professional schools to increase minority representation also began by first focusing on black Americans. As early as 1963, with the black civil rights movement nearing its zenith, the Law School Admission Council began a program to help "minority" admission to law schools. Minority meant blacks. They sponsored recruiting conferences, gave the LSAT for free at black colleges in the south, and waived application fees for "disadvantaged" students.[17]

In 1968, the American Association of Medical Colleges (AAMC) recommended that medical schools "admit increased numbers of students from geographical areas, economic backgrounds and ethnic groups that are now inadequately represented." The following year, the AAMC more narrowly defined what it meant by adequate representation and who the targeted students were: 12 percent of first-year medical school classes should be black by the 1975–76 year. More than one hundred schools responded to the recommendation by setting up programs to make it easier for black students to get into medical school.[18] In 1970, the AAMC expanded the targeted groups but (curiously) kept the percentage the same: the 12 percent should include blacks, Mexican Americans, Puerto Ricans, and American Indians (Asian Americans were left out). They failed in their goal, but not miserably: minority enrollments varied between 8.5 and 10.1 percent from 1971–72 to 1975–76.[19] Faculty members appeared to be early converts to the effort. At UCLA's medical school, where affirmative admissions began in 1967, one professor of radiology recalled, "There was a realization among the faculty that perhaps there had been injustices . . . We moved to revamp the [admissions] process."[20]

The Association of American Law Schools, the American Bar Association, the National Bar Association (an organization of black lawyers), and the Law School Admission Council used financial support from HEW to form the Council on Legal Education Opportunity in 1968. Its purpose was to increase the chances of "members of disadvantaged groups" to attend law school. The council recruited these students, promoted prelaw summer schools, and gave special financial aid and stipends. Despite the color-blind language of the program and a detailed socioeconomic definition of "disadvantaged," the thrust of the program was to gain proportional representation of black, Latino, American Indian, and Asian American lawyers.[21] Students were chosen for the program on the basis of official minority status and gained admission to law schools through some relaxing of prevailing standards.[22]

Different survey studies document the spread of affirmative action in admissions in professional schools, and the expansion beyond blacks to all the official minorities. One study found that by 1970, two-thirds of all medical schools and one-half of all law schools had some affirmative-admissions program.[23] Another study found that all ninety medical schools in a 1974 survey had some program to increase minority representation.[24] In 1970, one-half of approximately two thousand entering minority students were admitted to the nation's law schools with some preference.[25]

In 1968, 62 percent of medical schools targeted only blacks for preferential admissions, but by 1974, only 6 percent targeted this group exclusively. Surprisingly, the small Native American group was the next best represented in the preferences. Law schools used preferences more than medical schools, especially for Asian Americans, who were overrepresented in medical schools in proportion to their numbers in the national population. A 1978 Supreme Court decision (discussed below) that gave less-than-thumping support for preferences seemed to encourage their use (see Table 6.1).[26]

Available evidence thus suggests that medical and law schools did not simply copy the groups from the EEO-1 form, but they did not go beyond those groups. In other words, they borrowed the basic existing policy model of affirmative action but tailored it a little. Thus, for instance, the admissions committee at the University of Washington Law School eliminated the category of Asian Americans, but retained a preference for Filipino Americans on the belief that only this group among Asians would not achieve a proportional representation without some relaxed standards.[27]

The mostly voluntary transformation of professional schools was part of a broader change in moral culture encouraged by the minority rights revolution. Organizations that were overwhelmingly Euro-American developed a new meaning, a taint, that was entirely novel in American history. While the medical and law school associations hastened and standardized the spread of preferences, the individual schools often acted independently and willingly, apparently because of a genuine desire for increased equal representation.[28] The president of the University of Washington testified in a court case that "more and more it became evident to us that just an open door . . . seemed

Table 6.1 Categories of minorities targeted in medical and law school affirmative-action programs

	Blacks (%)	Hispanics (%)	Native Americans (%)	Asian Americans (%)
Medical Schools				
Pre-1978	85	64	71	18
Post-1978	90	69	77	16
Law Schools				
Pre-1978	93	85	82	70
Post-1978	95	93	89	81

Note: for medical schools, $N = 61$ before 1978, and $N = 68$ after. For law schools, $N = 67$ before 1978, and $N = 87$ after.

Source: Adapted from Susan Welch and John Gruhl, *Affirmative Action and Minority Enrollments in Medical and Law Schools* (Ann Arbor: University of Michigan Press, 1998), p. 77. Copyright by the University of Michigan, 1998.

insufficient to deal with what was emerging as the greatest internal problem of the United States of America, a problem which obviously could not be resolved without some kind of contribution being made not only by the schools, but obviously . . . the University of Washington."[29] "The situation in this country," explained Frederick Hart, president of the Law School Admission Council and dean of the New Mexico Law School, "demands that the law schools do something to increase the number of lawyers from minority groups."[30] For many, the statistics of official minority underrepresentation were an "obvious problem" and they "cry out for action by the law schools and by the legal profession."[31] Many universities, especially private elite schools, soon began to strongly support affirmative action, even though they had never even considered racial, ethnic, or female preferences for (in some cases) hundreds of years. Administrators often forgot that fear of black violence was the original rationale for affirmative admissions. They began to develop other rationales, though unlike the use of affirmative action policies in employment, there was rarely any pretense in admissions of preventing current discrimination practiced by the university.

Universities increasingly saw themselves as compensating for discrimination that took place in the past or currently in the wider society—"societal discrimination." Harry Reese, former president of the Law School Admission Council, told the US Commission on Civil Rights: "We cannot continue to penalize people because of the past educational deprivation. We cannot simply 'endorse' consequences of past discrimination. We must take into account that minorities have been denied educational opportunities available to others."[32]

While some minority students were being admitted with lower scores on standardized admissions tests, this was not a great concern to law school admissions officers, who increasingly were questioning the usefulness of the LSAT. Frederick Hart told law school admissions officers to be "suspicious of traditional predictors of success for minority applicants because of the strong possibility of bias."[33] In fact, official minority status was itself a kind of qualification. Reese explained that "minorities . . . frequently demonstrate a motivation and a commitment which is unusual, extraordinary" and this "motivational factor" is a predictor of future success.[34] The Association of American Medical Colleges joined in by arguing that "most medical schools believe that race is a very relevant personal characteristic which should be considered with other criteria to provide insight into the kind of physician the applicant will become."[35]

Seeing new positives in minority status, the professional schools began to think of their affirmative admissions as something that benefited all of the students by supplying "diversity." This rationale, articulated in a series of amicus briefs to the Supreme Court in the *Bakke* case (see below), was the creation of elites. "Diversity" was not a prominent part of the demands made by early student radicals. With it, the original targeting of the most economically disadvantaged minorities faded away, and simple minority status came to dominate discussion. The Association of American Law Schools argued that given "the importance of race in American life and the effect that it is certain to have for the indefinite future, it would be startling if faculties had not concluded that the absence of racial minorities in law schools, or their presence only in very small numbers, would significantly detract from the education experience of the student body."[36] (One wonders that if this was so obvious, why did it take black rioting in the cities and radical students on campus for the law faculty to develop this rationale?) A group of elite universities (Columbia University, Harvard University, Stanford University, and the University of Pennsylvania) maintained that diversity even aided the professors. "It has been the experience of many university teachers," they explained, "that the insights provided by the participation of minority students enrich the curriculum, broaden the teachers' scholarly interests, and protect them from insensitivity to minority perspectives."[37] The American Association of University Professors (AAUP) declared that minority diversity also aided the professional socialization of medical school students. Furthermore, "there is little doubt that for a subject, such as law, which must confront every pressing social issue, the participation of students of varied social and ethnic backgrounds provides vital additional perspectives and thus a fuller education than were the class socially and ethnically homogeneous."[38]

By the mid-1970s, then, university elites clearly were committed to reaching out to minority groups, and with zeal and creativity developed reasons why it was a good idea. Yet their creative and progressive thinking was without explanation limited by the affirmative-action policy paradigm. All minorities were equal and the same—there were no mixed-race persons—and all "whites" were the same—even "socially and ethnically homogeneous," as the AAUP had said. Only the official minorities were considered Others. Persons of British, Italian, Armenian, Greek, and Polish ancestry were all the same in their histories, past discrimination, and viewpoints. Protestants, Catholics, and Jews were the same as well. There was little mention of women, whose presence in the affirmative-action model was often tenuous.

Of course, women, while hardly pouring into the professional schools, did not need any special help in undergraduate admissions. The hurdle for women to overcome was not a difficulty in meeting university standards, but blatant official exclusion; this is discussed in Chapter 8. And there has never been a problem in getting enough Jewish students into the universities; on the contrary, many universities tried to keep them out. By the 1960s, however, Jewish students no longer faced the exclusions that limited their opportunities in the early decades of the twentieth century, and it is not surprising that universities saw no need to include them in programs of affirmative admissions. But universities showed no interest in helping eastern and southern Europeans or any other religious minorities, either to combat past or current societal discrimination or to increase diversity. The government had not deemed these groups as official minorities, and white ethnic students—excluded from Third World solidarity—did not press the point in radical campus demonstrations.

Affirmative Admissions and the Supreme Court

It was not long before university preferential admissions were challenged in court by Euro-Americans. In the 1974 case *DeFunis v. Odegaard*,[39] the Supreme Court turned down the opportunity to review a preferential admissions policy at the University of Washington Law School, since the original plaintiff by that time had been accepted and was nearing graduation. The lower federal courts were offering mixed messages. In *Flanagan v. Georgetown College* (1976),[40] a district court struck down a preferential financial aid program. The Georgetown Law Center had begun an affirmative action plan in 1967 to increase minority admissions, and when they saw that many of these students needed financial aid, they developed a plan to reserve 60 percent of financial aid for minority students. While technically available to Euro-American applicants, they would have to demonstrate their disadvantage, while black, Native American, Latino, and Asian American students were presumptively eligible. The court ruled this was discriminatory under Title VI of the Civil Rights Act of 1964. That same year, however, in *Alevy v. Downstate Medical Center*,[41] a New York court upheld on constitutional grounds minority preference in medical school admissions if the state could show a "substantial" interest in preferences and that a no less objectional alternative exists.

The most famous case concerning affirmative-action admissions policy involved the University of California at Davis Medical School, which was the focus of the Supreme Court decision in *Regents of University of California v. Bakke*.[42] The medical school was new, having opened in 1968, and growing. It doubled its incoming class to one hundred students in 1971. In those early years, the official minorities were poorly represented: the first class of fifty students included three Asian Americans but no African Americans, Latinos (the medical school counted only "Chicanos," the then-fashionable term for Mexican Americans), or American Indians. In 1972 and 1973, the faculty created a special program to increase the representation of these four groups, designated as "disadvantaged," though there was no formal definition of this term. Indeed, the program ostensibly allowed the admission of economically disadvantaged Euro-Americans, and more than a quarter of the applications for the special program were from this group in 1973 and 1974, though none were admitted. A special subcommittee dominated by blacks, Latinos, Asian Americans, and American Indians governed the program. They generally examined the same criteria as the regular admissions officers, including an applicant's overall grades and science course grades, score on the Medical College Admissions Test (MCAT), letters of recommendation, extracurricular activities, and performance in interviews. The main difference was that the disadvantaged students could be admitted at lower levels of achievement. The school set aside sixteen of the one hundred spaces for which only the disadvantaged students competed.

Alan Bakke, a Euro-American of Norwegian descent, applied to the school in 1973 and was rejected, despite having higher grades and MCAT scores than the averages among the special admittees. In 1974, he applied again. This time he was rejected despite scores and grades that on average were higher than both the special and the regular admittees. He had the misfortune of having as his interviewer the chairman of the admissions committee, to whom he had complained the previous year.[43]

While other well-qualified Euro-Americans were also turned away, it was Bakke who sued. He cited a violation of the Fourteenth Amendment's guarantee of equal protection of the laws and a violation of Title VI of the Civil Rights Act of 1964. This title prohibited discrimination on the bases of race, national origin, and religion by any program or activity receiving federal financial aid.

A trial court ruled the Davis plan an unconstitutional quota, but also that Bakke did not show that his race kept him from being admitted. Bakke and the medical school both appealed, and the California Supreme Court ruled in favor of Bakke: the Davis affirmative-action plan was unconstitutional, and the burden was on the school, not Bakke, to show that something other than his race prevented his admission. Davis then appealed to the Supreme Court.

In a famously tortured opinion, four justices (Brennan, White, Marshall, and Blackmun) ruled in favor of UC-Davis Medical School and against Bakke—the plan was fine. Another four (Rehnquist, Burger, Stewart, and Stevens) thought the plan—its quota and color-consciousness—were unconstitutional, and Bakke should be admitted. Justice Powell wrote the swing opinion, ruling that the plan was an unconstitutional quota, though race was constitutionally permissible to use as a factor in university admissions to promote educational objectives, since racial diversity aided the learning process. His ruling also stated that Bakke should be admitted.

Though the decision made no ruling on the constitutionality of government designation of particular groups as official minorities, it did address this issue. In assessing the program's legality, Powell was uncomfortable with the expansion of affirmative action as a way to compensate for "societal discrimination" because there were many groups that could claim "societal discrimination." In reviewing the intent of Congress in Title VI, he stated that "the problem confronting Congress was discrimination against Negro citizens at the hands of recipients of federal moneys."[44] But Powell pointed out that many groups in this "nation of minorities" had suffered and continued to suffer discrimination—including southern and eastern Europeans, Catholics and Jews—all of whom are protected by the Fourteenth Amendment.[45] Should some be more protected than others? He argued that "the difficulties entailed in varying the level of judicial review according to a perceived 'preferred' status of a particular racial or ethnic minority are intractable." The reason was that

> the white "majority" itself is composed of various minority groups, most of which can lay claim to a history of prior discrimination at the hands of the State and private individuals. Not all of these groups can receive preferential treatment and corresponding judicial tolerance of distinctions drawn in terms of race and nationality, for then the "majority" left would be a new minority of white Anglo-Saxon Protestants. There is no principled basis for deciding which groups would merit "heightened judicial solicitude" and which would not. Courts would be asked to evaluate the extent of the prejudice and consequent harm suffered by various minority groups. Those whose societal injury is thought to exceed some arbitrary level of tolerability then would be entitled to preferential classifications at the expense of other groups.

These problems would be compounded by the fact that new judicial rankings would be necessary as groups moved up in society as a result of the preferences.[46] In a footnote, Powell pointed out that "the University is unable to explain its selection of only the four favored groups—Negroes, Mexican Americans, American-Indians, and Asians—for preferential treatment. The inclusion of the last group is especially curious in light of the substantial numbers of Asians admitted through the regular admissions process."[47]

For Powell, the number of groups was key, and this allowed a rare discussion of gender preferences as being *simpler* than race issues: with gender classifications "there are only two possible classifications" and "there are no rival groups which can claim that they, too, are entitled to preferential treatment."[48] Powell therefore rejected official minority preferences as a way to help "certain groups whom the faculty of the Davis Medical School perceived as victims of 'societal discrimination,'" since "to hold otherwise would be to convert a remedy heretofore reserved for violations of legal rights into a privilege that all institutions throughout the Nation could grant at their pleasure to whatever groups are perceived as victims of societal discrimination."[49]

There was, on the other hand, another justification for minority preferences that could presumably avoid all of these problems. The goal of attaining a diverse student body "is clearly a constitutionally permissible goal for an institution of higher education," as it was part of academic freedom protected by the First Amendment. Relying heavily on the amicus brief filed by Columbia University, Harvard University, Stanford University, and the University of Pennsylvania, as well as literature supplied by Princeton University, Powell argued that selecting students as individuals, and assessing the various qualities they have to bring to the mix of that year's student body, can make a student's racial or ethnic backgrounds acceptable "plus factors." This was true with race and ethnicity just as it was with ability to play a musical instrument or agricultural background. For instance, "the applicant who loses out on the last available seat to another candidate receiving a 'plus' on the basis of ethnic background will not have been foreclosed from all consideration for that seat simply because he was not the right color or had the wrong surname."[50] In giving Supreme Court support for such an admissions program, Powell opened the door for universities to give a "plus factor" to all races or ethnicities and not just the official minorities. He gave an example where an Italian American might be preferred over an African American.[51]

The opinion by Justice Brennan in favor of the medical school gave little attention to the issue of who should be included in affirmative-action plans. He argued (among other things) that "the failure of minorities to qualify for admission at Davis under regular procedures was due principally to the effects of past discrimination," and therefore if there was not "societal discrimination," Bakke would not have been admitted anyway.[52] The minorities would have fared better. Powell had critiqued the logic of this argument, arguing that "if it may be concluded *on this record* (original emphasis) that each of the minority groups preferred by the petitioner's special program is entitled to the benefit of the presumption, it would seem difficult to determine that any of the dozens of minority groups that have suffered 'societal discrimination' cannot also claim it, in any area of social intercourse."[53] The Brennan opinion also did not address the issue whether all minorities faced the same level of societal discrimination.

Brennan—in a footnote—briefly discussed the issue of which groups were included in the Davis plan. He stated that "we are not asked to determine whether groups other than those favored by the Davis program should similarly be favored," but then developed an argument to protect an institution's selection of groups. Ignoring amicus curiae briefs submitted by Polish and Italian groups (discussed in Chapter 9), Brennan used the curious example of German Americans to argue that though whites as a class were obviously excluded from the Davis plan, it could not be concluded that German Americans (or any other group) were singled out for invidious treatment. If there were a differential impact on German Americans, a constitutional claim would require that discriminatory intent be shown. Failing this, "the only question is whether it was rational for Davis to conclude that the groups it preferred had a greater claim to compensation than the groups it excluded." Though no scheme was put forward for gauging the claims of various groups, the Brennan group was satisfied: "claims of rival groups . . . create relatively simple problems for the courts."[54]

Justice Marshall's separate opinion concurring with Brennan focused entirely on African Americans. It completely ignored the fact that Davis's plan included any other groups. "In light of the sorry history of discrimination and its devastating impact on the lives of Negroes," he argued, "bringing the Negro into the mainstream of American life should be a state interest of the highest order."[55] His opinion so emphasized the distinctiveness of the African American experience that it cast doubt on the constitutionality of the inclusion of the other groups, but Marshall did not explicitly express those doubts. The Rehnquist opinion, finding the whole program unconstitutional, obviously avoided the question of how far the minority rights revolution should go.

Conclusion

Like the other affirmative actions, affirmative admissions began as a policy for African Americans in the context of black riots in the cities. But without their having to demand affirmative admissions, and even before campuses were rocked by protest, universities began to offer preferences. And whether or not the African Americans were joined by the other official minorities in their protests, those nonblack official minorities became co-beneficiaries of the policy within a year or two.

The case of affirmative admissions shows that the development and expansion of affirmative action was not limited to the obscure administrative actions of the EEOC or the OFCC. Neither was it limited to the aggressive coalition-building on the part of the Nixon White House. University administrators often zealously joined in without government prodding. To be sure, various accrediting organizations gave them some encouragement and incentive, but they were preaching to the choir. There were no cases (that I could find) of mainstream universities actively bucking the new trend.[56]

The precise source of the choice of minority groups in affirmative admissions plans is obscure. Because the federal government did require universities to report the minority demographics of their student bodies, and because educational institutions had to report on their official minorities in their workforce, universities knew which groups the government was counting. As we saw, however, some of the accrediting organizations for professional schools promoted affirmative-admissions programs, and they came up with the same groups. The identity of America's minorities may have simply become a taken-for-granted part of American political culture.

Again, Asian Americans fit poorly into the black analogy, as did women. Unlike employment and minority-capitalism cases, however, there was obvious and overwhelming evidence that these groups did not need preference to succeed in higher education, and there was some effort to have Asian Americans excluded from affirmative-admissions programs. By the 1980s, the problem facing Asian Americans (or at least some of the Asian subgroups) were efforts to hold *down* their burgeoning admissions.[57] What may be more interesting is that Asian Americans remained in so many preference programs, including that of the UC-Davis Medical School—the center of the reverse discrimination controversy—and the majority of law school programs.

The Supreme Court rule in Bakke prompted some reflection on how institutions could justly select some groups as preferred. Powell's celebrated opinion, advocating "diversity" as a permissible rationale for affirmative admissions, evinced considerable discomfort with the standard four-minority scheme. But Powell did not push this line too hard, and most universities heard him as saying they could prefer the four minorities for diversity purposes.

It was easier to ignore the question of how far the minority rights revolution should expand. Justice Marshall mentioned only African Americans in his Bakke opinion—it was as if the other groups simply did not exist. The Brennan opinion discussed the issue with an example, but used German Americans as the example of a white ethnic group. The choice was ridiculous, given the assimilation of German Americans, second only to persons of British descent, and especially given the amicus curiae briefs submitted by white ethnic groups including Poles and Italians (see Chapter 9). In fact, the choice of example seemed designed to avoid the issue, to change the subject.[58] On the constitutionality of the minority rights revolution, the Court issued ambivalent and conflicting opinions, but on balance it approved.

7

"LEARN, AMIGO, LEARN!" BILINGUAL EDUCATION AND LANGUAGE RIGHTS IN THE SCHOOLS

Since the mid-1970s, bilingual education has been at the center of a storm over what it means to be an American, the proper role of government, and the nature of American culture. The policy itself, however, was created rapidly and with ease. It is usually debated in the context of discussions about Latinos in America because bilingual education and a federal right to accommodation of language difference came about primarily to benefit Latinos, and Latinos remain the largest beneficiaries of bilingual education.

It is not easy to define bilingual education because its implementation varies across districts—even within schools—and has changed over time.[1] It has always been grounded, however, on the idea that primary and secondary school students who do not speak English well or at all should be taught in some or all subjects in their native language while they learn English. The principal alternatives to bilingual education are "immersion" in an English-speaking classroom (the norm for most of American history), or special training in English (English as a Second Language, or ESL) without native-language instruction. Whether instruction in one's native language should continue throughout the student's schooling (language "maintenance") or simply until English has been mastered ("transition") is still a matter of contention, with the maintenance forces losing ground since the mid-1970s, the end of the minority rights revolution. Native-language instruction has always been paired with using other aspects of the student's native culture to the maximum extent possible. Bilingual education therefore is a precursor to what is now called multicultural education. Moreover, its advocates have also usually demanded, expected, or hoped that teachers would share the student's ethnic background.

Bilingual education is a case in which both federal politicians and bureaucrats suddenly showed great interest in a policy that previously had been controversial, perhaps even unthinkable. Before the 1960s, no one lobbied for federally provided bilingual education for language and culture maintenance.[2] Officially recognized languages other than English have always been very controversial. American icons such as Benjamin Franklin and Theodore Roosevelt saw foreign language use in everyday life as disloyal, and both were outspoken supporters of cultural unity founded on the English language.[3] Many immigrants during the early twentieth century faced active "Americanization" campaigns to reduce cultural differences as rapidly as possible.[4] It is therefore not surprising that politicians, even those from states with large Latino populations, did not offer policy recognition and special language education programs to address Latinos' higher than average poverty and poor educational achievement.

They did not, that is, until the late 1960s. Cultural taboos evaporated and there suddenly was a federal bilingual education policy. In 1968, Congress passed the Bilingual Education Act, offering money to school districts that wanted to develop programs for children with limited English proficiency (LEP). In 1970, the Office for Civil Rights (OCR) issued a memorandum explaining that there was a new right under Title VI of the Civil Rights Act of 1964. It informed school districts that received federal money—nearly all of them—that LEP children's needs must be accommodated. Federal courts began to order bilingual education, and the Supreme Court affirmed the OCR's ruling in 1974. A remarkable change had taken place. How did it happen?

The rise of bilingual education illustrates both of the primary sources of the minority rights revolution. Both national security and black civil rights left several legacies that opened the path to bilingual education. World War II and the Cold War left several important legacies. Perceived national-security imperatives broke down a cultural resistance to federal control of local education and set up a policy structure that favored categorical, specific aid programs. During World War II, there was federal aid for areas impacted by large but tax-exempt military bases. Fears of Soviet military superiority led the government to see education as part of national-security policy. In 1958 the National Defense Education Act gave money to local schools to further science education and also encouraged the teaching of foreign languages. Bilingualism then had a national-security meaning that it utterly lacked in the past.

In addition, war policy created new networks of education professionals, or what Peter Haas has called "epistemic communities."[5] The United Nations, created after World War II to prevent future cataclysmic world conflicts, established new institutions, such as the United Nations Educational, Scientific and Cultural Organization (UNESCO). This body brought American educators together with education professionals from around the world. Many of them believed in the value of bilingual education. The last war-related influence was the redefinition of refugees, specifically Cuban refugees, as part of national-security policy (as described in Chapter 2). The education of Cuban refugees set a precedent for the first federal involvement in bilingual education.

Civil rights policy for blacks also had legacies that were crucial in providing opportunity for advocates of bilingual education. First, black civil rights policy redefined concern for ethnic minorities as a legitimate federal government purpose, and (eventually) allowed formal recognition of ethnic minorities in policy. The dynamic here was similar to that in the expansion of affirmative action. The government had shown special interest in blacks, Latinos were *like* blacks, and therefore politicians and civil-rights administrators pursuing constituents or justice goals targeted this group with special policy initiatives. The initiatives were special because though Latinos were by then established as a minority like blacks, they were also different from blacks and had unique problems, in this case language.

Second, the black civil rights movement left a legacy for education policy for the disadvantaged. The Supreme Court ruling in *Brown v. Board of Education* established a model for education policy: practices that damaged the self-esteem of a student could lead to poor achievement, and equal opportunity required making a student feel good about his or her ethnic or racial group. Both of these factors were important in the passage of the Bilingual Education Act.

Third, and most important for a *right* to language accommodation, was Title VI of the Civil Rights Act—intended for blacks—and its creation, the OCR. Though staffed primarily by persons concerned with black issues, these administrators were by 1969 (like the EEOC) sympathetic to other disadvantaged groups they saw as analogous, especially Latinos. They were easily persuaded to interpret Title VI's prohibition against national origin discrimination to require accommodating the needs of children with limited English proficiency. Ultimately, the Supreme Court, with strong support from the Nixon administration, agreed.

This is a complex story to explain a complex policy. The chapter is organized in two main parts. First, I examine the ways national-security policy created interests and opportunity for advocates of bilingual education. Then I consider how legacies of black civil rights policy did the same. Each of these parts contains some unique features, but also examines some developments, such as the passage of the Bilingual Education Act, from both perspectives.

National Security and Federal Education Policy

Legitimating Aid to Education

For federal bilingual-education laws to come about, there first had to be federal involvement in education. It was war, and the specter of future war, that helped put the federal government in the education business in the first place. Of course, there has always been *some* federal support for education. The Survey Ordinance of 1785 and the Northwest Ordinance of 1787 both distributed land for the purpose of setting up schools.[6] Other examples include the Morill Act of 1862, creating the land grant colleges, and the Service Men's Readjustment Act (GI Bill of Rights), giving education aid to returning servicemen.[7]

However, though a more general aid to education had long had some supporters in Congress, it regularly failed. Three primary reasons account for this failure. First, and most general, many conservatives, especially in the Republican Party, voted against aid because it would lead to federal power over what was understood to properly be a local matter. The belief in local control of education was so taken for granted that it did not need to be explained or justified, and any policy that threatened to weaken local control was in trouble. Second, federal aid to education raised the issue of the constitutional separation of church and state. It did so because it threatened Catholic interests. With their extensive network of parochial schools—chosen for children by parents as part of their religious duty—Catholics saw it as "blatantly discriminating" and "unfair" (according to Catholic leader Cardinal Francis Spellman of New York) if aid only went to public schools. On the other hand, federal aid to Catholic schools was unacceptable to Protestant groups and many others as unconstitutional favoritism of a religious group. The third reason any attempt at general aid to education was frustrated related to racial inequality. Supporters of equal rights for blacks such as Harlem congressman Adam Clayton Powell could not bring themselves to support a bill buttressing an unjust segregated school system. Conversely, white southern Democrats feared that federal money could be used to encourage desegregation of the schools.[8]

The only way to get beyond the impasse was to categorize education aid as a matter of national security. Since the late 1940s, the Lanham Act of 1940, created during the buildup for World War II, had already linked war and education, though not in terms of national-security interests. Its purpose was to give aid to school districts "impacted" (the term used in the law) by military bases. The military installations did not pay the local taxes used by nearly all school districts to finance local education. The Lanham Act authorized federal payments to local schools for construction, maintenance, and operations. Not really considered federal aid, it bore a different meaning: impacted areas legislation simply corrected for a policy irrationality resulting from the structure of American tax revenue extraction.[9] A very popular policy, it was renewed, made permanent, and expanded to include money for teacher salaries in 1950. The Korean War caused new increases in federal installations, creating more local impact and prompting Congress to give more aid.[10]

By the 1950s, expanding federal aid for education became a pressing issue. The baby-boom generation started to overwhelm the schools. Enrollments skyrocketed. The nation, which had 2.2 million first graders in 1946, had 3.7 million in 1953—an increase of nearly 70 percent. Overall public school enrollment increased from 25.1 million in 1950 to 36.1 million in 1959.[11] In addition, public opinion showed majorities of Americans favoring federal aid throughout the early and middle 1950s.[12] Still, general federal aid for the whole country remained elusive.

All of this changed in October of 1957 when a small metallic sphere named "Sputnik" first circled the Earth. As the first man-made space satellite, Sputnik quickly exacerbated fears of American inadequacy in the face of surprising Soviet technological might. Sputnik was a symbol to the world that the Soviet system worked, it was modern, and it was possibly superior to that of the United States. More directly, Americans feared the implications Sputnik had for future warfare. Some public officials at the time, including Senate majority leader Lyndon Johnson, compared Sputnik to a second Pearl Harbor.[13] Sputnik helped change the meaning of federal aid to education. It was no longer seen as a federal power grab, but was a means to ensuring national security.

Before Sputnik, many Americans already felt American education was not contributing adequately to the nation's defense. In the spring of 1957, several months before Sputnik, President Eisenhower told the National Education Association that "our schools are strong points in our National Defense . . . more important than Nike [missile] batteries, more necessary than our radar warning nets, and more powerful even than the energy of the atom." Senator Lister Hill (D–AL) introduced an education bill designed to "enhance the security, defense and economic potential of the United States," and in June of 1957, Eisenhower's secretary of health, education and welfare (HEW) began work on a bill that would offer federal scholarships for those identified early on to have academic talent.[14]

Cold War considerations were thus already changing the meaning of federal education aid. Still, congressional supporters of federal aid to education knew that Sputnik allowed for compelling arguments that were not possible before October. With the help of scientists and educators, Lister Hill's staff assembled a new bill designed, in Hill's words, to "steer between the Scylla of race and the Charybdis of religion." One Senate staffmember told the political scientist Norman C. Thomas that putting the word "defense" in the title (the "National Defense Education Act") was part of the strategy to make the bill unassailable.[15] The strategy worked.

No one brought up the issues surrounding religion and education. Southern congressmen jumped on the education/defense bandwagon. The Eisenhower administration offered its own (similar) bill and five House Republicans ordinarily opposed to education aid switched sides. A majority of the senators of both parties supported it. Edith Green (D–OR), recalled later:

> [T]hat bill would never have passed the Congress if we had not put the word "defense" in it. If it had been called the National Education Act, we would never have secured the required number of votes on the floor to have it become law, because it was still not the thing to do to provide federal aid to education . . . [T]he word "defense" was very carefully placed in it and the appeal was made on the floor of the House and I participated in that and with no regrets and with no apologies to anybody, to win the votes of the people who would not see the importance of education to the nation, but who recognized the importance of defense and that if we placed more emphasis on education as the Russians were doing, we might, especially in science and those areas, we might then be able to retain our powers as the world leader . . . Our competition with the Russians by the launching of Sputnik did more for American education than the Congress was ever able to do up to that time. I am sure as anything in the world that if they hadn't launched Sputnik, we would never have gotten our education bill through in 1958.[16]

The preamble to the National Defense Education Act (NDEA) put the Congress on record with the declaration that "the security of the Nation requires the fullest development of the mental resources and technical skills of its young men and women . . . The national interest requires . . . that the federal government give assistance to education and programs which are important to our national defense."[17]

For the later development of bilingual education, the bill was important for establishing two precedents. Most obvious, in establishing money for financial aid and school programs, the NDEA put the federal government in the education business.[18] Second, though most of the program focused on science and math, the NDEA also put the government on the side of foreign language development. This was because, in addition to development of science and math skills, Titles II, III, VI, and XI of the law also gave aid to students specializing in modern foreign languages. Why was language part of national defense? America's lack of language instruction had been painfully apparent during World War II, as the United States had difficulty communicating with the non-English-speaking Allies. In response, the government began the Army Specialized Training Program to teach service personnel foreign languages.[19] In addition, during World War II some cities in the south and southwest promoted use of Spanish as part of a "hemispheric solidarity" project. The Texas state department of education initiated an experimental project in teaching Spanish to elementary school students in 1943 as part of the same project.[20]

Combating the Soviets, the lawmakers realized, would require being able to speak to allies and potential allies, as well as to enemies. There had been earlier efforts to develop language resources initiated by Cold War national-security policy, so this notion was hardly radical. The Office of Education was already involved in an effort to survey all living languages in the world and to find new experts for those not taught in the United States. It also commissioned a Survey of Language Resources of American Ethnic Groups, and beginning in 1952 encouraged teaching foreign languages in elementary schools.[21] Eisenhower by 1957 advocated foreign language training.[22]

The NDEA's Title II gave scholarship preference to students with talents in modern foreign languages along with math and science. Title III gave funds to assist foreign language instruction in addition to math and science, and Title VI of the NDEA provided for language development, including centers for research and language institutes for training teachers. A later Title XI shared this focus.

The foreign language program made an impact. By the summer of 1959, the NDEA had created twelve foreign language institutes to train 925 teachers. By 1963, it had trained 17,400 teachers, and by 1968, there were 106 foreign language and area studies centers receiving $18 million in federal aid.[23] In a pattern common in politics, long established by scholars working in institutionalist traditions, one legacy of this policy was the creation of lobbying groups oriented around the programs. Two professional groups formed: the American Council for the Teaching of Foreign Languages and the Teachers of English to Speakers of Other Languages.[24] Both groups would press for continued maintenance and expansion of foreign language training efforts.

The NDEA, in short, established a precedent, categorized education aid as security, and spawned new interest groups. By the 1960 election, the Republican and Democratic Party platforms described education as a Cold War weapon and argued that America needed representatives who understood foreign cultures.[25] In the words of the historian Hugh Davis Graham, the NDEA "explicitly asserted a legitimate *national* interest in the quality of

American education." In doing so, it "ran formidable interference" for future education legislation.[26] That future legislation was to be the massive aid package, the Elementary and Secondary Education Act (ESEA) in 1965. The ESEA funded early bilingual projects and served as the legislative vehicle for the Bilingual Education Act in 1968.

National security, of course, was not the only force in federal education policy, especially for the ESEA. It was certainly important that President Johnson had crushed Republican competitor Barry Goldwater in the 1964 election, and the Democrats had a majority in the Senate of sixty-eight compared to thirty-two for the hapless Republicans.[27] In the House, the Democrats' advantage was 295 to 140, and compounding the Republican loss was that many members with committee seniority were ousted.[28] But it is important to keep in mind that though the 1964 election unquestionably brought to power a "reform-oriented regime,"[29] it is also true that by the 1960s, many Republicans (as evidenced by their party platforms) along with the majority of the American people supported federal aid for education.

It still required Johnson's formidable legislative skill to pass such massive new federal education aid. While his new congressional majorities helped passage, Johnson also found a winning formula. One key idea was to use the wartime education bills as vehicles for further expansion. But Johnson did not use the threat of falling behind in the Cold War to push for education aid. Instead, supporters of what became the ESEA used the language of Johnson's Great Society initiative to frame what was initially an expansion of a wartime aid program.

In December of 1963, Johnson had an early success as Congress passed a bill that combined the popular NDEA with the impacted areas program and new initiatives in the area of vocational education, with special help for the handicapped.[30] In 1964, Congress passed some amendments to the NDEA that included federal grants to institutes for developing instruction for disadvantaged children.[31] Both Congress and the Johnson administration used a similar approach of linking impacted areas policy to education for the poor in creating the bill that became the ESEA. The new idea was to combine an expansion of the impacted program with categorical aid for poor children.[32] The ESEA, budgeted for $6.1 billion for two years, further eased the road for bilingual education because this format of categorical, specific aid for the disadvantaged facilitated a new program with a targeted beneficiary.[33]

Why Bilingualism? Why Latino Children?

As shown above, national-security policy and institutions spawned legacies that facilitated federal aid for education. Teaching and learning foreign languages became a matter of national security. But there were also legacies that facilitated movement specifically toward a bilingual–bicultural approach to aiding Latino LEP children. There have long been many ways of helping such children. Why focus on the Latino child's language and culture?

The UN and the international network of bilingual education advocates
One legacy of World War II that aided the development of bilingual education was the unprecedented international intellectual networks, or epistemic communities, created by the UN. Nations had always copied each other's technological and policy innovations, but UNESCO supplied a forum and an institutional base for new networks of policy specialists in a variety of fields, from medicine to agriculture to education, to rapidly transfer ideas. Well before the United States asserted a federal interest in bilingual education, international networks of education scholars and government education officials were advocating teaching immigrant or minority children in their mother tongue. An early UNESCO report, chronicling a meeting of international educators in Paris in 1951, stated bluntly that "it is axiomatic that the best medium for teaching a child is his mother tongue."[34] A resolution of by forty-nine Scandinavian professors in 1962 declared that "the extermination of a language, of a culture, and of a people are all one and the same thing."[35]

The American advocates of bilingual education were, not surprisingly, a cosmopolitan group. The professional teaching of foreign languages is by its very nature an enterprise with an international character. This fact, coupled with new UN institutions, put American teaching professionals into contact with others from far away lands who supported bilingual education. Theodore Andersson, a major (Swedish-born) American bilingual education advocate, moved easily between his directorship of the UNESCO Conference on the Teaching of Foreign Languages, his directorship of the Modern Language Association of America, and his chairmanship of the romance languages department at the University of Texas. His writings and statements at congressional hearings often emphasized his international perspective. Citing the UNESCO Institute for Education report from 1963, *Foreign Languages in Primary Education: The Teaching of Foreign or Second Languages to Younger Children,*[36] Andersson wrote in 1965 that "our need of language competence in this shrunken world is surely as great as that of European nations, where foreign languages—and usually more than one—are studied from four to ten years."[37] Foreign language interest groups spawned by the NDEA and persons with views like those of Andersson fought for federal funding from the ESEA to create in Texas the Office of International and Bilingual Education in early 1966. This organization was not only for bilingual education, but as Jose Vega has described, "was formed to promote the teaching of foreign languages, to gain expertise in the area of bilingual instructional methods, and to gather information on bilingual educational programs outside the United States."[38]

In short, the Allied effort to prevent future war—the UN—created worldwide institutions and networks among education professionals who believed in the value of bilingual education. American educators could learn from them, and then point to international advocacy of bilingual education when pressing for similar programs in the United States.

The Cuban refugees and the first federal bilingual education program

Cold War immigration policy also promoted bilingual education. As discussed in Chapter 2, refugee policy during that era took on a national-security meaning, exhibiting a "calculated kindness" in its selective honoring of the rules related to human rights.[39] One important aspect of this for bilingual education was the warm welcome the United States gave to the refugees from Communist Cuba.

In the early 1960s, President Kennedy granted Cuban refugees fleeing Castro's Communist regime special admission to Dade County, Florida. So many came that they would have overwhelmed the local school district. Because the refugee situation was created by federal policy, Kennedy promised federal money in relief. Overseen by the commissioner of education, the funding was based on the numbers of Cuban refugees served by the schools and not tied to any specific programs. The government spent approximately six hundred thousand dollars for elementary and secondary schooling for the 1960–61 school year, but after Congress created the Cuban Refugee Program, considerably more money became available: $3 million for 1961–62, $6 million for 1962–63, and $142 million for the period from 1960 to 1975.[40]

Since it was unknown how long the Cubans would be in the United States—and all were hopeful Castro's regime would not last—it did not make sense to immerse these students into the English language or to Americanize them in any other way. At the same time, as the superintendent of the Dade County public schools said, "Leaders of the community and of the school system, as well as the teachers, were sympathetic towards these homeless persons and were determined to demonstrate to them in a practical way that a democratic society could adjust to the problem."[41] Another problem regarded the ESL program the district was using to educate the children. Those materials could teach English reading to students who could already read in Spanish, but there were no materials for young students who could not read in any language. Though federal money was also being used, administrators applied for and received a special grant from the Ford Foundation in

January of 1963 entitled "Project in Bilingual Education of Cuban Refugee Pupils." This program, implemented at the Coral Way School in Miami, provided new materials for teaching English and Spanish reading, and sought the establishment of a bilingual school as one of its goals.[42] When the Ford grant ran out after three years, local funding and the federal Cuban Refugee Program picked up the tab.[43]

The Cuban refugee experience was significant because it further eroded the sense that had troubled many Americans from Franklin on that bilingualism was somehow "disloyal." Bilingual education advocates have often cited the Cuban program as a policy precedent legitimating bilingual education and helping to develop bilingual pedagogy.

Early bilingual pilot programs

Following the Cuban program, there were locally initiated bilingual demonstration projects in the mid-1960s in Texas and about a dozen in other states, including New Mexico, Arizona and California.[44] Though the origins of the Cuban program are clear, the initial development of similar programs in the southwest occurred with federal ESEA funding but without federal officials designing or pushing the policies. The sources of these local initiatives are obscure. Close to the center of both international bilingual pedagogy and Texas school districts, Theodore Andersson surmised that the impetus could have been the Miami program for Cubans, the new teaching of foreign languages in elementary schools promoted by the NDEA, bilingual schools in Latin America, or the *Brown* decision.[45]

National Security, the NDEA, and Support for Bilingual Education

In the early 1960s, some professional foreign-language education groups, created or strengthened by the NDEA, began to support and lobby for bilingual education for Latinos. These groups worked as meaning entrepreneurs, using the NDEA to link the Mexican American students to national-security considerations while stressing some of the policy irrationalities created by that Act—such as encouraging schools in the southwest to teach foreign languages to English speakers, even while they ignored or actively repressed (sometimes through punishment) Spanish use and proficiency among Latino students. For example, in October 1963, a *Texas Foreign Language Association Bulletin* article entitled "Texas Squanders Non-English Resources" argued it was a wasteful contradiction to promote foreign languages for Americans but not to develop Spanish speakers' preexisting skills. It pointed out that "the National Defense Education Act of 1958 identified FLs [foreign languages] as one of the three critical areas of shortage in US education, along with science and mathematics. Together with Chinese, Russian, Arabic, and a number of other languages, Spanish has been designated as one of the 'critical' languages from the point of view of US interest."[46] The Southwest Council of Foreign Language Teachers similarly passed a resolution in November 1965 calling for bilingual education and other measures to aid Latinos. The organization justified the call on both pedagogical grounds ("the early acquisition of literacy in the mother tongue is known to facilitate the learning of a second language") and national-security grounds ("our present educational policies, by preventing the full development of the bilingual child, squander language resources which are urgently needed by our Nation and which must be expensively replaced under the National Defense Education Act").[47]

This effort gathered great force when the National Education Association (NEA), the nation's largest organization of education professionals, began to develop a consensus around bilingual education for Latino students. The NEA justified its interest in the issue by arguing that these students were a seriously disadvantaged ethnic minority like blacks. If Latinos were like blacks, and if the nation was making an effort to help blacks, it should help Latinos too. A 1966 NEA report entitled *The Invisible Minority* showed that Latinos were overrepresented among school dropouts as well as other measures of poor achievement. Most disturbing was that 72 percent of total population males and 75 percent of females had completed one or more years of high school, but only 48.5 percent of Latino males and 52 of females had done so.[48]

Was this a problem requiring government action? The NEA clearly thought so, and it saw language difficulties as the source of Latino underachievement. *The Invisible Minority* rejected simply placing the students in class with non-Latino students, regardless of language ability. It also rejected a requirement that Latino students with limited English spend a year before first grade being taught English, as this would create an overage group of students. The NEA's interest was directed more toward the small number of local initiatives in the southwest, which it saw as "forward-looking" programs that would create students who were "truly bilingual and bicultural."

The NEA linked its argument to ideas from the black-civil rights movement (discussed below) and also to the irrationalities created by the NDEA's initiatives for foreign languages:

There is something sadly paradoxical about the schools' well-meaning effort to make the Mexican-American child "talk American"—to eradicate his Spanish. For they are at the same time working strenuously to teach Spanish to the Anglo-American student, acclaiming the advantages of being able to communicate fluently in a language other than one's own. The National Defense Education Act is providing funds to schools to strengthen the teaching of modern foreign languages as well as mathematics, science and other subjects. And so, while they strive to make the monolingual student bilingual, they are making—or trying to make—the bilingual student monolingual.[49]

The recognition of the national-defense implications of bilingual education shows that professional educators early on were interested in a program to maintain Latinos' culture and language. Unlike later years, however, when cultural diversity was seen as an end and value in itself, in 1966 it was a means to the end of national security. At the same time, NEA evaluations of the local bilingual projects often remarked on the pride in Mexican culture that students exhibited.

In October of 1966, on the heels of the *Invisible Minority* report, the NEA held its Third National Conference on Civil and Human Rights in Education in Tucson, Arizona. Its theme was "The Spanish-speaking Child in the Schools of the Southwest." The purpose of the conference was to publicize and catalyze actions being undertaken to aid Mexican American education. While they discussed various approaches, including ESL, NEA officials reserved most of their cheerleading for bilingual education. Indeed, page one of the conference report stated, "The urgent task—making bilingual programs like those discussed in *The Invisible Minority* the rule rather than the exception—lies before us."[50]

For most at the conference, the statistics of low Mexican American educational achievement made a need for bilingual education self-evident. Several federal officials speaking at the conference gave strong support to the purposes of the meeting and bilingual education in particular, sometimes linking the program to national security. Democratic Senator Ralph Yarborough of Texas argued that "bilingualism can mean a better approach to national and international affairs. It can offer a broader base for understanding among all people. Bilingualism is no longer a luxury in this world; it is a necessity."[51] Senator Joseph Montoya (D–NM) declared, "Our nation can no longer indulge in the luxury of letting its human resources go to waste! . . . Think of it—both heritages, both histories, and both languages producing tens of thousands of productive, stable, and capable personnel, utilizing the finest offered by both worlds."[52]

For other participants the national-security meaning of bilingual education was frequently implicit. Arizona governor Samuel Goddard held up a device that could measure radiation and argued melodramatically that "it's going to be our children who are going to determine whether we're going to exist through the atomic age," and therefore "this is the age when every child must have the best education possible."[53] Dr. Irvamae Applegate, president of the NEA, argued that America could not afford to waste any resource, and that "bilingualism" would benefit the foreign service.[54]

The strongest support for bilingual education and language maintenance came from Dr. A. Bruce Gaarder, chief of the Modern Foreign Language Section of the US Office of Education. Gaarder, of course, owed his position to the NDEA's promotion of foreign languages as part of national security, and his comments reflected a predictably, though not exclusively, international perspective: "The single greatest need seems to be for a strong statement of federal policy to the effect that the maintenance of all our nation's language resources is important and that any group that tries to maintain and develop these resources is serving the national interest." This applied to Spanish and also "at least 30 other languages spoken natively by groups of American citizens."[55] Gaarder cited studies from Puerto Rico and Mexico (where some Indian children were taught in their native Indian tongue) that indicated children learned better in their native languages.[56]

Bilingual Education for National Security in Congress

In American politics, it often takes years to get a new issue on the agenda, let alone passed into law. This was not the case with bilingual education. Within two years of the NEA's first promotion of the concept, bilingual education was formally a part of national policy as an amendment to the NDEA and to the ESEA's grab bag of categorical education aid packages.

The leading advocate of bilingual education in Congress was Senator Ralph Yarborough. He did not see himself as a Cold Warrior by supporting bilingual education. Before his death he told two scholars he simply thought bilingual education would be a good way to address a serious problem. His support also was prompted by the fact that his home state of Texas was among the nation's richest in natural resources but its high dropout rate among Latinos made it thirty-fourth in education.[57] There were, of course, political considerations—he was likely seeking the large Mexican American vote in Texas for an upcoming reelection campaign.[58] Like the anticipatory politics of those advocating minority capitalism during the Nixon administration, Yarborough assumed Latinos would like the new policy.

Yarborough introduced legislation for bilingual education on January 17, 1967, just three months after the NEA conference. He worked hard to make it clear both that he was trying to help his Mexican American constituents and that this was an all-American, nonradical initiative. As introduced, the Bilingual American Education Act was intended only for "the large numbers of students in the United States whose mother tongue is Spanish." If Yarborough was to reap Latino votes, they had to notice and see that his efforts were meant for them.

The bill proposed federal financial assistance for local bilingual education programs that taught Latino students Spanish and ESL, fostered "knowledge and pride in their ancestral culture and language," and attracted teachers of "Mexican or Puerto Rican descent." Yarborough cited the NEA for the notion that "it may be possible" that use of Spanish language and culture could aid adjustment and achievement. While he promoted the bill primarily as aiding the cause of justice (see below), Yarborough added that it had implications for national security and foreign policy. Recent experience in the Far East (Vietnam) showed how difficult it was for Americans to understand people of a different cultural background, he claimed, and future matters of foreign policy might be less difficult with a better understanding of Latin America.[59]

As with other policies of the minority rights revolution, especially those bearing meanings about national security, this was not to be a lonely crusade, or even a liberal Democratic one. Lawmakers from states with large Latino populations that might benefit lined up to co-sponsor the law, including Republicans John Tower of Texas (who had voted against the Civil Rights Act), Thomas Kuchel and George Murphy of California, Paul Fannin of Arizona, and Jacob Javits of New York.[60]

In Senate hearings for the bill, it became more clear how national security and the legacies of Cold War policies could render bilingual education more appealing than in the past, conferring an almost patriotic meaning to a policy that previously connoted disloyalty. Support for the bill was strong; opposition almost nonexistent. The main modification was to expand the bill's reach beyond Latinos to cover all children of limited English speaking ability.[61] Testimony repeated the arguments from the NEA conference with varying eloquence and force. Notably strong support for bilingual education and language and culture maintenance continued to come from A. Bruce Gaarder. In his written statement he cited the success of the Cuban refugee bilingual program and stressed other reasons to support the bill: "Our people's native competence in Spanish and French and Czech and all the other languages and the cultural heritage each language transmits are a national resource that we need badly and must conserve by every reasonable means."[62] Gaarder added:

The most obvious anomaly—or absurdity—of our educational policy regarding foreign language learning is the fact that we spend perhaps a billion dollars a year to teach languages—in the schools, the colleges and universities, the Foreign Service Institute, the Department of Defense, AID, USIA, CIA, etc. (and to a large extent to adults who are too old ever to master a new tongue)—yet virtually no part of the effort goes to maintain and to develop the competence of American children who speak the same languages natively. There are over four million native speakers of French or Spanish in our country and these two languages are the two most widely taught, yet they are the ones for which our Government recognizes the greatest unfilled need (at the levels, for example of the Foreign Service of the Department of State and the program of lectures and technical specialists sent abroad under the Fulbright-Hayes Act).[63]

Representative Edward R. Roybal (D–CA) emphasized this point as well, arguing in the House hearings that it is "absurd" that an estimated billion dollars a year were being spent to teach foreign languages but the abilities of native speakers were not maintained and developed. Talent that could be used for the national interest, Roybal argued, was being wasted.[64] Hector P. Garcia, founder of the GI Forum, a Latino veterans group, also emphasized national security, arguing that "in view of the present world situation we cannot afford to lose our Latin American friends. Bilingual education is the answer."[65]

The bill's national-security meaning also had a similar logic to civil rights and immigration reform: bilingual education could improve foreigners' opinions of the United States. William G. Carr, executive secretary of the NEA and secretary-general of the World Confederation of Organizations of the Teaching Profession, agreed that a valuable national asset was being wasted when Latino children lost their Spanish, but he added that the poverty of Latinos in the United States "is known by the citizens of the countries to the south of us." With bilingual education, "new opportunity for Latin-Americans in the North American society can have great impact on attitudes towards the United States in Central and South America . . . We could offset with [new bilingual programs] the propaganda of distrust and hostility planted among the students and others to the south who should be our best friends."[66]

To be sure, there were no representatives from the State Department making these claims, but the NDEA made available and plausible the national-security meaning of bilingual education, allaying the old fears of foreign languages in America. Indeed, nativism and even ethnic assimilationism were already in retreat. Throughout the hearings, government officials dismissed as an anachronism the idea of the United States as a "melting pot." Harold Howe, US commissioner of education, stated the apparently consensus view that the melting pot metaphor should be dropped. Howe claimed that the term "mosaic" is more accurate, since the "melting pot idea carries with it a kind of homogenization concept, which can be destructive."[67] Though Howe's comment suggested the later politics of multiculturalism and identity that would become major parts of the American political landscape, most of the supporters of a cultural or language dualism did so in a much more conservative light—as a means to an end. In the House hearings, Democrat Roman C. Pucinski of Illinois, chair of the General Subcommittee on Education, declared, "I am hopeful that as we succeed in enacting this legislation . . . that our action may ultimately become the forerunner of placing this Nation on a bilingual basis . . . We are living in a very small world . . . and it would be my hope that ultimately we will have a population that will be bilingual to assist us in meeting the problems of the world."[68]

Black Civil Rights and the Rise of Bilingual Education

Though the black civil rights movement obviously did not include bilingual education in its efforts, it was instrumental in the policy's development.[69] The demand for black civil rights and the government response to it were major factors creating policy legacies for the development of the Bilingual Education Act and also Latino language rights in education.

Black Civil Rights and the Bilingual Education Act

Perhaps most importantly, and most subtly, the federal response to the black civil rights movement made the problems of ethnoracial minorities a legitimate concern for government policy and made ethnic targeting acceptable. Before the late 1960s, positive ethnic targeting had occurred, but almost always indirectly and informally (the exception being American Indian programs). By 1967, national politicians advertised their targeting of ethnic groups to claim credit in anticipation of votes and support from these groups. For this brief period of American history, the old cultural prohibitions against ethnic targeting melted into air. Existing leaders of the minority groups noticed the new attention, and they and new groups that came into being seized opportunities. To win something like bilingual education, advocates for Latinos inside and outside the government had to stress both the analogy with blacks but also the unique problems of Latinos.

Latino interest groups and the Bilingual Education Act
Latino groups were newly energized to take advantage of the new political legitimacy of ethnic targeting. What was the message of these would-be beneficiaries—were they demanding bilingual education?

In fact, as we saw previously regarding the national-security meanings of bilingual education, Latino leaders did, on occasion, express support for bilingual education and other language rights. But what is striking is that they won the policy without having to make consistent demands for it. This is in great contrast to black groups, who maintained a remarkable consistency of demands in their most influential years between 1955 and 1965 but found success much more elusive. Latino groups also won new policy despite relatively poor organization and smaller numbers than the black groups.

The Latinos had talented leaders but no Martin Luther King. Perhaps the greatest American Latino leader was Cesar Chavez, who developed the United Farm Workers union in the years 1965–69. He organized a national boycott of grapes, went on a hunger strike to publicize his cause of improving the low wages and poor work conditions of fruit pickers in California, had his picture on the cover of *Time* magazine, and won agreements with half of California's grape growers. But Chavez, who modeled himself on Ghandi and King, rarely moved beyond these local issues. Though his cause attracted sympathy from Senator Robert Kennedy (D–NY), Chavez and the United Farm Workers never became a force for applying pressure on the government comparable to that exerted by the great black union leader A. Philip Randolph, who accomplished so much from the seemingly inconsequential position as head of the Brotherhood of Sleeping Car Porters.[70] In Denver in 1966, another Mexican American leader, Rodolfo "Corky" Gonzales, helped form the Crusade for Justice, which advocated "Chicano nationalism" and fought against school discrimination, police brutality, and other discrimination.[71] But Gonzales similarly did not lead a national movement.

Local Latino groups had earlier sought better education for their children, but there was no consensus for bilingual education. In the late 1950s, for example, a League of United Latin American Citizens (LULAC) chapter in Texas had promoted a program to teach basic English to Mexican American preschoolers.[72] In 1963, at least one local group (in East Los Angeles) demanded teaching in the Spanish language.[73]

By the 1960s, other groups representing Mexican Americans, Puerto Ricans, and Cubans were increasingly making their presence known to federal government officials. While it was not uncommon for them to trace their problems to language difficulties, there is little evidence of a sustained lobby for bilingual education. When Latino groups met with the federal government, they most frequently demanded Latino representation in the executive branch (especially the EEOC) and federal recognition of their importance (see Chapters 4 and 5).

Although they did not primarily focus their demands on bilingual education, by 1966 some Latino leaders were asking for federal recognition of their language and culture. Shortly after the NEA conference on bilingual education, President Johnson's domestic policy adviser Joe Califano received the report of an administration Task Force on Problems of Spanish-surnamed Americans. The report came out of meetings with Latino leaders, and outlined the priorities for federal aid to the Latino community. In the area of education (number ten in the list of priorities, below the standard demands for government jobs, a White House conference recognizing them, and the regulation of green-card commuters who depressed wages), the report called for bilingual education. It did not call for a new right, but for "flexibility and stronger leadership in the administration of education legislation." Mexican American leaders had grievances over the forced use of English in the schools. "One of the characteristics that marks the Spanish-speaking American is his legitimate claim to identification with a distinctive culture," the report declared, adding that "there is a definite need, at a minimum, for bi-lingual elementary schools and instruction which will bridge the gap from the Spanish-speaking background to the English-speaking culture." While a new and more conservative Congress in 1966 was thought to make legislation difficult, Johnson's task force still recommended that "legislation should be proposed to enable HEW to establish regional bi-cultural, education and training centers through grants either to public or private non-profit agencies." These centers would "have as their purpose the training of teachers in the language and culture of the children they are to serve; diagnostic and testing service for Spanish-speaking citizens needing remedial education; and remedial education for the Spanish-speaking."[74]

While the task force report suggested a growing interest in bilingual policy, this did not become a prominent or consistent demand. Unlike the NEA, which had a near consensus on the value of bilingual education by 1966, Mexican American educators remained split. For example, conferences held in California in August of 1966 and April of 1967 by a group of Mexican American educators, the Mexican American Education Research Project, promoted a diversity of approaches. While some wanted to teach the children's native language and culture, others believed that keeping the children "Mexican" in the United States was not in their best interest and advocated instead rapid assimilation.[75]

Meanwhile, Mexican American leaders began lobbying for a White House conference on Mexican American issues and problems. The Johnson White House had held two conferences on the problems of black Americans. The first was a general conference on civil rights called "To Fulfill These Rights" that had met in 1965; the other, in 1966, had focused on equal employment opportunity of black Americans. The possibility for such high-level recognition of a minority group's problems had a mobilizing and radicalizing effect on Mexican American leaders. Rudy Ramos, head of the GI Forum's Washington office, complained when Johnson gave financial aid to the Watts section of Los Angeles after blacks had rioted there, saying that East Los Angeles needed resources, and warned that Mexican Americans would demonstrate if not invited to the civil rights conference in 1966.[76] In May of 1966, Johnson met with leaders from the GI Forum, LULAC, and the Mexican American Political Association (MAPA), who asked for the appointment of a Mexican American White House aide and for inclusion in White House conferences. Johnson promised to help, but nixed the special White House aide, arguing that otherwise all groups would want one.[77] In August, Johnson's domestic policy aide David North began a "preplanning conference" for a future White House conference on Mexican American problems. He met with Mexican American leaders who requested a focus on a variety of issues, including greater participation in Great Society programs and a minimum wage for agricultural workers. They did not ask for bilingual education.[78]

The Johnson administration approached the proposed Mexican American conference with trepidation. In December, domestic policy adviser Harry McPherson sent a note to Johnson from Austin with a message that contradicted the semblance of coherence in the task force report described above. After four meetings with Mexican American leaders, McPherson had come away confused and frustrated. His main purpose was to further discuss possibilities and issues of a White House conference on the problems of the Mexican American. But such a conference should deal with federal issues, and on federal issues there was little lobbying. "In four meetings with various group leaders," McPherson wrote, "only moderate interest was shown in federal programs directed specifically toward Mexican American problems." The reason for this was partly "the relative immaturity of the movement—not much thought has been given to programs—but in another sense it probably comports with reality. The Mexicans want some of their people on police forces, highway patrols, in school systems—all matters within the states' and cities' power to give or withhold."[79]

The Johnson team desperately wanted to avoid a White House conference for fear that it would only be an occasion for posturing and criticizing the administration. They tried to dissuade the Latino leaders from demanding the conference. Yet the leaders seemed adamant about gaining public presidential recognition and attention for their group's problems. Their underlying message was always that Mexican Americans were like blacks but also had unique problems. They continued to apply pressure. McPherson told Johnson that the Mexican Americans "need the sense of self-importance it would give them." He added, "They are a major political factor in five states and we should not risk losing them; that risk is greater if we deny them the conference they think they are entitled to, than if some hell is raised." An exasperated Johnson returned McPherson's memo with a terse message of his own attached: "Keep this trash out of the White House. See me."[80]

Only a few days later, a MAPA group in California invited Johnson officials to their own "brown power" conference—organized out of frustration over delays by the administration. "Brown power" was clearly meant as a take on "black power" radicalism and served to reinforce the meaning of Mexican Americans as similar to but different from blacks. Their invitation contained a list of demands, several of which related to Latino language differences. The second education priority, after tuition-free state colleges and universities, was "Instruction in Spanish to Spanish-speaking children in the first three grades of school." (This was hardly a radical demand given that the NEA and several government officials were by then calling for Spanish language and cultural maintenance throughout all schooling.) They also advocated that teachers should be trained in the culture, tradition, and history of the Mexican Americans.[81]

The Johnson administration solved its Mexican American conference problem by meeting with moderate leaders in Texas instead of the White House. Identifying the "unique problems" (similar to problems faced by blacks but different) was the perfect way for politicians to show they were paying attention to Mexican Americans. In October 1967, President Johnson gave a speech to a distinguished group in El Paso as part of hearings conducted by the Inter-Agency Committee on Mexican American Affairs, chaired by new EEOC commissioner Vicente Ximenes. The event included Ximenes, several cabinet officials, leading members of Congress (including Ralph Yarborough), Diaz Ordaz, the president of Mexico, and Texas governor John Connally. Many Mexican American leaders also attended the conference, where they made plain their desire for greater official respect and consideration for Mexican American culture. Some Mexican American leaders, such as Carlos F. Truan of the Texas chapter of LULAC, argued passionately that the Mexican American was being ignored by the government:

> In the past, the Indian, the Negro, the Filipino, the Puerto Rican, and all the other peoples in a situation similar to that of the Mexican American have been the object of moral responsibility. Not so the Mexican American. He has been, and he continues to be, the most neglected, the least sponsored, the most orphaned major minority group in the United States.[82]

The Johnson administration did its best to reassure conference members of its concern for Latino problems. Johnson gave a fawning speech, praising the Mexican American people and recognizing their difficulties, while also bragging about his administration's achievements. He ticked off the accomplishments of what he called the "New Focus on Opportunity" for the Mexican American citizen, leading off with the government job representation that Mexican American leaders seemed to value most. This included Ximenes and "the first Mexican American to ever sit as a delegate of the United Nations," Dr. Hector García of the Texas GI Form, who the previous day "made a speech in Spanish to that great body." (This news led to "clapping, hoorahs" from the audience.) But Johnson also claimed that "we found programs that answered their special needs in language and education and economic development. And those programs respected their rich and unique cultural tradition." Johnson did not delve into specifics, and was content to extol Head Start and the increasing amount of federal money being spent on all education (from $4 billion to $12 billion).[83] The president's speech in this friendly setting showed that the administration was moving toward the "similar but different" meaning for Latinos: they should get special help like blacks, but that help should be tied to their unique problems.[84]

Meanwhile, on a local level, there were increasing signs of Mexican American discontent with education. An inchoate identity politics began to take hold, especially among Mexican American students, who more frequently called themselves "Chicanos." In 1968, East Los Angeles high school teacher Sal Castro led a Mexican American "blow out," in which fifteen thousand students simultaneously walked out of five Los Angeles schools to protest bad facilities and discrimination. Similar events followed in Denver and San Antonio. The following year, student groups such as the United Mexican American Students, the Mexican American Student Association, and MEChA (or Movimiento Estudiantil Chicano de Aztlan) began to demand Mexican American studies courses at universities and colleges in the southwest. An activist at San Jose City College said, "Our main goal is to orient the Chicano to *think* Chicano so as to achieve equal status with other groups, not emulate the Anglo." Activists started "Brown Power" newspapers, and high school students continued the blow outs and demanded bilingual education and other official recognition of Mexican American cultural differences. All this activity, however, almost always remained directed at local officials and not the national government.[85] In the assessment of historian Terry Anderson, the Brown Power movement did not gain significant national attention, and was hampered by a lack of clear objectives.[86]

Compared to the black civil-rights groups, the Latino groups were young and not well organized. While some sought to have Spanish language and Mexican culture recognized in social policy, they did not consistently make this demand, and when they did make it, it was usually a low priority or directed toward local officials. Thus, Latino groups were only indirect factors in the creation of the Bilingual Education Act. Though they could not produce the consistent mass mobilization of black leaders, they played a role as meaning entrepreneurs. Their message: Latinos were a minority like blacks and deserved equal—if distinctive—attention.

Black civil rights and the NEA's discovery of bilingual education: From Brown to bilingualism

As discussed above, the increasingly international character of pedagogy, courtesy of the UN, and the NDEA's stress on foreign language development led many American educators to espouse bilingual education. But there was another source of appeal of this heretofore ignored policy possibility. This was the notion that educational practices could damage—or repair—the minority child's self-esteem, and thereby affect education performance. This idea had been featured prominently in the struggle to end black school segregation. NEA advocates adapted the black education model to Latinos to justify federal bilingual education.

In 1954, persuaded in part by social science research on educational psychology,[87] Chief Justice Earl Warren writing for a unanimous Court struck down segregation in public schools in the landmark decision *Brown v. Board of Education*. He wrote that to separate black students "from others of similar age and qualifications solely because of their race generates a feeling of inferiority as to their status in the community that may affect their hearts and minds in a way unlikely ever to be undone."[88] This feeling of inferiority in turn damaged a child's motivation to learn. The result was that when the law sanctioned racially segregated schools, it created unequal schools.

The logic of this argument about the relation between self-esteem and education lived on after the *Brown* decision and found its way into the language of black civil-rights leaders, as the historian Daryl Michael Scott has amply documented.[89] After *Brown*, education scholars began to focus on the health of the black psyche outside of the Jim Crow south, such as in poor sections of Harlem. New interest developed in the "cultural deprivation" of poor (usually black) children. By the mid-1960s, social scientists such as Frank Riessman were gaining an attentive audience for their arguments that teachers should learn to respect the culture of the "deprived" child, that teaching methods should acknowledge the different communication styles of minority children, and that it was wrong to try to make poor children into cultural copies of middle-class children.[90]

NEA advocates for Latinos then extended this model to Latino language and cultural differences. Its explanation of poor Latino school performance had several steps. First, according to its 1966 report *The Invisible Minority*, the Spanish speakers were, to use a term that would gain later currency, a "conquered minority." Santa Fe was settled eleven years before Plymouth, and there were twenty-three thousand Spanish-speaking people in the area of the five southwestern states by 1790. Ignoring the relative smallness of this number, and that the vast majority of the Mexican American population in the 1960s were descended from later immigrants, the NEA reasoned that they were therefore "an alienated group," that "a cultural and linguistic gulf still exists between Mexican-Americans—the 'invisible minority,' as they have been called—and Anglo-Americans." They therefore resisted assimilation. The Mexican Americans also tended to be poorer than the average population in the southwest, leading to poor school achievement and high dropout rates.

But there was another factor directly implicating the school system. Latino students were forced, in the words of A. Bruce Gaarder, into a "form of masochism," forced to deny their own cultural heritage to fit into the dominant culture. Since 71 percent of Mexican American adults (according to a 1965 San Antonio survey) spoke only Spanish to each other, the typical Mexican American student spoke only some English, and did not use it often. Linguistic barriers led to psychological barriers. Further exacerbating these problems, the classroom lessons reflected a culture very different from that of the student. The NEA argued that the shock of sudden immersion into an alien culture may lead students to begin to see the Spanish language and community as a refuge, inhibiting learning. Culturally biased intelligence tests led Latino students to appear to be "low achievers," and they became stereotyped as such by school officials and teachers. All of this led to a damaged psyche:

> The harm done the Mexican-American child linguistically is paralleled—perhaps even exceeded—by the harm done to him as a person. In telling him that he must not speak his native language, we are saying to him by implication that Spanish and the culture which it represents are of no worth. Therefore (it follows) the people who speak Spanish are of no worth. Therefore (it follows again) this particular child is of no worth. It should come as no surprise to us, then, that he develops a negative self-concept—an inferiority complex. If he is no good, how can he succeed? And if he can't succeed, why try?[91]

The NEA's argument was plausible, but comparisons between the high- and low-achieving Mexican American students could have better identified causal factors of low achievement. The NEA instead simply transferred the damaged psyche model articulated in *Brown* and applied it to Latinos.

The perceived similarity between Latinos and African Americans made this transfer possible, though their differences were important as well. A kind of ethnic separatism was linked to Latino equal opportunity. Unlike the case of blacks, the Latino student's damaged self-image and inequality was shown to be the result not of segregated schools but of *overly integrated* schools. Also unlike the case of blacks, the importance of co-ethnic teachers was stressed from the beginning. When the NEA began to advocate bilingual education, it emphasized that teachers should know the local colloquial constructions and cultural background of the students, and strongly recommended that "Spanish teachers for native speakers of Spanish be themselves native speakers of Spanish. As much as possible, these persons should have a background similar to that of the students whom they are to teach."[92] This, of course, fit nicely with the Latino leaders' priority of getting Latinos on government payrolls.[93]

Bilingual education in Congress: Latinos as minorities

As described above, Texas Democratic senator Ralph Yarborough introduced the Bilingual American Education Act with little prodding or lobbying. The NEA's support for the bill was important not because of the push it could provide but because of the way it drew together the black civil rights movement's legitimation of ethnically targeted education policy, the policy to correct damage to minority students' self-esteem, and Cold War developments. Together these gave foreign language instruction a legitimacy and appropriateness it had lacked previously.

It is also clear that part of the appeal of bilingual education for a politician such as Yarborough was its "difference-recognizing" aspects: bilingual education told Latino citizens that the government cared specifically about them. Though national-security policy was the original impetus for the policy, Yarborough also presented bilingual education as a minority equal-opportunity initiative. He emphasized both the distinctiveness of Latino needs and (implicitly) their basic similarity with blacks. When he introduced the Bilingual American Education Act, Yarborough argued that "equality of economic opportunity" in the southwest was only "folklore." Repeating the NEA's misleading argument originally made in *The Invisible Minority,* he presented all of the Spanish-speaking people not as immigrants but as a conquered minority.[94]

Yarborough also followed the NEA's reasoning and the social psychology relied on in the *Brown* decision to explain Mexican American inequality. Mexican American children entering English-speaking schools were led to believe there was something wrong with them and their language, which "soon spreads to the image he has of his culture, of the history of his people, and of his people themselves." High dropout rates and low test scores showed the "psychological damage" resulting from the discriminatory educational system.[95]

The Senate and House hearings for the bill generally rehearsed these points, along with the national security arguments discussed above, and added an array of statistics showing high Latino drop out rates and low achievement. *No one* spoke out against bilingual education, either as a violation of American assimilationist ideals or as a pedagogy that would not or may not work. Latinos were prominent witnesses; indeed, in the Senate hearings in Washington, there were no representatives from any other groups that might benefit. Of the Latinos who took part in the hearings, the vast majority were Mexican American, with only a few Puerto Ricans. Roughly half of the 121 witnesses appearing were Latinos. Of those witnesses, however, less than a quarter represented Latino political or rights groups. By far, most were educators, including teachers, members of school boards, administrators, and representatives of groups like the NEA. Nearly half of all witnesses were education professionals, all supporting bilingual education.[96] In the House, the lineup of witnesses was different. More than half of those testifying were federal government officials, especially members of Congress or aides voicing their support, and there was one representative of the Bureau of Indian Affairs. No leaders of Mexican American rights organizations appeared.[97]

The House version of Yarborough's bill made its way to the House Labor and Public Welfare Committee, where it won a 20-5 vote. The Senate Labor and Public Welfare Committee attached Yarborough's bill to H.R. 7819, Amendments for the Elementary and Secondary Education Act of 1965. Bilingual education by itself was therefore never voted on by either chamber. On December 15, 1967, the conference committee reported out H.R. 7819, which the House adopted by a vote of 283-73; the Senate did the same by a 63-3 vote.[98]

The Johnson administration and final approval

The Johnson administration had been less than enthusiastic about the bill for bilingual education, mainly because of its cost. But a sampling of internal White House memos between White House aides, coupled with bipartisan congressional support, indicates the unquestioned legitimacy or appropriateness of using the federal government to affirm ethnic differences in the late 1960s. The administration went along for a variety of rather narrow reasons based mainly on politics and the belief that bilingual education was the best policy to help Latinos.

The memos show, first, that the Johnson administration supported bilingual education because they did not want to alienate Latino voters ("Are we on solid ground in opposing this bill? I understand the Latinos are upset w/ our position"; "this bill has been very well received in South Texas"). Further, Johnson officials believed the program worked ("Bilingual education has demonstrated its effectiveness for non-English speaking children"; "the evidence shows that this type of education—as compared with instruction only in English—is outstandingly successful for non-English speaking children"; "It is also clear that bilingual programs are almost the sine qua non of reaching non-English speaking children"). Johnson aides also had concerns that local officials would not act positively on their own ("A clue to local attitudes is that, until this year, California had a law forbidding the operation of bilingual programs in public schools, and Texas still has such a law although its repeal is expected"). Finally, the administration chose to support the bill because it felt there might be legal difficulties in using existing educational aid for the purpose of large-scale bilingual education programs. While accepting government reinforcement of ethnic language and culture, however, it is doubtful that the Johnson administration would have accepted a Latino-only bill. In a letter to Lister Hill (D–AL), the chair of the Senate Committee on Labor and Public Welfare, Johnson's secretary of HEW John Gardner described the original bill's focus on Spanish, on training teachers of Mexican or Puerto Rican descent, and its allotment formula based on number of persons with Spanish surnames:

> We firmly believe that the language of the legislation should avoid any restrictions to persons of particular ancestry or ethnic origin . . . Legislation should be directed to persons from non-English-speaking backgrounds because that factor—the language problem—has educational significance and that is the justification for legislation in the field of bilingual education. We believe it is an important principle that the statute should not provide that determinations be based upon consideration of ethnic or national origin (or surname) per se.[99]

When signing the law containing the Bilingual Education Act on January 2, 1968, however, Johnson made a point of mentioning some beneficiaries. He stated that the law "also contains a special program establishing bilingual education programs for children whose first language is not English. Thousands of children of Latin descent, young Indians, and others will get a better start—a better chance—in school."[100]

The stated purpose of the Bilingual Education Act was to "provide financial assistance to local educational agencies to develop and carry out new and imaginative elementary and secondary school programs designed to meet . . . the special educational needs of the large numbers of children of limited English-speaking ability in the United States." The law targeted limited English proficiency (LEP) students from families with annual incomes below three thousand dollars or receiving some poverty aid. Funds could be used for bilingual education, "programs designed to impart to students a knowledge of the history and culture associated with their languages," and other purposes not necessarily utilizing a bilingual component. The new law also amended the Higher Education Act of 1965 and the NDEA in ways designed to provide financial assistance for persons studying to teach LEP children.[101] Despite the lack of official ethnic targeting, Latinos, especially Mexican Americans, would be the primary beneficiaries. Mexican Americans would work in the federal government to run the program, and in its first year of funding, HEW distributed funds for seventy-six projects—90 percent of them for teaching in Spanish.[102]

Supporting the "richness of difference"?: Implementing the Bilingual Education Act

The legitimacy of bilingual education and the political interest in Latino votes did not mean the new program was a priority. After the bill's signing, Johnson officials lost interest in bilingual education, despite the efforts of his Latino appointee to the EEOC. Vicente Ximenes told Johnson aide Marvin Watson that the new law was almost "unheralded in the community," and called for a "major [signing] ceremony" with "heavy participation by Mexican American leaders, as well as the appropriate Congressmen and Senators." Watson dismissed him like he was a stranger: "The President is tremendously involved in the work for this year, therefore other parts of his schedule must be somewhat restricted."[103] Similarly, Ximenes's suggestions to the president about what he should mention in the 1968 state of the union address, which listed bilingual education at the top, were ignored by Johnson.[104]

In fact, Johnson, never an enthusiastic supporter of Yarborough or his bill's ethnic targeting, recommended no money at all for the new program. Congress authorized $15 million for 1968, and $400 million for the first six-year period. When it came time to distribute the funds, however, Congress apparently preferred mostly a symbolic law, giving bilingual education nothing for 1968, and only $7.5 million for 1969.[105]

Its immediate impact was even less than the paltry appropriation suggests because there were great problems in implementation. Despite the unquestioning confidence in bilingual education expressed by Congress and White House advisers, there were very few trained teachers, few texts, no established curricula, and no evaluation studies. It was not clear where to begin or how to proceed. Though speakers in the hearings had frequently described a language and culture maintenance program, the law did not push this idea, and it was unclear what the goals of bilingual education should be. When the administrators in the Office of Education tried to make bilingual education an ongoing policy, it became clear how rushed its passage really was.[106]

The HEW staff that wrote up the first "Manual for Project Applicants and Grantees" filled the void by putting a Latino culture and language maintenance spin on the new program. The importance of language and culture maintenance was now understood solely in terms of rectifying or avoiding damage to minority individuals' self-esteem; it was no longer categorized as national security. This understanding of the program was pervasive. Whereas the "Declaration of Policy" in the law only said it was to "meet these special educational needs" of the students, the manual clarified this by stating that the intention of the law was to develop competence in English while students "become more proficient in their dominant language." It explained that "the development of literacy in the mother tongue as well as in English should result in more broadly educated adults." The *Brown* decision's model of the damaged minority psyche lived on, as the manual stated that the history and culture of the mother tongue were part of the program, and that "a complete program develops and maintains the children's self-esteem and a legitimate pride in both cultures."[107]

A newly created Division of Bilingual Education at HEW's Office of Education issued guidelines to further elaborate on the concept of bilingual education and program development. These also stressed language maintenance. Students in the appropriate programs would "develop greater competence in English, and become more proficient in their dominant language."[108] Albar Peña, acting director of the division, wrote a letter to Senator Edward Kennedy (D–MA) on August 4, 1972 explaining HEW's view that "bilingual education projects are designed to use the child's first language as the medium of instruction until his competence in English permits the use of both languages in a balanced instructional program. An essential ingredient in all projects is the concurrent effort to develop and maintain the child's self esteem and a legitimate pride in both cultures."[109]

Armando Rodriguez of the Office of Education expressed the goals of bilingual program implementation in words that presaged multicultural education, which became popular in schools in the 1980s and 1990s: "The school must put into proper forms the . . . contributions of these citizens whose language and cultural values and customs differ from the majority." This would allow the minority child to feel respected and give to the majority child "sensitivity and comparison and understanding of the richness of difference." Children speaking foreign languages "must come to be accepted as a blessing, not a problem."[110]

"The Spanish-speaking make lousy Anglos": The politics of bilingual education in the Nixon administration

As described in Chapter 5, President Nixon, his political advisers, and several Republican members of Congress believed that while pursuit of the black vote could be futile or lead to alienation of white voters, Latinos were easier and safer prospects. This unreflectively led to support for bilingual education, which by 1969 had become part of the policy repertoire to appeal to these voters. This support was tempered, however, by concerns about inflation and its relation to the continually increasing education budget. Nixon wanted to require bilingual education but he did not want the federal government to pay for it through the Bilingual Education Act program. Throughout Nixon's six years in office, Latino leaders continued to lobby the White House. But the demands for bilingual education were never paramount or consistent.

Pressure and encouragement came early and from unlikely sources. On December 19, 1968, Cuban American entertainer Desi Arnaz, star of the *I Love Lucy* television show, sent Nixon a *Los Angeles Times* article describing a recent US Commission on Civil Rights hearing in San Antonio. The article, dated December 16, reported the Mexican American satisfaction with the hearing. As Bexar (San Antonio) County Commissioner Albert Pena said, the hearing recognized peculiar problems of the Mexican American in the southwest and could help "people across the country to realize we are here." Likely proposals resulting from the hearing included limitations on cheap Mexican labor in the border area and a "vast new bilingual educational program." The article also included Pena's hope that Nixon would fulfill his promise of a special White House conference and appointments for "Mexican Americans for significant positions in the Administration."[111]

There never was a White House conference as Nixon followed the Johnson precedent of regional meetings.[112] However, Congress created the Cabinet Committee on Opportunities for the Spanish Speaking (CCOSS) (see Chapter 5), allowing a place in the White House for Latino concerns. When signing the bill establishing the committee, Nixon explained that it would among other things "point up the need for a bilingual dimension in education."[113]

Following Nixon's meeting with CCOSS, in which he asked the new body to tell members of the cabinet to "get off their duffs," CCOSS chairman Henry Ramirez sent a round of letters to agency and cabinet heads telling them to do just that (also in Chapter 5). Among the grab bag of Latino policy items, Ramirez pushed bilingual education and other language accommodations. To HEW secretary Elliot Richardson, Ramirez called for more staff to monitor development of the Bilingual Education Act programs and, "since it is evident, and has been reiterated by educators time and time again, that bilingual/bicultural education is essential for Spanish speaking children," CCOSS recommended an increase in funding. The letter stressed the need not just for more bilingual teachers, but *bicultural* teachers as well to "manifest cultural expertise in the classroom." Ramirez sought to apply the model of bilingual policy to other areas, recommending development of a bilingual method to provide "an adequate means of communicating available health services so that they may be utilized effectively by the Spanish speaking," "[t]he continuation of cultural awareness seminars for those Social Security Administration personnel serving large numbers of Spanish speaking people," and "[c]ommunication of services to all Spanish speaking people via bilingual booklets, media, and active community orientation." The letter commended the Social Security Administration for already having offered Spanish information pamphlets and placed "bicultural persons" in offices where there were many Spanish-speaking people.[114]

That the Nixon White House supported this previously radical opinion in CCOSS says volumes about the state of discourse regarding ethnic politics in the early 1970s. Though not a policy-making body, CCOSS was a far-left voice for Latinos in a Republican White House. Consider a June 1971 CCOSS report on education that was laced with indignation and ethnic separatism. It boldly declared that "[t]he practice of cultural genocide must be stopped," and more mildly that "the 'America—love it or leave it' crowd must be convinced that their patriotism might better be reflected in the statement 'America, if you love it, let's help make it better!'" Making America better meant improving Latino school performance with bilingual education:

> [T]he utilization of a monolithic curriculum, as practiced in the United States, is based on the mistaken belief that humans can be homogenized like milk or mass-produced like appliances . . . As the statistics [of poor Latino school performance] support, this curriculum has never had applicability to the Spanish-speaking student. It is now even being questioned by the Anglo society itself. To continue to impose the traditional curriculum on a people for whom it was not designed is the height of folly.

Quoting an academic who offered testimony at the 1967 Inter-Agency Committee for Mexican American Affairs hearings, the CCOSS report stated that "the Spanish speaking make good soldiers, responsible taxpayers, in every way good citizens, but they make lousy Anglos." It concluded with (even then) unrealistic policy recommendations, foremost among them the presidential creation of an "Emergency Management and Technical Task Force" to design a program for "massive federal attention to Spanish-speaking education needs." Other recommendations included the mantra-like demand for increased Latino involvement in government decision making (in this case on education), and a new program to train an army of bilingual/bicultural teachers and administrators ("It is estimated that between 150,000 and 200,000 individuals will be required").[115]

Nixon officials did not squander the opportunity to use CCOSS and its push for bilingualism as a source of political gain for the 1972 election. In

October 1971, aides told Nixon of a meeting of CCOSS to take place in Texas with the purpose of helping "our candidates with the Mexican American vote and the Spanish-speaking vote." The choice of Texas made sense because there "it could be done in conjunction with a brand new pilot program of bilingual education taking place at an elementary school in Dallas." As with administrators creating affirmative action, the Nixon team simply assumed that Mexican Americans wanted bilingual education.[116] Domestic policy aide Ken Cole supported the CCOSS meeting in Texas along with Martin Castillo, former chairman of the Inter-Agency Committee on Mexican American Affairs, top domestic policy advisers John Ehrlichman and Leonard Garment, and public relations expert Jeb Magruder. They all advocated arranging the meeting to get "maximum mileage" for the administration's favored candidates.[117]

In 1971, Nixon's coalition-builder Charles Colson also worked on a strategy for winning Latino support. Along with an affirmative-action plan for public housing to ensure that more Latinos took advantage of that program, and increased efforts for the development of a Latino capitalist class, Colson gave great support to bilingual education. Though "budget priorities" limited new funding, this would not preclude an unfunded mandate: "We could require that bilingual education programs be components of any educational institution receiving funds with more than a 10 percent Spanish-speaking service population."[118] In fact, as described below, developments away from the White House, and not driven by electoral politics, were already moving the administration to precisely this policy.

The Nixon administration's support for bilingual education remained high even as support for the Bilingual Education Act weakened. This decline was related to cost and not the propriety of ethnic targeting or government-supported ethnic difference. On January 10, 1972 policy aide Ken Cole headed an examination of the feasibility of extending bilingual education. Cole expressed no ideological resistance to having the federal government pay to educate children in languages other than English. His concerns were limited to "the budget question involving bi-lingual education."[119] For the 1973 budget, the Nixon administration proposed $41 million for bilingual education, despite a report that according to the Office of Management and Budget (OMB) "there are serious questions about the effectiveness of this program." For the Nixon team, whether the program actually worked was not a concern. One aide's memo argued that "as far as appearance is concerned, a 17% increase in the program is not that bad," while another scribbled on the memo "How can we maximize credit w/the Spanish speaking?"[120]

How widespread was support for bilingual education in the Nixon administration? While not unanimous, support was very strong. In April of 1972, the administration planned further occasions to demonstrate Nixon's backing of bilingualism in preparation for the election. A group of seven top policy and public relations aides, including Colson and speechwriter William Safire, urged a half-hour event with Latino leaders and celebrities, including Fernando Lamas and Ricardo Montalban, "to show the President's interest in bilingual education." Again, they all took for granted the merits of bilingual education and the Latino community's support for it. Only press secretary Ron Ziegler opposed the occasion, on the grounds that the "proposed event is much too obvious."[121] Nevertheless, promotion of bilingual education became a favorite strategy to appeal to Latinos in the 1972 election.[122]

The politics surrounding the Bilingual Education Act show that by the first Nixon administration, this formerly controversial policy had fully matured. Now almost completely divorced from its national-security and black civil rights policy origins, its only meaning for Nixon officials was as part of the policy repertoire to win votes from the Latino groups. And this minority targeting was considered appropriate because Latinos were minorities—that is, analogous to blacks.

The Bilingual Education Act was only a program to provide federal financial aid for projects aimed at helping limited-English speakers. As the administrations' and congressional concerns for the budget show, it was only a benefit, not a right, and after gaining passage (and playing up its symbolic value for attracting Latino voters), Congress, Johnson, and Nixon all neglected it. Congress granted $21 million for 1970, $25 million for 1971, and $35 million for 1972. By 1975, however, the trend had greatly accelerated upward, as bilingual education received $70 million and benefited two hundred thousand children in 375 school districts. This was great expansion— but there were *5 million* LEP children in the country.[123]

Origins of the Civil Right to Language Accommodation in the Schools

There was another set of players attracted to bilingual education. Movement toward a *right* to language accommodation and eventually bilingual education began in the federal bureaucracy, was approved by the Nixon White House, and was sanctioned by the Supreme Court. Like many of the developments of the minority rights revolution, progress here came quietly, to the notice of very few and resistance of almost none, in behind-the-scenes bureaucratic rulings, initiatives, and decisions. The ease of the development of a right to language accommodation was, in various ways, due to the legacy inherited from black civil rights policy.

"Less of a political hot potato": Creating Latino language rights
The Civil Rights Act of 1964, based on the deceptively simple idea of nondiscrimination, developed in ways never foreseen by the congressional members

who voted for it. Title VI of that Act declared that no institution or program receiving federal aid could discriminate on the basis of race, national origin, or religion. The law created the Office for Civil Rights (OCR) within HEW to enforce Title VI. The central task was school desegregation for blacks, where little measurable progress had been made since the momentous decision in *Brown v. Board of Education.*

By 1969, OCR was moving from a color-blind, "freedom of choice" model of school desegregation to a result-oriented, proportional model that relied on bussing black and white students across cities and towns to achieve racially integrated schools. As part of an effort to win the support of the nominally Democratic south (the "Southern Strategy"), the Nixon administration opposed OCR's use of bussing. In this context of frustrated ambitions, OCR staffmembers began to look at the problems of Latinos. In May 1970, it issued the key "May 25 memorandum," which characterized the failure to accommodate LEP children as national-origin discrimination and a violation of Title VI where school districts received federal funds (which was everywhere).

How did this come about seemingly so easily? The first point to keep in mind is that OCR, like the EEOC, attracted persons committed to the cause of civil rights. Policies designed for black Americans gave positions of power to those who supported equality and minority rights generally. These included OCR's director, Leon Panetta, a liberal Republican from California who was proud to be part of the "party of Lincoln" and attracted attention for infuriating the Nixon administration with his determination to use the Civil Rights Act to desegregate southern schools. The son of Italian immigrants who knew firsthand the struggles facing those perceived as different, Panetta was sympathetic to minorities. One of his earliest memories was of his grandfather's being taken away from the family home in Monterrey during World War II by federal officials who suspected him of disloyalty to the United States. He also witnessed the plight of Mexican Americans in California, later learning more about their experience from a Mexican American roommate during his first year of law school at the University of Santa Clara. It was Panetta's decision to issue the May 25 memorandum.[124]

The nuts and bolts of the memorandum were mostly the work of Martin Gerry, special assistant to the director at OCR from 1970 to 1975. Gerry was another liberal Republican—a veteran of the 1963 Freedom Summer project in Mississippi, where white students worked with the black Student Nonviolent Coordinating Committee to register blacks to vote.[125]

The presence of Panetta and Gerry meant that minority leaders could find at OCR government officials with real power who believed in and were strongly committed to their cause. Latino groups therefore needed considerably less organization, resources, and lobbying to have their problems attended to. What was really required was a group meaning that was, to OCR, plausibly the same as that of blacks. While the black civil rights movement had spanned years of mass protest, violence, and marches on Washington involving hundreds of thousands of people, the right to foreign-language accommodation required only a few self-appointed advocates and several visits to the OCR and its officials.[126]

According to Panetta and Gerry, most important were a handful of visits from Mexican American leaders to the Washington office and with Panetta while he was visiting San Francisco. Among them was Father Henry Casso, a Catholic priest from San Antonio who was active in Texas and California efforts to improve education for Mexican American children.[127] These leaders described the difficulties of Mexican American children in school, and argued that the schools' failure to accommodate language and culture difference was part of the problem. None of them explicitly stressed the need for a bilingual approach, but demanded only that something be done. Panetta agreed that OCR should send a memo to school districts, informing them that nondiscrimination rights required some response to language discrimination.[128]

The civil-rights liberalism of Panetta and Gerry was not the only factor making for such easy persuasion on the matter of foreign-language accommodation. This new federal understanding of discrimination would have been a shocking departure from traditional understanding only a few years earlier. Looked at from the conventional model of discrimination, failure to provide language accommodation could not be a violation. Schools were, in theory, offering the same education to all children. And the policy of offering English education to all children was not founded on malicious intent to harm Mexican Americans or a belief in ethnic inferiority, as was the segregation of African Americans. Children of Mexican descent who spoke English were not being excluded by an English-only policy, and therefore, the crucial factor was language ability and not national origin. By 1969, however, the complaints of the Latino advocates clearly looked like discrimination.

This was because OCR officials had begun to see that intent was not always relevant to a finding of discrimination. Results, or the impacts of practices, were most important. School systems in the north that no longer segregated blacks by law nevertheless segregated them in fact. Panetta recalled that OCR was "beginning to look at school systems beyond the south that had developed discrimination, through employment practices, through residential discrimination, housing discrimination, and other forms of discrimination that ultimately resulted in school systems that were segregated." Similar to the "disparate impact" theory of discrimination that developed in employment law, the new understanding was that certain unintended practices could have adverse impacts on minority children, leaving them in segregated schools or otherwise harmed. OCR had developed regulations that focused on education administration or methods that had the *effect* of deterioration of educational service for blacks. It simply extended this policy model to Latinos in the southwest: "It was during this period that we began to also see the same problem with regard to schools in the southwest, [with] kids from Hispanic backgrounds either because of language problems or because of the same type of discrimination. This time [it was] based not so much on blacks as browns." The US Commission on Civil Rights, which had held widely publicized hearings in San Antonio in 1968 (discussed above), was also promoting such a view.

Therefore, meanings of discrimination that developed to understand the segregation of blacks made the problems of Latinos more visible. From there, OCR officials' commitment to rights could take over. Panetta's view was straightforward: "As a lawyer and as someone who believed in what this country was all about . . . I honestly believed that there is no right unless there is a remedy, and if in fact kids are suffering from discrimination or had been the victims of discrimination, then there has to be a remedy to correct that." Gerry also easily saw the Latino predicament as discrimination: "It was clear that simply providing these children the opportunity to sit in a room where a language they didn't understand was being spoken was not providing them an education . . . Actually there was very little discussion with either Leon or [Panetta's successor] Stan [Pottinger] about the basic assumptions which were that simply exposing kids to instruction that they couldn't benefit from was discriminatory."

There was another factor leading to the easy persuasion of the OCR officials that had its roots in the black civil rights movement. In July of 1969, Attorney General John Mitchell and HEW secretary Robert Finch issued a controversial statement declaring that the Nixon administration would avoid terminating federal education aid funds for still-segregated schools, and would concentrate on voluntary compliance with the threat of a lawsuit in reserve. A previous target date of the 1969–70 school year for desegregation was rescinded; there now was no target date. The statement outraged civil-rights advocates both in and outside the government. Of the one hundred lawyers in the Justice Department's Civil Rights Division, sixty-five signed a petition that said the new policy was "inconsistent with clearly defined legal mandates" and showed "a disposition on the part of responsible officials of the federal government to subordinate clearly defined legal requirements to non-legal considerations."[129] Civil-rights advocates began to prepare a lawsuit against the government for failing to enforce the Civil Rights Act. In October 1970, civil-rights activist Joseph Rauh and the NAACP Legal Defense

Fund—with the help of unhappy HEW officials—did file a lawsuit against HEW for failing to enforce Title VI.[130] This activity regarding black civil rights spurred the cause of language rights because OCR wanted to preempt similar litigation in this new area. Panetta recalled that language rights "was an area that we ought to get ahead of as opposed to being forced to deal with through some kind of lawsuit. It would have been to our advantage in OCR not to wait for legal action as we had in the dual (black–white) school systems but actually get ahead of the curve with a memorandum to address that problem."

While neither Panetta nor Gerry were politically motivated, HEW secretary Robert Finch shared the White House view that there were votes to be had in the Latino community. In February of 1969, he had announced a prompt, massive upgrading of bilingual education.[131] Finch later recalled:

> I wanted to make it clear that the course I was following at HEW was not motivated entirely by concern for good works or support for social programs. I was trying to deal with the cutting issues that were affecting the Republican party. I thought it was very important, for instance, that Republicans gain a foothold in the Chicano community.[132]

Finch's understanding of the new minority politics dictated support for the efforts of Panetta and Gerry.

There were no defenders of the status quo to slow down OCR, thus no real opposition. Some in the office believed that tackling national-origin discrimination would take away from the "real" mission, which was black–white school segregation, but this resistance was light and faded quickly. Panetta assigned most of the work on the May 25 memo to the young lawyer Gerry, who was then only in his midtwenties.

Gerry took to his task with zeal. He had meetings with HEW officials who had worked on the bilingual education program. He learned of work by the US Commission on Civil Rights on the practice of placing Latino LEP children into classes for the mentally retarded based on I.Q. tests in English—an obvious injustice.[133] Over a period of months in 1969, he made informal field visits to several school districts in South Texas with large Latino populations and also to New York City. There, he sat in on some classes and met with students, parents, and education experts. One expert was the superintendent of the Edgewood Independent School District near San Antonio, José Cárdenas, an education scholar and strong advocate of the idea that schools had to change their culture to be more "compatible" with the Mexican American child.

Latino politics and the political meaning of Latinos were entering new stages of similarity and differences with black politics. Whatever the views in the White House or at the top positions at HEW, at no time was there any great concern at OCR with the politics of language rights, either in the sense of winning Latino votes for Nixon or losing the votes of native-born or non-Latino Americans who objected to anything other than laissez faire or a strong assimilation policy. OCR was already working hard on the politically sensitive issue of school desegregation, and its leaders thought little of the political fallout from a new regulation to bring meaningful education to LEP children. There were no warnings from the White House, and no pressures from Congress. Panetta recalled that issues related to Latinos had a different politics than those related to blacks. In 1969 there was more sympathy for Latino problems in Congress, and Latino policy was "much less of a political hot potato" compared to black civil rights.

In February, Nixon decided that Panetta's ambition to desegregate southern black schools was alienating southern states from his administration, and he fired him. Nixon then installed J. Stanley Pottinger as director of OCR. Like Panetta and Gerry, Pottinger saw the language issue as straightforward. He signed Gerry's memo, and sent it to the office of Nixon's domestic adviser, John Ehrlichman, for approval. Gerry felt confident that the memo would encounter no problems, as Nixon had recently affirmed his commitment to equal educational opportunity in an Education Reform Message on March 9. Nixon's message was designed to deflect criticism over administration stands over busing, as he argued that support for "quality education" was not a "code word" for delay of desegregation. But Nixon also stated, "This administration is committed to the principle and the practice of seeing to it that equal educational opportunity is provided every child in every corner of this land."[134] And for Nixon, there were no problems with the OCR memorandum. On May 25, 1970, LEP children had a new civil right.

The May 25 memorandum began by evincing concern over OCR reports that had "revealed a number of common practices which have the effect of denying equality of educational opportunity to Spanish-surnamed pupils." Latinos were the main focus, but "similar practices which have the effect of discrimination on the basis of national origin exist in other locations with respect to disadvantaged pupils from other national origin-minority groups, for example, Chinese or Portuguese."

The memo spelled out four different areas of compliance with Title VI of the Civil Rights Act of 1964 relating to language. First, and most important, school districts would have to take "affirmative steps to rectify the language deficiency" to allow "effective participation" in district educational programs for students who could not speak or understand English. Second, tests that actually measured English language competency could not be the basis of assignments to classes for the learning disabled or exclusion from college preparatory classes. Third, grouping students by their ability as a way of dealing with language difficulties could only be temporary. This was to prevent the practice of permanently assigning LEP children to slow-learner groups. Last, "school districts have the responsibility to adequately notify national origin-minority group parents of school activities" if other parents are notified. In order to be adequate, these notices "may have to be provided in a language other than English."

It was an impressive expansion of rights, created by the power of bureaucratic memo. But there was a catch. Not *all* LEP children were included. So as not to be too burdensome on school districts, OCR sent the memorandum only to those districts in which more than 5 percent of the student population belonged to a national-origin minority group.[135]

Gerry and Panetta avoided declaring a civil right to bilingual education, though Gerry spoke regularly to believers in the new pedagogy. Panetta was not wedded to any particular approach. He recalled, "I think all of us recognized that the real challenge was how to take these kids and move them into an English-speaking society." There were other reasons to avoid mandating bilingual education. For one, Gerry did not encounter a consensus for bilingual education. Perhaps more important, Gerry recalled there was "some concern from the people in the Office of Education over anything that would imply the federal government would have to pay for all this education, because there wasn't enough money obviously. So we avoided that trap." For the minority rights revolution to progress smoothly, issues of funding were best avoided.

Implementation: A federal right to bilingual education?
Bilingual education became the favored approach. This was clear at the stage of implementation of the memo when Latino leaders and educators became closely involved.

At a May 21–22, 1971 symposium entitled "Mexican Americans and Educational Change," co-sponsored by the Office of Education and the Mexican-American Studies Program at the University of California at Riverside, Gerry announced to federal government officials, education scholars, and Latino studies professors from throughout the southwest that "outstanding Mexican American and Puerto Rican educators, psychologists, and community and civil rights leaders were invited to join" a task force to assist implementation of the May 25 memorandum.[136] While Gerry did not promise bilingual education, his presentation—"Cultural Freedom in the Schools: The Right of Mexican-American Children to Succeed"—fit comfortably with the other presentations during the symposium. A veteran of the civil rights movement, Gerry was among friends, even if the contributions of the Latino intellectuals more boldly celebrated bilingual education and Mexican-American cultural differences. One participant punctuated his discussion of "Chicano" cultural differences with earnest exhortations of "LEARN, AMIGO, LEARN!" for the "Anglos" in the audience.[137]

Similar educator-activists met with OCR officials in local meetings about implementation of the May 25 memo. Shortly after OCR issued the memo, it held a strategy conference in Denver. Unlike similar meetings on policy for expanding rights of women, which invariably invited groups hostile to those new rights, the conference brought together only Mexican American leaders, Mexican American educators, and psychologists to work with OCR officials in formulating implementation strategy. The group's emphasis in this Denver meeting was on preventing the erroneous placement of Mexican American LEP children into classes for the learning disabled. But a summary of the conference that Pottinger submitted to the new secretary of HEW Elliot Richardson showed an increasing interest in a civil right to multicultural education based on the well-established notion of the damaged minority psyche. It stated, "Equality of educational opportunity requires that special attention be given to the psychological needs of every child." These included needs for belonging, self-respect, affection, recognition, and achievement. To meet these needs, a school district "must provide differentiated staffing to facilitate individualized learning, it must offer suitable instructional materials, and it must employ instructional personnel of the same racial and ethnic background as that of the children." Further, "workshops must consider the distortion of history as found in our school textbooks, the contributions made by our ethnic minorities to the development of the United States, an analysis of social class, ethnocentrism, and other characteristics of complex societies." In this implementation stage, a right to bilingual education also began to take shape: "The school curriculum must also cover the above topics and provide bilingual-bicultural education so that children will be proud of their language and their heritage."[138]

At the OCR's urging, the Office of Education then established an Intradepartmental Advisory Committee that oversaw another meeting with Mexican American leaders, this time in San Diego on April 28–30, 1971. Their goal was to develop bilingual and bicultural educational programs for school districts that violated the rights outlined in the May 25 memorandum. Richardson, in a letter to Senator Walter Mondale, chair of the Senate's Subcommittee on Education, described the recommendations of the Advisory Committee. Though a longtime Republican who had worked at HEW in the Eisenhower administration, Richardson either wrote or signed a discussion that was indistinguishable from those of the NEA and the Latino educators supporting bilingual education. Richardson's basic message was of "the need for total institutional reposturing in order to incorporate, affirmatively recognize, and value the cultural environment of ethnic minority children so that the development of positive self-concept can be accelerated."[139]

While OCR bureaucrats worked on language rights as part of a new phase of civil rights and were guided by moral concerns in adopting the policy, the political benefits of the Latino rights efforts were not lost on the post-Panetta OCR leadership. In a memo to Richardson, OCR explained:

> Support for and confidence in the Office for Civil Rights in the Mexican-American and Puerto Rican communities is both widespread and at the highest point ever. While the Office has proceeded to develop, issue and operationalize the [May 25] Memorandum without public fanfare, the close working relationship the OCR has established with Mexican-American and Puerto Rican leaders and *opinion makers* has resulted in the quiet spreading of confidence in the community that the Office is both sincere and effective in its action goals.[140]

Events were moving fast, as members of Congress with large Latino constituencies also saw they could use the new right to force government action that could both help minorities and gain for themselves political advantage. In 1970, Jacob Javits asked HEW to investigate discrimination against New York City Puerto Ricans. The centerpiece of the investigation, according to Gerry, was the question "whether educational services being provided to children place them in educational and cultural environments which do not meet their linguistic needs, or include the use of curriculum materials which dictate a permanently lower level of educational achievement regardless of academic potential." More than language needs were examined. OCR launched a massive examination of every possible parameter of equality, including food service and recreational activities, square footage of counselor's offices, and the number of musical instruments available. When New York officials objected to the federal nosing about in local business and became uncooperative, the government filed suit to force school principals to fill out OCR's questionnaires. By the time the final reports were finished (OCR found discrimination in faculty hiring and other inequalities), New York City was already bound by a consent decree to provide bilingual education.[141]

Beginning in 1968, there were other developments that in time would add pressure for the implementation of the May 25 memorandum and a bilingual approach to education. The Mexican-American Legal Defense and Education Fund (MALDEF) was formed that summer and, as its name implies, was modeled on the NAACP Legal Defense Fund (LDF). It was developed with help from LDF lawyers and the Ford Foundation.[142] MALDEF would not fight for Mexican American legal rights alone, however—the federal government pushed equally hard for the same goals.[143] In August of 1970, Nixon's Department of Justice filed suit against the Texas Education Agency and the Austin Independent School District for discriminating against both black and Mexican American students.

The Justice Department's efforts were rewarded marvelously. On July 9, 1971, a Fifth Circuit Court ruled in *United States v. State of Texas*[144] that a Texas desegregation plan for the San Felipe Del Rio Independent School District had to take into account the needs of non-English speakers, and equal educational opportunity required special treatment for Latino language differences. The court also equated the situations of black and Mexican American children and required Texas to devise new programs for both.[145]

Five months later, a court ruling in the same case ordered bilingual education. The decision was a resounding endorsement of the right of students to have education in their own language, and to have their culture not just acknowledged in class, but celebrated throughout the school. The aptly named Judge William Justice's decision was apparently swayed by expert testimony, especially that of Dr. José Cárdenas and his theory of "cultural incompatibilities." In court, Cárdenas emphasized the Latinos-like-blacks-but-different line: "Mexican American children are a unique ethnic group, and they have unique characteristics, like Black children." These unique characteristics made them incompatible with the educational program. Cárdenas told the court that just as "there is no way that you can make a white out of black child," it was true that "there is no way that you can make an Anglo-Saxon out of a Mexican-American."[146] Cárdenas's complex theory, replete with diagrams and grids, ultimately focused on culture and language differences. Existing school techniques, curricula, and regulations were alien to the Mexican American child and created value conflicts. Comprehensive change was needed to repair damaged self-images and improve school performance.

At the same time, Gerry at OCR, working with lawyers from the Justice Department (who had "picked up the spirit of the [May 25] memo,")[147] as well as with Latino educators, formed the HEW Advisory Committee on Bicultural Education to assemble a preferred plan to be imposed on the school district as a remedy. The plan followed the basics of the Cárdenas theory, calling for an educational program that would "incorporate, affirmatively recognize, and value the cultural environment and language background of all of [the district's] children, so that the development of positive self-concepts in all children of the district can proceed apace."[148]

What Cárdenas's theory lacked in hard evidence it made up for in plausibility. Judge Justice wrote that "the Court was particularly impressed" by the testimony of Dr. Cárdenas. He agreed that the theory "demonstrated that

Mexican-American students exhibit numerous characteristics which have a causal connection with their general inability to benefit from an educational program designed primarily to meet the needs of so-called Anglo-Americans." Basing his ruling on a series of African American desegregation cases, Justice called for a thorough bicultural remaking of the schools to provide equal rights.[149]

What, then, did Texas need to do to meet the demand for equal opportunity? Following the plan urged by the HEW advisory committee, Texans in the district, including non-Latinos, needed to acknowledge the culture, language, and right to participation of Latinos. Thus, equal opportunity required "the Anglo-American students too must be called upon to adjust to their Mexican-American classmates, and to learn to understand and appreciate their different linguistic and cultural attributes." This was the key not only to "educational enrichment," but also to creating a unitary system.[150] The court order specified that Texas had to provide education that would, following HEW's language, "affirmatively recognize" Latino children's culture and language. The order, covering students from preschoolers through high school, called for language maintenance, cultural reinforcement, ethnic studies, and even "modification and expansion of home economics curriculum to respond to the life styles, family structures and needs of children in all cultures represented in the student body." There should be "vigorous recruitment" to make the school personnel mirror the ethnic composition of the community, the appointment of a multi-ethnic advisory committee to oversee staff development and handling of the new requirements, "cultural awareness training that will include School Board members, key community leaders, administrative staff, teaching personnel, counseling and guidance personnel and parents," and a new program so that school clubs, bands, mascots, songs, chants, cheers, and social activities reflected the "background and interests of all students in the consolidated district."[151] In short, to ensure equal opportunity, school life would have to be reinvented so that the Mexican American children would be a celebrated part. It was a stunning victory for a right to a minority group's language, culture, and participation in every aspect of schooling.

But victory in court did not necessarily mean victory in the school districts. Justice's ruling, like the May 25 memorandum, was an unfunded mandate. HEW came up with only a small amount of guaranteed money to fund its own recommended plan. School officials and—not surprisingly—many non-Latino parents did not support the plan. Some considered it unacceptable federal control of a local institution. Others thought it separatist. One parent commented, "These people are interested in building a new Quebec in South Texas." A few families left the district. Some thought studying Spanish was a waste of time for both Latinos and non-Latinos. Many monolingual teachers feared they would be replaced by bilingual teachers.[152]

The federal government's lack of funding made it easy to avoid implementation of the court order. Funding was available only on the basis of competitive proposals for Bilingual Education Act money, and all the school district officials had to do was to write ineffective proposals and they would be denied funding for a program that they did not want to implement in the first place. The Texas Education Agency did not push the district, and the district successfully transferred the case from Justice's court in Tyler, Texas to Judge John Wood's court in San Antonio. Wood was somewhat less inclined to follow Cárdenas's theory. After Cárdenas's testimony on his theory of cultural incompatibilities, Wood told the educator bluntly, "That is the stupidest thing I ever heard of."[153]

But despite the foot-dragging and accusations of stupidity, there was change in the district. By 1973 two thousand mostly Mexican American students were being taught by eighty bilingual teachers, and non-Latino students were learning Spanish.[154] The sweeping changes ordered by Judge Justice in a federal court also did much to legitimate a multicultural approach to education and embolden advocates to demand that more be done.[155]

The Supreme Court rules for language rights

Ultimately, the issue of language rights reached the Supreme Court. In the 1974 case *Lau v. Nichols,* the Court ruled that national-origin minorities did have certain language rights in education, though these rights were statutory—not constitutional—and the Court never mentioned bilingual-bicultural education. For many, however, the Court's ruling effectively did require bilingual education, and it gave increased legitimacy to advocates.

Despite the fact that language rights developed principally around the problems faced by Latinos, *Lau v. Nichols* concerned students of Chinese ancestry in San Francisco. A Chinatown legal services office first brought the case in 1970 to federal district court on behalf of the students. It claimed that the public schools were not properly educating the approximately three thousand non-English speaking Chinese American students, and arguing that this was a violation of Title VI of the Civil Rights Act of 1964 and the Fourteenth Amendment of the Constitution. Relying on *Brown v. Board of Education,* it argued that equality meant more than provision of equal books and the same school buildings. The state's hands were unclean, since California law mandated school attendance, use of English, and fluency in English for graduation. The lawsuit demanded that special English classes be established and taught by bilingual teachers.[156] The district court ruled against the Chinese American students, arguing that equal opportunity was satisfied by the equal availability of the same education that tens of thousands of other San Franciscans received.[157]

Despite a brief from the federal government arguing for relief, the Ninth Circuit court affirmed the earlier decision, stating that English language instruction was of great importance in schooling and that uniform use of English did not constitute illegal discrimination.[158] Both the district and appeals courts were sympathetic to the students, but both argued there was no constitutional or statutory claim for ordering the provision of special services.

At the Supreme Court level, Nixon's solicitor general Robert H. Bork and the Justice Department issued a brief arguing that San Francisco was violating both the Constitution and Title VI of the Civil Rights Act of 1964. Bork argued that San Francisco needed to implement HEW's (technically, OCR's) May 25 memorandum order that national-origin nondiscrimination required some kind of program to ensure equal opportunity. He pointed out that the Supreme Court had previously given great weight to HEW guidelines in black school-desegregation cases. Bork and the Justice Department (which now included ex-OCR head Stanley Pottinger as assistant attorney general) maintained that the Fourteenth Amendment and the Civil Rights Act "impose upon the school authorities in such circumstances an obligation to provide some special instruction to national origin-minority students" that would "allow them meaningfully to participate in the educational program which is readily accessible to their English-speaking classmates."

As in *United States v. State of Texas,* the argument for language accommodation was rooted in the black school-desegregation cases. Bork maintained that a school district that provides the same facilities and curriculum for all students, even though the district officials know that some students cannot benefit, is using a "narrow and mechanical view of equal educational opportunities" that "cannot be reconciled with this Court's holding" in a series of cases.[159] Citing the school-desegregation case *United States v. Jefferson County Board of Education,*[160] Bork argued that the school district's failure to provide special instruction led to a "[d]enial of access to the dominant culture."

The brief did not demand bilingual education. It argued that schools must do *something.* Bork used the May 25 memorandum and its "effect standard" of discrimination as a model: "The impact of that practice [of teaching in English] is upon a distinct segment of a national origin-minority group, whose members are affected on account of a national origin characteristic." However, a heavy reliance on cases dealing with racial discrimination against blacks caused a blurring of the differences between the issues of national origin and of race—the two had become the same. The brief argued, in the end, that "simple justice requires that public funds, to which all taxpayers of all races contribute, not be spent in any fashion which encourages, entrenches, subsidizes, or results in racial discrimination." Though the case dealt with national-origin discrimination—there are no racial languages—for the writers of the brief there was no meaningful difference between race and national-origin discrimination.[161]

The Supreme Court's *Lau* decision, written by Justice Douglas, rejected the constitutional argument with no dissents but otherwise followed Bork's brief: the Court did not order bilingual education, but it did decree that the Civil Rights Act assigned the state a responsibility to provide equal opportunity.[162] This implied the provision of some special programs for students who did not speak English. The Court declared that "there is no equality of treatment merely by providing students with the same facilities, textbooks, teachers, and curriculum." Non-English-speaking students were "effectively foreclosed from any meaningful education." Since basic English skills were "at the core of what these public schools teach," requiring that students already have these basic skills "is to make a mockery of public education."[163]

The Court made no great effort to justify the equation of national origin and language. Douglas acknowledged HEW's power to issue rules and regulations to implement the Civil Rights Act. He quoted with approval the May 25 memo and other HEW guidelines from school-desegregation cases that had established an "effect" standard of discrimination. For Douglas, it seemed "obvious that the Chinese-speaking minority receive fewer benefits than the English-speaking majority from respondents' school system which denies them a meaningful opportunity to participate in the educational program—all earmarks of the discrimination banned by the regulations."[164]

The Court was unreflectively siding with national-origin minorities. Was this issue really one of language and not the prohibited national-origin discrimination? Two years later, in *General Electric v. Gilbert*,[165] the Supreme Court faced a similar question regarding women's rights, but made a different judgment. Just as only some persons of Chinese national origin had trouble with English, only some women get pregnant. Firms could exclude pregnant women from disability coverage in insurance plans without sex discrimination, the Court argued, because nonpregnant workers include both males and females. Thus, in *Lau*, the Court could have argued that what was at issue was not national-origin discrimination (since English-speaking students included both Chinese and Euro-Americans), but language discrimination, which was not covered by the Civil Rights Act.[166] It did not. In *Lau*, the only notes of hesitation came in Justice Blackmun's concurring opinion. Blackmun affirmed his support of Douglas's decision but added: "We may only guess as to why [the Chinese American students] have had no exposure to English in their preschool years. Earlier generations of American ethnic groups have overcome the language barrier by earnest parental endeavor or by the hard fact of being pushed out of the family or community nest and into the realities of broader experience." He also underscored, following the May 25 memorandum, that this was a civil right that mattered only if there were sufficient numbers of LEP students. Blackmun wrote, "For me, numbers are at the heart of this case and my concurrence is to be understood accordingly."[167]

The legacy of Lau

While there were a handful of federal court decisions in the early 1970s that ordered bilingual education, *Lau*, even though it did not mandate bilingual or bicultural programs, was the most important for the policy's later development. Some federal courts interpreting *Lau* made the link that the Supreme Court did not, connecting the decision to bilingual education for Latinos.[168] The *Lau* decision also gave new impetus to a reauthorization of the Bilingual Education Act being led by Democratic senators Joseph Montoya of New Mexico, Edward Kennedy of Massachusetts, and Alan Cranston of California. When speaking to a Conference on Mexican American Education in Texas in March 1974, Montoya linked *Lau* to the *Brown* decision: "This time the Court said that a child whose language was different from that of the majority was still entitled to equal educational opportunity under our laws."[169] Kennedy declared from the Senate floor that to comply with *Lau* "it is clear that bilingual education will in most cases provide the fullest education opportunity."[170] While Kennedy was careful in choosing his words, it was easy to misconstrue the decision, as did Representative Mario Biaggi (D–NY) in hearings for the new authorization bill when he stated, "The Supreme Court of the United States already made clear in its decision on Chinese Americans in *Lau v. Nichols* that every American child has an unqualified right to bi-lingual education assistance if he needs it."[171]

The 1974 Bilingual Education Act amendments gave an official definition for bilingual education that the 1968 law lacked: bilingual education involved teaching in a student's native language and in English and incorporating the student's native culture as well. The reauthorization of the Act also did away with the former program's exclusive focus on poor children. Now any LEP child could benefit, and even English-dominant students could enroll voluntarily. Congress also authorized new funds for teacher training and research.[172]

Seven months after the *Lau* decision, Congress passed the Equal Educational Opportunity Act, aimed primarily at the then-raging controversy over bussing black and white children across town to integrate schools. The Act slowed down court-ordered bussing by declaring that while all public-school children are entitled to equal educational opportunities, a district's failure to achieve an integration balance does not necessarily imply unequal opportunity and "the neighborhood is the appropriate basis for determining public school assignments." This public controversy was also a perfect opportunity to expand rights for Latinos. A barely noticed amendment to the Act added on the House floor outlawed "the failure of an educational agency to take appropriate action to overcome language barriers that impede equal participation by its students in its instructional program." The formal effect of the provision was to expand the May 25 memorandum and *Lau* decision to all public schools, regardless of whether they received federal money, and to give a statutory basis to the memo. Courts have been mixed in ruling whether the Equal Educational Opportunity Act's "appropriate action" means bilingual education.[173]

Meanwhile, as the regulations became stronger, federal funding became more controversial. Under pressure from the Federal Reserve Board and concerned about rising inflation (among other pressing problems), the Nixon administration resisted government funding of bilingual education and other efforts, even ending up in court over an illegal impounding of funds appropriated for social programs.[174] Though the Nixon administration had avidly supported bilingual education in public and private statements and had produced the pivotal May 25 memorandum, by 1974 the under secretary of HEW, Frank C. Carlucci, expressed the preference for allowing local education officials to control their own pedagogy—and spend their own money. Further, bilingual education had not proven its effectiveness, and Carlucci resisted the increasingly bold demands for language and culture maintenance, by then completely severed from the Cold War arguments about national security that were common in the 1960s.[175]

Still, at the overworked OCR, they had not forgotten their Latino constituency. Martin Gerry recalled that OCR had a set of active cases from the May 25 memorandum, and there was a need for strong standardized guidelines to keep regional OCR offices from going their own way. Gerry wanted to use the leverage of the Supreme Court's imprimatur to develop powerful remedial guidelines.[176]

The new guidelines, called the *Lau* Remedies, were considerably more oriented around bilingual education than the May 25 memorandum had been, though they avoided outright mandates for a bilingual-bicultural approach. The comprehensiveness of the *Lau* Remedies showed the continued presence of minority-rights advocates in the government in 1974, while also making it clear how difficult it was to ensure an equal educational opportunity for each student. Though the *Lau* decision was directed at students with "linguistic deficiencies," the *Lau* Remedies were directed to students with a "primary or home language" that was not English. Determining this language involved very complex government regulations that apparently required school officials to follow children around with a pen and notepad. According to the directive, a school district was obligated "at a minimum" to

> determine the language most often spoken in the student's home, regardless of the language spoken by the student, the language spoken by the student in the home and the language spoken by the student in the social setting (by observation).
>
> These assessments must be made by persons who can speak and understand the necessary language(s). An example of the latter would be to determine, by observation, the language used by the student to communicate with peers between classes or in informal situations. These assessments must cross-validate one another. (Example: student speaks Spanish at home and Spanish with classmates at lunch). Observers must estimate the frequency of use of each language spoken by the student in these situations.

Local school districts were also to determine which "cognitive learning style" and "incentive motivational styles" these students better responded to (e.g., "competitive v. cooperative learning patterns"). For presecondary school students who were monolingual in a language other than English, or who spoke only a little English, the *Lau* Remedies stated that the students' language and culture should be maintained while English is taught. A "transitional bilingual education program" was also acceptable, but had extra requirements: "the district must provide predictive data which show that such student(s) are ready to make the transition into English and will succeed educationally in content areas and in the education program(s) in which he/she is to be placed." There were no guidelines on what kind of data was acceptable. For these younger children, however, the guidelines were emphatic that "an ESL program *is not* appropriate" (original emphasis). For secondary school students, the guidelines offered bilingual programs as well as other options.

Suggested compliance with the Civil Rights Act now also included multicultural education: "Required courses (example: American History) must not be designed to exclude pertinent minority developments which have contributed to or influenced such subjects." Regarding teachers, "Instructional personnel teaching the students in question must be linguistically/culturally familiar with the background of the students to be affected." In all, there were twenty-three pages of *Lau* Remedy guidelines, and given their complexity (how pertinent should those minority contributions to American history be for inclusion in the text? how does one determine if a teacher is adequately culturally familiar with the students' background?), they could—and perhaps should—have contained many more pages. Issued in the summer of 1975, the *Lau* Remedies were the zenith of the bilingual-education revolution.[177]

By 1978, OCR had identified 334 school districts, teaching approximately 1.1 million national-origin minority students, that would be targeted for investigation. While not technically requiring bilingual education or forbidding ESL instruction (these remedies were only guidelines), OCR made things difficult, if not impossible, for any district officials who wanted to try something different. They would have to prove that their method would be equally "effective to cure the violation." Yet, in 1975, there was no evidence that bilingual education offered equal education opportunity. A Seattle bilingual-education coordinator complained, "How can you prove something is equally as good as something else which nobody has proved the worth of? You come to a logical dead end on that one immediately."[178]

Conclusion

When the Mexican American education professor told the "Anglos" in his audience and in the teaching profession "LEARN, AMIGO, LEARN!" his point was emblematic of a great shift taking place. It was no longer the sole responsibility of immigrants to adapt or help their children adapt to America. With bilingual-bicultural education, it was "Anglo" America's responsibility to adapt to immigrants.

The story of the rise of bilingual education includes an act of Congress (the Bilingual Education Act), a bureaucratic order (the May 25 memorandum), and a Supreme Court ruling *(Lau v. Nichols)*. Support for these actions involved both political parties and the federal courts. They were achieved because of the inherited legacies of the policies for national security and black civil rights.

In some ways, the story told in this chapter seems to be an ordinary account of interest-group politics, but to see it only in this way is to overlook what makes the case of bilingual education interesting. First, Latinos were able to win a policy that represented a total break with a centuries-old "English-only" education policy without mass mobilization, protest, or consistent lobbying by their leaders. There was never any Latino march on Washington, and no Latino leaders could use the possibility of one as a threat as A. Philip Randolph had done as far back as 1941. While African Americans sometimes died in the struggle to end segregated schools, no blood was shed for federal bilingual education.[179] While a few local protests did take place, political leaders in Washington appeared oblivious to them.

This is not to say that Latino lobbying was irrelevant. Some Latino leaders joined with the NEA to fight for bilingual education. They used a strategy of meaning entrepreneurship, defining Latinos as a minority like blacks, but also different. Though inconsistent at first, after 1970 Latino leaders appeared to move to consensus on the merits of bilingual education for implementation of the memo-created civil right to language accommodation. But this stage was not marked by demonstrations or protest, and it did not even look like lobbying. Latino leaders worked so closely in consultations with OCR that one might be tempted to call the policy regime "corporatist."[180] Even that term would be misleading, however, because it would obscure the fact that language-rights activists not only consulted with the government, they were *in* the government. And when the government activists met with the Latino activists on how to implement language rights, they rarely invited groups who would foot the bill or might be opposed, a practice that was *de rigueur* for women's rights.

If OCR support for bilingual education was social-movement-style activism, the support from members of Congress or White House administrations looked more like a self-interested pursuit of reelection.[181] For this self-interest to kick in, the meaning of foreign languages had to have changed drastically, from something that implied disloyalty to something encouraging national security. This change took place courtesy of Sputnik and the National Defense Education Act. Also necessary were the legitimacy of minority politics and the perceptions of lawmakers and administrators of Latinos as deserving and politically valuable.

The politics of bilingual education showed signs of the "anticipatory politics" that characterized the expansion of minority capitalism. Policymakers, members of Congress, and both the Johnson and Nixon White Houses anticipated that Latinos across America really wanted bilingual education, an assessment that was based on the interests of just a few Latino leaders. So they gave it to them. In the late 1960s, Democrats and Republicans strongly played up their support of bilingual education for Latino audiences. In effect, they were meaning entrepreneurs, promoting themselves as friends of Latinos so they could win the suddenly available and valuable Latino vote. They did not necessarily have to concern themselves with funding when they could pass the problem to OCR, whose energetic administrators took the laws as far as they could go.

8

"I AGREE WITH YOU ABOUT THE INHERENT ABSURDITY": TITLE IX AND WOMEN'S EQUALITY IN EDUCATION

One of the most controversial but least-studied parts of the minority rights revolution was an obscure little law with a big impact. The law is so obscure that it has no familiar name by which it is identified, other than Title IX of the Education Amendments of 1972. Title IX's purpose was to grant equality to women in education. It did much to accomplish that purpose, while creating considerable national soul-searching and a firestorm of protest along the way.

Educational institutions today, particularly colleges and universities, are often thought of as bastions of progressivism, even criticized for going too far in pursuing egalitarian aspirations. In the late 1960s, however, they remained highly discriminatory toward women. The campaign of affirmative action for women would make strides in the area of employment by the early 1970s, but in other areas of the education process women continued to be discriminated against with impunity.

At that time, not surprisingly, women made up much smaller percentages of university students, administrators, and professors than they do today. Yet few women or men cared deeply about this. The modern women's movement was only just getting underway, and traditional views of what activities were appropriate for women sharply limited policy at the universities. Many universities had openly discriminatory policies toward women in key areas such as admissions, where women were held to higher standards and even then limited by exclusionary quotas. It was another area, however, that especially symbolized the exclusion of women and became the center of the political storm over Title IX. The new law's broad decree meant that men and women, boys and girls, must be given equal opportunity in school athletics.

Passed with Richard Nixon's signature, Title IX of the Education Amendments of 1972 stated that any schools receiving federal aid must not discriminate on the basis of sex. As for school athletics, however, the assumption had long been that sports were for men. Sex discrimination had gone unchallenged and almost unnoticed in sports that millions of Americans passionately loved, particularly football and basketball. Where women's sports did exist, they were mere afterthoughts, on the margins, unequally funded. Finding money for women's sports inevitably challenged the dominance of men's sports. Over the course of the 1970s and 1980s, Title IX helped create hundreds of thousands of women athletes—but it also led to the elimination of some men's sports and threatened others.

Although equalizing athletics became a lightening rod for hostility against the law in general, on this point there had been almost no lobbying at all. Before Title IX passed, there was almost no effort to increase women's participation in college and high school sports, and campuses were not obvious sites of frustrated female athletic aspirations. The lack of lobbying for Title IX, however, did not hinder its passage. Resistance to Title IX was almost nonexistent.

How, then, did the law come about? As with all aspects of the minority rights revolution, black civil rights left important legacies for the passage of Title IX. First, targeting minority groups for policy recognition and rights was a legitimate, appropriate activity of the federal government. Advocates for women's rights were able to claim that women were a minority just like blacks; they did not have the burden of legitimating minority targeting in principle. Furthermore, they could easily show their worthiness by using a method pioneered by advocates for black civil rights (especially in the EEOC) to show discrimination—namely, compiling statistics showing underrepresentation. These statistics obviated the need for a mass movement demanding the law.

If women were like blacks, it was appropriate that laws designed for blacks be extended and modified for women. Title IX was a modification of Title VI of the Civil Rights Act, which denied funding to any activity that received government aid and discriminated on the basis of race, national origin, or religion. Title VI provided a legitimated policy tool for any lawmaker wanting to express concern over the status of women (or other groups). Both those who believed in the cause and those more interested in using it for political gain could show they helped constituents with a relatively costless regulation, attaching strings to already appropriated funds, rather than a massive transfer of new resources.[1] Title IX adopted much of the Title VI language, but was written for sex discrimination and limited to education.

There was another, less direct way that the Civil Rights Act expedited passage of Title IX. A factor in the June 1972 enactment was Congress' vote the previous March for the Equal Rights Amendment (ERA). For decades, the ERA foundered on the split among women's groups (as described in Chapter 4) over the merits of protective legislation, all of which would be unconstitutional after the ERA. But the Civil Rights Act's Title VII, through EEOC and court rulings, already nullified protective legislation. Thus, women's leaders for the first time put forth a unified front. Though the Nixon administration was apprehensive, the ERA passed Congress easily. After that momentous event, Title IX, according to members of Congress, followed logically and attracted little notice. It did not matter that the ERA went on to failure during ratification in the states. Title IX lived on.

Yet there were, as in the case of affirmative action, some difficulties in arguing that women of all ethnicities were like blacks. The use of civil rights policies to benefit women was predicated on this analogy. Although the similarity of race and sex discrimination had a compelling logic on the surface, which made the law easy to pass, at the implementation stage the black analogy broke down. Administrators in the Office for Civil Rights (OCR), charged with writing implementing regulations, had to closely examine the implications of Title IX. They discovered that women and blacks were not so similar after all.

The real struggle therefore came during implementation, when the legislated revolution in athletics and other areas of gender relations became apparent. Unlike Latino advocacy for bilingual education, and despite their greater numbers and superior organization and mobilization, women advocates had to fight hard to have implementing regulations even written. The story of Title IX, then, is somewhat parallel to the story of women in affirmative action. The meaning of "woman" led to an uneven inclusion in the minority rights revolution. The legacies of the black civil rights movement and a superficial black analogy made the *formal* inclusion of women easy. But getting the implementing regulations to make the right a reality was difficult. Women's equality in education was finally established in a convoluted model of justice that combined classical liberalism for some policy areas and a difference-conscious "separate-but-equal" in others.

Contradictory Perceptions of Women during the First Nixon Administration: What Does Women's Equality Entail?

To trace the development of Title IX, we must first understand the early 1970s political perceptions of women, women's rights, and the significance of women in the legislative process. These are difficult to reproduce, but the often embarrassingly candid documents of the Nixon administration (as ever) provide valuable insights. They simultaneously show sexism and a perception of women's increasing power. They also show a tendency to equate women with blacks and other minority groups—and yet to see women as very different.

1969: Jokes, Rising Power, and "A Matter of Simple Justice"

Two small events in February 1969 reveal the contradictions in the politics of women's rights. By then, women were gaining positions of power and influence in the federal government, and astute politicians like President Nixon sensed political gain from being associated with women's rights.

Nixon had appointed a woman, Rita Hauser, as the US representative to the UN Human Rights Commission. He knew that a woman talking about rights had strong public relations benefits for the administration. On February 5, 1969, Hauser wrote Nixon that her appointment "has certainly generated publicity in the press and the media" and that she hoped thereby to "promote the image of your Administration in the field of human rights." She added, "I would be pleased to fill in any appearance in the human rights area that you may not be able to accept and for which you think I am suited." Nixon underlined this last offer, passing the note to chief of staff H. R. "Bob" Haldeman. He ordered him to "use her as extensively as possible—always non partisan. Particularly on T.V."[2]

The next day, however, Nixon publicly ridiculed a woman. At a February 6 press conference, the Washington bureau chief of the North American News Alliance, Vera Glaser, both Republican and female, asked Nixon if women were going to be neglected by his administration. She pointed out that only three of the administration's first two hundred top-level appointments were women. Rather than taking the opportunity to defend his record, rather than reaching out to potential women supporters in America, rather than showing the reporter respect, Nixon made a joke. "Would you be interested in coming to the government?" he asked. Everyone laughed—except, presumably, Vera Glaser.[3]

Such dismissive treatment of women periodically reappeared in Washington politics, but increasingly it became anachronistic as women's power and assertiveness in the government grew. Florence Dwyer (R–NJ) sent a letter to Nixon on February 26, 1969 asking him to appoint a special White House adviser on women's issues or create a new independent agency to strengthen "women's rights and responsibilities." The White House sent Dwyer a quiet reply but took no action.[4] In June, Dwyer wrote again, this time joined by three other GOP women representatives: Margaret Heckler (R–MA), Catherine May (R–WA), and Charlotte Reid (R–IL). They requested a meeting with Nixon "for the purpose of discussing a number of matters of direct and immediate concern to women generally." "We can provide you with information and ideas which should be of value in dealing with these problems," they explained.[5] Nixon aides simultaneously made light of the matter while taking it seriously. Political adviser Bryce Harlow told Nixon's appointments secretary, Dwight Chapin, of the meeting request and that appointing women was an important issue. Harlow said the women were "glinty about it" and they rejected speaking with anyone below Nixon on the matter. They "now want to beard the President instead." Still, Harlow wrote "their concern is vibrant and real. I strongly recommend that they be given a visit with the President."[6]

No visit was scheduled and the women became much more confrontational. In another letter, they chastised the president for having done "absolutely nothing of significance in the field of women's rights, responsibilities and opportunities." They charged that Nixon was presiding over "a retreat from the inadequate action of past Administrations" and that "not a single important policy decision or legislative recommendation [regarding women] has been made." Familiar charges of inadequate appointment of women to positions of responsibility followed, along with the accusation that Nixon's officials had dodged the whole issue and that "several are known to be positively anti-woman." It was strong stuff coming from Republicans, at least as critical as similar letters coming at nearly the same time from black Democrats who criticized Nixon on race issues.[7] The letter demanded, predictably, more women appointments, new laws sent to Congress, elimination of sex discrimination in government, support for the ERA, and support for new day care centers for the children of working mothers.[8]

In a later meeting with Nixon, the four Republican women told Nixon that (in the words of aide Peter Flanigan in follow-up notes to the meeting), "the President [must] realize the importance of the appointment of women, particularly in a generation when so many are college graduates." Nixon should "send a Message on the importance of women in the affairs of the country." Nixon immediately promised to appoint Reid to the Federal Communications Commission after her term in Congress expired, and "urged the ladies" to help find other women who "could be groomed through service in the lower levels in the judiciary to eventual appointment to the Supreme Court."[9] Nixon then appointed Helen Bently as head of the Maritime Commission, and 125 other women received high-ranking posts. He also issued for women a largely symbolic Executive Order 11478, calling on federal departments and agencies to "establish and maintain an affirmative action program of equal employment opportunity for all civilian employees and applicants."[10]

The archival evidence suggests that by the late summer of 1969, most politicians in Washington, including Republican men, recognized the political benefits to being perceived as supporting women's equality. Nixon's advisers were urged on by a Democrat, Nixon's house intellectual, Daniel Patrick Moynihan. He had been observing the growing grassroots women's movement, and on August 20, Moynihan predicted that "female equality will be a major cultural/political force of the 1970s." The former professor told Nixon of the alienation of young, politically liberal women from the student Left and the black radicals. Moynihan felt that the core issues—involving the exclusion of women from "the 'serious' things of American life"—would "spread and make this an increasingly prominent demand across the entire political spectrum." Some women's advocates were predicting "violence" if denied equality. Significantly, Moynihan highlighted "the general absence of women from higher education in America," since "it is considered too important for them." He pointed out the absence of women on university faculties, and argued that "male dominance is so deeply a part of American life that males don't even notice it." Nixon should "take advantage of this" through appointments "but perhaps especially in your pronouncements. This is a subject ripe for creative political leadership and initiative."[11]

Various (white male) members of Nixon's domestic policy staff were unanimous in agreement. Political adviser and speechwriter Jim Keogh said, "I do thoroughly agree with the conclusion and recommendation that the President take every opportunity in word and deed to champion female equality." Peter Flanigan, another political aide, wrote facetiously that "as a member of the staff who has borne the brunt of women's attack, I am well aware of the increasing use of violence," and said he was trying to find women for appointments and "major news coverage of such appointments." Bryce Harlow said, "Politically, it's gold" but cautioned that "we don't appear to have such a program, nor is one suggested here." In chief domestic policy adviser John Ehrlichman's summary for Nixon, he said that "politically this is a golden opportunity and that we should, whenever possible, champion female equality."[12] The women's rights revolution had arrived.

But how to respond? The Labor Department at the time was still resisting equating women with blacks for affirmative-action regulations, as described in Chapter 4. The meaning of women's equality for Nixon's team was only that it was "political gold." It had no policy substance. The Nixon team's decision was to follow the GOP women's suggestion and appoint a President's Task Force on Women's Rights and Responsibilities.[13] Nixon officially announced the new body on October 1, 1969, just two days after reading Moynihan's memo.[14] Like Kennedy's President's Commission on the Status of Women (see Chapter 4), the Nixon task force gave positions of authority to women and set up an agenda for progressive policy development. In doing so, it pushed Nixon to the left and put pressure on his administration to follow up.

The task force, which included journalist Vera Glaser, finished its report on December 15. Modestly entitled *A Matter of Simple Justice,* it called for a permanent Office of Women's Rights and Responsibilities and a special White House conference on the topic. More important were the calls for new laws.

The report is notable for Title IX's development both because of its strong support for the ERA, which eased the way for Title IX, and for its specific call for an end to discrimination in education. While not advocating the amendment of the Civil Rights Act's Title VI, its first recommendations included passage of the ERA, expansion of the Civil Rights Act's Title VII to give greater power to the EEOC, and amendments of Titles IV and IX of that Act to order the Office of Education to make a survey of sex discrimination in education and to authorize the attorney general to pursue litigation where it is found.[15] *A Matter of Simple Justice* stated, "Discrimination in education is one of the most damaging injustices women suffer. It denies them equal education and equal employment opportunity, contributing to a second class self image."[16]

The premise of the entire report, not explicit but obvious, was that efforts to fight sex discrimination should be equal to those used against race discrimination. The section on new legislation called mostly for expanding laws aimed at ending race discrimination to include sex discrimination. A section on enforcement stated, "The executive branch of the Federal government should be as seriously concerned with sex discrimination as with race discrimination."[17] Another part of the report used statistical evidence to support the claim that "sex bias takes a greater economic toll than racial bias." For example, "women with some college education, both white and Negro, earn less than Negro men with 8 years of education."[18] Accordingly, the government should not give blacks a priority over women in fighting employment discrimination, manpower training programs, or in the collection of economic and social statistics.

Though increasingly supportive, the Nixon team's understanding of what amounted to justice for women was muddled and contradictory. They were uncomfortable with these recommendations and initially tried to suppress the report of the task force to buy time and consider their options. After the report's prompt submission, Arthur Burns, a Columbia University economist in charge of various domestic policy reports for Nixon and head of the Council of Economic Advisors, told task force chair Virginia Allan it had been dutifully "filed."[19] The report, however, was leaked to Glaser's newspaper, the *Miami Herald,* which published *A Matter of Simple Justice* in its entirety and even sold reprints in April of 1970. The administration then formally released it.

Avoiding the Perplexing Politics of Women's Equality

The main reason for Nixon's discomfort and delay in releasing the report was its prominent support for the ERA. Despite his endorsement of the amendment in his 1960 and 1968 campaigns, he was no longer sure of his support. By 1970, the ERA was already becoming a dominant women's issue.

Republican advocates for women, both within and outside the government, pressured Nixon to give support to the amendment. Patricia Hitt, the assistant secretary for community and field services at HEW and one of Nixon's advisers on women's issues, told Ehrlichman in April that increasing percentages of the total presidential vote were being cast by women but declining percentages of women were voting Republican (from 51 percent in 1960 to 43 percent in 1968). "With the rising popularity of the women's 'Liberation' groups, and the increasing feminine interest in politics, as indicated by the statistics, it bothers me to see the Democrats taking the lead on the Equal Rights Amendment," she commented. This was a problem because "they are going to get all the credit if this measure passes." She urged a message to Congress from Nixon on the ERA and the official publishing of the women's task force report.[20] Meanwhile, Gladys O'Donnell, president of the National Federation of Republican Women, lobbied the White House for full support of the amendment in hearings on the ERA set to begin in May 1970, in Senator Birch Bayh's (D–IN) Judiciary Subcommittee on Constitutional Amendments.[21]

Nixon struggled with the issue. It was one thing to support the ERA when passage was unlikely and another thing entirely to support it when it had a very good chance. Ehrlichman laid out for Nixon all the complexities in a decision memo, offering as options endorsement, opposition, endorsement of a modified amendment, and delayed decision. Ehrlichman himself was noncommittal, but seemed to lean toward Nixon's endorsing the amendment, mainly because Nixon had endorsed it in both 1960 and 1968. Further, his vice president and his wife were both on record as supporting the ERA. But there was also other support for the ERA in the Nixon White House. Despite his foot-dragging on affirmative action for women, Labor Secretary George Shultz was in favor of it. Pat Hitt supported it, and Jacqueline Gutwillig, chair of the (now marginalized) Citizen's Advisory Council on the Status of Women, testified to Bayh's committee her support of the amendment. Leonard Garment, a supporter of other minorities, was lukewarm. Ehrlichman listed only Assistant Attorney General William Rehnquist as being against the ERA among administration officials. Rehnquist hyperbolically predicted that the amendment would lead to "the sharp reduction in importance of the family unit, with the eventual elimination of that unit by no means improbable."[22]

The perceived political strength of women was growing, and many in the Nixon administration were worried about it. On July 31, 1970, Ehrlichman and Haldeman learned of Bayh's accusation that the administration was "dragging its heels" on issues of women's rights, failing to "give a plain endorsement" of the ERA.[23] Nixon was beginning to seem antiwomen, and it was a problem.

For a president unsure of the meaning of women's equality, meetings and chit-chat with women seemed a safe way to win their support. In July, several top domestic policy aides were all recommending a simple gesture: a small private dinner with women serving in the administration "to show your concern for the interest of women in serving in responsible positions in government and in making meaningful contributions to our society." This was to be part of a series in which Nixon was to "touch base" with various interest groups. In this case, he would meet with the top eight women in his administration. Even this was a matter of debate. The mostly unconcerned speechwriter, Patrick Buchanan, argued that "all we have to do is be as concerned with the women vote, and with keeping women happy as we are with keeping the blacks happy; and then just do what comes naturally." Political strategist Charles Colson sounded a tone of alarm, however, claiming that "we are missing an opportunity in this area as well as allowing a negative issue to develop . . . There is no single area which would be more responsive and would result in so many political pluses at so little cost." Rogers Morton, a representative from Maryland and chair of the Republican National Committee, exemplified the contradictory perceptions of women as a growing political power and, by his language, of women as less than serious. He argued that "we have been fighting pretty much of a losing battle on the subject of the recognition of women in this Administration . . . The top women's organizations are beginning to unite in their promotion of the Equal Rights Amendment, and they are beginning to believe that ONLY the Democrats are interested . . . The gals have a tremendous influence on the outcome of any election." Nixon rejected the plan, and asked his aides to "look for a better way."[24]

Rita Hauser tried Moynihan's memo-writing strategy to change White House politics. She first just wanted Nixon to talk differently. In March of 1970, Hauser explained to speechwriter William Safire the dynamics of what she called the "Feminine Revolution": "The growing interest of American women in attaining their place in the sun is part of this national and world revolution" for equal opportunities for all people "to realize their full potential and be granted the dignity of a fellow human being." While new women's groups had small memberships, she explained, there was great sympathy for their goals, as evidenced by reports in popular magazines. Hauser recommended that Safire have Nixon recognize this broad-based sympathy in his speeches.[25]

A year later, Hauser tried to make the point directly to the president while putting a conservative spin on women's rights. She described a new phenomenon she called "Emergent Responsible Feminism" that could be seen across the country. She urged Nixon to talk to women as equals, and recommended a "'rap session' with selected women of different walks of life, the express purpose of which would be for you to learn why they feel as they do on a key issue and what, generally, they are about." She suggested special focus on "sex discrimination in employment, housing and public places; review of tax laws affecting the widow, divorcee and working mother; job training programs; government personnel policies; prospects for government-sponsored day care centers for children; abortion reforms; compulsory national service for women." Though these were only topics for discussion (not action), Hauser claimed they would be "productive for the country and beneficial to us in 1972."[26]

While Hauser's idea of "rap sessions" was kiboshed (Colson, for one, said it "would look extremely contrived" and "it is not something the President could do comfortably and I do not think it could be done well"), the general thrust of Hauser's memo was taken seriously and well received. Fred Malek, helping direct Nixon's reelection campaign, called for a "well thought out, well coordinated and well executed program to deal with the major issues of concern to women," because "it's time—given the growing concern and restlessness of women across the country, plus the upcoming 1972 election—to deal with these issues in an integrated way."

The apparent anachronism was Harry Dent, architect of Nixon's "Southern Strategy" to win over the formerly Democratic southern states. He saw women in light of their traditionally understood roles, and questioned the national appeal of women's rights advocates. He suggested a meeting with "average women in America—Mrs. Middle America, Mrs. Housewife, Mrs. Secretary, Mrs. Nurse, Mrs. Teacher." He cautioned against meeting with too many leaders, because "I just don't think most women in the country care about the Women Lib movement or anything relating to that" and "if we get too far out front with this matter we may wind up with another long list of demands being made to liberate all the women in the country." Feminists would have to be balanced by "good, average women." Dent suggested programming the meeting's outcome: "It would be good to have some women come out of that meeting saying we don't favor the women's lib movement and that we think the Nixon Administration is doing a great job for all the people and that's how we wanted to be treated, just like anybody else."[27]

What was remarkable about this and other White House discussions was the ratio of talk and concern to substance. No one advocated a single specific policy. And no one knew what the majority of women really wanted.

The Nixon papers show a continuing apprehension and indecision regarding this stage of the minority rights revolution, but they also clearly show the perception of the growing importance of women's issues in an administration generally thought of as conservative. Knowledge of the women's movement was impressionistic; Moynihan told of some grassroots encounters, while Hauser described magazine articles. Dent's view of women and what they wanted was totally different. But the papers also show that an analogy with blacks did not automatically shape perceptions of wise policy. The Nixon team was not for any specific policy, but they knew it was bad politics to appear antiwomen.

Women's Equality in Congress: More Action Than Thought

In contrast to the Nixon administration, where there was so much discussion and so little action, Congress took action and sometimes discussed little. Members of Congress seemed to believe that women had great influence in elections and should be full participants in a minority rights revolution. Title VII had eliminated the old factional fighting about protective legislation, and thus the primary basis of labor unions' previous resistance. Women's advocates put up a unified front in Congress as they pressed for passage of the ERA. With the leadership of Martha Griffiths (D–MI) and other feminists in Congress, support also came from such official women's groups as the National Organization for Women (NOW) and its spin-off, the Women's Equity Action League (WEAL), their unofficial networks in congressional staffs and elsewhere in government, and other allied groups, such as Common Cause.[28] On August 10, 1970, the ERA passed the House by the lopsided margin of 350-15. That year, the Senate argued over possible amendments, such as restricting women's eligibility for military service. In March of 1971, the House again passed the ERA, this time with a 354-23 vote. The Senate then approved it, 84-8, on March 22, 1972.[29]

Meanwhile, as Nixon agonized about the ERA, he signed a steady stream of legislation from Congress for women's equality. The pro-ERA politics in Congress would be a factor in making it difficult for Nixon or anyone else to oppose other women's-rights legislation. If you accept the ERA, how could you object to other classically liberal antidiscrimination measures aimed at increasing equality of opportunity? Martha Griffiths told political scientist Jo Freeman in an interview, "The ERA created a moral climate for reform. Once it was put through, everything else became logical."[30] Or as Birch Bayh later put it, "Once you get by the ERA, Title IX is a piece of cake."[31] Though there was lobbying and pressure for the ERA, on other women's issues, anticipatory politics reigned supreme.

Congress in the early 1970s showed unprecedented friendliness toward women's rights, even before the ERA. As described in Chapter 4, twenty members of Congress responded to WEAL's request to pressure the Nixon administration to enforce nondiscrimination and affirmative action by government contractors for women at American universities. Representatives Griffiths, Edith Green (D–OR), Shirley Chisholm (D–NY), and Patsy Mink (D–HI) were all members of WEAL, and they pushed women's equality toward new frontiers. Title IX was just one of several laws passed. Lesser-known prohibitions of sex discrimination were enacted, such as those in the Comprehensive Health Manpower Training Act of 1971 and the Nurses Training Act of 1971 (reaching approximately fourteen hundred hospitals and academic institutions). The ambitious Child Development Act, vetoed by Nixon for "fiscal irresponsibility, administrative unworkability, and family weakening implications," was intended to provide free day care for low-income families. Nixon instead supported an amendment to the Revenue Act of 1971 that allowed tax deductions of up to four hundred dollars per month for child-care expenses for low-income families. In an explicit recognition of women as minorities analogous to blacks, and in a move strongly supported by the Nixon administration, Congress expanded the jurisdiction of the US Commission on Civil Rights to include sex discrimination. Congress also passed a law that equalized employment benefits for federal employees who were married women.[32]

Without urging, Representative Bella Abzug (D–NY) added prohibitions of sex discrimination as a matter of course to as many new bills as possible, including the Public Works, Economic Development, and Appalachian Redevelopment Act and the Water Pollution Act. These were the laws that passed Congress. In 1972, Abzug and Griffiths introduced about twenty other measures, including various abortion bills and laws relating to social security, credit, and minimum wages for domestic workers and others.[33] Abzug later recalled that "1972 was a watershed year. We put sex discrimination provisions into everything. There was no opposition. Who'd be against equal rights for women? So we just kept passing women's rights legislation."[34]

Congress was legislating without pressure to do so, and without analysis or debate on how laws would be implemented, or what was appropriate for women's equal rights. The difference between Congress's activity and the Nixon administration's talking-but-no-action approach was actually less than it appears. Both knew that appearing antiwomen was bad politics. In Congress, however, there were strong advocates for women to force the issue, and members of both parties went along with them.

From Title VI to Title IX: The Origins of Women's Equality in Education

Edith Green's First Effort in the House

Title IX's origins most clearly reach back two years before the "watershed" of 1972. In 1970, Edith Green sought to add an amendment prohibiting sex discrimination to a law to aid higher education, the Omnibus Post-Secondary Education Act of 1970. Green was concerned about differences in salary between male and female professors, complaints by constituents regarding sex discrimination, and the ways that athletic scholarships worked to make higher education more accessible to men than women.[35]

Green held hearings on the amendment, Section 805, before her Special Subcommittee on Education. She wanted to use black civil rights policy as a vehicle to bring equality to women in education. Section 805 would amend Title VI of the 1964 Civil Rights Act; the title would then bar discrimination in federally funded programs on the basis of race, national origin, religion, *and* sex. This would reach nearly all public schools and universities.

Section 805 did not pass, but the hearings provided an occasion for Green to attack the Nixon administration on its initial failure to extend affirmative action to women, as discussed in Chapter 4. The hearings were important also because they publicized the problem of women's inequality.[36] Two themes were distinctive. The first was the overwhelming statistical basis of the arguments for the legislation. The second was the analogy of women with blacks.

While the use of statistics to highlight a social problem is common in modern politics (for example, using drop-out rates of Latinos to show the need for bilingual education), the rise of statistics to prove discrimination was firmly established by civil-rights administrators and court rulings on black civil-rights issues.[37] This made mass mobilization of supporters for a particular piece of proposed legislation less important; the faceless numbers told their own story. Advocates for women used this statistical strategy to great effect.

While some witnesses cited specific discriminatory rules or actions (such as the University of North Carolina's restriction limiting freshman admissions to women "who are especially well qualified"),[38] numbers formed the great bulk of evidence of sex discrimination. Green started the hearings on Section 805 with her own statistics framed in the language of modernity—the progress of nations. The United States had a lower proportion of women in the professions than most developed countries throughout the world, and "while the United States prides itself in being a leader of nations, it has been backward in its treatment of its working women." Women made up "only 9 percent of full professors, 8 percent of all scientists, 6.7 percent of all physicians, 3.5 percent of all lawyers, and 1 percent of all engineers." Women were at the bottom of earnings rankings, as both black and white women ranked below even black men: black women made an average of $3,677, white women made $4,700, black men made $5,603, and white men were on top with $8,014—and the gap was widening.[39] Throughout the hearings, those testifying offered other statistics related to sex discrimination in general and especially in education. They could point to employment and ranking in the federal civil service, employment and ranking in specific government offices and departments, representation in foreign service peace delegations, employment rates and pay as elementary and secondary school teachers, recipients of Ph.D.s and professional degrees, participation in federal job training programs such as the Job Corps, and on and on. The statistical evidence of underrepresentation was massive, almost mind numbing in its breadth and consistency.

But was statistical disparity the same thing as serious injustice? To lead others to answer that question affirmatively took some persuasion. By far the most prevalent way of establishing the injustice of women's inequality was not reference to specific instances of crushed aspirations, but rather the analogy of women with blacks. The logic of the comparison was simple: if American majorities saw race discrimination as intolerable and worthy of legislation (as polls by then showed they did) and women were similar to blacks as victimized minorities, then any resistance to the bill was as morally reprehensible as racism. While nearly every page of the hearings contains a statistic of inequality, almost as frequent are reiterations of this other major theme—the comparison of women to American blacks.

Perhaps most prominent here are the statements of government officials. Edith Green, for example, pointed to political trends among blacks of voting polarization and increased militancy, and predicted the same for women unless action was taken.[40] African American congresswoman Shirley Chisholm argued that black and female stereotypes were very similar:

The happy little homemaker, the dumb blonde, the bubble-brained secretary, are the same kind of distorted pictures, drawn by prejudice, as those of the contented old darky and black mammy and little pickaninnies down on the old plantation.

Blacks and women have both been taught from childhood, because our society is run by and for white males, that they are inherently inferior. To keep them in their place, the same, the very same, characteristics are imputed to women as to blacks—that they are more childish, emotional, and irresponsible than men, that they are of lower intelligence, that they need protection, that they are happiest in routine, undemanding jobs, that they lack ambition and executive ability.

The parallels are striking and almost frightening, aren't they?[41]

The most eloquent advocate of the analogy between blacks and women was the talented Yale legal scholar Pauli Murray, a woman and African American. In her testimony, she pointed out that most observers "would have us believe that the struggle against racism is the No. 1 issue of human relations in the United States and must take priority over all other issues." But Murray disagreed: "The struggle against sexism is equally urgent."[42] Sex discrimination against women "is just as degrading, dehumanizing, immoral, unjust, indefensible, infuriating and capable of producing societal turmoil as discrimination because of one's race."[43] Murray did not maintain that the experiences were identical, but that they were parallel. For example, "although it is true that manifestations of racial prejudice have often been more brutal than the subtler manifestations of sex bias," women experienced "the psychic counterpart of violence," which is ridicule.[44] Green, who was white, cited her black colleague in the House to take the argument even further: "I talked to Shirley Chisholm yesterday and she tells me very emphatically that she has suffered far greater discrimination as a woman than she has suffered as a black."[45]

Nixon administration officials at the hearings supported the principle of the law, and only quibbled with its structure. On July 31, for example, the assistant attorney general Jerris Leonard was a lonely figure when he implied the analogy with blacks did not work. By emphasizing that all single-sex colleges, dorms, and gyms should be allowed, he stated that for women, but not blacks, separate-but-equal justice was still appropriate.[46] No one paid much attention.

Green's proposed amendment did not progress any further as it was crowded off the calendar by other legislation. And though the attendance at the hearings by members of the subcommittee was spotty, the basic idea of the bill clearly had support. Both Democrats and Republicans introduced several similar bills in 1971. The Republican proposals, such as one introduced by Representative Albert Quie (R–MN) and supported by the Nixon administration, differed from the Democrats' in allowing discrimination where sex was found to be a bona fide ground for differential treatment. Edith Green came up with a new version for 1971, differing from the 1970 version only in that it followed a suggestion of the Nixon administration to bar sex discrimination only in federally assisted education programs, rather than amend Title VI, as well as to exempt substantially single-sex and religious institutions.[47] While Green tinkered, similar support emerged in the Senate.

The Not-Very-Deep Analysis of Women's Rights in the All-Male Senate

Though there were no women in the Senate in August of 1971, Indiana Democrat Birch Bayh supported a bill that would become Title IX. Bayh was chair of the Senate Judiciary Committee, and had attracted much attention for his hearings on the ERA. He was personally committed to the issue of women's equality. In an interview years later, Bayh credited his interest in women's equality to his hardworking grandmother, who helped run the family farm, and his wife, who after years of life as a homemaker decided to put her education degree to good use and began teaching. While he initially resisted his wife's intentions, Bayh relented, and later recalled, "Her ability to do so many things gave me an insight and I became familiar with some of the limitations that were placed on women that had that kind of talent."[48]

Bayh's vehicle to promote women's rights in education was a package of education amendments being debated in the Senate in February 1971. In the introduction to his amendment, Bayh recited the discriminatory rules against women in admissions and the statistics showing disparities in graduate degrees granted and professorships held; he described the charges made by WEAL against hundreds of universities; and he made the various links between women and blacks—with a real kicker: blacks had been protected for nearly twenty years, if one considered the Supreme Court's decision in *Brown* to be protection. But women still had no protection at all. Bayh linked his amendment to the Nixon administration by citing Nixon's Task Force on Women's Rights and Responsibilities, pointing out that his amendment followed some of its recommendations.[49] He used a passage of the report of that task force implying that women might riot as had blacks: "We have witnessed a decade of rebellion during which black Americans fought for true equality . . . Nothing could demonstrate more dramatically the explosive potential of denying fulfillment as human beings to any segment of our society."[50] Bayh was quiet about any radical implications of his bill, though he later maintained he was well aware of how nondiscrimination in education would have a great impact on athletics.[51]

A day later, however, the effects of gender equality on athletics came up in Senate colloquy, but only in passing. Senator Peter Dominick (R–CO) did a little probing on the applicability of the amendment. He wondered whether the amendment required quotas for women, what effect it had on military schools, and if it affected segregated dorms or athletic facilities. Bayh's answers suggested his intent was to be reasonable. But he was also vague. There was nothing radical, nothing to fear, no quotas. And regarding athletics, Bayh explained:

> I do not read this as requiring integration of dormitories between the sexes, nor do I feel it mandates the desegregation of football fields. What we are trying to do is provide equal access for women and men students to the educational process and the extracurricular activities in a school, where there is not a unique facet such as football involved. We are not requiring that intercollegiate football be desegregated, nor that the men's locker room be desegregated.[52]

The senators were touching on an issue that was to become tremendously controversial, one that soon enveloped cherished moral standards and American cultural tradition and identity. It was an issue, in fact, of incredible complexity. Was football unique? How could nondiscrimination mean both integration and separate-but-equal? If nondiscrimination for women and nondiscrimination for blacks might be very different, should the Congress not spell out precisely how and why they differ? And would women's sports take money from men's sports? What about revenue-producing men's sports; should these be exempt?

Rather moving directly to explore these issues, it was time for another joke. Even in 1971, women's rights, it seemed, were one step from vaudeville. Senator Dominick stated, "If I may say so, I would have had much more fun playing college football if it had been integrated." Bayh's retort: "The Senator from Indiana will resist the temptation to remark further on that point."[53]

While this exchange would suggest that Bayh had in mind a bill containing certain exceptions, he also provided a contradictory message by stressing that the amendment had language specifically taken from Title VI of the 1964 Civil Rights Act. Of course, there were no exceptions for dormitories or football in race-discrimination cases. Congress intended Title VI to *end* a separate-but-equal policy for blacks and whites. No one noticed the contradiction.

While Dominick was skeptical, the strongest opposition came from Strom Thurmond. The South Carolina Republican did not argue against specific provisions of the bill, but complained simply of the overreach of federal power. In his view, the amendment would create a situation in which the federal government could tell the states how to run their education systems, and he was concerned about those states that wanted to maintain all-women colleges. Bayh's response seemed to reinforce only the confusion with Title VI: "This is giving the Federal Government the same power—no more, no less— to prevent discrimination on the basis of sex that the Federal Government now has to prevent discrimination on the basis of race." At this point, with Thurmond envisioning a federal takeover and Bayh seeing only an adjustment to current race-discrimination law, Senate chair and Nevada Democrat Walter Cannon ruled that the sex-discrimination amendment was not germane to the bill under consideration, and was sustained with a 50-32 vote.[54]

"Don't Lobby for This Bill": The Final Steps to Passage

Edith Green tried again in the House, this time with better luck. Though Green and other House advocates for women were members of WEAL, they asked women's groups not to lobby on the issue. Bernice Sandler later recalled

> Mrs. Green's advice was: "Don't lobby for this bill." She was absolutely right. She said: "If you lobby, people are going to oppose it. Leave it. The opposition is not there right now so don't call attention to it." We knew it was going to cover athletics; it was not a surprise. We just didn't tell many people.[55]

At the first hurdle, the Special Subcommittee on Education, there was some resistance from Republicans. Nearly all of it was related to admissions policies of colleges (at the strong urging of several Ivy League institutions), and not to internal activities such as intercollegiate athletics.[56] Female congressional staff members and WEAL members Mink and Chisolm fought these changes,[57] but the House added an amendment by Illinois Republican John Erlenborn to exempt admissions policies of undergraduate institutions. The House sent the whole bill back to the Senate for consideration with what was then Title IX of the Education Amendments.[58]

When the Senate version of the entire bill came up for consideration before the full Senate in February of 1972, it lacked a sex-discrimination provision. Bayh stepped forward again with his proposal, now without such lonely support. He cited help from Senators Claiborne Pell (D–RI), Harrison Williams (D–NJ), and Jacob Javits (R–NY), as well as the Ford Foundation's "Report on Higher Education," declaring that "'discrimination against women, in contrast to that against minorities, is still overt and socially acceptable within the academic community.'"[59]

Bayh expressed concern about stereotypes that women were unwilling to work, and that colleges therefore should not waste admissions space on women. He pointed out that 70 percent of female college graduates secured jobs, and presented more statistics showing women's underrepresentation in academe.[60] This time, Bayh was more specific on exceptions, and brought up athletics in a discussion of implementing regulations to be issued by the federal government: "These regulations would allow enforcing agencies to permit differential treatment by sex only—very unusual cases where such treatment is absolutely necessary to the success of the program—such as in classes for pregnant girls or emotionally disturbed students, in sports facilities or other instances where privacy must be preserved."[61] He did not explain where and why privacy overrode nondiscrimination. Bayh again frequently cited *A Matter of Simple Justice*, produced by the Nixon task force, daring the Republicans to refute an official voice of the Republican administration.

There would be no more public statements on the meaning of women's equality in education until after the bill's passage. Bayh had his version attached to the Senate education amendments bill. A hybrid of the House and Senate versions became Title IX.

On May 22 and June 8, the Senate and House, respectively, passed the Education Amendments of 1972, a hodgepodge of provisions on a variety of education subjects, without protracted debate.[62] The key provision in Title IX stated innocuously that "[n]o person . . . shall, on the basis of sex, be excluded from participation in, be denied the benefits of, or be subjected to discrimination under any education program or activity receiving Federal financial assistance."[63] In addition, Title IX exempted military schools; exempted admissions policies of private undergraduate colleges, nonvocational elementary and secondary schools, and traditionally single-sex public undergraduate colleges; allowed a seven-year exemption for those institutions making a transition to coeducational learning; barred any preferential treatment on the basis of sex; and allowed for institutions to maintain separate living facilities on the basis of sex.

No one was thinking about football. In fact, Title IX was completely ignored during the final stages of passage. Its sweeping prohibition of sex discrimination in education slipped in without opposition, and without outside lobbying.[64] This was in part because Title IX benefited in an indirect way from the legacies of the black civil rights movement. The controversy over busing to achieve black and white school integration ran interference for Title IX, attracting attention to itself while lowering Title IX's visibility.

It is tempting to say that Title IX's low visibility was a major factor in its passage, but its superficial appropriateness was more important. Even during the minority rights revolution, if something did not look right, it was caught. As shown in Chapter 9, an extremely obscure Labor Department regulation for affirmative action for white ethnics was stopped dead in its tracks. Furthermore, the Nixon administration supported the principle behind Title IX, as evidenced by the support given at Edith Green's 1970 hearings. But it is also true that Nixon almost certainly never thought deeply about what Title IX would mean, and later called it a "monstrosity."[65] Still, the Nixon team was clearly distracted by aspects of the Education Amendments of 1972 having to do with busing of black and white school children to achieve racial integration. Nixon's June 23 signing statement does not mention women's rights at all. He lauded the bill's financial aid program for college loans and grants and the establishment of a new National Institute of Education within HEW for research on compensatory efforts for more equality in education. The bulk of his statement regarded the bill's "inadequate, misleading and entirely unsatisfactory" antibusing provisions. Nixon wanted restrictions, standards, and uniformity in court-ordered busing, but he believed Congress only offered rhetoric. He complained, "not in the course of this administration has there been a more manifest congressional retreat from an urgent call for responsibility."[66] But he was not referring to the complete lack of exploration of the meaning of women's equality in education. Like so many aspects of the minority rights revolution, in the case of women's equality in education, the revolution took place while no one was watching.

Preserving the Law: The Discovery of Difference

Title IX would have little impact until there were regulations stating what forbidding sex discrimination in education meant. It was during this process that the analogy with blacks faltered.

The Office for Civil Rights (OCR) had the unfortunate task of tracing out the radical implications of women's equality in education. When lawmakers discussed the law, especially in the Senate, the discussion seemed to assume that yes, there were exceptions, but that no, there were not very many. Nondiscrimination toward women on its face was a wonderful idea. And the black analogy seemed to work well superficially. But as OCR bureaucrats sat down and began to think about what guidelines for this simple idea might look like, paralysis set in. Outside of admissions policies, the legislative history of Title IX offered almost no guidance at all.

This was not a problem for language rights, though these were *never* considered in debates on the Civil Rights Act. The confidence and moral certainty that OCR exhibited on accommodation of language rights for Latinos was totally lacking in the matter of women's equality. Bureaucracies regularly pursue legitimacy based on cultural standards of supporting constituencies.[67] In looking for a direction to go, however, the OCR's first step always seemed to be squarely on a landmine.

Meeting (with Everyone) and Deciding (Nothing)

In July, 1972, OCR officials met to discuss Title IX regulations. Without any clear idea of what the regulations would entail, they decided to notify all education institutions under coverage of the new law. It was a legal notification, a warning, but it was also a cry for help. The memo, sent in August, said nothing about OCR's plans. It only contained the vague language of the statute.[68]

The memo served as the basis for meetings with more than fifty interested parties. This was similar to the quasicorporatism in writing the language-rights guidelines, but there was an important difference. With language rights, only Latino leaders and supporters of bilingual education were invited to take part. For women's rights, HEW and OCR officials met with national organizations representing a wide variety of interests such as professional education associations, school officials, student groups, athletic associations, and others. HEW also participated in a conference organized by various interested parties, including women's groups, athletic directors and coaches, and groups representing other educational professionals.

In addition, Nixon's new secretary of HEW, Caspar Weinberger, also met with a variety of representatives from groups including the NCAA, the Association of Intercollegiate Athletics for Women (AIAW), some women's groups, and university representatives.[69] These meetings achieved little progress. Weinberger later complained to a House education subcommittee of how hard it was to interpret congressional intent: "We have had conflicting suggestions from various authors of the bill."[70] It was "extraordinarily difficult, first, to interpret the intent of Congress and, second, to accommodate the concerns of a wide diversity of interest groups and individuals."[71]

In fact, OCR spent *two years* trying to determine what sex nondiscrimination in education meant. They got an early start, OCR official Peter Holmes later recalled, beginning to draft regulations in the fall of 1972 after all of those meetings with the various interested groups. But they continued, unsuccessfully, to look for suggestions from those groups on how to write the regulations.[72] They did not produce regulations for two years because "it simply took us that long to address many of the policy issues and other questions that we think arose and to draft the regulations."[73]

NOW was outraged at what they took to be HEW and OCR's plodding, cautious approach to women's rights. NOW's Project on Equal Education Rights (PEER) concluded a report on Title IX with a notion that HEW and OCR would not dispute: "The government has had a terrible time making decisions about Title IX and how it applies." However, PEER dismissed HEW's claims of being understaffed and underbudgeted, and instead put the blame on the bureaucrats themselves. PEER saw the lack of progress as the result of HEW and OCR's unfortunate placement at the center of the storm over the busing controversy. In this interpretation, black civil rights *hurt* women's rights, and "Title IX appeared likely to be a further source of trouble and dissension, and the agency's response was to slow everything down."[74] If this was true, it was a sharp contrast with OCR's role in the effort to secure language rights for Latinos, where Leon Panetta described the office's determination to "get ahead of the curve" on language rights (which Panetta saw as "less of a political hot potato") to avoid future trouble (see Chapter 7).

PEER's interviews with HEW staff also turned up another, familiar explanation: women's rights were not considered important. One insider reported that "not many [HEW] people see the urgency of sex discrimination." Another reported that "it's not respectable to work on Title IX in the agency."[75] While there were efforts to promote the importance of women's inequality and the analogy between women and blacks, it was true that OCR and HEW showed more concern for blacks and Latinos than for women.[76]

"I Agree with You about the Inherent Absurdity": Writing Regulations

In November of 1972, HEW's general counsel office circulated around the department and the White House a first draft of Title IX guidelines. They were vague modifications of the race-discrimination guidelines in Title VI. Since the main provision of Title IX was based on—indeed, almost identical to—Title VI, it seemed most logical to look at Title VI race-discrimination legal and administrative rulings to explain to the oblivious educational community what equal rights for women entailed. Yet reviews were very negative. Both other HEW offices and White House staff said the guidelines needed to be more specific. OCR's tiny legal staff began revisions. Weeks, and then months, and then more than a year passed.[77]

In June of 1973, as the Nixon administration increasingly became preoccupied with the Watergate scandal, the difficult issues surrounding sex discrimination finally began to bubble up from the writers of regulations to Secretary Weinberger. OCR staff sent Weinberger a memo presenting him with a series of issues in which the analogy between women and blacks did not seem to hold up. These included segregation in sports and physical education classes, personal privacy (restrooms, showers, and classes for sex hygiene), and the use of school facilities by private associations or clubs that practice sex discrimination, such as fraternities or boys or girls clubs. These issues had little clear legislative history, but the statute itself as well as Title VI precedents on race were quite clear. In Title VI, there was no tolerance for racially segregated sports, restrooms, classes, or use of school property by whites-only groups.

Weinberger tried to walk a blurry, middle line on the issues. He explained to his staff that women should have an equal opportunity to compete in sports. This would mean allowing women to try out for a place on teams in noncontact sports, but that the failure of females to make the team would not impose a duty on the school to establish a woman's team. Weinberger specifically stated that men-only football teams were not in violation of Title IX, but *also* said that physical education classes or sex education classes should be integrated—here, an act of Congress was needed for exemption. On the issue of the use of school facilities by private clubs, Weinberger took a conservative line. He told the OCR that a race-discrimination approach did not have to be followed. Simply allowing a group to use an auditorium was not supporting that group, so a narrower definition of "support" was required.[78]

Though it is not clear exactly when it started, a fierce lobbying campaign ensued, apparently as details of the proposed regulations began to leak. Suddenly, the opposition that was nonexistent during the law's passage and that HEW itself had alerted with its 1972 meetings began to weigh in assertively, putting pressure on members of Congress to urge Weinberger to issue regulations much more constrained than the letter of the law. Others pushed from the opposite direction. Weinberger's correspondence files for 1974 are stuffed with letters demanding that Title IX be interpreted broadly and narrowly. Much of the discussion was on athletics. For example, in March, Nixon's liaison to women, Anne Armstrong, sent Weinberger a memo with attached letters from women at Pennsylvania State University. They demanded that nondiscrimination in athletics be included in the regulations. Weinberger told Armstrong wearily, "There has been a great deal of comment, much of it from women college athletic instructors, urging the Department to retain an athletics section in the draft regulations. On the other side, male college athletic directors have commented in support of the National College Athletics Association position that the section should not be included."[79]

Some members of Congress sought to amend the law themselves. Though Republican senator John Tower was a co-sponsor of the Bilingual Education Act, he did not see similar electoral fortunes from support for women's rights, especially in his home state of Texas where football is a celebrated part of regional culture. So in May 1974, Tower proposed an amendment to Title IX as part of a new Education Amendments bill. His proposal stated Title IX should not apply to an intercollegiate athletic activity "to the extent that such activity does or may provide gross receipts or donations to the institution necessary to support that activity." He argued that Congress never intended to regulate athletics. Regulations that made all sports equal would mean that Title IX "would have thrown out the baby with the bath water." Tower's amendment primarily applied to football and basketball, but it could apply to other sports at different schools.

Tower's effort also came with a sign that resistance to and ridicule for women's equality was becoming anachronistic—Tower sold his amendment as *supporting* the women's-rights revolution. He declared that "the women in our colleges and universities have as great a stake in a strong financial base for their individual school's sports programs as do the men." Tower continued:

> I want to emphasize that one of the prime reasons for my wanting to preserve the revenue base of intercollegiate activities is that it will provide the resources for expanding women's activities in intercollegiate sports. I have a vested interest because I have a daughter who is a potential varsity tennis player, and I would like to see that she gets the opportunity.

The Senate adopted Tower's amendment by voice vote.[80] The House, however, did not pass a similar amendment.

In July, women's groups heavily lobbied the Conference Committee against Tower's amendment, and succeeded in replacing Tower's strong language with a compromise amendment suggested by women's advocate Jacob Javits. The New York Republican proposed that HEW have thirty days to publish regulations "which shall include with respect to intercollegiate athletic activities reasonable provisions considering the nature of particular sports." In addition, owing to the general political climate of suspicion between the Democrat-controlled Congress and the Nixon administration, created in part by the busing controversy, the 1974 Education Amendments contained a section that allowed greater congressional oversight.[81] Congress would have a forty-five-day window to disapprove HEW education guidelines by concurrent resolution.[82]

Meanwhile, OCR finally released for public comment the Title IX guidelines. With the few exceptions stated in the law, admissions were covered. OCR told vocational, professional, graduate and public undergraduate schools they must make equal recruitment efforts for male and female students. All employment opportunities and all aspects of educational employment, such as benefits, were to be equalized. Students were to be treated equally once admitted. This would mean, obviously, equal athletic opportunities.[83]

At a press conference, Weinberger announced that the time allotted for public comment would be quadrupled from one month to four. In response to repeated press questions, he quipped that college sports must be "the most important subject in the United States today." Queried also about the guidelines for sex education, where Weinberger uncharacteristically had ruled that they should not be segregated, the secretary became flustered, and soon changed his ruling. He ordered the guidelines be revised; coeducational sex education classes, Weinberger learned, invaded privacy and were inappropriate.[84]

HEW received an overwhelming response to the proposed regulations—more than nine thousand written comments rather than the usual handful.[85] Secretary Weinberger decided yet more meetings and consultations were needed. In the summer of 1974, HEW arranged public and press briefings on the regulations in Portland, Pittsburgh, Milwaukee, Boston, New York, Salt Lake City, Omaha, Houston, Atlanta, St. Louis, Miami, and Los Angeles. The briefings generated attention: 175 newspaper articles, plus fifteen editorials supporting the regulations, eleven that were opposed, and seven that were mixed or only offered summaries of the proposed guidelines.[86]

Congress's role was far from over. Lawmakers attempted to amend the law, though not by voting on a new provision to clarify their sloppy work. They instead hassled HEW, whose response was usually the same: HEW could not make exceptions to Congress's "no sex discrimination" law unless Congress did so. On August 16, for example, Weinberger responded to a letter from Representative Robin Beard (R–TN) on conflicts between Title IX and the hallowed tradition of exclusive collegiate fraternities and sororities. "I agree with you about the inherent absurdity of requiring fraternities and sororities to offer membership without sex discrimination," Weinberger explained. "But the law which we are required to implement does require such a result if the fraternity or sorority benefits substantially from funds, etc., donated by a college receiving Federal funds."[87] Athletics was the dominant issue, however. Four days later, Weinberger's deputy, Frank Carlucci, told Senator William L. Scott (R–VA) that the letter of Congress's law "required us to include athletics in the programs covered by Title IX. If athletics are to be exempted from Title IX, our General Counsel has advised me it will take an Act of Congress. Meanwhile we believe we have dealt with that in the least oppressive way possible consistent with the law."[88]

In September, Weinberger tried to justify equal athletic opportunities to Senator Wallace F. Bennett (R–UT), explaining that although "the proposed regulation expressly provides that equal aggregate expenditures for members of each sex are not required, . . . [w]here athletic opportunities for students of one sex have been limited, an institution must make affirmative efforts to inform members of that sex of the availability of equal opportunities and to provide support and training to enable them to participate." This was apparently HEW's attempted compromise: "[T]he Department has received a number of comments on the athletics section of the proposed regulation and they seem evenly divided between concerns that the section goes too far and other that is does not go far enough in assuring equal athletic opportunities for girls and women."[89]

Eventually, the lawmakers got the hint: they could not force HEW to violate blatantly the letter of their own law, at least not while women's advocates were watching closely. They would have to change the law. By the winter of 1974, some members of Congress were proposing new amendments for seemingly reasonable exemptions to Title IX as part of an effort to soften the radicalism of women's equality. In December, Birch Bayh himself joined in on the action. In what was apparently a preemptive move, he sponsored an amendment to exempt college fraternities and sororities from Title IX coverage (though professional fraternities were not exempted), as well as youth service organizations (such as Boy Scouts) for individuals younger than nineteen. The amendment passed in December of 1974.[90] A more serious effort came from Representative Marjorie Holt (R–MD), whose proposed amendment would have ended HEW's enforcement of both Title IX and its parent, Title VI, by barring HEW from gathering information on sex and race discrimination in schools. Holt's effort failed despite surprising support from Edith Green, who had become disillusioned with HEW's enforcement strategy.[91]

Three years after Congress passed Title IX, there were implementing regulations. In February 1975, Secretary Weinberger sent the "final" regulations and an explanatory memo to the new president Gerald Ford, who signed them on May 27, 1975. No one liked them. Women's groups called the rules "ineffective." Representatives of college sports said they were "destructive."[92] And the regulations still had to be approved by Congress. Weinberger did not help matters: he stoked the resentment of women by stating at a news conference that he did not believe that sex discrimination was as much of a problem as race or national-origin discrimination.[93]

The 1975 Regulations

The Title IX regulations were exceedingly long and detailed. Regulations for higher education were issued separately, and there was an array of exceptions and delays put in for various institutions, such as religious, military, or traditionally sex-segregated schools. Fraternities and sororities exempt from taxation were also exempt from Title IX, as were traditionally sex-segregated voluntary youth service organizations such as the Young Men's Christian Association, the Young Women's Christian Association, and the Girl and Boy Scouts.

The regulations required nonexempt educational institutions receiving federal funds to implement and publicize a policy of sex nondiscrimination. They could no longer treat student applicants differently on the basis of sex. They could not discriminate on the basis of pregnancy or childbirth- or pregnancy-related conditions. Nor could they make inquiries into marital status. Sex discrimination in all aspects of employment was forbidden, including recruitment, compensation, and benefits. In their programs and activities made available to students, educational institutions could not discriminate on the basis of sex in housing, facilities, access to courses, schools, counseling, financial assistance, employment assistance, health and insurance benefits and services, and—athletics.

On the troublesome matter of sports the regulations stated that "no persons shall, on the basis of sex, be excluded from participation in, be denied the benefits of, be treated differently from another person or otherwise be discriminated against in any interscholastic, intercollegiate, club or intramural athletics offered by recipient [of federal funds], and no recipient shall provide any such athletics separately on such basis."[94] In order to determine whether a recipient of federal funds was offering equal opportunity, the government would examine

> whether the selection of sports and levels of competition effectively accommodate the interests and abilities of members of both sexes; the provision of equipment and supplies; scheduling of games and practice time; travel and per diem allowance; opportunity to receive coaching and academic tutoring; assignment and compensation of coaches and tutors; provision of locker rooms, practice and competitive facilities; provision of medical and training facilities and services; provision of housing and dining facilities and services; and publicity.[95]

There was a statement that simultaneously sounded like threatening doubletalk to college athletics coaches and administrators, but seemed more of a pathetic retreat to women's rights advocates. The regulations also stated, "Unequal aggregate expenditures for member of each sex or unequal expenditures for male and female teams if a recipient operates or sponsors separate teams will not constitute non-compliance with this section, but the [OCR] Director may consider the failure to provide necessary funds for teams for one sex in assessing equality of opportunity for member of each sex."[96] In other words, universities did not *have* to spend equal money on women's and men's athletics. But if they did not, they might be in big trouble. This, of course, was how affirmative-action regulations worked: firms did not have to employ certain percentages of minorities, but failure to do so could be used against them.[97]

The premise underlying the entire Title IX regulations was that women were a minority like blacks, and discrimination against them was intolerable. But another premise was that they were different from blacks—witness, for example, the acceptance of separate-but-equal athletic opportunities. The regulations spelled out that separate teams were acceptable "where selection for such teams is based upon competitive skill or the activity involved is a contact sport." On the other hand, if there was only one team, both sexes must be able to try out "unless the sport is a contact sport." These included "boxing, wrestling, rugby, ice hockey, football, basketball and other sports the . . . major activity of which involves bodily contact."[98] In short, football teams could exclude women. There would be no female linebackers or wide receivers in the Big 10 Conference or elsewhere. But universities and schools would still have to make efforts to equalize opportunities in other sports. They would have to spend more money. Or they could cut some men's programs.

This was still a problem for football. In the final round of congressional hearings on the regulations, Darrell Royal, president of the American Football Coaches Association and coach at the University of Texas, and Tom Osborne, coach at the University of Nebraska, expressed their concern. Football teams were often celebrated parts of campus, state, and national culture. But the teams were large and their needs for equipment extensive. The use of expenditures as a measure of gender equality thus put this male-only sport in an ambiguous position. Football cost a lot. Including football in the calculation of expenditures would grossly skew the accounting ledger toward male sports, and equalization would require male sports that were not self-supporting to be dropped. But, the coaches insisted, football also *made* a lot of money. For this reason, they argued it should be excluded from the federal government's reach. Football was self-supporting and did not require federal funds. Those supporting the coaches' side were able to buttress their effort with quotations from Edith Green, who had made an astonishing turnabout. In November 1974, Green maintained that activities funded by tuition fees or tax dollars must not discriminate, "but intercollegiate sports financed by gate receipts is an entirely different matter and was not covered by Title IX."[99]

Defenders of the regulations, who by then included the previously critical women's groups, were in a better position. They were defending what had already been enacted and were trying to prevent further action, which is always easier than mobilizing forces of change. Leading the defense were Shirley Chisholm, Norma Raffel, a former president of WEAL and then head of WEAL's education committee, Bernice Sandler, then the director of the Project on the Status and Education of Women for the Association of American Colleges (and stalwart promoter of affirmative action for women), as well as Birch Bayh. They emphasized the black analogy, arguing that the race-discrimination guidelines had no exceptions similar to what the coaches were seeking. This was a weak argument that ignored the separate-but-equal pro-

visions in the law, such as the contact-sports exemption. These had no coun-
terparts in race-discrimination law—a fact noted by Albert Quie in the hearings.[100] More technically, Bayh dismissed the assertion that no direct money
went to some sports, because "if Federal aid benefits a discriminatory program by freeing funds for that program, the aid assists it, and I think that is
rather clear."[101]

Pointing out that female students were victims of second-class treatment,
regulation supporters also dismissed concerns about how gender equality
would affect funding of men's sports. Costs did not matter if one only had
faith that all would work out fine. Bayh said, "I would hope that a nation that
is as powerful and ingenious as ours, which has been able to perform miracles
in technology and science, ought to be able to let little girls and little boys
have equal opportunity to develop their athletic and physical talents without
destroying the major athletic events that we all enjoy."[102] Raffel waved off a
question about how funding would work, saying she really had no clear idea,
but that any money for sports should be distributed more equally. She called
for educational officials to "just do better sharing the facilities, and less inor-
dinate use of money for fancy uniforms and things like that."[103]

The coaches continued to lobby Congress for new amendments. They
even recruited University of Michigan coach Bo Schembechler in July of
1975 to lobby President Ford, who had played football at Michigan.[104] These
efforts failed to bring about any significant change. The mixed bag that was
women's equality in education—equal treatment, integration, and separate-
but-equal—had the force of law.

Conclusion

Without the prior development of black civil-rights protections, there would
be no Title IX. Black civil rights policy legitimated targeting policy at minorities, it provided a model for political strategy when seeking group support,
and it removed obstacles that had kept the women's movement divided. It
even provided a distraction to deflect attention from the perceived outra-
geousness of Title IX—the nation's agony over busing.

The politics of Title IX in Congress were similar to the "anticipatory politics" of minority capitalism and bilingual education. While many in Congress
and the White House were quite aware of a developing women's movement
and a change in the political and moral landscape, they had no evidence of a
groundswell of support for Title IX. There was no mass mobilization for the
law and—by design—no lobbying. Some members of Congress almost certainly knew what they were doing in enacting Title IX—they were members
of the women's group WEAL and at least one other, Birch Bayh, was strongly

committed to the cause. But other members of Congress who voted for Title IX appear not to have had a clear idea of what it would mean. Nixon recognized the importance of women as possible voters, but had no idea what that should mean in terms of policy. Politicians supported Title IX or at least did not oppose it because it had a surface plausibility and because they anticipated women would appreciate it and reward them for it.[105] As the ERA debate later showed (and Nixon's adviser Harry Dent correctly anticipated), many women opposed the goals of NOW and WEAL and later actively mobilized against them.[106] Such antirights countermobilization had no equal among any of the other minority groups.

The administrative politics of Title IX were completely different from the legislative politics. The contrast with the Latino cases are obvious. Affirmative action for Latinos developed with no resistance whatsoever. Bilingual education moved easily through Congress, and language rights developed quickly at OCR. The writing of language-rights regulations also was a smooth process, and almost immediately settled on bilingual and bicultural education as the basic goal. Federal bureaucrats simply met with Latino activists and educators, and wrote the strongest possible regulations. They did not meet with those who would have to pay for or bear the brunt of the new regulations, such as school districts or teachers' unions. Implementing women's equality in education reprised the pattern of employment civil rights and affirmative action for women at the EEOC and the Labor Department's OFCC. Unlike the Latino affirmative-action and bilingual-education cases, for women's rights there was a common practice of consulting with potential enemies of strong regulations. The EEOC and OFCC had continually met with groups hostile to women's equality before making rulings. Though Title IX had moved easily through Congress, at OCR and HEW it stalled. The boldness and confidence exhibited on language rights evaporated, and the regulation process was slowed by the perceived need to meet with all possible interested parties.[107] The three-year process of writing regulations involved much handwringing primarily because policymakers saw different meanings in women as a minority. When actual resources were at stake and they had to take a hard look at the black analogy, the analogy failed and policy went in different directions.

Did the difference in treatment of women as compared to Latinos have its basis in the fact that women were a larger group and their equality would have a more disruptive impact on society? This seemed to be a concern with the Labor Department's hesitancy to bring women within the ambit of its affirmative-action guidelines, and might explain why HEW was more circumspect with women than with Latinos, inviting interested parties to lobby against strong regulations. This factor may be relevant in some cases, but it ignores the massive disruption that was promised by some of the language-rights guidelines. These required complete reevaluations and sometimes transformations of schools, imposing significant burdens on existing staff and creating demands for new staff—all for children most of whose parents presumably *chose* to come to the United States. One of the first districts targeted was New York City—certainly a formidable adversary. And it is hard to argue that the Latino advocacy groups were stronger, better financed, or better organized that the women's groups. It seems clear that a cognitive failure of the analogy between women and blacks had its own effects, creating fear, indecision, or lack of concern.

This is made clearer when we recognize that Title IX implementation would not be the only instance when a hard look caused the analogy to fail. It failed also in the courts, even though judges are protected from political retribution. In the high stakes matter of Supreme Court constitutional law, where any change would require either a constitutional amendment or a new Court majority, the justices have had to take close looks of just this kind and their rulings have not equated women with blacks. This can be seen in the differing standards used in judicial review of laws making racial classifications and those making sex classifications. For racial classifications, the standard of strict scrutiny applies, where laws must be shown to be necessary and narrowly tailored to achieve a compelling government interest. It is rare for laws making these "suspect classifications" to pass this test. During the early and mid-1970s, the Court reviewed some sex classifications and apparently settled on a lesser standard of review for these "semisuspect" classifications. In the 1976 case *Craig v. Boren,* the Court established a legal rule that still governs sex classifications: they must be "substantially related" to an "important" government purpose. The terms are vague, but this standard would clearly allow more classifications than the strict scrutiny standard—and shows that in this important arena, the Court has *not* bought into the women–blacks analogy.[108]

Another revealing manifestation of the difference in perceived meaning between women and the other minorities was the joking manner that appeared time and again during discussions of women's rights and women's political activities. If policymakers were reluctant to push for women's rights because the impact would be too large, this sounds like a serious matter. Why, then, were women's rights so funny? The ridicule they received was a constant during the period, and the perceived hilarity of the topic and cuteness (for lack of a better word) of women in politics were significant barriers to women's advocates. No other group in this study faced such ridicule.

The historical record best preserves Nixon's transgressions. At a nationally televised news conference on June 1, 1971, Marianne Means of Hearst

Newspapers pointed out to Nixon that only 150 of the top 10,000 supervisory posts were women, and asked, "What are your goals for bringing more qualified women into Government and promoting them, and how do you personally feel about women's liberation?" Before describing the administration's efforts to bring women into government, Nixon's first response was to exclaim, "After that question, I am not going to comment upon women's liberation!"[109] The following day, there were two responses to Nixon's joking dismissal. Means herself wrote Nixon's press secretary, Ronald Ziegler, saying, "I was disappointed that he chose not to give a serious answer to a serious question about a serious social and economic development—i.e. women's liberation. Most well-educated women I know believe the President to be an old-fashioned advocate of woman's place is in the kitchen. I was hoping he would say it isn't so." Means wanted to do an interview with Nixon to dispel the bad image, but Ziegler brushed her off, saying only that the idea would remain "under active consideration."[110] The same day, a poignant note was sent to Nixon by Louella McCann, a HEW employee in the Office of Education. She told the president:

> As I usually do, I watched your press conference last evening. I am not normally moved to write letters to politicians, organizations, causes, etc. However, I feel I must express myself on one aspect of your conference last evening, and that is with respect to the question and answer regarding employment of women. It greatly disturbs me that this matter always seems to provoke laughter. If you were a woman, as I am, and if you were working to support yourself, as I am, it would not be quite so amusing.
>
> Let me emphasize that I do not now, nor do I intend to join the "Women's Lib" movement. I am proud of my femininity and will maintain it regardless of the cost. However, I feel very strongly about the rights of equal employment for women.[111]

Nixon's team would not learn. Of course, it was safer to ridicule women in front of predominately male audiences, as Nixon did at an August 5, 1971 meeting with the Cabinet Committee on Opportunities for Spanish-speaking Americans. Minutes of that meeting indicate that Nixon said, "We are making progress—I understand that the women are now a minority (laughter)." Later in the same meeting, Nixon played it straight, listing women along with blacks and Mexican Americans in a list of "all minority groups."[112] But jokes continued to be acceptable even in front of female audiences. In the prepared speech for Nixon's address to the National Federation of Republican Women, Nixon was to begin,

I note that I am the only male on this platform. Were it not for the fact that all 25 of these lovely ladies are good Republicans, I might feel threatened at this show of numbers and strength. You remember, I am sure, the story of the reporter who interviewed Winston Churchill, and asked him, 'What do you say, Sir, to the prediction that in the year 2000 women will be ruling the world?' To which the Prime Minister is said to have replied, 'They still will, eh?'"[113]

The essence of this humor was usually clear enough: the incongruity between the standard understanding of women and the notion that they had or could skillfully wield political power.[114] Precisely why only women were the targets of these jokes is not so obvious. The notion of blacks having political power would have offered a potentially humorous incongruity, but no political leaders made fun of blacks to their faces or made jokes about blacks with power. Of course, the typical Euro-American male lawmaker was more familiar with women, possibly having lived with a mother, sisters, spouse, and daughters. But they were also likely very familiar with a disabled person, especially a grandparent, yet it is harder to find examples of jokes about the disabled. The hilarity of women's rights was likely based in the perception that women's problems were not serious.

Whatever the reason, it was unique to women, and apparently part of some preconscious meanings informing politicians' thinking whenever they discussed women's issues. Those perceived meanings not only shaped boundaries of appropriateness regarding jokes. They guided the boundaries of the appropriateness, and thus the making of policy, for women. The case of Title IX shows that the policy dynamics of the minority rights revolution depended on the different ways policymakers saw the targets of their policies. This related to both the intrinsic meanings of the group in question, but also to how hard the policymakers even thought about what they were doing. If they did not think too hard, women were minorities just like blacks. When they thought hard, they looked very different, and were treated quite differently.

9

WHITE MALES AND THE LIMITS OF THE MINORITY RIGHTS REVOLUTION: THE DISABLED, WHITE ETHNICS, AND GAYS

Previous chapters have answered the question: Who is a minority? The question here is slightly different: Who is *not* a minority? To understand the minority rights revolution, we must understand its limits. And, for that, we have to examine whether any policies recognized white males as disadvantaged, and whether white maleness caused a failure of the analogy with blacks and thus exclusion from minority rights policies.

On the one hand, the answer is obviously no, because Latinos, at least a quarter of whom claimed to be white and male, were most easily analogized to African Americans.[1] However, as I showed in Chapter 4, this was because the government racialized Latinos. There was almost never explicit or implicit acknowledgment of the fact that Latinos could be white. The three cases to be considered here comprise groups that include white males and are not so easily racialized. All three groups could claim they had been victimized by discrimination, yet only one group won federal rights policy during the period. The cases highlight the importance of minority-group meanings in defining the boundaries of the minority rights revolution.

The successful case of Euro-American male inclusion is rights for the disabled. Section 504 of the Rehabilitation Act of 1973 ensured that programs receiving federal funds would not discriminate against disabled persons. Because the passage of this law has been ably analyzed by other scholars, I do not devote an entire chapter to it here. What the analysis shows is that at least in a case where a group was long the subject of public concern, a rights-based policy recognition that included Euro-American males was possible. Moreover, it was possible without lobbying, without outside leadership and without mass mobilization from social movements. Title IX, in other words, was no fluke. While the disabled were already a legitimate target of social policy, the 1964 Civil Rights Act's Title VI added a totally new approach to the politician's policy repertoire: linking nondiscrimination rights to federal disbursements was easy, inexpensive, communicated concern to the constituency, and promised real benefits. All this was possible because the disabled, government advocates argued, were a minority like blacks. In its simple, solidly legitimate language of nondiscrimination, Section 504 was difficult to oppose. As with all of the policies in this study, it was passed without controversy—that would come at the implementation stage, when it was discovered that the disabled were also very different from blacks. The case of disability rights shows that non-Latino white males were not disqualified from the minority rights revolution. It also shows that the failure of the analogy drawn with blacks at the stage of policy implementation was not a phenomenon unique to women.

Two other cases show the limits of the minority rights revolution. In the case of white ethnics, or the mostly Catholic, Orthodox Christian, and Jewish persons of eastern and southern European descent, widespread government perceptions of discrimination and/or disadvantage, lobbying for modification or inclusion in affirmative action, and intense political interest from the Nixon administration and in Congress did not lead to any significant policy recognition and rights.

White ethnics were excluded from minority rights policy recognition primarily for three reasons. First, civil-rights enforcement in the crucial employment arena was limited by resources and practical, administrative problems related to identifying ethnics. Indeed, a lack of personnel and resources meant that civil-rights enforcement did not even treat the official minorities with equal attention all the time (with Asian Americans especially falling out of the enforcement strategy). The lack of priority was related to the second factor. One frequently stated reason for denying white ethnics minority rights was that they simply had not suffered enough. In other words, there was a threshold of perceived discrimination that legitimated claims of oppression or victimhood, and white ethnics were just below that threshold. This caused a failure of the analogy sought with blacks. While plausible and defensible, it is striking that the civil-rights administrators—without any public debate, data, or legal basis—decided on an ethnoracial standard for victimhood and discrimination that officially divided the country into oppressed (blacks, Latinos, Native Americans, Asian Americans) and oppressors (all white non-Latinos). The third reason white ethnics were excluded from minority rights policies was that political elites, even while referring to this population as "ethnics," saw many different ways to appeal to them other than their ethnicity. Government officials, in other words, perceived ethnics as multifaceted—as ethnics, as Catholics, as union members, as cultural conservatives. This multiplicity of identities further undermined the analogy with blacks, who were seen principally in terms of race. Politicians' ethnic appeals therefore tapped a variety of political interests distinct from ethnicity.

The threshold of oppression may have kept white ethnics out, but it was not a general principle. Gays and lesbians were widely perceived to be discriminated against, but gay rights were never really in play. There was some mobilization from this group, some high-profile media attention, and some interest from lawmakers. But gay rights were a hard sell, harder, perhaps, than rights for any other disadvantaged group. This was because of the great weight of negative meaning attached to the group due to what most Americans perceived as its immorality, rendering in this case as well the analogy with blacks inappropriate.

This chapter examines first, rights for the disabled, followed by the case studies on ethnics and on gays and lesbians. Most attention is given to ethnics, where there were many reasons to expect success and much in the historical record to examine in understanding failure. Here, a group already formally covered by the Civil Rights Act's national origin and religion discrimination prohibitions was frozen out of the best techniques for ensuring nondiscrimination—affirmative action. Their case reveals the unspoken, extralegal principles that guided implementation of civil rights policy.

The Development of Rights for the Disabled

One of the most dramatic and revolutionary policies of the minority rights revolution was the innocuously named Section 504 of the Rehabilitation Act of 1973. This law followed the Civil Rights Act's Title VI (for blacks) and the Education Amendments of 1972's Title IX (for women) in denying federal funds to programs or activities that discriminated, in this case on the basis of disability. Section 504 was a major departure from previous policies for the disabled, none of which had the benefit of a minority-rights or nondiscrimination policy model. Because it was able to borrow from policies meant to protect black civil rights the definition of discrimination as disparate impact, thus focusing not on discriminatory intent but on unequal results, Section 504 led to profound and contentious changes. Its most controversial impact was on the federally funded public transportation systems of American cities, most of which could not be used by persons in wheelchairs. Equal access required fundamental changes in infrastructure and routine, demanded a "difference-consciousness," and meant the possibility of great expense. Section 504 was also the major precedent for the better-known, much-wider-reaching, but also much-delayed Americans with Disabilities Act, passed in 1990.

Section 504 was heir to the legacy of black civil rights policy, and depended on the black analogy for its success.[2]

Disability Policy before 1973

The earliest federal disability policy was aid to disabled veterans, which was greatly expanded after the Civil War.[3] Later, around 1900, states created programs of workers' compensation to give aid to workers injured on the job.[4] Both aid to disabled veterans and workers' compensation were based on a policy model that assumed the dependency of disabled persons, awarding financial support for persons unable to work and earn a living. In 1956, Congress created a larger program with a similar basis called Social Security Disability Insurance. Though administered through the states like workers' compensation, it was federally funded. Disability insurance was intended to support anyone over the age of fifty suffering from any kind of disability that prevented steady employment. In effect, it was an early retirement program, and it became the country's most expensive disability program. By the mid-1980s, it was spending around $30 billion in retirement and health benefits.[5]

Since the early part of the twentieth century, there was another strain in American policy that used a different model for the disabled, based on the notion that they should be helped to become working citizens. The federal government began to develop this approach with job training for disabled veterans after World War I. In 1920, Congress expanded these efforts to include vocational training, counseling, and job placement for all disabled citizens. The Social Security Act, passed in 1935, made authorizations for such rehabilitation a regular part of government—and a popular one. Johnson's Great Society expanded funding to states, so that with the Vocational Rehabilitation Amendments of 1965, there was $300 million for the states, additional money for experimental projects, and coverage expanded to include "socially handicapping conditions," such as juvenile delinquency.[6]

In the Johnson administration, special help for the disabled found great support. In a process largely driven by policy elites in Washington and encouraged by disability experts such as teachers and rehabilitation counselors, Johnson's Great Society encouraged the expansion of various programs. By the beginning of the Nixon administration, the historian Edward Berkowitz has noted, there were four areas of federal disability policy: Social Security Disability Insurance, the periodically reauthorized vocational rehabilitation acts, various programs created by the Elementary and Secondary Education Act, passed in 1965 and administered by the Office of Education, and various programs to aid mentally retarded children.[7] None of them had a civil-rights focus.

"The Right to Be a Mr. Somebody": The Origins of Section 504

There were signs before 1973 that an analogy between the disabled and African Americans, and thus the notion of disability rights, were possible or at least thinkable. In 1950, Representative Charles E. Bennett (D–FL) successfully amended a civil-rights bill to include "physical disability" as a forbidden ground of employment discrimination. He hoped this would make it harder for the bill to pass (he was right; the bill failed).[8] In 1958, the Rockefeller Brothers Fund sponsored a comprehensive report on national social policy that borrowed heavily from familiar arguments made on behalf of black civil rights. Echoing Truman's President's Committee on Civil Rights, it argued that racial discrimination had great economic costs, and was "perhaps the most dramatic example of waste of manpower in our economy." What was new was a seamless expansion of this argument to include the disabled.[9]

The black civil rights movement had made talk about rights an increasingly taken-for-granted part of American political discourse. By the late 1960s, it found its way to discussion of the disabled. Though profound, absolutist, and expansive in tone, such talk about rights seemed to come naturally, even for Republicans ostensibly cautious of the growth in federal government.[10] At the annual meeting in May of 1969 of the President's Committee on Employment of the Handicapped, Nixon's secretary of labor George Shultz declared that one of his basic premises was that if the United States was to remain "strong and vigorous," it needed to use all of its resources. But this was secondary to his sweeping, grandiloquent first premise:

> [E]very person in America should have the right to feel useful and to feel needed; the right to contribute to society as best he can and in whatever way he can; the right to dream, to aspire; the right to take whatever action he can to achieve his dreams and his aspirations. In short, every person in America should have the right to be a Mr. Somebody—or a Miss Somebody or a Mrs. Somebody. Ego-fulfillment, the psychologists call it . . . [E]very person who has the potential for work should have the right to seek and to find work. No door should be closed to him because of his color, his religion, his nationality—or his handicap, physical or mental.[11]

Though Shultz was suggesting a new minority-rights approach to disability policy, no one took action, and there was no disabled-rights movement in 1969. But Shultz's statement that year suggested that the disabled could be easily—at least in the formal sense—included in the minority rights revolution.

Some members of Congress thought as Shultz did but took action without the impetus of public pressure or lobbying. In January of 1972, Senator Hubert Humphrey (D–MN), one of the original sponsors of the Civil Rights Act of 1964, proposed an amendment to that Act. Humphrey wished to add "physical or mental handicap" to the list of race, color, and national origin as forbidden grounds for discrimination in Title VI. Similar to claims that Latinos were an "invisible minority," Humphrey said, "The time has come when we can no longer tolerate the invisibility of the handicapped in America." Humphrey pointed out that the "several million war veterans, the 22 million people with a severe physically disabling condition, the one in ten Americans who has a mental condition requiring psychiatric treatment, the six million persons who are mentally retarded, the hundreds of thousands crippled by accidents and the destructive forces of poverty, and the 100,000 babies born with defects each year" were barred from equal opportunity to participate in American society. Especially striking to Humphrey was that only 40 percent of handicapped children received special schooling and 1 million of the most handicapped received no schooling at all.[12] In other words, the problem was serious, and votes appeared plentiful.

Humphrey (the Democrat) echoed the rights talk of Shultz (the Republican), arguing that "these people have the right to live, to work to the best of their ability—to know the dignity to which every human is entitled." Humphrey underscored the legitimacy of his bill by mentioning recent court decisions creating disability rights.[13]

Charles Vanik (D–OH) proposed a counterpart bill in the House similar to Humphrey's, but more specific. He was concerned that wheelchair-bound travelers were not allowed on airplanes, and received constituent mail on other disability-related barriers to opportunity. His bill specifically would prevent airlines, buslines, and railroads from denying access or maintaining regulations that banned "persons who have malodorous conditions, gross disfigurement, or other unpleasant characteristics so unusual as to offend fellow passengers."[14]

These bills quickly found support—sixty members of the House and twenty in the Senate were co-sponsors—but died due to limited space on the legislative agenda. Disability rights did not have to amend the Civil Rights Act to become law, however. Another law being debated at the time, the Rehabilitation Act (reauthorizing and expanding federal aid for vocational training), became the vehicle for rights for the disabled.

Despite the complete lack of advocacy for these nondiscrimination rights in hearings for the overall bill, support was bipartisan, attracting liberal Republican senators such as Robert Stafford of Vermont and Jacob Javits of New York. In the House, Albert Quie of Minnesota offered help. But the real motive force in creating Section 504 and getting it into the bill was a group of energetic congressional staffmembers.

Why and how did they do it? The staff, many of whom had experience with civil rights and affirmative-action issues, clearly saw themselves as agents for positive, minority-oriented social change. As with other cases examined in this book, the social movement was *in* the government. In interviews conducted by the sociologist Richard Scotch, one staffmember explained how they viewed Nixon as "the enemy" since he was antagonistic toward 1960s programs, and that they should push for new legislation because "the initiative would not be taken elsewhere." Another explained:

> I'll tell you the frame of mind we all had. We had lived for three years under Richard Nixon, and under being told no, no, no, no, no by an executive branch which was totally unresponsive to the programs of the sixties, and to the things that were still felt important during that time of the seventies by the vast majority of the Congress . . . We were angry at the Nixon administration, and we wanted to do everything we could to do as much as we could to help people. Whether it be disabled people, minorities, poor people, you name it. Even the middle class.
>
> It was an important thread running through everything that was done at those times. It was: I'll get those sons of bitches [in the Nixon White House], they don't want to show any positive inclination toward doing things at all, then we're going to really stick it to them. And in the process, help people.[15]

It was these staffmembers who in 1972 added what became Section 504 to the Rehabilitation Act. Career aspirations and the committee-based organization of Congress helped the process along. Lisa Walker, a staffmember for Senator Harrison Williams, chair of the Labor and Public Welfare Committee since 1970, saw disability rights as "an obvious direction to take," as Harrison wanted new issues for the committee that no one else was working on.[16]

These staffmembers were also led to disability rights and the creation of Section 504 in particular because they were concerned that persons receiving training from rehabilitation programs were encountering employers reluctant to hire them. Someone—it is unclear precisely who—suggested copying Title VI of the Civil Rights Act, and a staffer who had recently worked on Title IX produced the Title VI language to use as a template.[17]

Section 504 stated: "No otherwise qualified handicapped individual in the United States . . . shall, solely by reason of his handicap, be excluded from the participation in, be denied the benefits of, or be subjected to discrimination under any program or activity receiving Federal financial assistance."[18] There were no details or explanations as to what this would mean and what limits might be placed on the potential remedies for exclusion. Section 504 was simply a part of the politicians' repertoire for addressing a group that they then saw as analogous to black Americans. No one paid any attention to what would become a revolutionary new policy. There was never any discussion of Section 504.

Shortly before the 1972 election, Nixon pocket-vetoed the bill. He disliked the $17 billion price tag and some other provisions in the bill far removed from the nondiscrimination regulations. Section 504, an unfunded regulation adding nothing to the bill's costs, escaped Nixonian comment.

Congress sent him an almost identical bill in 1973. By this point, Congress and the press viewed the Rehabilitation Act as a power struggle with the increasingly beleaguered president—a struggle that Congress knew it would win. As one indelicate lawmaker stated, "After all, there can't be too many folks who want to go on record as opposing aid to the crippled."[19] But Nixon vetoed again. The nondiscrimination provisions escaped comment a second time. The Senate failed to override the veto, but Congress was able to assemble a somewhat scaled-down version of the bill with the nondiscrimination provisions intact. Even after the two vetoes, Section 504, as Richard Scotch has pointed out, kept its place in the bill with no debate, lobbying, discussion, justification, or cost projection. And it remained untouched in the modified bill, which Nixon signed in September 1973, with strong bipartisan support.[20]

Section 504 and the official establishment of the disabled as a minority analogous to blacks was thus an act of the government. Robert Humphreys, one of the staffmembers, told Scotch that Section 504 was "essentially a self-generated item on the part of staff of the [Senate's Labor and Public Welfare] Committee." Fellow staffer Nik Edes recalled that the Senate staff were "the Martin Luther Kings of the disability movements on Capitol Hill and in the government . . . The movement [of disabled people] was stimulated by the acts of a very few individuals who were in the legislative branch."[21] Section 504 was another case of "anticipatory politics"—the staffers anticipated that the disabled would want what they were giving.

It is tempting to say that Section 504 passed because no one knew it was there. However, as will be seen in the later two cases, unless policymakers perceive the target of minority rights policy to have at least a surface similarity to African Americans, the policy will run into trouble very quickly. The disabled had such a surface similarity, as did women when Title IX passed. But as with women, a closer look at the disabled revealed they weren't so similar to blacks after all.

Implementation of Disability Rights: The Discovery of Difference

As with Title IX, easy, quiet passage of Section 504 was followed by delays and handwringing at the implementation stage. It was in trying to make the law a reality that policymakers discovered its revolutionary character. At passage, politicians apparently saw the disabled as just another minority group, with a meaning similar to blacks. No one seriously thought how they might be different, nor how equal opportunity for the disabled would be different. But once the law was looked at with an eye toward its implementation, it was clear that it might cost local districts, institutions, and programs a lot of money in ways that Title VI for blacks never did.

For this reason, HEW secretary Caspar Weinberger avoided having his department become involved. Weinberger's successor, David Matthews, felt the same way, arguing the law fell within the ambit of the Department of Justice's responsibilities. But Weinberger and Matthews were only delaying the inevitable. Section 504 was nearly identical to Title VI of the Civil Rights Act and Title IX of the Education Amendments for women's rights, both administered by the Office for Civil Rights at HEW. And OCR would again have to write the regulations.[22]

The delays allowed Matthews to punt the regulations in 1977 to the new administration of Jimmy Carter and a new secretary at HEW, Joe Califano. By this time, a government-created movement for disability rights was emerging with a clear, unifying grievance. Where, a number of demonstrators outside Califano's home asked, were the regulations implementing Section 504? Califano later wrote, "Nothing is likelier to evoke sympathy than the poignancy of a demonstration by the handicapped—people in wheelchairs, without sight or hearing, bodies crippled by accidents or genetic defects beyond their control."[23] Califano signed the regulations in April 1977, after a delay of almost four years.

By that time, affirmative-action and civil-rights law developed for blacks had established the idea that actions or practices could be considered discriminatory without having discriminatory intent. The key question was whether certain actions or practices had an adverse impact on a particular group. Given this understanding of discrimination as distinct from intent, the regulations implementing Section 504 declared that both attitudinal and architectural barriers to handicapped people (including lack of wheelchair ramps, among many others) would disqualify a program or activity from federal money.

Martin Gerry directed the regulation writing for Section 504. As described in Chapter 7, Gerry was a young, liberal Republican lawyer and veteran of the

Freedom Summer civil rights movement. He was a major force behind the memorandum of May 25, 1970 that created rights to language accommodation in the schools. For Gerry and others at the OCR, considerations of cost were a low priority, partly because of past experience with civil rights for blacks. Gerry pointed out in a later interview that "money was always kind of a red herring in race discrimination issues . . . There was all this stuff about how expensive it was going to be to eliminate the dual [race-segregated] school system. Well of course it saved money."[24] Another OCR administrator, Sally Foley, stated:

> In our office the party line was that it didn't cost anything, and I don't know what the hell we think it costs to even build a ramp. We constantly say that it doesn't cost anything. We constantly say the costs are exaggerated, exaggerated by the nasties out there who don't want the handicapped to have access.[25]

It is too simple to say that black civil rights policy taught the OCR that costs were irrelevant and not a barrier for making rights a reality. OCR officials were not consistent with this line of reasoning. The May 25 Memorandum, for example, granting language rights in schools to children of limited English-speaking ability, had the peculiar feature of linking individual rights to numbers—only school districts with 5 percent limited-English children had to comply. Presumably, this was due to cost considerations. Likewise, OCR was very reluctant to push Title IX regulations to their logical conclusions because of cost issues.

The disability rights regulations, written by Gerry and fellow lawyer John Wodatch, had a wider scope than either the language rights OCR enforced or Title IX. Those only affected education. Section 504 would affect 16,000 school systems, 7,000 hospitals, 6,700 nursing homes and home health agencies, 2,600 higher education institutions, and hundreds of day-care centers and libraries as well as public transit systems.[26] They defined "handicapped" broadly as those persons with physical problems or the appearance of problems. *Recovered* drug or alcohol addicts were covered, though persons with continuing addictions were not included. Regarding discrimination, the regulations stated that a person had to actually be qualified for the job to be able to charge discrimination (blind bus drivers, for example, would not have a claim). Nondiscrimination entailed comparable services for the disabled, and not necessarily services that integrated them with the able-bodied. Recipients of federal funds would have to make "reasonable accommodation" for the disabled but did not have to undertake measures imposing "undue hardship." The problems were complex and the legalisms vague, fleshed out by examples that implied undefined flexibility. For instance, the draft regulations stated that "a small day care center might not be required to expend more than nominal sum, but a large school district might be expected to provide a teacher's aide to a blind applicant for a teaching job."[27] But how large was "large?"

The real world presented many extremely difficult cases that today have become familiar, but that in the 1970s were quite novel. Students with sight, hearing, or reading disabilities were found to require special aides and more time to complete school work. Local officials reviewed their schools and hospitals to ensure that buildings and classrooms were accessible to wheelchairs, a process costing millions of dollars. In short, as Section 504 illuminated discrimination against the disabled, it was shown to be nearly everywhere.

Greatest controversy occurred in the area of public transportation systems—buslines, subways, and trains. These were all heavily dependent on federal subsidies, and solidly within the purview of Section 504. The chairman of New York City's Metropolitan Transit Authority, Richard Ravitch, complained about the cost—$100 million—of building elevators for its complex subway system. He pointed out that such costs siphoned money away from security and other upgrades. Ravitch argued that the expensive elevators of Washington, D.C.'s subway system only transported twenty-nine persons a day. Making buses accessible to the disabled generated similar problems where cost–benefit analysis clashed with the language of rights.[28]

Even while resistance to disability rights was growing, however, those rights were also expanding and gaining momentum through democratic politics. One effort targeted education for disabled children. Section 504 could help this cause, but a stronger force was the Education for All Handicapped Children Act of 1975, ordering school systems to provide a "free appropriate public education to *all* handicapped children" (emphasis added). This was obviously stronger than rights for children who had limited English proficiency, where the right kicked in only when those children reached 5 percent of the students in the school system. The law for disabled children required yearly conferences between school officials and parents to develop a program for each child. It also mandated that handicapped children be educated with nonhandicapped children to the greatest possible extent. The number of children in special education rose from 2.3 million in 1968 to 4.3 million in 1986.[29]

Again, unlike rights to language accommodation, the 1975 law mandated that a school with only one disabled child must take whatever steps necessary to educate that child, and a school with several children with varying handicaps must at local expense develop educational programs for each child. The law also passed with little controversy. As R. Shep Melnick has written, "Not one interest group opposed the bill. Only the White House and HEW Secretary Caspar Weinberger spoke against it. The bill passed both houses by margins so lopsided that President Ford decided not to veto it."[30]

The Meaning of the Disabled

Why did Section 504 come so easily? In some ways, the disabled are a group like none other in this study, as they have been the target of special aid for more than one hundred years. Yet this fact alone does not explain why and how they became minorities and part of the rights revolution.

In part, the story here is the same as with Title IX. Despite the inclusion of Euro-American men, politicians saw the disabled as a group similar to blacks. Because of this perception, and because of the prior passage of Title VI (and by then, Title IX), politicians who wanted to help the disabled and/ or wanted their votes could use the policy model of civil rights for blacks as part of an anticipatory politics strategy. Their inclusion in the minority rights revolution was, at first, remarkably easy and appropriate.

But as with the other minority groups, the disabled were both similar to yet different from blacks. At the stage of implementation, the OCR officials had to take a harder look at the groups in question than did the legislators. They saw that the disabled would require radically different and very expensive approaches to transportation, building, and schooling for equal opportunity and nondiscrimination—approaches that had no analogues with black civil rights.

Despite the foot-dragging and resistance during implementation, Congress proceeded to pass additional laws similar to Section 504. It also passed other women's rights legislation, another case with problems at implementation, though Republicans pulled back when a countermobilization developed.[31] The GOP, however, never stopped supporting rights for the disabled. And unlike Latinos' right to language accommodation in schools, Congress mandated expensive implementation of rights for even isolated individual disabled persons.

Among all the groups who were part of the minority rights revolution, these differences suggest that Americans—or at least their government leaders—see disabled Americans as the most deserving. This may be due to the fact, as R. Shep Melnick has pointed out, that unlike the other groups, any American can be forced to join the disabled due to illness or accident.[32] One cannot involuntarily become an African American, a woman, or a child of limited English-speaking ability. If this "open" nature of the group is relevant, however, we should recognize it as an extralegal, culture-based principle that nevertheless powerfully shapes the law. Moreover, it is mediated by complex group meanings. For example, anyone can become poor, but many

Americans have often thought of the poor as being responsible for their own plight.[33] The poor are lazy, while the disabled are victims. There has never been an effort to determine which disabled persons became so through their own irresponsibility, such as driving while intoxicated. Of course, it would be difficult if not impossible to prevent a former drunk driver in a wheelchair from using an access ramp. But policymakers do not even consider such divisions. The disabled evoke sympathy and the poor more often do not. It also should be noted that these meanings create policy in unconscious ways, rarely being voiced by policymakers themselves. As should be clear by now, politicians during the minority rights revolution did not think deeply and clearly about the differences among groups.

White Ethnics: The Almost-Minority

The "white ethnics" are one group that failed to secure a place in the minority rights revolution. Who are the white ethnics? As with the affirmative-action minority groupings, there never has been a clear definition of exactly who is in this category. The core groups are the mostly Catholic immigrants or persons with ancestry from eastern or southern Europe, such as Italians, Poles, Hungarians, and Slovaks. Orthodox Christians such as Greeks and Serbians are usually included, while Jews and Catholic Irish Americans are on the boundaries. American political commentators usually group Latinos separately, though they are often white. White ethnics are generally Americans of those nationalities that were disfavored but not excluded by American immigration policy between the early 1920s and 1965. WASPs and Scandinavians are therefore not in the category. According to the rather limited data from 1972, there were 8.8 million Italians out of a total American population of 204.8 million (4.3 percent), 5.1 million Polish Americans (2.5 percent), and about 5.9 million Jews (2.9 percent).[34]

Though members of these groups who were also women or disabled won new rights in the 1965–75 period, the category itself remained outside the minority rights revolution and did not receive policy recognition. Policies of minority rights reified some differences, but generally collapsed able-bodied Euro-American men into an undifferentiated and ostensibly privileged mass.

The ethnics, of course, technically did benefit from the classically liberal reforms of the 1965 Immigration Act. Eastern and southern Europeans could come to America on the same terms as northern and western Europeans. In 1965, however, there was less incentive to come to the United States since there were many opportunities in Europe (western European countries even imported "guest workers" for post–World War II rebuilding). Lawmakers also discovered that European immigration was disadvantaged as well by the preferences for family relatives; by the late 1960s many members of European groups had been in the United States so long that they no longer had close relatives in the old country. Most powerfully, few eastern Europeans could come even if they wanted to, as their countries were then ruled by totalitarian Communist governments.[35] Between 1965 and 1977, despite reform, immigration from Europe declined 38 percent (falling from 113,424 to 70,010). Immigration from all European countries fell with the exceptions of Portugal and Greece. In the same time period, overall immigration increased 56 percent (from 296,697 in 1965 to 462,315 in 1977), with immigration from Asia increasing 663 percent, from North America 48 percent (despite Canada's falling 67 percent), Africa 200 percent, Oceania 171 percent, and South America 6 percent.[36]

Bilingual education was therefore not a major benefit for white ethnics— there were simply not many new Euro-ethnic immigrants. Even those that were in the country did not benefit in any significant numbers. The vast majority of Bilingual Education Act funds went for Spanish speakers, the original intended beneficiaries. In 1973, 114 bilingual education grants went for Mexican Americans, 31 for Puerto Ricans, 2 for Cubans, 18 for mixed Spanish speakers, 16 for American Indians, 6 for French, 4 for Portuguese, 2 for Chinese, 1 for Guam (Chamorro language), 1 for Palauan/Ponopaean (Marina Islands), 1 for Yupik/Eskimo, and 13 for multilingual programs. Federal pressure for bilingual education based on Title VI of the 1964 Civil Rights Act also did not lead to programs for ethnic children—a fact noted with indignation by Italian American representative Mario Biaggi (D–NY). In House hearings in 1974 for amendments and reauthorization of the Bilingual Education Act, Biaggi diverged from the larger concerns of the bill to express outrage before an HEW official at the complete lack of programs for Italians, Greeks, and Albanians in New York. Biaggi also chastised OCR director Stanley Pottinger and his assistant Martin Gerry, creators of the Title VI program, for not even collecting data on European ethnic children.[37] Bilingual education remained a program primarily for Latinos and was never expanded to recognize white ethnic language or culture in any significant way.

In the 1965–75 period, white ethnics lobbied for recognition in other areas, and government officials treated them seriously, saw them as disadvantaged, and valued them as an electoral bloc. Yet ethnics made only insignificant and fleeting gains in difference-conscious policies. Some leaders sought to be included in affirmative action, and the OFCC issued affirmative-action draft guidelines directed at their "underutilization" in employment by government contractors, but the Nixon White House greatly weakened them and what remained was never enforced. White ethnics won, along with blacks, Latinos, and Asian Americans, the Ethnic Heritage Studies Act, but this program which would have recognized their ethnic identities never received anything more than token funding.

Were White Ethnics a Political Presence?

One possible reason white ethnics failed to win rights is that they were not mobilized and had no presence or tradition of a presence in federal politics. But in the late 1960s and early 1970s an extraordinary ethnic revival took place, especially in older northeastern and midwestern cities. Like Latinos and other groups, white ethnics formed organizations, lobbied, even engaged in some protest. The Ford Foundation gave them money, as it did the Latinos, and ethnics held conferences that attracted well-known politicians.

Ethnic political mobilization

Most eastern and southern Europeans came to America between 1880 and the early 1920s, when ethnic difference had no cachet whatsoever. Ethnicity was at best ignored and usually perceived as a stigma. Immigrants from eastern and southern Europe encountered pressures to assimilate that post-1965 immigrants did not, and their relatively pale skins and European features obviously gave them a better chance at "passing" than many Latino and Asian immigrants in the early twentieth century. They saw benefits to becoming "white" and certainly not from asserting difference from whites. Few ethnics gave up their religions, but many changed both their given and family names so they might blend more easily into the mainstream population. Some had their names changed for them by capricious immigration officers. Once arrived, native-born whites organized to encourage if not actually force the new ethnics to Americanize and assimilate.[38]

In the 1940s and 1950s, white ethnics began to assert their identities as whites in local political battles. The historian Thomas Sugrue has shown in his analysis of the decline of Detroit that ethnics who had achieved their small victory of homeownership formed white identities to contrast themselves with the encroaching poorer blacks. Though made up of a great variety of ethnic groups, Sugrue points out that "homeowners' and neighborhood groups shared a common bond of whiteness and Americanness—a bond that they asserted forcefully at public meetings and in correspondence with public officials."[39] Before the minority rights revolution of the mid-1960s, there was little to be gained by casting oneself as a victimized or oppressed group analogous to blacks. Consequently, like the Mexican American leaders Leo Grebler and his colleagues interviewed in 1964 (see Chapter 4), ethnics emphasized similarity, not difference, and linked themselves to the primary trait they shared with white elites—the color of their skins. Some conservative politicians, especially Alabama governor George Wallace during his failed presidential campaigns, had begun to appeal to ethnics as whites—*resentful* whites—on a national basis. In 1964 and again in 1968, Wallace, the former segregationist, had attracted ethnic support by advocating "law and order" and limits on black civil rights.[40]

A new pattern of white-ethnic politics emerged in the middle 1960s, along with the rise of affirmative action and other ethnoracially targeted policies. Many ethnic leaders began—as did Latinos, women, and other groups—to assert their difference, their past and present discrimination, and their present needs. It is difficult to date the rise in this ethnic political activity, but it developed most quickly after the rise of the black power movement and the federal designation of official minority groups and the institutionalization of affirmative action in 1965.

As with the case of other nonblack minority groups, advocacy inside the government developed before or in tandem with advocacy outside. In 1967, Robert C. Wood, the under secretary of Housing and Urban Development, gave a speech in Lincoln, Massachusetts focused on the problems of the "average white ethnic male." These related to the economic insecurity of being an easily dispensed with blue-collar worker, living adjacent to an expanding black ghetto, seeing the antiwar protests at the universities as violating deeply held values, and feeling neglected.[41]

In late 1967, Irving M. Levine, urban affairs director of the American Jewish Committee, began the National Project on Ethnic America (NPEA). Levine's goal was "to push whites off a strictly negative anti-black agenda" and to "make them conscious of their own realities." To do this, "a new breed of ethnic leaders has to be developed who are as visible as the demagogues trying to exploit ethnic fears."[42] In other words, Levine wanted to stop the trend for white ethnics to identify themselves in terms of their whiteness, reinforce their sense of difference, and have them see themselves as similar to blacks. The groups were by no means equally disadvantaged, but shared similar problems of inadequate schools, housing, and job prospects.

Levine pursued his goal by sponsoring conferences that later initiated various local projects. In 1968, the NPEA and Fordham University held a two-day National Consultation on Ethnic America, with participants from ethnic community organizations, academia, religious organizations, and labor unions. Also in 1968, the NPEA sponsored the Philadelphia Conference on the Problems of White Ethnic America. In 1969, it held another Consultation on Ethnicity, this time in Chicago. At these and similar conferences, the NPEA sought to train new leaders, discuss issues related to ethnicity such as ethnic studies in the schools, and develop strategies for ethnics to take control of their lives and to pressure local governments to improve their neighborhoods. Where possible, Levine fostered cooperation between blacks and ethnics. The Ford Foundation issued a two-year grant in January, 1971 for $260,000 to aid the effort.[43]

Catholic organizations also mobilized to attend to the mostly Catholic white ethnics. One influential Catholic leader was Monsignor Geno Baroni, an activist for black civil rights who helped organize the famous 1963 March on Washington.[44] In his view, ethnics were "economically, culturally, socially, and politically alienated and disillusioned."[45] Baroni believed that a cultural pluralism that recognized the distinctive white ethnic groups was key to social peace in the 1970s. With help from the Ford Foundation, Baroni established the National Center for Urban Ethnic Affairs at the Catholic University of America in Washington, D.C. Like Levine's NPEA, the center worked through conferences with academic, labor, religious, and local ethnic leaders. Like the National Education Association's conferences on bilingual education for Mexican Americans (see Chapter 7), it attracted the participation of powerful members of Congress. For example, a workshop in June, 1970 on "Urban Ethnic Community Development" was designed to analyze ethnic factors in urban strife, to explore different public and private policy options to address issues of economic and cultural development, and to encourage priests to become more involved in ethnic-community issues. The workshop speakers included Senator Edmund Muskie (D–ME, a Polish American whose original name was Edmund Sixtus Marciszewski), Senator Charles Percy (D–IL), Congressman Roman Pucinski (D–IL, another Polish American), as well as representatives of the Office of Economic Opportunity. The workshop received coverage from the *New York Times*, the *Washington Post*, and NBC's *Today Show*.

A 1971 conference on "New Directions for Urban America: Workshop on Ethnic and Working Class Priorities," also sponsored by the National Center for Urban Ethnic Affairs, brought together a range of speakers including Michael Novak, a Slovak American philosopher who was then writing *The Rise of the Unmeltable Ethnics*,[46] and Richard Scammon, a political consultant who with Ben Wattenberg had written an influential book on coalition building, *The Real Majority*.[47] The "New Directions" conference also attracted powerful members of Congress. Workshop participants were treated to a luncheon in the Senate Office Building, where speakers included Senators Edward Kennedy (D–MA), Jacob Javits (R–NY), Charles Percy (D–IL), Richard Schweiker (R–PA), and Congressman Roman Pucinski (D–IL).[48]

Another institution oriented around European ethnics was the Center for the Study of American Pluralism, established in 1971 under the directorship of the sociologist and Irish American Catholic priest Andrew Greeley.

Greeley had written a book entitled *Why Can't They Be Like Us?* that, along with Novak's *Unmeltable Ethnics,* was one of the central texts of the ethnic revival.[49] Greeley's center was part of the National Opinion Research Center, affiliated with the University of Chicago. Intended as an ethnic think tank, it sponsored a series of lectures at the university exploring the role of ethnicity in American life.

Greeley's center also benefited from a grant from the Ford Foundation, which was a major force in the minority rights revolution, underwriting, for example, the creation of the Mexican American Legal Defense and Education Fund. In announcing in January of 1971 a series of grants of nearly $1 million for action and research on the Euro-American working class, foundation president McGeorge Bundy stated that "it is clear that great numbers of working-class Americans have not been at the center of recent social concerns" and that the grants were intended to "deal with some of the problems of white working-class American communities" and "widen our understanding of the continuing role of ethnicity in American life."[50]

Though mass protest was not required for rights-oriented policy recognition, as the case of disabled rights demonstrates, there was some protest activity for ethnics. Perhaps the most notable demonstration took place on June 29, 1970, when Joseph Colombo Sr.'s Italian-American Civil Rights League staged an Italian American unity rally at Columbus Circle in Manhattan. Estimates of attendance varied between forty to one hundred thousand persons. *Time* magazine reported, "New York's waterfront was virtually shut down where many longshoremen took the day off for the ethnic celebration, and almost every politician in the city joined" the activities.[51] Italian Americans in New York were concerned about being neglected by a municipal government that seemed to them to pay more attention to blacks and Puerto Ricans. They wanted more control over schools, and were especially sensitive to the media's continual linking of Italian heritage and participation in organized crime. Colombo, despite his own strong ties to organized crime, had been able to persuade some moviemakers to stop using the term "mafia" and had begun a campaign to force corporations to stop using Italian stereotypes in advertising. His group was also beginning to set up summer camps for children. But the campaign was cut short when Colombo was assassinated by a young African American man at the Columbus Circle rally.[52]

While not engaging in mass protests, Polish American advocates were similarly sensitive in the late 1960s and early 1970s to the sudden, bizarre popularity of "Polish jokes," which had as their basis the portrayal of Polish people as oafs and buffoons.[53] In a time of rapidly increasing sensitivity toward racist portrayals of blacks in the media, the Polish jokes, spread by publications such as *It's Fun to Be a Polack,* enjoyed legitimacy in the mainstream media. As the historian John Bukowczyk has written, the special allowances that were made in American moral culture to ridicule Polish Americans caused them embarrassment and humiliation. In response, the Polish American Congress (PAC), a group created in the 1940s primarily to press foreign-policy issues related to Poland, complained to major television networks and newspapers, and the Polish president of a large food corporation donated five hundred thousand dollars to try to improve the image of Polish Americans.[54]

In addition to the mobilization, there was an explosion of writing about ethnics during the period, undertaken by both social scientists and journalists. The themes were almost always the same. One was the low economic achievement of the Catholic ethnics. Gerhard Lenski's 1961 study set the tone for seeing the group as disadvantaged by arguing that Catholics—because of something inherent in their religion—had less commitment to capitalism than either Jews or Protestants, and were most similar to black Protestants.[55] By the late 1960s, in the context of the minority rights revolution, economic deprivations suffered by ethnics took on a different meaning. In December 1970, *Newsweek* reported on the "Rising Cry: Ethnic Power," arguing that 40 million ethnics "are squeezed by inflation, frightened by crime at their doorsteps, outraged by jokes and movies stereotyping them as hardhat racists, and their homes and neighborhoods are threatened by bulldozers and blockbusters." *Newsweek,* which sent a reporter around the country specifically to examine the problem, stated other typical themes of the period: the WASP power structure ignored the ethnics, blacks outshouted them, and they were "caught in the middle." Their incomes were enough to be taxed but too much to take advantage of housing, job training, medical and legal-aid programs that *Newsweek* said were "run by and for the blacks in many big cities."[56] Two years later, the inside-the-beltway *Congressional Quarterly Weekly Report* offered a similar picture in an article called "Campaign '72: The Rising Voice of Ethnic Voters." It offered a demographic and political profile of the white ethnics, and described the leaders' demands for more housing, "job security and new opportunities," something to "allay fears that blacks will displace ethnics in jobs," stopping crime without calling the ethnics "bigots," tax reform and other issues.[57]

Ethnic lobbying for affirmative action
Ethnic organizations lobbied to be a part of the minority rights revolution. This was especially true in the development of affirmative action. For example, when EEOC officials were creating the EEO-1 form for firms to report the numbers of official minorities they had hired, representatives of Polish groups sought inclusion. EEOC administrator Herbert Hammerman

recalled that Polish representatives wanted a category of "Polonians" (a term some Polish leaders used to refer to Polish Americans) added, but that the EEOC firmly denied the request. The agency's stated explanation was mostly practical: there was no room for them on the form, Poles could not be identified by a visual survey, and "once we take care of them, where do we put Italians, Yugoslavs, Greeks, etc., who are sure to want to be separately identified?"[58]

Ethnic pressure on the federal government was light compared with that from blacks, women, and Latinos (who benefited from already being labeled minorities), yet it was *more* focused on affirmative action than the efforts of these official minorities. For example, in April of 1967, Vincent Trapani, state president of the New York Federation of Italian-American Democratic Organizations, told EEOC chair Stephen Shulman that the EEO-1 statistics "will disclose discrimination *but not for all minority groups* [original emphasis]. It is obvious that minority groups such as Italian-Americans, Polish-Americans, German-Americans, Irish-Americans, Jewish-Americans and others, will not be revealed." Trapani argued that these groups all suffered discrimination, and that excluding national origin categories from the EEO-1 violated the Civil Rights Act. Therefore, the current form was unacceptable. It discriminated against certain minority groups, was "wasteful" because it could not "ferret out discriminatory practices against the largest ethnic groups," and (echoing earlier arguments made by women and Latinos) was "not being used by government agencies themselves where major discriminatory practices do appear to exist." Trapani, who apparently was not invited to the 1965 hearings on the EEO-1, demanded hearings or a conference to revise the form, and threatened to complain to the US Commission on Civil Rights.[59]

Other groups also lobbied to be included on the EEO-1 form. Jewish leaders had been an important part of the early struggle for equal employment opportunity. Though only 8.7 percent of complaints to the wartime Fair Employment Practices Commission (FEPC) were based on religion, the Anti-Defamation League organized a campaign so that 72.7 percent of those were from Jews.[60] Prominent members of Truman's President's Committee on Civil Rights were Jewish, and Jews were mentioned more often than any other white ethnic group in the committee's final report, *To Secure These Rights*. Though almost completely ignoring discrimination against eastern and southern Europeans and Catholics, that report did describe discrimination against Jews in executive business positions and mentioned discrimination against Jews in higher education, housing sales (through "restrictive covenants" on home sales), and in some public recreation areas.[61] It also quoted the FEPC's final report as saying "the wartime gains of Negro, Mexican American, and Jewish workers are being lost through an unchecked revival of discriminatory practices."[62]

The inclusion of Jews as a minority continued into the 1950s. As described in Chapter 4, Eisenhower's President's Committee on Government Contracts originally named Jews as an official minority for reporting requirements. Contractors were supposed to count Negroes and "other minorities." The other minorities, according to the instructions for the survey, included the standard three minority groups of the later EEO-1 form, a mysterious "etc.," and Jews.

But black groups argued that Jews were not disadvantaged. David Mann, the committee's director of surveys, later recalled his agreement that "from the point of view of social recognition and economic progress, Jews had done well." Jewish groups, including the Anti-Defamation League, the American Jewish Congress, and the American Jewish Committee, did not object. They wished to maintain good relations with blacks and were concerned that official recognition in the workforce could be used to discriminate against them.[63]

By 1968, however, at least some Jewish groups had a change of heart. In a statement to the EEOC for that year's hearings in New York on discrimination in white-collar employment, Emanuel Muravchik, executive director of the Jewish Labor Committee, argued that Jews should be included on the EEO-1 form since such statistical information is needed to find discrimination:

> The claim that Jews are indistinguishable from other groups seeking and progressing in employment is belied by the common knowledge that, despite a goodly percentage of Jews being educated to high pursuits, they receive less than their fair share of advancement in white collar, technical, administrative, executive and professional employment.
>
> It is anomalous that reporting forms prepared by the government will give greater protection to persons who are readily identifiable minority members, such as Negroes and Puerto Ricans, than to Jews who are not readily identifiable. Thus, statistically, Jews are neither visibly detected as the victims of discrimination, nor do they appear in records for a pattern of discrimination to be traced out. In effect, they are left without governmental protection. Yet the employer, if only through his supervisory staff, knows they are Jewish and treats them accordingly.

Muravchik added, "We simply do think that in reality the employer has the information avialable [*sic*] to him. And we believe that just as the information must be reported by employers to the EEOC about other minority groups, a category for Jews should also be listed in the forms." He suggested experimenting with different methods of identification, such as using anonymous return post cards, or counting Rosh Hashanah and Yom Kippur absences.[64]

In fact, the EEOC did give some attention to Jewish underrepresentation at the hearing. Phyllis Wallace, the EEOC's chief of technical studies, pointed out that about 25 percent of the New York population was Jewish, 50 percent of college graduates in the city were Jews, that about 25 percent of all Ivy League college graduates were Jewish, and 15 percent of graduates of Harvard Business School were Jews. However, using statistics of Jewish surnames from a study of corporate officers and executives in New York conducted by the Anti-Defamation League in 1967, Jewish representation ranged from 1.5–12.1 percent, with an average of 4.5 percent. Wallace described a study by the American Jewish Committee that found that of the nine largest commercial banks in New York in 1966, only one of 173 senior officers was Jewish. Wallace also reported on an interview and questionnaire study of blacks, Puerto Ricans, and Jews in New York executive employment commissioned by the EEOC. This study of ten companies found underrepresentation of Jews, but data here was limited, since one of the companies refused to give any ethnoracial data and three of the ten refused to give information on Jews. Wallace concluded with a University of Michigan study that found that "a sizeable percentage" of personnel officers believed that their superiors consider social background of new employees, and stated, "The significant finding of all these studies is that there is a large under-representation of Jews at all levels of management."[65]

This was to be the high water-mark for affirmative action for Jews, however. Beginning in 1968, conflict erupted in New York City between Jews on the one hand and blacks and Puerto Ricans on the other in the area of public-education employment, a field in which Jews were overrepresented. Two years later, a court sided with NAACP Legal Defense Fund lawyers who argued that merit tests for supervisors were discriminatory and should be abolished, and that a quota system should be instituted.[66] Over the next two years, many Jewish groups lobbied the federal government *against* zealous enforcement of affirmative action for anyone. In the summer of 1970, several groups, including the American Jewish Committee, the American Jewish Congress, the Anti-Defamation League, the Jewish Labor Committee, and Agudath Israel went beyond New York and filed more than thirty complaints of reverse discrimination with HEW. White males, they argued, were being denied hiring and promotion opportunities because of HEW's affirmative-action policies in the university system. Of course, they were especially concerned about Jewish white males, who were statistically overrepresented in university employment and stood to lose more than any other white groups. Members of Congress representing New York stepped in, arguing that since the charges resulted from government action, an outside "ombudsman" was needed to investigate the issue. One was appointed, and more than three-fourths of the complaints were subsequently dismissed. Undaunted, the Jewish groups filed more than one hundred more complaints of reverse discrimination.[67]

Representatives of the groups met with HEW secretary Elliot Richardson and OCR director Stanley Pottinger to express their concern that the merit principle was being sacrificed in order to bring more official minorities into university employment.[68] On August 4, 1972, Philip Hoffman of the American Jewish Committee wrote a letter to President Nixon describing his "grave concern over a trend which is in sharp conflict with our longstanding commitment to the principle of equal opportunity." This was the "current widespread efforts and promises to achieve 'proportional representation' in our society" for minority groups in employment, education and government appointments. In his response, Nixon disavowed any interest in quotas or proportional representation, explaining that "the criteria for selection that I have employed and will continue to employ will be based on merit."[69] This issue of whether racial quotas were justified also led to conflict between Jewish groups and black groups within the civil-rights umbrella organization, the Leadership Conference on Civil Rights.[70]

On the issue of admissions to professional schools, Jewish groups also lobbied against preferences for official minorities. There is little evidence that admissions officers ever considered religious preferences for admission to professional schools, either for Jews or Catholics.[71] Of course, the possibility of obtaining preferences for Jews made little sense since Jews were already overrepresented in medical and law schools. Jewish groups were instead heavy contributors of amicus curiae briefs in the *Bakke* reverse discrimination case, arguing on the side of (Norwegian American) Allan Bakke.[72]

Other ethnic groups, however, continued the struggle that the Jewish groups dropped. They collected their own EEO-1-like data to demonstrate discrimination against white ethnics, but it received even less government attention than the Jewish groups' data. The Polish American Congress (PAC), like some Latino groups, also focused on government representation. In 1969, 1972 and 1977, PAC analyzed state government departments in Illinois, which has a large Polish American population, and the federal government, and found Polish American underrepresentation.[73] PAC's Illinois division and the Joint Civic Committee of Italian-Americans in Chicago requested a study by the Institute of Urban Life in Chicago on the representation of Poles, Italians, Latinos, and blacks in the upper levels of 106 of the largest Chicago corporations. The report found that the Italians and Poles were doing better on boards of directors and corporate officers than the officially recognized minorities, but only barely better. Blacks were clearly doing the worst, but Polish Americans were only barely above the levels of Latinos. For example, although Poles accounted for 6.9 percent of the area population, they made up only 0.3 percent of the "directors" in the study, and 0.7 percent of the "officers." "Latins" accounted for 4.4 percent of the population, but made up only 0.1 percent of the directors and officers. Fifty-five of the 106 corporations did not have any Poles, Italians, blacks, or Latinos as directors or officers. Ninety-seven had no Polish officers, while 104 had no Latinos. Italians fared somewhat better, but were also underrepresented.[74]

The backlash against affirmative action for ethnics

The EEOC never seriously responded to the issues raised by white ethnics,[75] but the OFCC did. On December 29, 1971, the *Federal Register* published new affirmative-action rules for notice and comment. The new rules were directed at "promoting and insuring equal employment opportunity for all persons without regard to religion or national origin." The proposed rules explained that "experience has indicated that members of various religious groups, primarily Jews and Catholics, and members of certain ethnic groups, primarily of Eastern, Middle, and Southern European ancestry, such as Italians, Greeks, and Slavic groups, continue to be excluded from executive, middle-management, and other job levels because of discrimination based on their religion and/or national origin. These guidelines are intended to remedy such unfair treatment." It is difficult to find information about the decision to issue the rules, but ethnic advocacy, as well as the increasing opposition by Jewish groups to the federal affirmative-action programs for the official minorities, likely played a part.

The proposed rules contained new obligations for employers with government contracts. These included internal communication of the commitment to equal opportunity and inclusive recruitment. The rules also stated that "if an underutilization of a particular religious or ethnic minority group is called to an employer's attention," the employer would be expected to initiate various steps to "remedy the underutilization of that particular religious or ethnic minority group." The guidelines did not state who would be calling attention to underutilization. Remedies included reviewing employment records to determine availability of members of that group for promotion, establishing "meaningful contacts with the appropriate religious and/or national origin-oriented organizations for purposes of referral of potential employees, advice, education, and technical assistance," using religious or ethnic press for advertising, recruiting from educational institutions with large numbers of the underutilized group, and discussing the employer's affirmative-action program with religious or ethnic leaders. Moreover, "whenever an underutilization of a religious or ethnic minority group is called to an employer's attention, the employer shall then make available for compliance review such information as may be reasonably obtainable on the approximate members of the various religious and ethnic minorities employed at the job levels in which a question of underutilization has been raised." Finally, employers were to make "reasonable accommodations" for employees who regularly observe Friday evening or Saturday Sabbath, or observe other religious holidays, and who are "conscientiously opposed to performing work or engaging in similar activity on such days."[76]

There was no clear analogy with blacks here. Unlike the previous affirmative-action regulations, there were no stated hiring goals or projected timetables for compliance, and the regulation was not self-executing. It apparently required initial action on the part of organizations or individuals. But there was a bigger difference: these regulations came under immediate attack, both from within and without the government. Surprisingly, the Nixon White House that had done so much to develop and expand affirmative action led the criticism. Political adviser Bryce Harlow objected to the recognition of religion, explaining, "I can't avoid the judgement that this is an inherently bad move and that somebody at the White House level needs to get a handle on this problem, too."[77] Another Nixon aide warned, "I have had many calls from both business and labor strongly objecting to this proposal and I think we would want to take a hard look at this and discuss it further with the Department of Labor."[78] Though the former labor secretary George Shultz himself defended the new affirmative action, declaring simply, "These guidelines are mild,"[79] others inside and outside the White House were opposed.

Jack A. Gleason, a Nixon operative engaged in controversial outside campaign fund-raising practices,[80] sent a detailed letter to Nixon aide John Dean complaining that the regulations required an invasion of privacy and violation of the principle of the separation of church and state. Apparently oblivious to or forgetting the EEO-1 form (now six years old), Gleason incorrectly added that "these requirements complete the full circle and return us to the use of the type of application blank and record keeping of 25 years ago which has been deemed discriminatory by other bodies as well as by court decision." Especially noxious to Gleason were the references to "underutilization" and employers' responsibility for correcting deficiencies. Gleason found the existing regulations acceptable, but "physical characteristics such as being black, male, white, oriental or female are permanent and not subject to change. Affirmative action in such areas can be accomplished and measured without undo complications or invasions or privacy."[81] The source of fundraiser

Gleason's interest in the issue is mysterious, and may have reflected donor dislike of the new regulation.

There is evidence of corporate leaders lobbying against affirmative action for ethnics. In January 1972, W. M. Bennett of the 3M Company fired off a letter to new labor secretary James D. Hodgson, explaining that "we have become pretty disturbed over the situation relative to the proposed guidelines developed by the Office of Federal Contract Compliance concerning the maintenance of records on an employee's religious preference and his national origin." Bennett, also apparently unaware of the EEO-1, had problems with the focus on both religion and national origin, based on principle and pragmatics:

> It was a major step forward in the elimination of discrimination when these questions were removed from the application forms and it is ironical that some people are now saying that they must be restored.
>
> Religious preference is a person's personal concern and it is an invasion of privacy to make such inquiry as well as of questionable constitutionality in our opinion.
>
> Information on national origin has many complications particularly for those of mixed backgrounds of which there are millions. Do we have to secure along with the application, a genealogy in such cases? This would be a nightmare.
>
> We hope you will give this your most serious consideration and remove it from the guidelines. It is onerous and really invites discrimination rather than helping it.[82]

Though dismissive of Gleason's letter (Dean explained incorrectly that trying to turn back the regulations would amount to White House interference of an independent regulatory agency),[83] the Nixon White House reacted to Bennett with concern. Nixon aide Peter Flanigan forwarded the note to the Office of Management and Budget, which was responsible for record-keeping matters.[84]

The unpublicized controversy grew to include a wide circle of Nixon domestic policy and politics aides. George T. Bell predicted "an endless donnybrook in highly controversial areas." "It could be a tool for harassment by disgruntled job seekers, professional ethnic and religious organizations and local politicians that would only cause burden on business and government," Bell explained, adding, "With all the other problems we have, why manufacture more?"[85]

An anonymous White House analysis memo gives more insight into why some on the Nixon team rejected this new type of affirmative action—and why the preferences for other groups were acceptable. Concerns of legality were greatest on the issues surrounding religion because the new regulations implied that the government would have to monitor the religious affiliations of the employees of government contractors, and employers would have to keep records on the various religions represented in their workforces. The memo made a variety of arguments against such practices. First, the regulations "raise serious legal questions concerning constitutional provisions regarding religious liberty and separation of church and state." Second, "they also raise legal questions in connection with Title VII of the Civil Rights Act of 1964 by requiring employers to consider religion as a factor in connection with employment, promotions and transfers." (This point was nonsensical, since affirmative action already required minority status as a factor in employment.) Third, "most state laws prohibit pre-employment inquiries which tend to reveal religion or national origin."

The memo emphasized that affirmative action for religious minorities introduced practical problems. For example, it was not clear how to go about determining who really belonged to a religious group. Would it be based on a person's professed affiliation, or would activity or formal certification be required? The matter was complicated by the fact that people change religious affiliations or have none. Moreover, the regulations would reverse trends that sought to make religious affiliation a less important part of political life, and "the reactions that could be expected as a result of special attention being given to so called 'appropriate' religious and ethnic groups to the exclusion of others, would be chaotic."

It was similarly complicated to define potentially mixed white ethnicities. The White House memo contrasted this situation with that of the official minorities:

Current affirmative action programs (Revised Order No. 4) which apply to minority groups and women concern people with *unchanging physical* attributes which are typically observable. Identifying such persons as targets for affirmative action is relatively simple. Matters of religion and national origin present totally different problems, ones of *changing beliefs* and inter-marriage . . . Through one or two generations of inter-marriage, national origin is changed or at least terribly confused (original emphasis).

Ultimately, however, the problem with affirmative action for these groups, the anonymous memo made clear, was that they simply had not suffered enough. There was some undefined standard of oppression or victimhood that guided national policy relating to affirmative action, and these groups did not reach it:

> There is no question that there has been religious and ethnic discrimination, however, there is no parallel between that discrimination and the discrimination suffered by Negroes, other minorities and women who are separately covered by Revised Order No. 4. Catholics, Jews and other groups mentioned in the proposed guidelines are not economically deprived groups, have not been educationally deprived, have not been deprived of voting, or suffered many of the other aspects of discrimination based on color or other identifiable physical characteristics . . . Because of these differences, the degree and type of affirmative action necessary is different for identifiable race and sex than for unidentifiable religious belief or national origin.[86]

The memo's argument was not based on any data or historical evidence, but the message was clear: the minority rights revolution was reaching a limit. Women, Asians, Latinos, and American Indians had suffered like blacks and thus could be analogized to them. White ethnics had not suffered enough and the analogy did not work.

In response, the OFCC retreated. On January 13, 1973, it published new regulations in the *Federal Register*. The primary difference between these and the previous set of regulations was that they completely excised the word "underutilization" and the section that required an employer, in the event of underutilization, to present data of ethnic and religious hiring for demonstrating compliance. In the new guidelines, all of the affirmative-action measures were placed under a new heading of "Outreach and Positive Recruitment." The government announced that contractors had to police themselves because the government was not going to. The regulations weakly stated, "It is not contemplated that employers necessarily will undertake all of the listed activities. The scope of the employer's efforts shall depend upon all the circumstances, including the nature and extent of the employer's deficiencies and the employer's size and resources." In other words, employers did not really have to do anything. The regulations remain today, adding pages to the Code of Federal Regulations, but nothing to the burden on business.[87]

It is not clear whether the ethnics or their advocates such as Pucinski were a part of these decisions. Given the remoteness of the decisionmaking and the small size and resources of ethnic groups, it is possible they missed the entire White House debate. Curiously, though white ethnics continued to lobby for inclusion in affirmative action, they never mentioned the OFCC regulations, and never lobbied to have them fully enforced.[88]

The continuing struggle: Bakke and beyond

Some Polish groups weighed in on the benchmark *Bakke* reverse discrimination case described in Chapter 6, making what would have been counterarguments to the Nixon administration's reasoning. A joint brief submitted by the PAC, a Polish lawyers' group (the National Advocates Society), and a Polish doctors' group (the National Medical and Dental Association) as amici curiae argued that current affirmative-action programs like that at the UC-Davis Medical School were unfair. The brief based its argument on the unsystematic designation of official minority groups. Its principal author, Leonard F. Walentynowicz, maintained that due process requires "an adequate data and analytical base" to justify affirmative-action programs that treat particular individuals and groups preferentially. The problem was that such programs began with a list of preferred groups already in mind without a comprehensive study of which ones had been discriminated against and should be preferred. UC-Davis, then, "chose to cast their attention only on select groups and fashioned a remedy not only constitutionally impermissible but patently unfair." There was "no reasoned explanation" why the four preferred groups were chosen, and though a full survey may show no underrepresentation of other groups, "common experience such as the defamation practiced against Americans of Polish descent and origin cause one to be skeptical unless such a finding is firmly established by evidence." "We know of no policy," the brief continued, "set by this Court, the Congress or the Executive which states that racial or any other type of discrimination deserves a higher priority than other prohibited types."

The brief went on to argue that if protections were to be given, they should be extended to all groups experiencing discrimination, and "such a decision should not be made simply because a group is more vocal, better organized, potentially possessed of more political leverage or by the emotion of the moment. It should be made by the full political process exploring in detail all that is involved so that public confidence can be secured and divisiveness avoided."

These Polish American advocates were unhappy with affirmative action because they saw themselves as discriminated against in a way analogous to the official minorities and hence deserving of protection. The brief pointed out the Institute of Urban Life report that revealed Polish and Italian underrepresentation in the higher levels of Chicago corporations; it argued that being called "Polack" was tantamount to a black being called "nigger"; and the brief asserted that it was unfair that groups that suffered discrimination such as Polish Americans, Italian Americans, Arab Americans, and Jewish Americans had to meet higher standards than recently arrived minority immigrants. The brief asked with obvious resentment, "Why are 'Whites' who never practiced discrimination, but fought for and championed equality, and who themselves suffered discrimination obliged to continue to suffer simply because other whites practiced racial discrimination? If Whites are to suffer for the 'greater good' then for how long and for whose benefit?"[89] While the claim that white ethnics never practiced discrimination was clearly inaccurate—many excluded blacks from construction unions and from their neighborhoods—the point was on target with respect to medical and law schools. Ethnics and their ancestors had little responsibility for any underrepresentation of black, Latino, Asian American, and American Indian doctors and lawyers.

Similar efforts on the parts of white ethnics followed. During his term as director of the OFCC from 1977 to 1981, Weldon J. Rougeau was lobbied by Polish and Italian leaders from Chicago and New York who complained of a glass ceiling in corporate employment. Rougeau believed that the government had a responsibility to address all discrimination, but rejected the ethnics' arguments. He explained later, "I don't think [discrimination against them] is as much a problem as is discrimination against black people, against Hispanics, and against women in this country."[90]

Through Walentynowicz's leadership, PAC persuaded the OMB to issue Circular No. 846 on May 12, 1977, authorizing the government to collect data on the federal government's hiring of various European ethnic groups. Walentynowicz also testified before the Civil Service Commission in December 1977, arguing for the inclusion of ethnics in its affirmative-action efforts. In February of 1978, he wrote to EEOC commissioner Eleanor Holmes Norton, cited a memorandum from President Jimmy Carter requesting departments and agencies to collect data for sixteen different groups, and called for the EEOC to collect similar data to enable discrimination complaints by ethnics.[91]

Other ethnic groups were also active. The National Federation of American Ethnic Groups adopted a resolution at their April 1979 convention that ethnic groups be included among the official minorities entitled to affirmative action. In testimony before the US Commission on Civil Rights, Lydio Tomasi, a priest and director of the Center for Migration Studies of New York, told of ethnics who could not obtain employment until they had changed their eastern European names to northern European ones. Tomasi also described the case of an Italian American lawyer who was being represented by the Catholic League for Religious and Civil Rights in his suit for discrimination brought against a prestigious law firm. During trial preparation they found that only 15 of 912 partners in the twenty largest New York law firms were of Italian descent. The Catholic League also gathered statistics showing Catholic underrepresentation in Chicago businesses and American universities, where Catholics accounted for only 10 percent of the faculty despite making up 25 percent of the national population. The New York State Italian American Legislators Caucus and the Association of Italian-American Faculty complained of Italian American underrepresentation at the City University of New York, where Italian Americans accounted for 25 percent of the students but only 4.5 percent of the faculty, concentrated in the assistant professor category.[92]

In 1981, PAC's Walentynowicz also addressed the Commission on Civil Rights during consultations for its official statement on affirmative action. Scheduled to appear as the last speaker, one month after the others, Walentynowicz made new attacks on the logic of the designation of official minorities, pointing out that many Latinos were white, and demanding an explanation as to why no other white groups were separately considered. He asked for a rationale why, if affirmative action's main purpose was to remedy historic discrimination, newly arrived immigrants and refugees could take part in affirmative-action programs.[93]

Walentynowicz was mainly concerned with how the government's stated policy and laws ensuring nondiscrimination coincided with the decision to collect data only on the official minorities. Without such data, it was extremely difficult for nonminorities to make the case that they too faced discrimination. This was especially true in the Small Business Administration program, which presumed eligibility for the official minorities, and nominally included any American who could show that he or she was from a disadvantaged group. Walentynowicz explained, "So then a Polish American comes up to me and he says, 'Well, where am I going to get the data [to prove disadvantage]? If I want a loan for $50,000, it may cost me $50,000 to get the information to prove that I need the loan.'" Walentynowicz wanted to scrap the current system and, after gathering data on all official minorities plus white ethnic groups, replace it with a system that could rank individuals in terms of the disadvantages that they faced, so that well-off minorities would not always be preferred over lower-class ethnics.[94]

Ethnic advocates in Congress

As with other minority groups, ethnics had their own advocates in government. Roman Pucinski went to the House floor to complain of the civil-rights enforcement practice of simply relying on unexamined, bureaucratic designations of the official minority groups in America. Pucinski apparently became aware of the new practice of minority designation in December 1969, though the EEOC's practice began in 1965. He summarized a memorandum that instructed government supervisors how to determine the minority makeup of their offices. Pucinski argued that employees should designate their own group identities and insisted that Euro-American ethnicities should be counted in addition to the other minorities since "it is contrary to the highest interests of equality in this country to arbitrarily select any one group of Americans for identification in their personnel records."[95]

In 1974 House subcommittee on education hearings on the civil rights obligations of higher education institutions, Mario Biaggi and Jack Kemp (R–NY) questioned EEOC chair John Powell Jr. on the place of Italian Americans and Polish Americans in EEOC civil-rights efforts. Following Powell's discussion of the use of hiring and promotion goals for the official minorities, including "Spanish-surnamed people," Biaggi and Kemp asked why people with Italian and Polish surnames were not included. Powell responded that "the complaints [of discrimination] that we have are complaints from people of Spanish-surnamed background in the national origin context" and that the groups on the EEO-6 form (which was the EEO-1 form modified for higher education) reflected the groups that in the Commission's experience had been discriminated against.[96]

This was inaccurate, as the group designations of the form preceded the existence of the EEOC. Powell's comment further contradicted the original purpose of the forms—the EEOC did not consider the number of complaints from a group to be a true measure of discrimination against that group. As discussed in Chapter 4, few in the EEOC believed that the number of complaints from blacks was an accurate measure of discrimination against this group; and while Latino leaders had argued that Latinos suffered discrimination, only a handful had ever complained to the EEOC in its first few years.

Echoing Latino advocates, Biaggi maintained that "if the government were to put the same emphasis on ethnic origins, the same emphasis, and communicate it to them, I am sure you would get more response from them because there is no question in my mind that the offense [of discrimination] is committed in other areas and I am sure you agree with that score and the moment you popularize the notion, there is a place they can obtain redress, you know they will return in hoards." But Powell was convinced there was a standard of discrimination and victimization and that ethnics had not reached it. Leaving out of the discussion the minorities that were most similar to white ethnics (Latinos and Asian Americans), he argued that there were "special problems" for blacks and women that "Polish people, in most contexts do not confront, although in some contexts undoubtedly face." Further, "if a black person applied to a public or private employer in the fifties and the application were for jobs which were not traditionally held by a black person, that type of person would be treated one way and the Polish person and Irish person and Italian person would be treated another, that is history."[97] In this case as in others, the explicit rejection of the analogy with blacks silenced the advocates for ethnics.

At House hearings on affirmative action and from the Senate floor, New York senator James Buckley of the Conservative Party also attacked the unequal status given to ethnics in affirmative-action programs, but did so in the context of an argument that the programs should be dismantled entirely. Buckley made the discovery that though affirmative-action regulations were based on the notion of "minorities," and in fact Revised Order No. 4 used the word "minority" sixty-five times, the regulations never defined what it meant and "the word 'minority' does not appear at all in Executive Order 11246 or in the 1964 Civil Rights Act." Buckley asked researchers at the Library of Congress to uncover the origin of the term, and with the help of some officials from the Civil Service Commission, they traced it to the censuses of government employment taken by the Kennedy administration.[98] Irving Kantor, assistant executive director of the Civil Service Commission, explained that Negroes, Spanish-surnamed Americans, American Indians, and Oriental Americans "appeared to be identifiable and significant enough to measure statistically," while counting other groups "would be impracticable" and "not particularly useful." Kantor's assistant added that "the minority groups selected are those which have historically suffered most discrimination and which have suffered discrimination continuously to the present."

Buckley challenged this reasoning, arguing that preferring some minorities over others violated the Civil Rights Act. In his view, an unspecified "identifiability" should not be the basis of special government treatment, and he charged that the civil-rights administrators simply did not care enough to make affirmative action for ethnics practicable.[99]

Other members of Congress also spoke up for ethnics. In 1979, Senator Jesse Helms (R–NC) and Representatives Barbara Mikulski (D–MD) and William Edwards (D–CA) were able to amend the section of the Civil Rights Act of 1957 that created the US Commission on Civil Rights to direct it to examine the status of ethnics. The fruit of this effort was a consultation on "Civil Rights Issues of Euro-Ethnic Americans in the United States: Opportunities and Challenges." Held on December 3, 1979 in Chicago, an array of ethnic leaders and academic experts presented arguments and exchanged views on the status of this group and the need for the Census Bureau to analyze them.[100]

"With All This Smoke There Must Be Some Fire": White Ethnics as a Political Constituency

Though the Johnson administration did not pursue the white ethnic vote as such, by 1969 both parties began to take great interest in them. Whatever the strength of their advocacy organizations, the ethnic rank and file wielded electoral clout augmented by their concentration in key industrial states (rich with electoral college votes) and Nixon's belief that he could attract these usually Democratic voters. In addition, like women and Latinos, ethnics had prominent spokespersons in the White House, such as Charles Colson, Michael Balzano, and Patrick Buchanan.

From its early days, the Nixon administration recognized ethnics as disadvantaged and considered it worthwhile to pursue their vote. But the administration was apparently confused as to the nature of this group's primary identity. Were they ethnics? Were they Catholics? Were they a class group? Were they union men? Were they patriotic Americans? Were they resentful whites?

In June of 1969, Secretary of Labor George Shultz gave his analysis of the problem to Nixon. Shultz was apparently prompted by an article in *New York* magazine by Pete Hamill on "The Revolt of the Lower White Middle Class" and by a *New York Times* article on how Roman Catholic voters tended to vote against candidates who were identified as sympathetic to minority-group problems. Shultz described the findings of Harris surveys in 1966 that low-income Catholic groups were "most resentful of contemporary social changes in the big cities." Shultz told Nixon:

> They are immigrants, or sons of immigrants, and feel insecure about their own place in the mainstream of American society. They tend to live in neighborhoods that the blacks are most likely to move into, and whose schools black children might attend. They sometimes have jobs that they feel blacks aspire to attain, and they get wages that are only slightly above liberal states' welfare payments. They suffer a real sense of "compression" on both the economic and social scales.
>
> Our review of this serious and growing problem indicates that two key factors underlie the tensions and frustrations. As these men reach their forties, they face an economic squeeze as a result of plateauing earnings and rising family budgets and college expenses. This money squeeze feeds racial hostility and creates a sense of being "forgotten men." The other side of the coin is the emotional and social hostility of working class whites towards minorities, and especially the blacks. These two factors interact and feed upon each other to worsen the overall tensions.[101]

Nixon built on this assessment in October of 1969, when he began to focus on creating what he would later call the "New Majority." The public's growing interest in these matters was stirred partly by increased media attention given to ethnics. *Newsweek* magazine published an article on "The Troubled American Majority" that devoted almost thirty pages to Euro-American discontent, focusing mostly on ethnics.[102] The article maintained that the "pendulum of public attention" was moving to "middle class whites," but went on to confuse the issue by describing the anger, and potential violence, welling up in blue-collar ethnic areas. *Newsweek* maintained that the greatest concern of this group was the US involvement in Vietnam, which most ethnics considered to be a mistake but were unsure how to correct. Other concerns included the decline in morality, criminal-justice reforms, excessive taxation, and the belief that blacks had a better chance of getting ahead than they did.

Newsweek never defined the "troubled American," but it was clear that he or she was typically a white ethnic. The article quoted Roman Pucinski as saying that the rise of black militancy led to a revival of ethnic identity, while a conservative intellectual explained that "the ethnics are discovering that you can't trust those Mayflower boys." Paul Deac, head of the National Confederation of American Ethnic Groups, complained that "we spend millions and the Negroes get everything and we get nothing." Deac told the magazine the ethnic vote was up for grabs. This was seconded by Leon Shull, executive director of the liberal Democrat group Americans for Democratic Action, who said that "any politician who ignores 40 million ethnics is a fool." The *Newsweek* article also described the argument of a controversial book by Republican campaign staffer Kevin Phillips that ethnics could and should become part of "the emerging Republican majority." According to the article, President Nixon told the magazine that he had not read the book.[103]

In fact, the White House was then discussing Phillips's book and developing an ethnic strategy. Administration thinking can be seen in a memo exchange between Harry Dent, the political adviser on the so-called Southern Strategy (the attempt to bring southerners to the Republican Party by slowing civil-rights enforcement), and Nixon. Dent had met with political and congressional leaders at Camp David to discuss strategies for reaching ethnics. Dent reported that a White House task force was being privately established "for the purpose of finding ways and means to reach the 'Forgotten Americans.'"[104] Nixon, inspired by the *Newsweek* article and tired of "talking to the [racial] minorities," asked his aides for "a list of ten items, each of the things we can do program wise and image wise to appeal to this group."[105]

The analysis of the ethnic situation by Dent and the task force was focused on how to reach what they sometimes called "Middle America." One week after the *Newsweek* article was published, he sent Nixon an analysis of a *Wall Street Journal* review of Phillips's *The Emerging Republican Majority*, an article series in the *Washington Star* on the "White Reaction," and a *Wall Street Journal* article on organized labor's strategy to maintain Democratic party control of Congress. Phillips's argument was that winning the presidency required Republicans to win the "swing" industrial states of Ohio, Illinois, Pennsylvania, New Jersey, and California, and to do that they needed to attract the "nominally Democrat white middle class vote." "According to Phillips," Dent explained, "this key group especially the Catholic element is becoming increasingly conservative and can be brought into the Republican camp by a moderately conservative policy." Dent's advice for the "Next Steps" (which Nixon labeled "OK") was to "disavow Phillips' book as party policy and assert we are growing in strength nationally because the public is increasingly conscious of the soundness of our philosophy . . . the sanctity of individual freedom, the evils of centralism, the importance of efficient fiscally sound government."[106]

Regarding the "White Reaction" series, Dent explained that though blacks remained unequal to whites in every measure, they had made great progress, and the improvement in their status had led whites to fear them. "This feeling is especially intense among blue-collar workers and lower middle class home owners who see the Negro as an immediate tangible adversary made even more formidable by lenient courts, militant white churchmen and self-seeking politicians," Dent explained to the president. Both races were losing faith in integration, and "both races see a prolonged period of racial polarization punctuated by conflicts over housing, education, and job discrimination." Dent's advice, also okayed by Nixon, was that

the Administration must proceed carefully through the mine field of contemporary race relations. The slightest misstep can cause an explosion both socially and politically devastating.

On the other hand, we must realize that old political loyalties have been dissolved by the racial situation and that we have an unprecedented opportunity to garner votes in large blocks. To capitalize on this opportunity we need a carefully conceived "master plan" for the Administration to implement.[107]

There never was a master plan, but by 1970, Nixon's interest in appealing to blacks declined.[108] In its place a concern for ethnics developed and became a regular part of Nixonian electoral strategy. In January, Nixon told chief of staff H. R. Haldeman that the administration should concentrate on building "our own new coalition based on [the] Silent Majority [of supporters of Nixon's Vietnam policy], blue collar, Catholic, Poles, Italians, and Irish."[109]

Nixon assigned Charles Colson the role of ethnic coalition builder. A Nixon campaign aide later recalled, "Colson picked up all sorts of secret missions and, as a result, built up an enormous empire in the White House." Respected as a strategic genius, he "had all sorts of groups: Catholics for Nixon, Labor for Nixon," and "was the one who came up with a lot of the thinking about the peripheral urban ethnics, and that drugs and crime were issues for the Republican Party."[110] Haldeman described Colson as an "advocate" who lobbied for the interests of ethnics and labor: "He fought for these causes; he was building a new coalition that Nixon was trying to leave as a legacy for the Republican Party."[111]

In November of 1970, Nixon wanted Colson and Donald Rumsfeld, a political aide and former director of the Office of Economic Opportunity, to decide which groups to focus on for the 1972 election. Colson suggested that "the group consisting of ethnic middle-class working family men is the one we should go after," while Rumsfeld suggested "the suburbanite, who is not a member of a labor union, and generally white collar." Nixon seemed more persuaded by Colson, telling Haldeman that (in Haldeman's words) "we should continue to cultivate Catholics clearly apart from whether they are labor or white collar, and that we should work hard on ethnics—particularly Eastern Europeans and Italians."[112]

Nixon struggled with the question of how to appeal to this group and held meetings with recent ethnic appointees for help. Rocco Siciliano, Nixon's deputy secretary of commerce, later recalled Nixon's concern with the ethnic vote with some puzzlement:

> On July 13, 1970, I was asked to come to the White House to meet with the president. When I arrived, [Secretary of Transportation and Italian American] John Volpe was there. We went into the Oval Office . . . and staff . . . were seated behind us. The president talked about minorities— about Italian-Americans and other ethnic groups. He wanted to know what we could do to get them more involved, to get them to understand what his administration was all about. It was a strange, strange meeting; he was quite agitated.[113]

Advocates within the administration pushed their own ideas. After Nixon said he would end the tradition of a "Jewish seat" on the US Supreme Court, speechwriter (and Catholic) Pat Buchanan urged Nixon to appoint an Italian American to the bench. "The Italians have never had one of their own on the United States Supreme Court," he pointed out, and "as the President used to say, 'the Italians in this country are coming into their own.'" Buchanan argued that "the elevation of a Catholic Italian-American to the Jewish seat on the Court would mean ten million Italians would light candles in their homes for the President." In addition, such an appointment would "remove some of the hurt Italian-Americans constantly feel as a result of Italian-Sicilian control of organized crime in the United States."[114]

There is considerable evidence that representatives of various white ethnic groups exerted pressure to be recognized as a political constituency, either through meetings, appointments, or special programs. These efforts were comparable to those made on behalf of women and Latinos. Laszlo Pasztor, the Hungarian American head of the Republican National Committee's

(RNC) Nationalities Division, communicated much of this pressure.[115] For example, in March of 1970, Pasztor told Harry Dent that he was "flooded with daily letters" from ethnics complaining about a lack of patronage. "We need to show them the kind of 'attention,'" Pasztor explained, "that will offset the constant publicity that blacks, Puerto Ricans and Mexicans and other minority poor are bombarded with."[116] In June, a political aide told Dent, "This ethnic thing continues to plague us as more and more letters come in from various unhappy groups. The head Pole went away from here mad last week, etc, etc. Pasztor is increasingly unhappy and vocal about it. With all this smoke, there must be some fire."[117] The following month, Pasztor sent another note regarding complaints about a lack of appointments, leading an exasperated Dent to write back, "Believe me, we are working on the problem."[118]

The appointment of ethnics to government posts was one area the Nixon administration put major effort into and found some success. As Michael Balzano, a Nixon aide and specialist on ethnic politics, put it later, "A series of agency directorships and assistant secretary positions began going to people whose names were difficult to spell and almost impossible to pronounce."[119] It was not long after the appointments were made before Charles Colson was complaining about insufficient publicity for them in the ethnic press.[120]

Still, it never seemed that enough had been accomplished in this area. Before transportation secretary John Volpe left for his new assignment as ambassador to Italy, he warned Nixon that "I have been receiving word, both directly and indirectly, that [Italian Americans] feel they are being ignored both by the Republican Party and the Administration." He recommended appointment of a person "with an appropriate power influence and authority" to be placed in a "lead position so they will not feel that the Administration has forgotten them." Nixon took the note seriously, asking Haldeman, "Why not more in Advisory Commissions, etc?"[121]

The Ethnic Heritage Studies Program Act: Symbolic politics and the limits of multiculturalism

In the late 1960s and early 1970s many ethnic leaders made it a priority to gain official acknowledgment and respect for their long-repressed cultures. Again, Italian and Polish groups, which suffered the most negative media portrayals, were the most active. On April 30, 1969, Roman Pucinski read on the House floor a proclamation by the Polish American Congress condemning ethnic stereotypes. The group saw themselves as victims of American media elites. Referring to "those who, by the use of vicious ethnic humor and malicious misrepresentation of our cultural heritage, deform and vilify our public image or the heritage and image of any other ethnic group," the PAC proclaimed that it would "on every possible occasion, expose, deplore, and denounce those powerful rulers of the pen and airwaves who violate our right to truth and accuracy."[122]

On November 13, 1969, Pucinski led a coalition of ethnics and official minorities in their push for a new federal law supporting ethnic studies. Pucinski (also a strong advocate for bilingual education for Latinos) introduced the bill, which was co-sponsored by African American John Conyers (D–MI), Mexican American Edward Roybal (D–NM), and Japanese American Spark Matsunaga (D–HI).[123] Pucinski argued that "this Nation thrives on a deep sense of ethnic community" and "we have oversold the value of homogenization, sacrificing the diversity of our pluralistic society for the sake of uniformity." Echoing arguments made on behalf of Latinos and bilingual education, Pucinski explained that "many of our ethnic groups have developed a profound sense of cultural inferiority" while others "have even totally forsaken their ethnic bonds." "The most serious casualties of this quasi-cultural obliteration have been the young," Pucinski explained, who are the "'Forgotten Young Americans,' with no feeling of belonging in our heterogeneous society." The remedy was to fund the creation of Ethnic Heritage Studies Centers in primary and secondary schools. These would develop curriculum materials on a particular group's "history, geography, society, literature, art, music, language, drama, economy and general culture" and on the group's "contributions to American heritage." In this way, "every one of the 51.5 million students in the primary grades and high school could study, in depth, about the ethnic culture of his own family and forefathers, and about their contributions to the American way of life." "Students," Pucinski added, "could also learn about other groups."[124] Senator Richard Schweiker (R–PA) introduced a similar bill in the Senate in January 1971.

Despite the fact that the push for the bill principally came from Pucinski and other ethnic leaders, the bill was never meant to be specifically or primarily for ethnics. It made no reference to which groups would get attention, or if there were requirements for balancing attention and funding equitably.[125] The bill would simply give money to the federal commissioner of education to make grants to public and private nonprofit educational agencies and organizations to assist in the creation of ethnic studies curricula (the notion of creating "centers" was deleted in favor of creating "programs").[126]

While the Nixon White House supported the ethnic studies bill, the president never made much of this support. Laszlo Pasztor took the matter seriously, however, telling the White House in April 1970 that "the Democrats openly admit that they realize that the 1968 elections were lost because a large number of nationalities voters deserted them," and warned of new

Democratic efforts to win them back. These included broadcasting on ethnic radio stations meetings with ethnic leaders in which the Democratic National Committee (DNC) chairman Larry O'Brien told of the 1932 birth of the committee's ethnic division and its new elite office adjacent to his own at the DNC. O'Brien also told ethnic radio listeners of Pucinski's proposed Ethnic Heritage Studies Centers Act—pointing out that the Republicans were doing nothing similar to benefit ethnics.[127]

In July of 1972, without White House involvement, Congress passed the Ethnic Heritage Studies Act as part of Title V of the Higher Education Amendments Act of 1972. The approach of the legislation clashed with Nixon's preferred regulatory strategy, which relied on unfunded mandates. The new law authorized grants for the creation of ethnic heritage studies programs in elementary and secondary schools, and for the establishment of a National Advisory Council on Ethnic Heritage Studies.[128]

Besides adding legitimacy to the politics of difference, the Act did little. Congress gave it only $8.3 million for four years. In May 1976, Rev. Andrew M. Greeley said in a speech at the HEW Office of Education that the program was "tokenism with a vengeance, a sop thrown at the ethnics to keep them quiet."[129]

The program could have been popular. John A. Carpenter, chief of the new Ethnic Heritage Studies branch of the Office of Education later wrote, "The national response to the Ethnic Heritage Studies Program has been immense. Despite the brief one-month period available for preparation of proposals, more than 1,000 plans were proposed to the United States Office of Education for only 42 grants." Eligible proposals would have required more than $84 million. While it is not clear which groups predominated in the proposals, every state sent applications, plus Puerto Rico, Guam, Samoa, and the Virgin Islands, and more than fifty ethnic groups were represented.[130]

To recognize ethnics, the Nixon White House preferred another (even less expensive) idea: a day on which ethnics were told they were important. Pasztor suggested to Harry Dent in May 1972 a presidential proclamation for a "National Heritage Day." This would "obviously be a non-political proclamation, but because of our organizational apparatus, we would be able to get the message across that it was a Republican President who initiated the idea . . . [I]t would have great appeal to the ethnic groups, for it would bring national attention to the fact that they are a large segment of the composite whole that is America."[131] Dent passed the memo on to Charles Colson with great enthusiasm for the idea, "particularly for this year 1972 with so many good ethnic voters out there." "At a meeting of the campaign strategy committee," Dent explained, "we found that the biggest single block of voters are the various nationality groups."[132] The administration's confidential proposal for the National Heritage Day proclamation described the great political benefits that would come from having Nixon tell ethnics they were important and that he celebrated their diversity.[133]

At the same time, representatives of ethnic groups were pressuring Michael Balzano for an audience with Nixon, though (like Latinos) they did not have clear demands. According to Colson, "These people want nothing more than an opportunity to meet with the President and to give him a token of their support." When a proposed signing ceremony for the Heritage Day proclamation was canceled, Colson sent an angry note to Haldeman. "There is a limit to how much we can do for the President without the support of these groups. Balzano tells me that we seem to be unable to deliver anything to the groups who are austensibly [sic] our friends." "Turn this thing around," Colson told chief of staff Haldeman, who was usually the one giving the orders. "Let us have a massive signing ceremony and reception large enough to symbolically do it up big."[134]

Despite all of the political importance assigned to ethnic voters, and despite all of the lobbying and demands for attention on the part of ethnic leaders, Nixon chose to forgo even a signing ceremony when he issued the National Heritage Day Proclamation on September 30. He did, however, extol the glories of all immigrants four days earlier in a dedication ceremony for the new Museum of Immigration on Liberty Island on September 26. Nixon stated that though America is described as a "melting pot," it "does not force its people into a narrow mold of conformity. America is a rich mosaic of many cultures and traditions, strong in its diversity."[135] One month later, Nixon gave a radio address on the topic of "One America" that contained typically mawkish and sycophantic statements about the great contributions made by immigrants. But he also used the opportunity to describe the "New Majority" that he envisioned, and to mention specifically some of the groups he thought were in this coalition: "the Polish-American, the Italian-American, the Mexican-American, the steelworker, the farmer." The speech was written to appeal to ethnic voters, as it emphasized the importance of a tough stand in Vietnam, "respect for the law," "belief in honest hard work, love of country, spiritual faith." Drawing a division in this One America, Nixon intoned a white ethnic credo: "America is the land of opportunity, not a land of handouts. Each of us deserves a fair chance to get ahead. But none of us has the right to expect a free ride—to remain idle, to take advantage of other men's labor."[136]

This sort of purely symbolic recognition of ethnicity continued through the second Nixon term. Michael Balzano was given much of the responsibility for appealing to ethnics. But rather than initiating a study of discrimination against ethnics, or making efforts to increase their representation in top law or medical schools, or establishing a project to break the glass ceiling facing ethnics in corporate America, or helping create more white-collar opportunities so that they would not cling to their union positions by excluding blacks, Balzano oversaw what were merely symbols and empty gestures. For example, one effort was to have Mrs. Nixon named honorary chair of the Polish War Veterans Benefit Ball.[137]

Why No Policy Recognition for Ethnics? What Does the Comparison Tell Us about the Minority Rights Revolution?

There were no significant, difference-conscious, rights-oriented policies for ethnics. They did not benefit from affirmative action in employment, education, or aid for businesses. Though eligible for bilingual education, their immigration numbers had shrunk from their old magnitude, and eastern and southern Europeans were only a tiny fraction of those in bilingual education programs. They certainly were not appealed to with such programs. The Ethnic Heritage Studies Act never received significant funding. Multicultural education developed in a way that completely ignored ethnics.[138] What was unique about the way policy elites perceived ethnics and tried to appeal to them? A comparison with ethnics along these lines can shed light on the crucial characteristics of the official minorities, including women and the disabled, that allowed for their inclusion in the minority rights revolution.

One possibility is that politicians did not see ethnics as sufficiently mobilized for pursuing minority status. On several occasions, civil-rights administrators had told Latino and women's leaders that the squeaky wheel gets the grease; it could be that ethnics were not squeaking enough. Indeed, if analyzed with the standard measures used by scholars of social movements, the white ethnic movement would likely show weak leadership, inconsistent goals, few protest events, poor organization, and (despite Ford Foundation efforts) limited resources. Arthur Mann, for example, has argued that the leadership distorted the nature of what ethnics really wanted because they were cut off from the majority ethnic views.[139] Nathan Glazer, long sympathetic to the cause, similarly agreed that the ethnic leaders' claims did not accurately reflect demands of the majority of ethnics: "It is hard to mourn the loss of a lost culture when one does not possess or recall it."[140] Compared to a movement like that seeking civil rights for blacks, the movement for white ethnics was a flash in the pan.

Even *if* public protest and "making noise" were the keys for inclusion in the minority rights revolution (and I do not believe they were for reasons described below), differences between ethnics and the official minorities on this score is an inadequate explanation for the failure of ethnics as a minority.

First, a balanced comparison between white ethnic political mobilization and that of the official minorities is impossible. As the PAC's Walentynowicz pointed out, the ethnic leaders operated with the enormous disadvantage of not having already been designated as a victimized minority group by the EEOC and OFCC and not having a collection of data at hand to show areas of underutilization.

Second, even with this disadvantage, the ethnic mobilization and activity was not that different. It is easy to exaggerate the level of mobilization of the nonblack minorities. None of them mass mobilized or showed the commitment and unity of purpose of black groups. They did not engage in anything like the mass violence that ran rampant in America's black neighborhoods in the late 1960s. Though Latinos had longer-lived groups and likely had more protest events than white ethnics, such as the "blowouts" in the schools demanding Chicano studies, there is little evidence those local protest events registered in Washington. Latino and women's mobilizations were usually discussed in the White House only as hearsay or news reports. But ethnics also had news reports on their activities, and while they certainly had fewer protest events, the Italian American rights effort in New York attracted an estimated forty to one hundred thousand people, and this was larger than any Latino or women's event in the period.

Moreover, the Latino leadership almost obsessively focused on patronage and group representation in policymaking positions, and *not* on the policies relating to affirmative action and bilingual education that they won. Compared to NOW and WEAL, the white ethnic leadership was disorganized, yet both movements had conflicting goals. White ethnic leaders both critiqued affirmative action and sought to be included. The demands of Women's leaders were less obviously but similarly conflicted. NOW and WEAL, for example, simultaneously sought to be included in affirmative action, sought to have women treated without regard to their sex, and sought some "separate-but-equal" institutions.

As Mann and Glazer make clear, another possible criticism of the white ethnic movement is that even had it been well financed and organized, the leaders did not speak for the rank-and-file ethnic citizens who may have preferred quiet assimilation. In short, the ethnic leaders had no constituency. While this argument has merit, similar assessments can be made of the other minority groups. As described in Chapter 4, many Mexican leaders avoided seeking to draw an analogy between their plight and that of blacks, choosing to portray their group as mostly white until the mid-1960s, when national policy brought a positive meaning to nonwhiteness. Even then, Latino leaders faced the embarrassing fact that almost no Latinos were complaining to the EEOC of discrimination. On other issues, the representativeness of Latino leaders is also questionable. Were Mexican American citizens really so concerned that they be the subject of more White House conferences and receive more government jobs, as Latino leaders demanded (Chapters 5 and 7)? Mexican American leaders sometimes fought for "brown power," ignoring the fact (as did everyone else) that about half of Mexican Americans consider themselves white even today. And at least one leading advocacy group, the Mexican American Legal Defense and Education Fund, had no constituency at all and is still entirely funded by outside donors. For these reasons, the political scientist Peter Skerry has referred to Mexican Americans as "the ambivalent minority."[141]

Women's leaders similarly had an uncertain status as leaders of a mass constituency. This was obvious throughout the 1970s and early 1980s, as NOW and WEAL were defeated by a countermobilization of women, led by Phyllis Schlafly, who sought to avoid ratification of the Equal Rights Amendment.[142] It also appears that Title IX created a broad interest in women's sports, and not the other way around.

These issues may not be important, however, because it is not clear that lobbying, protest, and movement leadership were important or necessary for inclusion in the minority rights revolution. As I have argued throughout this book, the legacies of the struggle for black civil rights greatly reduced the effort required to make policy gains for other groups. For example, American Indians were included in affirmative action without any lobbying at all. Title IX and Section 504 passed without lobbying. During their passage there were no howls of warning and complaint as there were when the OFCC quietly issued proposed regulations for white ethnic affirmative action in the *Federal Register*. The civil rights institutional homes created for African Americans allowed significant policy gains to flow from a few simple meetings of minority advocates and civil-rights administrators, as the right to educational language accommodation clearly showed. Thus, while the white ethnic movement was weak and conflicted, it cannot be said that the other movements I have considered were exemplars of powerful organization and mass protest, or needed to be to win rights.

Even if we grant that ethnics had a weak movement while they needed a strong one, there was another potential compensatory factor. Like the other groups, and perhaps even more so, white ethnics had patrons in Congress and in the White House who attended their rallies and conferences, met with their leaders, and very much wanted their votes. While they may have lacked strong leadership and mobilization outside of government, white ethnics undeniably had political clout inside.

The historical record points to three main reasons ethnics did not win minority rights. First, some policymakers saw practical problems in extending minority rights to ethnics, such as how to identify them and fears that people could change their identification. This is an important but not determining point. Visual identification mattered only in employment affirmative action to complete the EEO-1 forms. External identification was not a problem for affirmative action in minority capitalism and university admissions, where the policy relies on self-identification. Nevertheless, these programs did not go beyond the EEO-1's list of minorities.

Moreover, the Nixon officials who focused on the practical problems of employment affirmative action for ethnics exaggerated them while ignoring similar problems for the groups included in affirmative action. Employment affirmative action for blacks, for example, depended entirely on the continued maintenance of the so-called one-drop rule, which culturally defines anyone with at least some African ancestry as being black.[143] The edifice of affirmative action was built on an originally racist scheme of group categorization, and its administrative efficacy relied entirely on maintaining this scheme. No one noticed—or cared.

And what of groups with high intermarriage rates that are not subject to the one-drop rule? Or groups that appeared to be white? If the one-drop rule made African American categorization simple, this was not true of other groups. The issue of difficult categorizations and potentially changing identities excluded ethnics from affirmative action in 1972, but not American Indians, whose numbers curiously doubled between 1950 and 1970 and continued to rise afterward. The change was mostly the result of changing self-identification.[144] While American Indians were a small category, the same could not be said of Latinos, who were similarly left out of White House discussions on the practicality of affirmative action. Latinos, a category so complex that members of the group can be of any race, had no definitive group name in the late 1960s and early 1970s (government officials alternately referred to Spanish Americans, Spanish-surnamed Americans, Spanish-speaking Americans, Hispanics, Latinos, or simply used Mexican-American and usually left out other groups). They have typically exhibited high rates of intermarriage.[145]

Inclusion of Latinos, then, invites some of the same practical problems regarding identification. For example, in hearings held in Los Angeles in 1968 on minority employment, the EEOC confronted Anthony J. Frederick, vice president of Universal Studios, with statistics that showed an underrepresentation of Mexican Americans at Universal. Frederick argued in response that Mexican Americans were difficult to identify, stating, "I couldn't tell you a Mexican American, if I were to look at him. We are not permitted to ask a person his nationality, his national origin, in this state, and we don't and you cannot tell by surname." Mexican American commissioner Vicente Ximenes challenged him: "[A]ll you have to do is go through the roster, and you will find 'Garcia, Ramos, or Montes,' and it is going to be a Spanish surname." Of course, if ethnic identification was this easy, a similar method could work for ethnics. But it was not so easy. Frederick added:

> We have a fellow named Carbonas, and I could go on naming names, but, as I say, I cannot tell you all the Mexican Americans, and I have been around for a good many years. And we have one in production in particular who has the name of Harling, and I certainly would not recognize that as Mexican American than the man on the moon, and by looking at him you can't tell. We had a meeting the other day with a group of Mexican Americans, and they don't look any different than any of us do really.[146]

In short, there was precedent for ignoring the practical problems associated with ethnic affirmative action. If identifying Spanish surnames was a method for identifying Latinos, then there is little reason to believe that employers could not identify names like Takacs, Krasuski, Lopilato, Czlonka, or Balac.

A more important factor, then, was that civil-rights administrators (and, apparently, university admissions officers) had priorities. The priorities came from the belief that the official minorities suffered from greater discrimination both in the past and present. Constraints of time and resources reinforced the unspoken principle that there was a threshold of discrimination and victimhood that a group was required to meet before rights or policy recognition was available. Inadequate oppression as measured by some unspecified standard therefore caused the analogy with blacks to fail.

The sharp dividing line between white ethnics and the official minorities was easier to maintain because the critics of affirmative action for ethnics apparently had little knowledge of ethnic history in America. This ignorance (or indifference) was evident even in the 1947 President's Committee on Civil Rights report, written before federal policy had declared official minorities and not far removed in time from the most severe anti-ethnic discrimination. While ethnics were rarely treated as badly as the other groups, the treatment they received was often very severe. Indeed, at the turn of the twentieth century, ethnics were treated as something other than white—they were "dagoes," "polacks," "hunkies," and "guineas," slotted into the least desirable occupations.[147] Clear evidence of discrimination and ethnic discontent continued through World War II, provoking President Roosevelt to plead with employers to stop discriminating against those with "foreign-sounding names."[148] In 1950, the Soviet Union was beaming propaganda to Italy and Slavic countries, telling of discrimination against Italians and Slavs in America.[149] Moreover, critics of ethnic affirmative action stressing political disadvantages faced by official minorities in the past were ignorant of Progressive Era election reforms that had the effect of disenfranchising many eastern and southern European immigrants. Literacy tests disenfranchised European immigrants along with Asians, Mexicans, and blacks.[150] While none of this approached the oppression of African Americans or American Indians, it was closer to some of the discrimination suffered by Latinos or Asian Americans, at least in the twentieth century.

To be sure, white ethnics were showing signs of high social mobility by the 1970s.[151] Andrew Greeley, tirelessly trying to dispel ethnic stereotypes, published a study in 1976 that, astonishingly, showed both Jews and Catholic ethnics experiencing high educational mobility, and doing even better than the ostensibly privileged Protestants in measures of family income.[152] This pattern was confirmed in later research using 1980 census data.[153] The sociologist Richard Alba and his colleagues later demonstrated that during the 1980s ethnics were moving to the suburbs and intermarrying at high rates.[154]

On the other hand, political life is not based on reality, but on perceptions of reality. And the dominant perception was that there were millions of ethnics, they were urban, and they were disadvantaged. The perception matched at least some parts of ethnic reality. As with Asian Americans, there were statistics simultaneously showing success and disadvantage. For example, Nathan Glazer and Daniel Patrick Moynihan reported the results of a 1963 survey of New York City that found that while 9.5 percent of blacks were professionals, only 5 percent of Italians were in the professions.[155] A 1969 study by the Census Bureau of ethnic groups found that Italian Americans were near the bottom according to nearly every measure.[156] Roger Waldinger's research in New York City showed that Italians were concentrated in low-status "skilled but almost exclusively blue-collar" niches until the 1980s. Niches from previous decades lived on, as Italian Americans concentrated in apparel, construction, retail groceries, wholesale food, bakeries, and barber shops. Waldingers's data from 1970 showed that Italians had moved into government jobs, a step up, "but unlike the Jews, who worked for government as teachers, college professors, and accountants, the Italian civil servants clustered in the post office, in sanitation, and in transportation."[157] Greeley's study that showed ethnics were doing well economically also found the Catholic groups to be lower in occupational prestige than others, and especially had trouble turning college degrees into prestigious occupations with the ease of Protestants and Jews. Greeley pointed to discrimination as a possible cause.[158] Mark Levy and Michael Kramer's 1972 analysis of ethnicity in politics reported that less than half of Polish Americans had graduated from high school and were overwhelmingly concentrated in low-prestige, blue-collar occupations. Italians showed comparable disadvantage.

Forty percent of both groups were in labor unions.[159] In 1982, Richard Alba and Gwen Moore found underrepresentation of non-Irish Catholics in many elite positions in society, including business and politics.[160] This data is congruent with the dominant perception of the ethnics during this period, especially in the Nixon White House, though not shared in the civil-rights agencies.

Whatever the perceptions of policymakers, this unlegislated, undebated adherence to a discrimination threshold can also be but a partial explanation of why white ethnics were left out of the minority rights revolution. Discrimination was not the basis for all affirmative action. As shown in Chapter 5, the affirmative-action program for minority capitalists developed *without* a discrimination rationale. It was originally a measure to head off urban rioting, and its expansion grew as a result of anticipatory politics and a simple model of proportional-representation justice. Affirmative admissions in colleges and professional schools also spread without a clear discrimination rationale. Indeed, the "diversity" rationale for affirmative admissions logically should have included ethnics (Justice Powell even gave an Italian American as an example of an acceptable preference beneficiary), but no universities took this step.

The minority rights revolution did not include white ethnics for another reason, this one also related to group meanings: policymakers perceived more identities among ethnics than among the official minorities, which contributed to the failure of the black analogy.[161] As shown above, Nixon officials, and most likely congressional leaders as well, saw ethnics in terms of their ethnicity, but also in terms of their religion (mostly Catholicism), their class, and in other ways. Much more than members of the official minority groups, ethnics were multifaceted, and this shaped ethnic politics and policy, channeling strategic anticipatory politics away from minority rights and affirmative action.[162]

A document produced by the Nixon administration for the 1972 election reveals the polysemous quality of ethnics. Charles Colson and other aides working on political strategy created lengthy sociological and political analyses of various target voter groups in American society, such as Latinos, blacks, and ethnics. What the report based on these analyses had to say about ethnic American voters well represents administration thinking on this group, and highlights its differences with other groups.[163]

In the first place, the ethnic voter report stated that transportation secretary Volpe was to be the "administration's ethnic (not Blue-Collar) spokesman" and should be "talking constantly about the importance of ethnic heritage, national tradition, etc. and about concrete problems such as prejudice against ethnics." However, though the Nixon team knew that "ethnic identification among all population sectors appears to be on the upswing," ethnicity was not the only way to target ethnic voters. These voters could be appealed to in terms of economic class or other identities. "An ethnic appeal is one key to the lower middle-middle-class, Blue-Collar voter who was the 'swing' voter in both 1968 and 1970," but there were others. The Nixon administration saw the ethnic voter issues as essentially the same as blue-collar issues, "Middle American" issues, and issues that appealed to probable George Wallace supporters. The report went on to state that the ethnic voter, blue collar, and Middle America findings "should be considered together and interchangeable. Rarely would we find any voter in one category who could not also be placed in at least one of the other two."[164] Though Latinos were largely represented in blue-collar employment, and shared many of the conservative social views of ethnics and Middle Americans, the Nixon administration did not consider them interchangeable with a multiplicity of other identities. For example, the companion strategy report for Latinos racialized this group, stating, "Because of their language, ethnic pride and skin color, Spanish-speaking Americans have traditionally stood apart from the core of American Society."[165]

Perceiving ethnics as an economic class, as blue collar or union members, led to a distinct set of symbolic or policy appeals. Ethnics tended to be insecure about their economic status; they were not as poor as blacks or Latinos on average but they were not accumulating great wealth either. Consequently, Nixon officials believed that to win the ethnic vote "the unemployment issue is particularly important," and "the 'bread-and-butter' initiatives we have taken so far should be played strong. We cannot expect to gain substantial support from this group unless we are willing to do something substantial for them."

The importance of economic issues made the ethnics' identities as union members more salient. Nixon himself was strongly supportive of developing "strength with the labor unions and union leadership," and directed Haldeman to tell Colson that he was "most anxious to move hard, fast and extensively in this whole area" and "is counting on you to see that this is done."[166] Colson's response showed how the perceived identities of ethnics were mixed with their being seen as unionists, and the ways that the structure of unions focused efforts toward "cultivating" leaders rather than doing something of substance for union members. Colson explained that "we should not overlook the close relationship of the ethnic eastern European bloc to our whole labor activity. By and large we are talking about many of the same people." To win this bloc, Colson suggested encouraging support from the longshoremen's leader Teddy Gleason, but not the head of the United Auto Workers who was "a socialist who will never support us."

Colson argued that "our task . . . is to cultivate local leaders, who are strongly patriotic, anti-student and keenly aware of the race question."[167] In Haldeman's report of Nixon's orders for Colson, the emphasis was similarly on identifying possible friends in the labor leadership "who tend to lean our way and are worthy of nurturing," and "picking them off one by one."[168] While Colson felt that "romancing the union leadership" was not always sufficient to get the vote, sometimes it was enough.[169] In explaining why Nixon should meet union leader Peter Brennan, Colson argued:

> Far and away the most important reason of all is that Brennan really does control the Building Trades in New York. He is enormously powerful. In New York City alone there are 250,000 building tradesmen. Brennan contends that 90% voted for Humphrey in 1968, but that he can deliver 90% to our side in 1972. From the raw political standpoint this guy has to be regarded as one of the key labor contacts nationally because he could wield decisive power in New York which might well be a decisive state.[170]

Winning ethnic votes, then, required meeting with union leaders like Peter Brennan, but not giving ethnics affirmative action or ethnic heritage studies.

Then there was ethnics-as-Middle-Americans. Seeing them as vulnerable to the right-wing populism of Alabama governor George Wallace led to negative policies for other minorities. Rather than helping ethnics improve their position in society, Nixon could win their support by limiting the gains of blacks or the march of liberalism on a variety of cultural issues. This was similar to his policy toward the south—win allegiance by slowing down civil rights—and amounted to "nationalization of the Southern Strategy," as Paul Frymer and I have called it.[171] Haldeman wrote in his diary on July 21, 1971, "There are many ways to get the working people with us. Jobs is the main one, but the racial issue and a lot of others can also be used."[172] So similar were the appeals to the northern working class ethnics to those for southerners that, in a memo to Harry Dent, political strategist Kevin Phillips titled the subject of the memo as "Southern/Blue-Collar Strategy."[173] The political thinking in both cases was the same.

Thus, the ethnic voter report explained that though "housing is another key issue for this group," efforts to help ethnics gain new housing were not necessary. It meant only that the Nixon team had to ensure that blacks were not integrated too much in ethnic neighborhoods. Reports indicated that "HUD may be pursuing 'dispersal' housing contrary to the President's instructions. This should be investigated and stopped publicly." Additionally, "the President's strong 'law-and-order' position, and the actions that have followed from it, should be particularly popular among ethnics." The Democrats' nomination of liberal George McGovern certainly made this strategy to win ethnics easier. Nixon told Colson and Haldeman that though he had made gains among the ethnics, McGovern and his running mate Sargent Shriver were making "blatant" attempts to win back the ethnics. "The only way to keep them [McGovern and Shriver] from getting well," Nixon explained, "is not by defending our policy, but by hammering hard on those issues which irritate these people about McGovern." This meant "the blue collar issues, and the Catholic issues, where McGovern simply cannot be as appealing to them as we are."[174]

As Nixon's comment suggests, ethnics were overwhelmingly Catholic. The two categories tended to meld together, as evident in this July, 1971 Haldeman diary entry: "the place for us is not with the Jews and the Negroes, but with the white ethnics and [for] that we have to go after the Catholic thing."[175] This offered yet another way to win votes using policymaking that avoided reifying ethnic identities and was more symbolic than substantial. As the ethnic voter report explained:

> One of the most important set of secondary issues are those affecting the Catholic voter (The majority of ethnic voters are Catholic). The President has made important steps in support of parochial schools. These should be followed up with concrete support of a plan to support them through some kind of 'voucher' system . . . Also of note are the President's strong stand against abortion, his designation of Henry Cabot Lodge as his personal representative to the Vatican, and his two visits with Pope Pual [sic] since assuming the Presidency.

And of course, patronage worked well with Catholics, though Nixon and Haldeman sometimes guessed wrong as to who was a Catholic.[176]

As I describe in Chapter 2, one factor that worked to accord rights and recognition for other groups was the Cold War. Yet national security policy worked *against* granting minority rights for ethnics. Unlike other minority groups, ethnics often were fiercely anti-Communist owing to the Communist domination of many of their countries of origin or ancestry. This meant that unlike blacks, Latinos, women, or any other minority groups except Cuban Americans, ethnics could be appealed to with patriotic symbols and anti-Communist rhetoric in foreign policy.

The use of foreign policy to attract ethnic voters has a long pedigree in US history, as the historian Alexander DeConde has pointed out. For example, though Republicans were not ready to take serious action to support the failed 1956 Hungarian revolution, Congress encouraged and Eisenhower proclaimed a symbolic "Captive Nations Week," to be repeated annually until freedom was achieved.[177] Though the Nixon team's report on ethnic voters voiced concern that "those from the so-called 'captive nations' view our China initiative with considerable suspicion," it also seemed confident that patriotic appeals, criticism of hippie antiwar protesters, and any anti-Communist rhetoric would work to appeal to these voters.

In short, ethnics had everything that one would assume was required for being the beneficiary of rights-oriented, equal-opportunity-granting, difference-conscious policy. They had a Washington presence. They had advocates in Congress and in the White House. Politicians wanted their votes, and saw them as an economically disadvantaged group. But policymakers also saw that the disadvantages of ethnics never rose to some perceived threshold of oppression. Most important, unlike blacks, Latinos, the disabled, and—at least until the ERA debate in the 1970s—women, ethnics were seen in a more complex, multifaceted way, with multiple, equal identities. Left out of affirmative action, national policy therefore racialized ethnics as privileged whites and they remained close but just outside the minority rights revolution.

Why Not Gay Rights?

As described above, one of the reasons for the failure of minority rights for white ethnics was the existence of an unlegislated, undebated threshold of victimization and discrimination that shaped federal policy. While this threshold may have been a factor in the case of ethnics, comparison with another group suggests that it cannot explain the overall dynamics of the minority rights revolution. Indeed, the group that the greatest percentage of Americans perceived as targets of discrimination was also one of the groups that was left out of the minority rights revolution.

Like ethnics, gays and lesbians met the basic requirements for receiving validation as a minority group and protection from discrimination. There can be little doubt that this group suffers discrimination and did so during the height of the minority rights revolution in 1965–75, and it is almost certain that most Americans knew of this discrimination. A 1977 Harris poll found that more Americans thought gays suffered discrimination (55 percent) than thought blacks suffered discrimination (41 percent) (see Table 9.1).[178] However, despite their status as targets of discrimination, and the widespread perception of this group as such targets, neither President Johnson nor President Nixon promoted gay rights, and neither house of Congress passed legislation to recognize and protect gays and lesbians.

Gay rights failed at the federal level for a simple reason: the perceived meaning of the group. Gays and lesbians are like other minorities I have considered in that Americans perceive them as analogous to blacks in terms

Table 9.1 1977 Harris Poll: "Do you feel that *(read list)* are discriminated against more than most people, less, or no more than others?"

	More (%)	No more (%)	Less (%)	Not sure (%)
Homosexuals	55	24	3	18
Blacks	41	43	9	7
Puerto Ricans	33	45	3	19
Mexican Americans	32	46	4	18
Women	31	56	7	6
Jews	19	64	5	12
Japanese Americans	14	60	6	20
Chinese Americans	14	61	6	19
People of Italian descent	7	73	7	13
Catholics	5	76	8	11

Source: Connie de Boer, "The Polls: Attitudes toward Homosexuality," *Public Opinion Quarterly* 42 (1978), p. 272. Reprinted by permission of Harris Interactive.[SM]

of their being targets of discrimination and suffering unequal opportunity. Like Latinos, women, and the disabled, they also have special problems and seemed to require unique treatment. But here the black analogy failed. Gays and lesbians are unique in a way that puts them at a disadvantage relative to other groups. During the period of the minority rights revolution and continuing to the end of the twentieth century, many Americans and leaders in government saw gays as immoral or ill, sometimes both. The words "homosexual" or "gay" in the context of American politics connote both a minority-like status and yet a separation from other minorities. Gays therefore did not find strong advocates in the government, as did other groups, and the logic of client politics or anticipatory politics never extended to them. Any politician promoting gay rights risked their place in office in a way that advocacy for other groups did not, and strong advocacy of gay rights was and remains inappropriate in national politics.

Emergence of a Gay-Rights Movement

An active social movement was not necessary to win minority rights policies, but it could certainly help, and it is worth exploring whether there was a gay-rights movement during the 1965–75 period. In fact, a gay and lesbian underground culture existed throughout the twentieth century. The first gay-oriented political organization was the Mattachine Society, founded in 1951. A lesbian organization, the Daughters of Bilitis, formed in 1955. The peculiar names of these organizations highlight the fact that they were not rights-focused organizations. "Mattachine" referred to political satirists of medieval

Europe, while "Bilitis" alluded to Greek poetry celebrating the love between women. These organizations remained small and quiet, and there was little sense that they sought to mobilize gays as a minority like blacks. The groups limited their battles to such efforts as keeping the US mail open to their magazines, securing permission to serve alcohol at gay bars, and fighting police entrapment of gay men (all fifty states had antisodomy laws on the books).[179] By the mid-1960s, however, some gay leaders began to change their organizational model and goals after observing the government response to the black movement. As activist Frank Kameny explained, "We would be foolish not to recognize what the Negro rights movement has shown us is sadly so . . . that mere persuasion, information and education are not going to gain for us in actual practice the rights of equality which are ours in principle."[180]

It was not until the summer of 1969 that a significant homosexual-rights movement developed. The catalyzing event, now legendary among many gay leaders, occurred when the New York City police raided the Stonewall Inn, a well-established gay bar. Police raids were common at such places, though the triggering "crime" would vary. On this night, the infraction was said to be selling liquor without a license. While the raid was routine, the reaction was not: there was violent resistance. Police arrested thirteen persons and four police officers were injured. The following night, four hundred young people confronted police in the same area of the city, and a melee ensued as shouts of "I'm a faggot, and proud of it!" and "Gay Power!" echoed in the night.[181]

After Stonewall, new and more visible gay groups formed, such as the Gay Liberation Front. The quick acceptance of the phrase "coming out" for openly identifying oneself as homosexual reinforced the notion that being gay was a primary identity, similar to the way policymakers perceived a minority identity. More than eight hundred gay political groups formed across the country by 1973, an increase of 750 from 1968.[182] There were other manifestations of group emergence. The number of gay bars increased markedly, and in 1970, thousands paraded down New York's Sixth Avenue to commemorate the one-year anniversary of the Stonewall Inn incident.[183]

These events were not obscure. In October of 1969, *Time* magazine featured a cover story on "The Homosexual: Newly Visible, Newly Understood." The nation's leading news magazine announced there was a new minority in America: "Encouraged by the national climate of openness about sex of all kinds and the spirit of protest, male and female inverts [homosexuals] have been organizing to claim civil rights for themselves as an aggrieved minority." *Time* told Americans of the gay-rights movement's influence on elections in New York, San Francisco, and Los Angeles, and described demonstrations held at businesses, the White House, and the Pentagon demanding equal job opportunities and the right to serve in the military. It described research that showed 10 percent of gays had been blackmailed, and 25 percent robbed, with the robberies often accompanied by physical assaults. Following the logic of the *Brown v. Board of Education* school desegregation decision and some of the arguments for bilingual education, Kameny argued in a forum of experts (entitled "Are Homosexuals Sick?") that negative attitudes "are poisonous to the individual's self-esteem and self-confidence. The individual is brainwashed into a sense of his own inferiority, just as other minorities are." *Time* declared, "The case for greater tolerance of homosexuals is simple. Undue discrimination wastes talents that might be working for society. Police harassment . . . wastes manpower and creates unnecessary suffering."[184]

By 1971, annual celebrations of Stonewall had become international events, as Parisians and Londoners held their own commemorations.[185] Advocates for gays in the 1970s succeeded in having "homosexuality" removed from the American Psychiatric Association's list of mental illnesses, and political leaders increasingly began to argue that gays and lesbians were something like race and ethnic minorities.[186] The gay-rights advocate and historian Jonathan Katz gave voice to the ubiquitous emerging (nonblack) minority-rights claim of the period: "We have been the silent minority, the silenced minority—invisible women, invisible men."[187]

Though many of the radical groups flamed out, mainstream gay-rights organizations lived on and gays saw a rise in their political fortunes and national presence. Between 1969 and 1973, six states removed laws that had rendered same-sex sexual activity illegal.[188] At the 1972 Democratic Party Convention, gay advocates demanded nondiscrimination rights and the right to marry, and the New York delegation had nine affiliates of the Gay Liberation Front (three times the number of representatives from labor unions).[189] In 1973, gay activists created a national organization called the National Gay and Lesbian Task Force, which grew to ten thousand members by 1980 (not much smaller than NOW's fifteen thousand members in 1972).[190] Also, the Gay Rights National Lobby formed in 1976, the Human Rights Campaign in 1980, and the National Coalition of Black Lesbians and Gays in 1982. In short, gay rights had momentum and grew as a force in US politics throughout the 1970s.

Gays as a Political Constituency

Though this was a period of increasing recognition of minority rights as both a noble cause and smart electoral politics in Washington, gay rights simply were not an issue in Congress or the White House. Indeed, where gay power was perhaps the strongest, the 1972 Democratic Party convention, gay rights did not make it into the party platform. Instead there was only a vague exhortation that Americans avoid drifting into a bland homogeneity—a generalizing discourse that was often used in support of multiculturalism.[191]

Because gay rights had not emerged as a public issue during the Johnson years, it is not surprising that no gay initiatives emerged from his presidency. Indeed, one of Johnson's grand liberal initiatives, the Immigration Act of 1965, eliminating all ethnic discrimination from immigration law, retained an exclusion of "sexual deviants" among would-be immigrants. Johnson even assured worried members of Congress that the new bill would not eliminate this provision, which was used to exclude gays and lesbians since 1917 (it was not removed until 1990).[192]

The public issue became more salient during Nixon's first year in office. But despite prominority rights efforts on behalf of blacks, Latinos, American Indians, Asian Americans, women, and the disabled, there is little evidence of discussion of gay rights in the Nixon White House. While the *Newsweek* cover story on "the troubled American majority"—which really focused on a minority, the white ethnics—attracted Nixon White House discussion and analysis, the similar *Time* article on homosexuals did not.

Discussion of gays or lesbians in any capacity was rare in the Nixon White House. The bits of evidence of attention that were given to gays are as revealing as they are embarrassing. In his memoirs, John Ehrlichman tells of a 1969 report to Nixon from FBI director J. Edgar Hoover that Ehrlichman, Haldeman, and Dwight Chapin were gay lovers. Offending Ehrlichman, Nixon agreed to an investigation that "cleared" the three of them.[193] Another incident was revealed in the release of Nixon's tape-recorded conversations he had in the Oval Office. In a May 13, 1971 conversation with Ehrlichman and Haldeman, the three made disparaging comments about various minority groups. They discussed blacks (saying they will remain behind for hundreds of years) and Mexican Americans (currently untrustworthy, but a "different cup of tea" and improving due to strong family life), but saved their worst for gays. Nixon criticized the CBS television network for "glorifying homosexuality" on *All in the Family* (which he mistakenly identified as *Archie's Guys*), complaining that the show featured a hippie son-in-law to the blue-collar Archie who was "obviously queer—wears an ascot." Nixon declared, "I don't mind homosexuality . . . Nevertheless, goddamn, I don't think you glorify it on public television, homosexuality, even more than you glorify whores." Nixon feared damage to children, and argued that though "Aristotle was a homo," "homosexuality destroyed" the Greeks. He also attributed the fall of Rome to homosexuality, since "the last six Roman emperors were fags." Similarly, "the Catholic church went to hell three or four centuries ago" because "it was homosexual." While complaining about gay culture in San Francisco, Nixon also praised Soviet society for its "root 'em out" policy toward gays, and maintained that "homosexuality, dope, immorality, are the enemies of strong societies."[194] Although this conversation was obviously not a statement of policy—Nixon actively supported policies for African Americans even though he spoke ill of them—it does show the ways that the some of the most powerful shapers of domestic policy viewed gays. Even though they might discuss both gays and the official minorities in the same conversation, gays were different. They were immoral.

What about support for gay rights elsewhere in the executive branch? The civil-rights agencies might have shown the same creativity in fashioning rights for homosexuals as they did, for example, when finding language rights for Latinos in a statute that never mentioned language. Instead, the EEOC officially stated that sexual orientation was not covered by Title VII.[195] Better luck was had in the Department of Health, Education and Welfare, the parent of the OCR. On May 17, 1976, HEW very tentatively floated the idea in the *Federal Register* that homosexuals could be considered disabled and protected by the prohibitions on discrimination against disabled people contained in Section 504. HEW maintained that "it could be argued" that homosexuals qualified because its Section 504 regulations protected from discrimination persons who were not disabled but were nevertheless treated as disabled. HEW then rejected its own idea, but weakly added, "Comment is solicited with respect to this determination."[196] A few months later, the apparently anticipated negative response came in. HEW reported that the "overwhelming majority of comments" said that homosexuality should be excluded. The stated reasons for the rejection, presented without identifying authors in HEW's report, were manifold. First, homosexuality was (along with drug addiction, another possibility being proposed by HEW) "self-inflicted." Second, Section 504 was not "the proper vehicle" to protect homosexuals. Third, the concept of "'handicapped person' does not, from either an historical or popular viewpoint, connote . . . homosexuals." Fourth, homosexuals did not see themselves as handicapped. Last, protecting them would take away resources from the more "traditional" disabled.[197]

Gay-rights advocates did find some allies in Congress, but not congressional activists like those who fought for women, or for Latinos and bilingual education, or for nondiscrimination rights for the disabled. On June 27, 1974, Representatives Bella Abzug (D–NY) and Edward Koch (D–NY) submitted a bill, the Equality Act, to protect Americans from discrimination on the bases of sex, marital status, and sexual orientation.[198] A month later, Representative Robert Nix (D–PA) submitted another bill to outlaw sexual-orientation discrimination.[199] Neither bill was enacted.

Over the next few years, Abzug and Koch would try repeatedly to pass legislation on rights for homosexuals, and while they found increasing numbers of allies in the House, other members of Congress did not jump on the bandwagon as they did for other groups. In March of 1975, while working closely with members of the National Gay Task Force, Abzug and Koch submitted a bill that would have amended the Civil Rights Act of 1964 by including discrimination on the bases of "affectional or sexual preference" in its major titles. It would have banned discrimination against persons who manifest or have "an emotional or physical attachment to another consenting person or persons of either gender" in public accommodations, public education, employment, sale, rental and financing of housing, and education programs that receive federal financial aid. The bill would have made gays almost as protected as blacks.

Though members of Congress regularly make long speeches on the House floor promoting their submitted legislation, or even about such burning topics of national import as a recently deceased local high school football coach, Koch notably said little about his bill. He simply stated that he had written to the OCR about whether homosexuals were protected from discrimination, and that its director Peter Holmes had written back stating, "The Office for Civil Rights is aware that individuals are frequently denied education and employment opportunities on the basis of their status as homosexuals." Koch declared, "It is simply inequitable, indeed, immoral, that in this day and age there is no Federal law prohibiting discrimination against individuals on the basis of affectional or sexual preference." Koch added a quotation from Canadian prime minister Pierre Trudeau—that "the state has no business in the bedrooms of this nation"—and a modified statement of Thomas Jefferson: "Equal and exact justice to all men (and I would add 'women') of whatever state and persuasion."[200]

This time, the bill had twenty-three co-sponsors, with support coming most strongly from urban and minority members of congress, especially from California, Massachusetts, and New York. Prominent support from minorities included Herman Badillo (D–NY), a Puerto Rican; several African Americans, among them Shirley Chisholm (D–NY), Charles Rangel (D–NY), Parren Mitchell (D–MD), Robert Nix (D–PA), Ronald Dellums (D–CA), plus Washington, D.C. delegate Walter Fauntroy; and Japanese American Norman Mineta (D–CA). Support also came from two women—(Elizabeth Holtzman (D–NY) and Patricia Schroeder (D–CO)—as well as from Gerry Studds (D–MA), a still-closeted gay legislator.[201]

None of these bills went anywhere. It is difficult to understand the politics of gay rights in Washington at the time because there was never any debate. The lack of debate is in itself a clue. Members of Congress avoided the issue, and it never got on to committee agendas.[202] Even Abzug, presumably a strong supporter of gay rights, never even went to the floor of the House to explain why she supported the legislation in the early years. Koch's short speech was very weak, even incoherent: the Trudeau quotation about keeping the government out of bedrooms made sense for an effort to ban antisodomy laws, but its relationship to an antidiscrimination law that affected private citizens was obscure or nonsensical. In contrast, supporters for other minority rights considered in the preceding chapters made strong speeches in Congress. There was Martha Griffiths in the House defending women's right to be free of sex discrimination in employment in which she called the EEOC "Fantasyland," and later claimed with some justification that the speech helped launch the modern women's movement. In the Senate, Ralph Yarborough defended bilingual education for Latinos making nearly every conceivable argument to support the policy. Birch Bayh defended women's equality in education with skill and finesse. Hubert Humphrey defended equal rights for the disabled with similar ability. Even Pucinski and Schweiker said far more for white ethnics than did Abzug and Koch about gays and lesbians.

In summary, there was little perception of gays and lesbians as a political constituency during the minority rights revolution. The concept of federally protected gay rights is apparently so unthinkable even to scholars of the gay and lesbian movement that, despite the growing amount of work done in this area, there are no comprehensive studies of this struggle.

Why Did Gay Rights Fail?

Since the failure of gay-rights legislation in 1974, essentially the same bill has been reintroduced in every Congress since, but never with success.[203] Why didn't gays receive their share of minority-rights protections during the 1965–75 window of opportunity for making new initiatives? First, we might inquire about their lobbying and protest presence. These groups were new, they were not well organized, and they were not large—all of which undoubtedly limited their impact.[204] However, as noted above, while there was no massive Washington presence, gay-rights groups did demonstrate at the White House and they did lobby for action by Congress, many members of which were listening. Furthermore, they received national media attention.

I made the point earlier, however, that assessing the level of protest on the part of a group during the minority rights revolution is not crucial to understanding its political fortunes. Due to the legacies of black civil rights, strong and systematic lobbying was not necessary for at least some of the gains during the minority rights revolution. The failure of gay rights occurred *in* the government. Consider this issue in comparison with other efforts to achieve minority rights. Though gay rights could not even get on the agenda, the Bilingual Education Act sailed through Congress like boat on a calm sea. Title IX and Section 504 passed without lobbying. While OCR's regulation for gays was rescinded, it declared a right to language accommodation in the schools after only a few meetings of advocates for Latinos with government officials. Nixon pushed minority capitalism without urging because he anticipated political gain. So why didn't more politicians anticipate political support from gay rights?

One possible factor is that there were no statistics of the number of gay voters in the United States. As I showed in the previous chapters, government officials became keenly aware of the numbers of minorities during the 1960s. When advocating new policy, they often recounted to each other just how many blacks there were in America, or Latinos, or disabled people, or even ethnics, and whether they were concentrated in "key states." This was clear in internal Nixon White House documents and in speeches made in Congress. In contrast, the entire issue of counting gays and lesbians was and remains clouded by the ambiguity of homosexual identities and their relationship to the degree of same-sex attraction and the varying frequency of same-sex activity, and the imperfect relationship between the two.[205] If the minority rights revolution occurred partly because elected officials wanted the votes of minorities, it makes sense that gay rights were left out because gays were uncounted.

While this may be part of the explanation, it cannot be the whole story. There *were* some numbers that purported to represent the size of the gay and lesbian population. For example, the benchmark studies of human sexual behavior by Alfred Kinsey seemed to suggest that 10 percent of men and 5 percent of women were homosexual.[206] More accessibly, *Time* magazine's cover story estimated that there were 2.6 million exclusively gay men and 1.4 million exclusively lesbian women in the United States.[207] And national numbers arguably underestimated gay voting power, since gays, like Latinos, were concentrated in large, electorally significant states such as New York and California. Gay neighborhoods had developed in most major US cities, and lawmakers representing these districts did not need the Census Bureau to tell them there were a lot of gay voters among their constituents. Unlike the similarly concentrated Latinos, with gays there was something preventing other representatives from other districts or states from supporting the issue of protected rights for homosexuals.

Was there the sort of organized resistance to gay-rights initiatives like the Abzug bill as when business leaders attacked affirmative action for ethnics, or when college sports officials attacked the regulations to implement Title IX?

There is no evidence of any organized opposition to gay rights at the congressional level (though advocates for the disabled opposed OCR's "disability" rights for homosexuals). This does not mean, however, that opposition was not a factor.

It appears that the brake put on the inclusion of homosexuals in the minority rights revolution was the perception on the part of political elites of gays, the meaning of homosexuality, and its place in American moral culture. As with ethnics and to a lesser extent women, how the group was perceived—its meaning—prevented the easy analogy with blacks. The lack of effort to win the gay vote was the result of elite perceptions that active pursuit of success would lead to the emergence of an active opposition and perhaps damage to an elected official's standing. There was, then, a kind of anticipatory politics at play here, but instead of politicians' anticipating new rights policies would build coalitions, they anticipated gay rights would disrupt coalitions.[208] To be sure, it is difficult to make this argument because of the almost complete absence of discourse about gay rights by public officials during the period. Yet it seems clear that American moral culture and the meaning of gays and lesbians played a crucial role in the failure of federal gay rights, and this factor is even implicated in the small presence of gay-rights organizations. Before 1969, most gays lived their lives in secrecy or in subcultures because public organization might lead to uncomfortable public lives and even violent repression.

Even if American political culture of the day had allowed a massive, well-financed, and strongly organized gay-rights group to exist, it almost certainly would have failed. There is no public opinion data explicitly on the question of gays and their rights for the early 1970s, but the existing polls suggest public hostility. In 1969, *Time* magazine reported a Harris poll finding that 63 percent of Americans consider homosexuals to be "harmful to American life." *Time* explained that "most straight Americans still regard the invert with a mixture of revulsion and apprehension."[209] In fact, an Institute for Sex Research poll in 1970 found that 37.9 percent of Americans thought that for "all or almost all" gays and lesbians, homosexuality was a "sickness that can be cured." Twenty-four percent believed this was true for "more than half" of homosexuals.[210]

There were, to be sure, some positive poll results for gay rights. As mentioned previously, a 1977 Harris poll found that considerably more Americans believed that gays were discriminated against than any other group. Also, a majority of respondents, 55 percent, said they would "favor a law which outlawed discrimination against (homosexuals) in any job for which they were qualified."[211]

What is striking about this figure, however, is that despite the fact that

Table 9.2 1977 Harris Poll: "Would you favor or oppose a law which outlawed discrimination against *(read list)* in any job for which they were qualified?"

	Favor (%)	Oppose (%)	Not sure (%)
Women	76	15	9
Catholics	75	16	9
Jews	75	16	9
Mexican Americans	74	15	11
Italian Americans	74	16	10
Blacks	73	17	10
Puerto Ricans	73	16	11
Chinese Americans	73	16	11
Japanese Americans	73	16	11
Homosexuals	54	28	18

Source: Connie de Boer, "The Polls: Attitudes toward Homosexuality," *Public Opinion Quarterly* 42 (1978), p. 273. Reprinted by permission of Harris Interactive.[SM]

most Americans believed gays to be targets of discrimination, the 55 percent supporting a law to end the discrimination was by far the *least* amount of support given to a group perceived to suffer from discrimination (see Table 9.2). In 1977, homosexuals were about 20 percentage points behind every other group. Moreover, the Institute for Sex Research's 1970 poll found that majorities of Americans, between 67 and 77 percent, believed that homosexual men should not be allowed to be government officials, medical doctors, ministers, school teachers, or court judges. Majorities did support allowing them to enjoy certain apparently "gay-appropriate" occupations, such as beauticians, artists, musicians, and florists. Seven years later the Harris poll found that attitudes had become more accepting, as 53 percent thought it was acceptable for a "person who admits to being a homosexual" to be a congressman and 48 percent accepted a gay doctor, but between 48 and 63 percent still rejected admitted homosexuals as social workers, psychiatrists, ministers, priests, rabbis, school teachers, school principals, or camp counselors.[212]

Additional evidence of the importance of the meaning or understanding of gays as a group comes from the study of the local successes of the gay-rights movement by James Button, Barbara Rienzo, and Kenneth Wald. Some cities passed gay-rights ordinances, but only those with a political culture that did not stigmatize gay identities and allowed the crucial analogy with blacks to be drawn. Cosmopolitan college towns and big cities proved to be the most fertile ground. The first ordinance for gay rights passed in 1971 in East Lansing, Michigan, home to Michigan State University.[213] Button and his colleagues found that antidiscrimination laws for gays became more likely "(a) the larger and more diverse the community, (b) the greater the presence of supportive groups, (c) the better organized the local gay and lesbian community, and (d) the smaller the proportion of religious traditionalists." They found a common pattern for the mechanism of success, where advocates for gays first presented to political elites clear and consistent evidence of discrimination, emphasized the injustice of discrimination and increased the group's visibility, and compared gays to other minorities, especially African Americans.[214]

Homosexuals who suffered discrimination in places without such ordinances were left making creative arguments rooted in Title VII. Some gays argued that discrimination against them was essentially discrimination on the basis of sex on the grounds that employers might terminate the employment of men romantically involved with other men but not fire women similarly involved with men. This reasoning was at least as plausible as that making sexual harassment sex discrimination (see Chapter 10). But a Ninth Circuit court rejected the argument in a case in 1979, arguing that the matter was sexual preference, and not sex discrimination.[215]

Even advocates for liberal causes accepted the marginalization of gays and lesbians during the minority rights revolution. Leaders of the women's movement, for example, were wary of women's rights becoming identified too closely with lesbian rights, believing this would hurt their efforts. In the 1950s, several prominent women's leaders were lesbian, but this fact was never promoted. Lesbianism was still the stuff of charges and accusations, not a proud identity.[216] Later, while many radicals in the women's movement embraced the cause of lesbian rights, the more mainstream feminists, especially Betty Friedan, tried to distance the women's cause from the lesbians.[217] The issue came up at a national NOW conference in 1971, against the wishes of Friedan and other NOW members who feared, as Myra Marx Ferree and Beth B. Hess explain, "losing whatever legitimacy the fledgling organization had worked so hard to obtain." While the conference went ahead and endorsed a woman's right to be a lesbian and live as a lesbian, and recognized lesbian rights as part of the feminist cause, for years after, many feminists believed support of lesbian rights was, in the words of a NOW speaker at a 1977 conference, "an albatross around the neck of the movement."[218]

That gay rights and issues were taboo was most apparent in the struggle to pass the ERA. After lesbian groups marched in pro-ERA demonstrations with identifying banners, many of those opposed to the amendment used photos of the lesbians in their anti-ERA campaign. Some pro-ERA groups therefore banned lesbian participation and even instituted a dress code for demonstrations.[219] The bugaboo of gay rights, and especially gay marriage, was a major weapon wielded by anti-ERA forces. Even strident reformers like Martha Griffiths (D–MI) had to disavow the ERA–gay marriage link, deriding gay marriage as less than serious. In hearings on the amendment in the Senate in 1970, Griffiths countered arguments that the ERA would lead to gay marriage by calling the notion "ridiculous," adding that "marriage is protected in order to protect the propagation of the race." "I will admit that if any State were silly enough to sanction marriage between two men," she conceded, if the ERA passed "it would have to sanction it between two women."[220] Even in mainstream liberal political circles, gay rights were not considered a goal for American justice. They were silly.

If pushed with enough seriousness and energy, however, policymakers saw gay rights as threatening and evil. Gay rights produced enemies. In other words, if members of Congress or even the Nixon administration feared a loud, adverse reaction to promoting gay rights, their fears were well founded. There was, for example, the reaction to the OCR regulation bringing homosexuality under Section 504 disability rights. And, in a development that had an analogue in the campaign to defeat the ERA, local gay-rights efforts met resistance from Americans fighting for what they considered to be traditional values. In 1977, in Dade County, Florida—birthplace of bilingual education during the Cold War—singer Anita Bryant effectively led an organization called Save Our Children that sought and won the repeal of a local ordinance prohibiting discrimination on the basis of sexual orientation. The following year, a gay-rights ordinance was repealed in St. Paul, Minnesota.[221] In the history of the minority rights revolution, no major federal laws or policies have ever been repealed outright.[222] But as passage of gay-rights ordinances spread, so did opposition.[223]

One of the most decisive blows against the legitimacy of gay rights came in 1986 when the Supreme Court upheld antisodomy laws that were only enforced against gays. In *Bowers v. Hardwick,* the Court ruled that other rulings on rights to privacy, such as those dealing with procreation and family life, were different in nature from homosexual sodomy, and that there were no constitutional rights protecting this behavior, even though private. The Court rejected the argument that the majority's morality was an inadequate basis of law, stating bluntly, "We do not agree" because the laws are "constantly based on notions of morality," and therefore the Court was "unpersuaded that the sodomy laws of some 25 States should be invalidated on this basis."[224]

The reason for the failure of gay rights to be included in the minority rights revolution, then, was that the meaning of gays and lesbians placed them too far away from the American mainstream for policy attention and recognition. The issue of other identities, as was crucial with the pursuit of the ethnic vote, did not come into play. Though victimized, gays and lesbians were not *legitimate* victims. Though oppressed like blacks, they were not like blacks.

Conclusion

The cases analyzed in this chapter help us understand the boundaries of the minority rights revolution. Those boundaries were expansive. Women and the other official minorities constituted more than 60 percent of the nation's population. The addition of the disabled allowed the inclusion of some Euro-American males and pushed that majority of minorities even higher. Yet not every group that could claim disadvantage and discrimination could be included in policies that recognized difference to provide more equal opportunity. Despite widespread perceptions of disadvantage and discrimination, lobbying efforts on their behalf, all of the new agencies giving power to civil-rights advocates, and the easy availability of minority rights policy tools for politicians seeking new constituents, there was nevertheless a limit to how far the minority rights revolution could go.

A final point is in order on the question of whether the white ethnics or gays and lesbians simply did not mobilize enough. Anyone making this argument implies there is a threshold above which exerting pressure for being accorded rights receives a payoff. *Yet it would still be likely that this threshold would vary and vary significantly for each group.* Some disadvantaged groups can win without great organizational strength or mass mobilization. Chapter 2 showed that the Chinese and other Asians could win immigration rights without significant mobilization but rather through categorization of their goals as national security. Chapters 4, 7, and 8 showed that, if anything, women's groups were better organized and mobilized than were Latinos, and women's rights promised more votes than Latino rights, but that women's advocates faced more resistance. Each group is saddled with different meanings that variously advantage or disadvantage them in American politics.

Both white ethnics and gays and lesbians were excluded from the rights revolution by the perceived meanings of their respective groups and the failure to establish and maintain an analogy with blacks. Government officials saw white ethnics as insufficiently oppressed and also as multifaceted, which led to the appeals of ethnics being stretched to cover issues oriented around class, labor union membership, religion, and foreign policy considerations. They saw gays as violating the nation's morality, and unworthy of federal protection.

10

CONCLUSION:
THE RARE AMERICAN EPIPHANY

"The civil rights era," historian Hugh Davis Graham has written, "was a rare American epiphany."[1] Graham's assessment captures a defining aspect of the period: the profound cognitive shift that occurred among America's political elites, both on the Left and the Right and including America's staunchest conservatives. Recall from the opening chapter the note that Barry Goldwater sent to Nixon offering lessons, advice, and admonishment on the topic of how to appeal to Mexican Americans. Where, one wonders, was this sentiment during the previous years of Goldwater's political career?[2] Where was such a concern among *any* of Washington's politicians—Democrat or Republican, liberal or conservative—in the years before 1965? For a fantastic decade, politicians and policymakers sought to appeal to new constituent groups previously neglected but now understood as analogous to blacks. The "party of Lincoln" was alive and well in the late 1960s and early 1970s, joining with Democrats in creating America's minority-rights-oriented liberalism. Together they ended discrimination in immigration, fashioned affirmative action, expanded it aggressively, trumpeted bilingual education, and signed off on women's rights and rights for the disabled. In doing so, they brought America in line with the emerging global human-rights norms.

Group mobilization was sometimes a part of this process, but not always. The political dynamic of the 1965–75 period was characterized more by an anticipatory politics than a participatory one. With the exceptions of the black civil rights movement and to a lesser extent the 1965 immigration reform, policy was not promoted by the networks of federated interest groups that Theda Skocpol has studied in early veterans' organizations and the women's movement of the 1920s.[3] To win rights for Latinos, women, American Indians, Asian Americans, and the disabled, nothing like 1932's "Bonus Army" of poor veterans that occupied Washington demanding extra payments was needed. Neither was this the mass politics of the New Deal Era, such as the one-million-member Townsend movement for old-age pensions or the institutionalized, organized muscle of Big Labor. Nor was it the coordinated, courageous mass movement for basic, classically liberal black civil rights that culminated in 1965. The late 1960s were marked by massive black riots (some called them rebellions) but there was no violence by other groups that was remotely comparable. For the groups that policymakers saw as analogous to blacks, mass mobilization, civil disobedience, or rioting were simply not necessary.

How, then, did the nonblack minority social movements matter? It is hard to find evidence that the occasional grassroots mobilization had an impact at the national level in the cases presented here, though on occasion policymakers considered memos, such as those from Nixon advisers Daniel Patrick Moynihan or Rita Hauser, describing the apparently quite distant grassroots developments. The self-appointed leaders of the minority groups clearly mattered in forming policy, especially at the stages of implementation of language rights and Title IX. Still, no mass mobilization was necessary; policymakers usually took the leaders' claims at face value, simply anticipating that the minority citizens they claimed to represent wanted these new laws and programs.[4] It is also clear that policymakers created minority rights policies even if the leaders did not ask for them, especially in the cases of the expansion of affirmative action. However, assessing the impact of movement leaders is complicated by the fact that on many occasions, government officials *themselves* were the minority advocates or leaders. In many cases, it makes no sense to talk of the government and the movement as separate entities. It was activist government. And in all cases with the nonblack groups, there was a change in the meanings that politicians saw in particular groups; the previously ignored became new constituents that were theirs for the taking, and both the White House and Congress possessed the power to develop policy to appeal to them. The intense, almost-anything-goes political strategizing of Nixon's anticipatory politics was a forerunner of the current style of American politics, driven by polls and Svengali-like political consultants who make educated, semi-scientific, semi-artistic guesses as to what groups of Americans really want.[5]

Why did they so often choose to appeal to minorities with rights policies? Of course, the Bill of Rights established a rights approach, and Reconstruction lawmaking made rights the vehicle for bringing equality to African American citizens. But more important for the 1960s was that Franklin Roosevelt's promotion of human rights and the ensuing enemy propaganda strategy made rights talk a global language and minority rights an idea whose time had come. The black civil rights movement then established antidiscrimination law as part of the 1960s politicians' policy repertoire. Politicians, White

House and congressional staffmembers, and bureaucrats reached for new rights policies like an archer reaches for arrows in a quiver. They could confidently anticipate the policies would hit their targets, which they knew to be appropriate insofar as the target groups could legitimately be categorized as minorities like blacks. The "black analogy" governed the dynamic of policymaking. Moreover, with the exception of the Bilingual Education Act, these policies came easily because they cost the federal government so little. They were regulations that attached strings to money already being spent or that made someone else pay. The language of rights, with all of their hallowed glory in American politics, brilliantly obscured the costs—or made great costs seem irrelevant.[6]

Why did it end? What did it add up to? How should we interpret this rare American epiphany? In this final chapter, I first describe the rights counterrevolution of the 1980s and bring the story up to date for each of the policies described in Chapters 4–9. Next, I consider alternative explanations for the minority-rights movement and sum up what this revolution has to say about understanding political and social change, especially the importance of meanings and the place of African Americans in American politics. Last, I offer some possible visions for the future. Though minority rights policies are surprisingly resilient in the face of considerable criticism, there is an irony to the last century's turn toward minority-rights. The policies targeted at the group that helped start it all are the most vulnerable to retrenchment.

After 1975: Counterrevolution, Resilience, and Black Exceptionalism

What happened after 1975? With the old national-security meanings of minority rights only a fading memory and the *Federal Register* by then filled with hundreds of pages of new regulations, new initiatives were less compelling. Republican enthusiasm about rights for minority groups waned and that party's partnership in the revolution mostly ended by 1975. By the 1980s, many Republicans, led by President Ronald Reagan, engaged in what was primarily a rhetorical counterrevolution.

What had happened was another shift in meanings. In a process that had its beginnings in the Nixon administration, Republicans came to realize that many Euro-Americans, including many women, did not like the new minority rights policies, especially affirmative action. This discovery highlighted the uniqueness of the 1965–75 period. Then, politicians simply did not see political costs to pursuing minority rights policies, with women's rights the occasional exception. The political "gold," as Nixon's strategists sometimes referred to minority or ethnic voters, was theirs for the taking if they made the correct appeals. Slowly, however, evidence trickled in of the unpopularity of these policies.[7] They lost their place in the repertoire of Republican coalition builders; aggressive advocacy of the rights policies was instead seen to disrupt coalitions.[8] Thus rather than extending minority rights, critiquing them became the dominant way to appeal to Euro-American men and sometimes women.

Democrats shared this perception that aggressive support of many minority rights policies was politically unpopular. They did not push new initiatives except hate crime laws (which primarily only added increased punishments to acts that were already illegal) and more help for minority capitalists (which most voters did not even know about). During the 1980s, the Democrats mostly neglected their traditional constituency among white ethnic/blue collar voters[9] and switched to a conservative stance: rather than working to establish new programs, they simply defended the 1965–75 initiatives from Republican retrenchment efforts. In the 1990s, President Bill Clinton and the centrist Democratic Leadership Council reached out to lower-middle-class Euro-Americans and continued to avoid aggressive expansion of minority rights. Following President Ronald Reagan, many Republicans aggressively reasserted the conservative ideology that championed small federal government, local control, and traditional values. This ideology obviously left little room for the micromanagement required by federal minority rights regulations and congressional Republicans went on the attack. Despite the change in political climate, however, not all minority rights policies were equally vulnerable to retrenchment.

The Acceptance of Difference-Blind Policy and Disability Rights

Laws intended to stop intentional discrimination, that require treatment of individuals divorced from any group characteristics they might share, have been broadly and deeply accepted in the United States. Indeed, they are very nearly unassailable. Only a few academics criticize this classically liberal anti-discrimination law from the standpoint of economic theory.[10] Politicians swear their allegiance to federally guaranteed nondiscrimination on the basis of race, national origin, sex, religion, disability, and age.

This unassailability is perhaps most surprising in immigration law. During debates over the proposed Immigration Act of 1965, various advocates of the reform made predictions of its impact on America. They said that it would not significantly alter the source and the dynamics of immigration to the United States, maintained that immigration would remain in the area of 350,000 a year, and insisted that it would not impose any negative economic impact on Americans.[11] All of these predictions proved to be wrong, some almost laughably so. The share of European immigration was down to 34 percent by 1970, and immigration from specifically Northern and Western Europe, which was supposedly privileged by the family reunification preferences, was less than 12 percent of all immigration just five years after the predictions were made.[12] But overall numbers increased steadily, aided by more expansive policies, so that by the 1990s, America was receiving nearly one million mostly Latin American and Asian legal immigrants a year. Studies showed that the economic benefits were mixed, but that some immigration, especially immigration of the unskilled, depressed wages of unskilled workers.[13] By the late 1990s, chairman of the Federal Reserve Board Alan Greenspan was crediting immigration with helping fight inflation by holding down American wages.[14]

There have been various attempts to limit immigration since 1965, but these attempts have all failed.[15] The key point from the standpoint of the minority rights revolution, however, is not the failure to reduce the number of immigrants but the fact that during all of the debate over immigration policy since 1965, *no one* in Congress has attempted to bring back national-origin discrimination as part of immigration policy. This is true despite the now commonplace prediction on the basis of current trends that the United States will lose its Euro-American majority by 2050. No one expected this, no one has ever advocated it, and no one voted for it, but this grand demographic shift is the result of unequal demand to come to the United States, current immigration policy, and ethnically variable birth rates. Indeed, the family reunification provisions that were supposed to preserve a WASP domination now accelerate the decline of the Euro-American share of the total population.[16] That such a drastic change in a nation's population is not even a political issue is a forceful indication of at least one triumph of the minority rights revolution.

Joining difference-blind civil rights laws in their considerable resilience are the laws meant to protect the disabled from discrimination. While difference-blind on their face, disability rights in practice have required considerable difference-consciousness as accommodations are made for the disabled to access and use public facilities. Though coming later than rights for other groups, disability rights may be the most popular of all and were the subject of the only major legislation concerning minority rights enacted after 1975.

With bipartisan support, including that of Republican President George Bush, Congress enacted the Americans with Disabilities Act (ADA) in 1990. The law shared with Section 504 of the Rehabilitation Act basic concepts, such as the definition of disability and the requirement for "reasonable accommodation" of those disabilities, but expanded its coverage. Section 504 only touched institutions receiving federal funds—the local diner or dentist need not make any accommodations. In contrast, the ADA prohibited all discrimination against the disabled.[17] Even private firms under the ADA would have to make "reasonable accommodations" for disabled employees and customers. The Act also granted the right to sue employers or managers of any facility that is perceived not to follow the law. Compensatory and even punitive damages are possible.

Disability rights are implemented at sometimes enormous expense and siphon resources from other societal goals.[18] But it is very hard to find national politicians willing to publicly fight their implementation. Though poll data is hard to find, Carol Swain and her colleagues found in their focus group study stronger support for disability rights than rights for other minorities.[19] Disability rights transcend the politics of liberal and conservative and are here to stay as long as disability itself stays beyond the reach of medical science.

Another rights development that appears almost as accepted as standard difference-blind laws and disability rights are prohibitions against sexual harassment. This, too, has been a rare post-1975 rights development. Notably, no politicians risked their jobs by originating sexual-harassment law; it developed mostly in the courts and Congress affirmed it later. The move to outlaw sexual harassment had its beginnings in the mid-1970s when NOW and other groups sought to expand opportunities for working women. As the sociologist Abigail Saguy describes it, the American conception of sexual harassment was shaped by the prior development to Title VII to be understood as "discrimination" and built on case law dealing with race.[20] In 1977, federal courts defined "quid pro quo" sexual harassment—in which an employer threatens an employee's job or opportunities for advancement if the employee does not agree to sexual relations—as sex discrimination because it would not take place if the victim was the opposite gender.[21] In 1981, another court case expanded sexual harassment to include what are called "hostile environments." The opinion explained that "racial slurs, though intentional and directed at individuals, may still be just verbal insults, yet they too may create Title VII liability. How then can sexual harassment, which injects the most demeaning sexual stereotypes into the general work environment and which always represents an intentional assault on an individual's innermost privacy, not be illegal?"[22] Other courts, and eventually a unanimous Supreme Court, confirmed and strengthened this view.[23] The Civil Rights Act of 1991, which otherwise broke little new ground, did allow litigation for punitive and compensatory damages for emotional pain and suffering in cases of sexual harassment.[24]

The right to be free of sexual harassment is more controversial than difference-blind laws or disability rights, but controversy is limited to questions of employer liability, whether preventive efforts of the employer compromise individual privacy, and what precisely constitutes a hostile environment. Despite its novelty and its court-based genesis, there is now a consensus that sexual harassment is wrong, and any politician defending it would assuredly lose legitimacy.

The acceptance of difference-blind antidiscrimination law does not, however, extend to all groups. President Bill Clinton, elected in 1992, learned that despite increasingly favorable poll results, gay rights remained politically treacherous territory. In his first press conference, he announced his intention to repeal the ban on gays in the military. The opposition was overwhelming, and the new president suffered his first humiliating defeat. The effort was dead in six months.[25]

Though Clinton was wounded politically for waging this unpopular battle, in 1998 he quietly issued an executive order banning discrimination based on sexual orientation in the federal civilian workforce.[26] However, federal antidiscrimination rights for gays and lesbians similar to those for other minorities have remained elusive.[27] Similar to the some of the political struggles for local gay-rights ordinances, the farther the comprehensive federal gay-rights bill got on the congressional agenda, the more opposition it provoked from religious conservatives. They explicitly denied the analogy of gays with blacks, as in 1980 when Jerry Falwell complained that a gay-rights bill would establish homosexuality as a legitimate minority such as Hispanics and blacks.[28]

The public remained at best ambivalent about national political efforts to help gays and lesbians. Support for equal job opportunities for homosexuals has increased from 56 percent in 1977 to 71 percent in 1989 to 84 percent in 1996,[29] but other data points in another direction. A Pew Research Center poll found that 59 percent of Americans "personally believe homosexual behavior is morally wrong,"[30] and a New York Times/CBS poll found that only 46 percent believed that gay sex should be legal.[31] Or consider the summary by the political scientist James Button and his colleagues of their findings from the 1992 American National Election Study's "feeling thermometer" question: "The average rating for gays and lesbians was 15–30 points below such controversial groups as blacks, Jews, Hispanics, Asians, Christian fundamentalists, big business, feminists, and people on welfare. Measured by the percentage of respondents who assigned them the lowest possible rating of zero, gays and lesbians were even less popular than illegal immigrants."[32]

Evidence of the continued unpopularity of gays and lesbians also comes from Alan Wolfe's interview study of middle-class American moral culture. Wolfe found that, despite surprising moderation on a variety of social issues, homosexuality was one of the few issues that provoked strong views from Americans. While many Americans believe in "doing your own thing," they have profound difficulties with homosexuality and the notion of respect for homosexuals as a public value.[33] Opposition was so fierce that in 1993 Christian conservatives successfully led a referendum campaign to amend the state constitution of Colorado to prohibit local gay-rights ordinances in that state (later overturned by the Supreme Court).[34] Given the continuing negative meaning of homosexuality for many Americans, lawmakers will reasonably fear countermobilization if they push equal-rights initiatives too hard. Gays and lesbians are close but remain outside the minority rights revolution.

Controversies and Resilience: Title IX and Bilingual Education

Other laws of the minority rights revolution have produced more resistance and controversy than simple antidiscrimination laws. In a triumph for the revolution, however, almost no one argued for a return to the old days of legal discrimination or neglect. Legitimate critics of the new policies must always seek better ways of helping minorities, and never a return to the status quo.

For instance, Title IX—easy to pass but hard to implement—continued to have problems after 1975. Some schools openly scorned the implementing regulations for women's equality as an unwanted federal intrusion. In October 1975, Brigham Young University announced that it would ignore Title IX when it felt it should, especially regarding a regulation that required religious institutions seeking exemption to submit written explanations of how the regulations contradicted religious beliefs. The university argued that this procedure would "allow a bureaucrat in Washington to decide if we are sincere."[35] In November, Hillsdale College in Michigan declared that following the regulations was allowing "social engineers in Washington" to run the college. They therefore would not comply.[36] The "social engineers" at OCR did not help things when they issued controversial rulings that followed from the law but outraged the public, such as when they threatened to cut funds from one school that maintained a boy's choir.[37]

Meanwhile, as the historian Catherine Rymph has shown, feminism in the Republican Party was increasingly displaced by support for traditional women's roles, as represented by the anti-ERA efforts of conservative activist Phyllis Schlafly. The turning point was the National Women's Conference, held in Houston in 1977 with federal money. The goal was to develop an agenda modeled on the UN's International Women's Year in 1975. Republican women participated, but Schlafly held a "pro-family" counterconference that attracted media attention. In much-publicized comments, some Republican leaders sided with Schlafly. Representative Robert Dornan (R–CA) described those at the official conference as "sick, anti-God, pro-lesbian, and unpatriotic." The chairman of the Houston Republican Party referred to the delegates as a "gaggle of outcasts, misfits, and rejects."[38]

There was also controversy in the courts. In 1984, the Supreme Court ruled in *Grove City College v. Bell* that for Title IX compliance only the *specific* program receiving federal funds had to stop discriminating rather than the entire institution.[39] Reagan's Justice Department then expanded this interpretation to include Title VI, thus affecting race and ethnic minorities and even Section 504 for the disabled.

A bipartisan group mobilized legislation in Congress to reinstate the application of the law's regulations as originally enacted. In hearings, Reagan's assistant attorney general for civil rights argued the bill would "stretch the tentacles of the federal government to every crevice of public and private-sector activity" and it "uses the extension of the federal dollar as an excuse for opening virtually every entity in this country—public and private—to federal supervision, regulation, intervention, intrusion, and oversight."[40] The Civil Rights Restoration Act passed anyway. The 1988 law brought back the application of the original regulations, and "all of the operations" of school districts or universities, as well as any state or local government or any other kind of institution, would be covered if any part received some federal aid.[41]

Despite the controversy, Title IX is one of the success stories of the minority rights revolution. *No one* in national politics supports women's inequality in education or speaks disparagingly of women's sports. Differential standards for admission of women students are consigned to the dustbin of history, and women have actually become the majority of college students nationwide, and even the majority at some law schools.[42] Though Title IX is not the sole cause, there has been dramatic improvement even in women's athletics, where Title IX was most fiercely contested. Here the statistics, and the unit of measurement, are clear. In 1972, there were thirty-one thousand women participating in intercollegiate athletics. Twenty-five years later, the number had quadrupled.[43] In this area, separate-but-equal reigned supreme, but provided more opportunities for women and girls.

Other measures show similar impressive gains in Title IX's first quarter century. By 1997, women constituted 39 percent of all NCAA athletes (and 41 percent in 2002). Athletic scholarships for women nationwide increased in value from $100,000 in 1972 to $180 million by 1996. Men's athletics programs still accounted for 62 percent of Division I scholarship money and 60 percent of coaches' salaries in 1996, but there was a 71-percent growth in funds for recruiting female athletes.[44] The story was similar in high schools. While participation in boys athletics remained the same, girls' participation increased from 294,000 in 1971 to 2.4 million in 1995. In 1972, one in twenty-seven girls played high school sports, but by 1997, it was one in three.[45] The downside of these advances was fewer opportunities for men and boys. Many schools had to drop men's sports, especially men's gymnastics.

The number of NCAA men's teams fell from seventy-nine in 1981 to twenty-one in 2001. Wrestling also declined, from 363 teams to 234, as did men's fencing, from seventy-nine to thirty-seven, in the twenty-year period. While these declines are not due only to Title IX, many supporters of men's sports believe it to be the primary cause, keeping the controversy alive.[46]

Though it had a much smoother genesis than did Title IX, bilingual education faced rougher political waters after the mid-1970s. Other issues relating to language rights developed in areas such as provision of social services and voting instructions and ballots in non-English languages, but bilingual education became the most controversial.[47] There was less organized opposition compared to Title IX, but criticism was more direct and came from a variety of sources. It was impossible for politicians to ignore. Following the reauthorization and increased funding of the Bilingual Education Act in 1974, Nathan Glazer warned in the pages of *Commentary* that the nation's schools were becoming ethnically fragmented.[48] That same month, Stephen S. Rosenfeld wrote in the *Washington Post* that "with practically no one paying heed, the Congress has radically altered the traditional way by which immigrants become Americanized. No longer will the public schools be expected to serve largely as a 'melting pot,' assimilating foreigners to a common culture." Rosenfeld predicted that ethnic strife was increasingly likely.[49] Albert Shanker, president of the United Federation of Teachers, picked up on Rosenfeld's criticisms in his paid *New York Times* column. Shanker had a litany of complaints, including alleged defunding of programs to help black students to support bilingual programs and non-Latino teachers in Latino-majority schools being fired "on the assumption that if the teacher is not a member of the ethnic group, he or she cannot be as competent."[50] Bilingual education lost its status as a politically costless appeal for Latino votes.

This early criticism was probably disproportionate to the program's size, though it was greatly expanding beyond its meager beginnings. Noel Epstein, the education editor for the *Washington Post,* estimated that by 1977 $500 million had been spent on bilingual education.[51] In that year, the federal government was spending $115 million on bilingual education in 518 school districts, teaching more than three hundred thousand students.[52] These 518 bilingual education projects were taught in sixty-eight languages and dialects (including Arabic, Cherokee, Chinese, French, Greek, Italian, Japanese, Korean, Navajo, Pennsylvania Dutch, Polish, Portuguese, Punjai, Russian, Tagalog, Yiddish, and various Eskimo languages), though 80 percent of the students were learning in Spanish.[53]

The political picture further darkened when the results of a $1.3 million study commissioned by the Office of Education reported that students receiving bilingual education performed better in math but worse in English vocabulary and reading, and that many students in the program already spoke English. Noel Epstein wrote a widely cited book acknowledging the study's results and arguing that bilingual education was a boondoggle that amounted to federally sponsored "affirmative ethnicity."[54] Advocates for bilingual education attacked the study's methodology, beginning a war of studies measuring the policy's efficacy that continues to this day.

In 1978, Democratic senators Teddy Kennedy and Alan Cranston led a congressional effort to make the program more politically palatable. Their amendments to the Bilingual Education Act limited its scope and definition. The new version disavowed language and cultural maintenance and made the program expressly for transition to English—students were to receive native language instruction only "to the extent necessary to allow a child to achieve competence in the English language."[55] Meanwhile, federal regulations had made bilingual education a right. In the ten years after 1975, "approximately 500 school districts . . . negotiated Title VI compliance agreements with OCR requiring native language instruction based on the *Lau Remedies*."[56] By 1982, school districts were teaching more than eight hundred thousand students in their native language mostly at state and local expense through agreements under the Civil Rights Act. This was still a weakly implemented federal right—there were 3.6 million children with limited English-speaking ability.[57]

Meanwhile, the Lau Remedies were running into legal trouble. In 1978, school districts in the state of Alaska began litigation to stop their enforcement because the remedies, like the May 25 memorandum, had never been published in the *Federal Register* and allowed the customary period of public commentary. The Carter administration backed away from the bilingual education requirements, offering districts more choice of how to respond in a new set of guidelines. Latino bilingual education advocates wanted stronger rules, conservatives wanted weaker, and the controversy carried over to the Reagan administration. Reagan had supported bilingual education as governor of California, but was critical of the policy in public statements as president. In 1981, Reagan expressed his opposition, but did so in terms of the interests of children: "It is absolutely wrong and against American concepts to have a bilingual program that is now openly, admittedly dedicated to preserving their native language and never getting them adequate in English so they can go out into the job market and participate."[58] The administration cut spending on Bilingual Education Act programs by 40 percent, revoked the Lau Remedies, thus giving school districts the freedom to comply with language rights implied in the original May 25 memorandum, and school districts were one-ninth as likely to be targeted for a Title VI OCR review in 1981–86 as they were in 1976–81. But Reagan never tried to end the bilingual education program outright, and even campaigned in the southwest by mentioning his support for the program.[59]

Though responses were sensitive to how questions were worded, public opinion data suggested that majorities, including program beneficiaries, did not strongly support bilingual education. According to a 1988 Education Testing Service poll, Latino parents tended to be more supportive of bilingual education either for language maintenance or for transition to English than Asian parents (about 50 percent Latino support compared to 25 percent Asian support for both types), but for both groups, only a little more than 10 percent supported teaching in a non-English language if told that meant less time for teaching in English.[60] By the 1990s, however, bilingual education had developed a strong lobby of teachers whose livelihoods depended on the program. These educators, along with Latino-rights groups, defended bilingual education and considered all efforts at retrenchment to be anti-Latino, xenophobic, and racist. These powerful words eclipsed any political debate, so that even when the Republicans took control of Congress in 1995 with a fervor to shrink the federal government, they did not end federal support of bilingual education.

Sidestepping the powerful pro-bilingual education lobby, the California software entrepreneur Ron Unz single-handedly financed a campaign in 1997 to place a referendum on the state ballot for the repeal of state-supported bilingual education. As a private citizen, Unz had little to lose from being called a racist. The referendum, Proposition 227, would end bilingual education but replace it with mandatory English-language training for children. Notably, Unz called his campaign "English for the Children" and he explicitly projected it as a *benefit* to Latino children. Proposition 227 proved successful at the ballot box. A *Los Angeles Times*/CNN exit poll on June 2, 1998 found that among Euro-American voters, 67 percent supported the measure, joined by 57 percent of Asians, 48 percent of blacks, and 37 percent of Latinos (the total vote was 61 percent to 39 percent).[61] It was followed by another successful referendum repealing bilingual education in Arizona with 63 percent of the vote.

But referenda are very different from politics where elected representatives must protect their reputations. There were no signs of federal retrenchment by 2001. With the election of George W. Bush in 2000, Republicans picked up where the Nixon administration left off by reaching out even more prominently to Latino voters. Bush made a point of speaking Spanish in public addresses on Latino issues, and expressed support for working with Mexican president Vicente Fox to bring amnesty to 4 million undocumented aliens from Mexico. In this climate it is difficult to imagine any serious efforts at undoing a policy that symbolizes the rights of Latinos.

African Americans and Affirmative Action

The policy that has faced the most sustained and severe elite and public criticism has been the central, signature policy of the minority rights revolution—affirmative action. After doing so much to develop the policy, Nixon became one of its most vocal critics after the Democratic party embraced quota-like mechanisms to ensure proportional representation of minorities and other groups at its 1972 convention.[62] Influential political magazines and journals, including *Public Interest* and *Commentary,* published critical arguments that achieved their most developed form in Nathan Glazer's 1975 book *Affirmative Discrimination.*[63] Ronald Reagan stated his opposition to preferences in his 1980 presidential campaign: "We must not allow the noble concept of equal opportunity to be distorted into federal guidelines or quotas which require race, ethnicity, or sex—rather than ability and qualifications—to be the principal factor in hiring or education."[64] Reagan lost his nerve and never put an end to the policy, though he did weaken its enforcement, and criticism of affirmative action continued through the 1990s.[65] When the Republican party won both chambers of Congress in 1995, it made ending preferences an early priority. Senate majority leader Robert Dole (R–KS) introduced a bill on July 10, 1995 that prohibited the federal government from actions that "intentionally discriminate against" or "grant a preference to" "any individual or group based in whole or in part on race, color, national origin, or sex" in connection with federal contracts or subcontracts, federal employment or "any other federally conducted program or activity." A recurrent theme of those seeking the Republican nomination for president in 1996 was the promise to bring a swift end to preferential policies.[66] Dole was the eventual nominee, but he lost the election and his antipreference bill went nowhere.

Why have conservative politicians failed to end affirmative-action preferences? One part of the answer is that, as with bilingual education, there is no organized opposition pushing them. But politicians do not need a groundswell of support before they act, as this book has shown. The more important reason is the fear of being branded a racist. In my interviews with Republican congressional staff, these fears of the party's image, as portrayed by affirmative-action defenders and then broadcast by the news media, were the most frequently mentioned factor inhibiting major action on bills to end preferences. Public support for guarantees of equal opportunity is a legitimacy imperative.[67]

Failure to retrench in national politics did not mean there was no retrenchment elsewhere. In state politics, where interest groups may be less active and thus political calculations different, Governors Pete Wilson of California,

Mike Foster of Louisiana, and Jeb Bush of Florida took decisive action to end preferences. But it was still risky business, and Wilson's stance, coupled with his positions on other issues including opposition to state provision of health and education services to undocumented aliens and their children, may have cost him and California Republicans politically as Latinos have moved solidly to the Democrats in that state. As with bilingual education, antipreference campaigns used state referenda to sidestep the politicians' fears of appearing racist. In California, Proposition 209 reinforced Wilson's efforts to end race and gender preferences in firms with state contracts and in state employment and education.[68] The state of Washington passed a similar referendum in 1998.

Federal judges, also insulated from political repercussions, have placed limitations on racial preferences. With Republican appointees playing a leading role, courts have begun to use the "strict scrutiny" standard of judicial review to assess the constitutionality of preferences. It demands that legal classifications be narrowly tailored and necessary to achieve a compelling government purpose. Strict scrutiny limits laws relying on "suspect classifications" of persons. These classifications include race, national origin, and citizenship status.

Applying this standard to cases involving city and federal programs designed to enhance minority capitalism, the Supreme Court revealed increasing doubts about the constitutionality of preferences. The Court found no compelling interest for affirmative action without a specific showing of discrimination by the institution practicing the policy. Moreover, the policy had to be narrowly tailored—only groups that had been discriminated against could be included. For the first time, the government was casting a critical eye on the expansion of affirmative action beyond blacks.[69] In 1996, a Fifth Circuit court extended the standard of strict scrutiny to affirmative admissions. It ruled in *Hopwood v. Texas*[70] that the University of Texas Law School's affirmative-action admissions program was unconstitutional, rejected the university's "diversity" rationale (the law school claimed that racial preferences were necessary to maintain a diverse student body), and argued that a specific finding of discrimination is necessary for such a program. The Supreme Court refused to review the case. By 2001, other courts offered mixed rulings on race-conscious admissions, which has set the stage for a major Supreme Court decision in the coming years.[71]

Defenders of affirmative action can point to its economic benefits to the official minorities, though the picture is not entirely clear or rosy. Ironically, the benefits are most impressive in the area where the federal government plays almost no role—university admissions. Here, one can easily measure the gains of minority students because in some institutions the policy was ended. For example, when the law school ended admissions preferences at the University of California at Berkeley, the percentage of African American students among all students accepted dropped from 9.2 percent (1996) to 1.8 percent (1997), and Latinos dropped from 9.6 percent to 4.9 percent.[72]

Statistics also show that affirmative action directed at minority capitalism has conferred benefits. For example, in fiscal year 1995, 6,002 firms participated in the SBA's $5.8 billion Section 8(A) program to receive preference in federal procurement. Forty-seven percent of those firms were owned by African Americans, 25 percent by Latinos, 21 percent by Asian Americans, 6 percent by American Indians, and 1 percent by "other."[73] This represents a great amount of money that would not otherwise go to these firms. The program, however, requires firms to "graduate" out of the program after nine years, and it is not clear whether it helps firms to compete without the preferences after that period. Furthermore, though the minority-capitalism programs are not of great concern to the majority of Americans (who may not even know about them), they do generate much criticism and court challenges from firms that feel they lose government contracts because of the preferences.[74]

It has been more difficult to measure clearly the economic benefits in employment, the original target of affirmative action. Certainly, great changes have taken place in the nation's larger businesses, as the sociologist Frank Dobbin and has colleagues have shown, including the appointment of an affirmative-action officer in fifty percent of surveyed firms with 50 or more employees. Other changes include the establishment of internal grievance procedures, written equal employment opportunity policies, and an overall "legalization of the workplace."[75] Firms also dutifully fill out their EEO-1 forms to report on the numbers of minorities hired, and government contractors include goals and timetables of promised minority hiring with their bids. Because the enforcement pressure from the federal government has been inconsistent over time, many affirmative-action officers were led to redefine their job as "diversity management." The new rationale was that firms could become more profitable by hiring race-consciously because people of different races supposedly had unique viewpoints and could understand persons of their race better than could Euro-Americans.[76] Whether called affirmative action or diversity management, the practices are mostly the same and rely on recognition of ethnoracial and gender differences.

It is difficult to gauge the impact of employment affirmative action because it is not always clear what employers are actually doing and how much hard "preference" is going on, and it may indeed be very little.[77] On the one hand, there are clear signs of gains, at least among African Americans in some contexts. Jerome Karabel reported that "between 1970 and 1990, the number of black electricians more than tripled (from 14,145 to 43,276) and the number of black police officers increased almost as rapidly (from 23,796 to 63,855."[78] Also, in a review of aggregate studies of affirmative action's impact, Jennifer Hochschild concluded that the policy did contribute to the growth of the black middle class since 1970. On the other hand, less optimistically, the literature also shows that affirmative action had only slight positive effects on beneficiary groups.[79]

Critics of affirmative action have pointed out that African Americans were making gains prior to the middle 1960s, and these gains did not appreciably jump after the onset of the policy.[80] Even sympathetic observers have questioned the role of affirmative action in helping poor African Americans. For example, the sociologist William Julius Wilson has pointed out that affirmative action does not help the "truly disadvantaged" of the inner-city black poor.[81] And the economist Glenn Loury could point to continuing high rates of African American poverty, unemployment (about double that of whites throughout the civil-rights era), and welfare dependency and fairly comment that "the contribution of affirmative action to the reduction of racial inequality appears to be quite modest."[82]

Why so much critical attention to affirmative action by politicians and pundits? One reason, according to public opinion polls and focus group studies, is the continued unpopularity among Euro-Americans of preferences.[83] In addition, though civil-rights leaders before 1965 almost never made affirmative action as later understood one of their central demands, the policy nevertheless *became* civil rights—took on the meaning of civil rights—by virtue of its status as the implementing regulations or programs for classically liberal civil rights.[84] Another and related reason is that it touches such central aspects of the human experience—building a career, making a living, reaching one's potential, achieving one's dreams. Affirmative-action regulations and programs affect access to jobs, to promotions, to schools, and to resources for businesses.[85] As one Republican congressional staffer remarked, affirmative action "can apply in so many ways." Whereas civil-rights laws for schools, housing, and voting issues are relatively specific, a party's stance on affirmative action reveals its overall view on the question of race, and retrenchment says to minorities, "They don't want you in."[86] For its defenders, then, an attack on affirmative action is an assault on the core meaning of civil rights and equal opportunity. Criticism of its programs tells minorities that they are not wanted, which is tantamount to racism. But for critics, the policy is unacceptable precisely because of this defining centrality. They argue that civil rights and the road to success and dreams should be free of any government-sponsored discrimination. As *the* policy where America declares and manages its official minorities, affirmative action plays a powerful symbolic role in the culture war regardless of its economic impacts.[87]

Black Exceptionalism

There was a peculiar aspect to the controversy surrounding affirmative action: nearly all of the debate concerned African Americans. Few even mentioned Latino, Asian American, American Indian, and female participation. It was as if the other official minorities did not even exist.

This political pattern is especially surprising when viewed from a comparative perspective. India is a nation that has established preferential policies even more explicitly than has the United States. It has done so targeting its "untouchable" caste with great conflict. However, according to political scientist Sunita Parikh, most of this conflict is along the dividing line of the preferences. That is, the groups most resentful of the preferences are those lower in social status but *not* included in the preferences. The target of their resentment is not the most disadvantaged groups in Indian affirmative action, but those just within the threshold of necessary group disadvantage and victimhood.[88] By this logic, America's white ethnics should be most resentful of affirmative action and should direct most of their resentment at preferences for Asian Americans and Latinos. Instead, ethnics along with most Americans seem to ignore these groups.

We might also expect to see resentment directed toward affirmative action for women. After all, there had been much resistance to the initial inclusion of women. By the 1990s, however, complaints about affirmative action for women were hard to find. In fact, public opinion polls showed there was *more* general support for affirmative action and antidiscrimination law for women than for blacks. In part this reflected the greater support on the part of women for policies targeted for them, but it showed up in the views of Euro-American men as well. Polls also indicated that Americans who strongly believed in values of individualism and government nonintervention were less likely to support affirmative action for blacks, yet these values were unrelated to support for women.[89]

While there is no poll evidence that Euro-Americans give greater support for preferential hiring and promotion of Latinos, Asians, or Indians than of blacks, other research points to a principle of "black exceptionalism" in American politics and social life.[90] Indeed, evidence abounds attesting to what Glenn Loury has identified as the racial stigma, or unique "otherness," of black Americans.[91] In the preceding chapters, we saw policymakers plunging ahead with policies for Latinos, explicitly stating that they believed this was a safer move politically than policy development for blacks. More recent analysis of public opinion data shows that the bases of white attitudes toward policies for blacks are different than those for other groups. As David O. Sears and his colleagues have concluded, "Whites had more negative and more crystallized attitudes toward blacks than they did toward other minority groups . . . [T]hose anti-black attitudes also had a broader influence over whites' policy preferences, even affecting their preferences about policies that had almost nothing to do with blacks."[92] A study of factors that affect Euro-Americans' decision to buy a home found that the percentage of African Americans in the neighborhood had a significant effect, but that the percentage of Latinos or Asian Americans had no effect all.[93] Attitudes and action are not far apart. Residential segregation of blacks is far greater than that of other groups, including Latinos.[94] Euro-Americans are not alone in their perception of blacks as different. The sociologist Camille Zubrinsky-Charles found that even greater percentages of Latinos and Asians than Euro-Americans wished to live in neighborhoods with no blacks at all.[95] Other polls indicate that Euro-Americans, Latinos, and Asian Americans are all more likely to consider blacks to be lazy than they are to think of other groups in that way.[96] In William Julius Wilson's study of Chicago employers, 75 percent reported their beliefs that black workers were lazy and undependable, and preferred to hire Latinos and Asians, whom they saw as hardworking.[97] Jennifer Lee also found a preference for immigrants among New York and Philadelphia employers, including black immigrants over native-born African Americans.[98] Other research suggests informal preferences for immigrants are widespread.[99]

Other evidence of black stigma includes rates of minority intermarriage with Euro-Americans. These run considerably higher among Latino and Asian American groups than among blacks. For example, Filipino and Cuban Americans born in the United States have intermarriages rates as high as 60 percent, compared to 5 and 2 percent for black men and women, respectively.[100] A final example of black exceptionalism relates to the children of these unions. There is the simple but little-noticed fact that only blacks are defined by the one-drop rule that means any black ancestry at all makes a person black. Partial Latino or Asian ancestry generally does not make an American Latino or Asian unless the individual chooses that identity.[101] Though this appears to be changing, children with one African American parent are still much more likely to be classified simply as black. Blacks remain exceptional in American society and politics.

Meanings and Political Change

The New American Political System and the Minority Rights Revolution

Throughout this book, I have emphasized the importance of cultural meanings for understanding the minority rights revolution. There were more clearly structural changes in American politics that also had a major part in motivating political actors and accelerating the whole process. I have given considerable attention to some of these, especially the laws and new civil rights agencies created for African Americans. But there were other changes in American politics that eased the way for minority rights.

A convergence of factors originating in the New Deal Era found full form in the 1960s and led to what some social scientists have dubbed a "new American political system," one that allows for ambitious public policy that might aid previously neglected segments of society and might also go against public opinion.[102] The factors characterizing the new system are interrelated and include a stronger presidency and administrative government, declining parties, and a fragmented Congress.

Beginning with Franklin D. Roosevelt, argues the political scientist Sidney Milkis, those who sought the presidency developed their own campaigns for the most part independently of the parties, and looked for support mainly from coalitions or interest groups.[103] The presidency became a more active source of policymaking and unelected administrators gained more power. This process could be seen in the emergence of minority rights; for example, every president from Roosevelt through Nixon issued executive orders to create minority rights policies and bureaucracies. World War II and the Cold War reinforced this process of power consolidation in the presidency. The Cold War contributed to the rise of national security as a paramount value, which gave presidents even more policymaking authority—they were granted the freedom to pursue national security as they saw fit.[104] In Chapters 2 and 3, I described this presidential power to make national-security and related policies, including efforts to end discrimination (primarily against blacks) in defense industries, in government service at home and abroad, and in immigration and the admission of refugees. Later chapters described more free-wheeling presidential efforts, such as Nixon's strategy of expanding programs to enhance minority capitalism as a way to assembling a winning coalition.

The related decline of the power wielded by the political parties also aided the minority rights revolution. With presidents making so much policy and turning positions of political patronage into offices of civil service, parties had less to do and fewer stakes in the matter, and they lost vitality. Changes in party procedures hastened this decline. The rise of primaries for choosing presidential nominees led to entrepreneurial, candidate-centered campaigns. Party regulars and smoky backrooms lost their place in the candidate-selection process. It was in each candidate's interest to seek some distinctive policy platform that would separate him from the pack and help him put together a winning coalition. For example, though presidential-hopeful Senator Birch Bayh was personally motivated to help women, his prominent support for women's rights was also smart politics.[105] At the same time, as the Wallace candidacy showed, Americans' attachment to the political parties began to erode.[106] There were more constituents in play and more votes for the taking if the White House strategy teams played their cards right.[107] This fed the fervor to appeal to minorities, especially Latinos but also women, the disabled, and even white ethnics, with new policies as well as symbolic gestures. Moreover, parties began to lose their ability to provide cover for those opposed to minority rights at about the same time opposition became anachronistic. The news media's role in the process grew, perhaps also hastening the decline of the parties.[108]

Marc Landy and Martin Levin have noted the tendency in recent decades for the institutional fragmentation, especially in Congress, and the weakness of individual parts of American government to fail to prevent rapid policy development and actually encourage it. In their view, these factors "increase the competition for policy innovation and enhance the power of strategically placed policy entrepreneurs."[109] One instance of this phenomenon is the growth in congressional committees since the 1960s, which, they note, has opened the agenda for lawmaking.[110] An example I considered in Chapter 7 is the hastily constructed subcommittees on bilingual education that oversaw hearings on that issue. To be sure, this committee structure was not always necessary—Title IX became law as an amendment from the floors of Congress. But some of these laws, especially Section 504, benefited from another factor related to the institutional fragmentation of the late 1960s and 1970s. The political scientist David Mayhew, as well as Landy and Levin, point out that rather than producing policy gridlock, the divided government created when one party controls the White House and another controls the Congress encourages creative policymaking as the different branches compete with one another. Nixon was an especially independent and active policy maker. But when he spoke of slowing down the liberal policymaking of the Johnson years, or wrung his hands over women's rights, the Democratic-controlled Congress rolled up its sleeves and pushed new policies even harder. Minority rights policies were part of this productive period, which also created various laws to control pollution, the Occupational Safety and Health Act of 1970, and the Consumer Product Safety Act of 1972.[111]

All of this analysis of the new American political system is important, and all of it helps explain the speed of policy development. There are three reasons I do not place these factors up front in my account. First, they do not address the *world* revolution in minority rights. Was it a coincidence that the world traveled along the same path at the same time as the United States? Chapters 2 and 3 showed that it was not, that the world and America were closely linked at least in the crucial early stages, which added an important independent effect in pushing the US rights revolution forward. Indeed, the perceived national-security needs to initiate progressive race policies was in part a *cause* of the new American political system, as it forced a succession of presidents to create policy transcending party organizations and encouraged an adversarial relationship between the White House and Congress. Moreover, why should minority rights, especially ethnic minorities, be the focus for so much activity? The developing world human rights culture and foreign propaganda highlighting American racism forced the issue.

Second, the new American political system factors do not give enough credit to black civil rights in getting the ball rolling. It seems clear that without the international implications of black oppression and the black civil rights movement's creative strategies, there would not have been a minority rights revolution in America, or it would have taken a very different form. Evidence on this point is available from comparative studies of women's rights. These find that black civil-rights laws and institutions created an American women's movement that was very different from those in other Western countries. For example, Steven Teles shows that British feminism puts a priority on changing the male world, rather than being integrated into it through affirmative action or other means. Therefore, "British feminists typically push for welfare-state interventions such as paid family leave, that challenge the hegemony of the market over the sphere of the family and caregiving." The effects of affirmative action in this setting would be to draw women away from traditionally female roles when these feminists want the public sphere and men to draw closer to them.[112] The sociologist Myra Marx Ferree finds a similar pattern in Germany. Women's leaders there have supported issues based on the assumption that women play unique roles, and demand such things as pay for housework. Protective legislation retains a legitimacy and vitality in Germany that it lost in the United States after Title VII annihilated it.[113] Abigail Saguy's study of the development of sexual-harassment law in America and France shows how the US policy developed based on an antidiscrimination frame rooted in race and ethnic discrimination, while in France sexual harassment had its beginnings in penal law and was understood more as sexual violence—with links to socialist discourse emphasizing abuse of power and exploitation.[114]

Third, and most important, an analysis of the new American political system cannot explain why some minority rights policies found easy success, others found success but not so easily, and others found no success at all. Only by attending to the varying group meanings can we understand which groups the government was willing to designate and recognize as minorities. Great presidential and administrative strength, declining parties, and changes in Congress did not lead to minority rights and recognition for white ethnics and gays and lesbians. Again, it is the cognitive working of the black analogy that also helps us understand the different dynamics at different stages of policymaking for other groups. When policymakers had to actually mobilize resources to effect policies based on the black analogy, it forced them to look more closely at that analogy. In the process, previously ignored group differences came to the fore, and policy implementation broke down. This was most clear in the cases of Title IX and Section 504, which passed through Congress without a squabble but produced years of fighting and attempts at revision of the laws when OCR began to write implementing guidelines. In contrast, the writing of guidelines to implement language rights for Latinos—where costs were great, American culture deeply challenged, but the black analogy least contested—was bold and fast.[115]

Meaning Changes and Historical Contingencies

Can social scientists predict how meanings will matter and change? I do not believe that they can. The power to predict changes in meaning and its effects would amount to the power to control meanings and thus perceptions of reality. This would be a godlike power—or certainly an extremely lucrative one. The hit-or-miss meaning campaigns of consumer-product marketing professionals or political consultants, which pour millions of dollars into their efforts but which often fail miserably, supports my skepticism. Still, one can make a few points regarding meanings and their manipulation and change.

First, some controlled meaning change is possible. In this book I have documented some changes that occurred effortlessly, that were mass, uncontrolled shifts in perceptions or cognitive liberation. In other cases, however, meaning entrepreneurship was the source of change. Successful efforts involve sometimes great skills in the assessment of the enormously complex cultural and political landscape.[116] There is at times an impressive artistry here that separates the brilliant politicians from the mediocre. For example, Martha Griffiths knew that to be successful it mattered whether *she* offered the amendment to Title VII to prohibit sex discrimination (which would be seen as special pleading by a low-status member of Congress), or southerner Howard Smith offered it (making it an attempted legislative sabotage and appealing to southern enemies of the bill). Though social scientists can help clarify why some attempts to create policy are harder than others (as I have tried to do in Chapters 3 and 9), the possibility is not closed that in any instance of failure more skillful meaning entrepreneurs could have succeeded. On the other hand, bumblers can screw up even a seemingly unproblematic situation.

Culture is cohesive without being coherent, and this makes prediction difficult if not impossible. Consider one false start of the minority rights revolution. There were special, ethnically targeted policies for American Indians, even a Bureau of Indian Affairs, well before affirmative action for African Americans. There were efforts to hire Indians preferentially at the bureau.[117] There was also a very old precursor to efforts to enhance minority capitalism called the Buy Indian Act of 1910, which stated: "So far as may be practicable, Indian labor shall be employed and purchases of the products of Indian industry may be made in the open market at the direction of the Secretary of the Interior."[118] This bears a strong resemblance to the SBA and Nixon's minority-capitalism efforts, but I could not find a shred of evidence that Indian preferences were a model for the programs in the 1960s, or that Nixon and his team were even aware of them. Certainly no other groups pursued the "Indian analogy" in asking for targeted treatment.

Why not? American Indians remained a group apart *until* they were analogized with blacks. Blacks were not like Indians from 1910–65, but Indians were like blacks after 1965. Why did the analogy only work one way? Is it because the policies for African Americans were premised on equal rights, which logically brought in more groups? But minority-capitalism affirmative action was not originally premised on compensating or preventing discrimination. Did the black analogy work because the federal government had grown so much by the 1960s as compared to 1910? That is a possible factor, but it could logically work the other way. With the stakes smaller, a "Buy Black Act" could have been *easier* to achieve. Or if Big Government of the 1960s allowed for expansion whereas early Little Government Indian policies did not, then why not expand it even more? Why not include ethnics and gays and lesbians? Perhaps ethnics and gays "really" were different, and Latinos, Asian Americans, American Indians, women, and the disabled "really" were more like blacks. But what is the crucial criterion that links them and separates them from ethnics and gays? Is it identifiability? But as discussed in Chapter 9, the notion that Latinos are easily identifiable is a fiction, and in fact external identification only mattered in employment affirmative action; minority capitalism and affirmative admissions depended on self-identification. Moreover, consider the differences between the official minorities. Why did it *not* matter that only blacks were brought to America as slaves? The distinction between slaves and voluntary, fortune-seeking immigrants (as with Asian Americans and the vast majority of Latinos) could have been significant. It was not.

The search for coherence in meanings, for that magic formula that makes sense of it all, is futile. Just as we have to explain to persistent inquiries of foreign visitors or children, some things have no explanation. They simply *are*. Yet incoherence does not mean that meanings do not play a crucial role in politics. Scholars can show how these meanings shape decision-making, how they emerge and change, and how they interact with social structures and resources, even while making no "logical" sense.

The constraints on meaning entrepreneurship vary with context. The comparison of black civil rights and immigration reform with the failed case of women's rights as matters of national security suggests that meaning change was most easily accomplished where advocates could point to foreign propaganda. That propaganda did a lot of the meaning entrepreneurship work by promoting and categorizing ethnic and racial equality as national security. But similar propaganda on economic equality was apparently not enough; economic rights to a job or health care failed as national-security policy. It appears that the major constraint imposed on meaning entrepreneurs is the "original," or given, meaning of the thing, group, or policy in question. That is the starting point, and some starting points are closer or more simply related to the entrepreneur's goal than others.[119] Chapter 3 showed that economic rights were saddled with a meaning that placed them too near the taboo of socialism. As I described in subsequent chapters, because Latinos were understood as a racial group, it was not difficult to promote them as a minority. The meaning of "woman" was more complex, and somehow funny, and women's advocates faced a more difficult road. Meaning entrepreneurs for white ethnics and for gays had the most difficult task; their groups were saddled with meanings that led to visceral, immediate rejection of the black analogy in the case of white ethnics and separation from mainstream politics in the case of gays and lesbians.

Was there a strategy or formula to being defined as analogous to blacks, and thus as a minority?[120] Was there something that meaning entrepreneurs for white ethnics or gays and lesbians could have done differently? One strategy, used with great skill by women's advocates, was to catalog statistics of underrepresentation. Since the government itself had used such statistics as measures of discrimination against African Americans, the practice became legitimate for other groups as well. Advocates for Latinos did the same, especially regarding low educational achievement. Statistics were a double-edged sword for advocates for Asian Americans, however, who strenuously made the case of Asian American minorityhood to the US Commission on Civil Rights in 1979.[121] These leaders could point to statistics showing, for example, the continuing underrepresentation of Asian Americans in management positions.[122] But other statistics showed Asian Americans doing well relative to blacks and also whites, as the EEOC discovered when it analyzed data from its EEO-1 forms, and as university administrators could clearly see from their admissions statistics. Asian minorityhood therefore was a harder sell. For white ethnics and for gays, it was harder to find statistics of underrepresentation since the EEO-1 did not gather information for them.

Even without statistics, advocates for white ethnics could have had a much more compelling case if they compared themselves to nonblack minorities, such as the frequently white Latinos or the not-greatly-disadvantaged Asian Americans, rather than to African Americans. In other words, a Latino analogy or an Asian American analogy might have been the ticket to minority rights for ethnics. Indeed, the statistics that ethnic advocates gathered showed they faced a glass ceiling similar to that apparently faced by Asian Americans. At times, the Polish American Congress's Leonard Walentynowicz compared ethnics to nonblack minorities, as in his *Bakke* brief. Too often, ethnic leaders compared themselves to African Americans. Government officials could then reasonably reply that blacks faced far greater disadvantage and were more easily distinguishable. Another strategy would have been to change the context of or the audience for the claims being made. Not everyone sees things the same way all the time, and not everyone is equally persuadable. Thus, though they found almost total failure at the federal level and before the national audience, as described in Chapter 9, advocates for gays and lesbians were successfully able to make their case for being seen as analogous with blacks in some politically liberal cities and college towns.

Policy Change and "Racialization"

The interaction of politics and meanings is clearly a two-way street. The policies of minority rights in part flowed from the meanings of the groups in question, but policies also affected group meanings. The significance of the minority rights revolution is in part based on this dynamic.

This has important implications for research on "racialization," which is concerned with the process whereby groups are placed in categories based on some physical characteristics that are believed to have some social or behavioral significance.[123] Though this research has addressed the processes that allowed some groups to become white, it has hardly noted that the whiteness of ethnics was still contested during the white ethnic revival of the late 1960s and early 1970s.[124] It has also shown a totally unjustified disregard for affirmative action's impact on racialization.[125] More attention has gone to the racializing impact of the census. However, while the census is important as a tool for state measurement and management of the population, its idiosyncratic treatment of race does not mirror popular or folk understandings. The census treats Latinos as an ethnicity, and census racial and ethnic categories have undergone change every decade. The census also propagates the absurdity that various Asian ethnicities, such as Chinese, Vietnamese, and Korean, are in fact *races*.[126] In contrast, affirmative action's four basic racialized official minorities plus women have remain unchanged since 1965. Affirmative action mirrors, reinforces, and almost certainly helped create the folk "ethno-racial pentagon" described by the historian David Hollinger, which divides Americans into five "colors": the white Euro-Americans, the black African Americans, the brown Latinos, the yellow Asian Americans, and the red American Indians.[127] Scholars have similarly given unwarranted attention to the Office of Management and Budget's obscure "Directive 15," which standardized ethnic and racial data collection and management across the government in 1977. In fact, this directive was only reinforcing a long-running practice established by the EEO-1 and affirmative action's official minorities.[128]

It was through affirmative action that policymakers carved out and gave official sanction to a new category of American: the minorities. Without much thought given to what they were doing, they created and legitimized for civil society a new discourse of race, group difference, and rights. This new discourse mirrored racist talk and ideas by reinforcing the racial difference of certain ethnic groups, most incongruously Latinos. In this discourse race was real and racial categories discrete and unproblematic. By dividing the world into "whites" and "minorities" (or later "people of color") it sometimes obscured great differences among minority groups and among constituent groups within the pan-ethnic categories, so that Cubans and Mexicans officially became Latino, Japanese and Filipinos became Asian, and Italians, Poles, and Jews joined WASPs as white. Most profoundly, the minority rights revolution turned group victimhood into a basis of a positive national policy. Affirmative action led white ethnic leaders to lobby to be a minority, as well as various possibly Asian groups. As described in Chapter 5, Indians, Sri Lankans, and various Pacific Island groups found success, while Afghans and Middle Eastern peoples were rejected along with ethnics and Jews.

Affirmative action has become a means through which America incorporates immigrants from some parts of the world by racializing them.[129] With minority rights policy depending on the black analogy, in a political sense even women and the disabled were "racialized," or more specifically, African-Americanized. With federal policy dependent on a showing of group oppression, group advocates focused inward, pressed their distinctive claims, and the prospects for cross-race/ethnicity-coalition politics dimmed.[130]

Affirmative action specifically was the basis of the "identity politics" that characterized the late twentieth century. It created the group categories and legitimized the politics. By obliterating class distinctions, it cast even the lowliest Euro-American as a privileged oppressor, isolating the official minorities from a massive group of potential allies. Affirmative action brought immediate benefits to the official minorities but it may have foreclosed more comprehensive reforms.

The Continuing Legacies of the Minority Rights Revolution

From our standpoint at the beginning of the twenty-first century, some aspects of the minority rights revolution appear more durable than others. Classical liberalism in all probability will remain unassailable. Also most likely to survive are the rights policies for the disabled and for women. Those for ethnic and racial minorities have a less clear future. The spectacular growth of official minorities in the American population may have very different effects. It may render bilingual education and affirmative action impractical or politically vulnerable, or may further entrench them in American politics.

Americans are more supportive of women's rights, but the failure of the black analogy for women in constitutional law may ironically save women's rights from retrenchment in the courts. As legal scholar Deborah Malamud has pointed out, the courts may preserve affirmative-action preferences for women even while abolishing them for other official minorities. Laws that classify by gender receive less rigorous judicial scrutiny—the "intermediate" standard, which demands that laws be "substantially related" to an "important" government purpose (rather than "necessary" for a "compelling" purpose). This lighter standard of review makes it less likely that the courts would retrench affirmative action for women, and since national lawmakers fear to venture into this area, it may be safe for the foreseeable future. However, the coalition of women's and black groups that has worked to defend affirmative action could be increasingly strained.[131]

Changing demographics will not affect women's rights, but consider the problem of bilingual education in the 2000s. The 2000 census showed that due mostly to continuing immigration, Latinos now outnumber blacks. Immigration of other groups officially classified as minorities also continues in massive numbers. While Mexico still sends the greatest number of immigrants, the others hail from a dizzying variety of nations. Since they speak a corresponding variety of languages, and have very differing views on the wisdom of the policy, establishing bilingual education with qualified staff for all immigrants is growing more difficult.[132] It is becoming increasingly a Latino-only program; but if language accommodation is a right and linked to equal opportunities, how can we justify different policies for different groups?

In the area of affirmative action, increasing diversity may also lead to political and practical problems. Already there has been conflict over affirmative action as growing numbers of Latinos in search of jobs have confronted the established African Americans in government employment. In Los Angeles, where blacks were overrepresented in city government, Latino organizations demanded that city employment reflect Latino proportions in the population. On the federal level, Congressman Luis Gutierrez (D–IL), a Puerto

Rican from Chicago, asked for a Government Accounting Office study of affirmative action in the postal service. The report found that nationally African Americans were overrepresented in postal service employment by a factor of two, while Latinos (and Euro-Americans) were underrepresented. In Chicago, African Americans' presence in postal employment was four times greater than their proportion in the population, and in Los Angeles it was six. In contrast, Latino proportions were less than half. Meanwhile, blacks complained of Asian Americans displacing them in minority-capitalism programs.[133]

The potential practical problems in part stem from the high rates of intermarriage between Euro-Americans and Latinos and Asian Americans; these will lead to ever-increasing numbers of persons who can claim only partial minority ancestry. In response, the OMB issued new guidelines for the EEO-1 form for 2003: employers may no longer have to identify their official minorities by visual survey. Instead, depending on an EEOC decision still pending, employees may racialize themselves as bidders for government contract or SBA loan preferences and college applicants always have. The guidelines state that mixed-race persons will be able to check off any categories that apply to them, but anyone who picks a nonwhite or Hispanic background will be counted for civil-rights enforcement purposes as the nonwhite race or Hispanic. If the EEOC follows OMB, it will have extended the one-drop rule from African Americans to all of the official minority groups. This will simplify enforcement of affirmative action but will provide a picture of American society that does not square with dominant perceptions of mixed-race persons, including their perceptions of themselves. Moreover, because it comes with no mechanism to verify the choices, the rules would seem to invite deception.[134]

Eventually, in what will surely be a difficult and uncomfortable decision, policymakers or the courts will have to decide just how much of a minority one has to be to qualify and how the government can verify minority status. This decision will require what policymakers have avoided from the beginning: a massive study of which groups are actually discriminated against and to what degree—when, where, and how. For guidance, policymakers profitably may look to India, which undertook precisely this endeavor in deciding which disadvantaged groups should be eligible for preferences there.[135]

A related issue pending decision is whether the pan-ethnic categories are viable. White ethnic leaders, of course, always argued they were not, but new diversity among official minorities highlights this issue even more: when one Asian American group (Koreans) has the highest rate of business formation in the nation (including all Euro-American groups), and another (Laotians) has the lowest, the logic of grouping them together is certainly questionable.[136] Different rates of achievement among Latino groups (Cuban relative to Puerto Ricans or Mexican Americans) and blacks (American-born relative to West Indian or African) can also be observed in education and income.[137] This inequality within categories will result in most preferences and opportunities going to the most advantaged ethnicities within each category. Policymakers may just let some ethnic groups come to dominate representation within their respective ethnic categories, they may try to ensure ethnic proportionalism within them (impractical, especially in the employment arena, and certainly unfair to the excluded white ethnics or Middle Easterners), or they may come to embrace color-blind methods that could work to open doors to the disadvantaged without naming any groups. One example of this approach is the "percentage plans" adopted in Texas, Florida, and California in response to the ending of preferences in university admissions in those states. These plans guarantee admission to the states' top universities for all students who graduate in the top of their class (top 10 percent in Texas, 20 percent in Florida, and 4 percent in California). The presence of de facto segregated high schools thus leads to significant admissions of minorities to the universities, though critics complain that many are poorly prepared for university education.[138] For minority capitalism, one difference-blind approach would be to give preference in government contracts to firms that locate in areas with high concentrations of poverty or employ people from those areas.[139] Some have argued for a class-based approach in all questions of preferential treatment.[140]

It remains to be seen how the declining Euro-American segment of the population will view policies that use preferences to bring a proportional share of opportunities to the growing nonblack minority groups. The white ethnics, though denied recognition as an identity politics group, still have advocates who point out that despite the rhetoric of "diversity" in the elite universities, white ethnic students are almost nonexistent. They also continue to lobby for government appointments.[141] Barring a brilliant and as-yet unimagined public relations effort by high-status politicians, individuals, or groups, it is hard to imagine mainstream Euro-Americans embracing preferences for all groups.[142] "Black exceptionalism" may continue—Euro-Americans may remain oblivious to the changing demographics while they continue to focus resentment on African Americans. It is also possible they may begin to suffer a "diversity fatigue" and move out of the cities and inner suburbs to whiter and more distant fringe suburbs.[143] This action may be accompanied by resignation or increasing resentment.[144] Alternatively, continued high intermarriage rates may blur group boundaries and lessen tensions.[145] The blurring and absorbing may include African Americans, but current data suggests that blacks will remain isolated from the more residentially integrated and intermarrying Asian Americans, Latinos and Euro-Americans.[146]

Also unclear are the politics of the minorities themselves. African Americans regularly give support to affirmative action, though not overwhelmingly. Though there has been some Latino resentment of black domination of some affirmative action, polls show that Latinos give less support to affirmative action than blacks, and Asian Americans less still.[147] However, even if affirmative action is not a salient concern of African Americans or other minorities, a politician's stance on it may still carry meanings of his or her overall attitudes toward minorities, and rights groups will continue to label any retrenchment efforts as racist. In that case, support for affirmative action, bilingual education, other difference-conscious policies, and open immigration may be a litmus test for minority support, as has been the case with similar policies in India, and without challenges in the courts would likely become ever more entrenched in American politics.[148]

One legacy of the minority rights revolution is almost certain to endure. Since World War II, there has been a profound change in both US and world political culture. Respect for this twentieth-century invention—human rights—is a standard of legitimacy in world politics and American domestic politics. That does not mean that all nations and all politicians will always respect individual or minority rights. But it does mean they must be careful. Mass executions, deportations, or segregations and inequalities imposed on identifiable groups carry a different meaning now than they did before World War II. They are shameful anachronisms. American public opinion has undergone a massive shift toward the principle of equal opportunity for all.[149] Even if they dislike some of the specific policies, voters have rewarded politicians who support equal rights.[150]

If the minority rights revolution is to be undone at the federal level, it will most likely be at the hands of persons who do not have to worry about the next election—the nation's judges. If changes in minority rights policies are undertaken by a president or a joint action of Congress and the president, this effort will almost certainly take a form that affirms the revolution. Though the wild cards of historical contexts and varying skill levels of future political leaders make prediction extremely tricky, it is not likely that affirmative action, bilingual education, Title IX, Section 504, and related policies will be rescinded or replaced because they are believed to constitute excessive regulation. Neither will they be ended because they violate the principle of states' rights, because they are unfair to able-bodied Euro-American males, and certainly not because of any alleged group superiority. America is different now. Future actions will be done in the name of the beneficiaries, in the furtherance of their rights.

NOTES

1. Introduction

1. Barry M. Goldwater, *The Conscience of a Conservative* (New York: McFadden Books, 1964 [1960]).
2. Letter from Barry Goldwater to Ray Price, January 6, 1969, in Hugh Davis Graham, ed., *Civil Rights during the Nixon Administration, 1969–74* (Bethesda: University Publications of America, 1989), Part I, Reel 1, frame 21. Also see the letter from John Rhodes to Peter M. Flanigan, June 17, 1969, in Graham, *Civil Rights during Nixon*, Part I, Reel 2, frame 2.
3. The brief was for *Lau v. Nichols*, 94 U.S. 786 (1974), described in Chapter 7. In his 1996 book, Bork writes, "Part of our national lore, and glory, is the fact that youngsters speaking not a word of English were placed in public schools where only English was used and very shortly were proficient in the language. That was crucial to the formation of American identity." Bork goes on to criticize bilingual education without mentioning his own role in the establishment of federal language rights. See Robert H. Bork, *Slouching towards Gomorrah: Modern Liberalism and American Decline* (New York: Regan Books, 1996), pp. 300–3.
4. Work by the sociologist John Meyer and his colleagues has examined the world development of rights protections as a part of the modern state, but has not clearly traced the processes through which this has occurred in the United States. The most recent statement is John Boli and George M. Thomas, eds., *Constructing World Culture* (Stanford: Stanford University Press, 1999). Philip Epp's work has examined processes of change in a comparative perspective, but concentrates solely on developments in courts. Philip Epp, *The Rights Revolution* (Chicago: University of Chicago Press, 1997).
5. We have many sociological and historical studies of disadvantaged American groups that fought for and received new rights guarantees in the period, but this work usually concentrates on specific groups such as blacks or women, and usually does not examine the linkages between groups and the larger process. An exception is Hugh Davis Graham's *The Civil Rights Era: Origins and Development of National Policy* (New York: Oxford University Press, 1990). Scholars have begun to explore the links between the social-movement organizations of the various groups, but have not looked at policy and legal development regarding these links. See Sidney Tarrow, *Power in Movement* (New York: Cambridge

University Press, 1994), pp. 129–30, 156–57; Doug McAdam, "'Initiator' and 'Spin-Off' Movements: Diffusion Processes in Protest Cycles," in *Repertoires and Cycles of Collective Action,* ed. Mark Traugott (Durham: Duke University Press, 1995), pp. 217–39, p. 226; David S. Meyer and Nancy Whittier, "Social Movement Spillover," *Social Problems* 41 (1994): 27–98; and Debra C. Minkoff, "The Sequencing of Social Movements," *American Sociological Review* 62 (1997): 779–99.

6. Tarrow, *Power in Movement,* p. 129.

7. Ibid., pp. 156–57.

8. Ibid., p. 98.

9. The political-process or political-opportunity approach associated with Doug McAdam's *Political Process and the Development of Black Insurgency* (Chicago: University of Chicago Press, 1982), now the dominant social-movement theory, is designed to explain the emergence and decline of social-movement organizations. A recent look at outcomes is Marco Giugni, Doug McAdam, and Charles Tilly, *How Movements Matter* (Minneapolis: University of Minnesota Press, 1999).

10. For a rare dissenting view, see Mayer N. Zald and Michael A. Berger, "Social Movements in Organizations: Coup d'Etat, Insurgency, and Mass Movements," *American Journal of Sociology* 83 (1978): 823–61; and Mayer N. Zald, "Social Movements as Ideologically Structured Action: An Enlarged Agenda," *Mobilization* 5 (2000): 1–16.

11. A concise summary of this view is Sven H. Steinmo, "American Exceptionalism Reconsidered: Culture or Institutions?" in *The Dynamics of American Politics: Approaches and Interpretations* eds. Lawrence C. Dodd and Calvin Jillson (Boulder: Westview Press, 1994), pp. 106–31.

12. Theda Skocpol, *Protecting Soldiers and Mothers* (Cambridge, Mass.: Harvard University Press, 1992); Edwin Amenta, *Bold Relief* (Princeton: Princeton University Press, 1998).

13. The theory is elaborated in James Q. Wilson, *Political Organizations* (New York: Basic Books, 1973), Chapter 16; Wilson, *American Government: Institutions and Policies* (Lexington, Mass.: D. C. Heath, 1980), Part 4; and Wilson, "The Politics of Regulation," in James Q. Wilson, ed., *The Politics of Regulation* (New York: Basic Books, 1980), pp. 366–72.

14. Azza Layton extends social-movement political-process theory to link black civil rights to the international context, but does not explore the dynamics of that process beyond that case. Azza Layton, *International Politics and Civil Rights Policies in the United States, 1941–1960* (New York: Cambridge University Press, 2000).

15. Skocpol, *Protecting Soldiers and Mothers;* Paul Pierson, *Dismantling the Welfare State?* (New York: Cambridge University Press, 1994); Margaret Weir, *Politics and Jobs: The Boundaries of Employment Policy in the United States* (Princeton: Princeton University Press, 1992).

16. Scholars have long linked war with state building and policymaking. In social science, the importance of national security, or war, in state building was recognized since Max Weber's writing, but has been most developed in the

work of Charles Tilly. Charles Tilly, ed., *The Formation of National States in Western Europe* (Princeton: Princeton University Press, 1975); Tilly, "War Making and State Making as Organized Crime," in Peter B. Evans, Dietrich Rueschemeyer, and Theda Skocpol, eds., *Bringing the State Back In* (New York: Cambridge University Press, 1985), pp. 169–91. A more recent statement is Miguel Centeno, *Blood and Debt: War and the Nation-State in Latin America* (University Park: Pennsylvania State University Press, 2002). Michael Sherry's work surveys the relationship of national security to domestic politics. Michael Sherry, *In the Shadow of War* (New Haven: Yale University Press, 1994).

17. Chris Bonastia, "Why Did Affirmative Action in Housing Fail during the Nixon Era? Exploring the 'Institutional Homes' of Social Policies," *Social Problems* 47 (2000): 523–42.

18. The classic statement is Ann Swidler, "Culture in Action: Symbols and Strategies," *American Sociological Review* 51 (1986): 273–86. Elisabeth S. Clemens, *The People's Lobby* (Chicago: University of Chicago Press, 1997), Chapter 2, discusses repertoires as tool kits of organizational models. It is a simple adaptation to use the concept for models of policy. See Rogers Brubaker, *Citizenship and Nationhood in France and Germany* (Cambridge, Mass.: Harvard University Press, 1992), pp. 16–17, on the related concept of cultural "idioms." On "policy paradigms," a more cognitively oriented concept, see Frank Dobbin, *Forging Industrial Policy* (New York: Cambridge University Press, 1994).

19. I thank Steve Teles for this concept. He traces it to Daniel Patrick Moynihan, "The Professionalization of Reform," *Public Interest* 1 (1965): 6–16.

20. See, for example, James G. March and Johan P. Olsen, *Rediscovering Institutions: The Organizational Basis of Politics* (New York: Free Press, 1989); Clemens, *People's Lobby;* Robin Stryker, "Rules, Resources, and Legitimacy Processes: Some Implications for Social Conflict, Order and Change," *American Journal of Sociology* 99 (1994): 847–910; Michèle Lamont, *The Dignity of Working Men: Morality and the Boundaries of Race, Class and Immigration* (Cambridge, Mass.: Harvard University Press, 2000); Ronald L. Jepperson, Alexander Wendt, and Peter J. Katzenstein, "Norms, Identity, and Culture in National Security," in Peter J. Katzenstein, ed., *The Culture of National Security: Norms and Identity in World Politics* (New York: Columbia University Press, 1996), pp. 33–78.

21. For work dealing with the concept of frames in social movements, see Doug McAdam, John D. McCarthy, and Mayer N. Zald, "Introduction," in Doug McAdam, John D. McCarthy, and Mayer N. Zald, eds., *Comparative Perspectives on Social Movements* (New York: Cambridge University Press, 1996), pp. 1–22. Also see Tarrow, *Power in Movement;* David A. Snow, E. Burke Rochford Jr., Steven K. Worden, and Robert D. Benford, "Frame Alignment Processes, Micromobilization, and Movement Participation," *American Sociological Review* 45 (1986): 787–801.

22. Jeffrey Haydu, "Counter Action Frames: Employer Repertoires and the Union Menace in the Late Nineteenth Century," *Social Problems* 46 (1999): 313–31; Donald A. Schön and Martin R. Rein, *Frame Reflection: Toward the Resolution of Intractable Policy Controversies* (New York: Basic Books, 1994).

23. Francesca Polletta, "'It Was Like a Fever . . .': Narrative and Identity in Social Protest," *Social Problems* 45 (1998): 137–59; Polletta, "Contending Stories: Narrative in Social Movements," *Qualitative Sociology* 21 (1998): 419–46; Patricia Ewick and Susan Silbey, *The Common Place of Law* (Chicago: University of Chicago Press, 1998).

24. Work in this vein includes Erik Bleich, "From International Ideas to Domestic Policies: Educational Multiculturalism in England and France," *Comparative Politics* 31, no. 1 (October 1998): 81–100; Martha Derthick and Paul J. Quirk, *The Politics of Deregulation* (Washington, D.C.: Brookings Institution, 1985); Richard A. Harris and Sidney M. Milkis, *The Politics of Regulatory Change* (New York: Oxford University Press, 1989); the essays included in Sven Steinmo, Kathleen Thelen, and Frank Longstreth, eds., *Structuring Politics* (New York: Cambridge University Press, 1992), esp. Margaret Weir, "Ideas and the Politics of Bounded Innovation," pp. 188–216, and Desmond S. King, "The Establishment of Work-Welfare Programs in the United States and Britain: Politics, Ideas and Institutions," pp. 217–50.

25. In political science, see Rogers M. Smith, *Civic Ideals* (New Haven: Yale University Press, 1997); Smith, "Beyond Tocqueville, Myrdal, and Hartz: The Multiple Traditions in America," *American Political Science Review* 87 (1993): 549–66; and Desmond S. King, *Making Americans* (Cambridge, Mass.: Harvard University Press, 2000). In sociology, see Edward Shils, *Tradition* (Chicago: University of Chicago Press, 1981).

26. See the fascinating and beautifully illustrated book, Peter Menzel and Faith D'Aluisio, *Man Eating Bugs: The Art and Science of Eating Insects* (Berkeley: Ten Speed Press, 1998).

27. One suggestion is that Americans do not eat animals that are named, such as all pets, but do eat the unnamed. Marshall Sahlins, *Culture and Practical Reason* (Chicago: University of Chicago Press, 1976), p. 174, n. 6. This distinction holds because named animals are presumably more humanlike. Joseph Gusfield, "Nature's Body and the Metaphors of Food," in Michèle Lamont and Marcel Fournier, eds., *Cultivating Differences: Symbolic Boundaries and the Meaning of Inequality* (Chicago: University of Chicago Press, 1992), pp. 75–103, 80. While helpful, this line of reasoning can only take us so far. It is completely silent on why we eat only a small fraction of the unnamed animals. Americans do not eat unnamed apes and bonobos, which are humanlike, but they also do not eat bugs, rats, badgers, capybaras, and so on, which are not.

28. Marc K. Landy, "The New Politics of Environmental Policy," in Marc K. Landy and Martin A. Levin, *The New Politics of Public Policy* (Baltimore: Johns Hopkins University Press, 1995), pp. 207–27, 208.

29. For interesting discussions on this point, see Paul DiMaggio, "Culture and Cognition," *Annual Review of Sociology* 23 (1997): 263–87; George Lakoff and Mark Johnson, *Metaphors We Live By* (Chicago: University of Chicago Press, 1980); Eviatar Zerubavel, *The Fine Line* (New York: Free Press, 1991); and Zerubavel, *Social Mindscapes: An Invitation to Cognitive Sociology* (Cambridge, Mass.: Harvard University Press, 1997).

30. I base the concept of meaning entrepreneurs on Finnemore and Sikkink's dis-

cussion of "norm entrepreneurs." Martha Finnemore and Kathryn Sikkink, "International Norm Dynamics and Political Change," in Peter J. Katzenstein, Robert O. Keohane, and Stephen D. Krasner, eds., *Exploration and Contestation in the Study of World Politics* (Cambridge, Mass.: MIT Press, 1999), pp. 247–77, 257. Also see Barbara Ballis Lal, "Ethnic Identity Entrepreneurs: Their Role in Transracial and Intercountry Adoptions," *Asian and Pacific Migration Journal* 6 (1997): 385–413.

31. McAdam, *Political Process and the Development of Black Insurgency,* pp. 48–51.

32. DiMaggio, "Culture and Cognition," p. 280.

33. For a similar approach, see generally Peter J. Katzenstein, ed., *The Culture of National Security: Norms and Identity in World Politics* (New York: Columbia University Press, 1996). My main difference with this work regards range of application. In Katzenstein's definition, norms are "collective expectations for the proper behavior of actors with a given identity." Katzenstein, "Introduction," in ibid., pp. 1–32, 5. I do not believe norms should be attached only to actors; they are also linked to meanings of things.

34. As the economist Glenn Loury has written about racial groups, these meanings "bear on the identity, the status, and even the humanity of those who carry them" and "once established, these meanings may come to be taken for granted, enduring essentially unchallenged for millennia." Glenn Loury, *The Anatomy of Racial Inequality: Stereotypes, Stigma, and the Elusive Quest for Racial Justice* (Cambridge, Mass.: Harvard University Press, 2001).

35. See Lakoff and Johnson, *Metaphors We Live By,* p. 165, for a discussion of prototypes and how this process works on a cognitive level. On race and cognition, see Rogers Brubaker, Mara Loveman, and Peter Stamatov, "Reviving Constructivism: The Case for a Cognitive Approach to Race, Ethnicity and Nationalism," unpublished manuscript.

36. Other scholars have identified plural justices but have not linked them to specific meanings, instead identifying them with "spheres." Michael Walzer, *Spheres of Justice* (New York: Basic Books, 1983) ("spheres"); Jennifer Hoschschild, *What's Fair? American Beliefs about Distributive Justice* (Cambridge, Mass.: Harvard University Press, 1981) ("domains").

37. Lakoff and Johnson, *Metaphors We Live By,* pp. 141–46.

38. F. James Davis, *Who Is Black?* (University Park: Pennsylvania State University Press, 1991), p. 21.

39. Orlando Patterson, "Race by the Numbers," *New York Times,* May 8, 2001.

40. See, for example, Roger W. Cobb and Marc Howard Ross, "Agenda Denial: The Power of Competing Cultural Definitions," in Roger W. Cobb and Marc Howard Ross, eds., *Cultural Strategies of Agenda Denial* (Lawrence: University Press of Kansas, 1997), pp. 203–20; John W. Kingdon, *Agendas, Alternatives and Public Policies* (Boston: Little, Brown, 1984), pp. 115–19.

41. Max Weber, of course, focused on the meaning of work and the "calling" in his classic *The Protestant Ethic and the Spirit of Capitalism* (New York: Scribners, 1958). Clifford Geertz showed the utility of this approach in *The Interpretation of Cultures* (New York: Basic Books, 1973), and *Local Knowledge* (New York: Basic Books, 1983). More recent innovative scholarship in this tradition in-

cludes Richard Biernacki, *The Fabrication of Labor* (Berkeley: University of California Press, 1995); and Jason Andrew Kaufman, "Competing Conceptions of Individualism in Contemporary American AIDS Policy: A Re-Examination of Neo-Institutionalist Analysis," *Theory and Society* 27 (1998): 635–69. Keith Bybee offers a creative argument on judicial reasoning in political representation cases that shows how legal reasoning is shaped by how judges interpret the meaning of "the people." Keith J. Bybee, *Mistaken Identity: The Supreme Court and the Politics of Minority Representation* (Princeton: Princeton University Press, 1998), esp. Chapter 3.

42. Elisabeth Clemens and James Cook describe this process of innovation by quoting from William Sewell's analysis of the "transposition" of schemas to new settings: "Knowledge of a rule or schema by definition means the ability to transpose or extend it creatively. If this is so, then *agency* . . . the capacity to transpose and extend schemas to new contexts, is inherent in the knowledge of cultural schemas that characterizes all minimally competent members of society." William Sewell Jr., "A Theory of Structure: Duality, Agency, and Transformation," *American Journal of Sociology* 98 (1992): 1–29. Clemens and Cook go on to argue that "groups marginal to the political system" are most likely to innovate or experiment in part because marginal groups are "[d]enied the social benefits of current institutional configurations" and thus have "fewer costs associated with deviating from those configurations." Elisabeth S. Clemens and James M. Cook, "Politics and Institutionalism: Explaining Durability and Change," *Annual Review of Sociology* 25 (1999): 441–66, 452. While sound, this argument understates the tendency to experiment, which can be found in the most central political actors, such as presidents, depending on their aspirations or whether they perceive their situation as desperate and demanding risk. See Stephen Skowronek's discussion of the politics of preemption in Skowronek, *The Politics Presidents Make* (Cambridge, Mass.: Harvard University Press, 1993).

43. Robin Rogers-Dillon and John Skrentny, "Administering Success: The Legitimacy Imperative and the Administration of Welfare Reform," *Social Problems* 46 (1999): 13–29; Robin Rogers-Dillon, "Ending Welfare as We Know It," Ph.D. diss., University of Pennsylvania, 1998.

44. A similar integrative approach is used by Margaret Keck and Kathryn Sikkink. See Keck and Sikkink, *Activists beyond Borders: Advocacy Networks in International Politics* (Ithaca: Cornell University Press, 1998), p. 4.

45. Another possible comparative group is the elderly, which also obviously includes Euro-American men. Elderly Americans won simple, classically liberal difference-blind protection from discrimination in the Age Discrimination in Employment Act of 1967 and the Age Discrimination Act of 1975. The employment-focused law prohibits discrimination against those aged forty to sixty-five or seventy, depending on the category of employment. The Age Discrimination Act is yet another copy of Title VI, prohibiting age discrimination in federally assisted programs and activities, though with "reasonableness" exceptions. As usual, the law was based on the black analogy. Typically, Congress gave hapless HEW secretary Caspar Weinberger, then struggling with Title IX regulations, no guidance on what it meant by "reasonable." See Peter H. Schuck, "The

Graying of Civil Rights Law: The Age Discrimination Act of 1975," *Yale Law Journal* 89 (1979): 27–94, 28–45. I do not examine these rights laws because they do not recognize, highlight, or reify "agedness" in the way that affirmative action or disability rights reify differences. Moreover, rights for the elderly were not very disruptive to American society and less controversial. Therefore it is less surprising that they developed.

2. Racial Equality Becomes National Security

1. He was quoting from Victor Hugo's *Historie d'un crime*. Charles Whalen and Barbara Whalen, *The Longest Debate* (Washington, D.C.: Seven Locks Press, 1985), p. 185.

2. This interpretation mostly fits with and builds on recent work in international relations that emphasizes the constitutive role of culture in explaining state behavior. For example, Ronald Jepperson, Alexander Wendt, and Peter Katzenstein emphasize that cultural environments and state identity changes shape national security interests. Ronald L. Jepperson, Alexander Wendt, and Peter J. Katzenstein, "Norms, Identity, and Culture in National Security," in Peter J. Katzenstein, ed., *The Culture of National Security: Norms and Identity in World Politics* (New York: Columbia University Press, 1996), pp. 33–78, 54–60. This understanding fits the process traced in this chapter, where the new world culture of human rights, and America's identity as a champion of this culture, pointed government officials toward an interest in domestic minority-rights protection. Following Marc Lynch's adaptation of Habermas for international relations, this process can also be understood as the construction of a global public sphere. Citing the sociologist Craig Calhoun, Lynch describes the public sphere as "that site of interaction in which actors routinely reach understandings about norms, identities, and interests through public exchange of discourse." Lynch argues that if "state policymakers must defend, justify and explain their positions before a public sphere, behavior will tend to closely conform to the arguments being advanced, as each side attempts to establish its frame." For Lynch, as well as the interpretation of American behavior in this chapter, hypocrisy can be delegitimating. See Marc Lynch, *State Interests and Public Spheres: The International Politics of Jordan's Identity* (New York: Columbia University Press, 1999), pp. 11, 30, 39. On the public sphere, see Craig Calhoun, "Civil Society and the Public Sphere," *Public Culture* 5 (1995): 267–80.

   As described in the introductory chapter, this chapter also borrows from Martha Finnemore's notion of "norm entrepreneurs," who actively promote new moral/cultural standards of behavior. See Martha Finnemore, *National Interests in International Society* (Ithaca: Cornell University Press, 1996), pp. 12, 64–65; and Martha Finnemore and Kathryn Sikkink, "International Norm Dynamics and Political Change," in Peter J. Katzenstein, Robert O. Keohane, and Stephen D. Krasner, eds., *Exploration and Contestation in the Study of World Politics* (Cambridge, Mass.: MIT Press, 1999), pp. 247–77, 257. The account in this chapter differs from these accounts in the following respects. First, there is a tendency in the scholars associated with Katzenstein's "culture of national security" argument to see states as holistic entities. This is implicit in the concept of "identity" favored by these scholars. I argue for a more disaggregated view of the state, and present evidence that certain government officials (those most in interaction with other nations) were most likely to see American identity as tied in with human rights, and thus more likely to see minority rights as national-security policy. Second, the liabilities of hypocrisy are greatly dependent on the desire and ability of opponents to highlight hypocrisy, or the contradictions between stated meanings and goals and actual behavior; thus, Nazi, Japanese, and Soviet propaganda were crucial in giving national-security meanings to minority rights in the United States. This is demonstrated most clearly with the failed case of women's rights (Chapter 3). Last, as described in Chapter 1, I prefer the term "meaning entrepreneur" to "norm entrepreneur" because it is frequently the case that promoters of change are not promoting specific norms of behavior. When Roosevelt was promoting the meaning of the United States as a champion of equal rights, his main goal was to win support for his war effort. The norms his efforts helped to establish were totally unelaborated and secondary, and caused him and other presidents problems, as this chapter describes.

3. Steven A. Shull, *The President and Civil Rights Policy* (New York: Greenwood Press, 1989), pp. 189–90. Also see Milton Morris, *Immigration—The Beleaguered Bureaucracy* (Washington, D.C.: Brookings Institution, 1985), pp. 35–42, which notes the domestic orientation of Congress and the international orientation of the executive in the area of immigration policy.

4. Though the literature made occasional references to the positive impact of the Cold War on black civil rights, the first comprehensive treatment was Mary L. Dudziak, "Desegregation as a Cold War Imperative," *Stanford Law Review* 41 (1988): 61–120; later elaborated in Dudziak, *Cold War Civil Rights* (Princeton: Princeton University Press, 2000). Also see John Skrentny, "The Effect of the Cold War on African American Civil Rights, 1945–1968," *Theory and Society* 27 (1998): 237–85; Philip Klinkner and Rogers Smith, *The Unsteady March* (Chicago: University of Chicago Press, 1999); Azza Layton, *International Politics and Civil Rights Policies in the United States, 1941–1960* (New York: Cambridge University Press, 2000). For a theoretical statement, see Doug McAdam, "On the International Origins of Domestic Political Opportunities," in Anne Costain and Andrew McFarland, eds., *Social Movements and American Political Institutions* (Lanham, Md.: Rowman and Littlefield, 1998), pp. 251–67.

5. The main exception was Japan, which sought to prevent discrimination, segregation, and immigration prohibitions suffered by Japanese who had emigrated or sought to emigrate to the United States. Benjamin B. Ringer, *We the People and Others: Duality and America's Treatment of Its Racial Minorities* (New York: Routledge, 1983), Chapter 16.

6. In 1890, the United States and seventeen other nations signed and ratified the General Act of Brussels, condemning slavery and the slave trade. The League of Nations helped draft the International Slavery Convention of 1926. On international efforts to end slavery, see A. H. Robertson and J. G. Merrills, *Human Rights in the World*, 3rd ed. (Manchester, UK: Manchester University Press,

1972), pp. 14–17. On the Geneva Convention, see Finnemore, *National Interests in International Society,* Chapter 2. On other precursors, see Evan Luard, "The Origins of International Concern over Human Rights," in Evan Luard, ed., *The International Protection of Human Rights* (New York: Praeger, 1967), pp. 7–21.

7. Gerrit W. Gong, *The Standard of "Civilization" in International Society* (Oxford: Clarendon Press, 1984).

8. James Frederick Green, *The United Nations and Human Rights* (Washington, D.C.: Brookings Institution, 1959), p. 9; see also Louis Henkin, *The Age of Rights* (New York: Columbia University Press, 1990), p. 15.

9. Winthrop Jordan, *The White Man's Burden: Historical Origins of Racism in the United States* (New York: Oxford University Press, 1974).

10. Stephen Lawson, *Black Ballots: Voting Rights in the South, 1944–1969* (New York: Columbia University Press, 1976), pp. 22, 341. Poor whites in the south also had limited political rights. Edwin Amenta, *Bold Relief* (Princeton: Princeton University Press, 1998), pp. 65–66.

11. Samuel Krislov, *The Negro in Federal Employment* (Minneapolis: University of Minnesota Press, 1967), p. 20.

12. Howard Schuman, Charlotte Steeh, and Lawrence Bobo, *Racial Attitudes in America: Trends and Interpretations* (Cambridge, Mass.: Harvard University Press, 1985), pp. 119, 107, 74.

13. Harvard Sitkoff, *New Deal for Blacks* (New York: Oxford University Press, 1978), p. 46.

14. Margaret Keck and Kathryn Sikkink, *Activists beyond Borders* (Ithaca: Cornell University Press, 1998), pp. 81–83; Theodore A. Wilson, *The First Summit: Roosevelt and Churchill at Placentia Bay 1941* (Boston: Houghton Mifflin, 1969), p. 175.

15. Townsend Hoopes and Douglas Brinkley, *FDR and the Creation of the U.N.* (New Haven: Yale University Press, 1997), p. 23.

16. "Annual Message to the Congress," January 6, 1941, in *Public Papers and Addresses of Franklin D. Roosevelt, 1940* (New York: Macmillan, 1950), pp. 663–78, 672. Roosevelt's speechwriter Samuel Rosenman insists that Roosevelt was the sole source of the Four Freedoms. Samuel I. Rosenman, *Working with Roosevelt* (New York: Harper and Brothers, 1952), p. 263.

17. Hoopes and Brinkley, *FDR and the Creation of the U.N.,* p. 27.

18. Sumner Welles, *Where Are We Heading?* (New York: Harper and Brothers, 1946), p. 6.

19. Wilson, *First Summit,* pp. 177–78.

20. Ibid., p. 51.

21. Ibid., pp. 187, 206. See the full text at *http://www.ssa.gov/history/acharter2html.* At the outset of the war, Churchill had already said it was a war "to establish, on impregnable rocks, the rights of the individual." Inis L. Claude Jr., *National Minorities: An International Problem* (New York: Greenwood Press, 1955), p. 73.

22. Green, *United Nations and Human Rights,* p. 14; Hoopes and Brinkley, *FDR and the Creation of the U.N.,* p. 45.

23. Paul Lauren, *Power and Prejudice: The Politics and Diplomacy of Racial Discrim-*

ination (Boulder: Westview Press, 1988), p. 146. Also see Claude, *National Minorities*, p. 65.

24. Roosevelt was far from alone in promoting the United States as a champion of racial egalitarianism and human rights. His 1940 opponent in the presidential election, Wendell Willkie, prominently supported similar war aims and fought against discrimination at home. See Wendell L. Willkie, *One World* (New York: Simon and Schuster, 1943).

25. Gerald Horne, *Black and Red: W. E. B. Du Bois and the Afro-American Response to the Cold War, 1944–1963* (Albany: State University of New York Press, 1986), p. 36.

26. Brenda Gayle Plummer, *Rising Wind: Black Americans and U.S. Foreign Affairs, 1935–1960* (Chapel Hill: University of North Carolina Press, 1996), pp. 132, 139, 152.

27. Lauren, *Power and Prejudice*, p. 154; see also Howard Tolley Jr., *The U.N. Commission on Human Rights* (Boulder: Westview Press, 1987), pp. 4–5.

28. Green, *United Nations and Human Rights*, p. 17.

29. Jason Berger, *A New Deal for the World: Eleanor Roosevelt and American Foreign Policy* (New York: Columbia University Press, 1981), pp. 68–73; Tolley, *U.N. Commission on Human Rights*, p. 25.

30. Moses Moskowitz, *Human Rights and World Order: The Struggle for Human Rights in the United Nations* (New York: Oceana Publications, 1958), p. 25.

31. Available at *http://www.un.org/Overview/rights.html*.

32. Berger, *New Deal for the World*, p. 87.

33. Peter J. Kellogg, "Civil Rights Consciousness in the 1940s," *Historian* 42 (1979): 18–41, 31. Also see Russell Riley, *The Presidency and the Politics of Racial Inequality* (New York: Columbia University Press, 1999), pp. 145–54; Louis Ruchames, *Race, Jobs, and Politics: The Story of FEPC* (New York: Columbia University Press, 1953), p. 17; Daniel Kryder, *Divided Arsenal: Race and the American State during World War II* (New York: Cambridge University Press, 2000), pp. 55–66; Harold L. Ickes, *The Secret Diaries of Harold L. Ickes*, vol. 3: *The Lowering Clouds, 1939–1941* (New York: Simon and Schuster, 1954), p. 516.

34. Lauren, *Power and Prejudice*, p. 141.

35. Ibid.

36. Gerald David Jaynes and Robin M. Williams, eds., *A Common Destiny: Blacks and American Society* (Washington, D.C.: National Academy Press, 1989), p. 63; see also Richard M. Dalfiume, "The Forgotten Years of the Negro Revolution," *Journal of American History* 55 (1968): 90–106, 96–97; Ruchames, *Race, Jobs, and Politics*, p. 23; Jack Greenberg, *Crusaders in the Courts* (New York: Basic Books, 1994), p. 68.

37. Thomas Borstelmann, *Apartheid's Reluctant Uncle: The United States and Southern Africa in the Early Cold War* (New York: Oxford University Press, 1993), p. 41.

38. "Address to the Congress on the State of the Union," *Public Papers and Addresses of Franklin D. Roosevelt, 1942* (New York: Harper and Brothers, 1950), pp. 32–42, 39. See Rosenman, *Working with Roosevelt*, pp. 325–26, for a discussion.

39. Alonzo L. Hamby, *Beyond the New Deal: Harry S. Truman and American Liberalism* (New York: Columbia University Press, 1973), p. 115.

40. Lee Nichols, *Breakthrough on the Color Front* (New York: Random House, 1954), p. 9.

41. President's Committee on Civil Rights, *To Secure These Rights* (Washington, D.C.: Government Printing Office, 1947), p. 146. I thank Gerald Horne for pointing out the novelty of Acheson's civil-rights activism. See Gerald Horne, "Race from Power: US Foreign Policy and the General Crisis of 'White Supremacy,'" *Diplomatic History* 23, no. 3 (1999): 437–61, 456.

42. For efforts during the Truman years, see Lauren, *Power and Prejudice*, p. 189; *Hearings before a Special Subcommittee of the Committee on Education and Labor, House of Representatives, 1949: Hearings on H.R. 4453 and Companion Bills (Federal Fair Employment Practice Act)*, 81st Cong., 1st Sess. (Washington, D.C.: Government Printing Office), p. 114.

43. Dudziak, *Cold War Civil Rights*, p. 43.

44. Claude, *National Minorities*, pp. 149–50.

45. Dudziak, *Cold War Civil Rights*, pp. 26–42; Lauren, *Power and Prejudice*, p. 188. The United States would counteract some of the international criticism by highlighting discrimination in other countries. In 1947, for example, "sensing the country's extraordinary vulnerability on this matter of racial equality, the State Department sent out an unusual, confidential circular telegram to overseas missions asking diplomatic personnel to report back on 'any outstanding incidents of discrimination' that might be used as ammunition against their particular host country if its criticisms of the United States became too strong . . . 'Make no (repeat no) formal inquiries,' it directed." Lauren, *Power and Prejudice*, p. 191.

46. Donald R. McCoy and Richard T. Ruetten, *Quest and Response: Minority Rights and the Truman Administration* (Lawrence: University Press of Kansas, 1973), pp. 258–59; Dudziak, *Cold War Civil Rights*, p. 59.

47. *Shelley v. Kraemer*, 334 U.S. 1 (1948).

48. Brief for the United States as Amicus Curiae, *Shelley v. Kraemer*, in Michal R. Belknap, ed., *Civil Rights, the White House and the Justice Department, 1945–1968*, vol. 18: *Justice Department Briefs in Crucial Civil Rights Cases, 1948–1968* (New York: Garland Publishing, 1991), Part 1, pp. 92–100. The ACLU also cited the UN Charter in a brief for this case. Howard Tolley Jr., "Interest Group Litigation to Enforce Human Rights: Confronting Judicial Restraint," in *World Justice? U.S. Courts and International Human Rights*, ed. Mark Gibney (Boulder: Westview Press, 1991), pp. 123–48, 125. The ACLU, the American Association for the UN, the American Jewish Committee, B'nai B'rith, American Veterans Committee, the National Lawyers Guild, and the NAACP cited the UN Charter in briefs for cases against discrimination in education (*Sweatt v. Painter*, 339 U.S. 629 [1950]; *Bolling v. Sharp*, 347 U.S. 497 [1954]), transportation (*Bob-lo Excursion Co. v. Michigan*, 333 U.S. 28 [1948]), and employment (*Takahashi v. Fish & Game Comm'n*, 334 U.S. 410 [1948]). Ibid., p. 125.

49. *Henderson v. United States*, 339 U.S. 816 (1950).

50. Brief for the United States, *Henderson v. United States*, in Belknap, *Civil Rights, the White House and the Justice Department, 1945–1968*, vol. 18, Part 1,

pp. 184–86. Also see William C. Berman, *The Politics of Civil Rights in the Truman Administration* (Columbus: Ohio State University Press, 1970), p. 232; McCoy and Ruetten, *Quest and Response*, p. 342; Jack Greenberg, *Crusaders in the Courts* (New York: Basic Books, 1994), p. 73.

51. Walter White, *A Man Called White: The Autobiography of Walter White* (New York: Viking Press, 1969), p. 348.

52. Memorandum from David K. Niles to the President, February 16, 1948, and Attachment, in Belknap, *Civil Rights, the White House and the Justice Department, 1945–1968,* vol. 1: *Attitudes, Goals and Priorities,* pp. 34–40; Harry S. Truman, "Civil Rights Message," in David Horton, ed., *Freedom and Equality: Addresses by Harry S. Truman* (Columbia: University of Missouri Press, 1960), pp. 9–18.

53. Kenneth O'Reilly, *Nixon's Piano: Presidents and Racial Politics from Washington to Clinton* (New York: Free Press, 1995), p. 163.

54. Harry S. Truman, *Public Papers of the Presidents of the United States: Harry S. Truman, 1947* (Washington, D.C.: Government Printing Office, 1963), p. 91; McCoy and Ruetten, *Quest and Response*, pp. 92–94.

55. Minutes of President Truman's Committee on Civil Rights, February 5, 1947, in Belknap, *Civil Rights, the White House and the Justice Department, 1945–1968,* vol. 2: *Presidential Committees and White House Conferences,* p. 8. In hearings held in April, committee member and civil-rights leader Channing Tobias discussed how discrimination made international dialogue on the workings of the American system impossible, "particularly when we have in mind certain governments of different ideology." He stated that his "whole enthusiasm for the work of this Committee is that it shall lift American prestige in the world." Proceedings of the President's Committee on Civil Rights, April 3, 1947, in ibid., p. 66.

56. Dudziak, *Cold War Civil Rights,* pp. 85–86; Lee Nichols, *Breakthrough on the Color Front* (New York: Random House, 1954), pp. 175–79; Klinkner and Smith, *Unsteady March,* pp. 217–21, 236–37; Richard Polenberg, *One Nation Divisible: Class, Race, and Ethnicity in the United States since 1938* (New York: Pelican Books, 1980), p. 112.

57. Plummer, *Rising Wind,* 171–72; Horne, *Black and Red,* p. 75.

58. Dudziak, "Desegregation as a Cold War Imperative," 94–95; Plummer, *Rising Wind,* pp. 179–183; Horne, *Black and Red,* p. 80.

59. Horne, *Black and Red,* p. 80.

60. Civil Rights Congress, William L. Patterson, ed., *We Charge Genocide: The Historic Petition to the United Nations for Relief from a Crime of the United States Government against the Negro People* (New York: Civil Rights Congress, 1951), p. 5.

61. President's Committee on Civil Rights, *To Secure These Rights,* pp. 146–48.

62. Memorandum from Clark M. Clifford to the President, August 17, 1948, in Belknap, *Civil Rights, the White House and the Justice Department,* vol. 1, pp. 64–71; Hubert H. Humphrey, *Beyond Civil Rights: A New Day of Equality* (New York: Random House, 1968), p. 37.

63. Memorandum from David K. Niles to the President, February 16, 1948, and

Attachment, in Belknap, *Civil Rights, the White House and the Justice Department,* vol. 1, pp. 34–40.

64. Adolf A. Berle Jr., "Race Discrimination and the Good Neighbor Policy," in *Discrimination and National Welfare,* ed. R. M. MacIver (New York: Harper and Brothers, 1949), pp. 91–98, 91–92.

65. Roger N. Baldwin, "Our Standing in the Orient," in *Discrimination and National Welfare,* ed. R. M. MacIver (New York: Harper and Brothers, 1949), pp. 83–90, 89.

66. Alvin Z. Rubinstein, *Moscow's Third World Strategy* (Princeton: Princeton University Press, 1988), pp. 15–18; Joseph G. Whelan and Michael J. Dixon, *The Soviet Union in the Third World: Threat to World Peace?* (Washington, D.C.: Pergamon-Brassey's, 1968), p. 13.

67. For example, Martin Luther King, Adam Clayton Powell, Ralph Bunche, A. Philip Randolph, and Vice President Richard Nixon all attended independence ceremonies for Ghana in 1957. David J. Garrow, *Bearing the Cross: Martin Luther King, Jr., and the Southern Christian Leadership Conference* (New York: Vintage, 1986), p. 91.

68. Robert F. Burk, *The Eisenhower Administration and Black Civil Rights* (Knoxville: University of Tennessee Press, 1984), pp. 23–24; Nichols, *Breakthrough on the Color Front,* p. 174.

69. Dwight D. Eisenhower, *The White House Years: Waging Peace, 1956–1961* (Garden City, N.Y.: Doubleday, 1965), p. 136; see also John W. Henderson, *The United States Information Agency* (New York: Praeger, 1969), p. 52.

70. Dwight D. Eisenhower, *Public Papers of the Presidents of the United States: Dwight D. Eisenhower, 1955* (Washington, D.C.: Government Printing Office, 1959), p. 131.

71. O'Reilly, *Nixon's Piano,* p. 168.

72. E. Frederic Morrow, *Black Man in the White House: A Diary of the Eisenhower Years by the Administrative Officer for Special Projects, 1955–1961* (New York: Coward-McCann, 1963), pp. 125–56, 221, 267; Burk, *Eisenhower and Civil Rights,* pp. 70, 84; Dwight D. Eisenhower, *The White House Years: Mandate for Change, 1953–1956* (Garden City, N.Y.: Doubleday, 1963), p. 236.

73. See the thoughtful letter from Dwight D. Eisenhower to E. E. Hazlett, July 22, 1957, in Belknap, *Civil Rights, the White House and the Justice Department,* vol. 1, pp. 256–59; see also Arthur Larson, *Eisenhower: The President Nobody Knew* (New York: Scribner, 1968), p. 126; Herbert S. Parmet, *Eisenhower and the American Crusades* (New York: Macmillan, 1972), p. 439.

74. Telephone Conversation between the President and Attorney General, August 19, 1956, in Belknap, *Civil Rights, the White House and the Justice Department,* vol. 1, pp. 242–43.

75. Parmet, *Eisenhower,* pp. 277–80.

76. Eisenhower, *Mandate for Change, 1953–1956,* p. 234.

77. Eisenhower, *Waging Peace, 1956–1961,* p. 148.

78. Burk, *Eisenhower and Civil Rights,* pp. 45–46.

79. Policy Order of the District of Columbia Government Regarding Non-Discrimination, November 25, 1953, in Belknap, *Civil Rights, the White House and the*

Justice Department, vol. 4, p. 118; Burk, *Eisenhower and Civil Rights,* p. 50; Sherman Adams, *Firsthand Report: The Story of the Eisenhower Administration* (New York: Harper, 1961), pp. 333–34.

80. For a typical example from the Kennedy administration, see White House Meeting of Civil Rights Subcabinet Group, April 14, 1961, in Belknap, *Civil Rights, the White House and the Justice Department, 1945–1968,* vol. 1, p. 301.

81. Dudziak, *Cold War Civil Rights,* Chapter 4.

82. James A. Morone, *The Democratic Wish: Popular Participation and the Limits of American Government* (New York: Basic Books, 1990), p. 204. Also see Burk, *Eisenhower and Civil Rights,* p. 186.

83. Bruce Miroff, *Pragmatic Illusions: The Presidential Politics of John F. Kennedy* (New York: David McKay, 1976), p. 229; Theodore H. White, *The Making of the President 1960* (New York: Atheneum Publishers, 1961), pp. 202–3.

84. Richard M. Nixon, *The Challenges We Face* (New York: McGraw-Hill, 1960), pp. 186–88; Carl Brauer, *John F. Kennedy and the Second Reconstruction* (New York: Columbia University Press, 1977), p. 44; O'Reilly, *Nixon's Piano,* p. 197; Dudziak, *Cold War Civil Rights,* p. 155.

85. Taylor Branch, *Parting the Waters: America in the King Years, 1954–1963* (New York: Simon and Schuster, 1988), pp. 288–89, 579–83. *Parting the Waters* reprints the ad in its entirety.

86. Dean Rusk Oral History, John F. Kennedy Library, Boston, Mass., pp. 332–33. Also see O'Reilly, *Nixon's Piano,* p. 199. The flip side was concern with the negative impacts of high-level appointments of segregationists, such as Kennedy's first choice for secretary of state, Arkansas senator William J. Fullbright (who had signed a "Southern Manifesto" denouncing the *Brown v. Board of Education* decision). Kennedy changed his mind and appointed Dean Rusk—Fullbright's fellow southerner but without the taint—instead. Arthur M. Schlesinger Jr., *A Thousand Days: John F. Kennedy in the White House* (Boston: Houghton Mifflin, 1965), p. 140; Brauer, *Second Reconstruction,* p. 77.

87. Dean Rusk Oral History, pp. 335–36.

88. Letter from Dean Rusk to Attorney General Robert F. Kennedy, in Belknap, *Civil Rights, the White House and the Justice Department, 1945–1968,* vol. 9: *The Drive to Desegregate Places of Public Accommodation,* p. 37; Dudziak, *Cold War Civil Rights,* p. 167.

89. Harris Wofford Oral History, John F. Kennedy Library, Boston, Mass., p. 60; Brauer, *Second Reconstruction,* pp. 77–79; Harris Wofford, *Of Kennedys and Kings: Making Sense of the Sixties* (Pittsburgh: University of Pittsburgh Press, 1980), pp. 126–27; Duziak, *Cold War Civil Rights,* p. 169; Dean Rusk Oral History, pp. 326–29.

90. Dean Rusk Oral History, pp. 332–33.

91. Ibid., p. 338.

92. Gerald Rosenberg, *The Hollow Hope* (Chicago: University of Chicago Press, 1993), pp. 163–64.

93. Garrow, *Bearing the Cross,* p. 91.

94. Wofford, *Kennedys and Kings,* pp. 125, 153; O'Reilly, *Nixon's Piano,* p. 212.

95. Branch, *Parting the Waters,* p. 807.

96. *Hearings before the Subcommittee on Oversight of the Permanent Committee on Intelligence,* House of Representatives, 96th Congress, 2nd Sess., February 6, 19, 1980, pp. 207–8, 224.

97. Paul Burstein, *Discrimination, Jobs and Politics* (Chicago: University of Chicago Press, 1998).

98. John D. Skrentny, *The Ironies of Affirmative Action: Politics, Culture and Justice in America* (Chicago: University of Chicago Press, 1996), pp. 79–80.

99. Memorandum to Members of the Business Council and Cover Note by L. F. O., in Belknap, *Civil Rights, the White House and the Justice Department,* vol. 5, pp. 195–202.

100. The USSR ratified the race discrimination convention in 1969 and ratified the other covenants in 1973. Office of the UN High Commissioner for Human Rights, "Status of Ratifications of the Principal International Human Rights Treaties," July 16, 2001, p. 7.

101. David J. Garrow, *Protest at Selma* (New Haven: Yale University Press, 1978), pp. 52–53.

102. Lawrence H. Fuchs, *The American Kaleidoscope: Race Ethnicity, and the Civic Culture* (Hanover, Conn.: Wesleyan University Press, 1990), p. 188. Corky Gonzales considered a similar petition to the UN asking for a potentially independent territory for Mexican Americans in the Southwest. Ibid., p. 243. There was a precedent for such a petition to the UN on behalf of Mexican Americans from 1959, when the American Committee for the Protection of the Foreign Born claimed that the oppression of Mexican Americans violated the Declaration of Human Rights. David G. Gutiérrez, *Walls and Mirrors: Mexican Americans, Mexican Immigrants and the Politics of Ethnicity* (Berkeley: University of California Press, 1995), p. 176.

103. Skrentny, *Ironies of Affirmative Action,* p. 73.

104. Richard Shultz and Ray Godson, *Dezinformatsia: Active Measures in Soviet Strategy* (Washington, D.C.: Pergamon, 1984), pp. 57–60.

105. Skrentny, *Ironies of Affirmative Action,* p. 108.

106. See testimony of Edward L. Bernays and George Gallup in *The Future of United States Public Diplomacy, Hearings before the Subcommittee on International Organizations and Movements of the Committee on Foreign Affairs,* House of Representatives, 90th Cong., 2nd Sess. (1968), reprinted in Edward L. Bernays and Burnet Hershey, eds. *The Case for Reappraisal of U.S. Overseas Information Policies and Programs* (New York: Praeger, 1970), pp. 124, 129.

107. These efforts are detailed in Skrentny, *Ironies of Affirmative Action,* Chapter 4.

108. Riley, *Presidency and Racial Inequality,* pp. 157–64; Doug McAdam, *Political Process and the Development of Black Insurgency* (Chicago: University of Chicago Press, 1982), pp. 77–82.

109. As Rogers Smith has argued, there are liberal and illiberal "traditions" in American social policy, existing simultaneously. Rogers Smith, *Civic Ideals* (New Haven: Yale University Press, 1997).

110. Ringer, *We the People and Others,* pp. 609–80; Hyung-chan Kim, *A Legal History of Asian Americans, 1790–1990* (Westport, Conn.: Greenwood Press, 1994), Chapter 4.

374 | Notes to Pages 38–39

111. This part of American history is well known. See, for example, Richard Hofstadter, *Age of Reform* (New York: Vintage, 1955); Morton Keller, *Regulating a New Society* (Cambridge, Mass.: Harvard University Press, 1994); Ronald Takaki, "Reflections on Racial Patterns in America," in *From Different Shores,* ed. Ronald Takaki (New York: Oxford University Press, 1987), pp. 26–37; James R. Barrett and David Roediger, "Inbetween Peoples: Race, Nationality and the 'New Immigrant' Working Class," *Journal of American Ethnic History* 16 (1997): 3–44; John Higham, *Send These to Me* (New York: Atheneum, 1975); John Higham, *Strangers in the Land* (New Brunswick: Rutgers University Press, 1955); Desmond King, *In the Name of Liberalism* (New York: Oxford University Press, 1999).

112. Gabriel Chin, "The Civil Rights Revolution Comes to Immigration Law: A New Look at the Immigration and Nationality Act of 1965," *North Carolina Law Review* 75 (1996): 273–345, 280.

113. Maxine S. Seller, "Historical Perspectives on American Immigration Policy: Case Studies and Current Implications," in Richard Hofstetter, ed., *U.S. Immigration Policy* (Durham: Duke University Press, 1984), pp. 137–62, 154.

114. Peter Schuck, *Diversity in America: Keeping Government at a Safe Distance* (Cambridge, Mass.: Harvard University Press, 2003).

115. John A. Kromkowski, "Eastern and Southern European Immigrants: Expectations Reality and a New Agenda," *Annals of the American Academy of Political and Social Science* 487 (1986): pp. 57–78; Desmond King, *Making Americans* (Cambridge, Mass.: Harvard University Press, 2000), Chapter 7.
    Congress did not include immigration from the Western Hemisphere in its limitations. In the 1920s, immigration from the Caribbean and Central and South America was negligible, and that from Mexico was regulated with the Mexican government to supply cheap and temporary Mexican labor in western states. Marc Rosenblum, "At Home and Abroad: The Foreign and Domestic Sources of U.S. Immigration Policy," Ph.D. diss., University of California–San Diego, 2000, Chapter 3; Daniel Tichenor, "Regulating Community: Race, Immigration Policy and American Political Development, Ph.D. diss., Brandeis University, 1996, p. 254. Since most Mexicans did not permanently settle in the United States at that time, concerns about their Catholicism, loyalty, or perceived racial or cultural inferiority were muted. Ibid., pp. 334, 336.

116. Christopher Mitchell, "Introduction: Immigration and U.S. Foreign Policy toward the Caribbean, Central America, and Mexico," in Christopher Mitchell, ed., *Western Hemisphere Immigration and United States Foreign Policy* (University Park: Pennsylvania State University Press, 1992), pp. 1–30, 13.

117. Norman L. Zucker and Naomi Flink Zucker, "From Immigration to Refugee Redefinition: A History of Refugee and Asylum Policy in the United States," *Journal of Policy History* 4 (1992): 54–70, 54; Ellis Cose, *A Nation of Strangers: Prejudice, Politics and the Populating of America* (New York: William Morrow, 1992), p. 84.

118. Abba P. Schwartz, *The Open Society* (New York: Simon and Schuster, 1968), pp. 144–45.

119. Robert A. Divine, *American Immigration Policy* (New Haven: Yale University Press, 1957), p. 108.

120. Mass deportations of Mexicans had occurred in 1921–22, and occurred for the last time in 1954. Mitchell, "Immigration and Foreign Policy," p. 20; Fuchs, *American Kaleidoscope,* p. 121; Schwartz, *Open Society,* p. 150.

121. Divine, *American Immigration Policy,* p. 147.

122. Frederick Warren Riggs has identified various other factors that contributed to the repeal of the Chinese exclusion laws. In one section of his superb study, he describes "forces weakening the Anti-Chinese movement" on the west coast. These include economic changes that made the Chinese less of a threat to other workers, the decline of the Chinese share of the population (from 10 percent of the state of California in 1880 to one-half of 1 percent in 1940), and the increased assimilation of the Chinese (abandoning native Chinese clothes and hairstyles for western styles). Riggs also argues that the "traditional policy of the United States toward China" was to support "China's national integrity against the incursions of any major power." Further, there was a "growth of pro-Chinese sentiment," building on a "tradition of respect for China." This was led by missionaries who had spent time in China, and "old-China-hands," or persons who had lived in China for a time and returned to the United States to be spokespersons for the country. There was growing academic interest as well, as increasing numbers of universities offered courses in Chinese language and civilization. Pearl Buck's novel *The Good Earth,* among other books, also spread interest in China. Last, the immigration restriction laws of 1921 and 1924 had shown that immigration could be drastically reduced without total exclusion. Frederick Warren Riggs, *Pressures on Congress: A Study of the Repeal of Chinese Exclusion* (New York: Columbia University Press, 1950), Chapter 4. All of these are relevant and compelling parts of the explanation for repeal of Chinese exclusion, but national-security meanings stand out for their relevance to the timing of the end of Chinese exclusion, which occurred during World War II.

123. Divine, *American Immigration Policy,* p. 147.

124. Riggs, *Pressures on Congress,* p. 47; Roger Daniels, *Asian America: Chinese and Japanese in the United States since 1850* (Seattle: University of Washington Press, 1988), pp. 188, 193.

125. Chin, "Civil Rights Comes to Immigration," p. 284, n. 42.

126. Daniels, *Asian America,* P. 196.

127. Riggs, *Pressures on Congress,* p. 116. On Chiang's visit, also see Shih-shan Henry Tsai, *The Chinese Experience in America* (Bloomington: Indiana University Press, 1986), p. 114.

128. *Repeal of the Chinese Exclusion Acts, Hearings before the Committee on Immigration and Naturalization,* House of Representatives, 78th Cong., 1st Sess. (1943), p. 16.

129. Ibid., p. 78.

130. Ibid., pp. 249–50. Yarnell was an especially persuasive witness, according to the Immigration and Naturalization Service's monthly newsletter. Keith Fitzgerald, *The Face of the Nation* (Stanford: Stanford University Press, 1996), p. 187.

131. *House Chinese Exclusion Hearings,* p. 13.
132. Riggs, *Pressures on Congress,* p. 155.
133. Ibid., p. 50.
134. *House Chinese Exclusion Hearings,* p. 45.
135. Ibid., p. 38.
136. Ibid., p. 57.
137. Ibid., pp. 72–73.
138. It is not clear why Roosevelt waited so long to weigh in on the issue. It was typical, as described above, for presidents to support liberalization of immigration laws.
139. *Congressional Record,* October 11, 1943, pp. 8176, 8193; Riggs, *Pressures on Congress,* pp. 175, 210–11; Divine, *American Immigration Policy,* p. 150; Fuchs, *American Kaleidoscope,* p. 230; Cose, *Nation of Strangers,* p. 87.
140. Riggs, *Pressures on Congress,* pp. 65–75.
141. Divine, *American Immigration Policy,* p. 151; *Congressional Record,* October 11, 1943, pp. 8176, 8193, 8575, 8599, 9989.
142. *Bill to Grant a Quota to Eastern Hemisphere Indians, Hearings before the House Committee on Immigration and Naturalization,* House of Representatives, 79th Cong., 1st Sess. (1945), pp. 3–5; Reimers, *Still the Golden Door,* p. 15.
143. *House Indian Quota Hearings.*
144. *Congressional Record,* October 10, 1945, pp. 9521–32; January 14, 1946, p. 6918.
145. *Congressional Record,* June 14, 1946, p. 6933; April 17, 1945, p. 3454. See Divine, *American Immigration Policy,* p. 154; Reimers, *Still the Golden Door,* p. 17.
146. Chin, "Civil Rights Comes to Immigration," p. 287.
147. David M. Reimers, *Still the Golden Door* (New York: Columbia University Press, 1985), pp. 19–21.
148. Marion T. Bennett, "The Immigration and Nationality (McCarran-Walter) Act of 1952, as Amended to 1965," *Annals of the American Academy of Political and Social Science* 367 (September 1966): 127–136, p. 129–30; Divine, *American Immigration Policy,* p. 167. Also see *Congressional Record,* 1952, p. 5330.
149. Ringer, *We the People and Others,* pp. 932–38.
150. Divine, *American Immigration Policy,* p. 184.
151. Chin, "Civil Rights Comes to Immigration," p. 288.
152. Tichenor, *Regulating Community,* pp. 377–78.
153. *Whom We Shall Welcome: Report of the President's Commission on Immigration and Naturalization* (Washington, D.C.: Government Printing Office, 1953; reprint, New York: Da Capo, 1971), p. 13. The commission consisted of religious and government officials and was clearly stacked to give a pro-immigration report.
154. Ibid., p. 45.
155. Ibid., pp. 46–47.
156. Ibid., p. 47.
157. Ibid., p. 52.

158. Ibid., pp. 54–55.

159. Zucker and Zucker, "From Immigration to Refugee Redefinition," p. 58.

160. Gil Loescher and John A. Scanlan, *Calculated Kindness: Refugees and America's Half-Open Door, 1945–Present* (New York: Free Press, 1986), pp. xvii, 213.

161. Aristide R. Zolberg, "The Roots of U.S. Refugee Policy," in Robert W. Tucker, Charles B. Keely, and Linda Wrigley, eds., *Immigration and Foreign Policy* (Boulder: Westview, 1990), pp. 99–122.

162. Quoted in Loescher and Scanlan, *Calculated Kindness,* pp. 18–19; *Congressional Record,* June 10, 1948, p. 7872.

163. Schwartz, *Open Society,* p. 107.

164. Cose, *Nation of Strangers,* p. 103.

165. Zucker and Zucker, "From Immigration to Refugee Redefinition," p. 58.

166. Zolberg, "Roots of US Refugee Policy," p. 107.

167. Loescher and Scanlan, *Calculated Kindness,* p. 47.

168. Ibid., pp. 50–55, 60; Jethro K. Kieberman, *Are Americans Extinct?* (New York: Walker, 1968), p. 118; Eisenhower, *Waging Peace: 1956–1961,* p. 89.

169. Jorge I. Domínguez, "Cooperating with the Enemy? U.S. Immigration Policies toward Cuba," in Christopher Mitchell, ed., *Western Hemisphere Immigration and United States Foreign Policy* (University Park: Pennsylvania State University Press, 1992), pp. 31–88, 39. On the Cuban refugee program, also see Michael S. Teitelbaum, "Immigration, Refugees, and Foreign Policy," *International Organization* 38, no. 3 (summer 1984): 429–50; Robert A. Pastor, "U.S. Immigration Policy and Latin America," *Latin American Research Review* 19, no. 3 (1984): 35–56; Myron Weiner, "On International Migration and International Relations," *Population and Development Review* 11 (1985): 41–55.

170. Domínguez, "Cooperating with the Enemy," p. 40. Flights were suspended during the Cuban missile crisis; as Jorge Domínguez explains, the government then "sacrificed the ideological goal of having Cubans 'vote with their feet' against communism by emigrating to the United States in order to promote the strategic goal of isolating the Cuban government." Ibid.

171. Loescher and Scanlan, *Calculated Kindness,* p. 68.

172. Tichenor, *Regulating Community,* pp. 388–90.

173. Relevant sections are in *Congressional Record,* February 7, 1963, p. 2021.

174. John F. Kennedy, *A Nation of Immigrants,* rev. ed. (New York: Harper and Row, 1964 [1958]).

175. Memo for Mr. Frederick G. Dutton, through Ralph A. Dungan from L. D. Battle, Executive Secretary, Department of State, March 13, 1961, folder: 3-12-61-3-13-61, McGeorge Bundy file, Box 1, White House Staff Files, John F. Kennedy Library (JFKL).

176. See the folder LE/IM 1 in Box 483, White House Central Subject Files (WHCSF), JFKL. It is filled with letters of support for reform from ethnic groups, religious groups, and immigration organizations. Chinese, Polish, and Italian groups were especially active. Some groups linked their struggle to that of blacks for equal civil rights. For example, a September 27, 1961 letter to President Kennedy from the Chinese-American Democratic Club begins,

"Equal naturalization and residency rights is [*sic*] held to the same high degree of importance to the American Chinese as equal civil rights is [*sic*] to the American Negro."

177. Letter from Phillip Hart to Theodore Sorensen, December 14, 1962; Letter from Myer Feldman to Philip A. Hart, January 4, 1963, folder LE/IM 1, BOX 483, WHCSF, JFKL.

178. *Congressional Record,* February 7, 1963, p. 2022.

179. Ibid., p. 2024.

180. Letter to Myer Feldman, Deputy Counsel to the President, from William B. Welsh, Administrative Assistant to Senator Philip A. Hart, April 29, 1963, folder LE/IM, Box 482, WHCSF, JFKL.

181. Letter to President of the Senate and John W. McCormack, Speaker of the House, July 23, 1963, folder LE/IM, Box 482, WHCSF, JFKL.

182. Congressional Quarterly, *1965 Congressional Quarterly Almanac,* p. 468.

183. By 1963, the undesirability of the national-origins system was nearly a consensus principle in the executive branch, and therefore State's concerns on bills such as Hart's related to the way reform would reduce opportunities from those formerly favored Nordic lands, where in some cases such action would have "serious foreign policy repercussions." See the letter from Abba Schwartz to Myer Feldman, June 14, 1963; "Summary Report on the Anticipated Effect of the Proposed Elimination of the Asia–Pacific Triangle Provisions from Our Immigration Laws and Other Undated Documents," in folder Immigration [Legislation, 1963], files of Gordon Chase, Box 7, National Security Files, Lyndon B. Johnson Library (LBJL).

184. *Bills to Amend the Immigration and Nationality Act, Hearings before Subcommittee No. 1 of the Committee on the Judiciary,* House of Representatives, 88th Cong., 2nd Sess., on HR 7700 and 55 identical bills, Part 2, July 2, 1964, p. 385.

185. Ibid., p. 386.

186. Ibid. Between 1954 and 1963 inclusive, 694,643 aliens were issued nonquota visas from the Eastern Hemisphere and not as a part of the national origins quotas. The Refugee Relief Act of 1953 allowed 190,735 from 1954 through 1957. Ibid., p. 392.

187. Ibid., p. 389.

188. Ibid., p. 390.

189. Memo from Abba Schwartz to Jack Valenti, July 2, 1964, in folder Johnson Administration Redoubles the Effort, Legislative Background Immigration Law–1965, Box 1, LBJL.

190. Tichenor, *Regulating Community,* pp. 398, 401.

191. Press release statement of Robert Murphy, National Committee for Immigration Reform, June 14, 1965, in folder Legislation LE/HI-LE/LE 3, Confidential Files, Box 63, LBJL.

192. Statement of Purpose of the National Committee for Immigration Reform, in folder June 15, 1965, Remarks of the President to National Committee for Immigration Reform, Statements of Lyndon Baines Johnson, Box 150, LBJL.

193. National Committee for Immigration Reform Press Release, June 14, 1965, in ibid.; Letter to Mr. Henry Hall Wilson from Gladys Uhl, June 15, 1965, in ibid.

194. Chin, "Civil Rights Comes to Immigration," pp. 299–300.

195. For example, see Letter to the President from the Chinese Section of the Democratic National Committee Nationalities Division, December 30, 1963, folder EX LE/IM 11/22/63–4/30/64, Box 73, WHCSF, LBJL; Petition organized by Nello Ori, attorney at law, March 10, 1964, Highwood, Illinois (petition from people of Highland Park and nearby suburbs), in ibid. An Italian group brought the *Detroit Press*'s April 21, 1965 support to Johnson aide Jack Valenti's attention: "Aside from its fairness and its recognition of changing times—the most important reasons—revamping the law would provide one other bonus. It would put on the record, for the world to see, the ideal to which we have long given lip service—that all men are created equal, and that where a man is from and the color of his skin count for nothing against what he is." Letter from Anothon Maiullo to Jack Valenti, April 23, 1965, folder LE/IM 12/1/64–5/3/65, Box 73, WHCSF, LBJL.

196. Department of State, American Opinion Summary, n.d., in folder Immigration, Office Files of Frederick Panzer, Box 482, LBJL.

197. Memo from Hayes Redmon to Bill Moyers, July 21, 1965, in folder Immigration 1/13/65, Office Files of Bill Moyers, Box 1, LBJL. The poll was reported in the *Washington Post*, July 25, 1965. Also see Betty K. Koed, "Reform and Consequence: The Immigration Act of 1965," unpublished manuscript on file with author, p. 11. Somewhat less support was shown in a Harris poll published in the *Washington Post*, May 31, 1965, and printed in the *Congressional Record*, June 10, 1965, pp. A3014–15.

198. "OUR IMMIGRATION LAW UNDER ATTACK," copyright 1965 by the Independent American, in folder Anti-Immigration Legislation Propaganda, 1965, Papers of Abba P. Schwartz, Box 7, JFKL.

199. Department of State, American Opinion Summary, n.d., in folder Immigration, Office Files of Frederick Panzer, Box 482, LBJL.

200. U.S. Congress, Senate, S. Rep. 748, 89th Cong., 1st sess., pp. 52–56.

201. Memo from Nobert Schlei to the President, n.d., folder EX LE/IM 11/22/63–9/30/65, Box 73, WHCSF, LBJL.

202. Memo to the President from Jack Valenti, May 8, 1965; Memo to the Attorney General from Abba Schwartz, May 20, 1965 (the overall ceiling "would compound our problems with our Latin American neighbors, particularly in view of the Dominican situation and forthcoming inter-American conferences"); Memo from Perry Barber to Mr. Valenti, July 8, 1965 (Rusk "said he absolutely could not live with a numerical ceiling of any kind on the Western Hemisphere"); Memo to the President from Larry O'Brien, August 8, 1965, all in ibid.

203. Memo to Larry O'Brien from Mike Manatos, August 20, 1965, in ibid.

204. Larry O'Brien Oral History, Part 12, p. 18, LBJL.

205. Letter from Mike Masaoka to Senator Thomas Kuchel, September 17, 1965, reprinted in *Congressional Record*, September 20, 1965, pp. 24,502–4.

206. Congressional Quarterly, *1965 Congressional Quarterly Almanac*, pp. 464–65,

480; William S. Bernard, "A History of U.S. Immigration Policy," in Stephan Thernstrom and Ann Orlov, eds., *Dimensions of Ethnicity: Immigration* (Cambridge, Mass.: Harvard University Press, 1982), pp. 75–105, 103–4.

207. Lyndon Baines Johnson, *The Vantage Point: Perspectives on the Presidency, 1963–1969* (New York: Holt, Rinehart, and Winston, 1971).

208. Dean Rusk, *As I Saw It* (New York: Norton, 1990), p. 589.

209. Walker Connor, *The National Question in Marxist-Leninist Theory and Strategy* (Princeton: Princeton University Press, 1984), p. 207.

210. Frederick C. Barghoorn and Thomas F. Remington, *Politics in the USSR*, 3rd ed. (Boston: Little, Brown, 1986), p. 73.

211. M. G. Kirichenko, "National Equality in the Soviet Union," in William F. Mackey and Albert Verdoodt, eds., *The Multinational Society: Papers of the Ljubljana Seminar* (Rowley, Mass.: Newbury House Publishers, 1975), pp. 187–201, 190. For a fascinating account of a failed attempt to bring gender equality to Islamic women in the USSR, see G. J. Massell, "Law as an Instrument of Revolutionary Change in Traditional Milieu: The Case of Soviet Central Asia," *Law and Society Review* 2 (1968): 178–229.

212. Kirichenko, "National Equality in the Soviet Union," p. 191.

213. Albert Szymanski, *Human Rights in the Soviet Union* (London: Zed Books, 1984), pp. 54–56; Connor, *The National Question*, p. 212.

214. David Lane, *Politics and Society in the USSR*, 2nd ed. (New York: New York University Press, 1978 [1970]), p. 441.

215. Kirichenko, "National Equality in the Soviet Union," p. 194.

216. Ibid., p. 197; Connor, *The National Question*, pp. 215–16.

217. Connor, *The National Question*, p. 279.

218. Lane, *Politics and Society in the USSR*, pp. 455–56.

219. Frederick C. Barghoorn, *Soviet Foreign Propaganda* (Princeton: Princeton University Press, 1969), pp. 145–47. The USSR later executed Beria when the government thought he was aggravating nationalist tensions. Connor, *The National Question*, p. 282.

220. Paul Hollander, *Political Pilgrims: Travels of Western Intellectuals to the Soviet Union, China, and Cuba, 1928–1978* (New York: Oxford University Press, 1981), pp. 348, 372, 374.

221. Klaus von Beyme, *The Soviet Union in World Politics* (New York: St. Martin's Press, 1987), p. 118.

222. Szymanski, *Human Rights in the Soviet Union*, p. 68.

223. Joseph L. Nogee and Robert H. Donaldson, *Soviet Foreign Policy since World War II* (New York: Pergamon Press, 1988), p. 156.

224. Barghoorn, *Soviet Propaganda*, pp. 148–53.

225. Ibid., p. 158.

226. Baruch Hazan, *Soviet Impregnational Propaganda* (Ann Arbor, Mich.: Ardis, 1982), pp. 71–72.

227. Martin Ebon, *The Soviet Propaganda Machine* (New York: McGraw-Hill, 1987), pp. 275–76.

228. Peter Sager, *Moscow's Hand in India: An Analysis of Soviet Propaganda* (Bombay: Lalvani Publishing, 1966), p. 89.

229. Horne, "Race from Power," p. 456. Also see Alvin Z. Rubinstein, *The Soviets in International Organizations: Changing Policy toward Developing Countries, 1955–1963* (Princeton: Princeton University Press, 1964), pp. 290, 101.

230. Inis L. Claude Jr., *National Minorities: An International Problem* (New York: Greenwood Press, 1955), pp. 165–66.

231. Ibid., pp. 169–70.

232. Otto Klineberg, "The Study of Multinational Societies," in Mackey and Verdoodt, *The Multinational Society,* pp. 9–28, 22.

233. Barghoorn, *Soviet Propaganda,* pp. 65, 218.

234. Some social scientists have also argued that international human rights norms have differential impacts. Soysal argues that while "global discourses and models increasingly penetrate national frameworks" for migrant-worker policies, "polity-specific modes of membership still shape the patterns that incorporation takes in specific European countries." Yasemin Soysal, *The Limits of Citizenship* (Chicago: University of Chicago Press, 1994), p. 4. Research by Keck and Sikkink and by Gurowitz has shown that nations in the process of modernization and completing economic development are most likely to pay attention to international norms of human rights. In Gurowitz's view, nations secure in their place in the international system will be less open to the impact of global norms. See Margaret Keck and Kathryn Sikkink, *Activists beyond Borders* (Ithaca: Cornell University Press, 1998); Amy Gurowitz, "Mobilizing International Norms: Domestic Actors, Immigrants and the Japanese State," *World Politics* 51 (1999): 413–45; and Amy Gurowitz, "Mobilizing International Norms: Domestic Actors, Immigrants, and the State," Ph.D. diss., Cornell University, 1999. In this chapter, I emphasize the competition for world leadership between the United States and both the Axis powers and the USSR. The Third World was the crucial audience especially for American and Soviet actions, and propaganda was an important force in making the moral culture of these emerging nations factors in the strategic calculations of American and Soviet policymakers.

235. Usually, this process displays a more *internally* oriented dynamic than it did with regard to equal rights for blacks and immigrants, and growth of government can occur and did occur during World War II in ways not closely related to national security. Bartholomew Sparrow, *From the Outside In: World War II and the American State* (Princeton: Princeton University Press, 1996).

236. Gregory Hooks, *Forging the Military-Industrial Complex: World War II's Battle of the Potomac* (Urbana: University of Illinois Press, 1991), p. 82.

237. R. T. Maddock, *The Political Economy of the Arms Race* (London: Macmillan, 1990), pp. 22–24.

238. Rob Kitchin, *Cyberspace* (New York: Wiley, 1998), p. 29.

239. Michael Sherry, *In the Shadow of War* (New Haven: Yale University Press, 1994), p. 226.

240. Eisenhower, *Mandate for Change, 1953–1956,* p. 123.

241. Quoted in Sherry, *Shadow of War,* p. 226.

242. Walter A. McDougall, . . . *the Heavens and the Earth: A Political History of the Space Age* (New York: Basic Books, 1985), p. 180.

382 | Notes to Pages 63–68

243. Ibid., p. 303; Robert A. Divine, "Lyndon Johnson and the Politics of Space," in Robert A. Divine, ed., *The Johnson Years,* vol. 2: *Vietnam, the Environment, and Science* (Lawrence: University Press of Kansas, 1987), pp. 217–54, 232.

244. On highways and national security, see Ralph K. Banks, "An Historical Overview: National Defense and the National System of Interstate and Defense Highways," *Public Works* 115 (1984): 74–79; Henry Moon, *The Interstate Highway System* (Washington, D.C.: Association of American Geographers, 1994), pp. 6–8; Eisenhower, *Mandate for Change, 1953–1956,* pp. 501, 548–49; *Public Papers of the Presidents: Dwight D. Eisenhower, 1955* (Washington, D.C.: Government Printing Office, 1956), p. 276; John Kenneth White, *Still Seeing Red: How the Cold War Shapes the New American Politics* (Boulder: Westview Press, 1997), p. 113; Sherry, *In the Shadow of War,* pp. 206–7. Eisenhower also saw building the St. Lawrence Seaway to be a strategy for national defense. Eisenhower, *Mandate for Change, 1953–1956,* pp. 287, 301–2; Robert J. Donovan, *Eisenhower: The Inside Story* (New York: Harper and Brothers, 1956), pp. 77–78.

245. For the Nixonian perspective, see Stephen E. Ambrose, *Nixon: The Triumph of a Politician, 1962–1972* (New York: Simon and Schuster, 1989), Chapter 20.

246. Dean Rusk Oral History, pp. 338–41.

247. McAdam, *Political Process and Black Insurgency,* pp. 165, 227, and generally Chapter Eight.

248. David Kimche, *The Afro-Asian Movement: Ideology and Foreign Policy of the Third World* (Jerusalem: Israel Universities Press, 1973), p. 23.

249. Lauren, *Power and Prejudice,* pp. 208–9.

250. Tolley, *U.N. Commission on Civil Rights,* 61–68; Lauren, *Power and Prejudice,* pp. 252, 277. Also see generally Michael Banton, *International Action against Racial Discrimination* (Oxford: Clarendon Press, 1996).

251. Lauren, *Power and Prejudice,* p. 239. Also see Gary B. Ostrower, *The United Nations and the United States* (New York: Twayne, 1998), pp. 136–39.

252. For poll data, see Burstein, *Discrimination, Jobs and Politics;* Howard Schuman, Charlotte Steeh, and Lawrence Bobo, *Racial Attitudes in America: Trends and Interpretations* (Cambridge, Mass.: Harvard University Press, 1985).

253. Clem Brooks, "Civil Rights Liberalism and the Suppression of a Republican Political Realignment in the United Nations, 1972 to 1996," *American Sociological Review* 65 (2000): 483–505.

3. National Security and Equal Rights

1. For a skeptical view of World War II's impact on American race relations, see Daniel Kryder, *Divided Arsenal: Race and the American State during World War II* (New York: Cambridge University Press, 2000).

2. Kenneth O'Reilly, *"Racial Matters": The FBI's Secret File on Black America, 1960–1972* (New York: Free Press, 1989), pp. 122–23.

3. In 1976, Congress appointed a special committee to examine FBI abuses and singled out treatment of black leaders for special condemnation. Richard Gid

Powers, *Not without Honor: The History of American Anticommunism* (New York: Free Press, 1995), pp. 349–50.

4. O'Reilly, *"Racial Matters,"* pp. 137, 145.

5. Ibid., pp. 7, 132–33.

6. Paul Lauren, *Power and Prejudice: The Politics and Diplomacy of Racial Discrimination* (Boulder: Westview Press, 1988), p. 191.

7. Frantz Fanon, *The Wretched of the Earth* (New York: Grove Press, 1968 [1963]).

8. On this matter, the USSR and developing nations were in agreement. Michael Banton, *International Action against Racial Discrimination* (Oxford: Clarendon Press, 1996), p. 58.

9. Francisco O. Ramirez, Yasemin Soysal, and Suzanne Shanahan, "The Changing Logic of Political Citizenship: Cross-National Acquisition of Women's Suffrage Rights, 1890 to 1990," *American Sociological Review* 62 (1997): 735–45.

10. Lauren, *Power and Prejudice*, p. 197; Howard Tolley Jr., *The U.N. Commission on Human Rights* (Boulder: Westview Press, 1987), p. 45.

11. Tolley, *U.N. Commission on Human Rights*, p. 44.

12. David A. Kay, *The New Nations in the United Nations, 1960–1967* (New York: Columbia University Press, 1970), p. 45.

13. Lauren, *Power and Prejudice*, p. 229; Tolley, *U.N. Commission on Civil Rights*, p. 47.

14. Banton, *International Action against Racial Discrimination*, Chapter 4.

15. Lauren, *Power and Prejudice*, pp. 234–35.

16. Ibid., p. 227.

17. Clark M. Eichelberger, *UN: The First Twenty Years* (New York: Harper and Row, 1965), pp. 93–98; Kay, *The New Nations*, pp. 86–89; Louis Henkin, "The United Nations and Human Rights," *International Organization* 19, no. 3 (1965): 512; Thomas G. Weiss, David P. Forsythe, and Roger A. Coate, *The United Nations and Changing World Politics* (Boulder: Westview Press, 1994), p. 135.

18. Banton, *International Action against Racial Discrimination*, p. 56.

19. See generally Tolley, *U.N. Commission on Civil Rights*, Chapter 5.

20. Lauren, *Power and Prejudice*, pp. 222–23.

21. Theodore A. Wilson, *The First Summit: Roosevelt and Churchill at Placentia Bay 1941* (Boston: Houghton Mifflin, 1969), p. 123.

22. Townsend Hoopes and Douglas Brinkley, *FDR and the Creation of the U.N.* (New Haven: Yale University Press, 1997), p. 41.

23. Ibid., p. 70.

24. Ibid., p. 99.

25. Ibid., p. 119.

26. Thomas Borstelmann, *Apartheid's Reluctant Uncle: The United States and Southern Africa in the Early Cold War* (New York: Oxford University Press, 1993), p. 15.

27. Raymond F. Betts, *Decolonization: The Making of the Contemporary World* (New York: Routledge, 1998), p. 35; John D. Hargreaves, *Decolonization in*

Africa, 2nd Ed. (New York: Longman, 1996), pp. 96–97; Gabriel Kolko, *Confronting the Third World: United States Foreign Policy, 1945–1980* (New York: Pantheon, 1988), pp. 13, 112; W. David McIntyre, *British Decolonization, 1946–1997: When, Why and How did the British Empire Fall?* (New York: St. Martin's Press, 1998), p. 91. Also see Daniel Philpott, *Revolution in Soverignty: How Ideas Shaped Modern International Relations* (Princeton: Princeton University Press, 2001), pp. 180–86.

28. Borstelmann, *Apartheid's Reluctant Uncle,* p. 178.

29. Lauren, *Power and Prejudice,* 207. Also see Brenda Gayle Plummer, *Rising Wind: Black Americans and U.S. Foreign Affairs, 1935–1960* (Chapel Hill: University of North Carolina Press, 1996), pp. 176, 239. American leaders did not simply absorb the brunt of the criticism. To deflect it, they tried to delegitimize the Soviet Union on the colonialism issue by drawing attention to Soviet-style colonialism in its domination of eastern Europe, especially the brutal repression of Hungarian freedom fighters in 1956. Dwight D. Eisenhower, *The White House Years: Waging Peace, 1956–1961* (Garden City, N.Y.: Doubleday, 1965), p. 112.

30. Sara M. Evans, *Born for Liberty* (New York: Free Press, 1989), pp. 221–31.

31. Barbara Evans Clements, "Later Developments: Trends in Soviet Women's History, 1930 to the Present," in Barbara Evans Clements, Barbara Alpern Engel, and Christine D. Worobee, eds., *Russia's Women: Accommodation, Resistance, Transformation* (Berkeley: University of California Press, 1991), pp. 267–78, 271–72.

32. Ibid., p. 268. Also see Genia Browning, "Soviet Politics—Where Are the Women?" in Barbara Holland, ed., *Soviet Sisterhood* (Bloomington: Indiana University Press, 1985), pp. 207–36. Despite doing little to help women's equality, the Soviets and their supporters sometimes saw that a more egalitarian picture was better propaganda on the rare occasion women's rights were mentioned. For a view of Soviet society as a feminist paradise, see Pratima Asthana, *Soviet Women* (Agra, India: M. G. Publishers, 1992), Chapter 7.

33. Leila J. Rupp, *Worlds of Women: The Making of an International Women's Movement* (Princeton: Princeton University Press, 1997), p. 220.

34. Ibid., p. 223; Nitza Berkovitch, "The Emergence and Transformation of the International Women's Movement," in John Boli and George M. Thomas, eds., *Constructing World Culture: International Nongovernmental Organizations since 1875* (Stanford: Stanford University Press, 1999), pp. 100–26; 118.

35. James Frederick Green, *The United Nations and Human Rights* (Washington, D.C.: Brookings Institution, 1959), pp. 103–13; Tolley, *U.N. Commission on Human Rights,* p. 40.

36. Green, *United Nations and Human Rights,* p. 107. India's constitution contains prohibitions on discrimination against women, but the society has long been highly discriminatory toward women, including government practices. Charles R. Epp, *The Rights Revolution: Lawyers, Activists, and Supreme Courts in Comparative Perspective* (Chicago: University of Chicago Press, 1998), Chapters 5 and 6.

37. Green, *United Nations and Human Rights,* p. 109.

38. Ibid., p. 110.
39. The possibility of linkage became more remote after the mid-1960s when efforts in the UN's Commission on the Status of Women began to emphasize problems of women relating to economic development. Laura Reanda, "The Commission on the Status of Women," in Philip Alston, ed., *The United Nations and Human Rights: A Critical Appraisal* (Oxford: Clarendon Press, 1992), pp. 265–303, esp. 289–300.
40. Available at *http://turnerlearning.com/cnn/coldwar/sputnik/sput_re4.html*. For a discussion, see Emily S. Rosenberg, "Consuming Women: Images of Americanization in the 'American Century,'" *Diplomatic History* 23, no. 3 (1999): 479–97, 489.
41. Leila J. Rupp and Verta Taylor, *Survival in the Doldrums: The American Women's Rights Movement, 1945 to the 1960s* (New York: Oxford University Press, 1987), pp. 136–44.
42. Cynthia Harrison, *On Account of Sex* (Berkeley: University of California Press, 1988), pp. 57–58.
43. Ibid., p. 59. Eisenhower won a majority of the women's vote in both of his election victories. Anne Costain, *Inviting Women's Rebellion: A Political Process Interpretation of the Women's Movement* (Baltimore: Johns Hopkins University Press, 1992), p. 33.
44. Sidney Milkis, *The President and the Parties: The Transformation of the American Party System since the New Deal* (New York: Oxford University Press, 1993), pp. 38–43; Samuel I. Rosenman, *Working with Roosevelt* (New York: Harper, 1952), p. 171.
45. Alan Brinkley, *The End of Reform* (New York: Vintage, 1995), p. 143.
46. Roosevelt's speechwriter Samuel Rosenman argues that Roosevelt was inspired by a book (Samuel Grafton's *All Out*) that claimed an "economic bill of rights" was necessary to defeat Hitler. The Protestant and Roman Catholic churches in England had also advocated "that extreme inequalities of wealth be abolished" to prevent hatred. Rosenman, *Working with Roosevelt*, pp. 264–66.
47. Edwin Amenta, *Bold Relief* (Princeton: Princeton University Press, 1998), p. 128.
48. National Resources Planning Board, *National Resources Development, Report for 1942* (Washington, D.C.: Government Printing Office, 1942), p. 1.
49. Ibid., pp. 7–8.
50. National Resources Planning Board, *National Resources Development Report for 1943, Part II. Wartime Planning for War and Post War* (Washington, D.C.: Government Printing Office, 1943), p. 1.
51. Message to the Congress on the State of the Union, January 11, 1944, in *Public Papers of Franklin Delano Roosevelt*, vol. 13, *1944–45* (New York: Harper and Brothers, 1950), p. 33.
52. Ibid., p. 34.
53. Ibid., pp. 40–41.
54. Ibid., p. 41.
55. Campaign Address at Soldiers' Field, Chicago, Illinois, October 28, 1944, in *Public Papers of Franklin Delano Roosevelt*, vol. 13, *1944–45*, p. 371.

56. Bruce Bliven, Max Lerner, and George Soule, "Charter for America," *New Republic,* April 19, 1943, pp. 523–42; 523–24.

57. See Brinkley, *End of Reform,* pp. 144–45, who argues there was a decline of the New Deal reform impulse. For a dissenting view, see Milkis, *President and the Parties,* p. 137.

58. Milkis, *President and the Parties,* p. 152; Robert J. Donovan, *Conflict and Crisis: The Presidency of Harry S Truman, 1945–1948* (New York: Norton, 1977), p. 112.

59. Edwin Amenta and Theda Skocpol, "Redefining the New Deal: World War II and the Development of Social Provision in the United States," in Margaret Weir, Ann Shola Orloff, and Theda Skocpol, eds., *The Politics of Social Policy in the United States* (Princeton: Princeton University Press, 1988), pp. 81–122.

60. Ibid., p. 82. In Britain, there was an effort, similar to that of the NRPB, to link the creation of social rights to the war effort. William Beveridge, the author and promoter of an official government report on social insurance, argued that his plan would implement the guarantee of the "freedom from want" mentioned in the Atlantic Charter. Peter Flora and Arnold J. Heidenheimer, "The Historical Core and Changing Boundaries of the Welfare State," in Peter Flora and Arnold J. Heidenheimer, eds., *The Development of Welfare States in Europe and America* (New Brunswick, N.J.: Transaction Books, 1981), pp. 17–34, 20. Also see Jytte Klausen, *War and Welfare: Europe and the United States, 1945 to the Present* (New York: St. Martin's Press, 1998), p. 50.

61. Amenta and Skocpol, "Redefining the New Deal," pp. 105–7.

62. Ibid., pp. 109–10.

63. See, for example, Sven H. Steinmo, "American Exceptionalism Reconsidered: Culture or Institutions?" in *The Dynamics of American Politics: Approaches and Interpretations,* ed. Lawrence C. Dodd and Calvin Jillson (Boulder: Westview Press, 1994), pp. 106–31.

64. An excellent study is Stephen Kemp Bailey, *Congress Makes a Law* (New York: Vintage Books, 1950).

65. The reasons are not obvious. One may be that while regulations always impose costs, and sometimes great costs, the chain of causality by which they do so is not often readily apparent. On causality chains, see R. Douglas Arnold, *The Logic of Congressional Action* (New Haven: Yale University Press, 1990); Paul Pierson, *Dismantling the Welfare State? Reagan, Thatcher and the Politics of Retrenchment* (New York: Cambridge University Press, 1994).

66. Elizabeth A. Fones-Wolf, *Selling Free Enterprise: The Business Assault on Labor and Liberalism, 1945–60* (Urbana: University of Illinois Press, 1994).

67. I do not claim that social-rights policies are pure class politics, completely separate from color and sex discrimination. These have played important roles in the politics of social rights. For example, limited democracy in the south due to disenfranchised black voters undermined New Deal relief efforts, and evidence suggests discrimination against blacks created limits on social security policy. On southern democracy and the New Deal, see Amenta, *Bold Relief.* On race and the development of social security, see Robert C. Lieberman, *Shifting the Color Line* (Cambridge, Mass.: Harvard University Press, 1998).

68. As Gregory Hooks points out, "The same Congress that supplied billions of

dollars in excess of the military's needs abolished vulnerable New Deal agencies in the name of fiscal austerity." These included, besides the NRPB, other agencies that directly compromised the market economy by providing jobs, including the Works Progress Administration, the Civilian Conservation Corps, and the National Youth Administration. Congress also severely cut funding from the Rural Electrification Administration and Farm Security Administration. Hooks, *Military-Industrial Complex*, pp. 90–91.

69. Bailey, *Congress Makes a Law*, pp. 54–55, 107.
70. Ibid., p. 130.
71. Paul Starr, *The Social Transformation of American Medicine* (New York: Basic Books, 1982), p. 282.
72. Ibid., p. 283.
73. Ibid., p. 285.
74. Gary B. Ostrower, *The United Nations and the United States* (New York: Twayne, 1998), p. 71.
75. Paul Burstein, *Discrimination, Jobs and Politics* (Chicago: University of Chicago Press, 1998 [1985]).
76. This action had few risks regarding the nation's standing before the world, as America was at war with Japan; it is hard to imagine compelling Japanese propaganda being sent to China or elsewhere complaining about the internment. Further, what is often not acknowledged is that the Truman administration sought to compensate the Japanese Americans almost immediately after the war ended, when the president called for compensation in his bold 1947 Civil Rights Message. In 1948, Congress passed the Japanese-American Claims Act, a first effort to compensate those losses. Casting Japanese American compensation as a national-security issue, a report of the House Committee of the Judiciary explained that lack of redress "would provide ample material for attacks by the followers of foreign ideologies on the American way of life." Roger Daniels, *Asian America: Chinese and Japanese in the United States since 1850* (Seattle: University of Washington Press, 1988), pp. 283–97. The Claims Act only paid $25.5 million, but coming so soon after the hysterical policy of internment, any compensation at all was significant. Benjamin B. Ringer, *We the People and Others: Duality and America's Treatment of Its Racial Minorities* (New York: Routledge, 1983), pp. 914–19. In 1952, the Supreme Court referred to the UN Charter in striking down California's Alien Land Law, which prevented aliens, specifically Asians who were then denied the right to naturalize, from buying land. In *Oyama v. California*, 332 U.S. 633 (1948), Justices Black and Douglas explained that the "law stands as an obstacle to the free accomplishment of our policy in the international field." A concurring opinion by Justice Murphy made similar points. Green, *United Nations and Human Rights*, pp. 19–20, n. 23; Daniels, *Asian America*, p. 299.

4. Designating Official Minorities for Affirmative Action

1. For detailed studies of the development of affirmative action for blacks in employment, there is my own *Ironies of Affirmative Action* (Chicago: University of Chicago Press, 1996), as well as Hugh Davis Graham's influential study *The*

Civil Rights Era (New York: Oxford University Press, 1990). Also see Herman Belz, *Equality Transformed* (New Brunswick, N.J.: Transaction, 1991); Alfred Blumrosen, *Black Employment and the Law* (New Brunswick: Rutgers University Press, 1971), and Blumrosen, *Modern Law* (Madison: University of Wisconsin Press, 1993).

2. Steven Teles makes a similar argument in his analysis of the failure to develop American-style affirmative action in Britain—there, a "leading group" was lacking. See Teles, "Positive Action or Affirmative Action: The Persistence of Britain's Anti-Discrimination Regime," in John D. Skrentny, ed., *Color Lines* (Chicago: University of Chicago Press, 2001), pp. 241–69.

3. See Paul Starr's important essay on the sociology of official statistics, where he writes: "The classifications used in official statistics are cognitive commitments of a powerful kind. Once governments decide to use particular categories to count, the terms enter the language of administration and shape both private and governmental decisions. Official categories may help to constitute or divide groups and to illuminate or obscure their problems and achievements." Starr, "The Sociology of Official Statistics," in William Alonso and Paul Starr, eds., *The Politics of Numbers* (New York: Russell Sage, 1987), pp. 7–58, 53.

4. The term first appeared in the National Labor Relations Act in 1935. It is found in some of John F. Kennedy's executive orders relating to nondiscrimination by government contractors, but it remained vague and broad, including a wide variety of practices, until the EEOC and the OFCC fleshed out the concept. For example, in 1964, an interpretive memo in the Kennedy administration described the removal of segregated locker rooms and drinking fountains as examples of "affirmative action." John Skrentny, "Introduction," in Skrentny, *Color Lines,* pp. 1–28. There were precursor policies that were apparently unrelated to the 1960s developments. On developments from the New Deal era, see Paul D. Moreno, *From Direct Action to Affirmative Action: Fair Employment Law and Policy in America, 1933–1972* (Baton Rouge: Louisiana State University Press, 1997).

5. This part of the text is a condensed version of work that originally appeared in John D. Skrentny, "Pragmatism, Institutionalism and the Construction of Employment Discrimination," *Sociological Forum* 9 (1994): 343–69, and Skrentny, *The Ironies of Affirmative Action,* Chapter 5.

6. See Blumrosen, *Black Employment and the Law,* Chapter 8, for details.

7. The 1848 Treaty of Guadalupe Hidalgo gave citizenship to Mexicans living in the territory Mexico ceded to the United States. The Nationality Act of 1940 then gave naturalization rights to all persons of indigenous Western Hemisphere races. Gabriel Chin, "The Civil Rights Revolution Comes to Immigration Law: A New Look at the Immigration and Nationality Act of 1965," *North Carolina Law Review* 75 (1996): 273–345, 281. On Mexican American whiteness, see Matthew Frye Jacobson, *Whiteness of a Different Color* (Cambridge, Mass.: Harvard University Press, 1998), p. 230; Ian F. Haney López, *White by Law* (New York: New York University Press, 1996), p. 61.

8. Peter Skerry, *Mexican Americans: The Ambivalent Minority* (New York: Free Press, 1993), pp. 293–94.

9. Alonso S. Perales, *Are We Good Neighbors?* (New York: Arno Press, 1974 [1948]), pp. 57–63.

10. Juan Gómez-Quiñones, *Chicano Politics: Reality and Promise, 1940–1990* (Albuquerque: Univesity of New Mexico Press, 1990), pp. 60–62; Skerry, *Mexican Americans,* p. 117.

11. Of the 4,081 complaints that the FEPC received in fiscal year 1943–44, for instance, 80.8 percent of the complaints were based on race, almost all from blacks, while only 6.2 percent were based on national origin (71.9 of these were from Mexican Americans). President's Committee on Civil Rights, *To Secure These Rights* (Washington, D.C.: Government Printing Office, 1947), p. 54.

12. Gómez-Quiñones, *Chicano Politics,* p. 39.

13. Louis C. Kesselman, *The Social Politics of the FEPC: Study in Reform Pressure Movements* (Chapel Hill: University of North Carolina Press, 1948), pp. 110–12.

14. PCCR, *Secure These Rights,* pp. x, 14.

15. Ibid., p. 67.

16. Recent analyses of the American race problem, such as those by Desmond King and Matthew Frye Jacobson, have correctly noted that black–white problems were dominant and most important in America, but have not drawn attention to this quiet but important government understanding that there were other groups similar to blacks that suffered in analogous ways. Desmond King, *Making Americans* (Cambridge, Mass.: Harvard University Press, 2000), p. 242; Matthew Frye Jacobson, *Whiteness of a Different Color* (Cambridge, Mass.: Harvard University Press, 1998), p. 95.

17. PCCR, *Secure These Rights,* pp. 29, 33, 40, 59, 65, 68, 71, 74, 78.

18. Gómez-Quiñones, *Chicano Politics,* p. 91.

19. Ibid.

20. Leo Grebler, Joan W. Moore, and Ralph C. Guzman, *The Mexican-American People: The Nation's Second Largest Minority* (New York: Free Press, 1970), pp. 4–5, 389. Also see Skerry, *Mexican Americans,* p. 18.

21. Paul Burstein, *Discrimination, Jobs and Politics* (Chicago: University of Chicago Press, 1985), p. 106.

22. Ibid., pp. 20–21; Graham, *Civil Rights Era,* pp. 19–22.

23. See, for example, the testimony of Murray A. Gordon of the American Jewish Congress in *Hearings, Equal Employment Opportunity,* House General Subcommittee on Labor, 88th Cong., 1st Sess. (April 22, 30, May 3, 7, 21, 24, 27–29, June 6, 1963), pp. 117–20.

24. Theda Skocpol, *Protecting Soldiers and Mothers* (Cambridge, Mass.: Harvard University Press, 1992).

25. Cynthia Harrison, *On Account of Sex* (Berkeley: University of California Press, 1988), pp. 76–79, 111; Sara Evans, *Born for Liberty* (New York: Free Press, 1989), p. 274; Esther Peterson Oral History, p. 27, Lyndon B. Johnson Library; Ethel Klein, *Gender Politics* (Cambridge, Mass.: Harvard University Press, 1984), p. 22; Deborah Rhode, *Justice and Gender* (Cambridge, Mass.: Harvard University Press, 1990), p. 56.

26. Harrison, *On Account of Sex,* p. 162.

27. The Equal Pay Act was a rather muted first salvo of the minority rights revolution. Eighteen years after the original bill proposal, the Equal Pay Act became law as an amendment to the Fair Labor Standards Act. Its basic provision was to ensure that men and women doing the same work were paid equally. As passed, it excluded business and professional women, as well as low-paid women in agriculture and domestic service. Graham, *Civil Rights Era,* p. 207. Some argued that even where workers were covered, it did not represent a true triumph of women's interests at the expense of men's. In granting women equal pay, Congress also protected men from having their wages undercut by women. Further, the Equal Pay Act "increased job security for men by discouraging the replacement of men with lower paid women." Jo Freeman, *The Politics of Women's Liberation* (New York: Longman, 1975), p. 176 (Freeman's italics removed).

28. Evans, *Born for Liberty,* p. 275; Rhode, *Justice and Gender,* p. 57.

29. PCSW, *American Women* (Washington, D.C.: Government Printing Office, 1963), p. 30.

30. Harrison, *On Account of Sex,* p. 174.

31. Moreno, *From Direct Action to Affirmative Action,* p. 175; Graham, *Civil Rights Era,* p. 136.

32. Harrison, *On Account of Sex,* p. 147. There was a rare instance of an effort to add race-discrimination provisions to a sex-discrimination bill. During debate on 1963's Equal Pay Act, Charles S. Joelson (D–NJ) tried to add the words "or race" in all places where the word "sex" appeared, but this move "was disallowed on a point of order, raised by Edith Green, as not being 'germane.'" Ibid., p. 96.

33. Graham, *Civil Rights Era,* p. 136.

34. Esther Peterson Oral History, Lyndon B. Johnson Library (LBJL), p. 32.

35. Mary Keyserling Oral History, LBJL, p. 17.

36. Freeman, *Politics of Women's Liberation,* pp. 53–54.

37. *New York Times,* 9 February 1964, p. 1. It later was put into the bill, but was again eliminated in committee. Burstein, *Discrimination, Jobs and Politics,* p. 22.

38. Griffiths later recalled that "there weren't any great groups of women, and certainly not the National Women's Party, who were coming to support this . . . The National Women's Party never approached me on sex and the Civil Rights Act, and they never came to me afterwards and thanked me for the argument that I made that kept it in there. I know of nothing they did concerning it, absolutely nothing. They may have done it, but they never did it to my knowledge." Martha Griffiths Oral History, Oral History Collection of the Association of Former Members of Congress, Library of Congress, p. 118.

39. Evans, *Born for Liberty,* p. 276; Graham, *Civil Rights Era,* p. 137.

40. Freeman, *Politics of Women's Liberation,* p. 53.

41. Griffiths was under the impression that Smith would add the amendment to all titles in the bill, but when he only amended Title VII, Griffiths felt she had to go with that. Martha Griffiths Oral History, p. 73. See also Freeman, *Politics of Women's Liberation,* p. 53.

42. *Congressional Record,* February 8, 1964, p. 2577. See Harrison, *On Account of Sex,* p. 178, for a discussion.

43. Griffiths recalled that, "years later, I saw Smith after he had retired, gave him a hug, and said, 'We will always be known for *our* amendment.' And he said to me, 'Well, you know, I offered it as a joke.'" Martha Griffiths Oral History, p. 74.

44. *Congressional Record,* February 8, 1964, p. 2580.

45. Ibid., pp. 2577–2584.

46. *Congressional Record,* April 8, 1964, p. 7217. Clark gave broad interpretations of the BFOQ provisions that the EEOC and federal courts later ignored, as they preferred a much narrower approach. In their "Interpretive Memorandum of Title VII of H.R. 7152, Submitted Jointly by Senator Joseph S. Clark And Senator Clifford P. Case, Floor Managers," Clark and his colleague argued that "examples of such legitimate discrimination would be the preference of a French restaurant for a French cook, the preference of a professional baseball team for male players, and the preference of a business which seeks the patronage of members of particular religious groups for a salesman of that religion." Ibid., p. 7213.

47. There was a little behind-the-scenes wrangling. In a Republican strategy luncheon, Dirksen said he would try to delete the sex discrimination amendment, but Senator Margaret Chase Smith (R–ME) convinced him there was no reason to delete it and that she would oppose him if he tried. On the Democratic side, Betty Friedan and the Women's International League for Peace and Freedom also lobbied. Black civil-rights groups agreed to leave the amendment in, despite southern support, because keeping the Senate and House voting for the exact same bill would avoid more debate and mischief at the conference committee. Donald Robinson, "Two Movements in Search of Equal Employment Opportunity," *Signs* 4 (1979): 413–33, 419.

48. Burstein, *Discrimination, Jobs and Politics,* p. 74.

49. Ibid., p. 81.

50. 110 *Congressional Record* 1964, p. 6553.

51. "Radio and Television Remarks upon Signing the Civil Rights Bill," in *Public Papers of the Presidents of the United States: Lyndon B. Johnson, 1963–64,* vol. 2 (Washington, D.C.: Government Printing Office, 1965), pp. 842–44.

52. Quoted in Richard P. Nathan, *Jobs and Civil Rights: The Role of the Federal Government in Promoting Equal Opportunity in Employment and Training* (Washington, D.C.: Government Printing Office, Clearinghouse Publication No. 16, April, 1969), p. 55; US Commission on Civil Rights, *Federal Civil Rights Enforcement Effort: A Report of the US Commission on Civil Rights, 1970* (Washington, D.C.: Government Printing Office, 1970), p. 303, citing EEOC Annual Report, 1966, p. 5.

53. These include Grades 16–18. Aileen C. Hernandez, "E.E.O.C. and the Women's Movement, 1965–1975," paper prepared for the Symposium on the Tenth Anniversary of the US Equal Employment Opportunity Commission, November 28–29, 1975.

54. Julie Leinenger Pycior, *LBJ and Mexican Americans: The Paradox of Power* (Austin: University of Texas Press, 1997), p. 147.
55. This and the following material is from Harold Orlan's unpublished manuscript "The Origins of Protected Groups." Orlans conducted his study in 1985–86 while working at the US Commission on Civil Rights, with the assistance of Philip Lyons. Orlans's research is extremely valuable for its basis in interviews with Felipe de Ortega y Gasca, chairman of the National LULAC Heritage Commission, Michael Masaoka of the Japanese American Citizens League, and David Mann. I thank Harold Orlans for sharing his research with me.
56. There is another possible precedent for the EEO-1. Beginning in 1961, the Kennedy administration undertook a census of the total African American employment in government. In 1962, however, the census began to monitor African American and "Spanish-Speaking" employment, and in selected states, they also examined "American Indians, Mexican Americans, Puerto Ricans, and persons of Oriental origin." See Letter to James M. Quigley from Hobart Taylor Jr., February 6, 1964, in Steven F. Lawson, *Civil Rights during the Johnson Administration, 1963–1969* (Frederick, Md.: University Publications of America, 1984), Part 2, Reel 3, frame 829; "MINORITY GROUP STUDY," June, 1963, in Lawson, *Civil Rights during Johnson,* Part 1, Reel 7, frame 313; Memo for Lee C. White from John W. Macy, November 18, 1964 and DRAFT PRESS RELEASE, in Lawson, *Civil Rights during Johnson,* Part 1, Reel 7, frames 403–5.
57. President's Committee on Government Contracts, *Five Years of Progress, 1953–1958: A Report to President Eisenhower by the President's Committee on Government Contracts* (Washington, D.C.: Government Printing Office, 1958). Statistics on complaints of discrimination also showed that in the August 1953 to June 1958 period, the committee had received 717 total complaints, 446 of which were on the basis of race, 217 on religion, 29 on national origin, and 25 not specified. The Anti-Defamation League of B'nai B'rith brought 208 of the religious discrimination complaints. See p. 23 of the report.
58. I could not find any documents explaining this inclusion. Sex categories were most likely included on other Labor Department statistics forms, and were imported onto Form 40 as part of a script of what a proper labor statistics form should look like. There may also have been some interest in whether African Americans hired at a certain firm might be mostly women or not.
59. Title VII, Section 705(g)(5).
60. Ibid., Title VII, Section 709(c).
61. *Congressional Record,* April 8, 1964, p. 7214. I thank Alfred Blumrosen for directing me to this section of the *Record.*
62. Ibid., p. 7216.
63. Michael I. Sovern, *Legal Restraints on Racial Discrimination in Employment* (New York: Twentieth Century Fund, 1966), p. 86.
64. Ibid., pp. 122–27.
65. Alfred W. Blumrosen, *Black Employment and the Law* (New Brunswick: Rutgers University Press, 1971), p. 68.
66. *Federal Register* vol. 30, no. 228, Thursday, November 25, 1965, p. 14,658, in folder EEOC 1965, Box I:98, Papers of the Leadership Conference on Civil

Rights, Library of Congress.

67. Author interview with Charles Markham, June 15, 1998.

68. Ibid.

69. Blumrosen, *Black Employment,* pp. 70–71.

70. Author interview with Charles Markham, June 15, 1998. Also see Blumrosen, *Black Employment,* p. 73.

71. Graham, *Civil Rights Era,* p. 199. Walter White of the NAACP similarly objected to racial questions on Social Security applications. Robert C. Lieberman, *Shifting the Color Line* (Cambridge, Mass.: Harvard University Press, 1998), p. 81.

72. The notes are written on the *Federal Register* announcement of the EEO-1 in folder EEOC 1965, Box I:98, Papers of the Leadership Conference on Civil Rights, Library of Congress.

73. Personal correspondence with Herbert Hammerman, June 18, 1998.

74. Ibid.

75. Author interview with Charles Markham, June 15, 1998.

76. For example, see *EEOC Hearing on the Proposed Employer Reporting System,* December 16, 1965, in Lawson, *Civil Rights during Johnson,* Part 2, Reel 2, frame 433.

77. Ibid., frame 454. See also John David Skrentny, "State Capacity, Policy Feedbacks and Affirmative Action for Blacks, Women, and Latinos," *Research in Political Sociology* 8 (1998): 279–310.

78. Blumrosen, *Black Employment,* p. 117. The quotation is from Al Blumrosen's chapter, "The Many Faces of Job Discrimination," which is an excellent summary of the Equal Employment Report No. 1.

79. Ibid., pp. 119–20. I do not mean to suggest that this report was an accurate portrait of opportunity for Asian Americans or for any group. The EEO-1 was and is a very blunt instrument. It lacked any information on educational background or time of immigration. It contained detailed information only on minority-group representation. It contained no information at all on how aspirations and occupational preferences might vary between or within groups. Variations between ethnic groups within categories were lost. Government officials would have to infer that discrimination was the cause of all group variations.

80. EEOC Second Annual Report, in Lawson, *Civil Rights during Johnson,* Part 2, Reel 3, frame 414.

81. *New York Times,* August 21, 1965. The bunny problem is also discussed in "Sex and Nonsense" in the *New Republic,* September 4, 1965, p. 10.

82. Monroe W. Karmin, "Battling Job Bias: New U.S. Commission Plans Big Push to Open More Posts to Negroes," *Wall Street Journal,* October 13, 1965.

83. *New York Times,* July 21, 1965.

84. Letter from F. D. Roosevelt Jr. to the President regarding the activities of the first one hundred days of the EEOC, October 29, 1965, in Lawson, *Civil Rights during Johnson,* Part 2, Reel 1, frame 908.

85. Memo to Richard Graham from Franklin Roosevelt Jr., December 8, 1965, folder Inter-Office Memoranda, Records of Chairman Stephen Shulman, 1966–

1968, Box 2, RG 403, National Archives. Perhaps Roosevelt was trying to make up for a past blunder. Sylvia Danovitch claims that he was asked publicly what he thought about sex—in reference to sex discrimination—and the chairman said, "I'm in favor of it." Danovitch, "Humanizing Institutional History: Oral History at the EEOC," *Prologue* 27, no. 4 (1995): 335–47, 340.

86. Robin H. Rogers-Dillon and John David Skrentny, "Administering Success: The Legitimacy Imperative and the Implementation of Welfare Reform," *Social Problems* 46 (1999): 13–29; Robin Rogers-Dillon, "Ending Welfare as We Know It" (Ph.D. diss., University of Pennsylvania, 1998).

87. Nathan, *Jobs and Civil Rights*, p. 50.

88. Freeman, *Politics of Women's Liberation*, p. 185.

89. Quoted in ibid., p. 54.

90. Danovitch, "Oral History at the EEOC," p. 343.

91. Ibid., pp. 340–41.

92. Ibid., p. 342.

93. Memo from Aileen Hernandez to other commissioners and general counsel, September 6, 1966, folder Inter-Office Memoranda, Records of Chairman Stephen Shulman, 1966–1968, Box 2, RG 403, National Archives.

94. "Progress Report," March 6, 1967, folder TASK FORCE on Strengthening Staff Relations, Efficiency and Morale in EEOC, Records of Chairman Stephen Shulman, Box 6, RG 403, National Archives.

95. Letter from Kathryn Clarenbach, Betty Friedan, and Caroline East to Dick Berg, March 14, 1967, and attached note from R. K. Berg to Dr. Murray, March 16, 1967, folder NOW [National Organization for Women], Records of Chairman Stephen Shulman, 1966–1968, Box 7, RG 403, National Archives.

96. Hernandez, "EEOC and the Women's Movement," p. 8.

97. Ibid., p. 17–18; Nathan, *Jobs and Civil Rights*, p. 53. See *Rosenfeld v. Southern Pac. Co.*, 293 F. Supp. 1219 (C.D. Cal. 1968); *Weeks v. Southern Bell Tel. & Tel. Co.*, 408 F.2d 228 (5th Cir. 1969); *Bowe v. Colgate Palmolive Co.*, 416 F.2d 711 (7th Cir. 1969).

98. Author interview with Alfred Blumrosen, May 22, 1998.

99. Hernandez, "EEOC and the Women's Movement," pp. 26–28. The decision was still not unanimous—4 to 1—with Luther Holcomb dissenting.

100. In Title VII, the difference between race and sex discrimination was only expressed in the provision that allowed—in cases of alleged sex, national-origin and religious discrimination—for a defense that the alleged discrimination was the result of a "bona fide occupational qualification (BFOQ) . . . reasonably necessary to the normal operation of a particular business or enterprise." 42 U.S.C. Section 2000e-2(e) [1982].

101. Author interview with Alfred Blumrosen, May 22, 1998.

102. Hernandez, "EEOC and the Women's Movement," p. 10. The four women were Carol Cox from the Labor Department Office of the Solicitor, Beatrice Adams from Gardner Advertising Agency, Julia Thompson, American Nurses Association, and Laura Spencer of the Labor Department's Women's Bureau.

103. Patricia G. Zelman, *Women, Work and National Policy: The Kennedy–Johnson Years* (Ann Arbor: University of Michigan Research Press, 1982), Appendix B;

see also ibid., p. 98; Hernandez, "EEOC and the Women's Movement," pp. 11–13.

104. Memo from Luther Holcomb to Marvin Watson, Attention: Jim Jones, March 25, 1966; Memo from James R. Jones to W. Marvin Watson, March 25, 1966, in Lawson, *Civil Rights during Johnson*, Part 2, Reel 3, frames 102–03.

105. The letter is reprinted in 112 *Congressional Record,* June 20, 1966, pp. 13, 690.

106. Ibid.

107. Pauli Murray and Mary Eastwood, "Jane Crow and the Law: Sex Discrimination and Title VII," *George Washington Law Review* 34 (1965): 232–56.

108. 112 *Congressional Record,* June 20, 1966, pp. 13, 690–94. In a rare instance of national-security meanings of women's rights, "the CIA informed Griffiths that the Russians took her remarks as evidence of America's brutality to women." Emily George, R.S.M., *Martha W. Griffiths* (Washington, D.C.: University Press of America, 1982), p. 153.

109. Alfred Blumrosen recalls additional lobbying from businesses, mainly on the issues of preserving testing and joining with labor groups to preserve seniority. Author interview with Alfred Blumrosen, May 22, 1998. Aileen Hernandez recalled lobbying from the NAACP, the American GI Forum (a Latino advocacy group), the AFL-CIO, ANPA, and the Association of Employment Agencies. Hernandez, "EEOC and the Women's Movement," pp. 8–9.

110. Graham, *Civil Rights Era,* p. 207.

111. Evans, *Born for Liberty,* p. 277; Betty Friedan, *"It Changed My Life"* (New York: Random House, 1976), p. 99; Zelman, *Women, Work and National Policy,* p. 104. The Business and Professional Women's Clubs did call for public hearings on the classified ads fiasco, and the chair of the National Council of Women's "Title VII and Women" conference wrote Roosevelt on November 5, 1965 with appreciation for his comment that the time "for funny jokes" was over and the EEOC was going to begin opening job opportunities for women. Hernandez, "EEOC and the Women's Movement," p. 59, n. 11.

112. Hernandez, "EEOC and the Women's Movement," p. 28.

113. Evans, *Born for Liberty,* p. 277.

114. Griffiths proudly maintains that "that speech probably had more effect upon women in the United States than any other speech ever made in Congress. It was a speech which I understand created NOW. It was given to women who were going to a Status of Women meeting at the White House, and they were enraged, absolutely enraged, and from then you have a lot of activity." Martha Griffiths Oral History, p. 75, Oral History Collection of the Association of Former Members of Congress, Library of Congress.

115. Harrison, *On Account of Sex,* p. 195.

116. Ibid., p. 201.

117. Anne Costain, *Inviting Women's Rebellion* (Baltimore: Johns Hopkins University Press, 1992), p. 45.

118. NOW Statement of Purpose, folder NOW [National Organization for Women], Records of Chairman Stephen Shulman, 1966–1968, Box 7, RG 403, National Archives; Hernandez, "EEOC and the Women's Movement," p. 26.

119. Letter from Kathryn Clarenbach, Betty Friedan, and Caroline Davis to EEOC

Commissioners, November 11, 1966, folder NOW [National Organization for Women], Records of Chairman Stephen Shulman, 1966–1968, Box 7, RG 403, National Archives.

120. Klein, *Gender Politics,* p. 47.

121. Evans, *Born for Liberty,* p. 277; Freeman, *Politics of Women's Liberation,* p. 77; Klein, *Gender Politics,* p. 23.

122. Letter from Stephen Shulman to the President, March 23, 1967, in Lawson, *Civil Rights during Johnson,* Part 2, Reel 2, frame 192. Johnson had Shulman's letter forwarded to Henry Wilson with the notation, "Does this interest Martha Griffiths?" Ibid., Part 2, Reel 3, frame 190.

123. Letter from Stephen Shulman to the President, May 4, 1967, in Lawson, *Civil Rights during Johnson,* Part 2, Reel 3, frame 204. Shulman did not relate to Johnson the dominant point of view at the hearings, only that "the total reaction was favorable to the Commission for having held the hearings."

124. EEOC Administrative History, in Lawson, *Civil Rights during Johnson,* Part 3, Reel 1, frames 247–48; Graham, *Civil Rights Era,* p. 231.

125. Graham, *Civil Rights Era,* p. 231.

126. Freeman, *Politics of Women's Liberation,* p. 187.

127. Gómez-Quiñones, *Chicano Politics,* pp. 60–62.

128. EEOC Second Annual Report, in Lawson, *Civil Rights during Johnson,* Part 3, Reel 3, frame 414.

129. EEOC Administrative History, in Lawson, *Civil Rights during Johnson,* Part 3, Reel 1, frame 373.

130. Author interview with Alfred Blumrosen, May 22, 1998.

131. Letter from Carlos A. Rivera to Marvin Watson, August 30, 1965, in Lawson, *Civil Rights during Johnson,* Part 2, Reel 3, frame 48.

132. Memo from Franklin D. Roosevelt Jr. to Herman Edelsberg, December 24, 1965, folder Inter-Office Memoranda, Records of Stephen Shulman, 1966–68, Box 2, RG 403, National Archives.

133. Memo to Lee C. White from Herman Edelsberg, February 3, 1966, in Lawson, *Civil Rights during Johnson,* Part 2, Reel 3, frame 66.

134. Kaye Briegel, "The Development of Mexican-American Organizations," in Manuel P. Servín, ed., *The Mexican-Americans: An Awakening Minority* (Beverly Hills: Glencoe Press, 1970), pp. 160–78, 174.

135. MAPA press release, n.d. (received at the White House March 22, 1966), in Lawson, *Civil Rights during Johnson,* Part 2, Reel 3, frame 106. A similar emphasis on the importance of lobbying was voiced in 1969 by a lawyer in the Civil Rights Division of the Justice Department, speaking about women: "We respond to social turmoil," and "the fact that women have not gone into the streets is indicative that they do not take employment discrimination seriously." Freeman, *Politics of Women's Liberation,* p. 79.

136. Pycior, *LBJ and Mexican Americans,* p. 164.

137. Press release from the Southern California Delegation, n.d., in Lawson, *Civil Rights during Johnson,* Part 2, Reel 3, frame 108.

138. See the March 30, 1966 memo from Carlos Rivera to Marvin Watson, in Lawson, *Civil Rights during Johnson,* Part 2, Reel 3, frames 104–15.

139. Pycior, *LBJ and Mexican Americans,* p. 168.

140. Ibid., p. 164.

141. Memo from Edward C. Sylvester to Clifford L. Alexander, May 3, 1966, in Lawson, *Civil Rights during Johnson,* Part 2, Reel 3, frame 123.

142. Pycior, *LBJ and Mexican Americans,* p. 169.

143. Ibid., p. 166.

144. Letter from David S. North to Chairman Shulman, October 21, 1966, and attached letter from Rudy Ramos, folder White House, Records of Chairman Stephen Shulman, 1966–1968, Box 9, RG 403, National Archives.

145. Lamar Jones, Mexican Americans in the United States, folder Mexican Americans, Records of Chairman Stephen Shulman, 1966–1968, Box 7, RG 403, National Archives.

146. US Commission on Civil Rights, *Federal Enforcement Effort, 1970,* p. 304.

147. Dale L. Hiestand, "White Collar Employment Opportunities for Minorities in New York City," in Lawson, *Civil Rights during Johnson,* Part 2, Reel 2, frame 901.

148. EEOC Adminstrative History, Appendix J, in Lawson, *Civil Rights during Johnson,* Part 3, Reel 1, frames 444–45.

149. Ibid., Part 3, Reel 1, frames 450–1.

150. Transcripts of Meeting with Executives of the Pharmaceutical Industry, October 6, 1967, in Lawson, *Civil Rights during Johnson,* Part 1, Reel 1, frames 978–91.

151. Office of State and Community Affairs, EEOC, "Project Outline FY 1968," in Lawson, *Civil Rights during Johnson,* Part 3, Reel 1, frames 986, 991–92.

152. Harvey D. Shapiro, "Women on the Line, Men at the Switchboard," *New York Times Magazine,* May 20, 1973, p. 73.

153. Phyllis A. Wallace and Jack E. Nelson, "Legal Processes and Strategies of Intervention," in Phyllis A. Wallace, ed., *Equal Employment Opportunity and the AT&T Case,* (Cambridge, Mass.: MIT Press, 1976), pp. 243–52, 243.

154. Phyllis A. Wallace, "Equal Employment Opportunity," in Wallace, *The AT&T Case,* pp. 253–68, 253.

155. Herbert R. Northrup and John A. Larson, *The Impact of the AT&T–EEO Consent Decree: Labor Relations and Public Policy Series No. 20* (Philadelphia: Industrial Research Unit, Wharton School, 1979), pp. 2–3.

156. Shapiro, "Women on the Line," p. 75; Freeman, *Politics of Women's Liberation,* p. 189.

157. Freeman, *Politics of Women's Liberation,* p. 189, citing EEOC, "'A Unique Competence': A Study of Equal Employment Opportunity in the Bell System," Washington, D.C., n.d., p. 173.

158. Phyllis A. Wallace, "The Consent Decrees," in Wallace, *The AT&T Case,* pp. 269–76, 269.

159. Northrup and Larson, *Impact of the Consent Decree,* pp. 10–11. In 1974, AT&T also worked with the American Jewish Committee to increase Jewish representation at the level of management. Phyllis A. Wallace, "What Did We Learn?" in Wallace, *The AT&T Case,* pp. 277–82, 282.

160. Wallace, "The Consent Decrees," pp. 272–73.

161. Wallace and Nelson, "Strategies of Intervention," p. 249.

162. Wallace, "What Did We Learn?" p. 278–79.

163. Shapiro, "Women on the Line," p. 89–91.

164. According to the report, these priorities were determined by the number of incoming charges, prevailing patterns of discrimination from the EEO-1 data, lobbying, and determination of congressional intent. US Commission on Civil Rights, *Federal Civil Rights Enforcement Effort 1970: A Report of the United States Commission on Civil Rights*, (Washington, D.C.: Government Printing Office, 1970), p. 301. The Commission on Civil Rights's 1971 report also stated, "The Commission's three priority anti-discrimination activities have been concerned with blacks, and Spanish Americans, and women, in descending order of priority." Civil Rights Commission, *Enforcement Effort*, p. 97.

165. Herbert Hammerman, "'Affirmative-Action Stalemate': A Second Perspective," *Public Interest* (Fall 1988): 130–35, 131.

166. See the *Hearings before the United States Equal Employment Opportunity Commission on Discrimination in White Collar Employment*, New York, January 15–18, 1968, esp. pp. 446 and 464, and *Hearings before the United States Equal Employment Opportunity Commission on Utilization of Minority and Women Workers in Certain Major Industries*, Los Angeles, March 12–14, 1969.

167. Ibid., pp. 35, 102, 137.

168. *Hearings before the United States Equal Employment Opportunity Commission on Utilization of Minority and Women Workers in Certain Major Industries*, Houston, Texas, June 2–4, 1970, p. 669.

169. Letter from Willard Wirtz to the President, June 2, 1967, in Lawson, *Civil Rights during Johnson*, Part 2, Reel 7, frames 898–99.

170. Freeman, *Politics of Women's Liberation*, pp. 193–94.

171. Mary Keyserling Oral History, Part 1, pp. 21–22, LBJL.

172. Ibid., p. 35.

173. Ibid., Part 2, p. 3.

174. Judith Hole and Ellen Levine, *Rebirth of Feminism* (New York: Quadrangle Books, 1971), p. 45.

175. Theodore Hershberg, Alan Burstein, Eugene Ericksen, Stephanie Greenberg, and Willam Yancey, "A Tale of Three Cities: Blacks, Immigrants, and Opportunity in Philadelphia, 1850–1880, 1930, 1970," in Theodore Hershberg, ed., *Philadelphia: Work, Space, Family, and Group Experience in the 19th Century* (New York: Oxford University Press, 1981), Table 1, p. 465. In 1960, Philadelphia was 26.7 percent nonwhite (the category for that census year).

176. Memo to Heads of All Agencies from Arthur A. Fletcher, June 27, 1969, reprinted in *Congressional Record*, December 18, 1969, pp. 38, 951.

177. Memo to Heads of All Agencies from Arthur A. Fletcher and John L. Wilks, September 23, 1969, reprinted in ibid., pp. 39, 953.

178. Quoted in Graham, *Civil Rights Era*, pp. 342–43.

179. Mary Ann Millsap, "Sex Equity in Education," in Irene Tinker, ed., *Women in Washington: Advocates for Public Policy* (Beverly Hills: Sage, 1983), pp. 91–119, 94.

180. Freeman, *Politics of Women's Liberation*, p. 195.

181. Bernice Sandler, "A Little Help from Our Government: WEAL and Contract

Compliance," in Alice S. Rossi and Ann Calderwood, eds., *Academic Women on the Move* (New York: Russell Sage Foundation, 1973), pp. 439–62.

182. Ibid., p. 440; Hole and Levine, *Rebirth of Feminism*, p. 320.
183. Freeman, *Politics of Women's Liberation*, p. 195.
184. Emily George, *Martha W. Griffiths* (Washington, D.C.: University Press of America, 1982), p. 185.
185. Sandler, "Help from Our Government," p. 441; Freeman, *Politics of Women's Liberation*, p. 153.
186. Sandler, "Help from Our Government," p. 442.
187. Ibid., p. 456 (Appendix A); Freeman, *Politics of Women's Liberation*, pp. 196–97.
188. Quoted in Hole and Levine, *Rebirth of Feminism*, p. 322.
189. Freeman, *Politics of Women's Liberation*, pp. 196–97.
190. Ibid.
191. President's Task Force on Women's Rights and Responsibilities, *A Matter of Simple Justice* (Washington, D.C.: Government Printing Office, April 1970), p. v.
192. *Time*, July 10, 1972, p. 92.
193. The guidelines are reprinted in *Hearings, Discrimination against Women*, US House of Representatives, 2nd Sess., Special Subcommittee on Education of the Committee on Education and Labor, on Section 805 of H.R. 16098, June 17, 19, 26, 29, 30, July 1, 31, 1970], pp. 148–49; Hole and Levine, *Rebirth of Feminism*, p. 46. Also in June of 1970, "HEW issued a memorandum to all field personnel requiring them to routinely include sex discrimination in all contract compliance investigations," even if there was no complaint. Sandler, "Help from Our Government," p. 443.
194. Memo from Leonard Garment to Ken Cole, June 3, 1970, in Graham, *Civil Rights during Nixon*, Part 1, Reel 23, frame 181.
195. Hole and Levine, *Rebirth of Feminism*, p. 46.
196. The letter was presented by Scott at Edith Green's Special Subcommittee hearings, *Discrimination against Women*, p. 157.
197. Hole and Levine, *Rebirth of Feminism*, p. 46.
198. Sandler, "Help from Our Government," p. 451. On Mink, see Dean Kotlowski, *Nixon's Civil Rights: Politics, Principle, and Policy* (Cambridge, Mass.: Harvard University Press, 2002), p. 241.
199. *New York Times*, July 26, 1970.
200. Kotlowski, *Nixon's Civil Rights*, p. 241.
201. Ibid., p. 242.
202. Hole and Levine, *Rebirth of Feminism*, p. 46.
203. *Hearings, Discrimination against Women*, p. 689.
204. Ibid., pp. 694–95. Though very sensitive to possible differences between women and men, neither Shultz nor any Labor Department official ever questioned whether adult males of every ethnoracial category seek all occupations in equal percentages. Some critics of affirmative action have argued that this assumption, which lies at the heart of the regulations, is faulty. See Thomas Sowell, *Rhetoric or Rights?* (New York: William Morrow, 1984), pp. 53–56.

205. Hearings, *Discrimination against Women,* p. 695.

206. Ibid., p. 696.

207. Kotlowski, *Nixon's Civil Rights,* p. 242.

208. Ibid.

209. Letter from Secretary of Labor to Patsy Mink, October 7, 1970, folder 1/1/ 70–12/31/70, HU White House Subject Files, Box 22, Nixon Presidential Materials Project, National Archives.

210. Letter from Bradley H. Patterson, Assistant to Leonard Garment, to Miss Karen Keesling, February 16, 1971; Letter to Robert Dole from Frederick L. Webber, Special Assistant for Legislative Affairs, n.d.; Letter from Karen Keesling to Leonard Garment, February 5, 1971, folder: 1/1/71–9/30/71, HU White House Subject Files, Box 22, Nixon Presidential Materials Project, National Archives.

211. Sandler, "Help from Our Government," p. 451.

212. Kotlowski, *Nixon's Civil Rights,* p. 244.

213. As late as 1977, the Labor Department was still issuing separate guidelines for women's affirmative action (in this case, for the nearly all-male construction industry). Goals and timetables for the skilled trades were modest—only 6.9 percent women by the third year. Philip S. Foner, *Women and the American Labor Movement* (New York: Free Press, 1982), p. 463.

5. Expansion of Affirmative Action for Minority Capitalists

1. Especially active was the militant leader Roy Innis of the Congress of Racial Equality (CORE), who argued that "blacks must manage and control the institutions that service their areas" as part of his "separatist economics." Innis's vision, for which he was joined by liberals and conservative Republicans, was a model for the Community Self-Determination Act, proposed in 1969 but which failed in part due to conflicts within the black community. This plan would have set up community corporations and development banks to help blacks to gain this control. See Arthur I. Blaustein and Geoffrey Faux, *The Star-Spangled Hustle* (Garden City, N.Y.: Doubleday, 1972), Chapter 4, for an overview. For the CORE and Republican visions, see respectively, Roy Innis, "Separatist Economics: A New Social Contract," in *Black Economic Development,* ed. William F. Haddad and G. Douglas Pugh (Englewood Cliffs, NJ: Prentice-Hall, 1969), pp. 50–59; and John McClaughry, "Black Ownership and National Politics," in ibid., pp. 38–49.

2. Jennifer Lee, *Civility in the City: Blacks, Jews and Koreans in Urban America* (Cambridge, Mass: Harvard University Press, 2002).

3. John D. Skrentny, *The Ironies of Affirmative Action* (Chicago: University of Chicago Press, 1996), Chapter 4.

4. Jonathan J. Bean, *Big Government and Affirmative Action: The Scandalous History of the Small Business Administration* (Lexington: University Press of Kentucky, 2001), p. 43.

5. Howard J. Samuels, "Compensatory Capitalism," in *Black Economic Development,* pp. 60–73; also see Howard Samuels, "How to Even the Odds," *Saturday Review,* August 23, 1969, pp. 22–26; Blaustein and Faux, *Star-Spangled*

Hustle, p. 132; Bean, *Big Government and Affirmative Action,* pp. 65–66. On the origins of the SBA efforts generally, see US Commission on Civil Rights, *Minorities and Women as Government Contractors* (Washington, D.C.: Government Printing Office, May 1975), p. 35; and George La Noue and John C. Sullivan, "Presumptions for Preferences: The Small Business Administration's Decisions on Groups Entitled to Affirmative Action," *Journal of Policy History* 6 (1994): 439–67.

6. Hugh Davis Graham, *The Civil Rights Era: Origins and Development of National Policy* (New York: Oxford University Press, 1990), p. 314.

7. William Welsh, Assistant to the Vice President, March 26, 1968, "A National Program for Promoting Minority Entrepreneurs," pp. 4, 19, folder Minority Entrepreneurship (1), Gaither Papers, Box 21, Lyndon B. Johnson Library (LBJL).

8. Dean Kotlowski, "Black Power—Nixon Style: The Nixon Administration and Minority Business Enterprise," *Business History Review* 72 (Autumn 1998): 412–19.

9. Maurice H. Stans, "Nixon's Economic Policy toward Minorities," in *Richard M. Nixon: Politician, President, Administrator,* ed. Leon Friedman and William F. Levantrosser (New York: Greenwood Press, 1991), pp. 239–46, 239–40.

10. Blaustein and Faux, *Star-Spangled Hustle,* p. 16.

11. Skrentny, *Ironies of Affirmative Action,* p. 101.

12. Memo to the President from Howard Samuels, June 21, 1968, Subject: Proposed Response to the Poor People's Campaign, folder Minority Entrepreneurship (2), Gaither Papers, Box 21, LBJL.

13. On Abernathy's universalist goals, see Ralph David Abernathy, *And the Walls Came Tumbling Down* (New York: Harper and Row, 1989), pp. 414, 512. His memoirs do not even contain an index entry for affirmative action. Though Abernathy did support Indian claims that nineteenth-Century treaties be honored, he spurned demands of Mexican American leaders for bilingual education because it violated his desire to pursue issues of common interest. Ibid., pp. 518, 512.

14. Samuels claims that Johnson encouraged the color-conscious efforts in other writings. See Samuels, "Compensatory Capitalism," p. 71, and Samuels, "Even the Odds," p. 23. Congress later attributed the SBA's efforts to the Kerner Commission and executive orders by Johnson and Nixon, but there is no record of a Johnson executive order calling on the SBA to establish minority-capitalism programs that I could find. Senate Report 95-1070, Amending the Small Business Act and the Small Business Investment Act of 1958, 95th Cong., 2d Sess. (May 17, 1978), p. 14.

15. Memo from Howard J. Samuels to the President, June 22, 1968, folder Minority Entrepreneurship (2), Gaither Papers, Box 21, LBJL. On Samuels's efforts, also see John Lescott-Leszczynski, *The History of US Ethnic Policy and Its Impact on European Ethnics* (Boulder: Westeview Press, 1984), p. 143.

16. Kotlowski, "Black Power—Nixon Style," pp. 409–45, 416.

17. US Commission on Civil Rights, *Minorities and Women as Government Contractors,* p. 31, citing Executive Order 11518, 3 C.F.R. 907.

18. Hugh Davis Graham, "Affirmative Action for Immigrants? The Unintended

Consequences of Reform," in John Skrentny, ed., *Color Lines* (Chicago: University of Chicago Press, 2001), pp. 53–70, 55; La Noue and Sullivan, "Presumptions for Preferences," p. 442.

19. Senate Report 95-1070, p. 14.
20. US Commission on Civil Rights, *Minorities and Women as Government Contractors,* p. 37.
21. Kotlowski, "Black Power—Nixon Style," p. 426.
22. *Wall Street Journal,* 6 March 1969.
23. *Wall Street Journal,* 12 March 1969.
24. Kotlowski, "Black Power—Nixon Style," p. 421.
25. US Commission on Civil Rights, *Minorities and Women as Government Contractors,* p. 30.
26. Julian Bond, "Foreward," in *Black Business Enterprise,* ed. Ronald W. Bailey (New York: Basic Books, 1971), pp. vii–xi, x.
27. Kotlowski, "Black Power—Nixon Style," pp. 417–18, 427–28.
28. Skrentny, *Ironies of Affirmative Action,* p. 193.
29. Memorandum to John D. Ehrlichman from Maurice H. Stans, September 17, 1971, in Joan Hoff-Wilson, ed., *Papers of the Nixon White House* (Bethesda, Md.: University Publications of America, 1989), Part 6a, Fiche 173, frames 46–51.
30. Quoted in Gerald S. Strober and Deborah Strober, *Nixon: An Oral History of His Presidency* (New York: Harper Collins, 1994), p. 112.
31. Statement about a National Program for Minority Business Enterprise, March 5, 1969, *Public Papers of the Presidents of the United States, Richard Nixon, 1969* (Washington, D.C.: Government Printing Office, 1971), pp. 197–98; Executive Order 11,458, 34 *Federal Register,* p. 4937.
32. Memo from H. R. Haldeman to Mr. Dent, October 31, 1969, paraphrasing Nixon, in Hugh Davis Graham, ed., *Civil Rights during the Nixon Administration, 1969–1973,* (Bethesda, Md.: University Publications of America, 1989), Part 1, Reel 2, frame 129. Also see followup memo from Harry Dent to Ken Cole, November 3, 1969, in ibid., Part 1, Reel 2, frame 131. "[W]e are making progress among Mexican-Americans."
33. Memo from Martin Castillo to Herb Klein, December 17, 1969; Proposed statement upon signing S740 (Safire), December 29, 1969. See the series of form letters to be sent with signing pens to those who took part, dated January 16, 1970, all in folder EX FG 145, Inter-Agency Committee on Mexican-American Affairs/Cabinet Committee on Opportunities for Spanish Speaking Americans as of 12/30/69, Box 1, Nixon Presidential Materials Project (NPMP), National Archives.
34. "Statement on Signing the Bill Establishing the Cabinet Committee on Opportunities for Spanish-Speaking People, December 31, 1969," in *Public Papers of the Presidents of the United States, Richard Nixon 1969* (Washington, D.C.: Government Printing Office, 1971), pp. 1048–49; "Statement by the President," December 31, 1969, in Graham, *Civil Rights during Nixon,* Part 1, Reel 4, frame 423.
35. Memo from John Ehrlichman to the President, April 20, 1970, folder: CCOSS

File, White House Central Files (WHCF), Staff Member and Office Files (SMOF), Robert H. Finch, Box 15, NPMP, National Archives.

36. Memo to David Parker from Carlos d. Conde via Herb Klein, April 18, 1972; Memo for Herb Klein from David Parker, April 11, 1972; and Schedule Proposal from Herbert G. Klein via Dwight L. Chapin, March 9, 1972, in Graham, *Civil Rights during Nixon*, Part 1, Reel 4, frames 86, 88, 91, 92.

37. Peter Skerry, *Counting on the Census?* (Washington, D.C.: Brookings Institution, 2000), pp. 37–38. The move backfired somewhat. Nixon officials arranged to prevent publication of a Census Bureau report that showed that while Latinos had higher incomes than blacks, their education was worse and their incomes and education both lagged behind non-Latino whites. They believed that report could be used to criticize the administration's efforts to help Latinos, and that it could be seen as trying to exacerbate conflict between blacks and Latinos. *Hearings before the Select Committee on Presidential Campaign Activities*, US Senate, 93rd Cong., 1st Sess., Watergate and Related Activities, Phase III: Campaign Financing, Book 13, Washington, D.C., November, 1973, p. 5324. Also see ibid., pp. 5622, 5626, 5627, 5632.

38. "The President's News Conference of May 1, 1971," in *Public Papers of the Presidents of the United States: Richard M. Nixon, 1971* (Washington, D.C.: Government Printing Office, 1972), p. 613.

39. Memo from George Grassmuck to Clark MacGregor and George Shultz, May 10, 1971, in Graham, *Civil Rights during Nixon*, Part 1, Reel 3, frame 872.

40. Memo to Clark MacGregor from William Timmons, May 12, 1971 and attached Memo for Clark MacGregor and George Shultz from George Grassmuck, May 10, 1971, in Graham, *Civil Rights during Nixon*, Part 1, Reel 3, frame 871–73.

41. Memo to Ken Smith from George Grassmuck, July 30, 1971 and attached, "On the Spanish Speakers Caveats and Concerns," in folder WHCF: SMOF ROBERT H. FINCH GRASSMUCK, GEORGE L. -CCOSS [CFOA 328], Box 16, WHCF, SMOF Robert H. Finch, NPMP, National Archives.

42. "Confidential" untitled, undated, unauthored [probably Charles Colson] report in Graham, *Civil Rights during Nixon*, Part I, Reel 3, frames 902–3.

43. Draft minutes of Cabinet Committee meeting on Spanish-speaking, Remarks of the President, August 5, 1971, in ibid.

44. See the August 30, 1971 letters contained in folder Minutes of Meetings of the CCOSS [1 of 2], Box 17, WHCF, SMOF Robert H. Finch, NPMP, National Archives.

45. Memo to John D. Ehrlichman from Maurice H. Stans, September 17, 1971, in Hoff-Wilson, *Papers of the Nixon White House*, Part 6a, Fiche 173, frames 46–51.

46. Memo to the President from George Shultz, September 17, 1971, with handwritten comments by Nixon, in ibid., frames 32–38.

47. "Special Message to the Congress Urging Expansion of the Minority Business Enterprise Program, October 13, 1971," in *Public Papers of the Presidents of the United States: Richard M. Nixon, 1971*, pp. 1041–46.

48. Letter to Father Theodore Hesburgh (chair of the US Commission on Civil

Rights) from Leonard Garment, April 15, 1971, in Graham, *Civil Rights during Nixon,* Part 1, Reel 3, frame 290. Maurice Stans claimed the procurement for minority businesses reached $66 million for fiscal year 1971, and that government grants, loans, and guarantees for minorities increased from $200 million in 1969 to $550 million in 1971, and the number of franchises owned by minorities increased from 313 to 1,100 in those years, including an increase in auto dealerships from 14 to 87. Memorandum to John D. Ehrlichman from Maurice H. Stans, September 17, 1971, in Hoff-Wilson, *Papers of the Nixon White House,* Part 6a, Fiche 173, frames 46–51.

49. "Confidential," untitled, undated report on Latinos, in Graham, *Civil Rights during Nixon,* Part 1, Reel 3, frames 901–52, specifically 917–20.

50. Other suggested policies included HUD programs and public housing, which Colson said were not reaching Latinos in adequate percentages; he suggested a kind of affirmative action, or "an administrative goal of the number of housing units that can be reasonably provided to Spanish-speaking families under federal programs and that a time-frame be set up to fulfill that goal." Colson also pushed bilingual education, as discussed in Chapter 7. Memo from Charles W. Colson to John Ehrlichman, December 20, 1971, in ibid., frames 899–900. A 1972 campaign strategy memo justified allocating 33 percent of the next decade's $2 billion for minority contracts to Latinos not because Latino leaders demanded it, but simply because 33 percent of minorities were Latino. "Confidential," untitled, undated report on Latinos, in ibid., frames 901–52, specifically 917–20.

51. See the three memos to Ed Morgan from Ken Cole, January 10, 1972, on education, housing, and economic development, in ibid., frames 896–98.

52. *Hearings,* Watergate and Related Activities, pp. 5274–77.

53. Ibid., p. 5279. An original memo describing this strategy is reproduced in ibid., p. 5532.

54. Memo to Bob Brown, Bill Marumoto, Paul Jones, and Alex Armendariz from Fred Malek, March 3, 1972, in ibid., p. 5542.

55. All contained in the Weekly Activity Report for the Spanish Speaking (for Chuck Colson and Fred Malek from Bill Marumoto) on the cited dates, in ibid., pp. 5549, 5557, 5581, 5576.

56. Letter from Alex Armendariz to Frederick Malek, May 31, 1972, folder Ethnics [1 of 3], Box 62, White House Special Files (WHSF), SMOF, Charles W. Colson Papers, NPMP, National Archives. *Hearings,* Watergate and Related Activities, p. 5314.

57. Ibid., p. 5365.

58. Memo to Chuck Colson from Bill Marumoto, March 17, 1972, in ibid., p. 5543. This meeting involved officials from the Office of Economic Opportunity, formerly the cornerstone of Johnson's War on Poverty.

59. Blaustein and Faux's journalistic account describes a variety of approaches of giving minorities more control over their economic destinies and lists several groups or individuals calling for such things, and includes a Mexican American group, the Southwest Council of La Raza. Blaustein and Faux also describe a conference in December 1968 to discuss Roy Innis's Community Self-Determi-

nation Act, for which there were "Mexican-American organizers." They only mention the involvement of Alex Mercure, "director of a migrant worker education program in New Mexico," however. Blaustein and Faux, *Star-Spangled Hustle,* pp. 12, 46, 56.

60. Letter to President Nixon from Louis M. Cortez, State Chairman, California GI Forum, August 27, 1969, in Graham, *Civil Rights during Nixon,* Part 1, Reel 20, frame 92.

61. Memo to John Ehrlichman from Martin G. Castillo, September 20, 1969, in ibid., frame 82.

62. Letter to the Honorable Richard M. Nixon from Robert E. Gonzales, Board of Supervisors, San Francisco, August 21, 1970, in Graham, ibid., frames 96–97.

63. Press Release, November 5, 1970, folder Cabinet Committee on Opportunities for the Spanish-speaking, Box 13, WHSF: SMOF, Papers of John Dean, NPMP, National Archives.

64. Letter to the President from Herman Badillo and Edward R. Roybal, August 9, 1971, in Graham, *Civil Rights during Nixon,* Part 1, Reel 3, frames 852–53.

65. Administratively Confidential Memo to Ken Cole from Dan Kingsley, August 15, 1972, Memo to the President from Ken Cole, August 29, 1972, in Hoff-Wilson, *Papers of the Nixon White House,* Part 6a, Fiche 236, frames 45, 47.

66. Memo to IMAGE Chapter Chairmen and National Executive Board Members from Ed Valenzuela, National President, IMAGE, n.d., in Graham, *Civil Rights during Nixon,* Part 1, Reel 19, frames 472–73.

67. Other talking points instructed Nixon to show his "desire to improve economic development opportunities for the Hispanic with emphasis on the OMBE efforts at the Department of Commerce" while December's points included "increased involvement of the Spanish-speaking in economic development through SBA and OMBE actions as well as by awarding more '8a' contracts to Hispanic firms." Schedule Proposal from Anne Armstrong via David Parker, August 16, 1973, in ibid., Part 1, Reel 4, frames 875–76; Schedule Proposal from Anne Armstrong via David Parker, December 11, 1973, in folder EX FG 145, Cabinet Committee on Opportunities for Spanish-speaking People, 1/1/73–[8/9/74], CCOSS Papers, Box 1, NPMP, National Archives.

68. Letter to Anne Armstrong from Margaret Cruz, November 20, 1973, in Graham, *Civil Rights during Nixon,* Part 1, Reel 19, frames 446–7.

69. Letter to Anne Armstrong from Manual Banda, Chairman, Mexican American Issues Conference, November 20, 1973, and attached Resolution from the "Affirmative Action in Government Employment Workshop," October 21, 1973, in ibid., frames 448–50.

70. Confidential Discussion Summary, January 29, 1974, and Memo to Anne Armstrong from Fred Slight, February 4, 1974, in ibid., Reel 45, frames 883–89, 890.

71. Memo to Anne Armstrong from Ken Cole, June 20, 1974, in ibid., Reel 19, frames 539–44, 557–58.

72. Memo to David Parker from Anne Armstrong, April 10, 1973; Note to "Dave" from "Mary R.", n.d.; Letter to President Nixon from Fidel Gonzalez Jr., California State LULAC Director, March 29, 1973, in ibid., frames 398–403.

73. *Pasadena Star News,* September 2, 1973, in folder EX FG 145, Cabinet Committee on Opportunities for Spanish-speaking People, as of 1/1/73, Box 1, NPMP, National Archives.

74. La Noue and Sullivan, "Presumptions for Preferences," p. 445.

75. US Commission on Civil Rights, *Minorities and Women as Government Contractors,* pp. 32–35. The National Association of Women Business Owners (NAWBO) did not push for women in the SBA program because they believed that "technical and price competition is paramount to learning how to succeed in the procurement system and further because NAWBO believes such an action is politically infeasible." Laura Henderson, "Testimony of the National Association of Women Business Owners," in US Commission on Civil Rights, *Selected Affirmative Action Topics in Employment and Business Set-Asides: A Consultation/Hearing of the U.S. Commission on Civil Rights, March 6–7, 1985* (Washington, D.C.: Government Printing Office, 1985), pp. 252–62, 260. However, a different group, the National Association of Women Federal Contractors, did push the issue and won the Women's Business Ownership Act in 1988. It created a program similar to the 8(a) program but targeted at women. La Noue and Sullivan, "Presumptions for Preferences," p. 453. In 1994, Congress passed the Federal Acquisition Streamlining Act of 1994. This law set a goal of 5 percent of federal contracts for small, women-owned business enterprises.

76. Hugh Davis Graham, *Collision Course* (New York: Oxford University Press, 2002), p. 89.

77. 42 U.S.C. §6705(f)(2).

78. *Congressional Record,* February 23, 1977, p. 5097; February 24, 1977, pp. 5327–31; March 10, 1977, pp. 7155–56; John W. Sroka, "Minority and Women's Business Set-Asides: An Appropriate Response to Discrimination?" in US Commission on Civil Rights, *Selected Affirmative Action Topics in Employment and Business Set-Asides: A Consultation/Hearing of the United States Commission on Civil Rights, March 6–7, 1985,* vol. 1 (Washington, D.C.: Government Printing Office, 1985), pp. 90–108, 92; La Noue and Sullivan, "Presumptions for Preferences," p. 442.

79. La Noue and Sullivan, "Presumptions for Preferences," pp. 442–43.

80. Ibid., p. 464, n. 19. Nixon had left out Asians in one of his executive orders as well. In Executive Order 11625, issued on October 13, 1971, Nixon did some reorganizing and shuffling in the minority-capitalism program. He also defined a "minority business enterprise" as one that is "owned or controlled by one or more socially or economically disadvantaged persons. Such disadvantage may arise from cultural, racial, [or] chronic economic circumstances as background or other similar causes." This included, but was not limited to, "Negroes, Puerto Ricans, Spanish-speaking Americans, American Indians, Eskimos and Aleuts." 36 *Federal Register* pp. 19,967–70.

81. Graham, "Affirmative Action for Immigrants?" p. 55; George La Noue and John Sullivan, "Deconstructing Affirmative Action Categories," in Skrentny, *Color Lines,* pp. 71–86, 81.

82. Charles V. Dale, *A Brief Legal Overview of Federal Affirmative Action Statutes*

and Executive Orders (Washington, D.C.: Congressional Research Service, March 8, 1995).

83. La Noue and Sullivan, "Presumptions for Preferences," p. 462.
84. The 1960 census asked: "Is this person—White, Negro, American Indian, Japanese, Chinese, Filipino, Hawaiian, Part Hawaiian, Aleut, Eskimo, (etc.)?" The 1970 census asked respondents to check a race category, and included options for Chinese, Japanese, Korean, and Hawaiian.

6. Affirmative Admissions, Diversity, and the Supreme Court

1. John R. Hammond, "Affirmative Action in Historical Perspective," in Mildred García, ed., *Affirmative Action's Testament of Hope: Strategies for a New Era in Higher Education* (Albany: State University of New York Press, 1997), pp. 19–46, 31.
2. Robert M. O'Neil, "Preferential Admissions: Equalizing the Access of Minority Groups to Higher Education," *Yale Law Journal* 80 (1971): 699–768, 718.
3. John Aubrey Douglass, "Anatomy of Conflict: The Making and Unmaking of Affirmative Action at the University of California," in John Skrentny, ed., *Color Lines* (Chicago: University of Chicago Press, 2001), pp. 118–44, 125.
4. *Newsweek*, May 5, 1969, p. 28.
5. Ibid.
6. Ibid., p. 26; Terry Anderson, *The Movement and Sixties* (New York: Oxford University Press, 1995), p. 300; Nathan Glazer, *Ethnic Dilemmas, 1964–1982* (Cambridge, Mass.: Harvard University Press, 1983), pp. 11–13.
7. *Time*, May 9, 1969, pp. 22–23.
8. See Glazer's discussion of the "internal colonialsim" analogy in Glazer, *Ethnic Dilemmas*. Also see William Wei, *The Asian American Movement* (Philadelphia: Temple University Press, 1992). On the Vietnam War in the context of American race and ethnic history, see Gary Gerstle, *American Crucible: Race and Nation in the Twentieth Century* (Princeton: Princeton University Press, 2001), pp. 313–27.
9. Anderson, *The Movement and the Sixties*, pp. 294–99; University of California, San Diego, *Third College Twentieth Anniversary: Diversity, Justice, Imagination* (San Diego: UCSD Publications Office, 1990), pp. 6, 14–16, 28, 54.
10. Yen Le Espiritu, *Asian American Panethnicity: Bridging Institutions and Identities* (Philadelphia: Temple University Press, 1992), p. 44.
11. *Newsweek*, May 19, 1969, p. 69. Also see *Time*, May 16, 1969; *Newsweek*, June 9, 1969, p. 55; *Time*, June 6, 1969, p. 56.
12. *Newsweek*, May 5, 1969, p. 28.
13. As Peter Holmes, the director of the Office for Civil Rights (OCR), told a House subcommittee in 1974, though the OCR collected data on the admission of official minorities at universities, "the great increase in minority enrollment in institutions of higher education that has been witnessed in recent years derives, in great part, from affirmative admissions and assistance programs undertaken for minority students on a voluntary basis." *Hearings before the Special*

Subcommittee on Education of the Committee on Education and Labor, House of Representatives, 93rd Cong., 2nd Sess., Part 2A, Civil Rights Obligations, August 9, 1974, p. 72–75. The Department of Health, Education and Welfare (HEW) issued regulations on July 5, 1973 that specifically authorized affirmative action, even if an institution has not been guilty of discriminating. 45 C.F.R. 80.3(b)(6)(ii).

14. *Hearings,* Civil Rights Obligations, pp. 72–75. Educational institutions did not have to fill out EEO-1 forms until 1972, when Title VII was amended to expand coverage.

15. Carnegie Commission on Higher Education, *A Chance to Learn: An Action Agenda for Equal Opportunity in Higher Education, A Special Report and Recommendations* (New York: Mcgraw-Hill, 1970), p. 2. The report recommended open access at the undergraduate level and that "all institutions accept responsibility to serve the disadvantaged minorities at each of the levels at which they provide training, and that universities accept a special responsibility to serve a substantially greater representation of currently disadvantaged minorities in their graduate programs." Further, programs of ethnic studies should be instituted, though these should include "Southern Appalachian" along with black, Indian, Mexican American, and Puerto Rican. Ibid., pp. 14–18. Also see O'Neil, "Preferential Admissions," p. 750.

16. *Hearings,* Civil Rights Obligations, p. 209. Testimony of Representative Patricia Schroeder (D–CO).

17. Amicus Brief of the Law School Admission Council in *DeFunis v. Odegaard,* October Term, 1973, reprinted in *Hearings before the Special Subcommittee of Education of the Committee on Education and Labor,* House of Representatives, 93rd Cong., 2nd Sess., on H.R. 14673 to Amend Part D of Title IX of the Higher Education Act, Legal Education Opportunities, June 5, 1974, pp. 59–69, p. 60.

18. Joel Dreyfuss and Charles Lawrence III, *The Bakke Case: The Politics of Inequality* (New York: Harcourt, Brace, Jovanovich, 1979), p. 19.

19. Allan P. Sindler, *Bakke, DeFunis, and Minority Admissions: The Quest of Opportunity* (New York: Longman, 1978), p. 48.

20. US Commission on Civil Rights, *Toward Equal Educational Opportunity: Affirmative Admissions Programs at Law and Medical Schools* (Washington, D.C.: US Commission on Civil Rights Clearinghouse Publication 55, June 1978), p. 67.

21. The definition of disadvantaged came from the Higher Education Act, tit. iv, subpart 4, section 417(B)(b). It targeted low-income students with "cultural needs." In this view, persistent societal patterns lead to low aspirations and low self-esteem, lack of access to information and counseling for postsecondary careers, and isolation (physical or social) from the mainstream of society. This definition could have included poor southern whites or some European ethnic groups, such as Italians or Poles, but the program did not. Charles Saunders, acting assistant secretary of education, explained more simply that "minority groups and persons from disadvantaged backgrounds are woefully underrepresented in the legal profession and we believe a special effort must be made to

correct this imbalance." His statistics showed that only slightly more than 1 percent of the nation's lawyers were black and less than that were Latino, Asian
American, or American Indian. *Hearings,* Legal Education Opportunities,
pp. 11, 4.

22. Ibid., p. 17.

23. US Commission on Civil Rights, *Toward Equal Educational Opportunity,* p. 62.

24. Susan Welch and John Gruhl, *Affirmative Action and Minority Enrollments in
Medical and Law Schools* (Ann Arbor: University of Michigan Press, 1998),
p. 55, citing John S. Wellington and Pilar Montero, *Journal of Medical Education* 53 (August 1978): 633–39.

25. Robert O'Neil, *Discriminating against Discrimination: Preferential Admissions
and the DeFunis Case* (Bloomingtion: Indiana University Press, 1975), pp. 66–
67.

26. Welch and Gruhl, *Affirmative Action and Minority Enrollments,* p. 55, citing
John S. Wellington and Pilar Montero, *Journal of Medical Education* 53 (August 1978): 633–39.

27. See *DeFunis v. Odegaard,* 507 P.2d 1169, 1193 (1973).

28. Survey research by Susan Welch and John Gruhl asked 1970s' admissions officers what factors led them to institute affirmative admissions. Pressure from
professional organizations, rather than from students or civil-rights groups, appeared to be most important. The survey asked respondents if they felt pressure
to take race into account in admissions, and the source of that pressure. The
largest portion of medical school officers, 32 percent, felt pressure from an outside group such as the AAMC, which had power over accreditation; 24 percent felt pressure from accreditation agencies generally. Minority groups or student groups figured much lower in the survey. Forty-six percent of law schools
felt pressure from some outside group, and 31 percent identified accreditation
agencies. The term "pressure", however, is misleading. This outside "pressure"
was usually seen as welcome assistance by the admissions officers. Welch and
Gruhl, *Affirmative Action and Minority Enrollments,* p. 80.

29. *DeFunis v. Odegaard,* 507 P.2d at 1176.

30. *Hearings,* Civil Rights Obligations, p. 443.

31. Prepared Statement of Frederick M. Hart, President, Law School Admission
Council, in ibid., p. 402.

32. US Commission on Civil Rights, *Toward Equal Educational Opportunity,* p. 59.

33. Ibid., p. 60.

34. Ibid., p. 64.

35. Ibid., p. 67.

36. Ibid., p. 76.

37. Ibid., p. 76.

38. Ibid., p. 77.

39. 416 U.S. 312 (1974).

40. 417 F. Supp. 377 (D.D.C. 1976).

41. 39 N.Y.2d 326; 348 N.E.2d (1976).

42. 98 S. Ct. 2733 (1978).

43. Sindler, *Bakke, DeFunis,* p. 74.

44. Ibid., at 2745, 2746.
45. Ibid., at 2749.
46. Ibid., at 2751. Powell, at 2752 n. 37, cited favorably the view of Justice Douglas in *DeFunis v. Odegaard,* 416 U.S. 312, 337–40, 94 S. Ct. 1704, 1716–1717 (1974), in a dissenting opinion. Douglas considered group reservations to be "fraught with . . . dangers, for one must immediately determine which groups are to receive such favored treatment and which are to be excluded, the proportions of the class that are to be allocated to each, and even the criteria by which to determine whether an individual is a member of a favored group." Douglas argued that the state of Washington, which gave preferences only to Filipinos but not Japanese or Chinese Americans, would not solve its problems by including the latter two groups to make up for a history of discrimination, "for then Norwegians and Swedes, Poles and Italians, Puerto Ricans and Hungarians, and all other groups which form this diverse Nation would have just complaints."
47. 98 S. Ct. at 2758 n. 45.
48. Ibid., at 2755.
49. Ibid., p. 2758.
50. Ibid., at 2762.
51. Ibid., at 2762.
52. Ibid., at 2787.
53. Ibid., at 2751.
54. Ibid., at 2783, n. 35.
55. Ibid., at 2802.
56. The pressure, even if implicit, applied by accrediting agencies is what the organizational sociologists Paul DiMaggio and Walter Powell call "coercive isomorphism," where many organizations change to a new practice or form because of some outside influence (as opposed to pure market rationality). Paul J. DiMaggio and Walter W. Powell, "The Iron Cage Revisited: Institutional Isomorphism and Collective Rationality in Organizational Fields," *American Sociological Review* 48 (April 1983): 147–60.
57. Dana Y. Takagi, *The Retreat from Race: Asian-American Admissions and Racial Politics* (New Brunswick: Rutgers University Press, 1992).
58. Christopher Edley's otherwise excellent book on affirmation action does the same thing. In a very rare discussion of whether white ethnic groups should be targeted, he downplays the possibility with the bizarre example of Swedish Americans, a group always favored in immigration law (see Chapter 2), thus ignoring the more plausible candidates of Italians, Jews, Hungarians, and Poles. Christopher Edley Jr., *Not All Black and White* (New York: Hill and Wang, 1996), p. 175.

7. Bilingual Education and Language Rights

1. Christine H. Rossell and Keith Baker, *Bilingual Education in Massachusetts* (Boston: Pioneer Institute, 1996).
2. There were important local efforts, mostly in German, where Germans formed large portions of the community. See, for example, David B. Tyack, *The One Best*

System: A History of American Urban Education (Cambridge, Mass.: Harvard University Press, 1974), pp. 106–7; and Steven L. Schlossman, "Is There an American Tradition of Bilingual Education? German in the Public Elementary Schools, 1840–1919," *American Journal of Education* 92 (February 1983): 139–86; 148. Unlike modern bilingual education, Schlossman concludes that the Germans "never looked seriously to the public schools to preserve their powerful sense of cultural identity *(Deutschtum)*," that "Germans in America never viewed school language policy as the key to their children's overall adjustment to life in a new society," and points out that the programs were under constant attack.

3. On Franklin and Roosevelt and the language culture wars, see Stephen T. Wagner, "The Historical Background of Bilingualism and Biculturalism in the United States," in *The New Bilingualism: An American Dilemma,* ed. Martin Ridge (Los Angeles: University of Southern California Press, 1981), pp. 29–52, 30, 37–39; and Rebecca D. Freeman, *Bilingual Education and Social Change* (Philadelphia: Multilingual Matters, 1998), p. 37.

4. Robert H. Wiebe, *The Search for Order, 1877–1920* (New York: Hill and Wang, 1967), pp. 58, 156–57; Alan Dawley, *Struggles for Justice: Social Responsibility and the Liberal State* (Cambridge, Mass.: Harvard University Press, 1991), p. 115; Morton Keller, *Regulating a New Society: Public Policy and Social Change in America, 1900–1933* (Cambridge, Mass.: Harvard University Press, 1994), pp. 240–41; Richard Hofstadter, *Age of Reform* (New York: Vintage Books, 1955), p. 181; Wagner, "Background of Bilingualism," p. 42; John Higham, *Strangers in the Land: Patterns of American Nativism, 1860–1925* (New Brunswick: Rutgers University Press, 1994 [1955]), pp. 234–63.

5. Peter Haas, "Introduction: Epistemic Communities and International Policy Coordination," *International Organization* 46 (1992): 1–36.

6. Hugh Davis Graham, *The Uncertain Triumph: Federal Education Policy in the Kennedy and Johnson Years* (Chapel Hill: University of North Carolina Press, 1984), p. xvii.

7. Sidney W. Tiedt, *The Role of the Federal Government in Education* (New York: Oxford University Press, 1966); Frank J. Munger and Richard F. Fenno Jr., *National Politics and Federal Aid to Education* (Syracuse: Syracuse University Press, 1962); and Gilbert E. Smith, *The Limits of Reform: Politics and Federal Aid to Education, 1937–1950* (New York: Garland Publishing, 1982).

8. James L. Sundquist, *Politics and Policy: The Eisenhower, Kennedy and Johnson Years* (Washington, D.C.: Brookings Institution, 1968), p. 189.

9. See Paul Pierson's use of the policy irrationalities concept as limiting the retrenchment of welfare policy. Paul Pierson, *Dismantling the Welfare State?* (New York: Cambridge University Press, 1994), pp. 24–25.

10. Tiedt, *Federal Government in Education,* pp. 25–26; Eugene Eidenberg and Roy D. Morey, *An Act of Congress: The Legislative Process and the Making of Education Policy* (New York: Norton, 1969), p. 17; Norman C. Thomas, *Education in National Politics* (New York: David McKay, 1975), p. 20.

11. Stephen K. Bailey and Edith K. Mosher, *ESEA: The Office of Education Administers a Law* (Syracuse: Syracuse University Press, 1968), p. 4; Philip Meranto,

The Politics of Federal Aid to Education in 1965: A Study in Political Innovation (Syracuse: Syracuse University Press, 1967), p. 14.

12. Meranto, *Education in 1965,* p. 43.
13. Barbara Barksdale Clowse, *Brainpower for the Cold War: The Sputnik Crisis and the National Defense Education Act of 1958* (Westport, Conn.: Greenwood Press, 1981), pp. 9, 59, 63.
14. Sundquist, *Politics and Policy,* p. 175; Clowse, *Brainpower for the Cold War,* pp. 25–27.
15. Thomas, *Education in National Politics,* p. 24.
16. Oral History Collection of the Association of Former Members of Congress, Edith Green, pp. 62, 67, Library of Congress.
17. Sundquist, *Politics and Policy,* p. 179; Tyack, *One Best System,* pp. 275–76.
18. Tiedt, *Federal Government in Education,* p. 30.
19. Andersson, "Bilingual Education: The American Experience," p. 430.
20. Heinz Kloss, *The American Bilingual Tradition* (Rowley, Mass.: Newbury House, 1977), p. 35; Jose E. Vega, *Education, Politics and Bilingualism in Texas* (Washington, D.C.: University Press of America, 1983), pp. 34–35.
21. Kloss, *Bilingual Tradition,* pp. 35–36.
22. Clowse, *Brain Power for the Cold War,* pp. 56–57.
23. Ibid., pp. 151–59.
24. Arnold H. Leibowitz, "Language Policy in the United States," in Hernan LaFontaine, Barry Persky, and Leonard H. Golubchick, eds., *Bilingual Education* (Wayne, N.J.: Avery Publishing, 1978,), pp. 3–15, 8.
25. Donald Bruce Johnson and Kirk H. Porter, *National Party Platforms, 1940–1972* (Urbana: University of Illinois Press, 1973), pp. 614, 576.
26. Graham, *Uncertain Triumph,* p. 5.
27. Ibid., p. 71.
28. Eidenberg and Morey, *Act of Congress,* p. 34.
29. Edwin Amenta, *Bold Relief* (Princeton: Princeton University Press, 1998).
30. Graham, *Uncertain Triumph,* p. 51.
31. Bailey and Mosher, *ESEA,* p. 27. Meanwhile, poverty policy was moving toward education policy. Johnson's landmark Economic Opportunity Act of 1964 contained provisions to aid the education of poor children, creating the Office of Economic Opportunity and the popular Headstart program for preschoolers. Ibid., p. 33; Meranto, *Education in 1965,* pp. 15–16.
32. Bailey and Mosher, *ESEA,* p. 27; Graham, *Uncertain Triumph,* p. 76.
33. Graham, *Uncertain Triumph,* p. 129.
34. UNESCO, *The Use of Vernacular Languages in Education: Monographs on Fundamental Education, VIII* (UNESCO, 1953), quoted in Andersson and Boyer, *Bilingual Schooling in the United States,* vol. 1, p. 44.
35. Andersson and Boyer, *Bilingual Schooling in the United States,* vol. 1, p. 48.
36. *Foreign Languages in Primary Education: The Teaching of Foreign or Second Languages to Younger Children,* ed. H. H. Stern. Report on an International Meeting of Experts, April 1962 (Hamburg: International Studies in Education, UNESCO Institute for Education, 1963). The report offered psychological,

neurological, social, political, and economic grounds for early native-language teaching.

37. Theodore Andersson, "A New Focus on the Bilingual Child," in *Modern Language Journal* 49, no. 3 (March 1965): 659–664, 661.

38. Jose E. Vega, *Education, Politics and Bilingualism in Texas* (Washington, D.C.: University Press of America, 1983), p. 28.

39. Gil Loescher and John A. Scanlan, *Calculated Kindness: Refugees and America's Half-Open Door* (New York: Free Press, 1986).

40. William Francis Mackey and Von Nieda Beebe, *Bilingual Schools for a Bicultural Community: Miami's Adaptation to the Cuban Refugees* (Rowley, Mass.: Newbury House, 1977), pp. 140–41.

41. Ibid., p. 54. The generosity of the government to the Cubans would breed resentment among blacks in Florida. An October 13, 1965 letter to the mayor of Miami, Robert King High, from Donald Wheeler Jones (president of the Miami branch of the NAACP) complained about losing jobs to the Cubans. Jones explained that "we feel . . . that the Federal Government must exercise its responsibilities toward the economically oppressed of this community as well as toward the politically oppressed of Cuba. The average Negro citizen of this community who lost his job to a Cuban has, by and large, borne his burden in silence as a sacrificial lamb for the extension of freedom and democracy to refugees from another land." National Security File, Box 30, folder Cuba-Refugees 1/63–1/65, Lyndon B. Johnson Library (LBJL). Also see Garry Wills, *Nixon Agonistes: The Crisis of the Self-Made Man* (Boston: Houghton Mifflin, 1970), pp. 313–16.

42. Mackey and Beebe, *Bilingual Schools for a Bicultural Community*, p. 58.

43. Ibid., p. 141. Also see Theodore Andersson, "Bilingual Education: The American Experience," *Modern Language Journal* 51 (1971): 427–440, p. 428.

44. Andersson, "Bilingual Education: The American Experience," p. 429; Theodore Andersson and Mildred Boyer, *Bilingual Schooling in the United States,* vol. I (Austin: Southwest Educational Development Laboratory, 1970), p. 19.

45. Andersson and Boyer, *Bilingual Schooling in the United States,* vol. 1, p. 20. In the case of Laredo, Texas, a new superintendent, Harold C. Brantley, brought bilingual education to the district when he came in 1962. Encouraged by Andersson, Brantley also went to Florida to observe the program for Cubans. Robert L. Hardgrave Jr. and Santiago Hinojosa, *The Politics of Bilingual Education: A Study of Four Southwest Texas Communities* (Manchaca, Tex.: Sterling Swift, 1975), pp. 16–17.

46. The article was reprinted in *Hearings before the Special Subcommittee on Bilingual Education of the Committee on Labor and Public Welfare,* US Senate, 90th Cong., 1st Sess. (Washington, D.C.: Government Printing Office, 1968), p. 677.

47. Quoted in Andersson and Boyer, *Bilingual Schooling in the United States,* vol. 2, pp. 87–88.

48. *The Invisible Minority: Report of the NEA-Tucson Survey on the Teaching of Spanish to the Spanish-Speaking* (Washington, D.C.: National Education Association Department of Rural Education, 1966), pp. 6–7.

49. Ibid., pp. 10–11.
50. Elinor Hart, ed., *Third Annual Conference on Civil and Human Rights in Education: New Voices of the Southwest*, Symposium: The Spanish-Speaking Child in the Schools of the Southwest, Tucson, Arizona, October 30, 31, 1966 (Washington, D.C.: National Education Association, 1967), p. 1.
51. Ibid., p. 17.
52. Ibid. Morris Udall (D–AZ) seemed to stake out the position of the Johnson administration at the conference, which was supportive but unenthusiastic, as he mentioned that there were numerous laws on the books that could be used to aid Latino children, including the Elementary and Secondary Education Act of 1965, the General Cooperation Research Act, the National Defense Education Act of 1958, the Higher Education Act of 1965, the Vocational Education Act of 1963, and the Economic Opportunity Act of 1964. He also stressed the importance of expanding efforts beyond Mexican Americans: "We see these same conflicts of language and culture in trying to do something for our Indian children, the Cubans, and the Puerto Ricans." Ibid., pp. 14, 17.
53. Ibid., p. 16.
54. Ibid., p. 15.
55. Ibid., p. 15.
56. Ibid., pp. 4, 15–17.
57. Vega, *Bilingualism in Texas*, p. 30; Susan Gilbert Schneider, *Revolution, Reaction or Reform* (New York: Las Americas, 1976), p. 23.
58. Graham, *Uncertain Triumph*, p. 155.
59. *Congressional Record*, Senate, January 17, 1967, pp. 599–600.
60. Graham, *Uncertain Triumph*, p. 155.
61. While this muted the Latino-aid message of the bill, it was a wise political move, as it brought support from members of Congress without large Latino populations. Democratic Senator Edward Bartlett of Alaska, for example, sought and received in the Senate debate assurances that children speaking native dialects in his state would benefit. *Congressional Record*, December 11, 1967, p. 35,729.
62. *Senate Bilingual Education Hearings*, p. 47.
63. Ibid., p. 54. The quotation is from Gaarder's written statement. A less articulate orally presented version of the "absurdity" argument is transcribed on ibid., p. 50.
64. *Hearings before the General Subcommittee on Education of the Committee on Education and Labor*, U.S. House of Representatives, 90th Cong., 1st Sess. (Washington, D.C.: Government Printing Office, 1968), p. 143.
65. *Senate Bilingual Education Hearings*, p. 225.
66. Ibid., pp. 89–91.
67. *House Bilingual Education Hearings*, p. 56.
68. Ibid., p. 10. A survey conducted by the then doctoral student and acting director of HEW's new Office for Spanish-surnamed Americans, Gilbert Sanchez, gives more insight into how government officials and other supporters viewed bilingual education. Sanchez asked twenty of the major players in the passage of the Bilingual Education Act—including members of Congress, congressional staffmembers, educators, and Latino leaders—their perceptions of the new pro-

gram. Thirteen of the twenty saw it as "good for international relations," though by this time other meanings were more prominent. Nineteen of the twenty believed that bilingual education would be "helpful to the child in maintaining his ethnicity." Thirteen saw it as an aid for upward mobility. All of the respondents believed bilingual education would be "good for the child," "helpful in dropout prevention," and would provide "equal education opportunity." Gilbert Sanchez, "An Analysis of the Bilingual Education Act, 1967–68" (Ph.D. diss., University of Massachusetts, 1973), p. 140.

69. Major black civil-rights organizations did not demand bilingual education but supported the NEA conferences on the "invisible minority." Members of the External Advisory Committee of the "New Voices of the Southwest" conference included the Anti-Defamation League of B'Nai B'Rith, LULAC, the NAACP, the National Urban League (another black rights group), Martin Luther King Jr.'s Southern Christian Leadership Conference, as well as the US Commission on Civil Rights and the US Office of Education. See ibid., Appendix A.

70. Terry Anderson, *The Movement and the Sixties* (New York: Oxford University Press, 1995), pp. 302–4. A political strategy memo from the Nixon administration's 1972 campaign later described Chavez as the only Mexican American leader with support from blue-collar workers, "but Chavez is considered more of a moral than a political leader whose impact is limited largely to the farm labor issue." See the "Confidential" untitled, undated, unauthored (probably Charles Colson) report in Graham, ed., *Civil Rights during Nixon*, Part I, Reel 3, frame 928. On Chavez, also see Richard Griswold del Castillo and Richard A. Garcia, *César Chávez: A Triumph of Spirit* (Norman: University of Oklahoma Press, 1995). On Randolph, see Paula E. Pfeffer, *A. Philip Randolph: Pioneer of the Civil Rights Movement* (Baton Rouge: Louisiana State University Press, 1990).

71. Juan Gómez-Quiñones, *Chicano Politics* (Albuquerque: University of New Mexico Press, 1990), pp. 112–13.

72. See Guadalupe San Miguel Jr., *"Let All of Them Take Heed": Mexican Americans and the Campaign for Educational Equality in Texas, 1910–1981* (Austin: University of Texas Press, 1987), Chapter 6.

73. A group of parents in East Los Angeles organized the Mexican American Education Committee in 1963, and demanded that the school board recognize the Spanish language and Mexican culture, teach Spanish during elementary school, and teach Mexican history and literature. Rubén Donato, *The Other Struggle for Equal Schools: Mexican Americans during the Civil Rights Era* (Albany: State University of New York Press, 1997), p. 60.

74. Memo from David North to Joe Califano, November 15, 1966 and attached Report of the Task Force on Problems of Spanish Surnamed Americans, folder Spanish American, Box 325, Gaither files, LBJL.

75. Donato, *The Other Struggle*, p. 62.

76. Julie Leinenger Pycior, *LBJ and Mexican Americans: The Paradox of Power* (Austin: University of Texas Press, 1997), p. 163.

77. Ibid., p. 169.

78. Ibid., pp. 179–81.
79. Letter from Harry McPherson to the President, December 12, 1966, folder Mexican-Americans, Box 11, McPherson files, LBJL.
80. Memo from Harry McPherson to Joe Califano, February 17, 1967 and attached memos from LBJ and from McPherson to the President, both dated February 17, 1967, folder Mexican-Americans, Box 11, McPherson files, LBJL. According to Pycior, Johnson viewed the leaders, Herman Gallegos and Julian Samora, as "dissidents" and "Kennedy sympathizers." Pycior, *LBJ and Mexican Americans,* p. 187.
81. Memo from Joe Califano to Harry McPherson, February 21, 1967 and attached invitation to Brown Power Conference, February 10, 1967, and press release, February 12, 1967, folder Mexican-Americans, Box 11, McPherson files, LBJL. The conference, held on March 19 in Sacramento, was covered by the *Washington Post* which played up the group's radical nature. There was no mention of bilingual education. *Washington Post,* March 20, 1967, folder Mexican-Americans, Box 11, McPherson files, LBJL.
82. Quoted in Vega, *Bilingualism in Texas,* p. 32.
83. Memo for Will Sparks from Julia T. Cellini, December 19, 1967, and attachment, in Stephen F. Lawson, ed., *Civil Rights during Johnson, 1963–1969* (Frederick, Md.: University Publications of America, 1984), Part 2, Reel 3, frames 692–99. "One of the most important suggestions during the El Paso hearings," according to Ximenes, "was that the federal government help schools with bilingual education programs." Memo from Vicente Ximenes to Marvin Watson, n.d., folder EX LE/FA 2, 5/24/67–1/2/68, Box 39, White House Central Files (WHCF), LBJL.
84. Radical Mexican American groups protested the El Paso conference, and formed a new group, La Raza Unida, which quickly gathered momentum. At one of its first meetings—attended by twelve hundred persons representing fifty organizations—the group created the Plan de la Raza Unida, focusing on job training, education, housing, political representation, the Treaty of Guadalupe Hidalgo (some members believed that land had been illegally taken from Mexicans when the United States annexed the southwestern territory in 1848), police harassment, and cultural rights, but also pledging "loyalty to the Constitutional Democracy." La Raza Unida affected some Texas and California local elections in the 1970s. Gómez-Quiñones, *Chicano Politics,* p. 110–13; Peter Skerry, *Mexican Americans: The Ambivalent Minority* (New York: Free Press, 1993), Chapter 8; Lawrence Fuchs, *The American Kaleidoscope* (Hanover, N.H.: Wesleyan University Press, 1990), pp. 242–43, 259.
85. Anderson, *Movement and the Sixties,* pp. 305–7.
86. Ibid., pp. 309–10.
87. This research is discussed in Daryl Michael Scott, *Contempt and Pity: Social Policy and the Image of the Damaged Black Psyche, 1880–1996* (Chapel Hill: University of North Carolina Press, 1997), pp. 82, 96.
88. *Brown v. Board of Education,* 347 U.S. 483 (1954).
89. See, for example, Scott, *Contempt and Pity,* p. 138.
90. Diane Ravitch, *The Troubled Crusade* (New York: Basic Books, 1983), pp. 151–

55. There were court cases before *Brown* that facilitated seeing Latinos, or Mexican Americans at any rate, as analogous to blacks. In some parts of the country, Latinos were forced to attend segregated schools similar to those attended by blacks, and by the 1960s there was a tradition of federal court cases striking down discriminatory laws against Latinos. In *Mendez v. Westminister Sch. Dist. of Orange County*, 64 F. Supp. 544 (S.D. Cal. 1946), aff'd, 161 F.2d 774 (9th Cir. 1947), a federal district court in California struck down a "separate but equal" school system for Mexican Americans as a violation of the Fourteenth Amendment. The appeals court upheld the decision on statutory grounds only. Though the district court's finding relied on the argument tying together self-esteem and quality of education, it would seem to work against the implementation of bilingual education, as it stated: "The evidence clearly shows that Spanish-speaking children are retarded in learning English by lack of exposure to its use because of segregation, and that commingling of the entire student body instills and develops a common cultural attitude among the school children which is imperative for the perpetuation of American institutions and ideals. It is also established by the record that the methods of segregation prevalent in the defendant school districts foster antagonisms in the children and suggest inferiority among them where none exists" (64 F. Supp. at 549). In addition, two weeks before the *Brown* decision, the Warren Court issued an opinion, *Hernandez v. Texas*, 347 U.S. 475 (1954), finding Jackson County, Texas guilty of discriminating against Mexican Americans in jury selection. The court acknowledged the existence of segregated schools for Mexican American children in the county, and wrote that the "Fourteenth Amendment is not directed solely against discrimination due to a 'two-class theory'—that is, based upon differences between 'white' and 'Negro,'" (347 U.S. at 478). See Juan F. Perea, "The Black/White Binary Paradigm of Race: The 'Normal Science' of American Racial Thought," *California Law Review* 85 (1997): 1213.

91. *Invisible Minority*, pp. 1–11.

92. Ibid., pp. 31–32.

93. There was an undercurrent to the appeal of bilingual education that connected it with the Latino leaders' consistent demand for government jobs. For example, though Gaarder had his own well-developed pedagogical and geopolitical reasons for supporting bilingual education, he told the journalist Noel Epstein in 1977 that "what bilingual education is more than anything else, I believe, is a jobs program . . . It's fought for because it's a way of giving jobs and recognition and status to Spanish speakers, who traditionally have been at the lowest end of the socioeconomic pole. It's at that level that they fight for it and are going to keep on fighting for it." Epstein, *Language, Ethnicity and the Schools*, p. 38; Coleman Brez Stein Jr., *Sink or Swim: The Politics of Bilingual Education* (New York: Praeger, 1986), p. 31. Also see *New York Times*, June 21, 1976.

94. By the 1960s, the overwhelming majority of Mexican Americans were immigrants or descendants of immigrants. Estimates of the Spanish-speaking population of the southwestern states at the time of annexation vary between thirteen to fifty thousand. See A. J. Jaffe, Ruth M. Cully, and Thomas D. Boswell, *The Changing Demography of Spanish-Americans* (New York: Academic Press,

1980), p. 120; and Colin M. MacLachan and William W. Beezley, *El Gran Pueblo: A History of Greater Mexico* (Englewood Cliffs, N.J.: Prentice-Hall, 1994), p. 32. The *Invisible Minority* report itself claimed that there were only twenty-three thousand Spanish speakers in the southwest in 1790, but assumed all later Mexican Americans were part of this group and that this conquered status explained a perceived resistance to assimilation. *Invisible Minority*, p. 5. In hearings for the Bilingual American Education Act, Yarborough stuck to this argument that Mexican Americans were not immigrants, explaining to a critic: "There is . . . a basic difference between the Spanish-speaking and the other non-English-speaking groups. If you take the Italians, Polish, French, Germans, Norwegians, or other non-English-speaking groups, they made a definite decision to leave their old life and culture and come here to a new country and set up a way of life here in accordance with ours, and we assumed they were consenting at that time to give up their language, too . . . That wasn't true in the Southwest. We went in and took the people over, took over the land and culture. They had our culture superimposed on them. They did not consent to abandon their homeland and to come here and learn anew. They are not only the far more numerous group, but we recognize that they are entitled to special consideration." Quoted in Vega, *Bilingualism in Texas*, p. 45.

95. *Congressional Record*, Senate, January 17, 1967, pp. 599–600.
96. *Senate Bilingual Education Hearings*.
97. *House Bilingual Education Hearings*.
98. Sanchez traces the legislative history in Sanchez, "Bilingual Education Act," pp. 75–79.
99. Undated letter to Chairman Lister Hill from John Gardner; Memo to Mr. Cater from William B. Cannon, Chief, Education, Manpower, and Science Division, July 13, 1967; Memo from Barefoot (Sanders) to Joe (Califano), August 9, 1967; Memo to Mr. Gaither from Wilfred H. Rommel, August 9, 1967; Letter to Barefoot Sanders from Ben McDonald, August 10, 1967; Memo to Joe Califano from Jim Gaither, August 15, 1967; Memo to Mr. Gaither from Wilfred H. Rommel, August 14, 1967, folder EX LE/FA 2, Box 39, WHCF, LBJL.
100. "Statement of the President upon Signing the Elementary and Secondary Education Amendments of 1967," *Public Papers of the Presidents of the United States: Lyndon B. Johnson, 1968–69, Book I* (Washington, D.C.: Government Printing Office, 1970), pp. 15–17, 16.
101. Pub. L. No. 90-247 (1968).
102. Kloss, *Bilingual Tradition*, p. 37.
103. Memo from Marvin Watson to Vicente Ximenes, January 1, 1968, and memo from Ximenes to Watson, n.d., folder EX LE/FA 2, 5/24/67–1/2/68, Box 39, WHCF, LBJL.
104. Memo from Vicente Ximenes to the President, n.d. (received January 11, 1968), folder Interagency Committee on Mexican-American Affairs, EX FG 686/A, Box 386, WHCF, LBJL.
105. Stein, *Sink or Swim*, p. 32; Albar A. Peña, "Report on the Bilingual Education Program—Title VII, ESEA," in *Proceedings: National Conference on Bilingual*

Education, April 14–15, 1972 (New York: Arno Press, 1978), pp. 221–28, 222; Lloyd Bentsen, "Banquet Address," in ibid., pp. 241–51, 243.

106. Stein, *Sink or Swim*, p. 35. The problem of implementation was to last several years, particularly the difficulty of finding qualified teachers. Most agreed that there were simply not enough qualified teachers working in the programs. Epstein, *Language, Ethnicity, and the Schools*, p. 12.

107. Andersson, "Bilingual Education: The American Experience," p. 432, quoting Draft Manual No. 0–398–198 (Washington, D.C.: Government Printing Office, 1970).

108. Quoted in John C. Molina (director, Office of Bilingual Education), "National Policy on Bilingual Education: An Historical View of the Federal Role," in Hernan LaFontaine, Barry Persky, and Leonard H. Golubchick, eds., *Bilingual Education* (Wayne, N.J.: Avery Publishing, 1978), pp. 16–23, 17.

109. Quoted in Schneider, *Revolution, Reaction or Reform*, p. 33. This was a softer view than he expressed in 1971 to a friendlier audience of Mexican American professors and educators. Bilingual education, Peña said then, "may be the first desirable and attainable goal of a bilingual society which respects and fosters cultural pluralism. The two languages should be given equal status as symbols of both cultures." Albar A. Peña, "Creating Positive Attitudes towards Bilingual-Bicultural Education," in Castañeda, et al., *Mexican Americans and Educational Change*, pp. 363–72, 366.

110. Quoted in William Francis Mackey and Von Nieda Beebe, *Bilingual Schools for a Bicultural Community: Miami's Adaptation to the Cuban Refugees* (Rowley, Mass.: Newbury House, 1977), p. 4.

111. Clipping included in Letter to President Nixon from Desi Arnaz, December 19, 1968, in Graham, *Civil Rights during Nixon*, Part 1, Reel 1, frame 675.

112. Gareth Davies, "The Great Society after Johnson: The Case of Bilingual Education," *Journal of American History* 88 (2002): 1405–29.

113. Memo from Martin Castillo to Herb Klein, December 17, 1969; Proposed statement upon signing S740 (Safire), December 29, 1969; a series of form letters to be sent with signing pens to Edward Roybal, Barry Goldwater, Joseph Montoya, Paul Fannin, John Tower, George Bush, George Murphy, Manuel Lugan, and Jorge Cordova, dated January 16, 1970, all in folder EX FG 145, Inter-Agency Committee on Mexican-American Affairs/Cabinet Committee on Opportunities for Spanish Speaking Americans as of 12/30/69 through EX FG 145/A [1973–74], Nixon Presidential Papers Project (NPMP), National Archives; "Statement on Signing the Bill Establishing the Cabinet Committee on Opportunities for Spanish-Speaking People, December 31, 1969, in *Public Papers of the Presidents of the United States, Richard Nixon 1969* (Washington, D.C.: Government Printing Office, 1971), pp. 1048–49; Statement by the President, December 31, 1969, in Graham, *Civil Rights during Nixon, 1968–1973*, Part 1, Reel 4, frame 423.

114. Letter from Henry M. Ramirez to Elliot L. Richardson, August 30, 1971, in folder Minutes of Meetings of the CCOSS [1 of 2], Box 17, WHCF, Staffmember and Office Files, Robert H. Finch, NPMP, National Archives. Also, more effort behind the memorandum of May 25 concerning regulatory

effort (see below) was needed, though Ramirez emphasized notification and technical assistance to school districts, rather than tougher enforcement.

115. Cabinet Committee of Opportunities for the Spanish Speaking, Education Task Force, June 21–25, 1971, folder CCOSS Task Force Education, June 21–25, 1971 [CFOA 823], Box 22, Finch Files, WHCF, Staff Member and Office Files (SMOF), NPMP, National Archives.

116. Susan Gilbert Schneider reports of a survey undertaken by Nixon's campaign committee in Chicago, Los Angeles, New York, and San Antonio in April 1972 on Latino attitudes and policy preferences, which included questions on bilingual education. The survey found "a high level of support" for federal programs in this area. However, Schneider also points out that a strategy in response to the surveys was "to encourage support for bilingual-bicultural education." This suggests the government was creating the demand for bilingual education, rather than responding to it. Schneider, *Revolution, Reaction or Reform*, p. 101. Also see Davies, "The Great Society after Johnson: The Case of Bilingual Education," p. 1413. Moreover, most often Latino desire for bilingual education was more assumed than a matter of obvious fact as evidenced by mass mobilization. For example, a strategy memo for winning the Latino vote in 1972 argued for increased support and publicity for Nixon efforts for bilingual education to help Latino LEP children "develop their full potential as bilingual/bicultural Americans," explaining that "bilingual education is a concept close to the hearts of most Spanish-speaking people and it towers as a major example of government sensitivity and concern for equal educational opportunities for Spanish-speaking children." The same memo later stated that "to date, no substantial and controlled polling has been done on the attitudes, fears, and primary issues in Mexican-American communities." See the "Confidential" untitled, undated, unauthored (probably Charles Colson) report in Graham, *Civil Rights during Nixon*, Part I, Reel 3, frames 23, 48.

117. Memo to Richard Nixon from Hugh Sloan via Dwight Chapin, October 21, 1971, in folder EX FG 145 Cabinet Committee on Opportunities for Spanish Speaking People 1/71-[12/31/72], Box 1, EX FG 145 Inter-Agency Committee on Mexican-American Affairs as of 12/30/69 through EX FG 145/A [1973–74], NPMP, National Archives.

118. Memo from Charles W. Colson to John Ehrlichman, December 20, 1971, in Graham, *Civil Rights during Nixon*, Part 1, Reel 3, frames 899–900.

119. See Memo to Ed Morgan from Ken Cole, January 10, 1972; Memo to Ed Morgan from Ken Cole, January 10, 1972; Memo to Peter Flanigan from Ken Cole, January 10, 1972, in ibid., Part 1, Reel 3, frames 896–898.

120. Memo to Ken Cole via Edward L. Morgan from James B. Clawson, January 28, 1972, in ibid., Part 1, Reel 3, frames 887–888.

121. See Memo to David Parker from Ron Ziegler, April 18, 1972; Memo to David Parker from Dick Moore, April 14, 1972; Memo to Dick Moore, Bill Safire, Ron Ziegler from David Parker, April 13, 1972; Schedule Proposal from Herbert Klein via Dwight Chapin, April 11, 1972, in ibid., Part 1, Reel 4, frames 93, 96–98.

122. See, for example, Letter from Alex Armendariz to Frederick Malek, May 31,

1972, folder Ethnics [1 of 3], Box 62, White House Special Files (WHSF), SMOF, Charles W. Colson Papers, NPMP, National Archives; Undated campaign document, "Spanish-Speaking," in Graham, *Civil Rights during Nixon*, Part 1, Reel 4, frames 332–36.

123. John C. Molina, "Bilingual Education in the USA," in Rudolph C. Troike and Nancy Modiano, eds., *Proceedings of the First Inter-American Conference on Bilingual Education, November 20–22, 1974, Mexico City* (Arlington, VA: Center for Applied Linguistics, 1975), pp. 25–31, p. 30; Peña, "Report on the Bilingual Education Program," p. 224; Stein, *Sink or Swim*, p. 32.

124. Leon Panetta and Peter Gall, *Bring Us Together: The Nixon Team and the Civil Rights Retreat* (Philadelphia: Lippincott, 1971), pp. 14–15; author interview with Leon E. Panetta, August 3, 1999. All unattributed information below regarding Panetta's role in the creation of the May 25 memorandum is from this interview.

125. Author interview with Martin Gerry, May 22, 1998. All unattributed information regarding Gerry's role in the creation of the May 25 memorandum is from this interview. On this powerful aspect of the civil-rights movement, which had a formative experience on participants, see Doug McAdam, *Freedom Summer* (New York: Oxford University Press, 1988).

126. There were, in fact, a few protests occurring in schools in Texas in 1969, where Mexican American students were staging boycotts of the local public schools and demanding better treatment and bilingual and bicultural educational programs. In Abilene, Texas, an estimated 150 to 200 students walked out of schools on October 21 to protest discrimination. In Crystal City, Texas, a boycott staged by 1,600 Mexican American students began on December 9 in response to the faculty's discriminatory selection of a homecoming queen but based more broadly on school officials' denial of Latino student demands. See James V. Gambone, "Bilingual Bicultural Educational Civil Rights: The May 25th Memorandum and Oppressive School Practices," (Ph.D. diss., University of New Mexico, 1973), p. 4. Gambone maintains that OCR officials investigated the complaints, while Hardgrave and Hinojosa claim the officials were from the Justice Department, while students from Crystal City visited Yarborough as well as OCR officials. Hardgrave and Hinojosa, *Politics of Bilingual Education*, p. 57. In interviews with me, neither Panetta nor Gerry hinted that these were relevant to the OCR's interest in the issue.

127. In the 1969–71 period, Father Casso contributed to the Texas and California State Advisory Committees on Civil Rights in their efforts to understand discrimination against Mexican American children, and worked with other advisory committees created to aid HEW's Office of Education. Sanchez, *Bilingual Education Act*, p. 88.

128. Panetta described one meeting in Leon Panetta and Peter Gall, *Bring Us Together: The Nixon Team and the Civil Rights Retreat* (Philadelphia: Lippincott, 1971), pp. 335–36.

129. Stephen C. Halpern, *On the Limits of the Law: The Ironic Legacy of Title VI of the 1964 Civil Rights Act* (Baltimore: Johns Hopkins University Press, 1995), p. 89.

130. Ibid., p. 95.
131. Davies, "Great Society after Johnson," p. 1413.
132. Quoted in A. James Reichley, *Conservative in an Age of Change: The Nixon and Ford Administrations* (Washington, D.C.: Brookings Institution, 1981), p. 180.
133. See President's Committee on Mental Retardation, *The Six Hour Retarded Child: A Report on a Conference on Problems of Education of Children in the Inner City, Aug. 10–12, 1969, Airlie House, Warrentown, Virginia* (Washington: Government Printing Office, 1970).
134. Martin Gerry, "Cultural Freedom in the Schools: The Right of Mexican-American Children to Succeed," in Alfredo Castañeda, Manuel Ramírez III, Carlos E. Cortés, and Mario Barrera, eds., *Mexican Americans and Educational Change* (New York: Arno Press, 1974), pp. 226–54, 233.
135. Memo to School Districts with More Than Five Percent National Origin-Minority Group Children from J. Stanley Pottinger, May 25, 1970, in Graham, *Civil Rights during Nixon*, Part 1, Reel 3, frame 0889. For a discussion, see Iris C. Rotberg, "Some Legal and Research Considerations in Establishing Federal Policy in Bilingual Education," in *Harvard Educational Review* 52 (1982): 149–68.
136. Gerry, "Cultural Freedom in the Schools," p. 233.
137. See especially Juan A. Aragón, "The Challenge to Biculturalism: Culturally Deficient Educators Teaching Culturally Different Children," in *Mexican Americans and Educational Change*, pp. 258–67. Aragón was associate professor of education administration and director of the Cultural Awareness Center at the University of New Mexico.
138. "A Summary of the Denver Conference," report sent to Elliot Richardson from J. Stanley Pottinger, quoted in Gambone, "Educational Civil Rights," pp. 21–22.
139. Ibid., p. 23. Gambone, then a doctoral student at the University of New Mexico, took part in the San Diego meeting.
140. Quoted in ibid., p. 13, n. 19. Unfortunately, Gambone does not state the date of the memo or the author, though it was likely Pottinger. It is not clear whether the emphasis is Gambone's or in the original.
141. Gary Orfield, *Must We Bus?* (Washington: Brookings Institution, 1983), pp. 299–301, quoting Statement of Martin Gerry, *Bilingual Education Act, Hearings before the General Subcommittee on Education of the House Committee on Education and Labor*, 93rd Cong., 2nd Sess. (Washington, D.C.: Government Printing Office, 1974), p. 10.
142. Skerry, *Mexican Americans*, pp. 323–30; Jack Greenberg, *Crusaders in the Courts* (New York: Basic Books, 1994), pp. 487–88; Gómez-Quiñones, *Chicano Politics*, p. 112.
143. MALDEF worked closely with OCR, coordinating activities and sharing information. This was not difficult because many MALDEF lawyer-activists previously worked in the federal government and vice versa. Davies, "Great Society after Johnson," p. 1424.
144. 447 F.2d 441 (5th Cir. 1971).

145. Ibid., at 448.
146. José Cárdenas, *Multicultural Education: A Generation of Advocacy* (Needham Heights, Mass.: Simon and Schuster Custom Publishing, 1995), p. 42. Cárdenas reproduces his entire testimony in Chapter One.
147. Author interview with Gerry.
148. Plan quoted in Hardgrave and Hinojosa, *Politics of Bilingual Education*, p. 43.
149. *United States v. State of Texas*, 342 F. Supp. 24 (1971), at 26. In making his ruling, Justice cited *Green v. New Kent Country Bd. of Educ.*, 391 U.S. 430 (1968); *Alexander v. Holmes County Bd. of Educ.*, 391 U.S. 19 (1969); and *United States v. Jefferson County Bd. of Educ.*, 372 F.2d 836 (5th Cir. 1966). See *United States v. State of Texas*, 342 F. Supp. at 27–28.
150. *United States v. State of Texas*, 342 F. Supp. at 28.
151. Ibid., at 30–37.
152. Hardgrave and Hinojosa, *Politics of Bilingual Education*, p. 46.
153. Cárdenas, *Multicultural Education*, pp. 37–38.
154. Hardgrave and Hinojosa, *Politics of Bilingual Education*, p. 47.
155. Orfield, *Must We Bus?*, p. 207.
156. L. Ling-Chi Wang, "Lau v. Nichols: History of a Struggle for Equal and Quality Education," in Charles McLain, ed., *Asian Americans and the Law* (New York: Garland, 1994), pp. 422–45, 423.
157. *Lau v. Nichols*, 483 F.2d 791, 793 (9th Cir. 1973), *reh'g en banc denied*, 483 F.2d 805, from unreported district court opinion, Civil No. C-70, 627 LHB (N.D. Cal. May 26, 1970).
158. *Lau v. Nichols*, 483 F.2d 791, 798 (9th Cir. 1973).
159. These included *Brown, Sweatt v. Painter*, 339 U.S. 629 (1950), and *McLaurin v. Oklahoma State Regents* 339 U.S. 637 (1950).
160. 372 F.2d 836, 866 (5th Cir. 1956), *aff'd on reh'g en banc*, 380 F.2d 385 (5th Cir. 1967).
161. Bork's brief is reproduced in *House Bilingual Education Hearings*, pp. 10–19. Bork is listed as lead author, followed by Pottinger.
162. Initial drafts of the opinion were based on constitutional grounds, but Justices Blackmun, Burger, and White indicated that they would not join in the opinion if it had such a basis. They gave no reasons for their refusal in communications with Thurgood Marshall. Box 135, folder 12 72–6520 Lau v. Nichols, Thurgood Marshall Papers, Library of Congress.
163. *Lau v. Nichols*, 94 S.Ct. 786 (1974), at 788.
164. Ibid., at 789.
165. 429 U.S. 125 (1976).
166. American courts have been inconsistent in equating language discrimination with national-origin discrimination. See Herbert Teitelbaum and Richard J. Hiller, "Bilingual Education: The Legal Mandate," *Harvard Educational Review* 47 (1977): 138–70, p. 145, n. 36.
167. 94 S.Ct. at 791.
168. *Serna v. Portales Municipal Sch.*, 351 F. Supp. 1279 (N.D. Mex. 1972), *aff'd*, 499 F.2d 1147, 1154 (10th Cir. 1974); *Aspira of New York v. Board of Educ. of*

the City of New York, 72 Civ. 4002 (S.D.N.Y. Aug. 29, 1974) (unreported consent decree), 58 F.R.D. 62 (S.D.N.Y. 1973). See Teitelbaum and Hiller, "The Legal Mandate," pp. 146–49 for a discussion.

169. Schneider, *Revolution, Reaction or Reform,* p. 56.

170. Ibid., p. 54, citing US Congress, Senate, 93rd Cong., 2nd Sess., January 22, 1974, *Congressional Record* 120, p. 1231.

171. Ibid., citing *House Bilingual Education Hearings,* p. 366.

172. Rosemary C. Salomone, *Equal Education under Law: Legal Rights and Federal Policy in the Post-Brown Era* (New York: St. Martin's Press, 1986), p. 89.

173. Teitelbaum and Hiller, "The Legal Mandate," p. 146; Salomone, *Equal Education under Law,* pp. 60–61, 100–5.

174. Greene, *Limits of Power,* p. 72; Julie Roy Jeffrey, *Education for Children of the Poor: A Study of the Origins and Implementation of the Elementary and Secondary Education Act of 1965* (Columbus: Ohio State University Press, 1978), p. 203–7.

175. See Carlucci's testimony in *House Bilingual Education Hearings,* pp. 313–56.

176. Author interview with Martin Gerry.

177. "Task Force Findings Specifying Remedies Available for Eliminating Past Educational Practices Ruled Unlawful Under *Lau v. Nichols,*" Summer, 1975, in Donated historical papers, Shirley Hufstedler, Box 15, Lau Series, file: "Lau Regulations Background Book 1980," Jimmy Carter Library. I thank Hugh Graham for supplying me with this document. On the *Lau* Remedies, also see Rotberg, "Federal Policy in Bilingual Education," p. 152; Ravitch, *Troubled Crusade,* p. 274; Orfield, *Must We Bus?,* p. 306.

178. Graham, *Uncertain Triumph,* p. 218. Epstein, *Language, Ethnicity, and the Schools,* p. 15. The *Lau* Remedies were not published in the *Federal Register,* so there never was a period for public comment. This led to a court case, *Northwest Arctic Sch. Dist. v. Califano,* No. A-77–216 (D. Alaska Sept. 29, 1978), that argued the remedies were in violation of the Administrative Procedure Act. The result was a consent decree with HEW agreeing to publish the *Lau* Remedies in the *Federal Register* as a proposed regulation in 1980. Levin, "Regulating Bilingual Education," p. 39.

179. There was a Latino riot in east Los Angeles in August 1970. A demonstration that was intended to attract one hundred thousand participants instead attracted a crowd estimated between seven and twenty thousand, but turned violent with looting of stores and violent clashes with police. Two persons died. However, the issue for the "Chicano Moratorium" demonstration was the disproportionate Mexican American participation on the front lines of the Vietnam War. A later *New York Times* article investigating the situation found other Mexican American discontents, such as police brutality, difficulty in getting Latinos into elected offices, and education concerns related to language. Even if this was considered a bilingual education riot, however, it could not be said to have had a causal impact on the creation of federal policy because it came *after* the Bilingual Education Act and the May 25, 1970 memorandum. Richard Griswold del Castillo and Arnoldo de León, *North to Aztlan: A History of Mexican American*

in the United States (New York: Twayne, 1996), pp. 132–33; *New York Times,* August 30, 1970, August 31, 1970, and September 4, 1970.

180. Hugh Heclo has written that in the later part of the twentieth century, "there are corners of the realm in which corporatist-style consultation persists. But there is too much variation, conflict, and unpredictability to use the term *corporatism* to characterize the system as a whole or even its program sectors over time." Heclo, "The Emerging Regime," in Richard A. Harris and Sidney M. Milkis, eds., *Remaking American Politics* (Boulder: Westview Press, 1989), pp. 289–320, 312.

181. David R. Mayhew, *Congress: The Electoral Connection* (New Haven: Yale University Press, 1974).

8. Title IX and Women's Equality in Education

1. Hugh Davis Graham, "Since 1964: The Paradox of American Civil Rights Regulation," in Morton Keller and R. Shep Melnick, eds., *Taking Stock: American Government in the Twentieth Century* (New York: Cambridge, University Press, 1999), pp. 187–218.

2. Memo from Rita E. Hauser to the President, February 5, 1969, and handwritten note from the President to H [Haldeman], n.d., in Joan Hoff-Wilson, ed., *Papers of the Nixon White House* (Bethesda, Md.: University Publications of America, 1989), Part 6, Fiche 6a–7–44.

3. Hugh Davis Graham, *The Civil Rights Era* (New York: Oxford University Press, 1990), p. 397.

4. Ibid., p. 398.

5. Letter from Florence P. Dwyer, Catherine May, Charlotte T. Reid, and Margaret M. Heckler to Mr. President, June 9, 1969, in folder HU 2–5 women beginning 12/31/69, White House Subject Files (WHSF), Box 21, Nixon Presidential Materials Project (NPMP), National Archives.

6. Memo from Bryce Harlow to Dwight Chapin, June 23, 1969, in ibid.

7. On the Congressional Black Caucus, see Paul Frymer, *Uneasy Alliances* (Princeton: Princeton University Press, 1999), pp. 147–78.

8. Letter from Florence P. Dwyer, Catherine May, Charlotte T. Reid, and Margaret M. Heckler to Mr. President, July 8, 1969, in folder HU 2–5 women beginning 12/31/69, WHSF, Box 21, NPMP, National Archives.

9. Memo for the President's file, from Peter M. Flanigan, July 12, 1969, in Hoff-Wilson, *Papers of the Nixon White House,* Part 2, fiche 69–7–6.

10. Jo Freeman, *The Politics of Women's Liberation* (New York: McKay, 1975), p. 206–7. By 1972, Nixon had appointed 118 women to what the administration described as "top-level policy-making positions" and maintained that Johnson had only appointed twenty-seven to this high level. Joan Hoff, *Nixon Reconsidered* (New York: Basic Books, 1994), p. 99. The administration also continued increasingly anachronistic pursuits, such as meetings with the wives of administration officials as a means to "cultivate women power." The presi-

dential briefing with the wives would be "a way to get the Administration proposals on the women's pages of newspapers. The ladies could then intelligently discuss these subjects at their Alma Maters, Women's Organizations, etc." Schedule Proposal, from David N. Parker via Dwight L. Chapin, March 11, 1971, in Hugh Davis Graham, ed., *Civil Rights during the Nixon Administration* (Bethesda, Md.: University Publications of America, 1989), Part 1, Reel 23, frame 328. Nixon had earlier invited the wives of department secretaries to a cabinet meeting. Graham, *Civil Rights Era*, p. 398.

11. Memo from Daniel Patrick Moynihan for the President, August 20, 1969, in Graham, *Civil Rights during Nixon*, Part 1, Reel 23, frames 78–82.

12. Memo from John Ehrlichman to the President, September 29, 1969, and attached Memos for the Staff Secretary from Jim Keogh, August 26, 1969, Peter M. Flanigan, August 25, 1969, Bryce Harlow, September 20, 1969, and memo from Daniel Patrick Moynihan to the President, August 20, 1969, in ibid., Part 1, Reel 23, frames 73–82.

13. The peculiar name may have come from a suggestion of Representative Florence Dwyer, or from her original letter to Nixon, which suggested a new body to examine "women's rights and responsibilities." See above, this chapter at n. 4.

14. Graham, *Civil Rights Era*, p. 401.

15. President's Task Force on Women's Rights and Responsibilities, *A Matter of Simple Justice* (Washington, D.C.: Government Printing Office, 1970), pp. iii–v.

16. Ibid., p. 7.

17. Ibid., p. v.

18. Ibid., p. 18.

19. Graham, *Civil Rights Era*, p. 406.

20. Memo from Patricia Reilly Hitt to John Ehrlichman, April 15, 1970, in Graham, *Civil Rights during Nixon*, Part 1, Reel 23, frames 122–23.

21. Memo from Harry Dent to John Ehrlichman and Bill Timmons, May 7, 1970, in ibid., frame 132.

22. Memo from Leonard Garment to John Ehrlichman, May 25, 1970, and Memo from John Ehrlichman for the President, n.d., in ibid., frames 139–74. Ehrlichman's memo also mentioned that all presidents since Eisenhower had supported the amendment, and that Nixon's 1968 opponents, Hubert Humphrey and George Wallace, had joined him in support of the ERA during the 1968 election.

23. Memo from John R. Brown III to John Ehrlichman, c.c.: H. R. Haldeman, A. Butterfield, July 31, 1970, in Hoff-Wilson, *Papers of the Nixon White House*, Part 4, fiche 4–34–62.

24. Memo from Hugh Sloan to John Ehrlichman with handwritten comments by Nixon, July 17, 1970, in Graham, *Civil Rights during Nixon*, Part 1, Reel 23, frame 194; Memo from Hugh W. Sloan Jr. via Dwight L. Chapin for the President, July 17, 1970, in ibid., frames 217–18.

25. Memo from Rita E. Hauser to Mr. Bill Safire, March 2, 1970, in ibid., frames 116–19. A few weeks later, Ehrlichman tried to use women's rights as a way to harass *Newsweek* magazine, one of the Nixon administration's many enemies in

the press. Ehrlichman told an aide that some women employees at the magazine had filed complaints of sex discrimination to the EEOC, and that he wanted the Justice Department to consider a lawsuit against the magazine, writing, "I would like a highly confidential preparation of the necessary suit papers to be undertaken here, *not* in the U.S. Attorney's office in the southern office of New York, together with your memorandum to the President regarding the merits of such an action and the probable outcome." He added mischievously, "You may be aware of my long-standing advocacy of equal rights for women." Ehrlichman learned, however, that such a lawsuit would require an investigation that could not be kept confidential. Memo to Bud Krogh from John Ehrlichman, March 17, 1970; Memo to Egil [Bud] Krogh from Jerris Leonard, assistant attorney general, Civil Rights Division, March 25, 1970; Memo from Bud Krogh to John Ehrlichman, April 20, 1970, all in Graham, ibid., frames 128, 126, 125, respectively.

26. Memo to the President from Rita E. Hauser, April 12, 1971, in ibid., frames 333–35.

27. Memo from Len Garment to Bob Haldeman, April 19, 1971; Memo from Charles Colson to David Parker, cc: George Bell, Leonard Garment, Fred Malek, May 4, 1971; Memo from Fred Malek to Dave Parker, May 12, 1971; Memo to Dave Parker from Harry Dent, May 10, 1971; Schedule Proposal: "Rap Session" with selected women from different walks of life, July 7, 1971, all in ibid., frames 420, 418, 415, 417, 414, respectively.

28. Freeman, *Politics of Women's Liberation*, pp. 209–21; Anne Costain, *Inviting Women's Rebellion* (Baltimore: Johns Hopkins University Press, 1992), pp. 59–60.

29. Mary Frances Berry, *Why ERA Failed* (Bloomington: Indiana University Press, 1986), pp. 64–65.

30. Freeman, *Politics of Women's Liberation*, p. 222.

31. Author interview with Birch Bayh, May 12, 1998.

32. Freeman, *Politics of Women's Liberation*, pp. 202–3; Hoff, *Nixon Reconsidered*, pp. 110–11.

33. Freeman, *Politics of Women's Liberation*, pp. 203–4.

34. Quoted in Mary Ann Millsap, "Sex Equity in Education," in Irene Tinker, ed., *Women in Washington: Advocates for Public Policy* (Beverly Hills: Sage Publications, 1983), p. 94.

35. Fern S. Ingersoll, "Former Congresswomen Look Back," in ibid., p. 204. Green and her staff were in close contact with Bernice Sandler of WEAL, who helped supply witnesses and information for the hearings. Green invited Sandler formally to join the committee staff in August of 1970. Arvonne S. Fraser, "Insiders and Outsiders: Women in the Political Arena," in ibid., p. 126.

36. *Discrimination against Women, Hearings before the Special Subcommittee on Education of the Committee on Education and Labor,* House of Representatives, 91st Cong., 2d Sess., on Section 805 of H.R. 16098, Parts 1 and 2. Jo Freeman wrote that "the printed committee hearings have proved one of the most thorough compilations of material on women in higher education and have often

been used by feminists as a textbook—published at government expense." Freeman, *Politics of Women's Liberation*, p. 223. The hearings were published in an abridged form as Catharine R. Stimpson, ed., *Discrimination against Women: Congressional Hearings on Equal Rights in Education and Employment* (New York: R. R. Bowker, 1973).

37. John D. Skrentny, *The Ironies of Affirmative Action* (Chicago: University of Chicago Press, 1996), Chapter 5.

38. *Discrimination against Women Hearings*, p. 3.

39. Ibid., p. 2.

40. Ibid., p. 432.

41. Ibid., pp. 618–19. See also the statements of Frankie M. Freeman, commissioner of the US Commission of Civil Rights, ibid., p. 662, and Irving Kator, assistant executive director, Civil Service Commission, ibid., p. 704, among many others.

42. Ibid., p. 366.

43. Ibid., p. 365.

44. Ibid., p. 366.

45. Ibid., p. 365.

46. Ibid., p. 231.

47. Andrew Fishel and Janice Pottker, *National Politics and Sex Discrimination in Education* (Lexington, Mass.: D. C. Heath, 1977), pp. 96–97.

48. Author interview with Birch Bayh, May 12, 1998. Such publicity also had practical value in promoting his candidacy for a presidential campaign. Costain, *Inviting Women's Rebellion*, p. 133.

49. 117 *Congressional Record*, August 5, 1971, p. 30,155. Bayh's amendment was similar to Green's most recent effort. The major difference was it followed a recommendation of the Nixon task force and added an amendment to Title IV of the Civil Rights Act of 1964, which allowed the attorney general to bring a lawsuit on the behalf of persons denied college admission on the basis of sex. Senator George McGovern (D–SD) introduced a similar proposal that was later dropped in lieu of the Bayh amendment.

50. Ibid., p. 30,157.

51. Interview with Birch Bayh.

52. 117 *Congressional Record*, August 6, 1971, p. 30,407.

53. Ibid. Bayh told me in my interview with him that he regretted these comments.

54. Ibid., p. 30,412.

55. Quoted in Millsap, "Sex Equity in Education," p. 94.

56. Fishel and Pottker, *National Politics and Sex Discrimination*, pp. 101–2; Ingersoll, "Former Congresswomen Look Back," p. 205.

57. Ingersoll, "Former Congresswomen Look Back," p. 204.

58. Fishel and Pottker, *National Politics and Sex Discrimination*, pp. 101–2; Ingersoll, "Former Congresswomen Look Back," p. 205.

59. 118 *Congressional Record*, February 28, 1972, p. 5,803.

60. Ibid., pp. 5,804–5.

61. Ibid., p. 5,807.

62. Fishel and Pottker, *National Politics and Sex Discrimination,* pp. 102–3.

63. 20 U.S.C. § 1681(a) (1976).

64. Joyce Gelb and Marian Lief Palley, *Women and Public Policies* (Princeton: Princeton University Press, 1982), pp. 100–2.

65. Hoff, *Nixon Reconsidered,* p. 111.

66. Richard M. Nixon, "Statement on Signing the Education Amendments of 1972," in *Public Papers of the Presidents: Richard M. Nixon* vol. 4 (Washington, D.C.: Government Printing Office, 1973), pp. 701–3. Also see *Congressional Quarterly Weekly Report,* vol. 30, June 24, 1972, p. 1242.

67. Robin Rogers-Dillon and John D. Skrentny, "Administering Success: The Legitimacy Imperative and the Implementation of Welfare Reform," *Social Problems* 46 (1999): 13–29.

68. *Sex Discrimination Regulations: Hearings before the Subcommittee on Postsecondary Education of the House Committee on Education and Labor,* 94th Cong., 1st Sess. (1975), p. 437.

69. Ibid.

70. Ibid., p. 463.

71. Ibid., p. 463.

72. Fishel and Pottker, *National Politics and Sex Discrimination,* p. 106.

73. *Sex Discrimination Regulations Hearings,* p. 470.

74. Project on Equal Education Rights, NOW Legal Defense and Education Fund, *Stalled at the Start: Government Action on Sex Bias in the Schools* (Washington, D.C.: NOW Legal Defense and Education Fund, 1977), p. 34.

75. Ibid., p. 38.

76. In February of 1971, HEW secretary Elliot Richardson oversaw the creation of a "Women's Action Program" in HEW, with Bernice Sandler of WEAL—the guiding force behind the inclusion of women in Labor Department affirmative-action regulations—as the associate director. Judith Hole and Ellen Levine, *Rebirth of Feminism* (New York: Quadrangle, 1971), p. 47. For its report and Richardson's support, see Memo from Elliot Richardson to John Ehrlichman and attachment, January 12, 1972, in Graham, *Civil Rights during Nixon,* Part 1, Reel 23, frames 489–92. For one earnest response that equated women with the other minorities, see Report of Commissioner's Task Force, A Look at Women in Education: Issues and Answers for HEW, in *Women's Educational Equity Act: Hearings on H.R. 208 before the Subcommittee on Equal Opportunities of the House Committee on Education and Labor,* 93rd Cong., 1st Sess., Part 1, pp. 57–123.

77. Fishel and Pottker, *National Politics and Sex Discrimination,* pp. 106–7. Meanwhile, progress for women's rights in education was occurring on a constitutional basis in the courts, though there is surprisingly little evidence that OCR took notice. In most of the cases, total exclusion of females was the issue, such as in *Kirstein v. University of Virginia,* 309 F. Supp. 184 (E.D. Va. 1970), though differential admissions standards (making it more difficult for women) would also be struck down as violations of the Fourteenth Amendment. *Berkelman v. San Francisco Indep. Sch. Dist.,* 501 F.2d 1264 (9th Cir. 1974); *Bray v. Lee,* 337

F. Supp. 934 (D. Mass. 1972). Usually the courts ordered that women be admitted into the school or program at issue, but unlike constitutional race cases, separate-but-equal was acceptable. See Rosemary C. Salomone, *Equal Education under Law: Legal Rights and Federal Policy in the Post-Brown Era* (New York: St. Martin's Press, 1986), pp. 119–20, for a discussion.

More favorable results from the perspective of women's rights can be seen in the cases involving athletics, where Title IX encountered the most controversy. During the time of the writing of Title IX regulations, federal courts were ruling that it was a violation of the Fourteenth Amendment to completely exclude girls from school sports. *Reed v. Nebraska Sch. Activities Ass'n*, 341 F. Supp. 258 (D. Neb. 1972) (concerning golf); *Brenden v. Independent Sch. Dist.*, 457 F.2d 1292 (8th Cir. 1973) (cross country, skiing, running, and tennis); *Gilpin v. Kansas State High Sch. Activities Ass'n*, 377 F. Supp. 1233 (D. Kan. 1974) (cross country). Some courts stated that separate teams would be constitutional.

While courts and administrative agencies have cooperated in advancing law in other contexts, such as disability (R. Shep Melnick, *Between the Lines* [Washington, D.C.: Brookings Institution, 1994]), I could not find much evidence of OCR's using the courts to justify or shape its regulating activity.

78. Fishel and Pottker, *National Politics and Sex Discrimination*, pp. 109–11.
79. Memo to Caspar Weinberger from Anne Armstrong, March 27, 1972; Memo to Armstrong from Weinberger, May 8, 1974, in folder Education, proposed regulations re: Title IX Act of 72, August–September 74, RG 235 general records of the Department of Health, Education and Welfare, Office of the Secretary, Secretary's subject correspondence, 1956–1974, Box 427, National Archives.
80. 120 *Congressional Record*, May 20, 1974, pp. 15,322–23.
81. On Congress and the agencies, see R. Shep Melnick, "The Courts, Congress, and Programmatic Rights," in Richard A. Harris and Sidney M. Milkis, *Remaking American Politics* (Boulder: Westview Press, 1989), pp. 188–212, pp. 197–98.
82. Gelb and Palley, *Women and Public Policies*, p. 107; "Note: Sex Discrimination and Intercollegiate Athletics: Putting Some Muscle on Title IX," *Yale Law Journal* 88 (1979): 1254–79, 1255; Fishel and Pottker, *National Politics and Sex Discrimination*, pp. 113–14.
83. "Sex discrimination and Intercollegiate Athletics," p. 1257.
84. Fishel and Pottker, *National Politics and Sex Discrimination*, p. 113.
85. Ibid., p. 114; Gary Orfield, *Must We Bus?* (Washington, D.C.: Brookings Institution, 1978), p. 307.
86. Memo to the Secretary from Lewis M. Helm, Assistant Secretary for Public Affairs, August 13, 1974, in folder Education, proposed regulations re: Title IX Act of 72, August–September 74, RG 235 general records of the Department of Health, Education and Welfare, Office of the Secretary, Secretary's subject correspondence, 1956–1974, Box 427, National Archives.
87. Letter from Caspar Weinberger to Robin Beard, August 16, 1974, in ibid.
88. Letter from Acting Secretary Frank Carlucci to Senator William L. Scott, August 20, 1974, in ibid.

89. Letter from Caspar Weinberger to Senator Wallace F. Bennett, September 23, 1974, in ibid.
90. Fishel and Pottker, *National Politics and Sex Discrimination*, p. 117.
91. Ibid., pp. 114, 117.
92. *New York Times*, June 4, 1975.
93. The regulations were also released with a surprise: HEW announced that it would no longer investigate complaints of discrimination. HEW officials explained that they were trying to move away from the "mailbag" approach—investigating every complaint within ninety days—since this was overwhelming the small agency. OCR was investigating only 25 percent of all complaints that it received. Further, OCR director Peter Holmes argued that "complaints received by the department over the last few years have not been broadly representative of the spectrum of the department's civil rights enforcement program.

    "For example, more complaints involving sex discrimination in higher education academic employment are received than on any other subject, based, perhaps, in part upon the educational level of the affected persons.

    "In contrast, fewer complaints are received regarding national origin discrimination, of which the department has found substantial evidence, perhaps because the potential complainants speak and write English with difficulty." Some women's groups were outraged. "It's kind of like having a police department saying it won't respond to complaints because they are busy," argued a WEAL spokesperson, while Bernice Sandler predicted that women and minorities would go to the courts and bring lawsuits against educational institutions. *New York Times*, June 4, 1975.
94. *Sex Discrimination Regulations Hearings*, pp. 2–45, 39.
95. Section C(I)(ii) in ibid.
96. Ibid.
97. As Congressmen James O'Hara (D–MI) later complained, "This is the classic way of doing it. They don't say that you have to do this but they say one way that you can avoid having your university declared ineligible for Federal contracts and whatever is to do these things . . . So, in effect what it does is put a tremendous amount of pressure on you to comply with these things that they say you don't have to comply with because you recognize that if you do that you are safe." Ibid., p. 59.
98. Ibid., p. 39.
99. Ibid., p. 398. By 1975, Green had apparently lost interest in education legislation, including Title IX. Believing that "in 1973–74 there would be no new education legislation under Nixon," and that "the action would be on the Appropriations Committee," she moved to where the action was. Edith Green Oral History, Oral History Collection of the Association of Former Members of Congress, Library of Congress, p. 107.
100. *Sex Discrimination Regulations Hearings*, p. 54.
101. Ibid., p. 175.
102. Ibid., p. 183.
103. Ibid., p. 302.

104. Fishel and Pottker, *National Politics and Sex Discrimination,* p. 127.

105. As Anne Costain has written, "Members of women's groups had to see concrete legislative benefits coming out of Congress such as Title IX of the Education Amendments Act of 1972 . . . and the ERA before they were willing to commit the resources and take the risks inherent in participating in coordinated Washington lobbying." Costain, *Inviting Women's Rebellion,* p. 50. NOW's membership in 1972 was fifteen thousand (to balloon to 220,000 in 1982) but was increasingly becoming a "mass-membership organization, with most joiners only active enough to write a check." Myra Marx Ferree and Beth B. Hess, *Controversy and Coalition,* rev. ed. (New York: Twayne, 1995), p. 134. WEAL was an even more elite organization.

106. Jane Mansbridge, *Why We Lost the ERA* (Chicago: University of Chicago Press, 1986), pp. 133–37, 174–76.

107. This was true despite polls showing surprising—though perhaps superficial—support for women's equality in sports. A Gallup poll in September 1974 asked "Should girls be permitted to participate in noncontact sports—track, tennis, golf, baseball, and the like—*on the same teams as boys?* (Original emphasis.) Fifty-nine percent of Americans said yes. When asked "Should girls have equal financial support for their athletic activities as boys?" an even larger majority, 88 percent, agreed. George H. Gallup, "Participation in Sports by Girls," in Janice Pottker and Andrew Fishel, eds., *Sex Bias in the Schools* (Rutherford, N.J.: Fairleigh Dickinson University Press, 1977), p. 531.

108. On standards of review for sex classifications, see Deborah Rhode, *Justice and Gender* (Cambridge: Harvard University Press, 1991).

109. "The President's News Conference of June 1, 1971," *Public Papers of the Presidents, Richard M. Nixon,* vol. 3 (Washington, D.C.: Government Printing Office, 1972), pp. 688–97, 690.

110. Letter from Marianne Means to Ron [Ziegler], June 2, 1971, and Ziegler to Means, June 3, 1971, in folder hu 2–5 women 1/1171–12/31/71, WHSF, HU Box 21, NPMP, National Archives.

111. Letter from (Miss) Louella McCann to the President, June 2, 1971, in Hoff-Wilson *Papers of the Nixon White House,* Part 7, Fiche 87, frame 4.

112. Draft minutes of Cabinet Committee Meeting on Spanish-speaking, August 5, 1971, in folder GRASSMUCK, GEORGE L. -CCOSS, WHCF, SMOF, Files of Robert Finch, Box 16, NPMP, National Archives.

113. Suggested Remarks: National Federation of Republican Women, October 21, 1971, in Hoff-Wilson, *Papers of the Nixon White House,* Part 6a, Fiche 182, frame 6. According to the *Public Papers of the Presidents,* Nixon played it straight, though this record does not necessarily reflect what was actually said. "Remarks at the Convention of the National Federation of Republican Women, October 23, 1971," in *Public Papers of the Presidents, Richard M. Nixon,* vol. 3 (Washington, D.C.: Government Printing Office, 1972), pp. 1057–62.

114. On humor as incongruity, see Murray S. Davis, *What's So Funny? The Comic Conception of Culture and Society* (Chicago: University of Chicago Press, 1993), Part 1.

9. White Males and the Limits of the Revolution

1. Peter Skerry, *Mexican Americans: The Ambivalent Minority* (New York: Free Press, 1993), p. 16.
2. Though the United States was in step with the world in terms of its development of rights for the disabled—the UN issued a Declaration of the Rights of Disabled Persons in 1975—there is no evidence of a causal link between international and American developments.
3. Theda Skocpol, *Protecting Soldiers and Mothers* (Cambridge, Mass.: Harvard University Press, 1994), Chapter 2.
4. Edward D. Berkowitz, *Disabled Policy: America's Programs for the Handicapped* (New York: Cambridge University Press, 1987), Chapter 1; Lawrence M. Friedman and Jack Ladinsky, "Social Change and the Law of Industrial Accidents," in Lawrence M. Friedman and Harry N. Scheiber, eds., *American Law and the Constitutional Order,* enlarged ed. (Cambridge, Mass.: Harvard University Press, 1988 [1978]), pp. 269–82.
5. Berkowitz, *Disabled Policy* is an excellent source on the development of this program. On costs, see p. 2; on development see Chapters 2–4.
6. Ibid., p. 163.
7. Edward D. Berkowitz, "A Historical Preface to the Americans with Disabilities Act," in Hugh Davis Graham, *Civil Rights in the United States* (University Park: Pennsylvania State University Press, 1994), pp. 96–119, 101. The drive to rehabilitate the handicapped also led to the Architectural Barriers Act of 1968, mandating that all new federal construction projects be made accessible to the disabled. Richard K. Scotch, *From Good Will to Civil Rights: Transforming Federal Disability Policy* (Philadelphia: Temple University Press, 1984), pp. 29–30. Also see Stephen L. Percy, *Disability, Civil Rights, and Public Policy* (Tuscaloosa: University of Alabama Press, 1989). It was not linked to the discourse of discrimination and rights even though architectural barriers clearly had a disparate impact on some types of disabled persons.
8. Paul D. Moreno, *From Direct Action to Affirmative Action* (Baton Rouge: Louisiana State University Press, 1997), p. 175. In 1951, Truman's Government Contract Compliance Committee, created to ensure nondiscrimination among government contractors, drew analogies between blacks and women, children, and the handicapped to argue that all of these groups needed special treatment. Ibid., p. 179.
9. Rockefeller Brothers Fund, *Prospect for America* (New York: Doubleday, 1961), p. 316; see a discussion in Berkowitz, "Historical Preface," pp. 97–8.
10. For a critique of America's love affair with rights to the exclusion of duties, see Mary Ann Glendon, *Rights Talk* (New York: Free Press, 1991).
11. Minutes, Annual Meeting the President's Committee on Employment of the Handicapped, May 1–2, 1969, in folder 1969-committee-President's Committee on Employment of the Handicapped, RG 174 Records of the Secretary of Labor George P. Shultz, 1969–70, Box 67, Labor Department Papers, National Archives.

12. *Congressional Record,* January 20, 1972, p. 526.
13. In 1971, a district court in Alabama ruled that involuntarily institutionalized mental patients had a right to some individualized treatment that could realistically improve their condition. *Wyatt v. Hardin,* 325 F. Supp. 781 (M.D. Ala. 1971). Also in that year, a district court in Pennsylvania ruled in a Fourteenth Amendment case dealing with the education of the mentally retarded that the state had an "obligation to place each mentally retarded child in a free, public program of education and training appropriate to the child's capacity," and added that placement in a regular classroom was preferable to a special class. *Pennsylvania Ass'n for Retarded Children v. Commonwealth of Pennsylvania,* 324 F. Supp. 1257 (E.D. Pa. 1971). In 1973, a District of Columbia court extended the Pennsylvania ruling to cover physically disabled children as well. *Mills v. Board of Educ.,* 348 F. Supp. 866 (D.D.C. 1972). Members of Congress did not demonstrate similar respect for or even awareness of parallel court rulings for women's rights, many decided on constitutional principles.
14. Robert A. Katzmann, *Institutional Disability: The Saga of Transportation Policy for the Disabled* (Washington, D.C.: Brookings Institution, 1986), p. 46. The rest of this account of the origins of Section 504 is based on Scotch and Katzmann.
15. Scotch, *Good Will to Civil Rights,* p. 48.
16. Ibid., p. 51.
17. Ibid., pp. 51–52.
18. 87 Stat. 355, quoted in Katzman, *Institutional Disability,* p. 2.
19. Berkowitz, *Disabled Policy,* p. 178. The aggressiveness of Congress showed that the disabled were considered a minority group unlike all others in their deservingness. See Chapter 10.
20. Scotch, *Good Will to Civil Rights,* p. 53.
21. Ibid., p. 57.
22. Berkowitz, *Disabled Policy,* p. 213.
23. Joseph A. Califano Jr., *Governing America* (New York: Simon and Schuster, 1981), p. 260; *New York Times,* April 11, 1977.
24. Scotch, *Good Will to Civil Rights,* p. 76.
25. Ibid., pp. 76–77.
26. Katzmann, *Institutional Disability,* p. 100.
27. Berkowitz, *Disabled Policy,* p. 217, quoting the draft regulations.
28. Ibid., p. 219.
29. R. Shep Melnick, *Between the Lines* (Washington, D.C.: Brookings Institution, 1994), pp. 135–36.
30. Ibid., p. 150.
31. Catherine Rymph, "'Outcasts, Misfits, and Rejects': The Rise and Fall of Republican Feminism, 1972–1980," in Ken Cmiel and Casey Blake, eds., *Thinking through the Seventies* (Chicago: University of Chicago Press, forthcoming).
32. Melnick, *Between the Lines,* pp. 150–51.
33. Steven M. Teles, *Whose Welfare? AFCD and Elite Politics* (Lawrence: University Press of Kansas, 1996), Chapter 3.

34. Nathan Glazer, *Affirmative Discrimination: Ethnic Inequality and Public Policy* (Cambridge, Mass.: Harvard University Press, 1987 [1975]), pp. 173–74.

35. Hugh Davis Graham, *Collision Course* (New York: Oxford University Press, 2002), p. 94

36. David M. Reimers, "Post-World War II Immigration to the United States: America's Latest Newcomers," *Annals of the American Academy of Political and Social Science* 454 (March 1981): 1–12, 10. Also see John A. Kromkowski, "Eastern and Southern European Immigrants: Expectations, Reality and a New Agenda," *Annals of the American Academy of Political and Social Science* 487 1986: 57–78.

37. *Hearings before the General Subcommittee on Education of the Committee on Education and Labor,* House, 93rd Cong., 2nd Sess., on H.R. 1085, H.R. 2490, and H.R. 1146, bills to amend Title VII of the ESEA, 1974, pp. 34, 39, 332–333, 366.

38. James R. Barrett and David Roediger, "Inbetween Peoples: Race, Nationality and the 'New Immigrant' Working Class," *Journal of American Ethnic History,* 16 (1997): 3–44; John Higham, *Send These to Me* (New York: Atheneum, 1975); John Higham, *Strangers in the Land* (New Brunswick: Rutgers University Press, 1955).

39. Thomas J. Sugrue, *The Origins of the Urban Crisis: Race and Inequality in Postwar Detroit* (Princeton: Princeton University Press, 1996), p. 212.

40. Dan T. Carter, *The Politics of Rage* (New York: Simon and Schuster, 1995), p. 212; Thomas Byrne Edsall with Mary D. Edsall, *Chain Reaction* (New York: Norton, 1991), pp. 77–79; Mark R. Levy and Michael S. Kramer, *The Ethnic Factor: How America's Minorities Decide Elections* (New York: Simon and Schuster, 1972), pp. 18–19.

41. Peter Binzen, *Whitetown, U.S.A.* (New York: Random House, 1970), pp. 6–7, 33; Arthur Mann, *The One and the Many: Reflections on the American Identity* (Chicago: University of Chicago Press, 1979), p. 19.

42. Quoted in Perry L. Weed, *The White Ethnic Movement and Ethnic Politics* (New York: Praeger, 1973), pp. 19–20. On the Ford Foundation and the ethnic movement, also see Mann, *The One and the Many,* p. 20, and on the efforts of the American Jewish Committee, see ibid., p. 25. On the relationship between ethnics and blacks, also see Pete Hamill, "The Revolt of the White Lower Middle Class" and Andrew Hacker, "Is There a Republican Majority?" both in Louise Kapp Howe, ed., *The White Majority: Between Poverty and Affluence* (New York: Random House, 1970), pp. 10–22, 263–78.

43. Weed, *White Ethnic Movement,* Chapter 3.

44. Geno Baroni, "Ethnicity and Public Policy," in Michael Wenk, S. M. Tomasi, and Geno Baroni, eds., *Pieces of a Dream: The Ethnic Worker's Crisis with America* (New York: Center for Migration Studies, 1972), pp. 1–12. Also see Gary Gerstle, *American Crucible* (Princeton: Princeton University Press, 2001), pp. 333–34; and Lawrence M. O'Rourke, *Geno: The Life and Mission of Geno Baroni* (New York: Paulist Press, 1991), Chapters 8 and 9.

45. David R. Colburn and George E. Pozzetta, "Race, Ethnicity and the Evolution of Political Legitimacy," in David Farber, ed., *The Sixties: From Memory to*

History (Chapel Hill: University of North Carolina Press, 1994), pp. 119–48, 132.

46. Michael Novak, *The Rise of the Unmeltable Ethnics: Politics and Culture in the Seventies* (New York: Macmillan, 1972).

47. Richard Scammon and Ben Wattenberg, *The Real Majority: An Extraordinary Examination of the American Electorate* (New York: Coward-McCann, 1970).

48. Weed, *White Ethnic Movement*, pp. 27, 32, 118. Also see *Newsweek*, December 21, 1971, p. 27, on Baroni's activities.

49. Andrew M. Greeley, *Why Can't They Be Like Us? America's White Ethnic Groups* (New York: Dutton, 1971).

50. Quoted in Weed, *White Ethnic Movement*, p. 40.

51. *Time*, July 12, 1971, p. 15; Levy and Kramer, *Ethnic Factor*, pp. 159–60.

52. Weed, *White Ethnic Movement*, p. 51–62; *Time*, July 12, 1971, p. 15. On Italian American concern with the Mafia image, see Richard Gambino, *Blood of My Blood* (Garden City, N.Y.: Anchor Books, 1975 [1974]), Chapter 8.

53. The basis and origins of these jokes remain unclear. Murray's sociological analysis of humor (in which he uses many Polish jokes without comment to illustrate different dynamics of humor) does not analyze the issue. In a footnote, however, he mentions two views on why Poles were targeted. One view is that they are "the major lower class *white* group" while another (contradictory) view specifies their "*rising* economic status." Murray S. Davis, *What's So Funny?* (Chicago: University of Chicago Press, 1993), p. 349 n. 15.

54. John Bukowczyk, *And My Children Did Not Know Me : A History of the Polish-Americans* (Bloomington: Indiana University Press, 1987), Chapter 6. See also James J. Pula, "Image, Status, Mobility and Integration in American Society: The Polish Experience," *Journal of American History* 16 (1996): 75–95; Weed, *White Ethnic Movement*, p. 81; Helena Znaniecka Lopata, *Polish Americans*, 2nd rev. ed. (New Brunswick, N.J.: Transaction Publishers, 1994), pp. 125–26.

55. Gerhard Lenski, *The Religious Factor* (Garden City, N.Y.: Doubleday, 1961), pp. 115, 118. Similarly, in 1976, the social scientist Carmi Schooler argued that ethnics in the United States retained a distinctive peasant culture: "Ethnic groups with a long history of serfdom show the intellectual inflexibility, authoritarianism, and pragmatic legalistic morality typical of men working under such circumstances." Schooler, "Serfdom's Legacy: An Ethnic Continuum," *American Journal of Sociology* 81 (1976): 1265–86, 1281.

56. *Newsweek*, December 21, 1971, pp. 32–33.

57. Congressional Quarterly, "Campaign '72: The Rising Voice of Ethnic Voters," *Congressional Quarterly Weekly Report* 30 (1972): 531–34, 532.

58. Herbert Hammerman, personal correspondence, July 20, 1998.

59. Letter to Stephen Shulman from Vincent J. Trapani, April 21, 1967, in folder Research EEO-1, Papers of Chairman Stephen Shulman, Box 10, EEOC Papers, National Archives.

60. Data are from the 1943–44 fiscal year, as reported in President's Committee on Civil Rights, *To Secure These Rights* (Washington, D.C.: Government Printing Office, 1947), p. 54.

61. Ibid., pp. 56, 59, 63, 66, 78.

62. Ibid., p. 59.
63. Harold Orlans, "The Origins of Protected Groups," unpublished manuscript, 1986, p. 5.
64. *Hearings before the US Equal Employment Opportunity Commission on Discrimination in White Collar Employment,* New York, January 15–18, 1968, pp. 784–86.
65. At the hearing, the Jewish issues were mostly not pursued in questioning of New York business leaders, though Harvey Basham, senior vice president at Chemical Bank, was questioned why only "six or seven" of 140 vice presidents at the company were Jewish. Basham claimed that this was a "pipeline problem," and that all of the vice presidents had been with the company for fifteen to twenty years. *Hearings on Discrimination in White Collar Employment,* pp. 443–46, 464.
66. Roger Waldinger, *Still the Promised City? African-Americans and New Immigrants in Postindustrial New York* (Cambridge, Mass.: Harvard University Press, 1996), p. 225.
67. Jo Freeman, *The Politics of Women's Liberation* (New York: David McKay, 1975), pp. 200–1.
68. See the statement of Stanley Dacher, vice president of the Queens, N.Y. Jewish Community Council in *Hearings before the Special Subcommittee on Education of the Committee on Education and Labor, House of Representatives, 93rd Cong., 2nd Sess., on Federal Higher Education Programs Institutional Eligibility,* Civil Rights Obligations, Part 2A, 1974, pp. 489–90; and Freeman, *Politics of Women's Liberation,* pp. 200–1.
69. Letter from Philip E. Hoffman to President Nixon, August 4, 1972, and Letter from President Nixon to Philip E. Hoffman, August 11, 1972, in Hugh Davis Graham, ed., *Civil Rights during the Nixon Administration 1969–1974* (Bethesda, Md.: University Publications of America, 1989), Part 1, Reel 4, frames 276–78. See Nicholas Lemann, *The Big Test* (New York: Farrar, Straus, 1999).
70. See, e.g., the memo from Kenyon C. Burke, director of the National Urban Affairs Department, to David A. Schulte, chair of the Urban Affairs Committee, dated October 5, 1972, describing a September meeting of black and Jewish leaders on the quota issue. Papers of the Leadership Conference on Civil Rights, Box 114, folder Quota Hiring 1972 Affirmative Action, Library of Congress.
71. I could find almost no evidence of any discussion of preferences for religious groups in higher-education affirmative action. In hearings on a bill to limit affirmative-action preferences in the partially federally funded Council on Legal Education Opportunity (CLEO) program, James O'Hara (D–MI) grilled the dean of the law school at Catholic University (a supporter of the CLEO program) on how religion fit into his notion of a "representative" law school class. If there were too many Jews, would he support limiting their number so that other groups had more chances? The dean, E. Clinton Bamberger, tried to dodge the issue, then admitted "you are asking me very tough questions and I admit they are very tough" but that "I happen to come down on the side of thinking that we ought to make particular efforts in our law school to have a va-

riety of people involved there in learning and teaching." *Hearings before the Special Subcommittee on Education of the Committee on Education and Labor, House of Representatives*, 93rd Cong., 2nd Sess., on H.R. 14673, Legal Education Opportunities, 1974, p. 23.

In another round of hearings on affirmative action, Representative John Dellenback (R–OR) asked OCR director Peter Holmes why it did not look at religion in utilization analysis of institutions of higher education. Holmes simply stated that the OCR did not use religion in affirmative action "principally because the Department of Labor has not issued any specific guidance to the various agencies delegated the responsibility for enforcing the Executive Order with regard to the subject," though they had considered individual complaints of religious discrimination. *Hearings before the Special Subcommittee on Education of the Committee on Education and Labor, House of Representatives*, 93rd Cong., 2nd Sess., Part 2A, Civil Rights Obligations, 1974, p. 78.

72. Allan P. Sindler, *Bakke, DeFunis, and Minority Admissions* (New York: Longman, 1978), pp. 243–44; also see generally, Timothy J. O'Neill, *Bakke and the Politics of Equality: Friends and Foes in the Classroom of Litigation* (Middletown, Conn.: Wesleyan University Press, 1985).

73. Mary Patrice Erdmans, *Opposite Poles: Immigrants and Ethnics in Polish Chicago, 1976–1996* (University Park: Penn State University Press, 1998), p. 49.

74. Russell Barta, "Minority Report: The Representation of Poles, Italians, Latins and Blacks in the Executive Suites of Chicago's Largest Corporations," n.d. [1973 or 1974], in Graham, *Civil Rights during Nixon*, Part 1, Reel 19, frames 493–96. Barta updated the study in 1983, and continued to find low representation of all four groups. Percentage of directors: Poles (0.5), Italians (2.2), Hispanics (0.2), blacks (1.8), all others (95.3). Percentage of officers: Poles (2.6), Italians (2.9), Hispanics (0.1), blacks (0.5), all others (93.9). In the area population, Poles accounted for 11.2 percent, Italians, 7.3, Hispanics, 8.2, blacks, 20.1, and all others 53.2. See Kromkowski, "Eastern and Southern European Immigrants," pp. 75–76.

75. Alfred Blumrosen, a labor lawyer working in the EEOC in the middle 1960s and a major architect of affirmative action, later argued that ethnics, due to construction industry niches, were already viewed as beneficiaries of preferences: "Any recognition of depressed status for these groups, *qua* groups, would directly conflict with sought-for benefits for blacks, and to that extent cancel out the impact of the Civil Rights Act." White ethnics also benefited from seniority rights. For these reasons, recognition of white ethnic claims would have been inconsistent with the primary focus of the agency. Alfred Blumrosen, personal correspondence, May 2000. Blumrosen's basic point is sound, as the historian Thomas Sugrue has shown. See Sugrue, "Breaking Through: The Troubled Origins of Affirmative Action in the Workplace," in John Skrentny, ed., *Color Lines* (Chicago: University of Chicago Press, 2001), pp. 31–52. On the other hand, affirmative action to open up higher education and white-collar employment to ethnics would have lessened their resistance to integration of their labor unions.

76. *Federal Register*, vol. 36, no. 250, December 29, 1971, p. 25,165.

77. Memo from Bryce Harlow to George T. Bell, January 14, 1972, in folder Hu 2-

Equality [1971–74], White House Special Files (WHSF), Confidential Files (CF), Box 35, Nixon Presidential Materials Project (NPMP), National Archives.

78. Memo from Henry C. Cashen to Charles Perry, January 19, 1972, in ibid.
79. Memo from George Shultz to Henry Cashen, January 19, 1972, in ibid.
80. Gleason ran a secret $3 million slush fund from a Washington, D.C. townhouse basement. See *Washington Post,* February 16, 1980.
81. Letter from Jack A. Gleason to John Dean, January 20, 1972, in folder GEN FG 22–4 Federal Contract Compliance, Office of, [1971–72], WHCF Subject Files, Department of Labor, FG 22, Box 6, NPMP, National Archives.
82. Letter from W. M. Bennett to James D. Hodgson, January 27, 1972, in ibid.
83. John W. Dean to Jack Gleason, February 18, 1972, in ibid.
84. Letter from Peter M. Flanigan to W. M. Bennett, February 7, 1972, in ibid.
85. Memo from George T. Bell to Ken Cole, February 23, 1972, in folder Hu 2-Equality [1971–74], WHSF, CF, Box 35, NPMP, National Archives.
86. Unsigned, undated memo in ibid.
87. 41 C.F.R. Part 60–50 (7–1–97 ed.). In a phone call I placed to the Labor Department in 1998, I could not find anyone who knew these OFCC regulations existed.
88. Even the PAC activist Leonard Walentynowicz did not know of the regulations. Author interview with Leonard Walentynowicz, February 17, 2001.
89. Brief of the Polish American Congress, the National Advocates Society, and the National Medical and Dental Association as Amici Curiae, reprinted in *Regents of the University of California v. Allan Bakke: Complete Case Record,* vol. 2 (Englewood, Colo.: Information Handling Services, 1978).
90. See the testimony of Weldon J. Rougeau, US Commission on Civil Rights, *Consultations on the Affirmative Action Statement of the US Commission on Civil Rights, vol. 2: Proceedings, February 10 and March 10–11, 1981* (Washington, D.C.: Government Printing Office, 1982), p. 85.
91. *Civil Rights Issues of Euro-Ethnic Americans in the United States: Opportunities and Challenges, A Consultation Sponsored by the US Commission on Civil Rights,* Chicago, Illinois, December 3, 1979 (Washington, D.C.: Government Printing Office, 1980), pp. 385, 390, 444.
92. Ibid., pp. 493–97. Also see Philip Gleason, *Speaking of Diversity: Language and Ethnicity in Twentieth-Century America* (Baltimore, MD: Johns Hopkins University Press, 1992), p. 107; Patrick J. Gallo, *Old Bread, New Wine: A Portrait of the Italian-Americans* (Chicago: Nelson-Hall, 1981), p. 285.
93. Testimony of Leonard Walentynowicz, *Consultations on the Affirmative Action Statement,* pp. 158–71.
94. Ibid.
95. *Congressional Record,* December 15, 1969, pp. 39,062–63.
96. *Hearings before the Special Subcommittee on Education of the Committee on Education and Labor,* House of Representatives, 93rd Cong., 2nd Sess., Part 2A, Civil Rights Obligations, 1974, pp. 25–28.
97. Ibid. Kemp also questioned Representative Patricia Schroeder (D–CO), who was appearing as a pro-affirmative-action witness. Kemp asked if the sorts of Euro-ethnic groups that made up his district would be included in a utilization

analysis of hiring in higher education. Schroeder answered that "the biggest problems we have nationwide are including the female sex, including blacks, and including the Spanish speaking, because it is one of the bilingual, bicultural groups of our society today. In other words, the German-Americans, the Polish-Americans and the others have broken through and become absorbed." Ibid., p. 217.

98. See Chapter 4, n. 56.

99. Ibid., pp. 238–39. Buckley made similar arguments on the Senate floor. See Philip Gleason's discussion in *Speaking of Diversity,* Chapter 4, esp. p. 106.

100. US Commission on Civil Rights, *Civil Rights Issues of Euro-Ethnic Americans in the United States: Opportunities and Challenges, December 3, 1979* (Washington, D.C.: Government Printing Office, 1980).

101. Memo to the President from Secretary of Labor Shultz, June 26, 1969, in Graham, *Civil Rights during Nixon,* Part 1, Reel 2, frame 14.

102. *Newsweek,* October 6, 1969, p. 28.

103. Ibid., pp. 29–33. See Kevin Phillips, *The Emerging Republican Majority* (New Rochelle: Arlington House, 1969). The *Wall Street Journal* published a similar article in April 24, 1969. It quoted the president of the National Slovak Society, John Pankuch, as saying, "Naturally, there's bitter feeling on the part of white ethnics toward Negroes," since "there are more white poor than black, and very little has dribbled down to the white poor." Pankuch added, "But perhaps if the ethnics begin to speak as one voice maybe somebody will pay attention to us as well as them." The article reported that the National Confederation of American Ethnic Groups had 20 million members from sixty-seven different ethnic organizations. See Mann, *The One and Many,* p. 22.

104. Memo to the President from Harry S. Dent, September 26, 1969, in folder Memos to the President, 1969 [3 of 3], Staff Member and Office Files (SMOF), Papers of Harry S. Dent, Box 2, NPMP, National Archives.

105. Paul Frymer and John David Skrentny, "Coalition-Building and the Politics of Electoral Capture during the Nixon Administration: African Americans, Labor, Latinos," *Studies in American Political Development* 12 (spring 1998), 131–61, 151.

106. Memo to the President from Harry S. Dent, October 13, 1969, in folder Middle Americans, Dent, SMOF, Papers of Harry S. Dent, Box 8, NPMP, National Archives.

107. Ibid.

108. Frymer and Skrentny, "Coalition-Building," p. 150.

109. Ibid., p. 151.

110. Robert Reisner, quoted in Gerald S. Strober and Deborah Strober, *Nixon: An Oral History of His Presidency* (New York: Harper Collins, 1994), p. 277.

111. H. R. Haldeman, quoted in ibid., p. 274. Public relations aide Jeb Magruder saw Colson as the champion of Catholics and labor (as I describe below, these labels were interchangeable with "ethnics"). Jeb Stuart Magruder, *An American Life: One Man's Road to Watergate* (New York: Atheneum, 1974), p. 65.

112. Memo to Robert Finch from H. R. Haldeman, November 27, 1970, in folder

Catholic Vote–Charles Edison Youth Fund, WHSF, SMOF, Papers of Charles W. Colson, Box 46, NPMP, National Archives.

113. Quoted in Strober and Strober, *Nixon*, p. 82.

114. Memo to the President from Pat Buchanan, May 26, 1969, in Joan Hoff-Wilson, ed., *Papers of the Nixon White House* (Bethesda, Md: University Publications of America, 1989), Part 6a, Fiche 18, frames 52–3.

115. Both parties had created nationalities divisions in the 1880s, which made generally symbolic appeals to various ethnic groups by concentrating on foreign-policy issues. Especially in the aftermath of World War II and the subsequent Communist takeover of many eastern European nations, the interest in foreign policy began to dominate. The names of these divisions within the party institutions have changed over the decades. See Louis Gerson, *The Hyphenate in Recent American Politics and Diplomacy* (Lawrence: University of Kansas Press, 1964), esp. pp. 31–41.

116. Memo from Laszlo Pasztor to Harry S. Dent, March 19, 1970, in folder 1970 Nationalities and Minorities [2 of 2], WHSF, SMOF, Papers of Harry S. Dent 1969–70, Box 9, NPMP, National Archives.

117. Memo from Tom Lias to Harry S. Dent, June 1, 1970, in ibid.

118. Letter from Laszlo Pasztor to Harry S. Dent, July 31, 1970; Letter from Harry S. Dent to Laszlo Pasztor, August 10, 1970, in ibid.

119. Quoted in Skrentny, *Ironies of Affirmative Action,* p. 213.

120. Memo to Harry S. Flemming from Charles W. Colson, August 4, 1970, in Graham, *Civil Rights during Nixon*, Part 1, Reel 2, frame 952.

121. Letter to the President from John A. Volpe, February 1, 1973, in Hoff-Wilson, *Papers of the Nixon White House,* Part 6a, Fiche 264, frame 7.

122. *Congressional Record,* April 30, 1969, p. 10,867.

123. House Joint Resolution 983, *Congressional Record,* November 13, 1969, p. 34,165.

124. *Congressional Record,* November 21, 1969, pp. 35,435–36.

125. A Senate committee report did not define ethnicity because, according to Judith Herman, the committee did not want to unintentionally exclude any group. It listed as examples Italian Americans, Polish Americans, Mexican Americans, blacks, and "etc." Judith Herman, ed., *The Schools and Group Identity: Educating for a New Pluralism* (New York: Institute on Pluralism and Group Identity of the American Jewish Committee, 1974), p. 56.

126. *Congressional Record,* June 14, 1972, p. 20,805.

127. Memo from Harry Dent to Harry Flemming, April 28, 1970, ("Looks like we're going to have some competition here in the nationalities field"), and attached memo from Laszlo Pasztor to James N. Allison Jr., April 22, 1970, in folder Nationalities and Minorities [2 of 2], WHSF, SMOF, Papers of Harry S. Dent, 1969–70, Box 9, NPMP, National Archives.

128. *Congressional Quarterly Weekly Report,* vol. 30, July 22, 1972, p. 1837. See the discussion in Nathan Glazer, *Ethnic Dilemmas: 1964–1982* (Cambridge, Mass.: Harvard University Press, 1983), pp. 135–36.

129. Quoted in Noel Epstein, *Language, Ethnicity and the Schools: Policy Alterna-*

tives for Bilingual-Bicultural Education (Washington, D.C.: George Washington University Institute for Educational Leadership, 1977), pp. 38–39. Some ethnic groups found more success at the local or state level. For example, state legislatures created Polish American studies programs in higher-education institutions in Connecticut, Massachusetts, Michigan, and Wisconsin. Stanislaus A. Blejwas, "Polonia and Politics," in John J. Bukowczyk, ed., *Polish Americans and Their History* (Pittsburgh: University of Pittsburgh Press, 1996), pp. 121–51, 139. Also, in 1967, Illinois passed a law stating that "the teaching of history shall include a study of the role and contribution of American Negroes and other ethnic groups including but not restricted to Polish, Lithuanian, German, Hungarian, Irish, Bohemian, Russian, Albanian, Italian, Czechoslovakian, French, Scots, etc." No action was taken until 1972, when the state created the Office of Ethnic Studies. Herman, *Schools and Group Identity*, p. 58.

130. See Carpenter's "Foreword," p. 8, in Herman, *Schools and Group Identity*.
131. Memo to Harry Dent from Laszlo Pasztor, May 24, 1972, in folder [Events] National Heritage Day (Presidential Proclamation), WHSF, SMOF, Papers of Michael P. Balzano, Box 5, NPMP, National Archives.
132. Memo to Charles Colson from Harry Dent, May 26, 1972, in ibid.
133. Confidential, A Proposal, n.d., in ibid.
134. Memo to H. R. Haldeman from Charles Colson, September 25, 1972, in ibid.
135. "Remarks at the Dedication of the American Museum of Immigration on Liberty Island, September 26, 1972, and Statement about the Dedication of the American Museum of Immigration, September 26, 1972," in *Public Papers of the Presidents of the United States: Richard M. Nixon, 1972* (Washington, D.C.: Government Printing Office, 1973), pp. 913–16.
136. "Radio Address: One America, October 28, 1972," in *Public Papers of the Presidents of the United States: Richard M. Nixon, 1972* (Washington, DC: Government Printing Office, 1973), pp. 1054–57.
137. Memo to Susan Porter from Michael Balzano, February 21, 1973, in folder Events-Speaking Engagements, WHCF, SMOF, Papers of Michael P. Balzano, Box 5, NPMP, National Archives. This sort of thing was standard practice. In July of 1970, Nixon aide Dwight Chapin sought a study of the ethnic groups in the key states to determine special events or dates that should be exploited. "For example," Chapin continued, "in the State of Illinois, if there is a big Polish holiday between now and election day we would program someone in for that particular event." Memo to Murray Chotiner and Harry Dent from Dwight L. Chapin, July 25, 1970, in Graham, *Civil Rights during Nixon*, Part 1, Reel 2, frame 865.
138. Nathan Glazer, "Multiculturalism and a New America," in John Higham, ed., *Civil Rights and Wrongs* (University Park: Pennsylvania State University Press, 1997), pp. 119–33, 130; Nathan Glazer, *We Are All Multiculturalists Now* (Cambridge, Mass.: Harvard University Press, 1997), p. 14.
139. Mann, *The One and the Many*, pp. 34–44.
140. Glazer, *Affirmative Discrimination*, p. 183. Levy and Kramer argued that, at least among Poles, language and culture were alive and well in the early 1970s. Levy and Kramer, *Ethnic Factor*, p. 142. Glazer and Moynihan have made a dif-

ferent argument regarding the lack of effective minority politics from Italians. The failure of the Italian-American Anti-Defamation League, relative to the success of the Anti-Defamation League of B'nai B'rith, was due to the lack of an extensive network of intellectuals, scholars, and media connections that the Jews had in abundance. Nathan Glazer and Daniel Patrick Moynihan, *Beyond the Melting Pot,* Second 2nd ed. (Cambridge, Mass.: MIT Press, 1970 [1963]), p. lxviii.

141. Peter Skerry, *Mexican Americans: The Ambivalent Minority* (New York: Free Press, 1993). On differences between Latino and Asian leadership and rank-and-file citizens, see Christian Joppke, *Immigration and the Nation State* (New York: Oxford University Press, 1999), pp. 178–85.

142. See Chapter 10 on the decline in Republican interest in women's rights. On Schlafly's early career, see Catherine E. Rymph, "Neither Neutral nor Neutralized: Phyllis Schlafly's Battle against Sexism," in Linda K. Kerber and Jane Sherron De Hart, eds., *Women's America,* 5th ed. (New York: Oxford University press, 2000), pp. 501–7. On the failed effort to win the ERA, see Jane Mansbridge, *Why We Lost the ERA* (Chicago: University of Chicago Press, 1986); and Mary Frances Berry, *Why ERA Failed* (Bloomington: Indiana University Press, 1986).

143. See F. James Davis, *Who Is Black? One Nation's Definition* (University Park: Pennsylvania State University Press, 1991).

144. Karl Eschbach, "The Enduring and Vanishing American Indian: American Indian Population Growth and Intermarriage in 1990," *Ethnic and Racial Studies* 18 (1995): 89–108; Karl Eschbach, "Changes in Self-Identification of American Indians and Alaska Natives," *Demography* 30 (1993): 635–52.

145. Skerry, *Mexican Americans,* pp. 17–18.

146. EEOC, *Hearings before the United States Equal Employment Opportunity Commission on utilization of minority and women workers in certain major industries, Los Angeles, Calif., March 12–14, 1969,* pp. 130, 137.

147. James R. Barrett and David Roediger, "Inbetween Peoples: Race, Nationality, and the 'New Immigrant' Working Class," *Journal of American Ethnic History* 16, no. 3 (Spring, 1997): 2–44.

148. Franklin D. Roosevelt, "The President Condemns Discharging Loyal Aliens from Jobs," January 2, 1942, *Public Papers and Addresses of Franklin D. Roosevelt, 1942* (New York: Harper and Brothers, 1950), pp. 5–6; Richard W. Steele, "'No Racials': Discrimination against Ethnics in American Defense Industry, 1940–42," *Labor History* 32 (1991): 66–90.

149. Mary Dudziak, *Cold War Civil Rights* (Princeton: Princeton University Press, 2000), p. 35.

150. France Fox Piven and Richard Cloward, *Why Americans Don't Vote* (New York: Pantheon, 1985), pp. 86–87.

151. Mann, *The One and the Many,* pp. 41–44, argues that many if not most ethnics were middle-class suburbanites by the mid-1970s. Also see Glazer, *Affirmative Discrimination,* pp. 179–80. Jennifer Hochschild has compiled evidence showing rapid acceptance of Catholic and Jewish ethnics in the decades after the 1930s. Hochschild, *Facing Up to the American Dream* (Princeton: Princeton

University Press, 1995), pp. 241–43. On the differences between blacks and ethnics, see Stanley Lieberson, *A Piece of the Pie: Blacks and White Immigrants Since 1880* (Berkeley: University of California Press, 1980).

152. Andrew M. Greeley, *Ethnicity, Denomination, and Inequality* (Beverly Hills: Sage, 1976), pp. 52–53.

153. Stanley Lieberson and Mary C. Waters, *From Many Strands* (New York: Russell Sage Foundation, 1988).

154. Richard Alba, John R. Logan, and Kyle Crowder, "White Ethnic Neighborhoods and Assimilation: The Greater New York Region, 1980–1990," *Social Forces* 75 (1997): 883–909.

155. Glazer and Moynihan, *Beyond the Melting Pot,* p. lvi.

156. Gambino, *Blood of My Blood,* p. 245.

157. Waldinger, *Still the Promised City?* pp. 103–5.

158. Greeley, *Ethnicity, Denomination and Inequality,* pp. 56, 58–59. Also see Peter M. Blau and Otis Dudley Duncan, *The American Occupational Structure* (New York: Wiley, 1967), p. 233, for the finding of discrimination against the "less prestigeful" white ethnic groups.

159. Levy and Kramer, *Ethnic Factor,* pp. 143, 166.

160. Richard D. Alba and Gwen Moore, "Ethnicity in the American Elite," *American Sociological Review* 47 (1982): 373–383.

161. Nathan Glazer makes a similar point while focusing on ethnics' perceptions of themselves:

> When we consider the political orientations of any individual among these [ethnic] groups, it will not be easy to tell whether he responds as ethnic, as Catholic or Jew, Easterner or Midwesterner, as big-city-dweller as blue-collar or white-collar worker . . . The Polish blue-collar worker in an individually owned home in Detroit may see himself as Pole, Catholic, blue-collar worker, homeowner, Democrat, and defender of neighborhood turf, all in one.

Glazer, *Affirmative Discrimination,* p. 176.

162. More than other minority-group leaders, it was common in the politics of the late 1960s and early 1970s for white elites to treat ethnics and especially ethnic political leaders with contemptuous ridicule (different in nature than the light-hearted ridicule that women's leaders faced), though I found such attitudes expressed only rarely in the Nixon White House papers. For a sensitive discussion of the change in racial etiquette of the period, and the ways it worked to the detriment of white ethnics, see Glazer and Moynihan, *Beyond the Melting Pot,* pp. lxxii–lxxvi.

163. Untitled, undated report, in folder Ethnics, WHSF, SMOF, Papers of Charles Colson, Box 62, NPMP, National Archives.

164. The confusion of these categories was a constant theme in the 1965–75 period. In June of 1970, for example, speechwriter Patrick Buchanan urged appeals to the "forgotten minorities" concentrated in "labor, Catholic, and blue collar, etc." voters. H. R. Haldeman, *The Haldeman Diaries* (New York: G. P. Putnam's Sons, 1994), p. 177.

165. The report continued, "Their severe isolation is felt most strongly today in the

realm of government, education, and economic development. Because they have not yet been 'dealt in,' the Spanish-speaking consider themselves to be outsiders. As non-participants, they have had neither the opportunity nor the resources to work toward a productive solution to their many unique problems." See the "Confidential" untitled, undated, unauthored [probably Charles Colson] report in Graham, ed., *Civil Rights during Nixon,* Part I, Reel 3, frame 903.

166. Confidential Memo to Mr. Colson from H. R. Haldeman, September 8, 1970, in folder CF LA-7 Unions [1969–70], WHSF, CF, Box 38, NPMP, National Archives.

167. Memorandum to H. R. Haldeman from Charles Colson, September 14, 1970, in ibid.

168. Confidential Memo to Mr. Colson from H. R. Haldeman, September 8, 1970, in ibid.

169. Haldeman expressed great satisfaction after a fancy White House dinner with labor leaders, including AFL-CIO George Meany. Haldeman, *Haldeman Diaries,* pp. 191–92.

170. Memo to Dwight Chapin from Charles Colson, February 25, 1971, in folder Hard Hats—Building and Construction Trades, WHSF, SMOF, Papers of Charles Colson, Box 69, NPMP, National Archives.

171. Frymer and Skrentny, "Coalition Building," p. 150.

172. Haldeman, *Haldeman Diaries,* p. 326.

173. Memo to Harry Dent from Kevin P. Phillips, November 13, 1969, in folder 1970 Middle America [1 of 2], WHSF, SMOF, Papers of Harry S. Dent, 1969–70, Box 8, NPMP, National Archives.

174. Memo to Charles Colson and H. R. Haldeman from the President, August 9, 1972, in folder Memos August 1, 1972 to August 9, 1972, President's Personal File, Memoranda from the President, 1969–74, Box 4, NPMP, National Archives.

175. Haldeman, *Haldeman Diaries,* p. 370.

176. Erhlichman later recounted a story of Nixon's desire to reward Catholics for their support during the 1972 election that led to the appointment Claude Brinegar as secretary of transportation. Nixon thought Brinegar was an Irish Catholic, and his discussion with him one day about cardinals led first to confusion and then to Brinegar's admission, "I'm an Episcopalian." Italian appointments were a safer bet. Kenneth W. Thompson, ed., *The Nixon Presidency: Twenty-two Intimate Perspectives of Richard M. Nixon* (Lanham, Md: University Press of America, 1987), p. 135. Nixon also alienated AFL-CIO leader George Meany by bragging that Nixon's secretary was "a Catholic, too, George." Skrentny, *Ironies of Affirmative Action,* p. 282 n. 59. On Nixon and Catholics, also see Administratively confidential memo to Ken Cole and Ed Harper from Roy Morey, September 16, 1971, in folder Catholic Vote-Charles Edison Youth Fund, WHSF, SMOF, Papers of Charles W. Colson, Box 46, NPMP, National Archives.

177. Alexander DeConde, *Ethnicity, Race and American Foreign Policy: A History* (Boston: Northeastern University Press, 1992), pp. 89, 142–43.

178. Connie de Boer, "The Polls: Attitudes toward Homosexuality," *Public Opinion*

Quarterly 42 (1978): 265–76, 272. The Harris poll gave respondents a list of groups and asked, "Do you feel that [read list] are discriminated against more than most other people, less or no more than others?"

179. Steven Epstein, "Gay and Lesbian Movements in the United States: Dilemmas of Identity, Diversity, and Political Strategy," in Barry Adam, Jan Willem Duyvendak, and André Krouwel, eds., *The Global Emergence of Gay and Lesbian Politics: National Imprints of a Worldwide Movement* (Philadelphia: Temple University Press, 1998), pp. 30–90, 35.

180. Quoted in ibid., p. 79 n. 17.

181. Terry Anderson, *The Movement and the Sixties* (New York: Oxford University Press, 1995), p. 317.

182. James W. Button, Barbara A. Rienzo, and Kenneth D. Wald, *Private Lives, Public Conflicts* (Washington, D.C.: Congressional Quarterly, 1997), p. 25.

183. Estimates of the number of parade participants vary. Anderson, *The Movement and the Sixties*, p. 319, puts the number at ten thousand. Epstein, "Gay and Lesbian Movements," p. 39, estimates it at two thousand.

184. *Time,* October 31, 1969, pp. 56–67.

185. Epstein, "Gay and Lesbian Movements," p. 39.

186. Steven Epstein, "Gay Politics, Ethnic Identity: The Limits of Social Constructionism," *Socialist Review* 17 (May-August 1987), p. 12.

187. Anderson, *The Movement and the Sixties,* pp. 318–19.

188. Epstein, "Gay and Lesbian Movements," p. 41; Button, Rienzo, and Wald, *Private Lives,* p. 64.

189. Anderson, *The Movement and the Sixties,* pp. 397, 401.

190. Epstein, "Gay and Lesbian Movements," p. 44; Myra Marx Ferree and Beth B. Hess, *Controversy and Coalition,* rev. ed. (New York: Twayne, 1995), p. 134.

191. Donald Bruce Johnson and Kirk H. Porter, *National Party Platforms, 1940–1972* (Urbana: University of Illinois Press, 1973 [1956]); Urvashi Vaid, *Virtual Equality* (New York: Anchor Books, 1995), p. 110.

192. William B. Turner, "Lesbian/Gay Rights and Immigration Policy: Lobbying to End the Medical Model," *Journal of Policy History* 7 (1995): 208–25, 210.

193. John Ehrlichman, *Witness to Power* (New York: Simon and Schuster, 1982), pp. 159–60.

194. This conversation was transcribed from tapes by *Chicago Tribune* reporter James Warren and reprinted in *Harper's,* February, 2000, pp. 22–24.

195. Editors of the Harvard Law Review, *Sexual Orientation and the Law* (Cambridge, Mass.: Harvard University Press, 1989), p. 69–71.

196. *Federal Register,* vol. 41, no. 96, p. 20,299.

197. *Federal Register,* vol. 41, no. 38, p. 29,548. Jeremy Rabkin, "Office for Civil Rights," in James Q. Wilson, ed., *The Politics of Regulation* (New York: Basic Books, 1980), pp. 304–56, 330. Gay advocates may have been less than thrilled with the effort since they were simultaneously waging a campaign to have homosexuality no longer defined as an illness by the American Psychiatric Association.

198. *Congressional Record,* June 27, 1974, p. 21,713.

199. H.R. 16200, in *Congressional Record,* July 31, 1974, p. 26,187.

200. *Congressional Record,* March 25, 1975, p. 8548.
201. Studds "came out" in 1983. The other white males co-sponsoring the bill represented liberal districts, and were all Democrats except for one: George Brown (D–CA), Michael Harrington (D–MA), Fortney "Pete" Stark (D–CA), Frederick W. Richmond (D–NY), Benjamin Rosenthal (D–NY), Donald Fraser (D–MN), John L. Burton (D–CA), Paul McCloskey (R–CA), Stephen Solarz (D–NY), Jonathan Bingham (D–NY), and Henry Waxman (D–CA). For brief discussions of these congressional efforts, see Toby Marotta, *The Politics of Homosexuality* (Boston: Houghton Mifflin, 1981), pp. 324–25; Margaret Cruikshank, *The Gay and Lesbian Liberation Movement* (New York: Routledge, 1992), p. 79. The support of minority legislators may have resulted from their perception that gays were analogous to minorities, or from the large gay populations in their urban districts.
202. Chai R. Feldblum, "The Federal Gay Rights Bill: From Bella to ENDA," in John D'Emilio, William B. Turner, Urvashi Vaid, eds., *Creating Change: Sexuality, Public Policy, and Civil Rights* (New York: St. Martin's Press, pp. 149–87, 153–54.
203. The issue was finally examined in congressional hearings in 1980. See *Civil Rights Act Amendments of 1979: Hearings on H.R. 2074 before the Subcommittee on Employment Opportunities of the House Committee on Education and Labor,* 96th Cong., 2d Sess. (1980).
204. Feldblum, "Federal Gay Rights Bill," p. 154.
205. I thank Steven Epstein for this point.
206. See Mark Hertzog, *The Lavender Vote* (New York: New York University Press, 1996), p. 55. In fact, Kinsey's research was anything but clear on this point. The vast majority of his research on homosexuality focused on the incidence of homosexual encounters, rather than the prevalence of gay identities. Kinsey and his collaborators did say that 10 percent of men were "more or less" exclusively homosexual for at least three years between the ages of sixteen and fifty-five, and about half that were exclusively homosexual throughout their lives. Between 2 and 6 percent of unmarried females were "more or less" exclusively homosexual throughout their lives, while less than 1 percent of married females fell into this category. Alfred C. Kinsey, Wardell B. Pomeroy, and Clyde E. Martin, *Sexual Behavior in the Human Male* (Philadelphia: Saunders, 1948), p. 651; Institute for Sex Research, *Sexual Behavior in the Human Female* (Philadelphia: Saunders, 1953), p. 626.
207. *Time,* October 31, 1969, p. 56.
208. See Paul Frymer, *Uneasy Alliances* (Princeton: Princeton University Press, 1999), pp. 186–93.
209. Ibid., p. 61.
210. Connie de Boer, "The Polls: Attitudes toward Homosexuality," *Public Opinion Quarterly* 42 (1978): 265–76, 269.
211. Ibid., p. 275.
212. Ibid., pp. 271–72.
213. Button, Rienzo, and Wald, *Private Lives,* pp. 65–68.
214. Ibid., pp. 205–7. The comparison of gays to blacks is a theme running through

the analysis. See ibid., pp. 11, 25, 58, 62, 67, 209. For local ordinances, gay allies included human-rights groups, such as the American Civil Liberties Union, local bureaucracies administering human relations or civil rights, liberal religious groups, black civil-rights groups, women's rights groups, the Democratic Party, university or student organizations, businesses, and environmental groups. Ibid., p. 88. Similar groups were allies on the federal level. Toby Marotta, *The Politics of Homosexuality* (Boston: Houghton Mifflin, 1981), pp. 324–25.

215. *DeSantis v. Pacific Tel. & Tel. Co.*, 608 F.2d 327 (9th Cir. 1979). See Editors of the Harvard Law Review, *Sexual Orientation and the Law*, pp. 69–71, for a discussion.

216. Leila J. Rupp and Verta Taylor, *Survival in the Doldrums: The American Women's Rights Movement, 1945 to the 1960s* (New York: Oxford University Press, 1987), pp. 105–7, 123, 183.

217. Betty Friedan, *"It Changed My Life"* (New York: Random House, 1976), pp. 176, 200–1, 327.

218. Ferree and Hess, *Controversy and Coalition*, pp. 177–80.

219. Jane J. Mansbridge, *Why We Lost the ERA* (Chicago: University of Chicago Press, 1986), p. 131.

220. *Hearings before the Committee on the Judiciary*, Senate, 91st Cong, 2nd Sess., on S.J. Res. 61 and S.J. Res. 231, September 9–11, 15, 1970, p. 224.

221. Epstein, "Gay and Lesbian Movements," p. 47.

222. Even when the OFCC order creating affirmative action for white ethnics was weakened to the point of being useless, it was not completely eliminated.

223. Button, Rienzo, and Wald, *Private Lives*, Chapter 6.

224. *Bowers v. Hardwick*, 478 U.S. 186 (1986), at 196.

10. Conclusion

1. Hugh Davis Graham, *The Civil Rights Era* (New York: Oxford University Press, 1990), p. 476.

2. Goldwater rarely expressed interest in Mexican Americans despite this group's large presence in his home state. Peter Iverson, *Barry Goldwater: Native Arizonan* (Norman: University of Oklahoma Press, 1997), pp. 152–53.

3. Theda Skocpol, *Protecting Soldiers and Mothers* (Cambridge, Mass.: Harvard University Press, 1992).

4. Peter Skerry has decried this loss of a participatory element in minority politics in his many writings. See, for example, Peter Skerry, *Mexican Americans: The Ambivalent Minority* (New York: Free Press, 1993); Peter Skerry, *Counting on the Census?* (Washington, D.C.: Brookings Institution, 2000), Chapter 6. For an early assessment, see Daniel Patrick Moynihan, "The Professionalization of Reform," *Public Interest* 1 (1965): 6–16.

5. Larry J. Sabato, *The Rise of the Political Consultants* (New York: Basic Books, 1981).

6. R. Shep Melnick, "The Courts, Congress and Programmatic Rights," in Richard A. Harris and Sidney M. Milkis, eds., *Remaking American Politics* (Boulder:

Westview, 1989), pp. 188–212, 193; Thomas F. Burke, "On the Resilience of Rights," in Martin A. Levin, Marc K. Landy, and Martin Shapiro, eds., *Seeking the Center* (Washington, D.C.: Georgetown University Press, 2001), pp. 172–90, 178.

7. John D. Skrentny, *The Ironies of Affirmative Action* (Chicago: University of Chicago Press, 1996), Chapter 7.

8. Most prominently with black-oriented policies. See Paul Frymer, *Uneasy Alliances* (Princeton: Princeton University Press, 1999).

9. Thomas Byrne Edsall and Mary D. Edsall, *Chain Reaction* (New York: Norton, 1992).

10. As does Richard Epstein's *Forbidden Grounds* (Cambridge, Mass.: Harvard University Press, 1992), which argues that civil rights laws are inefficient and unnecessary because they distort markets.

11. Chin shows many in Congress *did* expect more previously disfavored immigrants to come, but it is doubtful that anyone predicted that 80 percent of immigrants would be Asian, Latin American, or from Africa and the West Indies. Gabriel Chin, "The Civil Rights Revolution Comes to Immigration Law: A New Look at the Immigration and Nationality Act of 1965," *North Carolina Law Review* 75 (1996): 273–345.

12. John A. Kromkowski, "Eastern and Southern European Immigrants: Expectations, Reality and a New Agenda," *Annals of the American Academy of Political and Social Science* 487 (1986): 57–78.

13. George J. Borjas, *Heaven's Door: Immigration Policy and the American Economy* (Princeton: Princeton University Press, 1999).

14. Relevant testimony from Greenspan on this point can be found online at the websites for both the opponents of expanded immigration *(http://www.fairus. org/html/07266008.htm)* and its supporters *(http://www.immigrationforum. org/CurrentIssues/economicprosperity/foi-1.htm)*.

15. The politics of immigration reform typically confound normal right–left coalitions. See Peter H. Schuck, "The Politics of Rapid Legal Change: Immigration Policy in the 1980s," in Marc K. Landy and Martin A. Levin, *New Politics of Public Policy,* Baltimore: Johns Hopkins University Press, 1995), pp. 47–87. On the failure of restrictionists, see David M. Reimers, *Unwelcome Strangers* (New York: Columbia University Press, 1998).

16. Hugh Davis Graham, *Collision Course: The Strange Convergence of Affirmative Action and Immigration Policy in America* (New York: Oxford University Press, 2002), Chapter 5.

17. Thomas F. Burke, "On the Rights Track: The Americans with Disabilities Act," in Pietro S. Nivola, ed., *Comparative Disadvantage: Social Regulations and the Global Economy* (Washington, D.C.: Brookings Institution, 1997), pp. 242–318.

18. It is difficult to find overall estimates of the costs of compliance with either Section 504 or the ADA. Though early studies estimated the cost to employers for accommodation to average five hundred dollars for the removal of physical barriers, there are other potential costs such as adjusting working hours, allowing sometime long absences for illnesses, and so on. Burke, "On the Rights Track,"

p. 284. The costs to maintain accessibility standards for buildings and mass transit have been the highest, and have led to hysterical complaints. In 1978, for example, a *Chicago Tribune* editorial on disability access for the city's mass transit system complained that the $1 billion price tag would work out to "more than half million dollars per [disabled] person." Quoted in Stephen L. Percy, *Disability, Civil Rights, and Public Policy* (Tuscaloosa: University of Alabama Press, 1989), p. 241. Philip K. Howard complained (without sources) in 1994 that less than 2 percent of the 43 million disabled were confined to wheelchairs, and most of those were in nursing homes, yet "billions are being spent to make every nook and cranny of every facility in America wheelchair-accessible [while] children die of malnutrition and finish almost dead last in math." Philip K. Howard, *The Death of Common Sense* (New York: Random House, 1994), p. 153. Such sentiments have led to litigation to lessen the cost burdens, but have not created a political movement to change the law.

19. Carol M. Swain, Kyra R. Greene, and Christine Min Wotipka, "Understanding Racial Polarization on Affirmative Action: The View from Focus Groups," in John D. Skrentny, *Color Lines* (Chicago: University of Chicago Press, 2001), pp. 214–37, 227.

20. Abigail C. Saguy, *Is This Sexual Harassment?* (Berkeley: University of California Press, forthcoming); Abigail C. Saguy, "Employment Discrimination or Sexual Violence? Defining Sexual Harassment in American and French Law," *Law and Society Review* 34 (2000): 1091–1128.

21. *Barnes v. Costle*, 561 F.2d 983 (D.C. Cir. 1977).

22. *Bundy v. Jackson*, 641 F.2d 934, 945 (D.C. Cir. 1981). In its opinion, the court followed the familiar practice of racializing Latinos—it based its opinion on a case (*Rogers v. EEOC*, 454 F.2d 234 [5th Cir. 1971]) dealing with discrimination against Hispanics, describing them as a racial and not ethnic group.

23. *Harris v. Forklift Sys.*, 510 U.S. 17 (1993).

24. Saguy, *Is This Sexual Harassment?*. Except for the provisions for litigation, the Civil Rights Act of 1991 did not advance rights but merely restored some guidelines for determining what constitutes discrimination that previous court rulings had narrowed. Skrentny, *Ironies of Affirmative Action*, p. 227.

25. For the details of this fascinating tale, see David Rayside, *On the Fringe: Gays and Lesbians in Politics* (Ithaca: Cornell University Press, 1998), Chapter Seven.

26. *San Francisco Chronicle*, August 6, 1998.

27. Gay-rights politics also collided for a time with policy in response to the epidemic of AIDS and HIV. While often linked to gay men due to their higher than average rates of the disease, this connection was never exclusive, as heterosexuals and intravenous drug users also were at risk. AIDS–HIV policy would take many forms, including efforts at prevention, identifying and testing for detection of the disease, treatment for those afflicted, and a rights-oriented initiative: antidiscrimination law for persons with AIDS. This latter law's symbolic victim was a boy, Ryan White, infected through a transfusion and not by a gay man. Jason Andrew Kaufman, "Competing Conceptions of Individualism in Contemporary American AIDS Policy: A Re-Examination of Neo-Institutionalist Analysis," *Theory and Society* 27 (1998): 635–69; Jason Andrew Kaufman, "Pol-

itics as Social Learning: Policy Experts, Political Mobilization, and AIDS Preventive Policy," *Journal of Policy History* 10 (1998): 289–329.

28. Chai R. Feldblum, "The Federal Gay Rights Bill: From Bella to ENDA," in John D'Emilio, William B. Turner, and Urvashi Vaid, eds., *Creating Change: Sexuality, Public Policy, and Civil Rights* (New York: St. Martin's Press, 2000), pp. 149–87, 163.

29. *New York Times*, August 2, 1998.

30. Ibid.

31. Paisley Currah, "Searching for Immutability: Homosexuality, Race and Rights Discourse," in Angelia R. Wilson, ed., *A Simple Matter of Justice? Theorizing Lesbian and Gay Politics* (London: Cassell, 1995), pp. 51–90, 56.

32. James W. Button, Barbara A. Rienzo, and Kenneth Wald, *Private Lives, Public Conflicts* (Washington, D.C.: Congressional Quarterly Press, 1997), p. 20, n. 5.

33. Alan Wolfe, *One Nation, After All* (New York: Viking, 1998), pp. 72–81.

34. *Romer v. Evans*, 517 U.S. 620 (1996). The mobilization of popular rejection of gay rights through referenda is the primary tool of anti-gay-rights activists. See Regina Werum and Bill Winders, "Who's 'In' and "Who's 'Out': State Fragmentation and the Struggle over Gay Rights, 1974–1999," *Social Problems* 48 (2001): 386–410.

35. Quoted in Andrew Fishel and Janice Pottker, *National Politics and Sex Discrimination in Education* (Lexington, Mass.: D. C. Heath, 1977), p. 128.

36. Ibid.

37. Joseph A. Califano Jr., *Governing America: An Insider's Report from the White House and the Cabinet* (New York: Touchstone, 1981), pp. 223–34.

38. Catherine E. Rymph, "Outcasts, Misfits and Rejects: The Rise and Fall of Republican Feminism, 1972–1980," in Ken Cmiel and Casey Blake, eds., *Thinking through the Seventies* (Chicago: University of Chicago Press, forthcoming).

39. Grove City College v. Bell, 104 S. Ct. 1211 (1984), at 1222.

40. Rosemary C. Salomone, *Equal Education under Law: Legal Rights and Federal Policy in the Post-Brown Era* (New York: St. Martin's Press, 1986), p. 133.

41. Hugh Davis Graham, "The Storm Over Grove City College: Civil Rights Regulation, Higher Education, and the Reagan Administration," *History of Education Quarterly* 38 (1998): 407–29, 424. Also see Salomone, *Equal Education under Law*, pp. 130–33.

42. Jerry A. Jacobs, "Women in the Workplace and Higher Education: Unanticipated Detours on the Road to Gender Integration," *Contexts*, forthcoming; *New York Times*, March 26, 2001.

43. *Time*, May 5, 1997, p. 79.

44. WIN [Women's International Network] News, 23 (1997), p. 66; *San Francisco Chronicle*, January 17, 2002.

45. *Time*, May 5, 1997, p. 79.

46. *New York Times*, August 7, 2001.

47. For an overview, see Bill Piatt, *¿Only English?: Law and Language Policy in the United States* (Albuquerque: University of New Mexico Press, 1990).

48. Nathan Glazer, "Ethnicity and the Schools," *Commentary* 58 (September, 1974), 55–59.

49. *Washington Post,* September 27, 1974.
50. *New York Times,* November 3, 1974.
51. Noel Epstein, *Language, Ethnicity and the Schools: Policy Alternatives for Bilingual-Bicultural Education* (Washington, D.C.: George Washington University Institute for Educational Leadership, 1977), pp. 2, 11.
52. Diane Ravitch, *The Troubled Crusade* (New York: Basic Books, 1983), p. 276.
53. Hugh Davis Graham, *Uncertain Triumph* (Chapel Hill: University of North Carolina Press, 1984), p. 218.
54. Epstein, *Language, Ethnicity and the Schools.*
55. Quoted in Salomone, *Equal Education under Law,* p. 91.
56. Ibid., p. 99.
57. *Washington Post,* April 24, 1982. Despite its ambitions, OCR was a poorly funded and weak agency. On the strange story of its ambitions despite its weakness, see Jeremy Rabkin, "Office for Civil Rights," in James Q. Wilson, ed., *The Politics of Regulation* (New York: Basic Books, 1980), pp. 304–56.
58. Rebecca D. Freeman, *Bilingual Education and Social Change* (Philadelphia: Multilingual Matters, 1998), pp. 46–47; James Crawford, *Hold Your Tongue* (New York: Addison Wesley, 1992), p. 43; Gareth Davies, "The Great Society after Johnson: The Case of Bilingual Education," *Journal of American History* 88 (2002): 1405–29, 1410. In 1985, Reagan's education secretary William Bennett was similarly unsympathetic, complaining that $1.7 billion of federal money had been spent on bilingual education. William Bennett, *The De-Valuing of America* (New York: Touchstone, 1992), p. 54.
59. Califano, *Governing America,* pp. 312–14; Rachel F. Moran, "The Politics of Discretion: Federal Intervention in Bilingual Education," *California Law Review* 76 (1988): 1249–1352, 1293–39; Colman Brez Stein Jr., *Sink or Swim: The Politics of Bilingual Education* (New York: Praeger, 1986), 76.
60. See Christine H. Rossell and Keith Baker, *Bilingual Education in Massachusetts* (Boston: Pioneer Institute, 1996), Chapter 7, for a review of poll data.
61. *Los Angeles Times Poll Alert,* October 15, 1997 (Study #400); *Politico,* vol. 1, February 16, 1998; *http://www.onenation.org/0598/051298an2.html.*
62. Skrentny, *Ironies of Affirmative Action,* pp. 216–17.
63. Nathan Glazer, *Affirmative Discrimination* (New York: Basic Books, 1975).
64. Quoted in Gary L. McDowell, "Affirmative Inaction: The Brock–Meese Standoff on Federal Racial Quotas," *Policy Review* (1989): 32–37, p. 32.
65. Hugh Davis Graham, "The Politics of Clientele Capture: Civil Rights Policy in the Reagan Administration," in Neal Devins and Douglas Davison, eds., *Redefining Equality* (New York: Oxford University Press, 1997), p. 103.
66. John D. Skrentny, "Walking a Fine Line: Republican Efforts to End Affirmative Action," in Marc Landy, Martin Levin, and Martin Shapiro, eds., *Seeking the Center* (Washington, D.C.: Georgetown University Press, 2001), pp. 132–71.
67. Skrentny, "Republicans and Affirmative Action," p. 148.
68. On the California effort, see Lydia Chavez, *The Color Bind* (Berkeley: University of California Press, 1997); Nicholas Lemann, *The Big Test* (New York: Farrar, Straus and Giroux, 2000).

69. *Richmond v. Croson,* 488 U.S. 469 (1989); *Adarand Constructors v. Peña,* 515 U.S. 200 (1995).

70. 78 F.3d 932 (1996).

71. In Michigan, federal courts upheld affirmative admissions at the University of Michigan, *Gratz v. Bollinger,* 122 F.Supp.2d 811 (E.D. Mich. 2000), but struck down a similar program at the university's school of law. (*Grutter v. Bollinger,* 137 F.Supp.2d 821 (E.D. Mich. 2001). Meanwhile, in *Smith v. University of Washington Law Sch.,* 233 F.3d 1188 (9th Cir. 2000), an appeals court upheld preferences for diversity.

72. *Sacramento Bee,* May 15, 1997.

73. Hugh Davis Graham, "Affirmative Action for Immigrants? The Unintended Consequences of Reform," in Skrentny, *Color Lines,* pp. 53–70, 64.

74. See the testimony in *Review of SBA's Business Development Programs, Hearings before the Committee on Small Business,* House, 104th Cong., 1st Sess., March 6, 1995.

75. Erin Kelly and Frank Dobbin, "From Affirmative Action to Diversity Management," in Skrentny, *Color Lines,* pp. 87–117, 110; Frank Dobbin and John R. Sutton, "The Strength of a Weak State: The Employment Rights Revolution and the Rise of Human Resources Management Division," *American Sociological Review* 104 (1998): 441–76; Frank Dobbin, John R. Sutton, John W. Meyer, and W. Richard Scott, "Equal Opportunity Law and the Construction of Internal Labor Markets," *American Journal of Sociology* 99 (1993): 396–427; John R. Sutton, Frank Dobbin, John W. Meyer, and W. Richard Scott, "The Legalization of the Workplace," *American Journal of Sociology* 99 (1994): 944–71.

76. Kelly and Dobbin, "From Affirmative Action to Diversity Management." Also see Frederick Lynch, *The Diversity Machine* (New York: Free Press, 1997). The diversity rationale, while popular, was of dubious legality and possibly limited minorities to those jobs in which they worked with minorities. Michael Lichter and Roger Waldinger, "Producing Conflict: Immigration and the Management of Diversity in the Multiethnic Metropolis," and Deborah C. Malamud, "Affirmative Action and Ethnic Niches: A Legal Afterward," both in Skrentny, *Color Lines,* pp. 147–67 and pp. 313–45.

77. Barbara Reskin, *The Realities of Affirmative Action* (Washington, D.C. American Sociological Association, 1998).

78. Quoted in Jennifer Hochschild, "Race in the Culture Wars: The Symbolic use of Affirmative Action," in Michèle Lamont, ed., *The Cultural Territories of Race: White and Black Boundaries* (New York: Russell Sage Foundation and Chicago: University of Chicago Press, 1999), pp. 343–68, 360, n. 13.

79. Hochschild, "Affirmative Action as Culture War," pp. 348–49. Even some of the more celebrated successes showed meager progress. For example, the EEOC's ballyhooed 1973 consent decree with AT&T did not revolutionize hiring at that giant company. By 1979, blacks had increased their share of "Officials and Managers" from 2.8 percent of the workforce in 1973 to 5.7 percent, though in all white-collar jobs, they only increased from 12.2 percent to 13.9 percent. "Other minorities" increased from 1.4 percent of officials and manag-

ers to 3.1, and from 3.7 of all white-collar jobs to 5.4 percent. Women increased in the officials and managers category from 24.5 to 29.1 percent, and in the blue-collar jobs, from which they had been mostly excluded, they increased from 6.6 to 11.6 percent. Herbert R. Northrup and John A. Larson, *The Impact of the AT&T–EEO Consent Decree: Labor Relations and Public Policy Series No. 20* (Philadelphia: Industrial Research Unit, Wharton School, 1979), pp. 38–44.

80. Stephen Thernstrom and Abigail Thernstrom, *America in Black and White* (New York: Simon and Schuster, 1997), p. 187.

81. William Julius Wilson, *The Truly Disadvantaged* (Chicago: University of Chicago Press, 1987), pp. 110–11.

82. Glenn Loury, *One by One from the Inside Out* (New York: Free Press, 1995), p. 109. The economist Barbara Bergmann agrees with this pessimistic assessment, but uses it to call for "a far more rigorous application of affirmative action techniques than has yet occurred." Barbara R. Bergmann, *In Defense of Affirmaive Action* (New York: Basic Books, 1996), p. 27.

83. Skrentny, *Ironies of Affirmative Action,* pp. 4–5; Skrentny, "Republican Efforts," p. 133; Swain, Greene and Wotipka, "Racial Polarization," pp. 221–23.

84. Skrentny, *Ironies of Affirmative Action,* Chapter 6.

85. Hence Lawrence Bobo has argued the debate is about group interests rather than moral principles. Lawrence Bobo, "Race, Interests, and Beliefs about Affirmative Action: Unanswered Questions and New Directions," in Skrentny, *Color Lines,* pp. 191–213.

86. Skrentny, "Republican Efforts," p. 150.

87. Orlando Patterson, *The Ordeal of Integration* (Washington, D.C.: Civitas, 1997), p. 149; Jennifer Hochschild, "Race in the Culture Wars: The Symbolic Use of Affirmative Action," in Michèle Lamont, ed., *The Cultural Territories of Race: White and Black Boundaries* (New York: Russell Sage Foundation, 1999).

88. Sunita Parikh, "Affirmative Action, Caste and Party Politics in Contemporary India," in Skrentny, *Color Lines,* pp. 297–312, 309.

89. Dara Z. Strolovitch, "Playing Favorites: Public Attitudes toward Race- and Gender-Targeted Anti-discrimination Policy," *NWSA Journal* 10 (1998): 27–53.

90. Euro-American support for the preferential hiring of blacks and Latinos varies between 10 and 15 percent, depending on the year, according to the Los Angeles County Social Survey. Euro-American support for preferences for Asian Americans is somewhat lower, at around 5 percent. David O. Sears, Jack Citrin, Sharmaine V. Cheleden, and Colette van Laar, "Cultural Diveristy and Multicultural Politics: Is Ethnic Balkanization Psychologically Inevitable?" in Deborah A. Prentice and Dale T. Miller, eds., *Cultural Divides* (New York: Russell Sage Foundation, 1999), pp. 35–79, 51; David O. Sears, Jack Citrin, Sharmaine Vidanage, Nicholas Valentino, "What Ordinary Americans Think about Multiculturalism," paper presented at the Annual Meeting of the American Political Science Association, 1994, table 3. On black exceptionalism, see David Hollinger, *Post-Ethnic America* (New York: Basic Books, 2000 [1995]), pp. 176–78.

91. Glenn Loury, *The Anatomy of Racial Inequality: Stereotypes, Stigma, and the Elusive Quest for Racial Justice* (Cambridge, Mass.: Harvard University Press, 2001), Chapter 2.

92. Sears et al., "Multicultural Politics," p. 65.

93. Michael O. Emerson, George Yancey, and Karen Chai, "Does Race Matter in Residential Segregation? Explaining the Preferences of White Americans," *American Sociological Review* 66 (2001): 922–35.

94. Douglas Massey and Nancy Denton, *American Apartheid* (Cambridge: Harvard University Press, 1992), p. 87.

95. Camille Zubrinsky-Charles, "Neighborhood Racial-Composition Preferences: Evidence from a Multiethnic Metropolis," *Social Problems* 47 (2000): 379–407.

96. Sears et al., "Multicultural Politics," p. 56.

97. William Julius Wilson, *When Work Disappears* (New York: Random House, 1996), pp. 11–46.

98. Jennifer Lee, "The Racial and Ethnic Meaning behind Black: Retailers' Hiring Practices in Inner-City Neighborhoods," in *Color Lines,* pp. 168–86.

99. Kathryn M. Neckerman and Joleen Kirschenman, "Hiring Strategies, Racial Bias and Inner-City Workers," *Social Problems* 38 (1991): 433–47; Philip Kasinitz and Jan Rosenberg, "Missing the Connection: Social Isolation and Employment on the Brooklyn Waterfront," *Social Problems* 43 (1996): 180–96; Harry J. Holzer, *What Employers Want: Job Prospects for Less-Educated Workers* (New York: Russell Sage Foundation, 1996).

100. Jerry Jacobs and Teresa Labov, "Gender Differentials in Intermarriage among Sixteen Race and Ethnic Groups," *Sociological Forum,* forthcoming.

101. F. James Davis, *Who Is Black?* (University Park: Pennsylvania State University Press, 1991).

102. Anthony King, ed., *The New American Political System,* 2d ed. (Washington, D.C.: AEI Press, 1990). Skerry provides an excellent summary in Skerry, *Counting on the Census?,* Chapter 6.

103. Sidney Milkis, *The President and the Parties* (New York: Oxford University Press, 1993), pp. 9–12.

104. Arthur Schlesinger Jr., *The Imperial Presidency* (New York: Houghton Mifflin, 1973), Chapter 6.

105. The perceived political wisdom of supporting women's rights—even before women's mobilization—is a major theme in Anne Costain's work. In assessing the Equal Rights Amendment, for example, Costain notes that there were 214 introductions of the amendment in 1969 though there was little coverage of the women's movement in the media at the time. Anne Costain, *Inviting Women's Rebellion* (Baltimore: Johns Hopkins University Press, 1992), p. 57.

106. A. James Reichley, *The Life of the Parties: A History of American Political Parties* (New York: Free Press, 1992), pp. 6–12.

107. Larry Sabato argues political consultants gained influence as party power waned, and began to develop first in California—Nixon's home state—because the party system was so weak there. Sabato, *Rise of Political Consultants,* pp. 10–11.

108. Everett Carl Ladd Jr. and Charles D. Hadley, *Transformations of the American Party System* (New York: Norton, 1975), p. 336.

109. Marc K. Landy and Martin A. Levin, "The New Politics of Public Policy," in Landy and Levin, *The New Politics of Public Policy,* pp. 277–98, 278.

110. Ibid., p. 280.

111. David R. Mayhew, *Divided We Govern* (New Haven: Yale University Press, 1991), Chapter 5; Landy and Levin, "New Politics," pp. 278–79.

112. Steven M. Teles, "Positive Action or Affirmative Action? The Persistence of Britain's Antidiscrimination Regime," in Skrentny, *Color Lines,* pp. 241–69, 258.

113. Myra Marx Ferree, "Equality and Autonomy: Feminist Politics in the United States and West Germany," in Mary Fainsod Katzenstein and Carol McClurg Mueller, eds., *The Women's Movements of the United States and Western Europe: Consciousness, Political Opportunity, and Public Policy* (Philadelphia: Temple University Press, 1987), pp. 175–80.

114. Saguy, "Employment Discrimination or Sexual Violence?" p. 1120.

115. Congressional reluctance to fully fund the Bilingual Education Act appeared to reflect not resistance to the policy—there were no complaints about bilingual education in the early years—but a belief that political credit could be claimed without movement of resources.

116. In an influential article, William H. Sewell Jr. describes a process through which "schemas," or taken-for-granted rules or assumptions, can be transposed or extended to "new situations when the opportunity arises." William H. Sewell Jr., "A Theory of Structure: Duality, Agency, and Transformation," *American Journal of Sociology* 98 (1992): 1–29, 8. Sewell does not offer a theory of the limits of this transposing. I do not offer one here, but the cases in this study suggest this ability is limited in complex ways by the meanings of the things in question and the skills of the actor.

117. Steven J. Novak, "The Real Takeover of the BIA: The Preferential Hiring of Indians," *Journal of Economic History* 50 (1990): 639–54.

118. US Commission on Civil Rights, *Minorities and Women as Government Contractors* (Washington, D.C.: Government Printing Office, May 1975), pp. 63–64.

119. This basic principle applies to any policy that a politician would like to sell to the American people. Some are simply more difficult to make appealing than others. As one political adviser in the Clinton administration told me, in a remark he attributed to Lyndon Johnson, "You can't shine shit."

120. Though the importance of boundaries and categorizations has been a major theme in the work of cultural sociologists such as Michèle Lamont (*Money, Manners and Morals* [Chicago: University of Chicago Press, 1992], *The Dignity of Working Men* (Cambridge, Mass.: Harvard University Press, 2000]) and Eviatar Zerubavel (*The Fine Line* [New York: Free Press, 1991]), there is less work on how these boundaries change. Some promising research on the related "pathways to credibility" comes from the sociology of science. Steven Epstein, *Impure Science* (Berkeley: University of California Press, 1996), pp. 334–37; and Kelly Moore, *Disrupting Science: Social Movements and Institutional Change* (Princeton: Princeton University Press, forthcoming).

121. US Commission on Civil Rights, *Civil Rights Issues of Asian and Pacific Americans: Myths and Realities* (Washington, D.C.: Government Printing Office, May 8–9, 1980).

122. For example, at California Blue Shield 23 percent of the employees were Asian

American. While one of every six white employees was a manager or supervisor, only one of thirty-nine Asians was at this rank. None of the top nineteen decisionmaking positions were occupied by Asian Americans. Ibid., p. 420.

123. The most influential theoretical statement remains Michael Omi and Howard Winant, *Racial Formation in the United States,* 2nd ed. (Philadelphia: Temple University Press, 1994). Also see Robert C. Lieberman, "The Political Construction of Race," *American Political Science Review* 89 (1995): 437–41.

124. A classic statement on transitions to whiteness is David R. Roediger, *The Wages of Whiteness: Race and the Making of the American Working Class* (New York: Verso, 1991). The white ethnic revival sits uncomfortably within the "whiteness" literature in general because it tends to argue that the racialization to whiteness occurred well before 1965. For example, see Matthew Frye Jacobson, *Whiteness of a Different Color* (Cambridge: Harvard University Press, 1998). Roediger has elsewhere treated white ethnics as an interstitial category at least through the 1950s, but has not offered analysis of the late 1960s period. David Roediger, *Towards the Abolition of Whiteness* (New York: Verso, 1994), Chapter 11 generally, esp. p. 183.

125. Even where Omi and Winant identify state practices as important "sources of racial change," creating pan-ethnic labels such as "Asian American," they ignore affirmative action's role in the process. Omi and Winant, *Racial Formation,* p. 89. An exception is Felix M. Padilla, *Latino Ethnic Consciousness* (Notre Dame: University of Notre Dame Press, 1985), pp. 84–89. Espiritu's influential study acknowledges the role of affirmative action in constructing race. Yen Le Espiritu, *Asian American Pan-Ethnicity* (Philadelphia: Temple University Press, 1992), p. 13.

126. Skerry, *Counting on the Census?* p. 14.

127. David Hollinger, *Post-Ethnic America* (New York: Basic Books, 2000 [1997]). Padilla shows how affirmative action unified and mobilized various Latino groups in Chicago. Padilla, *Latino Ethnic Consciousness,* p. 85.

128. Hollinger, *Post-Ethnic America,* p. 33; also see Christian Joppke, *Immigration and the Nation-State* (New York: Oxford University Press, 1999), p. 156. Directive 15 had an impact, but it certainly did not create the official minorities. Skerry, *Counting on the Census?,* pp. 69–70.

129. Joppke, *Immigration and the Nation-State,* Chapter 5; Hugh Davis Graham, *Collision Course: The Strange Convergence of Affirmative Action and Immigration Policy in America* (New York: Oxford University Press, 2002). Peter Skerry, "The Racialization of Immigration Policy," in Morton Keller and R. Shep Melnick, eds., *Taking Stock: American Government in the Twentieth Century* (New York: Cambridge University Press, 1999), pp. 81–122.

130. As Ralph Abernathy was perhaps the first to find when Latinos' pursuit of bilingual education disrupted his "Poor Peoples' Campaign." See Chapter 5. For one scholar-activist's pursuit of cross-race coalitions, see William Julius Wilson's *The Bridge over the Racial Divide* (Berkeley: University of California Press, 1999).

131. Deborah Malamud, "Affirmative Action and Ethnic Niches: A Legal Afterword," in Skrentny, *Color Lines,* pp. 313–45, 314–16.

132. *New York Times*, February 24, 2001.

133. Graham, *Collision Course*, pp. 159–60; Graham, "Affirmative Action for Immigrants?" pp. 64–66. Also see Joppke, *Immigration and the Nation-State*, pp. 162–64; Peter Skerry, *Mexican Americans: The Ambivalent Minority* (New York: Free Press, 1993).

134. Graham, *Collision Course*, p. 194; Joshua R. Goldstein, J. R. Morning, and Ann Morning, "Back in the Box: The Dilemma of Using Multiple-Race Data for Single-race Laws", paper presented at September 22–23, 2000 conference, "Multiraciality: How Will the New Census Data Be Used?" Jerome Levy Economic Institute, Bard College, Annandale-on-Hudson (updated March 2001). For a critical discussion see Peter H. Schuck, "Affirmative Action: Past, Present and Future," *Yale Law and Policy Review* 20 (2002): 1–96, 15–17. The old rules for mixed race individuals were very vague: "The category that most closely reflects the individual's recognition in his community should be used for purposes of reporting on persons who are of mixed racial and/or ethnic origins." OMB, "Directive No. 15: Race and Ethnic Standards for Federal Statistics and Administrative Reporting," *Federal Register*, vol. 43, May 4, 1978, p. 19,269. This rule also lacked any mechanism for verification.

135. Clark D. Cunningham, Glenn C. Loury, and John David Skrentny, "Passing Strict Scrutiny: Using Social Science to Design Affirmative Action Programs," *Georgetown Law Journal* 90 (2002): (forthcoming).

136. George La Noue and John Sullivan, "Deconstructing Affirmative Action Categories," in *Color Lines*, pp. 71–86, 81.

137. Graham, *Collision Course*, pp. 144, 192; and see generally Alejandro Portes, ed., *The New Second Generation* (New York: Russell Sage Foundation, 1996).

138. For an analysis of this approach, see David Orentlicher, "Affirmative Action and Texas' Ten Percent Solution: Improving Diversity and Quality," *Notre Dame Law Review* 74 (1998): 181–210. William Bowen and Derek Bok argue that this policy will admit students who are unprepared. William Bowen and Derek Bok, *The Shape of the River* (Princeton: Princeton University Press, 1998), pp. 271–74.

139. Though originally a Democratic idea, this was suggested by some Republicans as a replacement for preferences but rejected by Congress. Skrentny, "Republican Efforts," p. 153.

140. Richard D. Kahlenberg, *The Remedy: Class, Race and Affirmative Action* (New York: Basic Books, 1997).

141. Jonathan Tilove, "Christian at Harvard Says Paper Nailed Him to the Cross," *New Orleans Times Picayune*, February 28, 1999; David R. Colburn and George E. Pozzetta, "Race, Ethnicity and the Evolution of Political Legitimacy," in David Farber, ed., *The Sixties: From Memory to History* (Chapel Hill: University of North Carolina Press, 1994), pp. 119–48, 134.

142. John D. Skrentny, "Affirmative Action and the Failure of Presidential Leadership," in Stanley Renshon, ed., *One America?* (Washington, D.C.: Georgetown University Press 2001), pp. 103–29.

143. Jonathan Tilove, "2000 Census Finds America's New Mayberry is Exurban and Overwhelmingly White," *New Orleans Times Picayune*, May 12, 2001, p. 22.

144. Carol Swain, *Challenges to an Integrated America: The Emerging White Nationalist Movement* (New York: Cambridge University Press, 2002).

145. Graham, *Collision Course,* p. 196.

146. Herbert J. Gans, "The Possibility of a New Racial Hierarchy in the Twenty-First-Century United States," in Lamont, *Cultural Territories of Race,* pp. 371–90.

147. Patterson, *Ordeal of Integration,* pp. 150, 153; Sears et al, "Multicultural Politics," p. 51 (mixed results on Latinos); Swain et al., "Racial Polarization," pp. 225–29; Lawrence Bobo, "Race, Interests, and Beliefs about Affirmative Action: Unanswered Questions and New Directions," pp. 191–213, 199.

148. Parikh, "Affirmative Action in India," p. 308.

149. Howard Schuman, Charlotte Steeh, and Lawrence Bobo, *Racial Attitudes in the United States* (Cambridge, Mass.: Harvard University Press, 1985).

150. Clem Brooks, "Civil Rights Liberalism and the Suppression of a Republican Realignment in the United States, 1972–1996," *American Sociological Review* 65 (2000): 483–505.

INDEX

Abernathy, Ralph, 147
Abzug, Bella, 241, 319–322
Acheson, Dean, 28, 45
Affirmative action, 143, 340–344, 348, 350, 352–355, 357
AFL-CIO, 150
African Americans, 23–24, 27–37, 87–89, 100–101, 144–150, 166–173. *See also* black capitalism; black exceptionalism
Afro-Asian Peoples' Solidarity Organization, 60, 71
Agudath Israel, 284
Alba, Richard, 309–310
Alevy v. Downstate Medical Center, 173
Alexander, Clifford, 129
Alienza, 102
All African Peoples' Conference, 71
All in the Family, 318
Allan, Virginia, 236
Allen, A. Leonard, 43
Amenta, Edwin, 80–81
American Association of Medical Colleges (AAMC), 169
American Association of University Professors (AAUP), 172
American Association of University Women, 116
American Banker's Association, 148
American Bar Association, 169
American Civil Liberties Union (ACLU), 31, 50
American Council for the Teaching of Foreign Languages, 185
American Federation of Labor (AFL), 43
American Immigration and Citizenship Conference, 50

American Indians, 17–18, 85–87, 90–92, 94, 101, 103–104, 107, 109–110, 125–126, 128–129, 132, 140–142, 144–146, 150, 155, 156, 159, 163, 169, 173–175, 264, 290, 292, 307, 309, 318, 328, 342, 344–345, 350, 353
American Jewish Committee, 278, 283–285
American Jewish Congress, 283–284
American Legion, 43
American Medical Association (AMA), 82
American National Election Study of 1992, 334
American Newspaper Publishers Association, 115–116
American Women, 95
Americans with Disabilities Act (ADA), 265, 332–333
Americans for Democratic Action, 297
Amin, Idi, 72
An Appeal to the World (NAACP petition to the Commission on Human Rights), 30
Anderson, Terry, 200
Andersson, Theodore, 187, 189
Andrews, George, 99
Anti-Defamation League, 282–284
Applegate, Irvamae, 192
Arab League, 64–65
Armendariz, Alex, 157–158
Armenian ancestry, persons of, 172
Armstrong, Anne, 160–161, 252
Arnaz, Desi, 208
Asia and the Americas, 40
Asian-African Conference, 71
Asian Americans, 17–18, 69, 73, 85–86, 88–90, 92, 94, 96, 100–101, 103–112, 114, 116–118, 126–127, 130, 132–133, 142,